Dictionary of Literary Biography

Dictionary of Literary Biography Documentary Series

Dictionary of Literary Biography Yearbooks

1980 edited by Karen L. Rood, Jean W. Ross, and Richard Ziegfeld (1981)

1981 edited by Karen L. Rood, Jean W. Ross, and Richard Ziegfeld (1982)

1982 edited by Richard Ziegfeld; associate editors: Jean W. Ross and Lynne C. Zeigler (1983)

1983 edited by Mary Bruccoli and Jean W. Ross; associate editor Richard Ziegfeld (1984)

1984 edited by Jean W. Ross (1985)

1985 edited by Jean W. Ross (1986)

1986 edited by J. M. Brook (1987)

1987 edited by J. M. Brook (1988)

1988 edited by J. M. Brook (1989)

1989 edited by J. M. Brook (1990)

1990 edited by James W. Hipp (1991)

1991 edited by James W. Hipp (1992)

1992 edited by James W. Hipp (1993)

1993 edited by James W. Hipp, contributing editor George Garrett (1994)

1994 edited by James W. Hipp, contributing editor George Garrett (1995)

1995 edited by James W. Hipp, contributing editor George Garrett (1996)

1996 edited by Samuel W. Bruce and L. Kay Webster, contributing editor George Garrett (1997)

1997 edited by Matthew J. Bruccoli and George Garrett, with the assistance of L. Kay Webster (1998)

1998 edited by Matthew J. Bruccoli, contributing editor George Garrett, with the assistance of D. W. Thomas (1999)

1999 edited by Matthew J. Bruccoli, contributing editor George Garrett, with the assistance of D. W. Thomas (2000)

2000 edited by Matthew J. Bruccoli, contributing editor George Garrett, with the assistance of George Parker Anderson (2001)

2001 edited by Matthew J. Bruccoli, contributing editor George Garrett, with the assistance of George Parker Anderson (2002)

Concise Series

Concise Dictionary of American Literary Biography, 7 volumes (1988–1999): *The New Consciousness, 1941–1968; Colonization to the American Renaissance, 1640–1865; Realism, Naturalism, and Local Color, 1865–1917; The Twenties, 1917–1929; The Age of Maturity, 1929–1941; Broadening Views, 1968–1988; Supplement: Modern Writers, 1900–1998.*

Concise Dictionary of British Literary Biography, 8 volumes (1991–1992): *Writers of the Middle Ages and Renaissance Before 1660; Writers of the Restoration and Eighteenth Century, 1660–1789; Writers of the Romantic Period, 1789–1832; Victorian Writers, 1832–1890; Late-Victorian and Edwardian Writers, 1890–1914; Modern Writers, 1914–1945; Writers After World War II, 1945–1960; Contemporary Writers, 1960 to Present.*

Concise Dictionary of World Literary Biography, 10 volumes projected (1999–): *Ancient Greek and Roman Writers; German Writers; African, Caribbean, and Latin American Writers; South Slavic and Eastern European Writers.*

Dictionary of Literary Biography® • Volume Two Hundred Sixty-Nine

Nathaniel Hawthorne:
A Documentary Volume

Dictionary of Literary Biography® • Volume Two Hundred Sixty-Nine

Nathaniel Hawthorne: A Documentary Volume

Edited by
Benjamin Franklin V
University of South Carolina

A Bruccoli Clark Layman Book

GALE®

Detroit • New York • San Diego • San Francisco • Cleveland • New Haven, Conn. • Waterville, Maine • London • Munich

THOMSON
GALE

Dictionary of Literary Biography
Volume 269: Nathaniel Hawthorne:
A Documentary Volume
Benjamin Franklin V

© 2003 by Gale. Gale is an imprint of
The Gale Group, Inc., a division of
Thomson Learning, Inc.

Gale and Design™ and Thomson Learning™
are trademarks used herein under license.

For more information, contact
The Gale Group, Inc.
27500 Drake Rd.
Farmington Hills, MI 48331-3535
Or you can visit our Internet site at
http://www.gale.com

LIBRARY OF CONGRESS CATALOGING-IN-PUBLICATION DATA

Nathaniel Hawthorne : a documentary volume / edited by Benjamin Franklin V.
    p. cm. — (Dictionary of literary biography ; v. 269)
"A Bruccoli Clark Layman book."
Includes bibliographical references and index.
        ISBN 0-7876-6013-2
        1. Hawthorne, Nathaniel, 1804–1864.
        2. Novelists, American—19th century—Biography.
    I. Franklin, Benjamin, 1939–   . II. Series.

PS1881 .N38 2002
813'.3—dc21   2002013278

Printed in the United States of America
10 9 8 7 6 5 4 3 2 1

To the memory of C. E. Frazer Clark Jr., Hawthornian

Contents

Plan of the Series

. . . Almost the most prodigious asset of a country, and perhaps its most precious possession, is its native literary product— when that product is fine and noble and enduring.

Mark Twain*

The advisory board, the editors, and the publisher of the *Dictionary of Literary Biography* are joined in endorsing Mark Twain's declaration. The literature of a nation provides an inexhaustible resource of permanent worth. Our purpose is to make literature and its creators better understood and more accessible to students and the reading public, while satisfying the needs of teachers and researchers.

To meet these requirements, *literary biography* has been construed in terms of the author's achievement. The most important thing about a writer is his writing. Accordingly, the entries in *DLB* are career biographies, tracing the development of the author's canon and the evolution of his reputation.

The purpose of *DLB* is not only to provide reliable information in a usable format but also to place the figures in the larger perspective of literary history and to offer appraisals of their accomplishments by qualified scholars.

The publication plan for *DLB* resulted from two years of preparation. The project was proposed to Bruccoli Clark by Frederick G. Ruffner, president of the Gale Research Company, in November 1975. After specimen entries were prepared and typeset, an advisory board was formed to refine the entry format and develop the series rationale. In meetings held during 1976, the publisher, series editors, and advisory board approved the scheme for a comprehensive biographical dictionary of persons who contributed to literature. Editorial work on the first volume began in January 1977, and it was published in 1978. In order to make *DLB* more than a dictionary and to compile volumes that individually have claim to status as literary history, it was decided to organize volumes by topic, period, or

From an unpublished section of Mark Twain's autobiography, copyright by the Mark Twain Company

genre. Each of these freestanding volumes provides a biographical-bibliographical guide and overview for a particular area of literature. We are convinced that this organization—as opposed to a single alphabet method— constitutes a valuable innovation in the presentation of reference material. The volume plan necessarily requires many decisions for the placement and treatment of authors. Certain figures will be included in separate volumes, but with different entries emphasizing the aspect of his career appropriate to each volume. Ernest Hemingway, for example, is represented in *American Writers in Paris, 1920–1939* by an entry focusing on his expatriate apprenticeship; he is also in *American Novelists, 1910–1945* with an entry surveying his entire career, as well as in *American Short-Story Writers, 1910–1945, Second Series* with an entry concentrating on his short fiction. Each volume includes a cumulative index of the subject authors and articles.

Since 1981 the series has been further augmented by the *DLB Yearbooks*, which update published entries, add new entries to keep the *DLB* current with contemporary activity, and provide articles on literary history. There have also been nineteen *DLB Documentary Series* volumes which provide illustrations, facsimiles, and biographical and critical source materials for figures, works, or groups judged to have particular interest for students. In 1999 the *Documentary Series* was incorporated into the *DLB* volume numbering system beginning with *DLB 210: Ernest Hemingway.*

We define literature as the *intellectual commerce of a nation:* not merely as belles lettres but as that ample and complex process by which ideas are generated, shaped, and transmitted. *DLB* entries are not limited to "creative writers" but extend to other figures who in their time and in their way influenced the mind of a people. Thus the series encompasses historians, journalists, publishers, book collectors, and screenwriters. By this means readers of *DLB* may be aided to perceive literature not as cult scripture in the keeping of intellectual high priests but firmly positioned at the center of a nation's life.

DLB includes the major writers appropriate to each volume and those standing in the ranks behind them. Scholarly and critical counsel has been sought in deciding which minor figures to include and how full their entries should be. Wherever possible, useful references are made to figures who do not warrant separate entries.

Each *DLB* volume has an expert volume editor responsible for planning the volume, selecting the figures for inclusion, and assigning the entries. Volume editors are also responsible for preparing, where appropriate, appendices surveying the major periodicals and literary and intellectual movements for their volumes, as well as lists of further readings. Work on the series as a whole is coordinated at the Bruccoli Clark Layman editorial center in Columbia, South Carolina, where the editorial staff is responsible for accuracy and utility of the published volumes.

One feature that distinguishes *DLB* is the illustration policy–its concern with the iconography of literature. Just as an author is influenced by his surroundings, so is the reader's understanding of the author enhanced by a knowledge of his environment. Therefore *DLB* volumes include not only drawings, paintings, and photographs of authors, often depicting them at various stages in their careers, but also illustrations of their families and places where they lived. Title pages are regularly reproduced in facsimile along with dust jackets for modern authors. The dust jackets are a special feature of *DLB* because they often document better than anything else the way in which an author's work was perceived in its own time. Specimens of the writers' manuscripts and letters are included when feasible.

Samuel Johnson rightly decreed that "The chief glory of every people arises from its authors." The purpose of the *Dictionary of Literary Biography* is to compile literary history in the surest way available to us–by accurate and comprehensive treatment of the lives and work of those who contributed to it.

The *DLB* Advisory Board

Introduction

After becoming a writer following his graduation from college, Nathaniel Hawthorne published fiction for almost a decade before becoming known and celebrated as an author. He received no acclaim initially because his work, which mostly appeared in periodicals, was published anonymously or pseudonymously. With the 1837 publication of the collection of tales and sketches *Twice-Told Tales,* however, Hawthorne's life dramatically changed because he allowed his name to appear on the title page. The book impressed reviewers and readers generally, as did, mostly, his subsequent publications. At mid century Hawthorne became known and admired principally as a novelist, and as such he remains most famous. Nevertheless, such tales as "Young Goodman Brown," "The Minister's Black Veil," "The Birth-mark," and "My Kinsman, Major Molineux" are also regarded as among the greatest short stories ever written. At his death on 19 May 1864, he was widely considered the major American fiction writer. In eulogizing Hawthorne in *The Atlantic Monthly,* Oliver Wendell Holmes is not hyperbolic in stating that Hawthorne "left enough [superior fiction] to keep his name in remembrance as long as the language in which he shaped his deep imaginations is spoken by human lips."

Hawthorne wrote fiction for a little more than three decades, from the 1828 publication of the novel *Fanshawe,* which he quickly renounced, until the 1860 appearance of his last completed novel, *The Marble Faun.* His career had two major stages: from the beginning until 1850 he wrote mostly tales and sketches; from 1850 until the end of his life, novels, or, as he called them, romances, a distinction he discusses in the preface to *The House of the Seven Gables.* Hawthorne's transition from a writer of short fiction to novelist coincided with the beginning of one of the most impressive six-year periods in American literary history. In 1850 appeared Hawthorne's *The Scarlet Letter,* Herman Melville's *White-Jacket,* and Ralph Waldo Emerson's *Representative Men;* in 1851, Hawthorne's *The House of the Seven Gables* and *The Snow-Image* and Melville's *Moby-Dick;* in 1852, Hawthorne's *The Blithedale Romance,* Melville's *Pierre,* and Harriet Beecher Stowe's *Uncle Tom's Cabin;* in 1853, Hawthorne's *Tanglewood Tales;* in

1854, Melville's "The Encantadas" and Henry David Thoreau's *Walden;* in 1855, Melville's "Benito Cereno," Walt Whitman's *Leaves of Grass,* and Henry Wadsworth Longfellow's *Hiawatha.* Largely, but not exclusively, because of the volumes Hawthorne published during this period (but not including *Tanglewood Tales,* a collection of stories for children), he has long been considered—in company with Melville, because of *Moby-Dick,* a novel Hawthorne helped inspire—the most significant antebellum American writer of fiction.

At his best, Hawthorne (like his friend Melville) investigated the human psyche. The most popular authors when Hawthorne began writing, Washington Irving and James Fenimore Cooper, did not plumb psychic depths. Only Hawthorne's contemporary Edgar Allan Poe consistently probed the psyche, as such poems as "The Raven" and "To Helen" and such tales as "William Wilson" and "The Fall of the House of Usher" show. But Hawthorne's characters are more memorable than Poe's, and the motivations for their behavior are at least as fascinating and enigmatic as those of Poe's characters. Why, really, does Reverend Hooper conceal his face in "The Minister's Black Veil"? In "The Birth-mark," why is Aylmer compelled to remove the mark from Georgiana's face? What ultimately motivates Beatrice's father and Baglioni in "Rappaccini's Daughter"? Why does the husband leave his wife in "Wakefield"? Part of Hawthorne's appeal results from his implicitly raising such questions as these and not answering them, although he leaves clues for responding to them at least tentatively. Anyone interested in human motivation delights in characters such as the ones he creates.

Among the many other reasons for Hawthorne's appeal is his examination of the effects of guilt, a topic of interest to any reflective person. Hawthorne's fascination with the theme is evident in his earliest published tale, "The Hollow of the Three Hills" (1830), in which the main character presumably dies because of her guilt. In "Young Goodman Brown," Faith's husband feels guilty for spending a night away from his wife; partly as a result of this guilt, the remainder of his life is bleak. Because moral weakness keeps Arthur Dimmesdale from acknowledging himself as Hester's

Bronze statue on Hawthorne Boulevard in Salem (by Bela Pratt, 1925)

lover and Pearl's father in *The Scarlet Letter,* he feels guilty; and his guilt ultimately kills him. The Pyncheons' familial guilt drives the plot of *The House of the Seven Gables.*

Such topics as these—investigation of the psyche and concern with guilt, presented in graceful, poetic prose—help explain Hawthorne's sustained popularity. Even in this age of canon expansion and the devaluing of a group of writers known as "dead white males," to which Hawthorne belongs, his works remain staples in high school and college classrooms. He is one of the American authors about whom scholars write most frequently and from whom other writers continue to draw inspiration. John Updike, for example, wrote a trilogy updating the characters in *The Scarlet Letter*: *A Month of Sundays* (1975), about Arthur Dimmesdale; *Roger's Version* (1986), about Roger Chillingworth; and *S.* (1988), about Hester Prynne. Recently, "The Minister's Black Veil" inspired Rick Moody's *The Black Veil: A Memoir with Digressions* (2002). Every bookstore stocks several

Hawthorne titles. Movies have been made about Hawthorne's books, including more than one about *The Scarlet Letter.*

Dictionary of Literary Biography 269: Nathaniel Hawthorne: A Documentary Volume presents a detailed overview of mostly critical but also some personal responses to Hawthorne's work through 1904, the hundredth anniversary of his birth. It features scores of illustrations, including examples of his manuscripts; photographs and portraits of him, his family, and friends; images of places important to him; depictions of scenes from his fiction; facsimiles of title pages of his books; copies of pages from the Salem Athenaeum charge books that indicate volumes he withdrew and presumably read; and Thoreau's survey of The Wayside, Hawthorne's Concord residence, the only home the author ever owned. Therefore, this book—text and illustrations—provides a means of gaining insight into the world of Nathaniel Hawthorne, the author and the man.

—Benjamin Franklin V

Acknowledgments

This book was produced by Bruccoli Clark Layman, Inc. Karen L. Rood is senior editor. George Parker Anderson was the in-house editor.

Production manager is Philip B. Dematteis.

Administrative support was provided by Ann M. Cheschi and Carol A. Cheschi.

Accountant is Ann-Marie Holland.

Copyediting supervisor is Sally R. Evans. The copyediting staff includes Phyllis A. Avant, Caryl Brown, Melissa D. Hinton, Philip I. Jones, Rebecca Mayo, Nancy E. Smith, and Elizabeth Jo Ann Sumner. Freelance copyeditors are Brenda Cabra, Thom Harman, and Alice Poyner.

Editorial associates are Michael S. Allen, Michael S. Martin, Catherine M. Polit, and Amelia B. Lacey.

Permissions editor and database manager is Amber L. Coker.

Layout and graphics supervisor is Janet E. Hill. The graphics staff includes Zoe R. Cook and Sydney E. Hammock.

Office manager is Kathy Lawler Merlette.

Photography supervisor is Paul Talbot. Photography editor is Scott Nemzek.

Digital photographic copy work was performed by Joseph M. Bruccoli.

Systems manager is Marie L. Parker.

Typesetting supervisor is Kathleen M. Flanagan. The typesetting staff includes Patricia Marie Flanagan, Mark J. McEwan, and Pamela D. Norton. Freelance typesetters are Wanda Adams and Rebecca Mayo.

Walter W. Ross did library research. He was assisted by Jo Cottingham and the following other librarians at the Thomas Cooper Library of the University of South Carolina: circulation department head Tucker Taylor; reference department head Virginia W. Weathers; reference department staff Brette Barron, Marilee Birchfield, Paul Cammarata, Gary Geer, Michael Macan, Tom Marcil, Rose Marshall, and Sharon Verba; interlibrary loan department head John Brunswick; and interlibrary loan staff Robert Arndt, Hayden Battle, Alex Byrne, Bill Fetty, Marna Hostetler, and Nelson Rivera.

In preparing this volume, the editor has benefited especially from the work of John L. Idol Jr., Buford Jones (*Nathaniel Hawthorne: The Contemporary Reviews*), Brian Harding (*Nathaniel Hawthorne: Critical Assessments*), and Rita Gollin (*Portraits of Nathaniel Hawthorne: An Iconography*). He acknowledges, with gratitude, the assistance of his friend and colleague Donald J. Greiner.

Nathaniel Hawthorne:
A Documentary Volume

Dictionary of Literary Biography

Books by Nathaniel Hawthorne

See also the Hawthorne entries in *DLB 1: The American Renaissance in New England, DLB 74: American Short-Story Writers Before 1880; DLB 183: American Travel Writers, 1776–1864;* and *DLB 223: The American Renaissance in New England, Second Series.*

Fanshawe, A Tale (Boston: Marsh & Capem, 1828; London: Kegan Paul, Trench, 1883);

Twice-Told Tales (1 volume, Boston: American Stationers Company, 1837; revised and enlarged edition, 2 volumes, Boston: Munroe, 1842; abridged edition, 1 volume, London: Kent & Richards, 1849);

Peter Parley's Universal History, on the Basis of Geography, edited and written by Hawthorne and Elizabeth Hawthorne (Boston: American Stationers Company / London: Parker, 1837); republished, abridged, and modified as *Peter Parley's Common School of History* (Boston: American Stationers Company, 1838);

The Sister Years: Being the Carriers Address, to the Patrons of the Salem Gazette, for the First of January, 1839 (Salem, 1839);

Grandfather's Chair: A History for Youth (Boston: E. P. Peabody / New York: Wiley & Putnam, 1841 [i.e. 1840]; revised and enlarged edition, Boston: Tappan & Dennet, 1842); republished in *True Stories from History and Biography* (Boston: Ticknor, Reed & Fields, 1851; London: Low, 1853);

Famous Old People: Being the Second Epoch of Grandfather's Chair (Boston: E. P. Peabody, 1841); republished in *True Stories from History and Biography* (Boston: Ticknor, Reed & Fields, 1851; London: Low, 1853);

Liberty Tree: With the Last Words of Grandfather's Chair (Boston: E. P. Peabody, 1841); republished in *True Stories from History and Biography* (Boston: Ticknor, Reed & Fields, 1851; London: Low, 1853);

Biographical Stories for Children (Boston: Tappan & Dennet, 1842; London: Sonnenschein, [1883]); republished in *True Stories from History and Biography* (Boston: Ticknor, Reed & Fields, 1851; London: Low, 1853);

The Celestial Rail-Road (Boston: Wilder, 1843; London: Houlston & Stoneman, 1844);

Mosses from an Old Manse, 2 volumes (New York & London: Wiley & Putnam, 1846; revised and enlarged edition, Boston: Ticknor & Fields, 1854);

The Scarlet Letter, A Romance (Boston: Ticknor, Reed & Fields, 1850; London: Bogue/Hamilton/Johnson & Hunter/ Washbourne; Edinburgh: Johnston & Hunter/Oliver & Boyd; Dublin: McGlashan, 1851);

The House of the Seven Gables, A Romance (Boston: Ticknor, Reed & Fields, 1851; London: Bohn, 1851);

A Wonder-Book for Girls and Boys (Boston: Ticknor, Reed & Fields, 1852 [i.e., 1851]; London: Bohn, 1852);

The Snow-Image, and Other Twice-Told Tales (Boston: Ticknor, Reed & Fields, 1852 [i.e., 1851]; London: Bohn, 1851);

The Blithedale Romance (2 volumes, London: Chapman & Hall, 1852; 1 volume, Boston: Ticknor, Reed & Fields, 1852);

Life of Franklin Pierce (Boston: Ticknor, Reed & Fields, 1852; London: Routledge, 1853);

Tanglewood Tales, for Girls and Boys: Being a Second Wonder-Book (London: Chapman & Hall, 1853; Boston: Ticknor, Reed & Fields, 1853);

Transformation: or, The Romance of Monte Beni, 3 volumes (London: Smith, Elder, 1860); republished as *The Marble Faun: or, The Romance of Monte Beni,* 2 volumes (Boston: Ticknor & Fields, 1860);

Our Old Home: A Series of English Sketches (1 volume, Boston: Ticknor & Fields, 1863; 2 volumes, London: Smith, Elder, 1863);

Pansie: A Fragment (London: Hotten, 1864);

Passages from the American Note-Books, 2 volumes, edited by Sophia Peabody Hawthorne (Boston: Ticknor & Fields, 1868; London: Smith, Elder, 1868);

Passages from the English Note-Books, 2 volumes, edited by Sophia Peabody Hawthorne (Boston: Fields, Osgood, 1870; London: Strahan, 1870);

Passages from the French and Italian Note-Books, 2 volumes, edited by Sophia Peabody Hawthorne (London: Strahan, 1871; Boston: Osgood, 1872);

Septimus, A Romance, edited by Una Hawthorne and Robert Browning (London: King, 1872); republished as *Septimus Felton; or The Elixir of Life* (Boston: Osgood, 1872);

Fanshawe and Other Pieces (Boston: Osgood, 1876);

The Dolliver Romance and Other Pieces (Boston: Osgood, 1876; London: Kegan Paul, Trench, 1883);

Doctor Grimshawes Secret, A Romance, edited by Julian Hawthorne (Boston: Osgood, 1883; London: Longmans, Green, 1883);

Alice Doanes Appeal, Chiefly about War Matters, and Life of Franklin Pierce, volume 24 of the *Wayside Edition* (Boston & New York: Houghton, Mifflin, 1884);

The Ghost of Doctor Harris (N.p., 1900);

Twenty Days with Julian and Little Bunny (New York: Privately printed, 1904);

The American Notebooks, edited by Randall Stewart (New Haven: Yale University Press, 1932);

The English Notebooks, edited by Stewart (New York: Modern Language Association of America, 1941);

Hawthorne as Editor; Selections from the Writings in the American Magazine of Useful and Entertaining Knowledge, edited by Arlin Turner (Baton Rouge: Louisiana State University Press, 1941);

The American Notebooks, edited by Claude M. Simpson, volume 8 of *The Centenary Edition of the Works of Nathaniel Hawthorne* (Columbus: Ohio State University Press, 1973);

The Snow Image and Uncollected Tales, edited by J. Donald Crowley and Fredson Bowers, volume 11 of *The Centenary Edition of the Works of Nathaniel Hawthorne* (Columbus: Ohio State University Press, 1974);

The American Claimant Manuscripts: The Ancestral Footstep, Etherege, Grimshawe, edited by Edward H. Davidson, Simpson, and L. Neal Smith, volume 12 of *The Centenary Edition of the Works of Nathaniel Hawthorne* (Columbus: Ohio State University Press, 1977);

The Elixir of Life Manuscripts: Septimus Felton, Septimus Norton, and The Dolliver Romance, edited by Davidson, Simpson, and Smith, volume 13 of *The Centenary Edition of the Works of Nathaniel Hawthorne* (Columbus: Ohio State University Press, 1977);

Hawthorne's Lost Notebook, 1835–1841, edited by Hyatt H. Waggoner and Barbara S. Mouffe (University Park: Pennsylvania State University Press, 1978);

The French and Italian Notebooks, edited by Thomas Woodson, volume 14 of *The Centenary Edition of the Works of Nathaniel Hawthorne* (Columbus: Ohio State University Press, 1980).

Collection: *The Centenary Edition of the Works of Nathaniel Hawthorne,* 23 volumes (Columbus: Ohio State University Press, 1962–1997).

OTHER: *Journal of an African Cruiser; Comprising Sketches of the Canaries, the Cape de Verds, Liberia, Madeira, Sierra Leone, and Other Places of Interest on the West Coast of Africa. By an Officer of the U.S. Navy* [Horatio Bridge], edited by Nathaniel Hawthorne (New York & London: Wiley & Putnam, 1845).

Portrait of Hawthorne in 1840 by Charles Osgood
(Peabody Essex Museum)

Nathaniel Hawthorne:
A Chronology of His Life and Writings

This listing of the events that shaped Nathaniel Hawthorne's life includes information on the first publication of all of his significant writings. The sources for this chronology are Nathaniel Hawthorne: A Descriptive Bibliography *(1978), by C. E. Frazer Clark Jr., and the chronology found in the twenty-three-volume* Centenary Edition of the Works of Nathaniel Hawthorne *(1962–1997), edited by William L. Charvat, Thomas Woodson, and others.*

1804

4 July   Nathaniel Hathorne is born in Salem, Massachusetts, the second child of Elizabeth Clarke Manning Hathorne and Nathaniel Hathorne, mariner. The couple's first child, Elizabeth Manning Hathorne, had been born on 7 March 1802.

1808

Winter   Hathorne's father dies in Surinam (Dutch Guiana).

9 January   Hathorne's sister Maria Louisa Hathorne is born.

April   Hathorne family moves in with grandfather Richard Manning at Herbert Street, Salem.

1809

21 September   Sophia Amelia Peabody is born in Salem.

1813

19 April   Richard Manning dies. Hathorne's uncle Robert Manning becomes his guardian.

10 November   Hathorne injures his foot; he is lame for fourteen months.

1816

Summer   Hathornes spend season at Manning property in Maine.

1818

Late October   Hathornes move to Raymond, Maine.

1819

5 July   Hathorne enters school in Salem.

1821

Early October   Hathorne enrolls at Bowdoin College in Brunswick, Maine.

1825

26 August   "The Ocean," a poem Hathorne signs as "C.W.," is published in the *Salem Gazette;* it is his first known publication.

7 September   Hathorne is graduated from Bowdoin. He returns to family home at Herbert Street, Salem, and devotes himself to writing.

1827

Hathorne adds the letter *w* to his surname.

1828

Late October   Hawthorne publishes *Fanshawe* anonymously and at his own expense; he soon attempts to disassociate himself from the novel. His family moves to a house on Dearborn Street, Salem.

1830

2 November   "The Battle Omen," an unsigned poem attributed to Hawthorne, is published in the *Salem Gazette*.

12 November   "The Hollow of the Three Hills," unsigned, is published in the *Salem Gazette;* it is Hawthorne's first published tale.

23 November   "Sir William Phips," unsigned, is published in the *Salem Gazette*.

7 December   "Mrs Hutchinson," unsigned, is published in the *Salem Gazette*.

21 December   "An Old Woman's Tale," unsigned, is published in the *Salem Gazette*.

1831

"Sights from a Steeple," unsigned, and three other stories attributed to Hawthorne—"The Fated Family," unsigned; "The Haunted Quack. A Tale of a Canal Boat—By Joseph Nicholson"; and "The New England Village," unsigned—are published in *The Token; A Christmas and New Year's Present,* edited by S. G. Goodrich.

11 January   "Dr. Bullivant," unsigned, is published in the *Salem Gazette*.

1832

Hawthorne's family returns to the Herbert Street home; he travels alone to New Hampshire and Vermont.

"The Wives of the Dead," signed "F. . . . . ."; "My Kinsman, Major Molineux—By the Author of 'Lights [*sic*] from a Steeple'"; "Roger Malvin's Burial," unsigned; "The Gentle Boy," unsigned; "My Wife's Novel," attributed to Hawthorne; and "David Whicher—a North American Story," unsigned, attributed to Hawthorne, are published in *The Token; A Christmas and New Year's Present,* edited by S. G. Goodrich.

1833

"The Seven Vagabonds—By the Author of 'The Gentle Boy'"; "A Cure for Dispepsia," an unsigned story attributed to Hawthorne; "Sir William Pepperell—By the Author of 'Sights from a Steeple'"; and "The Canterbury Pilgrims," unsigned, are published in *The Token and Atlantic Souvenir. A Christmas and New Year's Present,* edited by S. G. Goodrich.

1834

November   "The Story Teller. No. I," unsigned, is published in the *New-England Magazine*.

December   "The Story Teller. No. II," unsigned, is published in the *New-England Magazine*.

1835

"The Haunted Mind—by the Author of Sights from a Steeple," "Alice Doane's Appeal—By the Author of the Gentle Boy," and "The Mermaid: A Reverie," unsigned, are published in *The Token and Atlantic Souvenir. A Christmas and New Year's Present,* edited by S. G. Goodrich.

"Little Annie's Ramble. By the Author of 'The Gentle Boy'" is published in *Youth's Keepsake. A Christmas and New Year's Gift for Young People.*

January   "The Gray Champion," a story signed "By the Author of 'The Gentle Boy,'" is published in the *New-England Magazine*.

February   "Old News. No. I," unsigned, and "My Visit to Niagara," signed "By the Author of 'The Gray Champion,'" are published in the *New-England Magazine*.

March   "Old News. No. II. The Old French War," unsigned, is published in the *New-England Magazine*.

April   "Young Goodman Brown," signed "By the Author of 'The Gray Champion,'" is published in the *New-England Magazine*.

May   "Old News. No. III. The Old Tory," unsigned, and "Wakefield," signed "By the Author of 'The Gray Champion,'" are published in the *New-England Magazine*.

June   "The Ambitious Guest," signed "By the Author of 'The Gray Champion'"; "Graves and Goblins," unsigned; and "A Rill from the Town-Pump," unsigned, are published in the *New-England Magazine*.

July   "The Old Maid in the Winding Sheet," signed "By the Author of 'The Gray Champion,'" is published in the *New-England Magazine*.

August   "The Vision of the Fountain," signed "By the Author of 'The Gray Champion,'" is published in the *New-England Magazine*.

November   "Sketches from Memory. By a Pedestrian. No. I," unsigned, and "The Devil in Manuscript," signed "By Ashley A. Royce," are published in the *New-England Magazine*.

December   "Sketches from Memory. By a Pedestrian. No. II," unsigned, is published in the *New-England Magazine*.

1836

"The Wedding Knell—By The Author of 'Sights from a Steeple,'" "The May Pole of Merry Mount—By the Author of 'The Gentle Boy,'" and "The Minister's Black Veil—By the Author of 'Sights from a Steeple'" are published in *The Token and Atlantic Souvenir. A Christmas and New Year's Present,* edited by S. G. Goodrich.

January   Hawthorne moves to Boston to accept his first employment: editorship of *The American Magazine of Useful and Entertaining Knowledge;* the first issue he edits is published in March.

February   "Old Ticonderoga. A Picture of the Past," unsigned, is published in *The American Monthly Magazine*.

23 February   "The Outcast, and other Poems; by S. G. Goodrich," review signed "H," is published in *Boston Daily Atlas*.

May	Hawthorne and his sister Elizabeth agree to write and edit *Peter Parley's Universal History, on the Basis of Geography.*
August	Hawthorne resigns as editor of *The American Magazine* and returns to Salem.

1837

	"Monsieur du Miroir–by the Author of Sights from a Steeple"; "Mrs. Bullfrog–by the Author of Wives of the Dead"; "Sunday at Home–by the Author of the Gentle Boy"; "The Man of Adamant," unsigned; "David Swan," unsigned; "The Great Carbuncle," unsigned, "Fancy's Show Box," unsigned; and "The Prophetic Pictures," unsigned, are published in *The Token and Atlantic Souvenir. A Christmas and New Year's Present,* edited by S. G. Goodrich.
January	"The Fountain of Youth," an unsigned story, is published in *Knickerbocker, or New-York Monthly Magazine;* it is collected as "Dr. Heidegger's Experiment."
March	"A Bell's Biography," signed "By the author of *Twice-Told Tales,* 'The Fountain of Youth,' etc.," is published in *Knickerbocker, or New-York Magazine.*
6 or 7 March	*Twice-Told Tales,* a collection of eighteen previously published stories, is published as "By Nathaniel Hawthorne."
29 July	*Peter Parley's Universal History,* edited by Hawthorne and his sister Elizabeth, is deposited for copyright; it is soon published.
September	"Edward Fane's Rosebud," an unsigned story, is published in *Knickerbocker, or New-York Magazine.*
October	"The Toll-Gatherer's Day. A Sketch of Transitory Life," signed "By the Author of Twice-told Tales," is published in *United States Magazine and Democratic Review.*
11 November	Hawthorne and his two sisters call on the Peabody sisters in Salem. Hawthorne is subsequently introduced to Sophia Peabody.

1838

	"Sylph Etherege," unsigned; "Peter Goldthwait's Treasure–by the Author of 'Twice-told Tales'"; "Endicott and the Red Cross," unsigned; "Night Sketches, beneath an Umbrella," unsigned; and "The Shaker Bridal–by the Author of 'Twice-told Tales'" are published in *The Token and Atlantic Souvenir. A Christmas and New Year's Present,* edited by S. G. Goodrich.
January	"Foot-Prints on the Sea-Shore," signed "By the Author of 'Twice-Told-Tales,'" is published in *United States Magazine and Democratic Review.*
	"Thomas Green Fessenden," signed "By Nathaniel Hawthorne," is published in *The American Monthly Magazine.*
1 January	*Time's Portraiture,* an address that is collected in *The Dolliver Romance,* is published as a broadside for patrons of the *Salem Gazette.*
February	"Snow-Flakes," signed "By the Author of 'Twice-Told Tales,'" is published in *United States Magazine and Democratic Review.*
March	"The Threefold Destiny. A Faëry Legend," signed "By Ashley Allen Royce," is published in *The American Monthly Magazine.*
May	"Tales of the Province-House. No. I. Howe's Masquerade," signed "By the Author of 'Twice Told Tales,'" is published in *United States Magazine and Democratic Review.*

July	"Tales of the Province-House. No. II. Edward Randolph's Portrait," signed "By the Author of 'Twice Told Tales,'" is published in *United States Magazine and Democratic Review*.
September	"Chippings with a Chisel," signed "By the Author of 'Twice Told Tales,'" and "Biographical Sketch of Jonathan Cilley," signed "By Nathaniel Hawthorne Esq.," are published in *United States Magazine and Democratic Review*.
December	"Tales of the Province-House. No. III. Lady Eleanore's Mantle," signed by Nathaniel Hawthorne, is published in *United States Magazine and Democratic Review*.

1839

January	"Tales of the Province-House. No. IV. Old Esther Dudley," signed "By Nathaniel Hawthorne," is published in *United States Magazine and Democratic Review*.
1 January	*The Sister Years,* unsigned, is published as a pamphlet for patrons of the *Salem Gazette*.
11 January	Hawthorne accepts the position of measurer at the Boston Custom House; he begins work on 17 January.
19 January	"The Lily's Quest," signed "By Nathaniel Hawthorne," is published in *The Southern Rose*.
24 July	Hawthorne becomes engaged to Sophia Peabody.

1840

	"The Man with the ____. A mystery," an unsigned story attributed to Hawthorne, is published in *Moral Tales*.
March	"John Inglefield's Thanksgiving," signed "By Rev. A. A. Royce," is published in *United States Magazine and Democratic Review*.
August	Sophia Peabody and her family move to Boston.
November	Hawthorne resigns from the Boston Custom House effective January.
3 December	*Grandfather's Chair: A History for Youth,* signed "By Nathaniel Hawthorne. Author of Twice-Told Tales," is published.

1841

Mid January	Hawthorne leaves the Boston Custom House and returns to Salem.
18 January	*Famous Old People: Being the Second Epoch of Grandfather's Chair,* signed "By Nathaniel Hawthorne. Author of Twice-Told Tales," is published.
March	*Liberty Tree: With the Last Words of Grandfather's Chair,* signed "By Nathaniel Hawthorne. Author of Twice-Told Tales," is published.
12 April	Hawthorne moves to the experimental community of Brook Farm in West Roxbury, Massachusetts.
Late August	Hawthorne changes his status at Brook Farm, becoming a paying boarder who is not required to do physical labor.
29 September	Hawthorne buys two shares in the Brook Farm project as part of a plan to build a home there.
Late October	Hawthorne leaves Brook Farm for Boston.

1842

13 January	The second, enlarged edition of *Twice-Told Tales* is published.

April	*Biographical Stories for Children,* signed "By Nathaniel Hawthorne," is published.
May	"A Virtuoso's Collection," signed "By Nathaniel Hawthorne," is published in *Boston Miscellany of Literature and Fashion.*
9 July	Hawthorne marries Sophia Peabody and moves to the Old Manse in Concord, Massachusetts.
17 October	Hawthorne resigns from the Brook Farm project and requests that the money he invested be returned.

1843

January	"The Old Apple-Dealer," signed "By Nathaniel Hawthorne, Author of 'Twice-Told Tales,'" is published in *Sargent's New Monthly Magazine of Literature, Fashion, and the Fine Arts.*
Early February	Sophia Hawthorne miscarries.
February	"The Antique Ring," signed "By Nathaniel Hawthorne," is published in *Sargent's New Monthly Magazine of Literature, Fashion, and the Fine Arts.*
	"The New Adam and Eve," signed "By Nathaniel Hawthorne," is published in *United States Magazine and Democratic Review.*
	"The Hall of Fantasy," signed "By Nathaniel Hawthorne," is published in *The Pioneer.*
March	"Egotism; or, The Bosom Serpent, From the Unpublished 'Allegories of the Heart,'" signed "By Nathaniel Hawthorne," is published in *United States Magazine and Democratic Review.*
	"The Birth-mark," signed "By Nathaniel Hawthorne," is published in *The Pioneer.*
April	"The Procession of Life," signed "By Nathaniel Hawthorne," is published in *United States Magazine and Democratic Review.*
May	"The Celestial Railroad," signed "By Nathaniel Hawthorne," is published in *United States Magazine and Democratic Review.*
June	"Buds and Bird-Voices," signed "By Nathaniel Hawthorne," is published in *United States Magazine and Democratic Review.*
August	"Little Daffydowndilly," signed "By Nathaniel Hawthorne," is published in *Boys' and Girls' Magazine.*
December	"Fire-Worship," signed "By Nathaniel Hawthorne," is published in *United States Magazine and Democratic Review.*

1844

January	"The Christmas Banquet. From the Unpublished Allegories of the Heart," signed "By Nathaniel Hawthorne," is published in *United States Magazine and Democratic Review.*
February	"A Good Man's Miracle," signed "By Nathaniel Hawthorne," is published in *The Child's Friend.*
March	"The Intelligence Office," signed "By Nathaniel Hawthorne," is published in *United States Magazine and Democratic Review.*
3 March	Una, the Hawthornes' first child, is born.
May	"Earth's Holocaust," signed "By Nathaniel Hawthorne," is published in *Graham's Lady's and Gentleman's Magazine.*

June	"The Artist of the Beautiful," signed "By Nathaniel Hawthorne," is published in *United States Magazine and Democratic Review*.
July	"A Select Party," signed "By Nathaniel Hawthorne," is published in *United States Magazine and Democratic Review*.
	"Drowne's Wooden Image," signed "By Nathaniel Hawthorne, Author of 'Twice Told Tales,'" is published in *Godey's Magazine and Lady's Book*.
November	"A Book of Autographs," signed "By Nathaniel Hawthorne," is published in *United States Magazine and Democratic Review*.
December	"Writings of Aubépine," signed "By Nathaniel Hawthorne," is published in *United States Magazine and Democratic Review;* it is collected as "Rappaccini's Daughter."

1845

April	"P.'s Correspondence," signed "By Nathaniel Hawthorne," is published in *United States Magazine and Democratic Review*.
20 June	*Journal of an African Cruiser,* a book by his friend Horatio Bridge that Hawthorne edits, is published.
September	Hawthorne and his family live with his mother and sisters on Herbert Street in Salem.
6 September	Hawthorne sues to recover the remainder of his investment in Brook Farm.

1846

25 March	"Wiley & Putnam's Library of American Books, Nos. XIII and XIV," an unsigned review of Melville's *Typee,* is published in *Salem Advertiser*.
April	Sophia Hawthorne moves to 77 Carver Street, Boston; Hawthorne joins her in May.
9 April	Hawthorne is sworn in as surveyor, or chief administrator, of the Salem Custom House.
29 April	"Scenes and Thoughts in Europe," unsigned review of George H. Calvert's *Scenes and Thoughts in Europe* and Charles Dickens's *Traveling Letters,* is published in *Salem Advertiser*.
2 May	"Views and Reviews in American History . . . ," an unsigned review of Simm's *Views and Reviews* and Hood's *Poems,* is published in *Salem Advertiser*.
Early June	*Mosses from an Old Manse,* a collection of tales and sketches signed "By Nathaniel Hawthorne," is published.
22 June	Julian, the Hawthornes' second child and only son, is born.
August	The Hawthornes rent a house on Chestnut Street in Salem.

1847

17 April	"The Supernaturalism of New England, By J. G. Whittier. New York: Wiley & Putnam's Library of American Books," an unsigned review, is published in *The Literary World*.
27 September	Hawthorne rents a home on Mall Street, Salem, where he and his wife and children live downstairs while his mother and sisters occupy the upstairs.
13 November	"Evangeline; by Henry Wadsworth Longfellow," an unsigned review, is published in *Salem Advertiser*.

1849

                "Main-street,–N. Hawthorne, Esq." is published in *Æsthetic Papers,* edited by Elizabeth P. Peabody.

7 June   Hawthorne is dismissed as surveyor at the Salem Custom House.

21 June   Letter to George S. Hillard, Salem, 18 June 1849, signed "Nath'l Hawthorne," is published in *The Boston Daily Advertiser.*

31 July   Hawthorne's mother dies.

1850

5 January   "The Unpardonable Sin. From an Unpublished Work," signed "By Nathaniel Hawthorne," is published in *Boston Weekly Museum;* it is collected as "Ethan Brand: A Chapter from an Abortive Romance."

24 January   "The Great Stone Face," signed "By Nathaniel Hawthorne," is published in *National Era.*

16 March   *The Scarlet Letter* is published.

Late May   The Hawthornes move to Lenox, Massachusetts, where they live in a red cottage owned by William and Caroline Sturgis Tappan.

5 August   Hawthorne meets Herman Melville at a picnic.

17 and
24 August   Melville's laudatory essay "Hawthorne and his Mosses," signed "By a Virginian Spending July in Vermont," is published in the *Literary World.*

1 November   "The Snow-Image," signed "By Nathaniel Hawthorne," is published in *International Miscellany of Literature, Art and Science.*

1851

9 April   *The House of the Seven Gables* is published.

20 May   Rose, the Hawthornes' third and last child, is born.

8 November   *A Wonder-Book for Girls and Boys* is published.

Mid November Hawthorne moves with his family to West Newton, Massachusetts.

18 or
20 December   *The Snow-Image, and Other Twice-Told Tales,* Hawthorne's last collection of stories, is published.

1852

1 February and
1 March   "Feathertop: A Moralized Legend," signed "By Nathaniel Hawthorne," is published in *International Miscellany of Literature, Art and Science.*

2 April   Hawthorne buys Bronson Alcott's house in Concord and land across from it from Ralph Waldo Emerson and Samuel Sewell.

Late May   The Hawthornes move to their new home, which they name "The Wayside."

14 July   *The Blithedale Romance* is published.

27 July   Hawthorne's sister Louisa dies in a steamboat accident.

11 September	*Life of Franklin Pierce*, the presidential campaign biography of Hawthorne's friend from Bowdoin, is published.

1853

17 April	President Pierce appoints Hawthorne as consul to the port of Liverpool, England. His appointment is confirmed by the Senate on 26 March.
6 July	Hawthorne sails with his family from Boston to Liverpool.
17 July	The Hawthornes arrive in Liverpool and settle temporarily into a boardinghouse in Duke Street.
1 August	Hawthorne begins consulship.
24 August	"Antaeus and the Pygmies," signed "By Nathaniel Hawthorne," is published in *The New York Evening Post*.
Late August	*Tanglewood Tales* is published.
1 September	The Hawthornes move into Rock Park, a three-story stone house in the Rock Ferry section of Liverpool, where they reside for nearly two years.

1855

1 January	Dr. Nathaniel Peabody, Hawthorne's father-in-law, dies.
18 June	The Hawthornes leave Rock Park to reduce living expenses and to facilitate travel. The family lives a nomadic existence for much of the following five years, traveling in the United Kingdom and on the Continent.
5 September	Hawthorne visits London for the first time.

1857

13 February	Hawthorne resigns his consulship, effective 31 August 1857.
April	"Lichfield and Uttoxeter," signed "By Nathaniel Hawthorne," is published in *Harper's New Monthly Magazine*.
April	"A Preface by Nathaniel Hawthorne" is published in Delia Bacon's *The Philosophy of the Plays of Shakspere*.
21 July	Hawthorne and his family move to Old Trafford, a suburb of Manchester. Hawthorne commutes to Liverpool.

1858

5–6 January	The Hawthornes travel to Paris.
January	The Hawthornes arrive in Italy where they travel. They settle in Rome in October and remain there until the end of May 1859.
24 October	Una first becomes ill with malaria, a disease from which she nearly dies in April 1859.

1860

28 February	*Transformation*, the English title for *The Marble Faun*, is published.
7 March	*The Marble Faun* is published.

16 June	Hawthorne and his family sail for Boston.
28 June	The Hawthornes arrive in Boston and return to The Wayside in Concord.
October	"Some of the Haunts of Burns by a Tourist Without Imagination or Enthusiasm," unsigned, is published in *Atlantic Monthly*.

1861

October	"Near Oxford," unsigned, is published in *Atlantic Monthly*.

1862

January	"Pilgrimage to Old Boston," unsigned, is published in *Atlantic Monthly*.
6 March	Hawthorne and William D. Ticknor leave Concord on a trip to Washington, D.C.
13 March	Hawthorne meets President Abraham Lincoln at the White House.
July	"Chiefly About War-Matters," signed "By a Peaceable Man," is published in *Atlantic Monthly*.
October	"Leamington Spa," signed "By a Peaceable Man," is published in *Atlantic Monthly*.
December	"About Warwick," unsigned, is published in *Atlantic Monthly*.

1863

January	"Recollections of a Gifted Woman," unsigned, is published in *Atlantic Monthly*.
March	"A London Suburb," unsigned, is published in *Atlantic Monthly*.
May	"Up the Thames," unsigned, is published in *Atlantic Monthly*.
July	"Outside Glimpses of English Poverty," unsigned, is published in *Atlantic Monthly*.
August	"Civic Banquets," unsigned, is published in *Atlantic Monthly*.
19 September	*Our Old Home* is published.

1864

29 March	Hawthorne leaves on a trip to New York with William D. Ticknor, who dies in Philadelphia on 10 April; Hawthorne returns to Concord.
18 May	Hawthorne dies in Plymouth, New Hampshire, while on a trip with Franklin Pierce. He is buried in Sleepy Hollow Cemetery in Concord, Massachusetts.

From Obscurity to Fame: *Fanshawe, Twice-Told Tales,* and *Mosses from an Old Manse*

Nathaniel Hawthorne was born Nathaniel Hathorne in Salem, Massachusetts, on 4 July 1804. (He added the letter w to his surname around the year 1827.) His place of birth is important because of his family's involvement in the history of the area. The first Hathorne in America, William, held various official positions, including deputy of the House of Delegates, although in time he became best remembered for ordering the whipping of a Quaker woman. William's son John was notorious for his unrepentant participation in the witchcraft trials. *The Puritan society of these ancestors influenced Hawthorne profoundly, as may be seen in some of his most impressive stories and novels, including "Young Goodman Brown," "The Minister's Black Veil," "The Gentle Boy,"* The Scarlet Letter *(1850), and* The House of the Seven Gables *(1851).*

Hawthorne's birthplace, 21 Union Street, Salem

Headstone in Salem cemetery for Hawthorne's great-grandfather, a judge at the witchcraft trials of 1692

Young Hawthorne

Publisher James T. Fields knew Hawthorne well professionally and personally, beginning in the late 1840s. Fields was partner in Ticknor, Reed, and Fields (later Ticknor and Fields), an important Boston firm of the mid nineteenth century that published authors such as Ralph Waldo Emerson, Henry David Thoreau, and Henry Wadsworth Longfellow, as well as Hawthorne. The house published all four of Hawthorne's mature novels, in addition to other titles. In the following excerpts from his memoir Yesterdays with Authors *(1872), Fields gives an impressionistic account of the author from childhood to young adulthood.*

There is a charming old lady, now living two doors from me, who dwelt in Salem when Hawthorne was born, and, being his mother's neighbor at that time (Mrs. Hawthorne then lived in Union Street), there came a message to her intimating that the baby could be seen by calling. So my friend tells me she went in, and saw the little winking thing in its mother's arms. She is very clear as to the beauty of the infant, even when only a week old, and remembers that "he was a pleasant child, quite handsome, with golden curls." She also tells me that Hawthorne's mother was a beautiful woman, with remarkable eyes, full of sensibility and expression, and that she was a person of singular purity of mind. Hawthorne's father, whom my friend knew well, she describes as a warm-hearted and kindly man, very fond of children.

He was somewhat inclined to melancholy, and of a reticent disposition. He was a great reader, employing all his leisure time at sea over books.

Hawthorne's father died when Nathaniel was four years old, and from that time his uncle Robert Manning took charge of his education, sending him to the best schools and afterwards to college. When the lad was about nine years old, while playing bat and ball at school, he lamed his foot so badly that he used two crutches for more than a year. His foot ceased to grow like the other, and the doctors of the town were called in to examine the little lame boy. He was not perfectly restored till he was twelve years old. His kind-hearted schoolmaster, Joseph Worcester, the author of the Dictionary, came every day to the house to hear the boy's lessons, so that he did not fall behind in his studies.

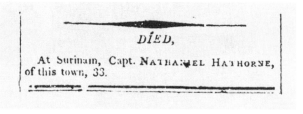

Etching of Hawthorne's father and the notice of his death in winter 1808

Moderate Views

With passions unruffled untainted by pride.

By reason my life let me square.

The wants of my nature are cheaply supplied

And the rest are but folly and care.

How vainly through infinite trouble and strife,

The many their labours employ,

Since all that is truly delightful in life,

Is what all if they please may enjoy.

Nathaniel Hathorne.

Salem February 13th 1817

Poem written by eight-year-old Hawthorne (from Kenneth W. Cameron, Hawthorne among His Contemporaries, *1968)*

Salem Thursday December 9 1813

Dear Uncle

I hope you are well
and I hope Richard is too My foot is no
better Louisa has got so well that she has
begun to go school but she did not go
this forenoon because it snowd Maam is
going to send for Doctor Kitridge to day
when William Cross comes home at 12
o cloch and may be he will do some good
for Doctor Barstow has not and I dont
know as Doctor Kitridge will it is
know 4 weeks Yesterday. since I have
been to school and I dont know but
but it will be 4 weeks longer before I

Hawthorne's earliest extant letter, written to his uncle Robert Manning on 9 December 1813. The nine-year-old Hawthorne mentions a foot injury that resulted in a long period of lameness. In the letter, Hawthorne refers to his uncle Richard Manning. Louisa is Hawthorne's sister, Louisa Hathorne. Maam is Hawthorne's mother, Elizabeth Clarke Manning Hathorne. Doctor Kitridge is probably Oliver Kittredge, the Manning family doctor. William Cross was a young clerk at the stage line owned by his father, Hawthorne's uncle Samuel Manning, and Holton Dale. Gideon Barstow was married to Hawthorne's cousin Nancy Forrester. Hannah Lord was a niece of Hawthorne's grandmother Miriam Manning. Elizabeth is Hawthorne's sister (from Kenneth Cameron, Hawthorne Among his Contemporaries, 1968).

go again I have been out in the office
two or three times and have set down
on the step of the door and once I
hopped out into the street. yesterday I
went out in the office and had a cake
Hannah carried me out once but not
then Elizabeth and Louisa send their
love to you I hope you will write
to me soon but I have nothing more
to write so good bye dear Uncle your
affectionate Nephew
                    Nathaniel Hathorne

Robert Manning, one of Hawthorne's four maternal uncles, who became a father figure for his nephew.
The other uncles were Richard, William, and Samuel (Peabody Essex Museum).

[There is a tradition in the Manning family that Mr. Worcester was very much interested in Maria Manning (a sister of Mrs. Hawthorne), who died in 1814, and that this was one reason of his attention to Nathaniel.] The boy used to lie flat upon the carpet, and read and study the long days through. Some time after he had recovered from this lameness he had an illness causing him to lose the use of his limbs, and he was obliged to seek again the aid of his old crutches, which were then pieced out at the ends to make them longer. When a little child, and as soon almost as he began to read, the authors he most delighted in were Shakespeare, Milton, Pope, and Thomson. The "Castle of Indolence" was an especial favorite with him during boyhood. The first book he bought with his own money was a copy of Spenser's "Faery Queen."

One who watched him during his childhood tells me, that "when he was six years old his favorite book was Bunyan's 'Pilgrim's Progress': and that whenever he went to visit his Grandmother Hawthorne, he used to take the old family copy to a large chair in a corner of the room near a window, and read it by the hour, without once speaking. No one ever thought of asking how much of it he understood. I think it one of the happiest circumstances of his training, that nothing was ever explained to him, and that there was no professedly intellectual person in the family to usurp the place of Providence and supplement its shortcomings, in order to make him what he was never intended to be. His mind developed itself; intentional cultivation might have spoiled it. . . . . He used to invent long stories, wild and fanciful, and tell where he was going when he grew up, and of the wonderful adventures he was to meet with, always ending with, 'And I'm never coming back again,' in quite a solemn tone, that enjoined upon us the advice to value him the more while he stayed with us."

When he could scarcely speak plain, it is recalled by members of the family that the little fellow would go about the house, repeating with vehement emphasis and gestures certain stagy lines from Shakespeare's Richard III., which he had overheard from older persons about him. One line, in particular, made a great impression upon him, and he would start up on the most unexpected occasions and fire off in his loudest tone,

Stand back, my Lord, and let the coffin pass."

On the 21st of August, 1820, No. 1 of "The Spectator, edited by N. Hathorne," neatly written in printed letters by the editor's own hand, appeared. A prospectus was issued the week before, setting forth that the paper would be published on Wednesdays, "price 12 cents per annum, payment to be made at the end of the year." Among the advertisements is the following:–

"Nathaniel Hathorne proposes to publish by subscription a NEW EDITION of the MISERIES OF AUTHORS, to which will be added a SEQUEL, containing FACTS and REMARKS drawn from his own experience."

Six numbers only were published. The following subjects were discussed by young "Hathorne" in the Spectator,–"On Solitude," "The End of the Year," "On Industry," "On Benevolence," "On Autumn," "On Wealth," "On Hope," "On Courage." The poetry on the last page of each number was evidently written by the editor, except in one instance, when an Address to the Sun is signed by one of his sisters. In one of the numbers he apologizes that no deaths of any importance have taken place in the town. Under the head of Births, he gives the following news, "The lady of Dr. Winthrop Brown, a son and heir. Mrs. Hathorne's cat, seven kittens. We hear that both of the above ladies are in a state of convalescence." One of the literary advertisements reads:–

"Blank Books made and for sale by N. Hathorne."

While Hawthorne was yet a little fellow the family moved to Raymond in the State of Maine; here his out-of-door life did him great service, for he grew tall and strong, and became a good shot and an excellent fisherman. Here also his imagination was first stimulated, the wild scenery and the primitive manners of the people contributing greatly to awaken his thought. At seventeen he entered Bowdoin College, and after his graduation returned again to live in Salem. During his youth he had an impression that he would die before the age of twenty-five; but the Mannings, his ever-watchful and kind relations, did everything possible for the care of his health, and he was tided safely over the period when he was most delicate. Professor Packard told me that when Hawthorne was a student at Bowdoin in his freshman year, his Latin compositions showed such facility that they attracted the special attention of those who examined them. The Professor also remembers that Hawthorne's English compositions elicited from Professor Newman (author of the work on Rhetoric) high commendations.

When a youth Hawthorne made a journey into New Hampshire with his uncle, Samuel Manning.

Hawthorne's verse, recorded in his copybook circa 1815 (American Art Association Anderson Galleries catalogue, Rebecca B. Manning, sale number 3927, 19–20 November 1931; reprinted in Hawthorne at Auction, *p. 232)*

The home of Hawthorne's mother in Raymond, Maine, where her son "ran quite wild." The family moved to this house in October 1818 (Peabody Essex Museum).

They travelled in a two-wheeled chaise, and met with many adventures which the young man chronicled in his home letters. Some of the touches in these epistles were very characteristic and amusing, and showed in those early years his quick observation and descriptive power. The travellers "put up" at Farmington, in order to rest over Sunday. Hawthorne writes to a member of the family in Salem: "As we were wearied with rapid travelling, we found it impossible to attend divine service, which was, of course, very grievous to us both. In the evening, however, I went to a Bible class, with a very polite and agreeable gentleman, whom I afterwards discovered to be a strolling tailor, of very questionable habits."

When the travellers arrived in the Shaker village of Canterbury, Hawthorne at once made the acquaintance of the Community there, and the account which he sent home was to the effect that the brothers and sisters led a good and comfortable life, and he wrote: "If it were not for the ridiculous ceremonies, a man might do a worse thing than to join them." Indeed, he spoke to them about becoming a member of the Society, and was evidently much impressed with the thrift and peace of the establishment.

This visit in early life to the Shakers is interesting as suggesting to Hawthorne his beautiful story of "The Canterbury Pilgrims," which is in his volume of "The Snow-Image, and other Twice-Told Tales."

A lady of my acquaintance (the identical "Little Annie" of the "Ramble" in "Twice-Told Tales") recalls the young man "when he returned home after his collegiate studies." "He was even then," she says, "a most noticeable person, never going into society, and deeply engaged in reading everything he could lay his hands on. It was said in those days that he had read every book in the Athenæum Library in Salem." This lady remembers that when she was a child, and before Hawthorne had printed any of his stories, she used to sit on his knee and lean her head on his shoulder, while by the hour he would fascinate her with delightful legends, much more wonderful and beautiful than any she has ever read since in printed books.

The traits of the Hawthorne character were stern probity and truthfulness. Hawthorne's mother had many characteristics in common with her distinguished son, she also being a reserved and thoughtful person. Those who knew the family describe the son's affection for her as of the deepest and tenderest nature, and they remember that when she died his grief was almost insupportable. The anguish he suffered from her loss is distinctly recalled by many persons still living, who visited the family at that time in Salem.

—Yesterdays with Authors, pp. 42–47

. . . .

Later in his reminiscence Fields returned to Hawthorne as a young man.

I have lately met an early friend of Hawthorne's, older than himself, who knew him intimately all his life long, and I have learned some additional facts about his youthful days. Soon after he left college he wrote some stories which he called "Seven Tales of my Native Land." The motto which he chose for the title-page was "We are Seven," from Wordsworth. My informant read the tales in manuscript, and says some of them were very striking, particularly one or two Witch Stories. As soon as the little book was well prepared for the press he deliberately threw it into the fire, and sat by to see its destruction.

When about fourteen he wrote out for a member of his family a list of the books he had at that time been reading. The catalogue was a long one, but my informant remembers that The Waverly Novels, Rousseau's Works, and The Newgate Calender were among them. Serious remonstrances were made by the family touching the perusal of this last work, but he persisted in going through it to the end. He had an objection in his boyhood to reading much that was called "true and useful." Of history in general he was not very fond, but he read Froissart with interest, and Clarendon's History of the Rebellion. He is remembered to have said at that time "he cared very little for the history of the world before the fourteenth century." After he left college he read a great deal of French literature, especially the works of Voltaire and his contemporaries. He rarely went into the streets during the daytime, unless there was to be a gathering of the people for some public purpose, such as a political meeting, a military muster, or a fire. A great conflagration attracted him in a peculiar manner, and he is remembered, while a young man in Salem, to have been often seen looking on, from some dark corner, while the fire was raging. When General Jackson, of whom he professed himself a partisan, visited Salem in 1833, he walked out to the boundary of the town to meet him,—not to speak to him, but only to look at him. When he came home at night he said he found only a few men and boys collected, not enough people, without the assistance he rendered, to welcome the General with a good cheer. It is said that Susan, in the "Village Uncle," one of the "Twice-Told Tales," is not altogether a creation of his fancy. Her father was a fisherman living in Salem, and Hawthorne was constantly telling the members of his family how charming she was, and he always spoke of her as his "mermaid." He said she had a great deal of what the French call *espièglerie*.

There was another young beauty, living at that time in his native town, quite captivating to him, though in a different style from the mermaid. But if his head and heart were turned in his youth by these two nymphs in his native town, there was soon a transfer of his affections to quite another direction. His new passion was a much more permanent one, for now there dawned upon him so perfect a creature that he fell in love irrevocably; all his thoughts and all his delights centred in her, who suddenly became indeed the mistress of his soul. She filled the measure of his being, and became a part and parcel of his life. Who was this mysterious young person that had crossed his boyhood's path and made him hers forever? Whose daughter was she that could thus enthrall the ardent young man in Salem, who knew as yet so little of the world and its sirens? She is described by one who met her long before Hawthorne made her acquaintance as "the prettiest low-born lass that ever ran on the greensward," and she must have been a radiant child of beauty, indeed, that girl! She danced like a fairy, she sang exquisitely, so that every one who knew her seemed amazed at her perfect way of doing everything she attempted. Who was it that thus summoned all this witchery, making such a tumult in young Hawthorne's bosom? She was "daughter to Leontes and Hermione," king and queen of Sicilia, and her name was Perdita! It was Shakespeare who introduced Hawthorne to his first real love, and the lover never forgot his mistress. He was constant ever, and worshipped her through life. Beauty always captivated him. Where there was beauty he fancied other good gifts must naturally be in possession. During his childhood homeliness was always repulsive to him. When a little boy he is remembered to have said to a woman who wished to be kind to him, "Take her away! She is ugly and fat, and has a loud voice."

When quite a young man he applied for a situation under Commodore Wilkes on the Exploring Expedition, but did not succeed in obtaining an appointment. He thought this a great misfortune, as he was fond of travel, and he promised to do all sorts of wonderful things, should he be allowed to join the voyagers.

One very odd but characteristic notion of his, when a youth, was, that he should like a competent income which should neither increase nor diminish, for then, he said, it would not engross too much of his attention. Surrey's little poem, "The Means to obtain a Happy Life," expressed exactly what his idea of happiness was when a lad. When a school-boy he wrote verses for the newspapers, but he ignored their existence in after years with a smile

Hawthorne's 7 March 1820 letter to his mother in Raymond, Maine. When Hawthorne returned to Salem to attend school in summer 1819, his mother and sisters remained in Raymond, where the mother hoped to live permanently. In Salem, Hawthorne lived with his mother's sister, Mary Manning, and mother, Miriam Manning. Hawthorne's mother returned to Salem in 1822. The fifteen-year-old asks, "Should you want me to be a Minister, Doctor or Lawyer? A Minister I will not be" (Peabody Essex Museum).

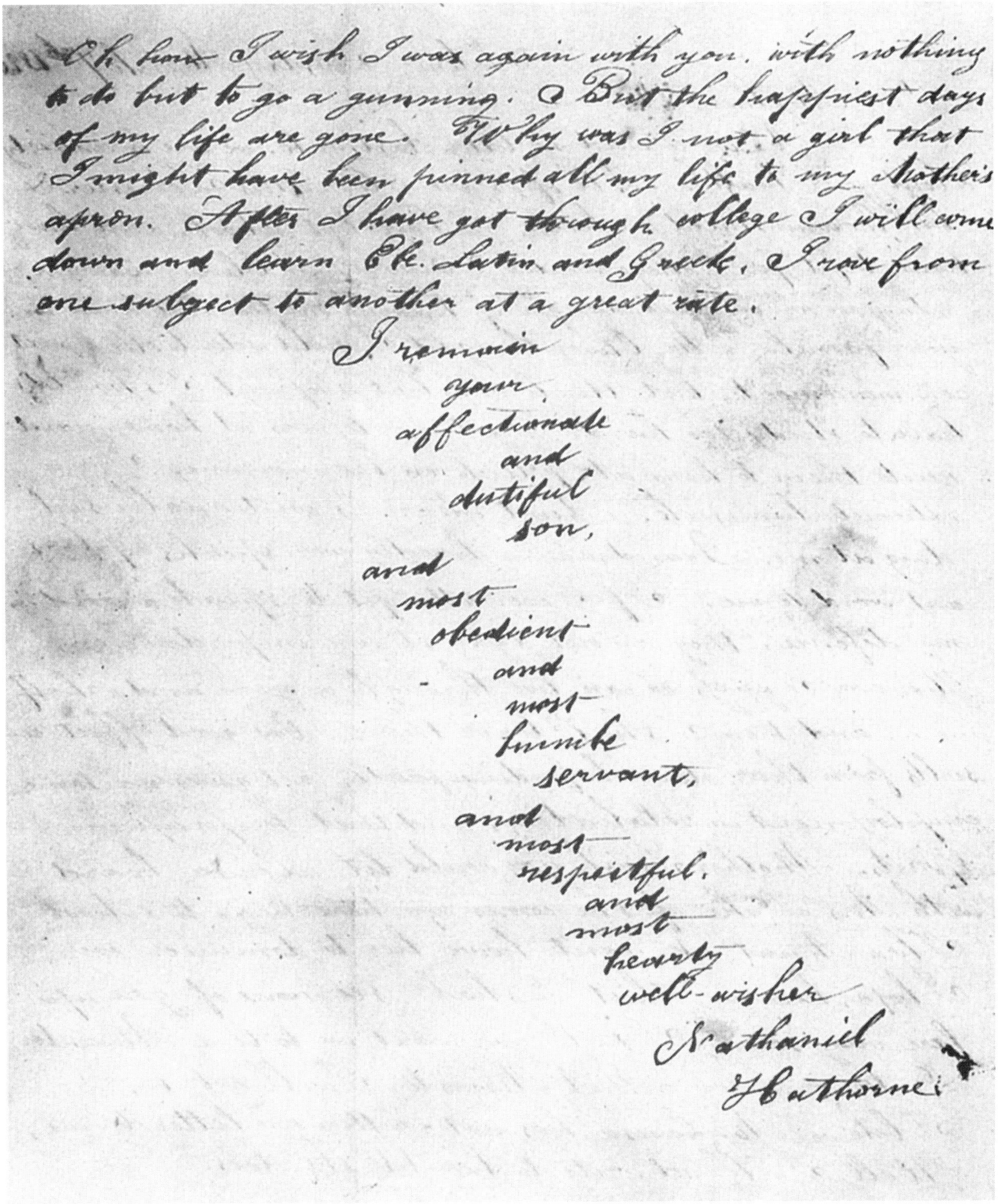

Oh how I wish I was again with you, with nothing
to do but to go a gunning. But the happiest days
of my life are gone. Why was I not a girl that
I might have been pinned all my life to my Mother's
apron. After I have got through college I will come
down and learn Ek. Latin and Greek, I rove from
one subject to another at a great rate.

    I remain
      your,
      affectionate
       and
       dutiful
        son,
    and
     most
      obedient
       and
       most
       humble
        servant,
    and
     most
      respectful,
       and
      most
       hearty
       well-wisher
        Nathaniel
        Hathorne

of droll disgust. One of his quatrains lives in the memory of a friend, who repeated it to me recently:—

"The ocean hath its silent caves,
   Deep, quiet, and alone;
Above them there are troubled waves,
   Beneath them there are none."

When the Atlantic Cable was first laid, somebody, not knowing the author of the lines, quoted them to Hawthorne as applicable to the calmness said to exist in the depths of the ocean. He listened to the verse, and then laughingly observed, "I know something of the deep sea myself."

In 1836 he went to Boston, I am told, to edit the "American Magazine of Useful Knowledge," for which he was to be paid a salary of six hundred dollars a year. The proprietors soon became insolvent, so that he received nothing, but he kept on just the same as if he had been paid regularly. The plan of the work proposed by the publishers of the magazine admitted no fiction into its pages. The magazine was printed on coarse paper and was illustrated by engravings painful to look at. There were no contributors except the editor, and he wrote the whole of every number. Short biographical sketches of eminent men and historical narratives filled up its pages. I have examined the columns of this deceased magazine, and read Hawthorne's narrative of Mrs. Dustan's captivity. Mrs. Dustan was carried off by the Indians from Haverhill, and Hawthorne does not much commiserate the hardships she endured, but reserves his sympathy for her husband, who was *not* carried into captivity, and suffered nothing from the Indians, but who, he says, was a tender-hearted man, and took care of the children during Mrs. D.'s absence from home, and probably knew that his wife would be more than a match for a whole tribe of savages.

When the Rev. Mr. Cheever was knocked down and flogged in the streets of Salem and then imprisoned, Hawthorne came out of his retreat and visited him regularly in jail, showing strong sympathy for the man and great indignation for those who had maltreated him.

Those early days in Salem,—how interesting the memory of them must be to the friends who knew and followed the gentle dreamer in his budding career! When the whisper first came to the timid boy, in that "dismal chamber in Union Street," that he too possessed the soul of an artist, there were not many about him to share the divine rapture that must have filled his proud young heart. Outside of his own little family circle, doubting and desponding eyes looked upon him, and many a stupid head wagged in derision as he

passed by. But there was always waiting for him a sweet and honest welcome by the pleasant hearth where his mother and sisters sat and listened to the beautiful creations of his fresh and glowing fancy. We can imagine the happy group gathered around the evening lamp! "Well, my son," says the fond mother, looking up from her knitting-work, "what have you got for us to-night? It is some time since you read us a story, and your sisters are as impatient as I am to have a new one." And then we can hear, or think we hear, the young man begin in a low and modest tone the story of "Edward Fane's Rosebud," or "The Seven Vagabonds," or perchance (O tearful, happy evening!) that tender idyl of "The Gentle Boy!" What a privilege to hear for the first time a "Twice-Told Tale," before it was even *once* told to the public! And I know with what rapture the delighted little audience must have hailed the advent of every fresh indication that genius, so seldom a visitant at any fireside, had come down so noiselessly to bless their quiet hearthstone in the sombre old town. In striking contrast to Hawthorne's audience nightly convened to listen while he read his charming tales and essays, I think of poor Bernardin de Saint-Pierre, facing those hard-eyed critics at the house of Madame Neckar, when as a young man and entirely unknown he essayed to read his then unpublished story of "Paul and Virginia." The story was simple and the voice of the poor and nameless reader trembled. Everybody was unsympathetic and gaped, and at the end of a quarter of an hour Monsieur de Buffon, who always had a loud way with him, cried out to Madame Neckar's servant, "Let the horses be put to my carriage!"

Hawthorne seems never to have known that raw period in authorship which is common to most growing writers, when the style is "overlanguaged," and when it plunges wildly through the "sandy deserts of rhetoric," or struggles as if it were having a personal difficulty with Ignorance and his brother Platitude. It was capitally said of Chateaubriand that "he lived on the summits of syllables," and of another young author that he was so dully good, that he made even virtue disreputable." Hawthorne had no such literary vices to contend with. His looks seemed from the start to be

"Commercing with the skies,"

and he marching upward to the goal without impediment. I was struck a few days ago with the untruth, so far as Hawthorne is concerned, of a passage in the Preface to Endymion. Keats says: "The imagination of a boy is healthy, and the mature imagination of a man is healthy; but there is a space of life between, in

The Pin Society

Be it remembered, that on the 10 day of June, in the year of our Lord 1820, we, the undersigned Subscribers, have conglomerated ourselves into a Corporation, under the name of *The Pin Society*, and have consented to the following rules of the said Society.

                    Nathaniel Hathorne
                    M L Hathorne

First page of the rules of The Pin Society, which comprised Hawthorne and his sister Maria Louisa (American Art Association Anderson Galleries catalogue, Rebecca B. Manning, sale number 3927, 19–20 November 1931; reprinted in Hawthorne at Auction, *p. 234)*

The first page of the initial issue of Hawthorne's manuscript newspaper that he distributed to his family. Probably produced on 14 August 1820, this two-page number was followed by six more, all four pages long, that he delivered on Wednesdays (Peabody Essex Museum).

which the soul is in a ferment, the character unde-cided, the way of life uncertain, the ambition thick-sighted." Hawthorne's imagination had no mid-dle period of decadence or doubt, but continued, as it began, in full vigor to the end.

                    – *Yesterdays with Authors,* pp. 65–71

. . . .

After he returned from the funeral of Mrs. Franklin Pierce, Hawthorne on a December 1863 afternoon spoke to Fields of his mother's home in Maine.

The same day, as the sunset deepened and we sat together, Hawthorne began to talk in an autobio-graphical vein, and gave us the story of his early life, of which I have already written somewhat. He said at an early age he accompanied his mother and sister to the township in Maine, which his grandfather had purchased. That, he continued, was the happiest period of his life, and it lasted through several years, when he was sent to school in Salem. "I lived in Maine," he said, "like a bird of the air, so perfect was the freedom I enjoyed. But it was there I first got my cursed habits of solitude." During the moon-light nights of winter he would skate until midnight all alone upon Sebago Lake, with the deep shadows of the icy hills on either hand. When he found him-self far away from his home and weary with the exertion of skating, he would sometimes take refuge in a log-cabin, where half a tree would be burning on the broad hearth. He would sit in the ample chimney and look at the stars through the great aperture through which the flames went roaring up. "Ah," he said, "how well I recall the summer days also, when, with my gun, I roamed at will through the woods of Maine. How sad middle life looks to people of erratic temperaments. Everything is beau-tiful in youth, for all things are allowed to it then."

The early home of the Hawthornes in Maine must have been a lonely dwelling-place indeed. A year ago (May 12, 1870) the old place was visited by one who had a true feeling for Hawthorne's genius, and who thus graphically described the spot.

"A little way off the main-travelled road in the town of Raymond there stood an old house which has much in common with houses of its day, but which is distinguished from them by the more evi-dent marks of neglect and decay. Its unpainted walls are deeply stained by time. Cornice and window-ledge and threshold are fast falling with the weight of years. The fences were long since removed from all the enclosures, the garden-wall is broken down, and the garden itself is now grown up to pines where shadows fall dark and heavy upon the old

and mossy roof; fitting roof-trees for such a man-sion, planted there by the hands of Nature herself, as if she could not realize that her darling child was ever to go out from his early home. The highway once passed its door, but the location of the road has been changed; and now the old house stands solitarily apart from the busy world. Longer than I can remember, and I have never learned how long, this house has stood untenanted and wholly unused, except, for a few years, as a place of public worship; but, for myself, and for all who know its earlier history, it will ever have the deepest interest, for it was *the early home of Nathaniel Hawthorne.*

"Often have I, when passing through that town, turned aside to study the features of that landscape, and to reflect upon the influence which his sur-roundings had upon the development of this author's genius. A few rods to the north runs a little mill-stream, its sloping bank once covered with grass, now so worn and washed by the rains as to show but little except yellow sand. Less than half a mile to the west, this stream empties into an arm of Sebago Lake. Doubtless, at the time the house was built, the forest was so much cut away in that direc-tion as to bring into view the waters of the lake, for a mill was built upon the brook about half-way down the valley, and it is reasonable to suppose that a clearing was made from the mill to the landing upon the shore of the pond; but the pines have so far regained their old dominion as completely to shut out the whole prospect in that direction. Indeed, the site affords but a limited survey, except to the northwest. Across a narrow valley in that direction lie open fields and dark pine-covered slopes. Beyond these rise long ranges of forest-crowned hills, while in the far distance every hue of rock and tree, of field and grove, melts into the soft blue of Mount Washington. The spot must ever have had the utter loneliness of the pine forests upon the borders of our northern lakes. The deep silence and dark shadows of the old woods must have filled the imagination of a youth possessing Hawthorne's sensibility with images which later years could not dispel.

"To this place came the widowed mother of Hawthorne in company with her brother, an origi-nal proprietor and one of the early settlers of the town of Raymond. This house was built for her, and here she lived with her son for several years in the most complete seclusion. Perhaps she strove to con-ceal here a grief which she could not forget. In what way, and to what extent, the surroundings of his boyhood operated in moulding the character and developing the genius of that gifted author, I leave to the reader to determine. I have tried simply to draw a faithful picture of his early home."

                    – *Yesterdays with Authors,* pp. 113–115

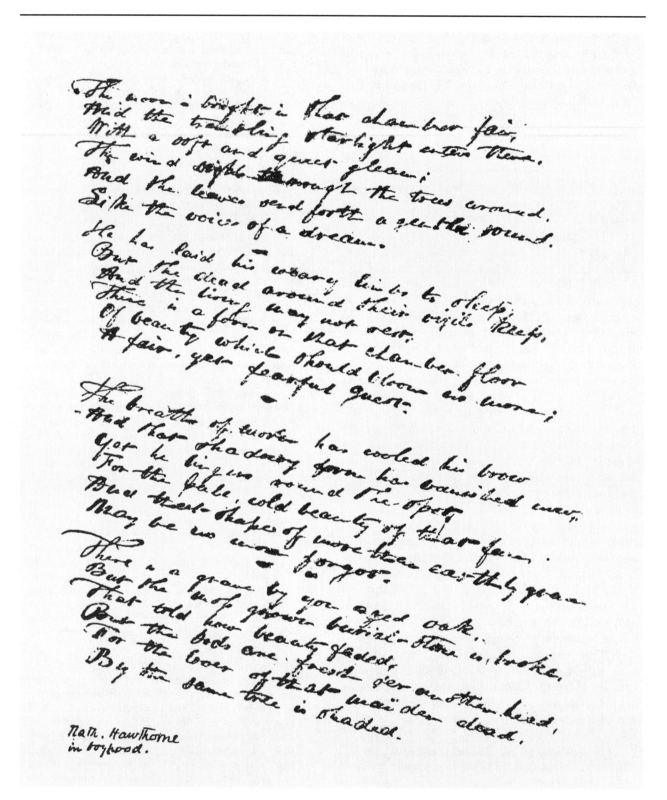

A poem Hawthorne wrote at age sixteen. In 1865 the author's sister Elizabeth wrote of the poem to one of her nieces: "These verses have not much merit;
they were written merely for amusement, and perhaps for the pleasure of seeing them in print,—for some like this he sent to a Boston newspaper."
Julian Hawthorne added the note "Nath. Hawthorne in boyhood" at the bottom left of the page (American Art Association
Anderson Galleries catalogue, Julian Hawthorne, sale number 4283, 9–10 December 1936;
reprinted in Hawthorne at Auction, p. 276).

Bowdoin College and *Fanshawe*

Hawthorne attended Bowdoin College in Maine from October 1821 until his graduation on 7 September 1825, when he returned to live with his family in Salem. Three years after his graduation Hawthorne paid for the publication of his first novel, Fanshawe, *which involves a love triangle and an attempted kidnapping, set at a fictional college that is clearly based on Bowdoin.*

Some one thousand copies of Fanshawe *were published anonymously in late October 1828 by Marsh and Capen in Boston. Hawthorne later regretted its existence to the degree that he would not acknowledge the novel as his creation. Today, this first American college novel is one of the rarest books by a major American writer.*

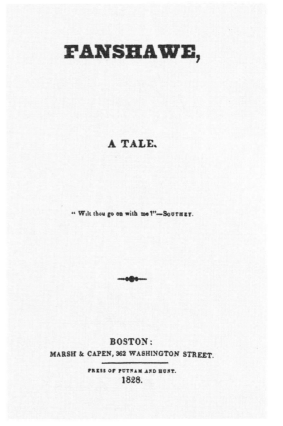

FANSHAWE,

A TALE.

" Wilt thou go on with me?"—SOUTHEY.

BOSTON:
MARSH & CAPEN, 362 WASHINGTON STREET.
PRESS OF PUTNAM AND HUNT.
1828.

Title page for Hawthorne's first novel, one of the rarest editions of any book by a major American writer. Although some one thousand copies of the novel were printed, most were destroyed by a fire in the publisher's warehouse (C. E. Frazer Clark Jr., Nathaniel Hawthorne: A Descriptive Bibliography, *1978).*

An engraving of Bowdoin College, circa 1821

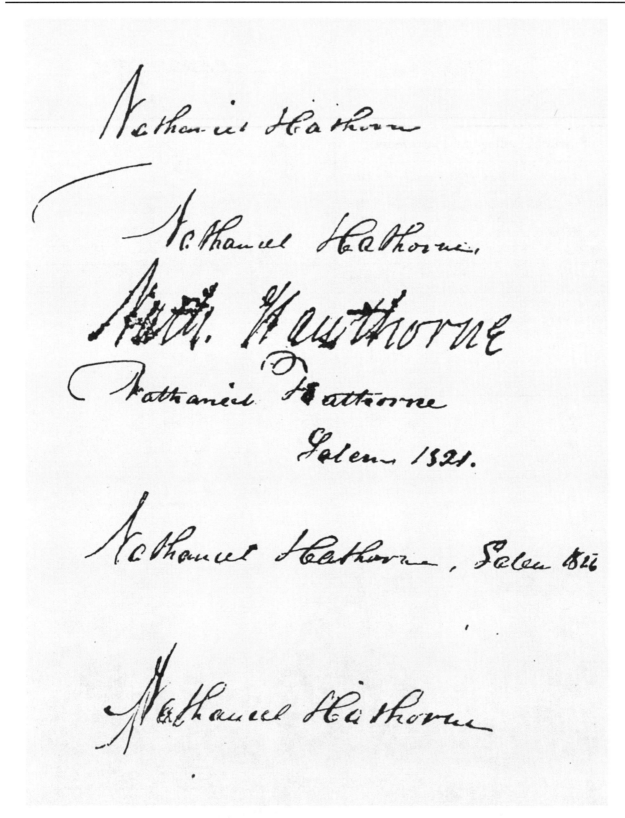

Hawthorne's signatures on the flyleaf of his copy of an edition of the writings of the Roman historian Sallust
(from Kenneth W. Cameron, Hawthorne among His Contemporaries*)*

Hawthorne's 12 August 1823 letter to Robert Manning, in which he discusses college and family (Peabody Essex Museum)

An Anonymous Novel

Although it was preceded by a few notices of Fanshawe, *William Leggett's review is the first substantial criticism of any work by Hawthorne. At the end of his review, Leggett, an author, newspaperman, and abolitionist, guesses that the author of the novel is N. P. (Nathaniel Parker) Willis, a well-known poet from Maine.*

Review of *Fanshawe, a Tale*
William Leggett
The Critic (New York), 1 (22 November 1828): 53–55

Who wrote this book? Yet what need is there to know the name of the author, in order to pronounce a decision? Be he whom he may, this is not his first attempt, and we hope it will not be his last. The mind that produced this little, interesting volume, is capable of making great and rich additions to our native literature; and it will, or we shall be sadly mistaken. The author is a scholar, though he makes no ostentatious display of scholarship; he is a poet, though there are not two dozen metrical lines in the volume with which to substantiate the assertion; he is a gentleman, though the nearest approach to gentlemen in his pages, are two country college boys; and he possesses a heart alive to the beauties of nature, and the beauties of sentiment, and replete with all those kindly feelings which adorn and dignify human nature. His story is told in language, simple, chaste and appropriate; describing, so that the eye of the reader sees them, all the beautiful and varied traits of the landscape in which he has chosen to locate his narrative; describing the heavens in all their different aspects of storm and sunshine, in the gray twilight of morning, the sleepy splendour of noonday, and the gorgeous effulgence of sunset; and describing (a more difficult thing than all) the human heart, both as it lightly flutters in a young, pure, happy maiden's bosom, and as it heavily beats beneath the yellow and shrivelled skin of an octogenarian virago; both as it animates the dark recesses of a ruffian's breast, and the young, ardent, impetuous bosom of an honourable and thoughtless lad of eighteen. It takes a poet to do this. The delicacy of Fanshawe's attachment; the nice propriety of conduct which both he and his rival observe towards the object of their affection, and towards each other; the frankness with which one asked, and the refined and courteous manner in which the other granted, his forgiveness, after some harsh words had escaped between them—and a thousand other circumstances—are convincing proofs that the author is a

William Leggett

gentlemen; for none but a gentleman understands these things. There is no parade of manners, no mock sentiment, no stuff, about him; but there is sincerity, and ease, and urbanity, and an ever wakeful regard for others' feelings, all of which he imparts to his characters, giving them an irresistible attraction. Though we do not exactly subscribe to the sentiment of Dr. Johnson's humorous parody, 'Who drives fat oxen, should himself be fat;' yet we are fully persuaded that it takes a gentleman to describe a gentleman. Your common writers make such stiff, such tape and buckram creatures of them, that they are truly insupportable. That the author is a scholar, there is much evidence; though the reader does not every here and there meet with a Greek or a Latin, or a Hebrew quotation; an affection of learning which an intolerable ignoramus may use, as well as one of real information. The true scholar shows his literary, as men ought to show their pecuniary wealth in their expenditures, not by sudden bursts of profusion, but by continual and salutary munificence. Such are the evidences of scholarship which we find in *Fanshawe*.

But the book has faults. The plot lacks probability; there is too much villany in some of the characters; or rather, there are too many bad characters introduced; their number is disproportioned to that

*Cover for the constitution and "bye lawes" of the Bowdoin College "Potato" social club, to which Hawthorne belonged
(Hawthorne-Longfellow Library, Bowdoin College)*

of the good ones. The flight of the heroine is without sufficient motive, especially as her nature was but little spiced with romance; her rescue is effected by improbable means; and finally, the gullibility and unsophisticatedness of the amiable principal of Harley College, is rather a caricature than a portrait.

We will not impair the interest of such of our readers as may intend perusing this delightful little volume, by giving a synopsis of its fable; for those who do not, could derive but little edification from such a proceeding, which is no more calculated to give a true idea of the merit of the story, than the argument to one of Milton's books of *Paradise Lost*, is like to create a proper estimate of the poem. But we will extract one passage, that our remarks may be accompanied by proof that we have not eulogized without cause. It is a death-bed scene, at which the villain of the piece had been led to be present; the place is the cot in which he was born, and the dying female, his mother, whom he had forsaken in his youth, and never saw after, till the period described in the extract.

Ellen had no heart to continue the conversation; and they rode on in silence, and through a wild and gloomy scene . . . Thus saying, he threw the purse upon the table, and without trusting himself again towards the dead, conducted Ellen out of the cottage. [p. 109–14.]

We have quoted the most sombre scene in the volume. There is a great deal of gayety and buoyancy of spirit evinced by the writer, in other parts; but when poor Fanshawe occupies the page, he will sometimes excite the reader's tears in despite of himself. We love to read, and love to review a work like this, where one can conscientiously shake hands with the author, and bid him, All hail, and be sure on leaving him, that no unkindly feelings have been created, to rankle in his breast, making both the critic and the criticised unhappy. Beside those already mentioned, we have no fault to find with the author of *Fanshawe*; but we shall have, if he does not erelong give us another opportunity of reading one of his productions. Is it not quite possible the Willis wrote this book? We merely *guess*.

Pages showing Hawthorne's different spellings of his name: left, page from his copy of The American Book-Keeper *(The Anderson Auction Company* catalogue, *Jacob Chester Chamberlain, sale number 725, 16–17 February 1909; reprinted in* Hawthorne at Auction, *p. 68); right, title page of Hawthorne's copy of* Laws of Bowdoin College *(Hawthorne-Longfellow Library, Bowdoin College)*

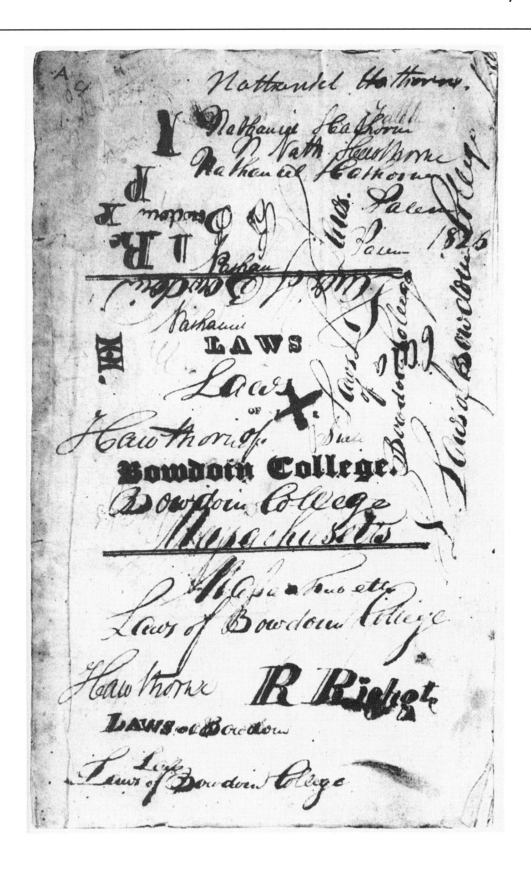

First page of the sheet music for Hawthorne's first publication, "The Ocean," which originally appeared in the Salem Gazette *on 26 August 1825. The musical setting of the poem was deposited for copyright with the District Court for the Eastern District of Pennsylvania in 1836 (Peabody Essex Museum).*

Repudiating *Fanshawe*

Hawthorne, who burned much of his early writings, was careful of his literary reputation, as this reminiscence by Fields shows.

In 1828 Hawthorne published a short anonymous romance called Fanshawe. I once asked him about this disowned publication, and he spoke of it with great disgust, and afterwards he thus referred to the subject in a letter written to me in 1851: "You make an inquiry about some supposed former publication of mine. I cannot be sworn to make correct answers as to all the liter-ary or other follies of my nonage; and I earnestly recommend you not to brush away the dust that may have gathered over them. Whatever might do me credit you may be pretty sure I should be ready enough to bring forward. Anything else it is our mutual interest to conceal; and so far from assisting your researches in that direction, I especially enjoin it on you, my dear friend, not to read any unacknowledged page that you may suppose to be mine."

—Yesterdays with Authors, p. 48

Bindings for some of the publications Hawthorne contributed to between 1831 and 1850. Shown are The Token, The Mariner's Library,
Youth's Keepsake, Autumn Leaves, The Picturesque Pocket Companion, The Boston Book, The Moss Rose, *and* The
Child's Friend *(C. E. Frazer Clark Jr.,* Nathaniel Hawthorne: A Descriptive Bibliography, *1978).*

Accumulating a Collection

After finishing at Bowdoin College, Hawthorne spent the next dozen years living with his family in Salem, a difficult period during which he developed his craft. "In this dismal and squalid chamber FAME was won"—so reads an 1836 notebook entry Hawthorne made about the house on Herbert Street. Part of his development involved extensive reading, which he did from books borrowed from the Salem Athenaeum.

Almost immediately after the publication of Fanshawe, *Hawthorne identified subjects that truly interested him. In tales and sketches that were published in newspapers, gift books, and annuals, he discovered his literary voice. Some of the earliest of these publications contain themes and techniques that became hallmarks of his writing. For example, "The Hollow of the Three Hills" (1830), one of his shortest tales, introduces such enduring themes as guilt and its effect on people, isolation from family and society, and adultery—all presented in the rich ambiguity that is the hallmark of Hawthorne's style. At approximately this time Hawthorne also began writing about the American past. This interest, which would endure, is obvious in the sketch "Sir William Phips" and the tale "Dr. Bullivant." At or near the beginning of his career he also addressed the subjects of initiation*

("My Kinsman, Major Molineux"), love ("The Gentle Boy"), and religion ("Mrs. Hutchinson"). Seven years after the appearance of his first short prose publications, Hawthorne gathered some of his tales and sketches for publication in Twice-Told Tales *(1837, enlarged 1842).*

Of the approximately forty-five tales and sketches Hawthorne published before the appearance of Twice-Told Tales, *not one bears his name as author. These works are unsigned, signed with a pseudonym (the author of "The Devil in Manuscript" is identified as Ashley A. Royce, for example), or signed according to his authorship of other works, as in "By the Author of 'The Gentle Boy,'" "By the Author of 'Sights from a Steeple,'" or "By the Author of 'The Gray Champion.'" Because of such practices, Hawthorne was generally unknown as a writer until his name appeared on the title page of* Twice-Told Tales *in March 1837. Addressing his inability to make a living or gain fame as a storywriter, he declares himself, at the beginning of the preface to this book, "the obscurest man of letters in America." If this was his situation before the publication of the collection, the response to it changed his status. With the appearance of uniformly positive reviews, Hawthorne became known not only as an author but also as a serious and significant one.*

Pages from the Salem Athenaeum register showing books withdrawn by Mary Manning (spring 1827), who checked out books for her nephew, and by Hawthorne (1834–1835) after the library privileges had been passed to him. Both lists include Joseph Strutt's The Sports and Pastimes of the People of England, *which Hawthorne cited in the headnote to "The May-Pole of Merry Mount" to authenticate the events of the story (Peabody Essex Museum).*

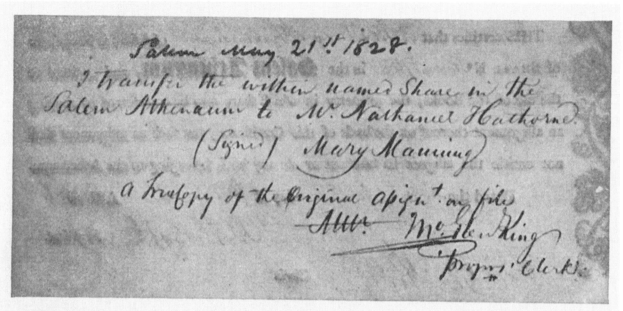

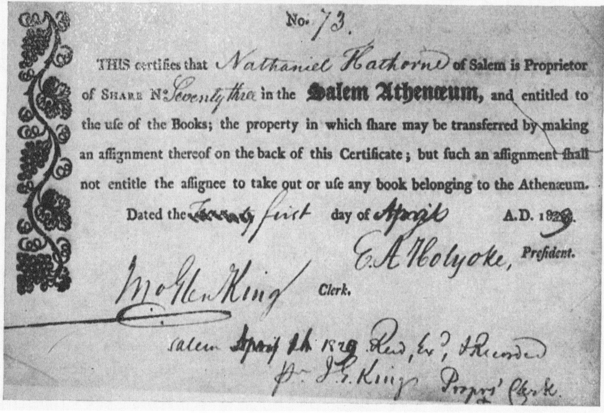

Transfer (top) and certificate passing Mary Manning's membership in the Salem Athenaeum, a subscription library, to her nephew
(Peabody Essex Museum)

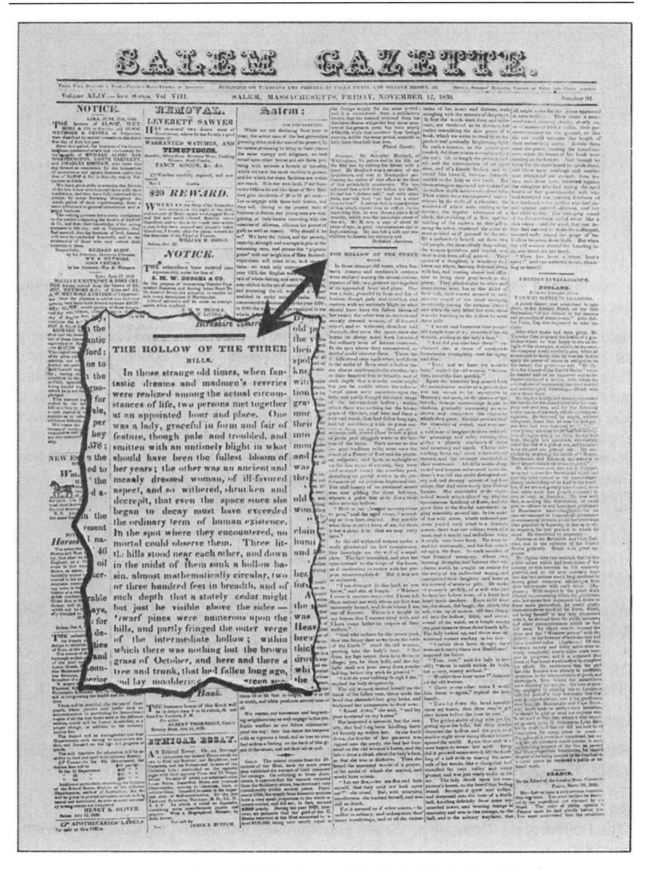

Front page of the 12 November 1830 issue of the Salem Gazette, *with Hawthorne's third unsigned contribution to the newspaper*

EDITORIAL NOTICE.

Owing to circumstances unforeseen when we assumed the charge of this periodical, (in March last,) the present Number will probably terminate our connection with it. The brevity of our continuance in the Chair Editorial will excuse us from any lengthened ceremony in resigning it. In truth, there is very little to be said on the occasion. We have endeavoured to fill our pages with a pleasant variety of wholesome matter. The reader must judge how far the attempt has been successful. It is proper to remark that we have not had full controul over the contents of the Magazine ; inasmuch as the embellishments have chiefly been selected by the executive officers of the Boston Bewick Company, or by the engravers themselves ; and our humble duty has consisted merely in preparing the literary illustrations. In some few cases, perhaps, the interests of the work might have been promoted by allowing the Editor the privilege of a veto, at least, on all engravings which were to be presented to the Public under his auspices, and for which his taste and judgment would inevitably be held responsible. In general, however, the embellishments have done no discredit either to the artists or their employers. Any causes, which may hitherto have impeded the prosperity of the concern, will probably be done away in future, and the Magazine be rendered worthier of the public favour, both as regards Literature and Art.

Hawthorne's August 1836 notice terminating his editorship of the American Magazine. *Hawthorne moved to Boston to edit the magazine for Samuel G. Goodrich in January 1836 but soon became dissatisfied with the hard work and inadequate pay.*

*Portrait of Horatio Bridge by Eastman Johnson
(Bowdoin College Museum of Art)*

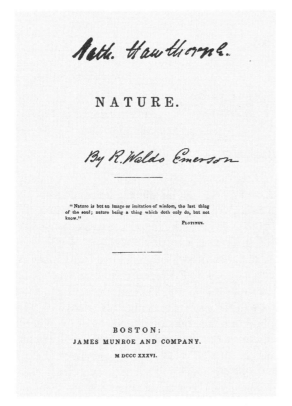

*Title page for the copy of the first edition of Emerson's anonymously
published first book, owned and signed by Hawthorne. A former
owner wrote "By R. Waldo Emerson" under the title (American
Art Association Anderson Galleries catalogue,
sale number 3911, 29 April 1931; reprinted in
Hawthorne at Auction, p. 218).*

Reviews of *Twice-Told Tales*

The first edition of Twice-Told Tales, *published in one volume on 6 or 7 March 1837, comprises eighteen stories, all of which had been previously printed: "The Gray Champion," "Sunday at Home," "The Wedding Knell," "The Minister's Black Veil," "The May-Pole of Merry Mount," "The Gentle Boy," "Mr. Higginbotham's Catastrophe," "Little Annie's Ramble" (listed as "Little Anne's Ramble" in the table of contents), "Wakefield," "A Rill from the Town Pump," "The Great Carbuncle," "The Prophetic Pictures," "David Swan," "Sights from a Steeple," "The Hollow of the Three Hills," "The Vision of the Fountain," "Fancy's Show Box," and "Dr. Heidegger's Experiment" (first appeared as "The Fountain of Youth"). One thousand copies of the volume, priced $1, were printed; Hawthorne received $100 from profits.*

Horatio Bridge, Hawthorne's Bowdoin classmate and friend thereafter, guaranteed funding for the publication of Twice-Told Tales. *Bridge's comparison of Hawthorne to English authors doubtless pleased Hawthorne, who hoped that his writings would be "praised by the reviewers as equal to the proudest productions of the scribbling sons of John Bull." Hawthorne edited Bridge's* Journal of an African Cruiser *(1845) and dedicated* The Snow-Image *(1851) to his friend.*

Review of *Twice-Told Tales*
Horatio Bridge
Age, 6 (5 April 1837): 3

We take great pleasure in noticing a volume under the above title, from the pen of an author, whose name is now for the first time, given to the public. The contents of this book consist of writings heretofore published in different Magazines and Annuals—writings which have been extensively read and admired in this country, as well as copied frequently and with high praise, by several of the literary periodicals of England. In this notice, we can only touch upon the most prominent traits in the volume under consideration, and advise those who would know it more intimately, to read and judge for themselves.

The style of this writer is remarkable for ease grace and delicacy; in which qualities, as well as in purity and classical finish, it will compare advantageously with that of the best living English writers. In the adaptation of a style appropriate to the subject on which he writes, Mr Hawthorne is peculiarly happy. When portraying the times of the Puritans, for instance, the style is in such perfect accordance with the subject, that the reader fancies himself carried back to the age and presence of those stern and

CONTENTS.

Table of contents for The Token *(1837), with Hawthorne's contributions marked*

self-denying men. Probably we have no writer, more deeply versed in the early literature and history of this country, or who can so well describe the manners and customs of the Pilgrim Fathers.

One of the greatest merits of this author, is originality of conception. The reader cannot fail to perceive that the pieces in this volume are perfectly distinct conceptions, differing among themselves and unlike what other writers have conceived; and this too, without any unnatural straining after originality, but the natural effect of a mind that forms its own combinations, and takes its own views respecting them.

There is much of strong thought and deep feeling in this book, though there is little or none of what is often termed powerful writing, i.e. ranting, and foaming at the mouth—lacerating the reader's nerves, and as it were, taking his sympathies by storm. The author sometimes gives too free a rein to Fancy, but never leaves entirely the range of human sympathies. There is

a pervading warmth in all his stories, which proves them to be, in a certain sense, true to nature.

One of the faults, or rather misfortunes, of this author is, that he is at times, too ideal and refined, to please the great mass of readers. The web of his fancy is too aerial to strike a careless eye. Yet this very fault is, to a delicate taste, one of the greatest beauties. Another obstacle to the success of some of these writings is, that they have too little relation to real life, or to matters that are interesting to the public. Of all the tales, the beautiful fiction entitled "The Rill of the Town Pump" is likely to be the most popular, because it embodies the prevailing public sentiment upon a topic of universal interest. If the author will imbue his future productions with the same spirit, he will assuredly become one of our most popular writers.

To characterize a few of the articles, we should say that "The Gray Champion" shows a massive simplicity of conception, and that its coloring is som-

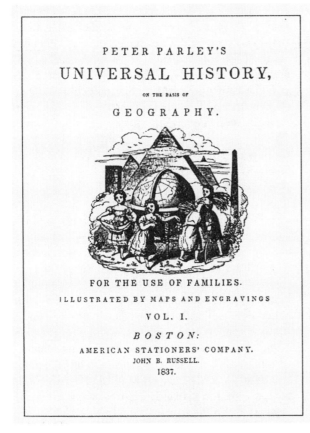 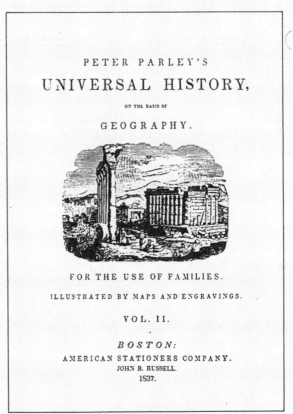

Title pages for the two-volume history Hawthorne edited with his sister Elizabeth (from C. E. Frazer Clark Jr.,
Nathaniel Hawthorne: A Descriptive Bibliography, *1978)*

A Children's Author

Writing for children was a significant part of Hawthorne's career. After contributing with his sister Elizabeth to Samuel G. Goodrich's Peter Parley series, Peter Parley's Universal History, on the Basis of Geography *(1837), Hawthorne considered devoting himself to literature for children. He went on to write* Biographical Stories for Children *(1841),* A Wonder-Book for Girls and Boys *(1851), and* Tanglewood Tales *(1853). The beginning of "Little Annie's Ramble," originally published in 1835, shows the evident satisfaction Hawthorne found in the company of children.*

Ding Dong! Ding-dong! Ding-dong!

The town crier has rung his bell, at a distant corner, and little Annie stands on her father's doorsteps, trying to hear what the man with the loud voice is talking about. Let me listen too. Oh! He is telling the people that an elephant, and a lion, and a royal tiger, and a horse with horns, and other strange beasts from foreign countries, have come to town, and will receive all visiters who choose to wait upon them. Perhaps little Annie would like to go. Yes; and I can see that the pretty child is weary of this wide and pleasant street, with the green trees flinging their shade across the quiet sunshine, and the pavements and the sidewalks all as clean as if the housemaid had just swept them with her broom. She feels that impulse to go strolling away–that longing after the mystery of the great world–which many children feel, and which I felt in my childhood. Little Annie shall take a ramble with me. See! I do but hold out my hand, and, like some bright bird in the sunny air, with her blue silk frock fluttering upwards from her white pantalettes, she comes bounding on tiptoe across the street.

Smooth back your brown curls, Annie; and let me tie on your bonnet, and we will set forth! What a strange couple to go their rambles together! One walks in black attire, with a measured step, and a heavy brown, and his thoughtful eyes bent down, while the gay little girl trips lightly along, as if she were forced to keep hold of my hand, lest her feet should dance away from the earth. Yet there is sympathy between us. If I pride myself on anything, it is because I have a smile that children love; and, on the other hand, there are few grown ladies that could entice me from the side of little Annie; for I delight to let my mind go hand in hand with the mind of a sinless child. So, come, Annie; but if I moralize as we go, do not listen to me; only look about you, and be merry!

–*Twice-Told Tales,* The Centenary Edition,
volume IX, pp. 121–122

bre, as befitted the people and times. It was an original and a fortunate idea, that of making the old man the type of the hereditary spirit of New England, and connecting his reappearance with the great occasions on which that spirit is, and shall be manifested. "The Gentle Boy" is beautifully written, and in it the author has struck a vein of the deepest pathos. The boy is a character of tenderness and beauty, more fit for Heaven than for the world, and therefore inevitably crushed by human sufferings and wrongs. "Sunday at Home," ["]Little Annie's Ramble" and "Sights from a Steeple," may form one class, the merit of which consists in a graphic representation of visible objects, and connecting those objects with thoughts, images and sentiments appropriate to each, so that nothing passes before the eye without being turned to some purpose in the mind. "David Swan," aptly termed "a Fantasy," is a conception which will impress some readers very strongly, while others will see little merit in it. The execution of this piece is admirable: the dreamlike flow of those events which we neither see, nor hear, nor are otherwise sensible of, was to be illustrated, and the author has ingeniously done it in such a manner, that, while the passing scenes are distinctly painted, they seem rather like visions sweeping past the sleeping David than like realities.

Having thus imperfectly criticised the volume, it remains only to recommend it to our readers, as one which will richly repay them for its perusal, and to express the hope that Mr Hawthorne will continue his literary labors. By so doing, he cannot fail to confer credit upon the literature of his country, and to derive honor and profit to himself.

Henry Wadsworth Longfellow was a college classmate of Hawthorne, but they were not close friends. At the time of his review of Twice-Told Tales, *Longfellow was a Harvard professor. Although he had published poems, he had not yet published* Evangeline (1847), The Song of Hiawatha (1855), *and* The Courtship of Miles Standish (1858). *These and other poems helped him become the most famous American poet of the nineteenth century.*

Review of *Twice-Told Tales*
Henry Wadsworth Longfellow
North American Review, 45 (July 1837): 59–73

When a new star rises in the heavens, people gaze after it for a season with the naked eye, and with such telescopes as they may find. In the stream of thought, which flows so peacefully deep and clear, through the pages of this book, we see the bright reflection of a spiritual star, after which men will be fain to gaze 'with the naked eye, and with the spy-glasses of criticism.' This star is but newly risen; and ere long the observations of numerous stargazers, perched up on arm-chairs and editors' tables, will inform the world of its magnitude and its place in the heaven of poetry, whether it be in the paw of the Great Bear, or on the forehead of Pegasus, or on the strings of the Lyre, or in the wing of the Eagle. Our own observations are as follows.

To this little work we would say, 'Live ever, sweet, sweet book.' It comes from the hand of a man of genius. Every thing about it has the freshness of morning and of May. These flowers and green leaves of poetry have not the dust of the highway upon them. They have been gathered fresh from the secret places of a peaceful and gentle heart. There flow deep waters, silent, calm, and cool; and the green trees look into them, and 'God's blue heaven.' The book, though in

Hawthorne's presentation inscription to his uncle in Peter Parley's Universal History *(American Art Association Anderson Galleries catalogue, Rebecca B. Manning, sale number 3927, 19–20 November 1931; reprinted in* Hawthorne at Auction, *p. 226)*

prose, is written nevertheless by a poet. He looks upon all things in the spirit of love, and with lively sympathies; for to him external form is but the representation of internal being, all things having a life, an end and aim. The true poet is a friendly man. He takes to his arms even cold and inanimate things, and rejoices in his heart, as did St Bernard of old, when he kissed his Bride of Snow. To his eye all things are beautiful and holy; all are objects of feeling and of song, from the great hierarchy of the silent, saint-like stars, that rule the night, down to the little flowers which are 'stars in the firmament of the earth.' . . .

There are some honest people into whose hearts 'Nature cannot find the way.' They have no imagination by which to invest the ruder forms of earthly things with poetry . . . But it is one of the high attributes of the poetic mind, to feel a universal sympathy with Nature, both in the material world and in the soul of man. It identifies itself likewise with every object of its sympathy, giving it new sensation and poetic life, whatever that object may be, whether man, bird, beast, flower, or star. As to the pure mind all things are pure, so to the poetic mind all things are poetical. To such souls no age and no country can be utterly dull and prosaic. They make unto themselves their age and country; dwelling in the universal mind of man, and in the universal forms of things. Of such is the author of this book.

There are many who think that the ages of Poetry and Romance are gone by. They look upon the Present as a dull, unrhymed, and prosaic translation of a brilliant and poetic Past. Their dreams are of the days of Eld; of the Dark Ages, of the days of Chivalry, and Bards, and Troubadours and Minnesingers . . . We also love ancient ballads. Pleasantly to our ears sounds the voice of the people in song, swelling fitfully through the desolate chambers of the past, like the wind of evening among ruins. And yet this voice does not persuade us that the days of balladry were more poetic than own. The spirit of the past pleads for itself, and the spirit of the present likewise. If poetry be an element of the human mind, and consequently in accordance with nature and truth, it would be strange indeed, if, as the human mind advances, poetry should recede. The truth is, that when we look back upon the Past, we see only its bright and poetic features. All that is dull, prosaic, and common-place is lost in the shadowy distance . . . With the Present it is not so. We stand too near to see objects in a picturesque light. What to others at a distance is a bright and folded summer cloud, is to us, who are in it, a dismal, drizzling rain. Thus to many this world, all beautiful as it is, seems a poor, working-day world . . . Thus has it been since the world began. Ours is not the only Present, which has seemed dull, common-place, and prosaic.

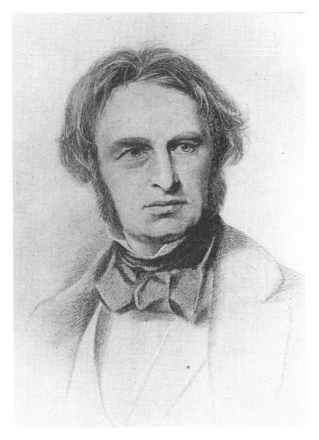

Henry Wadsworth Longfellow, Hawthorne's Bowdoin classmate

The truth is, the heaven of poetry and romance still lies around us and within us. If people would but lay aside their 'abominable spectacles,' the light of The Great Carbuncle would flash upon their sight with astonishing brightness. So long as truth is stranger than fiction, the elements of poetry and romance will not be wanting in common life. If, invisible ourselves, we could follow a single human being through a single day of its life, and know all its secret thoughts, and hopes, and anxieties, its prayers, and tears, and good resolves, its passionate delights and struggles against temptation,—all that excites, and all that soothes the heart of man,—we should have poetry enough to fill a volume. Nay, set the imagination free, like another Bottleimp, and bid it lift for you the roofs of the city, street by street, and after a single night's observation you shall sit you down and write poetry and romance for the rest of your life.

We deem these few introductory remarks important to a true understanding of Mr Hawthorne's character as a writer. It is from this point that he goes forth; and if we would go with him, and look upon life and nature as he does, we also must start from the same spot. In order to judge of the truth and beauty of his sketches, we must at

First page of Hawthorne's two-page manuscript of a story published by the Salem Gazette on 1 January 1838 as a broadside to be distributed by the newspaper carriers. In the upper left corner Hawthorne's sister-in-law attests his authorship in a note dated 7 February (American Art Association Anderson Galleries catalogue, Walter Thomas Wallace, 23–25 March 1920; reprinted in Hawthorne at Auction, p. 145)

Broadside of a story that was not collected in a book until 1876 in The Dolliver Romance and Other Pieces
(from C. E. Frazer Clark Jr., Nathaniel Hawthorne: A Descriptive Bibliography, *1978)*

least know the point of view, from which he drew them. Let us now examine the sketches themselves.

The *Twice-told Tales* are so called, we presume, from having been first published in various annuals and magazines, and now collected together, and told a second time in a volume by themselves. And a very delightful volume do they make; one of those, which excite in you a feeling of personal interest for the author. A calm, thoughtful face seems to be looking at you from every page; with now a pleasant smile, and now a shade of sadness stealing over its features. Sometimes, though not often, it glares wildly at you, with a strange and painful expression . . .

One of the most prominent characteristics of these tales is, that they are national in their character. The author has wisely chosen his themes among the traditions of New England; the dusty legends of 'the good Old Colony times, when we lived under a king.' This is the right material for story. It seems as natural to make tales out of old tumbledown traditions, as canes and snuff-boxes out of old steeples, or trees planted by great men. The puritanical times begin to look romantic in the distance . . . Truly, many quaint and quiet customs, many comic scenes and strange adventures, many wild and wondrous things, fit for humorous tale, and soft, pathetic story, lie all about us here in New England. There is no tradition of the Rhine nor of the Black Forest, which can compare in beauty with that of the Phantom Ship. The Flying Dutchman of the Cape, and the Klabotermann of the Baltic, are nowise superior. The story of Peter Rugg, the man who could not find Boston, is as good as that told by Gervase of Tilbury, of a man who gave himself to the devils by an unfortunate imprecation, and was used by them as a wheelbarrow; and the Great Carbuncle of the White Mountains shines with no less splendor, than that which illuminated the subterranean palace in Rome, as related by William of Malmesbury . . .

Another characteristic of this writer is the exceeding beauty of his style. It is as clear as running waters are. Indeed he uses words as mere steppingstones, upon which, with a free and youthful bound, his spirit crosses and recrosses the bright and rushing stream of thought. Some writers of the present day have introduced a kind of Gothic architecture into their style. All is fantastic, vast, and wondrous in the outward form, and within is mysterious twilight, and the swelling sound of an organ, and a voice chanting hymns in Latin, which need a translation for many of the crowd. To this we do not object. Let the priest chant in what language he will, so long as he understands his own mass-book. But if he wishes the world to listen and be edified, he will do well to choose a language that is generally understood.

Elizabeth Palmer Peabody in middle age

Elizabeth Palmer Peabody was the elder sister of Sophia Peabody. She met Hawthorne in late 1837, so she knew him before writing her review of Twice-Told Tales, *in which she implies her unfamiliarity with him. An associate of William Ellery Channing and Bronson Alcott, she edited* Aesthetic Papers, *where Hawthorne's "Main-Street" was published. She was a social reformer, bookstore owner, and, with her sister Mary, the founder of the first American kindergarten.*

Review of *Twice-Told Tales*
Elizabeth Palmer Peabody
The New Yorker, 5 (24 March 1838): 1–2

The Story without an End, of which all true stories are but episodes, is told by Nature herself. She speaks now from the depths of the unmeasured heavens, by stars of light, who sing in a distance that the understanding cannot measure, but which the spirit realises; now from clouds, that, dropping sweetness, or catching light—to soften it to weak eyes—bend with revelations of less general truth over particular regions of earth's surface; and now from the infinitely varied forms, and hues, with which vegetable life has clothed the nakedness of the dark unknown of this rock-ribbed earth, (whose secrets who may tell?) And not only does she speak to the eye and ear, but to the heart of man; for taking human voice and form, she tells of love, and desire, and hate; of grief, and joy, and remorse; and even of human wilfulness and human caprice, when, as sometimes, these break the iron chains of custom, and

The Peabody family home in Salem

Sophia Peabody in 1830, seven years before she met Hawthorne
(portrait by Chester Harding; from Louise Hall Tharp,
The Peabody Sisters of Salem, *1988)*

Calling on the Peabodys

On Saturday, 11 November 1837, Elizabeth Palmer Peabody invited to her family's Salem home Nathaniel Hawthorne, author of the recently published Twice-Told Tales, *who was accompanied by his two sisters, Elizabeth and Louisa. According to Peabody's recollection, she entertained the visitors for some time until she was able to find a pretext for going upstairs to confide in her younger sister: "Oh, Sophia, Mr. Hawthorne and his sisters have come, and you never saw anything so splendid—he is handsomer than Lord Byron! You must get up and dress and come down." Sophia, who was ill at the time, responded, "If he has come once he will come again." Upon his next visit to the Peabody home shortly thereafter, Hawthorne did meet Sophia Amelia Peabody, to whom he became secretly engaged late in the next year. The couple married on 9 July 1842 and first resided at the Old Manse in Concord. They had three children: Una, born 3 March 1844; Julian, born 22 June 1846; and Rose, born 20 May 1851.*

scatter, with the breath of their mouths, the cobwebs of conventionalism.

Therefore must every true story-teller, like the child of the German tale, go out of his narrow hut into Nature's universal air, and follow whatsoever guides may woo him: her humble-bee, her butterfly, her dragon-fly, each in their turn; lying down in her caverns, and with heart couchant on her verdant breast, ever listening for her mighty voice. If, like one class of modern novelists, he prefers to listen to his own narrow individuality, to generalise his own petty experience, to show us the universe through the smoky panes of a Cockney window, he shall not give us any of that immortal story; its sphere-music will be drowned in that discord. Or if, like another class, he is mainly intent on some theory of political economy—some new experiment in social science—the dogmas of some philosophical or theological sect, he shall not make a work of art—he shall not open or clear up the eye of Reason, but rather thicken that crowd of phenomena that overwhelms it with fatigue. The confessions of egotism, and the demonstrations of modern science, have their place, but not where the true story-teller—who is the ballad- singer of the time—has *his*. He sits at the fountain-head of national character, and he must never stoop below the highest aim, but for ever seek the primal secret—for ever strive to speak the word which is answered by nothing less than a creation.

Pencil sketch of Hawthorne by Sophia Peabody, his future wife, circa 1838 (Collection of Manning Hawthorne)

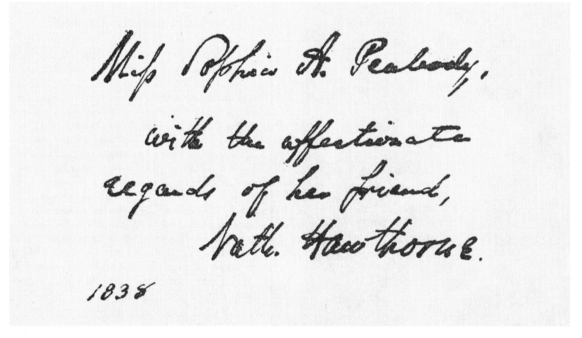

Hawthorne's inscription to his fiancée in a copy of Twice-Told Tales *(American Art Association Anderson Galleries catalogue, Stephen H. Wakeman sale, 28–29 April 1931)*

In this country, the state of things is so peculiarly unfavorable to that quiet brooding of the spirit over the dark waters, which must precede the utterance of a word of power;—our young men are so generally forced into the arena of business or politics before they have ever discriminated the spirit that they are, from the formless abyss in which they are, that it argues a genius of a high order to soar over the roaring gulf of transition in which the elements of society are boiling, into the still heaven of beauty. Such genius, however, there is amongst us. The harmonies of Nature, like the musical sounds in the ancient rites of Cybele, so fill the souls of her chosen priests, that they are insensible to all meaner sounds; and one of these true priests is the sweet storyteller, with the flowery name, whose little book of caged melodies we are now to review.

We have heard that the author of these tales has lived the life of a recluse; that the inhabitants of his native town have never been able to catch a glimpse of his person; that he is not seen at any time in the walks of men. And, indeed, his knowledge of the world is evidently not the superficial one acquired by that perpetual presence in good society—so called—which is absence from all that is profound in human feeling and thought; but, on the contrary, it is the wisdom which comes from knowing some few hearts well—from having communed with the earnest spirits of the past, and mainly studied in the light of that Pythian temple 'not built with hands—eternal in the spirit,' whose initiation is—'know thyself.' There is throughout the volume a kindliness and even heartiness of human sympathy—a healthy equilibrium of spirits, and above all, a humor, so exquisitely combined of airy wit and the 'sad, sweet music of humanity,' that it contradicts the notion of misanthropical or whimsical seclusion. We will venture our reputation for sagacity on the assertion that he is frank and communicative in his character, winning thereby the experience of whatsoever hearts come in his path, to subject it to his Wordsworthian philosophy.

Wordsworthian philosophy we say, and with consideration; not that we would imply that he has taken it from Wordsworth. We mean to speak of the kind of philosophy, which cannot be learnt except in the same school of Nature where Wordsworth studied, and by the same pure light. We mean that he illustrates the principle defended by Wordsworth in his prose writings, as well as manifested by him in his metrical compositions, viz: that the ideal beauty may be seen clearest and felt most profoundly in the common incidents of actual life, if we will but 'purge our visual ray with euphrasie and rue.' Mr Hawthorne

THE

SISTER YEARS;

BEING THE

CARRIER'S ADDRESS,

TO THE PATRONS

OF THE

SALEM GAZETTE,

FOR THE

FIRST OF JANUARY,

1839.

SALEM.
1839.

Title page for a story that was originally published as a pamphlet and collected in the enlarged 1842 edition of Twice-Told Tales *(The Anderson Auction Company catalogue, Frank Maier, sale number 782, 16–17 November 1909; reprinted in* Hawthorne at Auction, *p. 95)*

seems to have been born to this faith. His stories, generally speaking, have no dramatic pretension. Their single incident is the window through which he looks 'into the mind of man—/*His* haunt, and the main region of *his* song.'

In none of the little pieces before us has he succeeded more completely in suggesting the most general ideas, than in the 'Sunday at Home,' the 'Sights from a Steeple,' and 'Little Annie's Ramble.' These pieces also exhibit in perfection the objective power of his mind. With what a quiet love and familiar power he paints that sunrise stealing down the steeple opposite his chamber window! We turn to this passage, as we do to a painting upon canvass, for the pleasure it affords to the eye. The motion and sentiment so mingled with the forms and hues do not obscure the clear outlines—the sharp light and shade. What a living as well as tangible being does that

Frontispiece by Sophia Peabody for the separate 1839 publication of The Gentle Boy *(courtesy of Special Collections, Thomas Cooper Library, University of South Carolina)*

meeting-house become, even during its week-day silence! The author does not go to church, he says; but no one would think he stayed at home for a vulgar reason. What worship there is in his stay at home! How livingly he teaches others to go, if they do go! What a hallowed feeling he sheds around the venerable institution of public worship! How gentle and yet effective are the touches by which he rebukes all that is inconsistent with its beautiful ideal! His 'Sunday at Home' came from a heart alive through all its depths with a benignant Christian faith. '*Would that the Sabbath came twice as often, for the sake of that sorrowful old soul!*' This is worth a thousand sermons on the duty of going to church. It quickens the reader's love of religion; it shows the adaptation of Christianity to our nature, by adding to the common phenomena of the sacred day the pathos and grace which are

to be drawn up from the wells of sympathy, and reproduces the voice that said 'the Sabbath is made for man,' in its very tones of infinite love, even to our senses. And 'Little Annie's Ramble,' though still lighter in execution, is no less replete with heart-touching thought. We feel as if to dwell upon it in our prosaic manner would be to do some injury to its airy structure. The more times we have read it, the more fully we have realised the force of its last paragraph:

> Sweet has been the charm of childhood on my spirit throughout my ramble with little Annie! Say not that it has been a waste of precious moments, an idle matter, a babble of childish talk, and a reverie of childish imaginations, about topics unworthy of a grown man's notice. Has it been merely this? Not so—not so. They are not truly wise who would

An 1839 view of Salem showing the town pump, the narrator of "A Rill from the Town Pump" (from Hawthorne, Little Daffydowndilly and Other Stories, *1887; Thomas Cooper Library, University of South Carolina)*

affirm it. As the pure breath of children revives the life of aged men, so is our moral nature revived by their free and simple thoughts, their native feeling, their airy mirth for little cause or none, their grief soon roused and soon allayed. Their influence on us is at least reciprocal with ours on them. When our infancy is almost forgotten, and our boyhood long departed, though it seems but as yesterday;–when life settles darkly down upon us, and we doubt whether to call ourselves young any more, then it is good to steal away from the society of bearded men, and even of gentle woman, and spend an hour or two with children. After drinking from these fountains of still fresh existence, we shall return into the crowd, as I do now, to struggle onward, and do our part in life, perhaps as fervently as ever, but, for a time, with a kinder and purer heart, and a spirit more lightly wise. All this by thy sweet magic, dear little Annie!

Not so grave is the effect of the 'Vision of the Fountain.' But who would ask for more than meets the eye and touches the heart in that exquisite little fancy? 'Sure, if our eyes were made for seeing,/Then Beauty is its own excuse for being.'

But nothing about our author delights us so much as the quietness–the apparent leisure, with which he lingers around the smallest point of fact, and unfolds therefrom a world of thought, just as if

nothing else existed in the outward universe but that of which he is speaking. The hurried manner that seems to have become the American habit–the spirit of the steam-engine and railroad, has never entered into him. He seems to believe and act upon what is seldom ever apprehended, that every man's mind is the centre of the whole universe–the *primum mobile*– itself at rest, which wheels all phenomena, in lesser or greater circles, around it. Thus, 'David Swan' goes down from his father's house in the New Hampshire hills, to seek his fortune in his uncle's grocery in Boston; and being tired with his walk, lies down by a fountain near the way-side for an hour's repose. Our philosophic, or, more accurately, our poetical story-teller, marks him for his own, and sitting down by his side, notes the several trains of phenomena which pass by and involve the unconscious sleeper; and comparing these with that train in which he is a conscious actor, reads the great lesson of superintending Providence, with the relation thereto of the human foresight. Again, his eye is struck with an odd action related in a newspaper, and his attentive mind is awakened, and may not rest until he has harmonised it with the more generally obeyed laws of human nature. Thus we have 'Wakefield,' and the terror-striking observation with which it closes: 'Amid the seeming confusion of our mysterious

The Boston Custom House, where Hawthorne worked from 11 January 1839 until January 1841

A Weigher and Gauger

Active in Democratic politics, George Bancroft not only appointed Hawthorne to his job at the Boston Custom House but also played a role in the author's obtaining his position at the Salem Custom House. Fields in his memoir writes of Hawthorne's work in Boston.

When Mr. George Bancroft, then Collector of the Port of Boston, appointed Hawthorne weigher and gauger in the custom-house, he did a wise thing, for no public officer ever performed his disagreeable duties bet-ter than our romancer. Here is a tattered little official document signed by Hawthorne when he was watching over the interests of the country: it certifies his attendance at the unlading of a brig, then lying at Long Wharf in Boston. I keep this precious relic side by side with one of a similar custom-house character, signed *Robert Burns.*

—Yesterdays with Authors, p. 48

Hawthorne's 31 August 1840 letter to Caleb Foote, the editor of the Salem Gazette, *in which he begins, "Professor Longfellow and myself contemplate establishing a paper in Boston; and we are desirous of gaining some lights upon the subject, from your experience." Nothing became of this project (Peabody Essex Museum).*

world, individuals are so nicely adjusted to a system, and systems to one another, and to a whole, that *by stepping aside for a moment*, a man exposes himself to a fearful risk of losing his place for ever. Like Wakefield, he may become, as it were, the outcast of the universe.'

'The Rill from the Town Pump' has been praised so much—not too much, however—that we have hardly anything left to say. It shows that genius may redeem to its original beauty the most hackneyed subject. We have here what would make the best temperance tract; and it is a work of the fine arts too—something we could hardly have believed possible beforehand.

'The Gray Champion,' 'The Maypole of Merry Mount,' and 'The Great Carbuncle,' form another class of stories, for which it has often been said that this country gives no material. When we first read them, we wanted to say to the author, 'This is your work:—with the spirit of the past, chrystallized thus, to gem the hills and plains of your native land; especially let every scene of that great adventure which settled and finally made free our country, become a symbol of the spirit which is too fast fading—the spirit that in Hugh Peters and Sir Henry Vane laid down mortal life, to take up the life which is infinitely communicable of itself.' But, on second thought, we feel that we cannot spare him from the higher path, to confine him to this patriotic one; although we would recommend him frequently to walk in it. Why will he not himself give us the philosophical romance of Mt Wallaston, of which he speaks? We can see but one objection; and that is, that into his little tale of 'The Maypole,' he has already distilled all the beauty with which he might have garnished the volume. 'The Great Carbuncle' combines the wild imagination of Germany, and its allegoric spirit, with the common sense that the English claim as their characteristic; and these diverse elements are harmonized by the reliance on natural sentiment which we love to believe will prove in the end to be the true American character. The story awakens first that feeling and thought which is too fine in its essence for words to describe. A practical philosophy of life, that gives its due place and time to imagination and science, but rests on the heart as a solid foundation, is the light that flashes from the 'Great Carbuncle' upon the true soul; which absorbing it, leaves the outward rock only 'opaque stone, with particles of mica glittering on its surface.'

The momentous questions with which 'Fancy's Show Box' commences, and the 'sad and awful truths' interwoven with its light frame-work, and the expressed hope with which the author relieves these at the end, where he suggests 'that all the dreadful consequences of sin may not be incurred unless the act have

set its seal upon the thought,' would make the story interesting, even if it were not half so well done. Yet it does not denote a character of genius so high as the others that we have mentioned. It is as much inferior to the 'Great Carbuncle' as the faculty of fancy is below the imagination. In quite an opposite vein is Mr Higginbotham's catastrophe; but the variety of power proves the soundness of the author's mind. Where there is not the sense and power of the ludicrous, we always may fear weakness.

'The Gentle Boy' we have not neglected so long because we like it least. It is more of a story than any of the rest; and we, perhaps, are the most fond of it, because it was the first of the author's productions we saw. We took it up in the Token, where it was first told, not expecting much, and found ourselves charmed by a spell of power. That sad, sweet, spiritual Ilbrahim, with 'eyes melting into the moonlight,' seeking a home on the cold tomb of his murdered father, while his deluded mother is wandering over the earth to awaken, with the concentrated force of all human passions that she has baptized into the name of the Holy Ghost, the spiritually dead to spiritual life, is worth a thousand homilies on fanaticism in all its forms, contrasted with the divinity of the natural sentiments, and the institutions growing therefrom. In this angelic child, we see human nature in its perfect holiness, its infinite tenderness, its martyr power, pleading, with all the eloquence of silent suffering, against the time-hallowed sins and ever renewed errors of men. On the judgment seat sits Time; and he shows himself, as usual, a very Pilate, delivering up the innocent victim to the furies of the present. They crucify him, and bury him in its stony bosom. Bury him, did we say? No—we saw his feet 'pressing on the soil of Paradise,' and again his soothing spirit coming 'down from heaven, to teach his parent a true religion.'

We have now spoken, as we could, of our chief favorites in this volume. A few more stories are left, which are indeed treated with great skill and power, and with as severe a taste as their subjects admit—especially the 'Prophetic Pictures,' a masterpiece in its way. As specimens of another vein of the author's art, we would not give them up. But we cannot avoid saying that these subjects are dangerous for his genius. There is a meretricious glare in them, which is but too apt to lead astray. And for him to indulge himself in them, will be likely to lower the sphere of his power. First-rate genius should leave the odd and peculiar, and especially the fantastic and horrible, to the inferior talent which is obliged to make up its own deficiency by the striking nature of the subject matter. Doubtless, we are requiring of genius some self-denial. These very tales are probably the most effective of the volume, at least with readers of Tokens and Magazines. They are the first read and oftenest spo-

Lithograph of a painting of Brook Farm by M. G. Cutter (from Mary Caroline Crawford, Romantic Days in Old Boston, *1910)*

George Ripley

Hawthorne and Brook Farm

In 1841 the Unitarian minister George Ripley established Brook Farm in West Roxbury, Massachusetts, as a place where like-minded people could apply Christian and transcendental values to practical living. A fundamental goal was for the members to live cooperatively as a means of developing as fully as possible their physical, moral, and educational potential. They believed that farming for a few hours each day would permit the artistically inclined among them ample time to pursue their artistic endeavors. Visitors to Brook Farm included Margaret Fuller, Ralph Waldo Emerson, and Theodore Parker; among the members were Ripley, Charles A. Dana, and Hawthorne. The community began as a joint-stock company with twenty-four shares sold at $500 each. Tired of toiling at the Boston Custom House, Hawthorne bought two shares in the hope he would live comfortably there with Sophia Peabody, who would soon become his wife. Hawthorne moved to Brook Farm in April 1841. He soon discovered, though, that he was incapable of writing there and that life at Brook Farm would not satisfy the newlyweds, so he departed the community in November. In 1845 the financially strapped Hawthorne tried legally to force Ripley to return some of the money Hawthorne had paid toward the building of a Brook Farm home for him and Sophia. Although Hawthorne won the case, he never collected the money due him.

Hawthorne's 16 July 1841 letter to George S. Hillard, who was editing the 1842 Token, in which the author blames his inability to complete a story on his Brook Farm experience: "You cannot make a silk purse out of a sow's ear; nor must you expect pretty stories from a man who feeds pigs."
A lawyer, Hillard later represented Hawthorne in his suit against Ripley, the founder of Brook Farm
(from C. E. Frazer Clark Jr., Hawthorne at Auction, *1972).*

ken of, perhaps, by all persons; and yet, we would venture to say, they are the least often recurred to. They never can leave the reader in so high a mood of mind as the 'Sunday at Home,' or 'Little Annie's Ramble.' The interest they excite, in comparison with the latter, is somewhat analogous to the difference between the effect of Byron and Wordsworth's poetry.

But it is with diffidence we offer counsel to Mr Hawthorne. We prefer to express gratitude. Can we do it more strongly, than to say, 'We would hear more and more and forever'? Nor do we doubt that we shall hear more. Talent may tire in its toils, for it is ascending a weary hill. But genius wells up at the top of the hill; and in this instance descends in many streams—and the main stream is augmented and widened and deepened at every conflux. As it approaches the dwelling places of men, and spreads out to bear the merchandise of nations on its bosom, may it preserve the sweetness and purity of its fountains, far up in the solitudes of nature! We can wish nothing better for Mr Hawthorne or for ourselves. He will then take his place amongst his contemporaries, as the greatest artist of his line; for not one of our writers indicates so great a variety of the elements of genius.

And this is a high quarry at which to aim. The greatest artist will be the greatest benefactor of our country. Art is the highest interest of our state, for it is the only principle of conservatism our constitution allows—a beauty which at once delights the eye, touches the heart, and projects the spirit into the world to come, will be something too precious to be weighed against the gains of a breakneck commerce, or the possible advantages held out by empirical politicians. While all the other excitements of the time tend to change and revolution, this will be a centre of unity. Let the poetic storyteller hasten, then, to bind with the zone of Beauty whatever should be permanent amongst us. In order to discharge his high office worthily, he will draw his materials from the wells of nature, and involve the sanctities of religion in all his works. Being, thinking, loving, seeing, uttering himself, without misgiving, without wearisomeness, and, like the spirit which hangs the heavens and clothes the earth with beauty, for ever assiduous; he yet need do nothing with special foresight. We would not yoke Pegasus to the dray-cart of utility; for the track of his footsteps will be hallowed, and every thing become sacred which he has touched.—Then, and not till then, we shall have a country; for then, and not till then, there will be a national character, defending us alike from the revolutionist within, and the invader without our borders.

The Enlarged *Twice-Told Tales*

The second, enlarged edition of Twice-Told Tales *(1842), totaling thirty-nine tales, was published in two volumes in December 1841; as was the case with the first edition of the collection, all of the stories had been previously printed. The first volume had the same contents as the 1837 edition but with the addition of "The Toll-Gatherer's Day." The second volume comprises twenty stories: "Legends of the Province House: No. I.–Howe's Masquerade," "No. II.–Edward Randolph's Portrait," "No. III–Lady Eleanore's Mantle," "No. IV.–Old Esther Dudley," "The Haunted Mind," "The Village Uncle," "The Ambitious Guest," "The Sister Years," "Snow Flakes," "The Seven Vagabonds," "The White Old Maid," "Peter Goldthwaite's Treasure," "Chippings with a Chisel," "The Shaker Bridal," "Night Sketches," "Endicott and the Red Cross," "The Lily's Quest," "Foot-Prints on the Sea-Shore," "Edward Fan's Rosebud," and "The Threefold Destiny." Hawthorne's contract with the publisher James Munroe specified "one edition not exceeding fifteen hundred copies"; the author received a 10 percent royalty on the book, which sold for $2.25.*

By the time of his review of Twice-Told Tales, *Edgar Allan Poe was well known as a writer of tales, as a poet, and as a literary critic. Of all the stories written in the United States by 1850, those by Hawthorne, Poe, and Washington Irving are the*

Edgar Allan Poe

most enduring. Poe's review of the collection is marred by his absurd charge of plagiarism in regard to Hawthorne's "Howe's Masquerade" (1838), which was published before Poe's "William Wilson" (1839). Poe accused several authors, including Longfellow, of plagiarizing his works.

Review of *Twice-Told Tales*
Edgar Allan Poe
Graham's Magazine, 20 (May 1842): 298–300

We said a few hurried words about Mr Hawthorne in our last number, with the design of speaking more fully in the present. We are still, however, pressed for room, and must necessarily discuss his volumes more briefly and more at random than their high merits deserve.

The book professes to be a collection of *tales,* yet is, in two respects, misnamed. These pieces are now in their third republication, and, of course are thrice-told. Moreover, they are by no means *all* tales, either in the ordinary or in the legitimate understanding of the term. Many of them are pure essays; for example, 'Sights from a Steeple,' 'Sunday at Home,' 'Little Annie's Ramble,' 'A Rill from the Town-Pump,' 'The Toll-Gatherer's Day,' 'The Haunted Mind,' 'The Sister Years,' 'Snow-Flakes,' 'Night Sketches,' and 'Foot-Prints on the Sea-Shore.' We mention these matters chiefly on account of their discrepancy with that marked precision and finish by which the body of the work is distinguished.

Of the Essays just named, we must be content to speak in brief. They are each and all beautiful, without being characterised by the polish and adaptation so visible in the tales proper. A painter would at once note their leading or predominant feature, and style it *repose.* There is no attempt at effect. All is quiet, thoughtful, subdued. Yet this repose may exist simultaneously with high originality of thought; and Mr Hawthorne has demonstrated the fact. At every turn we meet with novel combinations; yet these combinations never surpass the limits of the quiet. We are soothed as we read; and withal is a calm astonishment that ideas so apparently obvious have never occurred or been presented to us before. Herein our author differs materially from Lamb or Hunt or Hazlitt—who, with vivid originality of manner and expression, have less of the true novelty of thought than is generally supposed, and whose originality, at best, has an uneasy and meretricious quaintness, replete with startling effects unfounded in nature, and inducing trains of reflection which lead to no satisfactory result. The Essays of Hawthorne have much of the character of Irving, with more of originality, and less of finish; while, com-

pared with the Spectator, they have a vast superiority at all points. The Spectator, Mr Irving, and Mr Hawthorne have in common that tranquil and subdued manner which we have chosen to denominate *repose;* but, in the case of the two former, this repose is attained rather by the absense of novel combination, or of originality, than otherwise, and consists chiefly in the calm, quiet, unostentatious expression of commonplace thoughts, in an unambitious unadulterated Saxon. In them, by strong effort, we are made to conceive the absence of all. In the essays before us the absence of effort is too obvious to be mistaken, and a strong under-current of *suggestion* runs continuously beneath the upper stream of the tranquil thesis. In short, these effusions of Mr Hawthorne are the product of a truly imaginative intellect, restrained, and in some measure repressed, by fastidiousness of taste, by constitutional melancholy and by indolence.

But it is of his tales that we desire principally to speak. The tale proper, in our opinion, affords unquestionably the fairest field for the exercise of the loftiest talent, which can be afforded by the wide domains of mere prose. Were we bidden to say how the highest genius could be most advantageously employed for the best display of its own powers, we should answer, without hesitation—in the composition of a rhymed poem, not to exceed in length what might be perused in an hour. Within this limit alone can the highest order of true poetry exist. We need only here say, upon this topic, that, in almost all classes of composition, the unity of effect or impression is a point of the greatest importance. It is clear, moreover, that this unity cannot be thoroughly preserved in productions whose perusal cannot be completed at one sitting. We may continue the reading of a prose composition, from the very nature of prose itself, much longer than we can persevere, to any good purpose, in the perusal of a poem. This latter, if truly fulfilling the demands of the poetic sentiment, induces an exaltation of the soul which cannot be long sustained. All high excitements are necessarily transient. Thus a long poem is a paradox. And, without unity of impression, the deepest effects cannot be brought about. Epics were the offspring of an imperfect sense of Art, and their reign is no more. A poem *too* brief may produce a vivid, but never an intense or enduring impression. Without a certain continuity of effort—without a certain duration or repetition of purpose—the soul is never deeply moved. There must be the dropping of the water upon the rock. De Béranger has wrought brilliant things—pungent and spirit-stirring—but, like all immassive bodies, they lack *momentum,* and thus fail to satisfy the Poetic Sentiment. They sparkle and excite, but, from want of

Concluding page from Sophia Peabody's 19 June 1842 letter to Mary W. Foote, the wife of the editor of the Salem Gazette, *in which she writes of her upcoming 9 July marriage, "This most bountiful month, so rich in treasures of verdure & fulness will find us bound by earthly as we long have been bound by heavenly ties. The ceremony is nothing—our true marriage was three years ago"* (American Art Association Anderson Galleries catalogue, Julian Hawthorne, sale number 4283, 9–10 December 1936; reprinted in Hawthorne at Auction, *p. 281*).

continuity, fail deeply to impress. Extreme brevity will degenerate into epigrammatism; but the sin of extreme length is even more unpardonable. *In medio tutissimus ibis.*

Were we called upon however to designate that class of composition which, next to such a poem as we have suggested, should best fulfil the demands of high genius—should offer it the most advantageous field of exertion—we should unhesitatingly speak of the prose tale, as Mr Hawthorne has here exemplified it. We allude to the short prose narrative, requiring from a half-hour to one or two hours in its perusal. The ordinary novel is objectionable, from its length, for reasons already stated in substance. As it cannot be read at one sitting, it deprives itself, of course, of the immense force derivable from *totality.* Worldly interests intervening during the pauses of perusal, modify, annul, or counteract, in a greater or less degree, the impressions of the book. But simple cessation in reading would, of itself, be sufficient to destroy the true unity. In the brief tale, however, the author is enabled to carry out the fulness of his intention, be it what it may. During the hour of perusal the soul of the reader is at the writer's control. There are no external or extrinsic influences—resulting from weariness or interruption.

A skilful literary artist has constructed a tale. If wise, he has not fashioned his thoughts to accommodate his incidents; but having conceived, with deliberate care, a certain unique or single *effect* to be wrought out, he then invents such incidents—he then combines such events as may best aid him in establishing this preconceived effect. If his very initial sentence tend not to the outbringing of this effect, then he has failed in his first step. In the whole composition there should be no word written, of which the tendency, direct or indirect, is not to the one pre-established design. And by such means, with such care and skill, a picture is at length painted which leaves in the mind of him who contemplates it with a kindred art, a sense of the fullest satisfaction. The idea of the tale has been presented unblemished, because undisturbed; and this is an end attainable by the novel. Undue brevity is just as exceptionable here as in the poem; but undue length is yet more to be avoided.

We have said that the tale has a point of superiority even over the poem. In fact, while the *rhythm* of this latter is an essential aid in the development of the poem's highest idea—the idea of the Beautiful—the artificialities of this rhythm are an inseparable bar to the development of all points of thought or expression which have their basis in *Truth.* But Truth is often, and in very great degree, the aim of the tale.

Making Arrangements

The Reverend James Freeman Clarke saved this brief note from Hawthorne and gave it to Fields as he was preparing his essay on the author.

54 PINCKNEY STREET, Friday, July 8, 1842.
MY DEAR SIR,—Though personally a stranger to you, I am about to request of you the greatest favor which I can receive from any man. I am to be married to Miss Sophia Peabody; and it is our mutual desire that you should perform the ceremony. Unless it should be decidedly a rainy day, a carriage will call for you at half past eleven o'clock in the forenoon.
Very respectfully yours,
Nath. Hawthorne.
REV. JAMES F. CLARKE, Chestnut Street.

—Yesterdays with Authors, p. 118

Some of the finest tales are tales of ratiocination. Thus the field of this species of composition, if not in so elevated a region on the mountain of Mind, is a table-land of far vaster extent than the domain of the mere poem. Its products are never so rich, but infinitely more generous, and more appreciable by the mass of mankind. The writer of the prose tale, in short, may bring to his theme a vast variety of modes or inflections of thought and expression—(the ratiocinative, for example, the sarcastic or the humorous) which are not only antagonistical to the nature of the poem, but absolutely forbidden by one of its most peculiar and indispensable adjuncts; we allude of course, to rhythm. It may be added, here, *par parenthèse,* that the author who aims at the purely beautiful in a prose tale is laboring at great disadvantage. For Beauty can be better treated in the poem. Not so with terror, or passion, or horror, or a multitude of such other points. And here it will be seen how full of prejudice are the usual animadversions against those *tales of effect* many fine examples of which were found in the earlier numbers of Blackwood. The impressions produced were wrought in a legitimate sphere of action, and constituted a legitimate although sometimes an exaggerated interest. They were relished by every man of genius: although there were found many men of genius who condemned them without just ground. The true critic will but demand that the design intended be accomplished, to the fullest extent, by the means most advantageously applicable.

We have very few American tales of real merit—we may say, indeed, none, with the exception of *The Tales of a Traveller* of Washington Irving, and these

Twice-told Tales of Mr Hawthorne. Some of the pieces of Mr John Neal abound in vigor and originality; but in general, his compositions of this class are excessively diffuse, extravagant, and indicative of an imperfect sentiment of Art. Articles at random are, now and then, met with in our periodicals which might be advantageously compared with the best effusions of the British Magazines; but, upon the whole, we are far behind our progenitors in this department of literature.

Of Mr Hawthorne's Tales we would say, emphatically, that they belong to the highest region of Art—an Art subservient to genius of a very lofty order. We had supposed, with good reason for so supposing, that he had been thrust into his present position by one of the impudent *cliques* which beset our literature, and whose pretensions it is our full purpose to expose at the earliest opportunity; but we have been most agreeably mistaken. We know of few compositions which the critic can more honestly commend than these *Twice-told Tales*. As Americans, we feel proud of the book.

Mr Hawthorne's distinctive trait is invention, creation, imagination, originality—a trait which, in the literature of fiction, is positively worth all the rest. But the nature of originality, so far as regards its manifestation in letters, is but imperfectly understood. The inventive or original mind as frequently displays itself in novelty of *tone* as in novelty of matter. Mr Hawthorne is original at *all* points.

It would be a matter of some difficulty to designate the best of these tales; we repeat that, without exception, they are beautiful. 'Wakefield' is remarkable for the skill with which an old idea—a well-known incident—is worked up or discussed. A man of whims conceives the purpose of quitting his wife and residing *incognito,* for twenty years, in her immediate neighborhood. Something of this kind actually happened in London. The force of Mr Hawthorne's tale lies in the analysis of the motives which must or might have impelled the husband to such folly, in the first instance, with the possible causes of his perseverance. Upon this thesis a sketch of singular power has been constructed.

'The Wedding Knell' is full of the boldest imagination—an imagination fully controlled by taste. The most captious critic could find no flaw in this production.

'The Minister's Black Veil' is a masterly composition of which the sole defect is that to the rabble its exquisite skill will be *caviare.* The *obvious* meaning of this article will be found to smother its insinuated one. The *moral* put into the mouth of the dying minister will be supposed to convey the *true* import of the

narrative; and that a crime of dark dye, (having reference to the 'young lady') has been committed, is a point which only minds congenial with that of the author will perceive.

'Mr Higginbotham's Catastrophe' is vividly original and managed most dexterously.

'Dr Heidegger's Experiment' is exceedingly well imagined, and executed with surpassing ability. The artist breathes in every line of it.

'The White Old Maid' is objectionable, even more than the 'Minister's Black Veil,' on the score of its mysticism. Even with the thoughtful and analytic, there will be much trouble in penetrating its entire import.

'The Hollow of the Three Hills' we would quote in full, had we space;—not as evincing higher talent than any of the other pieces, but as affording an excellent example of the author's peculiar ability. The subject is commonplace. A witch subjects the Distant and the Past to the view of a mourner. It has been the fashion to describe, in such cases, a mirror in which the images of the absent appear; or a cloud of smoke is made to arise, and thence the figures are gradually unfolded. Mr Hawthorne has wonderfully heightened his effect by making the ear, in place of the eye, the medium by which the fantasy is conveyed. The head of the mourner is enveloped in the cloak of the witch, and within its magic folds there arise sounds which have an all-sufficient intelligence. Throughout this article also, the artist is conspicuous—not more in positive than in negative merits. Not only is all done that should be done, but (what perhaps is an end with more difficulty attained) there is nothing done which should not be. Every word *tells,* and there is not a word which does *not* tell.

In 'Howe's Masquerade' we observe something which resembles a plagiarism—but which *may* be a very flattering coincidence of thought. We quote the passage in question.

> *With a dark flush of wrath* upon his brow they saw the general *draw his sword* and *advance to meet* the figure *in the cloak* before the latter had stepped one pace upon the floor.
> *'Villain, unmuffle yourself,'* cried he, 'you pass no farther.'
> The figure, without blenching a hair's breadth from the sword which was pointed at his breast, made a solemn pause, and *lowered the cape of the cloak* from his face, yet not sufficiently for the spectators to catch a glimpse of it. But Sir William Howe had evidently seen enough. The sternness of his countenance gave place to a look of wild amazement, if not horror, while he recoiled several steps from the figure, and *let fall his sword* upon the floor.—See Vol. 2, page 20.

The idea here is, that the figure in the cloak is the phantom or reduplication of Sir William Howe; but in an article called 'William Wilson,' one of the *Tales of the Grotesque and Arabesque*, we have not only the same idea, but the same idea similarly presented in several respects. We quote two paragraphs, which our readers may compare with what has been already given. We have italicized, above, the immediate particulars of resemblance.

The brief moment in which I averted my eyes had been sufficient to produce, apparently, a material change in the arrangement at the upper or farther end of the room. A large mirror, it appeared to me, now stood where none had been perceptible before: and as I stepped up to it in extremity of terror, mine own image, but with features all pale and dabbled in blood, *advanced* with a feeble and tottering gait to meet me.

'Thus it appeared I say, but was not. It was Wilson, who then stood before me in the agonies of dissolution. Not a line in all the marked and singular lineaments of that face which was not even identically mine own. *His mask and cloak lay where he had thrown them, upon the floor*–Vol. 2, p. 57.

Here it will be observed that, not only are the two general conceptions identical, but there are various *points* of similarity. In each case the figure seen is the wraith or duplication of the beholder. In each case the scene is a masquerade. In each case the figure is cloaked. In each, there is a quarrel–that is to say, angry words pass between the parties. In each the beholder is enraged. In each the cloak and sword fall upon the floor. The 'villain, unmuffle yourself,' of Mr H. is precisely paralleled by a passage at page 56 of 'William Wilson.'

In the way of objection we have scarcely a word to say of these tales. There is, perhaps, a somewhat too general or prevalent *tone*–a tone of melancholy and mysticism. The subjects are insufficiently varied. There is not so much of *versatility* evinced as we might well be warranted in expecting from the high powers of Mr Hawthorne. But beyond these trivial exceptions we have really none to make. The style is purity itself. Force abounds. High imagination gleams from every page. Mr Hawthorne is a man of the truest genius. We only regret that the limits of our Magazine will not permit us to pay him that full tribute of commendation, which, under other circumstances, we should be so eager to pay.

Reviews of *Mosses from an Old Manse*

Mosses from an Old Manse (1846) enhanced the reputation Hawthorne had achieved with Twice-Told Tales, *but his stories did not enable him to make a living from writing. With marriage and the responsibilities of fatherhood, Hawthorne's need for money became more acute, and he was relieved when President James K. Polk, on the recommendation of George Bancroft, nominated him for the position of surveyor of the Salem Custom House at $1,000 per year. He was sworn in at the customhouse on 9 April 1846, two months before the publication of his collection.*

Mosses from an Old Manse (1846), comprising twenty-three tales and sketches, was published in two volumes, each bound with paper wrappers and sold individually for 50¢ or as a set; the two volumes were also bound together in cloth and sold for $1.25. All of the pieces had been previously printed, except for "The Old Manse," which appeared for the first time in print and led off the collection. The first volume comprises "The Old Manse," "The Birthmark," "A Select Party," "Young Goodman Brown," "Rappaccini's Daughter,"

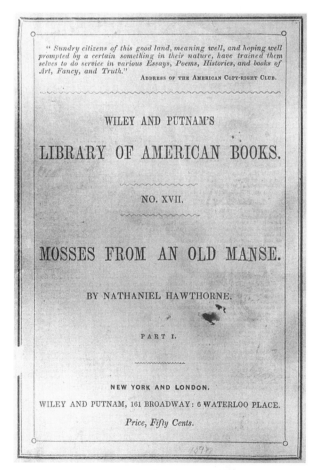

Front wrapper for Hawthorne's contribution to the Library of American Books, a short-lived series intended to publicize American authors (American Antiquarian Society, Worcester, Massachusetts)

"Mrs. Bullfrog," "Fire-Worship," "Buds and Bird-Voices," "Monsieur du Miroir," "The Hall of Fantasy," "The Celestial Railroad," and "The Procession of Life." The second volume comprises "The New Adam and Eve," "Egotism; or the Bosom Friend [Serpent]," "The Christmas Banquet," "Drowne's Wooden Image," "The Intelligence Office," "Roger Malvin's Burial," "P.'S Correspondence," "Earth's Holocaust," "The Old Apple Dealer," "The Artist of the Beautiful," and "A Virtuoso's Collection." An unknown number of copies of the collection were published about 5 June 1846.

Margaret Fuller was probably the most important nineteenth-century American literary woman before Emily Dickinson. A friend of Elizabeth Palmer Peabody, Hawthorne's sister-in-law, Fuller was a feminist who expressed her views in Woman in the Nineteenth Century *(1845). Fuller edited* The Dial, *the transcendentalist magazine, and also visited Brook Farm.*

Margaret Fuller, 1846

Review of *Mosses from an Old Manse*
Margaret Fuller
New-York Daily Tribune, 22 June 1846, p. 1

We have been seated here the last ten minutes, pen in hand, thinking what we can possibly say about this book that will not be either superfluous or impertinent.

Superfluous, because the attractions of Hawthorne's writings cannot fail of one and the same effect on all persons who possess the common sympathies of men. To all who are still happy in some groundwork of unperverted Nature, the delicate, simple, human tenderness, unsought, unbought and therefore precious morality, the tranquil elegance and playfulness, the humor which never breaks the impression of sweetness and dignity, do an inevitable message which requires no comment of the critic to make its meaning clear. Impertinent, because the influence of this mind, like that of some loveliest aspects of Nature, is to induce silence from a feeling of repose. We do not think of any thing particularly worth saying about this that has been so fitly and pleasantly said.

Yet it seems unfit that we, in our office of chronicler of intellectual advents and apparitions, should omit to render open and audible honor to one whom we have long delighted to honor. It may be, too, that this slight notice of ours may awaken the attention of those distant or busy who might not otherwise search for the volume, which comes betimes in the leafy month of June.

So we will give a slight account of it, even if we cannot say much of value. Though Hawthorne has now a standard reputation, both for the qualities we have mentioned and the beauty of the style in which they are embodied, yet we believe he has not been very widely read. This is only because his works have not been published in the way to insure extensive circulation in this new, hurrying world of ours. The immense extent of country over which the reading (still very small in proportion to the mere working) community is scattered, the rushing and pushing of our life at this electrical stage of development, leave no work a chance to be speedily and largely known that is not trumpeted and placarded. And, odious as are the features of a forced and artificial circulation, it must be considered that it does no harm in the end. Bad books will not be read if they are bought instead of good, while the good have an abiding life in the log-cabin settlements and Red River steamboat landings, to which they would in no other way penetrate. Under the auspices of Wiley and Putnam, Hawthorne will have a chance to collect all his own public about him, and that be felt as a presence which before was only a rumor.

The volume before us shares the charms of Hawthorne's earlier tales; the only difference being that his range of subjects is a little wider. There is the same gentle and sincere companionship with

The Old Manse, Concord, where the Hawthornes lived from July 1842 through September 1845. During this period Hawthorne wrote many of the stories that were included in Mosses from an Old Manse *(1846), and the couple's first child, Una, was born.*

Nature, the same delicate but fearless scrutiny of the secrets of the heart, the same serene independence of petty and artificial restrictions, whether on opinions or conduct, the same familiar, yet pensive sense of the spiritual or demoniacal influences that haunt the palpable life and common walks of men, not by many apprehended except in results. We have here to regret that Hawthorne, at this stage of his mind's life, lay no more decisive hand upon the apparition—brings it no nearer than in former days. We had hoped that we should see, no more as in a glass darkly, but face to face. Still, still brood over his page the genius of revery and the nonchalance of Nature, rather than the ardent earnestness of the human soul which feels itself born not only to see and disclose, but to understand and interpret such things. Hawthorne intimates and suggests, but he does not lay bare the mysteries of our being.

The introduction to the "Mosses," in which the old Manse, its inhabitants and visitants are portrayed, is written with even more than his usual charm of placid grace and many strokes of his admirable good sense. Those who are not, like ourselves,

familiar with the scene and its denizens, will still perceive how true that picture must be; those of us who are thus familiar will best know how to prize the record of objects and influences unique in our country and time.

"The Birth Mark" and "Rappaccini's Daughter" embody truths of profound importance in

The Hawthornes in Concord

Upon their marriage, Sophia and Nathaniel Hawthorne lived in Concord at the Old Manse, which was available because of the death of its previous occupant, Dr. Samuel Ripley. One of their neighbors was Ralph Waldo Emerson, with whom Sophia had been friendly before her marriage. He became a frequent Concord visitor to their home. Hawthorne also became friendly with such other illustrious Concord residents as Amos Bronson Alcott, Ellery Channing, and Henry David Thoreau. The Hawthornes first lived in Concord from 1842 to 1845; upon returning there in 1852, they bought the Hillside (which they renamed Wayside) from Alcott. This is the only home they ever owned.

shapes of aerial elegance. In these, as here and there in all these pieces, shines the loveliest ideal of love and the beauty of feminine purity, (by which we mcan no mere acts or abstinences, but perfect single truth felt and done in gentleness) which is its root.

"The Celestial Railroad," for its wit, wisdom, and the graceful adroitness with which the natural and material objects are interwoven with the allegories, has already won its meed of admiration. "Fire-worship" is a most charming essay for its domestic sweetness and thoughtful life. "Goodman Brown" is one of those disclosures we have spoken of, of the secrets of the breast. Who has not known such a trial that is capable indeed of sincere aspiration toward that only good, that infinite essence, which men call God. Who has not known the hour when even that best-beloved image cherished as the one precious symbol left, in the range of human nature, believed to be still pure gold when all the rest have turned to clay, shows, in severe ordeal, the symptoms of alloy. Oh hour of anguish, when the old familiar faces grow dark and dim in the lurid light—when the gods of the hearth, honored in childhood, adored in youth, crumble, and nothing, nothing is left which the daily earthly feelings can embrace—can cherish with unbroken Faith! Yet some survive that trial more happily than young Goodman Brown. They are those who have not sought it—have never of their own accord walked forth with the Tempter into the dim shades of Doubt. Mrs. Bull-Frog is an excellent humorous picture of what is called to be "content at last with substantial realities"!! The "Artist of the Beautiful" presents in a form that is, indeed, beautiful, the opposite view as to what *are* the substantial realities of life. Let each man choose between them according to his kind. Had Hawthorne written "Roger Malvin's Burial" alone, we should be pervaded with the sense of the poetry and religion of his soul.

As a critic, the style of Hawthorne, faithful to his mind, shows repose, a great reserve of strength, a slow secure movement. Though a very refined, he is also a very clear writer, showing, as we said before, a placid grace, and an indolent command of language.

And now, beside the full, calm yet romantic stream of his mind, we will rest. It has refreshment for the weary, islets of fascination no less than dark recesses and shadows for the imaginative, pure reflections for the pure of heart and eye, and, like the Concord he so well describes, many exquisite lilies for him who knows how to get at them.

In a review article of Wiley and Putnam's American Library series, the anonymous critic for the Edinburgh-based monthly Blackwood's Magazine *considers William Gilmore Sims's* Views and Reviews of American Literature *and* The Wigwam, and The Cabin, *Fuller's* Papers on Literature and Art, *and Poe's* Tales *before coming to* Mosses from an Old Manse. *At the beginning of the article the reviewer recommends Hawthorne's work and laments its comparative unavailability:*

> we shall be able to introduce to our readers (should it be hitherto unknown to them) one volume, at least, which they will be willing to transfer from the American to the English library. The "Mosses from an old Manse," is occasionally written with an elegance of style which may almost bear comparison with that of Washington Irving; and though certainly it is inferior to the works of that author in taste and judgment, and whatever may be described as artistic talent, it exhibits deeper traces of thought and reflection. What can our own circulating libraries be about? At all our places of summer resort they drug us with the veriest trash, without a spark of vitality in it, and here are tales and sketches like these of Nathaniel Hawthorne, which it would have done one's heart good to have read under shady coverts, or sitting—no unpleasant lounge—by the seas-side on the rolling shingles of the beach.

In his more specific remarks on the stories, however, the reviewer faults the improbability of plot in some of the stories.

The American Library: *Mosses from an Old Manse*
Blackwood's Magazine, 62 (November 1847): 587–592

Mosses from an Old Manse, by Nathaniel Hawthorne, is the somewhat quaint title given to a series of tales, and sketches, and miscellaneous papers, because they were written in an old manse, some time tenanted by the author, a description of which forms the first paper in the series. We have already intimated our opinion of this writer. In many respects he is a strong contrast to the one we have just left. For whereas Mr Poe is indebted to whatever good effect he produces to a close detail and agglomeration of fact, Mr Hawthorne appears to have little skill and little taste for dealing with matter of fact or substantial incident, but relies for his favourable impression on the charm of style, and the play of thought and fancy.

The most serious defect in his stories is the frequent presence of some palpable improbability which mars the effect of the whole—not improbability, like that we already remarked on, which is intended and wilfully perpetrated by the author—not improbability of incident even, which we are not disposed very rigidly to inquire after in a novelist—but improbability in the main motive and state of mind which he has undertaken to describe,

Two of Hawthorne's Concord neighbors: Ralph Waldo Emerson (left) and Henry David Thoreau (right)

and which forms the turning-point of the whole narrative. As long as the human being appears to act as a human being would, under the circumstances depicted, it is surprising how easily the mind, carried on by its sympathies with the feelings of the actor, forgets to inquire into the probability of these circumstances. Unfortunately, in Mr Hawthorne's stories, it is the human being himself who is not probable, nor possible.

It will be worth while to illustrate our meaning by an instance or two, to show that, far from being hypercritical, our canon of criticism is extremely indulgent, and that we never take the bluff and surly objection—it cannot be!—until the improbability has reached the core of the matter. In the first story, 'The Birth Mark,' we raise no objection to the author, because he invents a chemistry of his own, and supposes his hero in possession of marvellous secrets which enable him to diffuse into the air an ether or perfume, the inhaling of which shall displace a red mark from the cheek which a beautiful lady was born with; it were hard times indeed, if a

---

An Afternoon of Ice Skating

In a 30 December 1842 letter to Mrs. Caleb Foote, Sophia Hawthorne described her husband's afternoon outing with two of their Concord neighbors.

One afternoon, Mr. Emerson and Mr. Thoreau went with him down the river. Henry Thoreau is an experienced skater, and was figuring dithyrambic dances and Bacchic leaps on the ice—very remarkable, but very ugly, methought. Next him followed Mr. Hawthorne who, wrapped in his cloak, moved like a self-impelled Greek statue, stately and grave. Mr. Emerson closed the line, evidently too weary to hold himself erect, pitching headforemost, half lying on the air.

–Rose Hawthorne Lathrop,
Memories of Hawthorne, p. 53

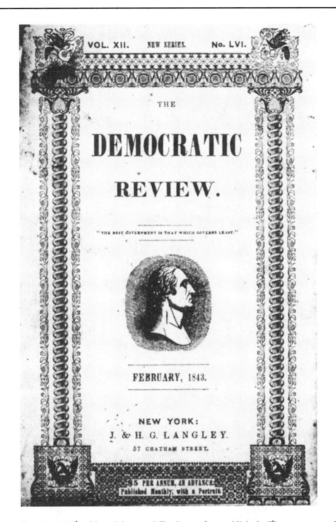

Front wrapper for the periodical in which "The New Adam and Eve" was first published. The story was collected in Mosses from an Old Manse *(American Art Association Anderson Galleries* catalogue, Stephen H. Wakeman sale, 28–29 April 1931).

novelist might not do what he pleased in a chemist's laboratory, and produce what drugs, what perfumes, what potable gold or charmed elixir, he may have need of. But we do object to the preposterous motive which prompts the amateur of science to an operation of the most hazardous kind, on a being he is represented as dearly loving. We are to believe that a good *husband* is afflicted, and grievously and incessantly tormented by a slight red mark on the cheek of a beautiful woman, which, as a *lover*, never gave him a moment's uneasiness, and which neither to him nor to anyone else abated one iota from her attractions. We are to suppose that he braves the risk of the experiment—it succeeds for a moment, then proves fatal, and destroys her—for what? Merely that she who was so very beautiful should attain to an ideal perfection. 'Had she been less beautiful,' we are told, 'it might have heightened his affection. But, seeing her otherwise so perfect, he found this one defect grow more and more intolerable, with

every moment of their united lives.' And then, we have some further bewildering explanation about 'his honourable love, so pure and lofty that it would accept nothing less than perfection, nor miserably make itself contented with an earthlier nature than he had dreamed of.' Call you this 'pure and lofty love,' when a woman is admired much as a connoisseur admires a picture, who might indeed be supposed to fume and fret if there was one little blot or blemish in it. Yet, even a connoisseur, who had an exquisite picture by an old master, with only one trifling blemish on it, would hardly trust himself or another to repair and retouch, in order to render it perfect. Can anyone recognise in this elaborate nonsense about ideal perfection, any approximation to the feeling which a man has for the wife he loves? If the novelist wished to describe this egregious connoisseurship in female charms, he should have put the folly into the head of some insane mortal, who, reversing the enthusiasm by which some men have loved a picture or

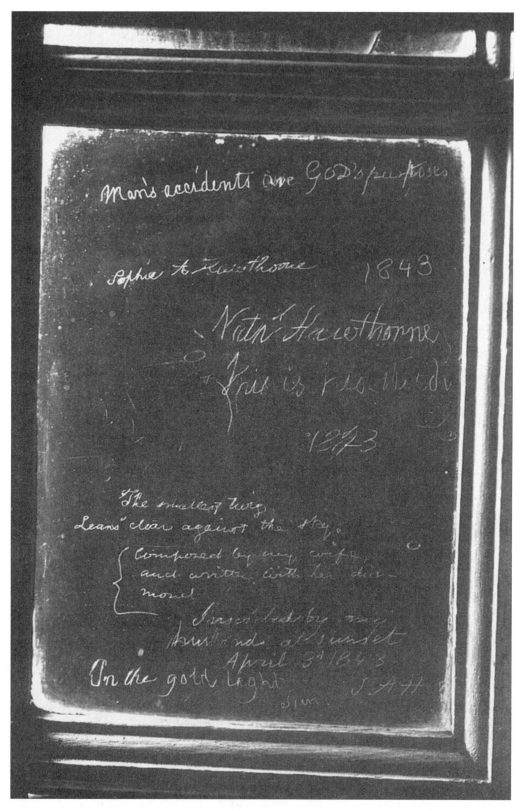

Window at the Old Manse that the Hawthornes incised with a diamond ring. The sentence "Man's accidents are God's purposes" is believed to refer to Sophia's miscarriage, the result of a fall after she slipped on ice (from Edwin Haviland Miller, Salem Is My Dwelling Place, *1991).*

First page of Hawthorne's manuscript setting copy for a story initially published in the June 1843 issue of The United States Magazine and Democratic Review. *It was collected in* Mosses from an Old Manse *(Peabody Essex Museum).*

Sophia Peabody Hawthorne at age thirty-six (etching by S. A. Schoff; Collection of Joel Myerson)

a statue as if it were a real woman, had learned to love his beautiful wife as if she were nothing else than a picture or a statue.

Again, in the 'Story of the Artist of the Beautiful,' we breathe not a word about the impossibility of framing out of springs and wheels so marvellous a butterfly, that the seeming creature shall not only fly and move its antennæ, and fold and display its wings like the living insect, but shall even surpass the living insect by showing a fine sense of human character, and refusing to perch on the hand of those who had not a genuine sentiment of beauty. The novelist shall put what springs and wheels he pleases into his mechanism, but the springs and wheels he places in the mechanist himself, must be those of genuine humanity, or the whole fiction falls to the ground. Now the mechanist, the hero of the story, the 'Artist of the Beautiful,' is described throughout as animated with the feelings proper to the artist, not to the mechanician. He is a young watchmaker, who, instead of plodding at the usual and lucrative routine of his trade, devotes his time to the structure of a most delicate and ingenious toy. We all know that a case like this is very possible. Few men, we should imagine, are more open to the impulse of emula-

tion, the desire to do that which had never been done before, than the ingenious mechanist; and few men more completely under the dominion of their leading passion or project, because every day brings some new contrivance, some new resource, and the hope that died at night is revived in the morning. But Mr Hawthorne is not contented with the natural and very strong impulse of the mechanician; he speaks throughout of his enthusiastic artisan as of some young Raphael intent upon 'creating the beautiful.' Springs, and wheels, and chains, however fine and complicate, are not 'the beautiful.' He might as well suppose the diligent anatomist, groping amongst nerves and tissues, to be stimulated to *his* task by an especial passion for the beautiful.

The passion of the ingenious mechanist we all understand; the passion of the artist, sculptor, or painter, is equally intelligible; but the confusion of the two in which Mr Hawthorne would vainly interest us, is beyond all power of comprehension. These are the improbabilities against which we contend. Moreover, when this wonderful butterfly is made—which he says truly was 'a gem of art that a monarch would have purchased with honours and abundant wealth, and have treasured among the jewels of his kingdom, as the most unique and wondrous of them all,'—the artist sees it crushed in the hands of a child and looks 'placidly' on. So never did any human mechanist who at length had succeeded in the dream and toil of his life. And at the conclusion of the story we are told, in not very intelligible language,—'When the artist rose high enough to achieve the Beautiful, the symbol by which he made it perceptible to mortal senses became of little value to his eyes, while his spirit possessed itself in the enjoyment of the reality.'

It is not, perhaps, to the *stories* we should be disposed to refer for the happier specimens of Mr Hawthorne's writing, but rather to those papers which we cannot better describe than as so many American *Spectators* of the year 1846—so much do they call to mind the style of essay in the days of Steele and Addison.

We may observe here, that American writers frequently remind us of models of composition somewhat antiquated with ourselves. While, on the one hand, there is a wild tendency to snatch at originality at any cost—to coin new phrases—new *probabilities*—to '*intensify*' our language with strange '*impulsive*' energy—to break loose, in short, from all those restraints which have been thought to render style both perspicuous and agreeable; there is, on the other hand—produced partly by a very intelligible reaction—an effort somewhat too apparent to be classical and correct. It is a very laudable effort, and we should be justly accused of fastidiousness did we mention it as in the least blameworthy. We would merely observe that an effect is sometimes produced upon an English ear as if the writer belonged to a previous era of our literature, to an epoch when to produce smooth and well modulated sentences was something rarer and more valued than it is now. It will be a proof how little of censure we attach to the characteristic we are noticing, when we point to the writings of Dr Channing for an illustration of our meaning. They have to us an air of formality, a slight dash of pedantry. We seem to hear the echo, though it has grown faint, of the Johnsonian rhythm. They are often not ineloquent, but the eloquence seems to have passed under the hands of the composition-master. The clever classical romance, called 'The Letters from Palmyra,' has the same studied air. It is here, indeed, more suited to the subject, for every writer, when treating of a classical era, appears by a sort of intuitive propriety to recognise the necessity of purifying to the utmost his own style.

In some of Mr Hawthorne's papers we are reminded, and by no means disagreeably, of the manner of Steele and Addison. 'The Intelligence Office' presents, in some parts, a very pleasing imitation of this style. This central intelligence office is one open to all mankind to make and record their various applications. The first person who enters inquires for 'a place,' and when questioned what sort of place he is seeking, very naïvely answers, 'I want my place!–my own place!–my true place in the world!–my thing to do!' The application is entered, but very slender hope is given that he who is running about the world in search of his place, will ever find it.

> The next that entered was a man beyond the middle age, bearing the look of one who knew the world and his own course in it . . .
> . . . Very probably, the next possessor may acquire the estate with a similar encumbrance, but it will be of his own contracting, and will not lighten your burden in the least.'

Mr Hawthorne is by no means an equal writer. He is perpetually giving his reader, who, being pleased by parts, would willingly think well of the whole, some little awkward specimen of dubious taste. We confess, even in the above short extract, to having passed over a sentence or two, whose absence we have not thought it worth while to mark with asterisks, and which would hardly bear out our Addisonian compliment.

> But again the door is opened. A grandfatherly personage tottered hastily into the office, with such

Crayon drawing of Hawthorne by Eastman Johnson that was commissioned by Longfellow. Hawthorne sat for Johnson several times from fall 1846 to spring 1847 (Longfellow National Historic Site).

an earnestness in his infirm alacrity that his white hair floated backward, as he hurried up to the desk. This venerable figure explained that he was in search of To-morrow.

'I have spent all my life in pursuit of it,' added the sage old gentleman, 'being assured that To-morrow has some vast benefit or other in store for me. But I am now getting a little in years, and must make haste; for unless I overtake To-morrow soon, I begin to be afraid it will finally escape me.'

'This fugitive To-morrow, my venerable friend,' said the man of intelligence, 'is a stray child of Time, and is flying from his father into the region of the infinite. Continue your pursuit and you will doubtless come up with him; but as to the earthly gifts you expect, he has scattered them all among a throng of Yesterdays.'

There is a nice bit of painting, as an artist might say, under the title of 'The Old Apple-dealer.' We have seen the very man in England. We had marked it for quotation, but it is too long, and we do not wish to mar its effect by mutilation.

In the 'Celestial Railroad,' we have a new Pilgrim's Progress performed by *rail*. Instead of the slow, solitary, pensive pilgrimage which John Bunyan describes, we travel in fashionable company,

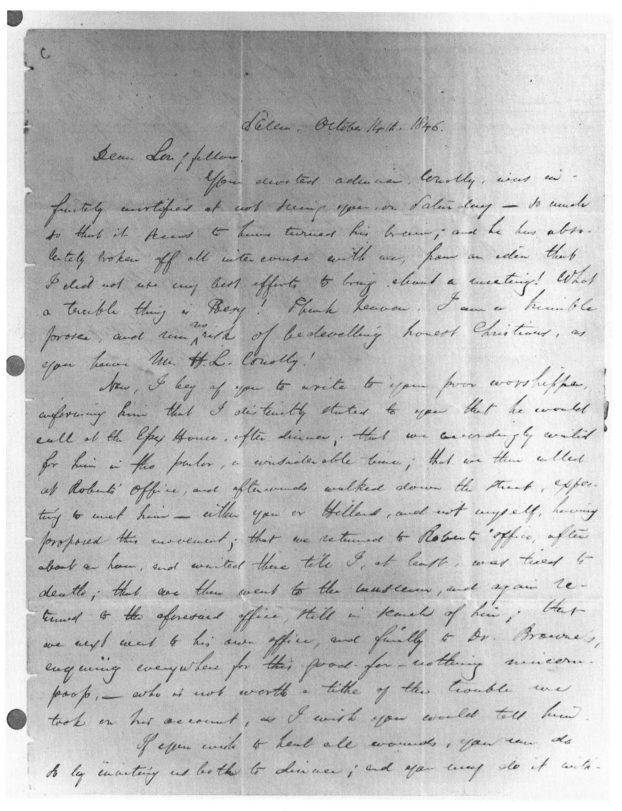

Hawthorne's 14 October 1846 letter to Longfellow, in which he writes, "What a terrible thing is Poesy! Thank heaven, I am a humble proser, and run no risk of bedevelling honest Christians, as you have Mr. H. L. Conolly!" H. L. (Horace) Conolly was the adopted son of Suzy Ingersoll, a relative of Hawthorne. He edited the Salem Advertiser, *for which Hawthorne occasionally wrote (Peabody Essex Museum).*

out dread of consequences; for I hereby bind myself
most positively and unmitigably to refuse to come with
him, on the score of his having behaved like a jackass.
It would gratify me much to have such an opportunity of
punishing him.

      If you will speak to Mr. Johnson, I will
call on him the next time I visit Boston, and make
arrangements about the portrait. My wife is much delighted with the idea — all previous attempts at my
"lineaments divine" having resulted unsuccessfully.

                Your friend,
                  Nath¹. Hawthorne.

If you invite us, let it be for some particular day.

The only surviving daguerreotype of Hawthorne, circa 1848, by John Adams Whipple (Library of Congress) and a wood engraving by J. Barry based on it that was published in Ballou's Pictorial Drawing-Room Companion *in 1855*

and in the most agreeable manner. A certain Mr Smooth-it-away has eclipsed the triumphs of Brunel. He has thrown a viaduct over the Slough of Despond; he has tunnelled the hill Difficulty, and raised an admirable causeway across the valley of Humiliation. The wicket gate, so inconveniently narrow, has been converted into a commodious station-house; and whereas it will be remembered there was a long standing feud in the time of Christian between one Prince Beelzebub and his adherents (famous for shooting deadly arrows) and the keeper of the wicket gate, this dispute, much to the credit of the worthy and enlightened directors, has been pacifically arranged on the principle of mutual compromise. The Prince's subjects are pretty numerously employed about the station-house. As to the fiery Apollyon, he was, as Mr Smooth-it-away observed, 'The very man to manage the engine,' and he has been made chief stoker.

'One great convenience of the new method of going on pilgrimage we must not forget to mention. Our enormous burdens, instead of being carried on our shoulders, as had been the custom of old, are all snugly deposited in the luggage-van.' The company, too, is most distinguished and fashionable; the conversation liberal and polite, turning 'upon the news

of the day, topics of business, politics, or the lighter matters of amusement; while religion, though indubitably the main thing at heart, is thrown tastefully into the background.' The train stops for refreshment at Vanity Fair. Indeed, the whole arrangements are admirable—up to a certain point. But it seems there are difficulties *at the other terminus* which the directors have not hitherto been able to overcome. On the whole, we are left with the persuasion that it is safer to go the old road, and in the old fashion, each one with his own burden upon his shoulders.

The story of 'Roger Malvin's Burial' is well told, and is the best of his narrative pieces. 'The New Adam and Eve,' and several others, might be mentioned for an agreeable vein of thought and play of fancy. In one of his papers the author has attempted a more common species of humour, and with some success. For variety's sake, we shall close our notice of him, and for the present, of 'The American Library,' with an extract from 'Mrs Bullfrog.'

Mr Bullfrog is an elegant and fastidious linen-draper, of feminine sensibility, and only too exquisite refinement. Such perfection of beauty and of delicacy did he require in the woman he should honour with the name of wife, that there was an

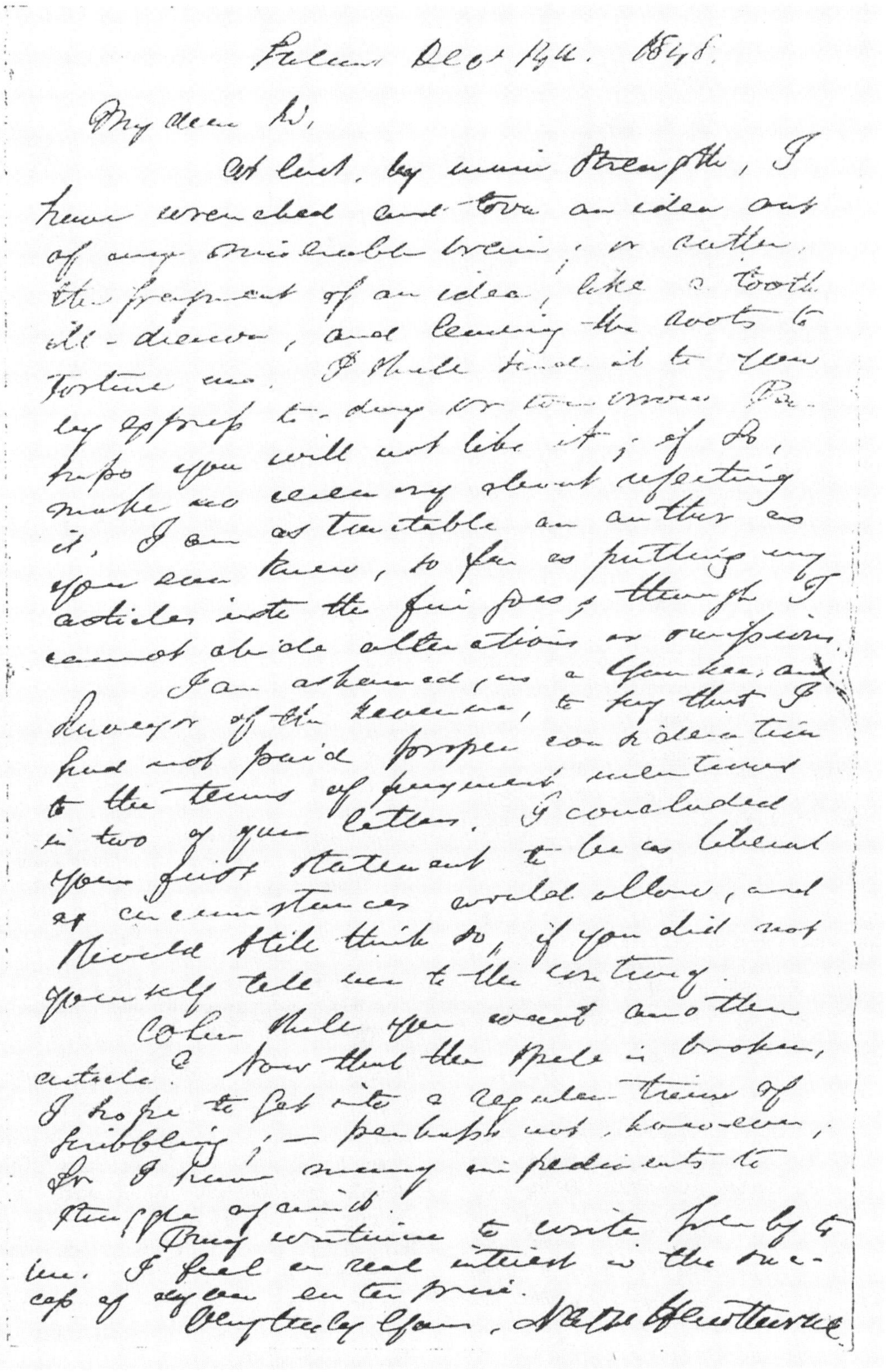

Salem Dec 14th. 1848.

My dear W,

At last, by main strength, I have wrenched and torn an idea out of my miserable brain; or rather, the fragment of an idea, like a tooth ill-drawn, and leaving the roots to torture me. I shall send it to you by Express to-day or tomorrow. Perhaps you will not like it; if so, make no ceremony about rejecting it. I am as tractable an author as you ever knew, so far as putting my articles into the fire goes; though I cannot abide alterations or omissions.

I am ashamed, as a Yankee and Surveyor of the Revenue, to say that I had not paid proper consideration to the terms of payment mentioned in two of your letters. I concluded your first statement to be as liberal as circumstances would allow, and should still think so, if you did not yourself tell me to the contrary.

When shall you want another article? Now that the spell is broken, I hope to get into a regular train of scribbling; — perhaps not, however, for I have many impediments to struggle of mind.

Pray continue to write freely to me. I feel a real interest in the success of your enterprise.

Very truly Yours, Nathl Hawthorne

Hawthorne's 15 December 1848 letter to editor Charles Walker Webber, which accompanied the author's submission of "Ethan Brand" (Collection of Stephen Rudin, Manhassat, New York)

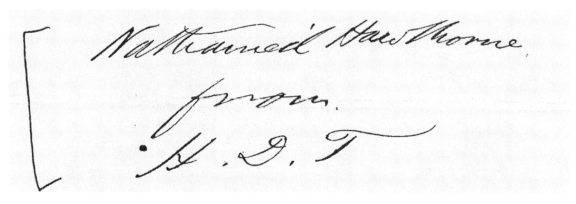

Thoreau's inscription in A Week on the Concord and Merrimack Rivers, *published in 1849 (American Art Association Anderson Galleries catalogue, Stephen H. Wakeman sale, 28–29 April 1931)*

awful chance of his obtaining no wife at all; when he happily fell in with the amiable and refined person, who in a very short time became Mrs Bullfrog.

An unlucky accident, an upset of the carriage on their wedding trip, giving rise to a strange display of masculine energy on the part of Mrs B. and disarranging her glossy black ringlets and pearly teeth, so as to occasion their disappearance and reappearance in a most miraculous manner, has excited a strange disquietude in the else happy bridegroom.

> 'To divert my mind,' says Mr Bullfrog, who tells his own story, 'I took up the newspaper which had covered the little basket of refreshments, and which now lay at the bottom of the coach, blushing with a deep red stain, and emitting a potent spirituous fume, from the contents of the broken bottle of *kalydor* . . .
> . . . Nay, since the result has been so fortunate, I rejoice at the wrongs which drove thee to this blessed lawsuit–happy Bullfrog that I am!'

Poe was probably the most important American literary critic in the first half of the nineteenth century, as may be seen in such a piece as "The Philosophy of Composition" (1846) and in reviews, including those about Hawthorne. This 1847 essay appeared in Godey's Lady's Book, *edited by Sarah Josepha Hale (now perhaps best remembered as the author of the poem "Mary's Lamb," which became known as "Mary Had a Little Lamb"). Although this publication published articles about fashion and society, it also published work by such serious authors as Hawthorne ("Drowne's Wooden Image") and Poe ("The Cask of Amontillado"). In the first sentence of this 1847 essay about Hawthorne, Poe refers to "The Literati of New York City," also published in* Godey's Lady's Book.

Tale-Writing–Nathaniel Hawthorne
Edgar Allan Poe
Godey's Lady's Book, 35 (November 1847): 252–256

In the preface to my sketches of New York Literati, while speaking of the broad distinction between the seeming public and real private opinion respecting our authors, I thus alluded to Nathaniel Hawthorne:–

> For example, Mr Hawthorne, the author of *Twice-told Tales*, is scarcely recognized by the press or by the public, and when noticed at all, is noticed merely to be damned by faint praise. Now, my own opinion of him is, that although his walk is limited and he is fairly to be charged with mannerism, treating all subjects in a similar tone of dreamy *innuendo*, yet in this walk he evinces extraordinary genius, having no rival either in America or elsewhere; and this opinion I have never heard gainsaid by any one literary person in the country. That this opinion, however, is a spoken and not a written one, is referable to the facts, first, that Mr Hawthorne is a poor man, and secondly, that he *is not* an ubiquitous quack.

The reputation of the author of *Twice-told Tales* has been confined, indeed, until very lately, to literary society; and I have not been wrong, perhaps, in citing him as *the* example, *par excellence*, in this country, of the privately-admired and publicly-unappreciated man of genius. Within the last year or two, it is true, an occasional critic has been urged, by honest indignation, into very warm approval. Mr Webber, for instance (than whom no one has a keener relish for that kind of writing which Mr Hawthorne has best illustrated,) gave us, in a late number of *The American Review*, a cordial and certainly a full tribute to his talents; and since the issue of the *Mosses from an Old Manse*, criticisms of similar tone have been by no means infrequent in our more authoritative journals. I can call to mind few reviews of Haw-

Emerson's inscription in Nature, Addresses, and Lectures, *published in 1849 (American Art Association Anderson Galleries catalogue, Stephen H. Wakeman sale, 28–29 April 1931)*

thorne published *before* the *Mosses*. One I remember in *Arcturus* (edited by Matthews and Duyckinck) for May, 1841; another in the *American Monthly* (edited by Hoffman and Herbert) for March, 1838; a third in the ninety-sixth number of the *North American Review*. These criticisms, however, seemed to have little effect on the popular taste—at least, if we are to form any idea of the popular taste by reference to its expression in the newspapers, or by the sale of the author's book. It was never the fashion (until lately) to speak of him in any summary of our best authors. The daily critics would say, on such occasions, 'Is there not Irving and Cooper, and Bryant and Paulding, and—Smith?' or, 'Have we not Halleck and Dana, and Longfellow and—Thompson?' or, 'Can we not point triumphantly to our own Sprague, Willis, Channing, Bancroft, Prescott and—Jenkins?' but these unanswerable queries were never wound up by the name of Hawthorne.

Beyond doubt, this inappreciation of him on the part of the public arose chiefly from the two causes to which I have referred—from the facts that he is neither a man of wealth nor a quack;—but these are insufficient to account for the whole effect. No small portion of it is attributable to the very marked idiosyncrasy of Mr Hawthorne himself. In one sense, and in great measure, to be peculiar is to be original, and than the true originality there is no higher literary virtue. This true or commendable originality, however, implies not the uniform, but the continuous peculiarity—a peculiarity springing from ever-active vigor of fancy—better still if from ever-present force of imagination, giving its own

hue, its own character to everything it touches, and, especially, *self impelled to touch everything*.

It is often said, inconsiderately, that very original writers always fail in popularity—that such and such persons are too original to be comprehended by the mass. 'Too peculiar,' should be the phrase, 'too idiosyncratic.' It is, in fact, the excitable, undisciplined and child-like popular mind which most keenly feels the original. The criticism of the conservatives, of the hackneys, of the cultivated old clergymen of the *North American Review*, is precisely the criticism which condemns and alone condemns it. 'It becometh not a divine,' saith Lord Coke, 'to be of a fiery and salamandrine spirit.' Their conscience allowing them to move nothing themselves, these dignitaries have a holy horror of being moved. 'Give us *quietude*,' they say. Opening their mouths with proper caution, they sigh forth the word '*Repose*.' And this is, indeed, the one thing they should be permitted to enjoy, if only upon the Christian principle of give and take.

The fact is, that if Mr Hawthorne were really original, he could not fail of making himself felt by the public. But the fact is, he is *not* original in any sense. Those who speak of him as original, mean nothing more than that he differs in his manner or tone, and in his choice of subjects, from any author of their acquaintance—their acquaintance not extending to the German Tieck, whose manner, in *some* of his works, is absolutely identical with that *habitual* to Hawthorne. But it is clear that the element of the literary originality is novelty. The element of its appreciation by the reader is the reader's sense of the new. Whatever gives him a new and insomuch a pleasurable emotion, he considers original, and whoever frequently gives him such emotion, he considers an original writer. In a word, it is by the sum total of these emotions that he decides upon the writer's claim to originality. I may observe here, however, that there is clearly a point at which even novelty itself would cease to produce the legitimate originality, if we judge this originality, as we should, by the effect designed: this point is that at which *novelty becomes nothing novel*; and here the artist, *to preserve his originality*, will subside into the common-place. No one, I think, has noticed that, merely through inattention to this matter, Moore has comparatively failed in his 'Lalla Rookh.' Few readers, and indeed few critics, have commended this poem for originality—and, in fact, the effect, originality, is not produced by it—yet no work of equal size so abounds in the happiest originalities, individually considered. They are so excessive as, in the end, to deaden in the reader all capacity for their appreciation.

These points properly understood, it will be seen that the critic (unacquainted with Tieck) who reads a single tale or essay by Hawthorne, may be justified in thinking him original; but the tone, or manner, or choice of subject, which induces in this critic the sense of the new, will—if not in a second tale, at least in a third and all subsequent ones—not only fail of inducing it, but bring about an exactly antagonistic impression. In concluding a volume, and more especially in concluding all the volumes of the author, the critic will abandon his first design of calling him 'original,' and content himself with styling him 'peculiar.'

With the vague opinion that to be original is to be unpopular, I could, indeed, agree, were I to adopt an understanding of originality which, to my surprise, I have known adopted by many who have a right to be called critical. They have limited, in a love for mere words, the literary to the metaphysical originality. They regard as original in letters, only such combinations of thought, of incident, and so forth, as are, in fact, absolutely novel. It is clear, however, not only that it is the novelty of *effect* alone which is worth consideration, but that this effect is *best* wrought, for the end of all fictitious composition, pleasure, by shunning rather than by seeking the absolute novelty of combination. Originality, thus understood, tasks and startles the intellect, and so brings into undue action the faculties to which, in the lighter literature, we least appeal. And thus understood, it cannot fail to prove unpopular with the masses, who, seeking in this literature amusement, are positively offended by instruction. But the true originality—true in respect of its purposes—is that which, in bringing out the half-formed, the reluctant, or the unexpressed fancies of mankind, or in exciting the more delicate pulses

of the heart's passion, or in giving birth to some universal sentiment or instinct in embryo, thus combines with the pleasurable effect of *apparent* novelty, a real egoistic delight. The reader, in the case first supposed, (that of the absolute novelty,) is excited, but embarrassed, disturbed, in some degree even pained at his own want of perception, at his own folly in not having himself hit upon the idea. In the second case, his pleasure is doubled. He is filled with an intrinsic and extrinsic delight. He feels and intensely enjoys the seeming novelty of the thought, enjoys it as really novel, as absolutely original with the writer—*and* himself. They two, he fancies, have, alone of all men, thought thus. They two have, together, created this thing. Henceforward there is a bond of sympathy between them, a sympathy which irradiates every subsequent page of the book.

There is a species of writing which, with some difficulty, may be admitted as a lower degree of what I have called the true original. In its perusal, we say to ourselves, not 'how original this is!' nor 'here is an idea which I and the author have alone entertained,' but 'here is a charmingly obvious fancy,' or sometimes even, 'here is a thought which I am not sure has ever occurred to myself, but which, of course, has occurred to all the rest of the world.' This kind of composition (which still appertains to a high order) is usually designated as 'the natural.' It has little external resemblance, but strong internal affinity to the true original, if, indeed, as I have suggested, it is not of this latter an inferior degree. It is best exemplified, among English writers, in Addison, Irving and *Hawthorne*. The 'ease' which is so often spoken of as its distinguishing feature, it has been the fashion to regard as ease in appearance alone, as a point of really difficult attainment. This idea, however, must be received with some reservation. The natural style is difficult only to those who should never intermeddle with it—to the unnatural. It is but the result of writing with the understanding, or with the instinct, that the *tone*, in composition, should be that which, at any given point or upon any given topic, would be the tone of the great mass of humanity. The author who, after the manner of the North Americans, is merely at *all* times *quiet*, is, of course, upon *most* occasions, merely silly or stupid, and has no more right to be thought 'easy' or 'natural' than has a cockney exquisite or the sleeping beauty in the waxworks.

The 'peculiarity' or sameness, or monotone of Hawthorne, would, in its mere character of 'peculiarity,' and without reference to what *is* the peculiarity, suffice to deprive him of all chance of popular appreciation. But at his failure to be appreciated, we can, *of course*, no longer wonder, when we find him monotonous at decidedly the worst of all possible points—at that point which, having the least concern with Nature, is the farthest removed from the popular intellect, from the popular sentiment and from the popular taste. I allude to the strain of allegory which completely overwhelms the greater number of his subjects, and which in some measure interferes with the direct conduct of absolutely all.

In defence of allegory, (however, or for whatever object, employed,) there is scarcely one respectable word to be said. Its best appeals are made to the fancy—that is to say, to our sense of adaptation, not of matters proper, but of matters improper for the purpose, of the real with the unreal; having never more of intelligible connection than has something with nothing, never half so much of effective affinity as has the substance for the shadow. The deepest emotion aroused within us by the happiest allegory, *as* allegory, is a very, very imperfectly satisfied sense of the writer's ingenuity in overcoming a difficulty we should have preferred his not having attempted to overcome. The fallacy of the idea that allegory, in any of its moods, can be made to enforce a truth—that metaphor, for example, may illustrate as well as embellish an argument—could be promptly demonstrated: the converse of the supposed fact might be shown, indeed, with very little trouble—but these are topics foreign to my present purpose. One thing is clear, that if allegory ever establishes a fact, it is by dint of overturning a fiction. Where the suggested meaning runs through the obvious one in a *very* profound under-current, so as never to interfere with the upper one without our own volition, so as never to show itself unless *called* to the surface, there only, for the proper uses of fictitious narrative, is it available at all. Under the best circumstances, it must always interfere with that unity of effect which, to the artist, is worth all the allegory in the world. Its vital injury, however, is rendered to the most vitally important point in fiction—that of earnestness or verisimilitude. That *The Pilgrim's Progress* is a ludicrously over-rated book, owing its seeming popularity to one or two of those accidents in critical literature which by the critical are sufficiently well understood, is a matter upon which no two thinking people disagree; but the pleasure derivable from it, in any sense, will be found in the direct ratio of the reader's capacity to smother its true purpose, in the direct ratio of his ability to keep the allegory out of sight, or of his *in*ability to comprehend it. Of allegory properly handled, judiciously subdued, seen only as a shadow or by suggestive glimpses, and making its nearest approach to truth in a not obtrusive and therefore not unpleasant *appositeness*, the *Undine* of De La Motte Fouqué is the best, and undoubtedly a very remarkable specimen.

The obvious causes, however, which have prevented Mr Hawthorne's *popularity*, do not suffice to con-

---

Longfellow's *Evangeline*

Fields included this anecdote of Hawthorne and Longfellow in his memoir. Hawthorne reviewed Evangeline *in the 13 November 1847 issue of the* Salem Advertiser.

Hawthorne dined one day with Longfellow, and brought with him a friend from Salem. After dinner the friend said: "I have been trying to persuade Hawthorne to write a story, based upon a legend of Acadie, and still current there; a legend of a girl who, in the dispersion of the Acadians, was separated from her lover, and passed her life in waiting and seeking for him, and only found him dying in a hospital, when both were old." Longfellow wondered that this legend did not strike the fancy of Hawthorne, and said to him: "If you have really made up your mind not to use it for a story, will you give it to me for a poem?" To this Hawthorne assented, and moreover promised not to treat the subject in prose till Longfellow had seen what he could do with it in verse. And so we have "Evangeline" in beautiful hexameters,—a poem that will hold its place in literature while true affection lasts. Hawthorne rejoiced in this great success of Longfellow, and loved to count up the editions, both foreign and American, of this now world-renowned poem.

—Yesterdays with Authors, pp. 64–65

---

demn him in the eyes of the few who belong properly to books, and to whom books, perhaps, do not quite so properly belong. These few estimate an author, not as do the public, altogether by what he does, but in great measure—indeed, even in the greater measure—by what he evinces a capability of doing. In this view, Hawthorne stands among literary people in America much in the same light as did Coleridge in England. The few, also, through a certain warping of the taste, which long pondering upon books as books merely never fails to induce, are not in condition to view the errors of a scholar as errors altogether. At any time these gentlemen are prone to think the public not right rather than an educated author wrong. But the simple truth is, that the writer who aims at impressing the people, is *always* wrong when he fails in forcing that people to receive the impression. How far Mr Hawthorne has addressed the people at all, is, of course, not a question for me to decide. His books afford strong internal evidence of having been written to himself and his particular friends alone.

There has long existed in literature a fatal and unfounded prejudice, which it will be the office of this age to overthrow—the idea that the mere bulk of a work must enter largely into our estimate of its merit. I do not suppose even the weakest of the Quarterly reviewers weak enough to maintain that in a book's size or mass, abstractly considered, there is anything

Lowell on Hawthorne

One measure of Hawthorne's reputation before composing The Scarlet Letter *is his inclusion in James Russell Lowell's satire* A Fable for Critics *(1848). Lowell puts Hawthorne in the company of American authors such as Ralph Waldo Emerson, Edgar Allan Poe, and William Cullen Bryant.*

. . . There is Hawthorne, with genius so shrinking and rare
That you hardly at first see the strength that is there;
A frame so robust, with a nature so sweet,
So earnest, so graceful, so lithe and so fleet,
Is worth a descent from Olympus to meet;
'Tis as if a rough oak that for ages had stood,
With his gnarled bony branches like ribs of the wood,
Should bloom, after cycles of struggle and scathe,
With a single anemone trembly and rathe;
His strength is so tender; his wildness so meek,
That a suitable parallel sets one to seek,–
He's a John Bunyan Fouqué, a Puritan Tieck;
When Nature was shaping him, clay was not granted
For making so full-sized a man as she wanted,
So, to fill out her model, a little she spared
From some finer-grained stuff for a woman prepared,
And she could not have hit a more excellent plan
For making him fully and perfectly man.
The success of her scheme gave her so much delight,
That she tried it again, shortly after, in Dwight;
Only, while she was kneading and shaping the clay,
She sang to her work in her sweet childish way,
And found, when she'd put the last touch to his soul,
That the music had somehow got mixed with the whole . . .

–A Fable for Critics, pp. 134–135

which especially calls for our admiration. A mountain, simply through the sensation of physical magnitude which it conveys, does, indeed, affect us with a sense of the sublime, but we cannot admit any such influence in the contemplation even of *The Columbiad.* The Quarterlies themselves will not admit it. And yet, what else are we to understand by their continual prating about 'sustained effort?' Granted that this sustained effort has accomplished an epic—let us then admire the effort, (if this be a thing admirable,) but certainly not the epic on the effort's account. Common sense, in the time to come, may possibly insist upon measuring a work of art rather by the object it fulfils, by the impression it makes, than by the time it took to fulfil the object, or by the extent of 'sustained effort' which became necessary to produce the impression. The fact is, that perseverance is one thing and genius quite another; nor can all the transcendentalists in Heathendom confound them.

Full of its bulky ideas, the last number of the *North American Review,* in what it imagines a criticism on Simms, 'honestly avows that it has little opinion of the mere tale;' and the honesty of the avowal is in no slight degree guaranteed by the fact that this Review has never yet been known to put forth an opinion which was *not* a very little one indeed.

The tale proper affords the fairest field which can be afforded by the wide domains of mere prose, for the exercise of the highest genius. Were I bidden to say how this genius could be most advantageously employed for the best display of its powers, I should answer, without hesitation, 'in the composition of a rhymed poem not to exceed in length what might be perused in an hour.' Within this limit alone can the noblest order of poetry exist. I have discussed this topic elsewhere, and need here repeat only that the phrase 'a long poem' embodies a paradox. A poem must intensely excite. Excitement is its province, its essentiality. Its value is in the ratio of its (elevating) excitement. But all excitement is, from a psychal necessity, transient. It cannot be sustained through a poem of great length. In the course of an hour's reading, at most, it flags, fails; and then the poem is, in effect, no longer such. Men admire, but are wearied with the *Paradise Lost*; for platitude follows platitude, *inevitably*, at regular interspaces, (the depressions between the waves of excitement,) until the poem, (which, properly considered, is but a succession of brief poems,) having been brought to an end, we discover that the sums of our pleasure and of displeasure have been very nearly equal. The absolute, ultimate or aggregate effect of any epic under the sun is, for these reasons, a nullity. 'The Iliad,' in its form of epic, has but an imaginary existence; granting it real, however, I can only say of it that it is based on a primitive sense of Art. Of the modern epic nothing can be so well said as that it is a blindfold imitation of a 'come-by-chance.' By and by these propositions will be understood as self-evident, and in the meantime will not be essentially damaged as truths by being generally condemned as falsities.

A poem *too* brief, on the other hand, may produce a sharp or vivid, but never a profound or enduring impression. Without a certain continuity, without a certain duration or repetition of the cause, the soul is seldom moved to the effect. There must be the dropping of the water on the rock. There must be the pressing steadily down of the stamp upon the wax. De Beranger has wrought brilliant things, pungent and spirit-stirring, but most of them are too immassive to have *momentum*, and, as so many feathers of fancy, have been blown aloft only to be whistled down the wind. Brevity, indeed, may degenerate into epigrammatism, but this danger does not prevent extreme length from being the one unpardonable sin.

Were I called upon, however, to designate that class of composition, which, next to such a poem as I have suggested, should best fulfil the demands and serve the purposes of ambitious genius, should offer it the most advantageous field of exertion, and afford it the fairest opportunity of display, I should speak at once of the brief prose tale. History, philosophy, and other matters of that kind, we leave out of the question, of course. *Of course*, I say, and in spite of the graybeards. These graver topics, to the end of time, will be best illustrated by what a discriminating world, turning up its nose at the drab pamphlets, has agreed to understand as *talent*. The ordinary novel is objectionable, from its length, for reasons analogous to those which render length objectionable in the poem. As the novel cannot be read at one sitting, it cannot avail itself of the immense benefit of *totality*. Worldly interests, intervening during the pauses of perusal, modify, counteract and annul the impressions intended. But simple cessation in reading would, of itself, be sufficient to destroy the true unity. In the brief tale, however, the author is enabled to carry out his full design without interruption. During the hour of perusal, the soul of the reader is at the writer's control.

A skillful artist has constructed a tale. He has not fashioned his thoughts to accommodate his incidents, but

Hawthorne and Melville

The Hawthornes moved to Lenox, Massachusetts, in spring 1850. On 5 August of that year Hawthorne attended a picnic at Monument Mountain that had been organized for the purpose of bringing together notable people of the area. These included Oliver Wendell Holmes, Evert Duyckinck, Henry Sedgwick, James T. Fields, and Herman Melville. Hawthorne and Melville had not met before this picnic, though Hawthorne had reviewed Melville's Typee *in 1846. These two men quickly became friends, and Melville was liked by the entire Hawthorne family. As a result of his relationship with Hawthorne and understanding the depth of Hawthorne's mind, Melville reworked a nearly-finished manuscript about whaling. Hawthorne therefore might be seen as liberating the genius in Melville that permitted him to rewrite the whaling book as* Moby-Dick, *which he dedicated to Hawthorne ("In Token of my admiration for his genius, This book is inscribed to Nathaniel Hawthorne"). The men's relationship continued until November 1851, when the Hawthornes moved from Lenox to West Newton, Massachusetts. Hawthorne and Melville met for the last time in 1856, when Hawthorne was American consul to Liverpool, England.*

The "little red house," where the Hawthornes lived from May 1850 until November 1851

Portrait of Herman Melville by Asa W. Twitchell,
circa 1847 (Berkshire Athenaeum)

can be commended as a whole. In many of them the interest is subdivided and frittered away, and their conclusions are insufficiently *climacic*. In the higher requisites of composition, John Neal's magazine stories excel–I mean in vigor of thought, picturesque combination of incident, and so forth–but they ramble too much, and invariably break down just before coming to an end, as if the writer had received a sudden and irresistible summons to dinner, and thought it incumbent upon him to make a finish of his story before going. One of the happiest and best-sustained tales I have seen, is 'Jack Long; or, The Shot in the Eye,' by Charles W. Webber, the assistant editor of Mr Colton's *American Review*. But in general skill of construction, the tales of Willis, I think, surpass those of any American writer–with the exception of Mr Hawthorne.

I must defer to the better opportunity of a volume now in hand, a full discussion of his individual pieces, and hasten to conclude this paper with a summary of his merits and demerits.

He is peculiar and *not* original–unless in those detailed fancies and detached thoughts which his want of general originality will deprive of the appreciation due to them, in preventing them forever reaching the *public* eye. He is infinitely too fond of allegory, and can never hope for popularity so long as he persists in it. This he will not do, for allegory is at war with the whole tone of his nature, which disports itself never so well as when escaping from the mysticism of his Goodman Browns and White Old Maids into the hearty, genial, but still Indian-summer sunshine of his Wakefields and Little Annie's Rambles. Indeed, *his* spirit of 'metaphor run-mad' is clearly imbibed from the phalanx and phalanstery atmosphere in which he has been so long struggling for breath. He has not half the material for the exclusiveness of authorship that he possesses for its universality. He has the purest style, the finest taste, the most available scholarship, the most delicate humor, the most touching pathos, the most radiant imagination, the most consummate ingenuity; and with these varied good qualities he has done *well* as a mystic. But is there any one of these qualities which should prevent his doing doubly as well in a career of honest, upright, sensible, prehensible and comprehensible things? Let him mend his pen, get a bottle of visible ink, come out from the Old Manse, cut Mr Alcott, hang (if possible) the editor of 'The Dial', and throw out of the window to the pigs all his odd numbers of *The North American Review*.

having deliberately conceived a certain *single effect* to be wrought, he then invents such incidents, he then combines such events, and discusses them in such tone as may best serve him in establishing this preconceived effect. If his very first sentence tend not to the outbringing of this effect, then in his very first step has he committed a blunder. In the whole composition there should be no word written of which the tendency, direct or indirect, is not to the one pre-established design. And by such means, with such care and skill, a picture is at length painted which leaves in the mind of him who contemplates it with a kindred art, a sense of the fullest satisfaction. The idea of the tale, its thesis, has been presented unblemished, because undisturbed–an end absolutely demanded, yet, in the novel, altogether unattainable.

Of skillfully-constructed tales–I speak now without reference to other points, some of them more important than construction–there are very few American specimens. I am acquainted with no better one, upon the whole, than the 'Murder Will Out' of Mr Simms, and this has some glaring defects. The 'Tales of a Traveler,' by Irving, are graceful and impressive narratives–'The Young Italian' is especially good–but there is not one of the series which

Melville's review of Mosses from an Old Manse *is one of the most significant statements of cultural nationalism in the nineteenth century. In* Herman Melville: A Biography *(1996) Hershel Parker suggests that because "Melville expressed openly Hawthorne's impact on him" he chose to "protect himself by ascribing the essay to 'a Virginian Spending July in Vermont.'"*

Herman Melville's essay, in which he compares Hawthorne to William Shakespeare and focuses on the darkness of some of the stories in Mosses from an Old Manse, *so pleased Nathaniel and Sophia Hawthorne that they expressed their delight to Evert A. Duyckinck, the editor for the American Library series who had published Melville's essay in* The Literary World.

Hawthorne and His Mosses

By a Virginian Spending July in Vermont
The Literary World, 7 (17 and 24 August 1850): 125–127, 145–147

A papered chamber in a fine old farm-house, a mile from any other dwelling, and dipped to the eaves in foliage—surrounded by mountains, old woods, and Indian ponds,—this, surely, is the place to write of Hawthorne. Some charm is in this northern air, for love and duty seem both impelling to the task. A man of a deep and noble nature has seized me in this seclusion. His wild, witch-voice rings through me; or, in softer cadences, I seem to hear it in the songs of the hill-side birds that sing in the larch trees at my window.

Would that all excellent books were foundlings, without father or mother, that so it might be we could glorify them, without including their ostensible authors! Nor would any true man take exception to this; least of all, he who writes, 'When the Artist rises high enough to achieve the Beautiful, the symbol by which he makes it perceptible to mortal senses becomes of little value in his eyes, while his spirit possesses itself in the enjoyment of the reality.'

But more than this. I know not what would be the right name to put on the title-page of an excellent book; but this I feel, that the names of all fine authors are fictitious ones, far more so than that of Junius; simply standing, as they do, for the mystical, ever-eluding spirit of all beauty, which ubiquitously possesses men of genius. Purely imaginative as this fancy may appear, it nevertheless seems to receive some warranty from the fact, that on a personal interview no great author has ever come up to the idea of his reader. But that dust of which our bodies are composed, how can it fitly express the nobler intelligences among us? With reverence be it spoken, that not even in the case of one deemed more than man, not even in our Saviour, did his visible frame betoken anything of the augustness of

the nature within. Else, how could those Jewish eyewitnesses fail to see heaven in his glance!

It is curious how a man may travel along a country road, and yet miss the grandest or sweetest of prospects by reason of an intervening hedge, so like all other hedges, as in no way to hint of the wide landscape beyond. So has it been with me concerning the enchanting landscape in the soul of this Hawthorne, this most excellent Man of Mosses. His *Old Manse* has been written now four years, but I never read it till a day or two since. I had seen it in the book-stores—heard of it often—even had it recommended to me by a tasteful friend, as a rare, quiet book, perhaps too deserving of popularity to be popular. But there are so many books called 'excellent,' and so much unpopular merit, that amid the thick stir of other things, the hint of my tasteful friend was disregarded; and for four years the Mosses on the Old Manse never refreshed me with their perennial green. It may be, however, that all this while the book, likewise, was only improving in flavor and body. At any rate, it so chanced that this long procrastination eventuated in a happy result. At breakfast the other day, a mountain girl, a cousin of mine, who for the last two weeks has every morning helped me to strawberries and raspberries, which, like the roses and pearls in the fairy tale, seemed to fall into the saucer from those strawberry-beds, her cheeks—this delightful creature, this charming Cherry says to me—'I see you spend your mornings in the haymow; and yesterday I found there "Dwight's Travels in New England." Now I have something far better than that, something more congenial to our summer on these hills. Take these raspberries, and then I will give you some moss.' 'Moss!' said I. 'Yes, and you must take it to the barn with you, and good-by to "Dwight".'

With that she left me, and soon returned with a volume, verdantly bound, and garnished with a curious frontispiece in green; nothing less than a fragment of real moss, cunningly pressed to a fly-leaf. 'Why, this,' said I, spilling my raspberries, 'this is the *Mosses from an Old Manse.*' 'Yes,' said cousin Cherry, 'yes, it is that flowery Hawthorne.' 'Hawthorne and Mosses,' said I, 'no more: it is morning: it is July in the country: and I am off for the barn.'

Stretched on that new mown clover, the hill-side breeze blowing over me through the wide barn-door, and soothed by the hum of the bees in the meadows around, how magically stole over me this Mossy Man! and how amply, how bountifully, did he redeem that delicious promise to his guests in the Old Manse, of whom it is written—'Others could give them pleasure, or amusement, or instruction—these could be picked up anywhere—but it was for me to give them rest. Rest, in a life of trouble! What better could be done for weary and world-worn spirits? What better could be done for anybody, who came within our magic circle, than to throw the spell of a magic spirit over him?' So all that day, half-buried in the new clover, I watched this Hawthorne's 'Assyrian dawn, and Paphian sunset and moonrise, from the summit of our Eastern Hill.'

The soft ravishments of the man spun me round about in a web of dreams, and when the book was closed, when the spell was over, this wizard 'dismissed me with but misty reminiscences, as if I had been dreaming of him.'

What a wild moonlight of contemplative humor bathes that Old Manse!—the rich and rare distilment of a spicy and slowly-oozing heart. No rollicking rudeness, no gross fun fed on fat dinners, and bred in the lees of wine,—but a humor so spiritually gentle, so high, so deep, and yet so richly relishable, that it were hardly inappropriate in an angel. It is the very religion of mirth; for nothing so human but it may be advanced to that. The orchard of the Old Manse seems the visible type of the fine mind that has described it—those twisted and contorted old trees, 'that stretch out their crooked branches, and take such hold of the imagination, that we remember them as humorists and odd-fellows.' And then, as surrounded by these grotesque forms, and hushed in the noon-day repose of this Hawthorne's spell, how aptly might the still fall of his ruddy thoughts into your soul be symbolized by 'the thump of a great apple, in the stillest afternoon, falling without a breath of wind, from the mere necessity of perfect ripeness!' For no less ripe than ruddy are the apples of the thoughts and fancies in this sweet Man of Mosses—

Buds and Bird-voices—

What a delicious thing is that! 'Will the world ever be so decayed, that Spring may not renew its greenness?' And the 'Fire-Worship.' Was ever the hearth so glorified into an altar before? The mere title of that piece is better than any common work in fifty folio volumes. How exquisite is this:—

> Nor did it lessen the charm of his soft, familiar courtesy and helpfulness, that the mighty spirit, were opportunity offered him, would run riot through the peaceful house, wrap its inmates in his terrible embrace, and leave nothing of them save their whitened bones. This possibility of mad destruction only made his domestic kindness the more beautiful and touching. It was so sweet of him, being endowed with such power, to dwell, day after day, and one long, lonesome night after another, on the dusky hearth, only now and then betraying his wild nature, by thrusting his red tongue out of the chimney-top! True, he had done much mischief in the world, and was pretty certain to do more,

but his warm heart atoned for all; he was kindly to the race of man.

But he has still other apples, not quite so ruddy, though full as ripe;—apples, that have been left to wither on the tree, after the pleasant autumn gathering is past. The sketch of 'The Old Apple-Dealer' is conceived in the subtlest spirit of sadness; he whose 'subdued and nerveless boyhood prefigured his abortive prime, which, likewise, contained within itself the prophecy and image of his lean and torpid age.' Such touches as are in this piece cannot proceed from any common heart. They argue such a depth of tenderness, such a boundless sympathy with all forms of being, such an omnipresent love, that we must needs say that this Hawthorne is here almost alone in his generation,—at least, in the artistic manifestation of these things. Still more. Such touches as these,—and many, very many similar ones, all through his chapters—furnish clues whereby we enter a little way into the intricate, profound heart where they originated. And we see that suffering, sometime or other and in some shape or other,—this only can enable any man to depict it in others. All over him, Hawthorne's melancholy rests like an Indian-summer, which, though bathing a whole country in one softness, still reveals the distinctive hue of every towering hill and each far-winding vale.

But it is the least part of genius that attracts admiration. Where Hawthorne is known, he seems to be deemed a pleasant writer, with a pleasant style,—a sequestered, harmless man, from whom any deep and weighty thing would hardly be anticipated—a man who means no meanings. But there is no man, in whom humor and love, like mountain peaks, soar to such a rapt height as to receive the irradiations of the upper skies;—there is no man in whom humor and love are developed in that high form called genius; no such man can exist without also possessing, as the indispensable complement of these, a great, deep intellect, which drops down into the universe like a plummet. Or, love and humor are only the eyes through which such an intellect views this world. The great beauty in such a mind is but the product of its strength. What, to all readers, can be more charming than the piece entitled 'Monsieur du Miroir;' and to a reader at all capable of fully fathoming it, what, at the same time, can possess more mystical depth of meaning?—yes, there he sits and looks at me,—this 'shape of mystery,' this 'identical Monsieur du Miroir.' 'Methinks I should tremble now, were his wizard power of gliding through all impediments in search of me, to place him suddenly before my eyes.'

How profound, nay appalling, is the moral evolved by the Earth's Holocaust; where—beginning

Painting of Monument Mountain by Asher Brown Durand (Detroit Institute of Arts)

A Literary Picnic

Fields provides this account of the 5 August 1850 picnic at which Hawthorne and Melville first met.

One beautiful summer day, twenty years ago, I found Hawthorne in his little red cottage at Lenox, surrounded by his happy young family. He had the look, as somebody said, of a banished lord, and his grand figure among the hills of Berkshire seemed finer than ever. His boy and girl were swinging on the gate as we drove up to his door, and with their sunny curls formed an attractive feature in the landscape. As the afternoon was cool and delightful, we proposed a drive over to Pittsfield to see Holmes, who was then living on his ancestral farm. Hawthorne was in a cheerful condition, and seemed to enjoy the beauty of the day to the utmost. Next morning we were all invited by Mr. Dudley Field, then living at Stockbridge, to ascend Monument Mountain. Holmes, Hawthorne, Duyckinck, Herman Melville, Headley, Sedgwick, Matthews, and several ladies, were of the party. We scrambled to the top with great spirit, and when we arrived, Melville, I remember, bestrode a peaked rock, which ran out like a bowsprit, and pulled and hauled imaginary ropes for our delecta-

tion. Then we all assembled in a shady spot, and one of the party read to us Bryant's beautiful poem commemorating Monument Mountain. Then we lunched among the rocks, and somebody proposed Bryant's health, and "long life to the dear old poet." This was the most popular toast of the day, and it took, I remember, a considerable quantity of Heidsieck to do it justice. In the afternoon, pioneered by Headley, we made our way, with merry shouts and laughter, through the Ice-Glen. Hawthorne was among the most enterprising of the merry-makers; and being in the dark much of the time, he ventured to call out lustily and pretend that certain destruction was inevitable to all of us. After this extemporaneous jollity, we dined together at Mr. Dudley Field's in Stockbridge, and Hawthorne rayed out in a sparkling and unwonted manner. I remember the conversation at table chiefly ran on the physical differences between the present American and English men, Hawthorne stoutly taking part in favor of the American. This 5th of August was a happy day throughout, and I never saw Hawthorne in better spirits.

—Yesterdays with Authors, pp. 52–53

Bryant's Mountain

The following passage from William Cullen Bryant's poem describes the top of Monument Mountain.

There is a precipice
That seems a fragment of some mighty wall,
Built by the hand that fashioned the old world,
To separate its nations, and thrown down
When the flood drowned them. To the north, a path
Conducts you up the narrow battlement.
Steep is the western side, shaggy and wild
With mossy trees, and pinnacles of flint,
And many a hanging crag. . . .

—"Monument Mountain"

with the hollow follies and affectations of the world,—all vanities and empty theories and forms are, one after another, and by an admirably graduated, growing comprehensiveness, thrown into the allegorical fire, till, at length, nothing is left but the all-engendering heart of man; which remaining still unconsumed, the great conflagration is naught.

Of a piece with this, is the 'Intelligence Office,' a wondrous symbolizing of the secret workings in men's souls. There are other sketches still more charged with ponderous import.

'The Christmas Banquet,' and 'The Bosom Serpent,' would be fine subjects for a curious and elaborate analysis, touching the conjectural parts of the mind that produced them. For spite of all the Indian-summer sunlight on the hither side of Hawthorne's soul, the other side—like the dark half of the physical sphere—is shrouded in a blackness, ten times black. But this darkness but gives more effect to the ever-moving dawn, that for ever advances through it, and circumnavigates his world. Whether Hawthorne has simply availed himself of this mystical blackness as a means to the wondrous effects he makes it to produce in his lights and shades; or whether there really lurks in him, perhaps unknown to himself, a touch of Puritanic gloom,—this, I cannot altogether tell. Certain it is, however, that this great power of blackness in him derives its force from its appeals to that Calvinistic sense of Innate Depravity and Original Sin, from whose visitations, in some shape or other, no deeply thinking mind is always and wholly free. For, in certain moods, no man can weigh this world without throwing in something, somehow like Original Sin, to strike the uneven balance. At all events, perhaps no writer has ever wielded this terrific thought with greater terror than this same harmless Hawthorne. Still more: this black conceit pervades him through and through. You may be witched by this sunlight,—transported by the bright gildings in the skies he builds over you; but there is the blackness of darkness beyond; and even his bright gildings but fringe and play upon the edges of thunder-clouds. In one word, the world is mistaken in this Nathaniel Hawthorne. He himself must often have smiled at its absurd misconception of him. He is immeasurably deeper than the plummet of the mere critic. For it is not the brain that can test such a man; it is only the heart. Yet cannot come to know greatness by inspecting it; there is no glimpse to be caught of it, except by intuition; you need not ring it, you but touch it, and you find it is gold.

Now, it is that blackness in Hawthorne, of which I have spoken, that so fixes and fascinates me. It may be, nevertheless, that it is too largely developed in him. Perhaps he does not give us a ray of his light for every shade of his dark. But however this may be, this blackness it is that furnishes the infinite obscure of his back-ground,—that background, against which Shakspeare plays his grandest conceits, the things that have made for Shakspeare his loftiest but most circumscribed renown, as the profoundest of thinkers. For by philosophers Shakspeare is not adored as the great man of tragedy and comedy.—'Off with his head; so much for Buckingham!' This sort of rant, interlined by another hand, brings down the house,—those mistaken souls, who dream of Shakspeare as a mere man of Richard-the-Third humps and Macbeth daggers. But it is those deep far-away things in him; those occasional flashings-forth of the intuitive Truth in him; those short, quick probings at the very axis of reality;—these are the things that make Shakspeare, Shakspeare. Through the mouths of the dark characters of Hamlet, Timon, Lear, and Iago, he craftily says, or sometimes insinuates the things which we feel to be so terrifically true, that it were all but madness for any good man, in his own proper character, to utter, or even hint of them. Tormented into desperation, Lear, the frantic king, tears off the mask, and speaks the same madness of vital truth. But, as I before said, it is the least part of genius that attracts admiration. And so, much of the blind, unbridled admiration that has been heaped upon Shakspeare, has been lavished upon the least part of him. And few of his endless commentators and critics seem to have remembered, or even perceived, that the immediate products of a great mind are not so great as that undeveloped and sometimes undevelopable yet dimly-discernible greatness, to which those immediate products are but the infallible indices. In Shakspeare's tomb lies infinitely more than Shakspeare ever wrote. And if I magnify Shakspeare, it is not so much for what he did do as for what he did not do, or refrained from doing. For in this world of lies, Truth is forced to fly like a scared white doe in the woodlands; and only by cunning glimpses will she reveal herself, as in Shakspeare and other masters of the great Art of Telling the Truth,—even though it be covertly and by snatches.

But if this view of the all-popular Shakspeare be seldom taken by his readers, and if very few who extol him have ever read him deeply, or perhaps, only have seen him on the tricky stage (which alone made, and is still making him his mere mob renown)—if few men have time, or patience, or palate, for the spiritual truth as it is in that great genius;—it is then no matter of surprise, that in a contemporaneous age, Nathaniel Hawthorne is a man as yet almost utterly mistaken among men. Here and there, in some quiet armchair in the noisy town, or some deep nook among the noiseless mountains, he may be appreciated for something of what he is. But unlike Shakspeare, who was forced to the contrary course by circumstances, Hawthorne (either from simple disinclination, or else from inaptitude) refrains from all the popularizing noise and show of broad farce and blood-besmeared tragedy; content with the still, rich utterance of a great intellect in repose, and which sends few thoughts into circulation, except they be arterialized at his large warm lungs, and expanded in his honest heart.

Nor need you fix upon that blackness in him, if it suit you not. Nor, indeed, will all readers discern it; for it is, mostly, insinuated to those who may best understand it, and account for it; it is not obtruded upon every one alike.

Some may start to read of Shakspeare and Hawthorne on the same page. They may say, that if an illustration were needed, a lesser light might have sufficed to elucidate this Hawthorne, this small man of yesterday. But I am not willingly one of those who, as touching Shakspeare at least, exemplify the maxim of Rochefoucault, that 'we exalt the reputation of some, in order to depress that of others;'—who, to teach all noble-souled aspirants that there is no hope for them, pronounce Shakspeare absolutely unapproachable. But Shakspeare has been approached. There are minds that have gone as far as Shakspeare into the universe. And hardly a mortal man, who, at some time or other, has not felt as great thoughts in him as any you will find in Hamlet. We must not inferentially malign mankind for the sake of any one man, whoever he may be. This is too cheap a purchase of contentment for conscious mediocrity to make. Besides, this absolute and unconditional adoration of Shakspeare has grown to be a part of our Anglo-Saxon superstitions. The Thirty-Nine articles are now Forty. Intolerance has come to exist in this matter. You must believe in Shakspeare's unapproachability, or quit the country. But what sort of a belief is this for an American, a man who is bound to carry

republican progressiveness into Literature as well as into Life? Believe me, my friends, that men, not very much inferior to Shakspeare, are this day being born on the banks of the Ohio. And the day will come when you shall say, Who reads a book by an Englishman that is a modern? The great mistake seems to be, that even with those Americans who look forward to the coming of a great literary genius among us, they somehow fancy he will come in the costume of Queen Elizabeth's day; be a writer of dramas founded upon old English history or the tales of Boccaccio. Whereas great geniuses are parts of the times; they themselves are the times, and possess a correspondent coloring. It is of a piece with the Jews, who, while their Shiloh was meekly walking in their streets, were still praying for his magnificent coming; looking for him in a chariot, who was already among them on an ass. Nor must we forget that, in his own lifetime, Shakspeare was not Shakspeare, but only Master William Shakspeare of the shrewd, thriving, business firm of Condell, Shakspeare & Co., proprietors of the Globe Theatre in London; and by a courtly author, of the name of Chettle, was looked at as an 'upstart crow,' beautified 'with other birds' feathers.' For, mark it well, imitation is often the first charge brought against real originality. Why this is so, there is not space to set forth here. You must have plenty of sea-room to tell the Truth in; especially when it seems to have an aspect of newness, as America did in 1492, though it was then just as old, and perhaps older than Asia, only those sagacious philosophers, the common sailors, had never seen it before, swearing it was all water and moonshine there.

Now I do not say that Nathaniel of Salem is a greater than William of Avon, or as great. But the difference between the two men is by no means immeasurable. Not a very great deal more, and Nathaniel were verily William.

This, too, I mean, that if Shakspeare has not been equalled, give the world time, and he is sure to be surpassed, in one hemisphere or the other. Nor will it at all do to say, that the world is getting grey and grizzled now, and has lost that fresh charm which she wore of old, and by virtue of which the great poets of past times made themselves what we esteem them to be. Not so. The world is as young to-day as when it was created; and this Vermont morning dew is as wet to my feet, as Eden's dew to Adam's. Nor has nature been all over ransacked by our progenitors, so that no new charms and mysteries remain for this latter generation to find. Far from it. The trillionth part has not yet been said; and all that has been said, but multiplies the avenues to what remains to be said. It is not so much paucity as superabundance of material that seems to incapacitate modern authors.

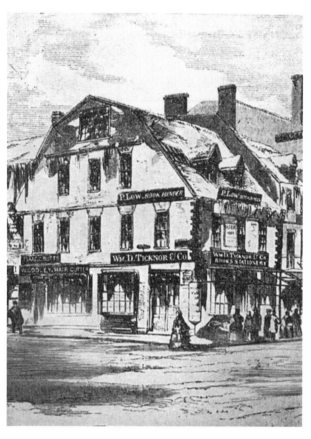

The Ticknor and Fields Old Corner Bookstore at Washington and School streets, Boston, which was frequented by Hawthorne and other writers such as Emerson, Oliver Wendell Holmes, Longfellow, and James Russell Lowell

Let America, then, prize and cherish her writers; yea, let her glorify them. They are not so many in number as to exhaust her good-will. And while she has good kith and kin of her own, to take to her bosom, let her not lavish her embraces upon the household of an alien. For believe it or not, England, after all, is in many things an alien to us. China has more bonds of real love for us than she. But even were there no strong literary individualities among us, as there are some dozens at least, nevertheless, let America first praise mediocrity even, in her own children, before she praises (for everywhere, merit demands acknowledgment from everyone) the best excellence in the children of any other land. Let her own authors, I say, have the priority of appreciation. I was much pleased with a hotheaded Carolina cousin of mine, who once said,—'If there were no other American to stand by, in literature, why, then, I would stand by Pop Emmons and his *Fredoniad,* and till a better epic came along, swear it was not very far behind the *Iliad.*' Take away the words, and in spirit he was sound.

Not that American genius needs patronage in order to expand. For that explosive sort of stuff will expand though screwed up in a vice, and burst it, though it were triple steel. It is for the nation's sake, and not for her authors' sake, that I would have America be heedful of the increasing greatness among her writers. For how great the shame, if other nations should be before her, in crowning her heroes of the pen! But this is almost the case now. American authors have received more just and discriminating praise (however loftily and ridiculously given, in certain cases) even from some Englishmen, than from their own countrymen. There are hardly five critics in America; and several of them are asleep. As for patronage, it is the American author who now patronizes his country, and not his country him. And if at times some among them appeal to the people for more recognition, it is not always with selfish motives, but patriotic ones.

It is true, that but few of them as yet have evinced that decided originality which merits great praise. But that graceful writer, who perhaps of all Americans has received the most plaudits from his own country for his productions,—that very popular and amiable writer, however good and self-reliant in many things, perhaps owes his chief reputation to the self-acknowledged imitation of a foreign model, and to the studied avoidance of all topics but smooth ones. But it is better to fail in originality, than to succeed in imitation. He who has never failed somewhere, that man cannot be great. Failure is the true test of greatness. And if it be said, that continual success is a proof that a man wisely knows his powers,—it is only to be added, that, in that case, he knows them to be small. Let us believe it, then, once for all, that there is no hope for us in these smooth, pleasing writers that know their powers. Without malice, but to speak the plain fact, they but furnish an appendix to Goldsmith, and other English authors. And we want no American Goldsmiths: nay, we want no American Mil-

tons. It were the vilest thing you could say of a true American author, that he were an American Tompkins. Call him an American and have done, for you cannot say a nobler thing of him. But it is not meant that all American writers should studiously cleave to nationality in their writings; only this, no American writer should write like an Englishman or a Frenchman; let him write like a man, for then he will be sure to write like an American. Let us away with this leaven of literary flunkeyism towards England. If either must play the flunkey in this thing, let England do it, not us. While we are rapidly preparing for that political supremacy among the nations which prophetically

---

In Praise of a Virginian

Both Sophia and Nathaniel Hawthorne wrote to Evert Duyckinck shortly after Melville's essay on Hawthorne's work appeared in The Literary World. *At the beginning of her letter Sophia evidently comments on designs for Washington Irving's* The Sketch Book *by F. O. C. Darley, who later illustrated Hawthorne's writing. Although both letters mention Melville's books, neither of the Hawthornes then knew that he was the "Virginian" who had written the essay.*

My dear Sir,

I thank you very much for these admirable outlines. I am such a profound admirer of Flaxman, & the severe beauty of his classic style is so particularly in accord with my love of sculpture, that I thought I could not like any other outlines. Retzsch never had for me the charm which obtains with so many persons. But I think these are superior to those of Retzsch. I am weary of his consumptive profiles. Rip Van Winkle himself is wonderfully fine, I think. The fathomless goodnature, the patience, gentleness & mild sufferance of his face & figure transcend Irving's conception.

But, my dear Mr Duyckinck, I cannot speak or think of any thing now but the extraordinary review of Mr Hawthorne, in the Literary World. The Virginian is the first person who has ever in *print* apprehended Mr Hawthorne. I keep constantly reading over & over the inspired utterances, & marvel more & more that the word has at last been said which I have so long hoped to hear, & so well said. There is such a generous, noble enthusiasm as I have not before found in any critic of any writer. While bringing out the glory of his subject, (excuse me, but I am speaking as an indifferent person) he surrounds himself with a glory. The freshness of primeval nature is in that man, & the true Promethean fire is in him. Who can he be, so fearless, so rich in heart, of such fine intuition? Is his name altogether hidden?

We have been very much interested in Mr Melville's books, & we are very much obliged to you for them. Mr Hawthorne has read them all on the new hay in the

barn, which is a delightful place for the perusal of worthy books.

Truly yours,
S. A. Hawthorne

E. A. Duyckinck Esq.
Aug. 29 1850

* * *

Lenox, August 29th. 1850.

My dear Sir,

I have read Melville's works with a progressive appreciation of the author. No writer ever put the reality before his reader more unflinchingly than he does in "Redburn," and "White Jacket." "Mardi" is a rich book, with depths here and there that compel a man to swim for his life. It is so good that one scarcely pardons the writer for not having brooded long over it, so as to make it a great deal better.

You will see by my wife's note that I have all along had one staunch admirer; and with her to back me, I really believe I should do very well without any other. Nevertheless, I must own that I have read the articles in the Literary World with very great pleasure. The writer has a truly generous heart; nor do I think it necessary to appropriate the whole magnificence of his encomium, any more than to devour everything on the table, when a host of noble hospitality spreads a banquet before me. But he is no common man; and, next to deserving his praise, it is good to have beguiled or bewitched such a man into praising me more than I deserve.

Sincerely Yours,
Nath Hawthorne

E. A. Duyckinck, Esq.
New York

—pp. 361–363

awaits us at the close of the present century, in a literary point of view, we are deplorably unprepared for it; and we seem studious to remain so. Hitherto, reasons might have existed why this should be; but no good reason exists now. And all that is requisite to amendment in this matter, is simply this: that while fully acknowledging all excellence everywhere, we should refrain from unduly lauding foreign writers, and, at the same time, duly recognise the meritorious writers that are our own;—those writers who breathe that unshackled, democratic spirit of Christianity in all things, which now takes the practical lead in this world, though at the same time led by ourselves—us Americans. Let us boldly contemn all imitation, though it comes to us graceful and fragrant as the morning; and foster all originality, though at first it be crabbed and ugly as our own pine knots. And if any of our authors fail, or seem to fail, then, in the words of my Carolina cousin, let us clap him on the shoulder, and back him against all Europe for his second round. The truth is, that in one point of view, this matter of a national literature has come to such a pass with us, that in some sense we must turn bullies, else the day is lost, or superiority so far beyond us, that we can hardly say it will ever be ours.

And now, my countrymen, as an excellent author of your own flesh and blood,—an unimitating, and, perhaps, in his way, an inimitable man whom better can I commend to you, in the first place, than Nathaniel Hawthorne. He is one of the new, and far better generation of your writers. The smell of your beeches and hemlocks is upon him; your own broad prairies are in his soul; and if you travel away inland into his deep and noble nature, you will hear the far roar of his Niagara. Give not over to future generations the glad duty of acknowledging him for what he is. Take that joy to yourself, in your own generation; and so shall he feel those grateful impulses on him, that may possibly prompt him to the full flower of some still greater achievement in your eyes. And by confessing him you thereby confess others; you brace the whole brotherhood. For genius, all over the world, stands hand in hand, and one shock of recognition runs the whole circle round.

In treating of Hawthorne, or rather of Hawthorne in his writings (for I never saw the man; and in the chances of a quiet plantation life, remote from his haunts, perhaps never shall); in treating of his works, I say, I have thus far omitted all mention of his *Twice-told Tales* and *Scarlet Letter*. Both are excellent, but full of such manifold, strange and diffusive beauties, that time would all but fail me to point the half of them out. But there are things in those two books, which, had they been written in England a century ago, Nathaniel Hawthorne had utterly displaced many of the bright names

we now revere on authority. But I am content to leave Hawthorne to himself, and to the infallible finding of posterity; and however great may be the praise I have bestowed upon him, I feel that in so doing I have more served and honored myself, than him. For, at bottom, great excellence is praise enough to itself; but the feeling of a sincere and appreciative love and admiration towards it, this is relieved by utterance; and warm, honest praise, ever leaves a pleasant flavor in the mouth; and it is an honorable thing to confess to what is honorable in others.

But I cannot leave my subject yet. No man can read a fine author, and relish him to his very bones while he reads, without subsequently fancying to himself some ideal image of the man and his mind. And if you rightly look for it, you will almost always find that the author himself has somewhere furnished you with his own picture. For poets (whether in prose or verse), being painters of nature, are like their brethren of the pencil, the true portrait-painters, who, in the multitude of likenesses to be sketched, do not invariably omit their own; and in all high instances, they paint them without any vanity, though at times with a lurking something that would take several pages to properly define.

I submit it, then, to those best acquainted with the man personally, whether the following is not Nathaniel Hawthorne;—and to himself, whether something involved in it does not express the temper of his mind,—that lasting temper of all true, candid men—a seeker, not a finder yet:—

> A man now entered, in neglected attire, with the aspect of a thinker, but somewhat too roughhewn and brawny for a scholar. His face was full of sturdy vigor, with some finer and keener attribute beneath; though harsh at first, it was tempered with the glow of a large, warm heart, which had force enough to heat his powerful intellect through and through. He advanced to the Intelligencer, and looked at him with a glance of such stern sincerity, that perhaps few secrets were beyond its scope.
>
> 'I seek for Truth,' said he.

Twenty-four hours have elapsed since writing the foregoing. I have just returned from the hay-mow, charged more and more with love and admiration of Hawthorne. For I have just been gleaning through the *Mosses*, picking up many things here and there that had previously escaped me. And I found that but to glean after this man, is better than to be in at the harvest of others. To be frank (though, perhaps, rather foolish) notwithstanding what I wrote yesterday of these *Mosses*, I had not then culled them all; but had, nevertheless, been sufficiently sensible of the subtle essence in them, as to write as I did. To what infinite height of loving wonder and admiration I may yet be borne, when by repeatedly banqueting on these *Mosses*, I shall have thoroughly incorporated their whole stuff into my being,– that, I cannot tell. But already I feel that this Hawthorne has dropped germinous seeds into my soul. He expands and deepens down, the more I contemplate him; and further and further, shoots his strong New England roots into the hot soil in my Southern soul.

By careful reference to the 'Table of Contents,' I now find that I have gone through all the sketches; but that when I yesterday wrote, I had not at all read two particular pieces, to which I now desire to call special attention,–'A Select Party,' and 'Young Goodman Brown.' Here, be it said to all those whom this poor fugitive scrawl of mine may tempt to the perusal of the 'Mosses,' that they must on no account suffer themselves to be trifled with, disappointed, or deceived by the triviality of many of the titles to these sketches. For in more than one instance, the title utterly belies the piece. It is as if rustic demijohns containing the very best and costliest of Falernian and Tokay, were labelled 'Cider,' 'Perry,' and 'Elder-berry wine.' The truth seems to be, that like many other geniuses, this Man of Mosses takes great delight in hood-winking the world,– at least, with respect to himself. Personally, I doubt not that he rather prefers to be generally esteemed but a so-so sort of author; being willing to reserve the thorough and acute appreciation of what he is, to that party most qualified to judge–that is, to himself. Besides, at the bottom of their natures, men like Hawthorne, in many things, deem the plaudits of the public such strong presumptive evidence of mediocrity in the object of them, that it would in some degree render them doubtful of their own powers, did they hear much and vociferous braying concerning them in the public pastures. True, I have been braying myself (if you please to be witty enough to have it so), but then I claim to be the first that has so brayed in this particular matter; and therefore, while pleading guilty to the charge, still claim all the merit due to originality.

But with whatever motive, playful or profound, Nathaniel Hawthorne has chosen to entitle his pieces in the manner he has, it is certain that some of them are directly calculated to deceive–egregiously deceive, the superficial skimmer of pages. To be downright and candid once more, let me cheerfully say, that two of these titles did dolefully dupe no less an eager-eyed reader than myself; and that, too, after I had been impressed with a sense of the great depth and breadth of this American man. 'Who in the name of thunder' (as the country-people say in this neighborhood), 'who in the name of thunder, would anticipate any marvel in a piece entitled "Young Goodman Brown?"' You would

of course suppose that it was a simple little tale, intended as a supplement to 'Goody Two Shoes.' Whereas, it is deep as Dante; nor can you finish it, without addressing the author in his own words–'It is yours to penetrate, in every bosom, the deep mystery of sin.' And with Young Goodman, too, in allegorical pursuit of his Puritan wife, you cry out in your anguish:

> 'Faith!' shouted Goodman Brown, in a voice of agony and desperation; and the echoes of the forest mocked him, crying–'Faith! Faith!' as if bewildered wretches were seeking her all through the wilderness.

Now this same piece, entitled 'Young Goodman Brown,' is one of the two that I had not all read yesterday; and I allude to it now, because it is, in itself, such a strong positive illustration of that blackness in Hawthorne, which I had assumed from the mere occasional shadows of it, as revealed in several of the other sketches. But had I previously perused 'Young Goodman Brown,' I should have been at no pains to draw the conclusion, which I came to at a time when I was ignorant that the book contained one such direct and unqualified manifestation of it.

The other piece of the two referred to, is entitled 'A Select Party,' which, in my first simplicity upon originally taking hold of the book, I fancied must treat of some pumpkin-pie party in old Salem, or some chowder-party on Cape Cod. Whereas, by all the gods of Peedee, it is the sweetest and sublimest thing that has been written since Spenser wrote. Nay, there is nothing in Spenser that surpasses it, perhaps nothing that equals it. And the test is this: read any canto in *The Faery Queen*, and then read 'A Select Party,' and decide which pleases you most,–that is, if you are qualified to judge. Do not be frightened at this; for when Spenser was alive, he was thought of very much as Hawthorne is now,–was generally accounted just such a 'gentle' harmless man. It may be, that to common eyes, the sublimity of Hawthorne seems lost in his sweetness,–as perhaps in that same 'Select Party' of his; for whom he has builded so august a dome of sunset clouds, and served them on richer plate than Belshazzar when he banqueted his lords in Babylon.

But my chief business now, is to point out a particular page in this piece, having reference to an honored guest, who under the name of 'The Master Genius,' but in the guise 'of a young man of poor attire, with no insignia of rank or acknowledged eminence,' is introduced to the man of Fancy, who is the giver of the feast. Now, the page having reference to this 'Master Genius,' so happily expresses much of what I yesterday wrote, touching the coming of the literary Shiloh of America, that I cannot but be charmed by the coinci-

First page of Melville's 8 January 1852 letter to Sophia Hawthorne, in which he acknowledges her appreciation of Moby-Dick.
Melville's dedication is: "In Token of My Admiration for his Genius, This Book is Inscribed to Nathaniel Hawthorne"
(American Art Association Anderson Galleries catalogue, *Cortland F. Bishop sale, 25–27 April 1938).*

dence; especially, when it shows such a parity of ideas, at least in this one point, between a man like Hawthorne and a man like me.

And here, let me throw out another conceit of mine touching this American Shiloh, or 'Master Genius,' as Hawthorne calls him. May it not be, that this commanding mind has not been, is not, and never will be, individually developed in any one man? And would it, indeed, appear so unreasonable to suppose, that his great fullness and overflowing may be, or may be destined to be, shared by a plurality of men of genius? Surely, to take the very greatest example on record, Shakspeare cannot be regarded as in himself the concretion of all the genius of his time; nor as so immeasurably beyond Marlow, Webster, Ford, Beaumont, Jonson, that these great men can be said to share none of his power? For one, I conceive that there were dramatists in Elizabeth's day, between whom and Shakspeare the distance was by no means great. Let anyone, hitherto little acquainted with those neglected old authors, for the first time read them thoroughly, or even read Charles Lamb's Specimens of them, and he will be amazed at the wondrous ability of those Anaks of men, and shocked at this renewed example of the fact, that Fortune has more to do with fame than merit,—though, without merit, lasting fame there can be none.

Nevertheless, it would argue too ill of my country were this maxim to hold good concerning Nathaniel Hawthorne, a man, who already, in some few minds, has shed 'such a light, as never illuminates the earth save when a great heart burns as the household fire of a grand intellect.'

The words are his,—'in the Select Party;' and they are a magnificent setting to a coincident sentiment of my own, but ramblingly expressed yesterday, in reference to himself. Gainsay it who will, as I now write, I am Posterity speaking by proxy—and after times will make it more than good, when I declare, that the American, who up to the present day has evinced, in literature, the largest brain with the largest heart, that man is Nathaniel Hawthorne. Moreover, that whatever Nathaniel Hawthorne may hereafter write, *The Mosses from an Old Manse* will be ultimately accounted his masterpiece. For there is a sure, though a secret sign in some works which proves the culmination of the powers (only the developable ones, however) that produced them. But I am by no means desirous of the glory of a prophet. I pray Heaven that Hawthorne may *yet* prove me an impostor in this prediction. Especially, as I somehow cling to the strange fancy, that, in all men, hiddenly reside certain wondrous, occult properties—as in some plants and minerals—which by some happy but very rare accident (as bronze was discovered by the melting of the iron and brass at the burning of Corinth) may chance to be called forth here on earth; not entirely waiting for their better discovery in the more congenial, blessed atmosphere of heaven.

Once more—for it is hard to be finite upon an infinite subject, and all subjects are infinite. By some people this entire scrawl of mine may be esteemed altogether unnecessary, inasmuch 'as years ago' (they may say) 'we found out the rich and rare stuff in this Hawthorne, whom you now parade forth, as if only *yourself* were the discoverer of this Portuguese diamond in our literature.' But even granting all this—and adding to it, the assumption that the books of Hawthorne have sold by the five thousand,—what does that signify? They should be sold by the hundred thousand; and read by the million; and admired by every one who is capable of admiration.

"A Hell-Fired Story": *The Scarlet Letter*

Hawthorne's years of relative obscurity as a writer of tales and sketches ended with the 1850 publication of The Scarlet Letter— *which, he told his friend Horatio Bridge, "is positively a h–l-fired story, into which I found it almost impossible to throw any cheering light." As early as the mid 1830s Hawthorne conceived of characters and situations similar to those in* The Scarlet Letter. *He had been appointed as the surveyor of the customhouse in Salem—the chief administrative officer of the port—and during the writing of the novel, the author was deeply affected by the loss of his government position on 7 June 1849. He was then shaken by the death of his mother the next month on 31 July. Hawthorne wrote the novel quickly, in part because he was jobless and needed the money the book would generate. The sketch Hawthorne used as a preface for his novel, "The Custom-House," brought him notoriety in Salem; the story of Hester Prynne and Arthur Dimmesdale earned him a national and interna-*tional reputation, although many of the author's contemporaries deplored his material. "One cannot but wonder," reviewer Anne W. Abbott wrote, why such a gifted author "should not choose a less revolting subject than this of* The Scarlet Letter, *to which fine writing seems as inappropriate as fine embroidery." After an initial press-run of 2,500 copies on 9 March, Ticknor, Reed and Fields published a second edition of 2,500 copies on 22 April and a third edition of 1,000 copies on 9 September 1850; for all three editions, each priced at 75¢, Hawthorne received a 15 percent royalty. Hawthorne received $1,500 in royalties for* The Scarlet Letter. *This amount might pale in comparison with the money Harriet Beecher Stowe received for* Uncle Tom's Cabin *(1852), for example, but it was substantial for Hawthorne, whose writing before 1850 had generated little income.*

Portrait of Hawthorne by Cephas Thompson, 1850. William D. Ticknor bought the painting two years later and presented it to the Hawthornes for their Concord home; it was the only oil portrait of himself Hawthorne ever owned. Engravings made from this painting were the first published portraits of the author (Grolier Club).

Termination

Hawthorne's being replaced at the Salem Custom House was reported and editorialized about in the Salem Register, *a Whig paper.*

The Salem Custom House
Salem Register, 11 June 1849

Here shall the Pages the PEOPLE'S RIGHTS maintain,
Unawed by INFLUENCE and unbribed by GAIN.
Here Patriot TRUTH her glorious precepts draw,
Pledged to RELIGION, LIBERTY, and LAW.

The lightning has struck at last, and in so unexpected a quarter as to create great consternation among the *ins,* who felt themselves so safe. The electric telegraph announced on Friday, that Capt. ALLEN PUTNAM had been appointed Surveyor of the port of Salem, in place of Nathaniel Hawthorne, Esq., the present incumbent. Capt. Putnam is a highly respectable shipmaster, every way qualified for the office, and will discharge its duties with great honor to himself, and advantage to the public interests. He will undoubtedly prove a very efficient and popular officer.

We are not informed when the new commission is to take effect, and are ignorant of the circumstances connected with this change. The Salem Custom House needs a reform badly enough, every body knows, who is acquainted with its history and conduct. For twenty years, at least, it has been a complete house of refuge for locofoco politicians, of the most offensive cast.—The active electioneerers of the party have gone there to roost, with as much impudent assurance as though they had a life-lease of the premises, and supposed they could bleed Uncle Sam till they were surfeited. Here were the headquarters of the political managers, who contrived to keep the party *"conveniently small,"* and well enough in check to enable them to apportion the offices to suit themselves; and here they concocted their party schemes with a single eye to their own interests. They seemed to consider themselves fixtures in the Custom House, incapable of removal without a total demolition of the building, and dead ruin to Uncle Sam. We rather think they are beginning to rub their eyes, with an incipient suspicion that they have made a sad mistake. They are really

Hawthorne's desk at the Salem Custom House (The Salem Maritime Historical Society)

A receipt signed by Hawthorne in his capacity as the surveyor of the Salem Custom House
(The House of the Seven Gables Historic Site)

in a fair way to be suitably impressed with the conviction that *some* things can be done as well as others.

Mr. Hawthorne is not, that we are aware of, particularly obnoxious on the score of any of the above charges. Certainly he is not to be classed with the crew who have ruled in the Custom House so long and with whom he has been forced to hold companionship, so uncongenial, probably, with his refined tastes and brilliant literary turn of mind. He may congratulate himself, when he is freed from these disturbing influences, that he can turn his undivided attention to the cultivation of his fine talents, by which he can confer a higher and more lasting benefit on the public, than by his services as Surveyor. Personally we have none but the kindest feelings towards Mr. Hawthorne, and the warmest wishes for his prosperity, and we should be sorry to rank him with his temporary associates, the clique of plotters who have made themselves so offensive as public officers. But he is too old a soldier—and too much impregnated with the doctrines of the Democratic Review, which he has contributed so powerfully, by the

exercise of his talents, to sustain—to whine at the fortunes of war. Undoubtedly he holds religiously to the doctrine of the great idol of his party, Gen. Jackson, who, in his first Annual Message, said:—

In a country where offices are created solely for the benefit of the people, *no one man has any more intrinsic right to official station than another. Offices were not established to give support to particular men, at the public expense. No individual wrong is therefore done by removal, since neither appointment to nor continuance in office is matter of right.* The incumbent became an officer with a view to public benefits; and when these require his removal, they are not to be sacrificed to private interests. It is the people, and they alone who have a right to complain, when a bad officer is substituted for a good one. *He who is removed has the same means of obtaining a living, that are enjoyed by the millions who never held office.* The proposed limitation would destroy the idea of property, now so generally connected with official station; and although individual distress may be sometimes produced, it would, by promoting *that rotation* which constitutes a leading principle in the republican creed, give healthful action to the system.

There is a moral to be deduced from this change which comes home to the bosoms, and, what will touch them most, the *pockets,* of sundry individuals who have been long browsing on the public clover, but were seized with a very sudden palpitation of the heart, on Friday last. It is simply this: "If the Surveyor isn't safe, WHEN AM I TO GO?" Wait patiently, gentlemen, and the answer will come.

Publishing *The Scarlet Letter*

In this excerpt from his memoir, publisher James T. Fields tells the story of how he came to publish Hawthorne's masterpiece.

In the winter of 1849, after he had been ejected from the custom-house, I went down to Salem to see him and inquire after his health, for we heard he had been suffering from illness. He was then living in a modest wooden house in Mall Street, if I remember rightly the location. I found him alone in a chamber over the sitting-room of the dwelling; and as the day was cold, he was hovering near a stove. We fell into talk about his future prospects, and he was, as I feared I should find him, in a very desponding mood. "Now," said I, "is the time for you to publish, for I know during these years in Salem you must have got something ready for the press." "Nonsense," said he; "what heart had I to write anything, when my publishers (M. and Company) have been so many years trying to sell a small edition of the 'Twice-Told Tales'?" I still pressed upon him the good chances he would have now with something new. "Who would risk publishing a book for *me,* the most unpopular writer in America?" "I would," said I, "and would start with an edition of two thousand copies of anything you write." "What madness!" he exclaimed; "your friendship for me gets the better of your judgment. No, no," he continued; "I have no money to indemnify a publisher's losses on my account." I looked at my watch and found that the train would soon be starting for Boston, and I knew there was not much time to lose in trying to discover what had been his literary work during these last few years in Salem. I remember that I pressed him to reveal to me what he had been writing. He shook his head and gave me to understand he had produced nothing. At that moment I caught sight of a bureau or set of drawers near where we were sitting; and immediately it occurred to me that hidden away somewhere in that

James T. Fields in 1870

article of furniture was a story or stories by the author of the "Twice-Told Tales," and I became so positive of it that I charged him vehemently with the fact. He seemed surprised, I thought, but shook his head again; and I rose to take my leave, begging him not to come into the cold entry, saying I would come back and see him again in a few days. I was hurrying down the stairs when he called after me from the chamber, asking me to stop a moment. Then quickly stepping into the entry with a roll of manuscript in his hands, he said: "How in Heaven's name did you know this thing was there? As you have found me out, take what I have written, and tell me, after you get home and have time to read it, if it is good for anything. It is either very good or very bad,—I don't know which." On my way up to Boston I read the germ of "The Scarlet Letter"; before I slept that night I wrote him a note all aglow with admiration of the marvellous story he had put into my hands, and told him that I would come again to Salem the next day and arrange for its pub-

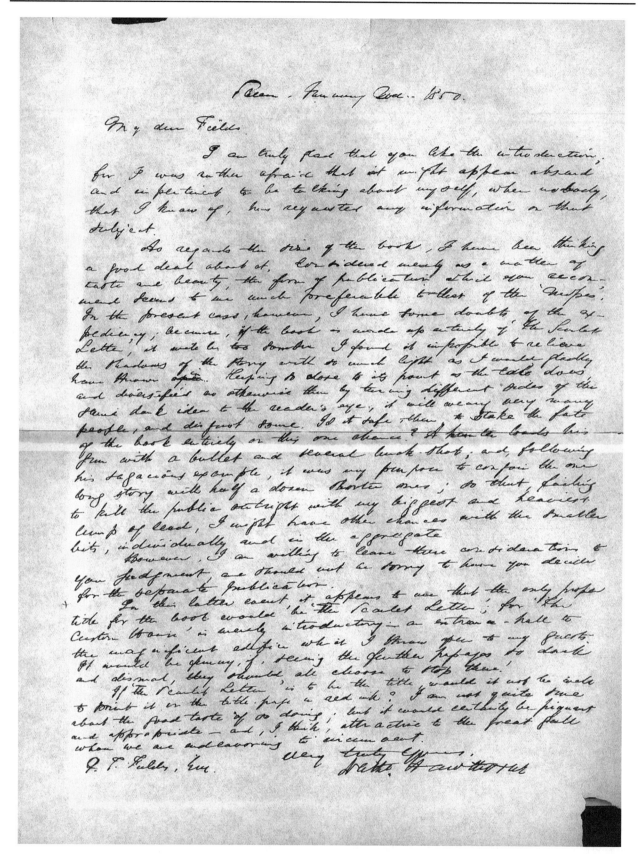

Hawthorne's 20 January 1850 letter to publisher Fields in which he discusses the advisability of publishing The Scarlet Letter *without other pieces (from Fields's* Yesterdays with Authors, *1900)*

lication. I went on in such an amazing state of excitement when we met again in the little house, that he would not believe I was really in earnest. He seemed to think I was beside myself, and laughed sadly at my enthusiasm. However, we soon arranged for his appearance again before the public with a book.

This quarto volume before me contains numerous letters, written by him from 1850 down to the month of his death. The first one refers to "The Scarlet Letter," and is dated in January, 1850. At my suggestion he had altered the plan of that story. It was his intention to make "The Scarlet Letter" one of several short stories, all to be included in one volume, and to be called

OLD-TIME LEGENDS:
TOGETHER WITH SKETCHES,
EXPERIMENTAL AND IDEAL.

His first design was to make "The Scarlet Letter" occupy about two hundred pages in his new book; but I persuaded him, after reading the first chapters of the story, to elaborate it, and publish it as a separate work. After it was settled that "The Scarlet Letter" should be enlarged and printed by itself in a volume he wrote to me:—

"I am truly glad that you like the Introduction, for I was rather afraid that it might appear absurd and impertinent to be talking about myself, when nobody, that I know of, has requested any information on that subject.

"As regards the size of the book, I have been thinking a good deal about it. Considered merely as a matter of taste and beauty, the form of publication which you recommend seems to me much preferable to that of the 'Mosses.'

"In the present case, however, I have some doubts of the expediency, because, if the book is made up entirely of 'The Scarlet Letter,' it will be too sombre. I found it impossible to relieve the shadows of the story with so much light as I would gladly have thrown in. Keeping so close to its point as the tale does, and diversified no otherwise than by turning different sides of the same dark idea to the reader's eye, it will weary very many people and disgust some. Is it safe, then, to stake the fate of the book entirely on this one chance? A hunter loads his gun with a bullet and several buckshot; and, following his sagacious example, it was my purpose to conjoin the one long story with half a dozen shorter ones, so that, failing to kill the public outright with my biggest and heaviest lump of lead, I might have other chances with the smaller bits, individually and in the aggregate. However, I am willing to leave these considerations to your judg-

ment, and should not be sorry to have you decide for the separate publication.

"In this latter event it appears to me that the only proper title for the book would be 'The Scarlet Letter,' for 'The Custom-House' is merely introductory,—an entrance-hall to the magnificent edifice which I throw open to my guests. It would be funny if, seeing the further passages so dark and dismal, they should all choose to stop there! If 'The Scarlet Letter' is to be the title, would it not be well to print it on the title-page in red ink? I am not quite sure about the good taste of so doing, but it would certainly be piquant and appropriate, and, I think, attractive to the great gull whom we are endeavoring to circumvent."

—*Yesterdays with Authors,* pp. 49–52

Assaying the Custom House

In "The Custom-House," which serves as the introduction to The Scarlet Letter, *Hawthorne complains about being removed from his position as surveyor—the consequence of the election of the Whig Party candidate, Zachary Taylor, in the 1848 presidential election. (The Whigs were the more conservative of the two major parties of the time, and Hawthorne was aligned with their opponents, the Democrats.) Hawthorne's depiction of his former Whig associates struck many as unflattering and prompted the ire of the anonymous reviewer for the* Salem Register.

The Scarlet Letter Prefix
Salem Register, 25 March 1850, p. 2

We find that we are not *entirely* alone in lamenting that Hawthorne has allowed personal exasperation and private resentment to dim the lustre of his undeniably fine talents, and expose some of the weak points in his character. Papers out of Salem have begun to discover the discreditable nature of his introductory chapter, and, while universally yielding a merited tribute to his genius, do not hesitate to speak of his Custom House Reminiscences as unmanly, illiberal and censurable. The Lowell *Courier* says: "The long introductory chapter, containing reminiscences of the Salem Custom House, is quite interesting, though we can not but think that it shows rather too much sensitiveness on the part of the author, in reference to his removal or decapitation. It would have been better to have omitted all his charges and insinuations against the Whig party."

The Salem Custom House, where Hawthorne served as surveyor of the port from April 1846 until June 1849. He discusses his experiences there in "The Custom-House," the introductory sketch to The Scarlet Letter.

John D. Howard, who wrote the following letter to Hawthorne, was, like the author, appointed to a position at the customhouse because he was a Democrat. In "The Custom-House," Hawthorne describes Howard (whom he does not name) as an "excellent fellow" with whom he would talk about Napoleon and Shakespeare.

SALEM, March 23, 1850.

MY DEAR HAWTHORNE,—I feel an inexplainable delicacy in addressing you, for I am altogether incapable of describing the sensations which seem to sway and control me in connection with my subject. I have just concluded the reading of "The Scarlet Letter," and am perfectly spellbound in view of the true and vivid picture of human life which is presented in its pages. I can no more tell you of the mighty influence this romance produced on me, than a child can explain a flash of lightning. I can only estimate the power and beauty of the production by its effect on my imperfect and humble powers of judgment. I have never throughout my life been so highly excited in reading a book, as this afternoon by "The Scarlet Letter." My mind has been taken captive, and carried through its scenes, as though I actually lived in its time and participated in its events. I should not have told you of this but that I thought it might possibly give you some little satisfaction. However this may be, I know you will accept this tribute in the spirit that has dictated it,—that of the sincerest friendship and good-will.

I have spent many hours in your society, probably for the first and only time on this side the grave. May Heaven bless you wherever fate or choice may lead you, and may your children and your children's children be blessed, and share the fame your townsmen may deny to you. But what matters it what Salem may do?—the world and all time must feel the power of your mighty and mysterious genius. I do not speak to flatter. I hate flattery and hypocrisy as I do the pains of hell. Write me, if you feel like it: I should be very highly pleased to have a line from you. I thank you for your notice of me in your introduction, although in so close proximity to "Joe." The "Old Inspector" was faithfully portrayed, and, as I understand, the galled jade winces, and wishes he was young for your sake!

Yours truly,

JOHN D. HOWARD.

—Hawthorne and his Wife, pp. 364–366

The Preface to the Second Edition

Hawthorne responded to the criticism of "The Custom-House" in his preface to the second edition of The Scarlet Letter. *The "certain venerable personage" the author refers to is believed to be the Reverend Charles Wentworth Upham, the Whig leader chiefly responsible for his removal from the surveyor post. Upham is also thought to be a model for Judge Pyncheon in* The House of the Seven Gables.

Much to the author's surprise, and (if he may say so without additional offence) considerably to his amusement, he finds that his sketch of official life, introductory to *The Scarlet Letter*, has created an unprecedented excitement in the respectable community immediately around him. It could hardly have been more violent, indeed, had he burned down the Custom-House, and quenched its last smoking ember in the blood of a certain venerable personage, against whom he is supposed to cherish a peculiar malevolence. As the public disapprobation would weigh very heavily on him, were he conscious of deserving it, the author begs leave to say, that he has carefully read over the introductory pages, with a purpose to alter or expunge whatever might be found amiss, and to make the best reparation in his power for the atrocities of which he has been adjudged guilty. But it appears to him, that the only remarkable features of the sketch are its frank and genuine good-humor, and the general accuracy with which he has conveyed his sincere impressions of the characters therein described. As to enmity, or ill-feeling of any kind, personal or political, he utterly disclaims such motives. The sketch might, perhaps, have been wholly omitted, without loss to the public, or detriment to the book; but, having undertaken to write it, he conceives that it could not have been done in a better or a kindlier spirit, nor, so far as his abilities availed, with a livelier effect of truth.

The author is constrained, therefore, to republish his introductory sketch without the change of a word.

SALEM, March 30, 1850.

– *The Scarlet Letter,* The Centenary Edition,
vol. 1, pp. 1–2

The *Boston Bee* remarks:–

"We have not had time to peruse this much vaunted production, but hear that its preamble is replete with personal reflections on the functionaries at the Salem Custom House, and illiberal flings of censure at the Whig party. This is censurable in an author whose literary position should place him above the dictates of revenge because he, in his turn, was a victim to change of administration."

The *Boston Journal* concludes a highly complimentary notice of *The Scarlet Letter*, by saying:–

"We can not but regret that the author did not take counsel with discreet friends, before prefixing to his charming romance some sixty pages, in the shape of a preface, of matter as entirely irrelevant as would be a description of the household arrangements of the Emperor of China. Under the text of Reminiscences of the Salem Custom House, the author has dragged before the public, and held up to ridicule, individuals, whose greatest peculiarity was that they could not sympathize with the dreamy thoughts and the literary habits of the author. Mr. Hawthorne evidently keenly feels that his talents and personal importance were not appreciated by his fellow-officials and by the citizens of Salem, and he takes a paltry revenge in lampooning his former associates. There is a vein of bitterness running through this portion of the work, which, though covered under an assumed playfulness of language, is by no means concealed. The whole chapter, from beginning to end, is a violation of the courtesies of life, and an abuse of the privileges of common intercourse."

Even the *Transcript* ventures to whisper that

"Mr. Hawthorne seems to have given great offence to the good people of Salem, by his portraits of the gentlemen with whom he was associated in the custom-house."

The *Mail* expresses itself thus:–

"The Romance itself is considered a good one–first rate, indeed; but the author has seen fit to preface it with some fifty pages of extraneous matter, in which he makes covert attacks on private individuals in Salem, apparently in revenge of some of his own private griefs and disappointments. This is wrong, and the publishers ought to have insisted upon its being expunged from the work. If Mr. Hawthorne wishes to 'write a book' against his enemies, let him do so manfully and openly, and not interlope his attacks in a Romance, intended for universal circulation among those who have no desire to be troubled with his private connections or personal peccadilloes."

The *New York Express* of Friday, says:

"Nathaniel Hawthorne has written a book, called *The Scarlet Letter*, attracting much comment and little commendation, from the fact, it is said, that he has introduced the affairs of private life to public discussion. If so, it is a matter of deep regret, for no writer, of his class, in the nation, enjoyed a more enviable position than N. H."

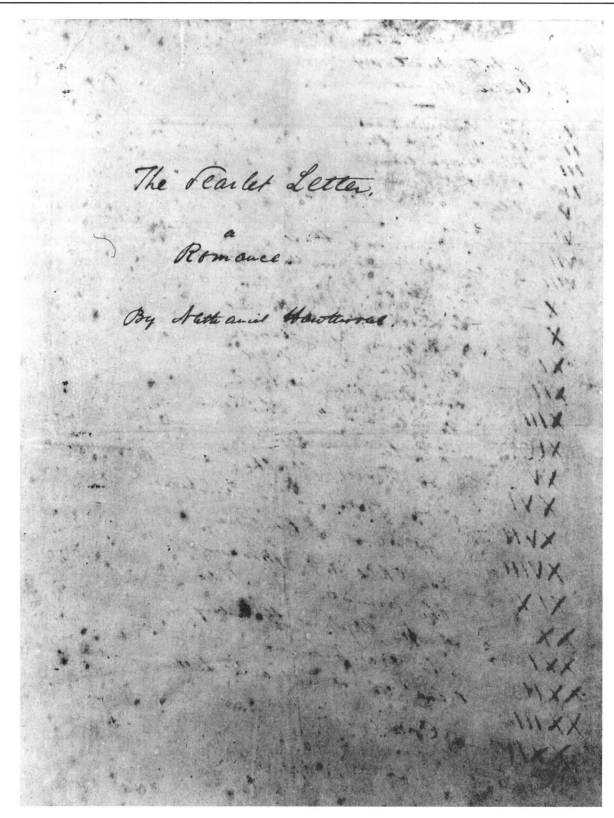

Title page on the only surviving leaf of the manuscript for Hawthorne's second novel
(The Pierpont Morgan Library, New York. MA 571)

Edwin Percy Whipple

Author, lecturer, and critic E. P. Whipple was one of the major American literary figures of the mid nineteenth century. He was a friend of James T. Fields, Hawthorne's publisher. Despite admiring Hawthorne, Whipple was not reluctant to mention what he perceived as shortcomings in Hawthorne's work. Hawthorne so valued Whipple's opinion that he sent the critic a copy of the manuscript of The Blithedale Romance.

Reviews of *The Scarlet Letter*

Review of *The Scarlet Letter*
E. P. Whipple
Graham's Magazine, 36 (May 1850): 345–346

In this beautiful and touching romance Hawthorne has produced something really worthy of the fine and deep genius which lies within him. The *Twice-told Tales* and *Mosses from an Old Manse,* are composed simply of sketches and stories, and although such sketches and stories as few living men could write, they are rather indications of the possibilities of his mind than realizations of its native power, penetration, and creativeness. In *The Scarlet Letter* we have a complete work, evincing a true artist's certainty of touch and expression in the exhibition of characters and events, and a keen-sighted and far-sighted vision into the essence and purpose of spiritual laws. There is a pro-

found philosophy underlying the story which will escape many of the readers whose attention is engrossed by the narrative.

The book is prefaced by some fifty pages of auto-biographical matter, relating to the author, his native city of Salem, and the Custom House, from which he was ousted by the Whigs. These pages, instinct with the vital spirit of humor, show how rich and exhaustless a fountain of mirth Hawthorne has at his command. The whole representation has the dreamy yet distinct remoteness of the purely comic ideal. The view of Salem streets; the picture of the old Custom House at the head of Derby's wharf, with its torpid officers on a summer's afternoon, their chairs all tipped against the wall, chatting about old stories, 'while the frozen witticisms of past generations were thawed out, and came bubbling with laughter from their lips'—the delineation of the old Inspector, whose 'reminiscences of good cheer, however ancient the date of the actual banquet, seemed to bring the savor of pig or turkey under one's very nostrils,' and on whose palate there were flavors 'which had lingered there not less than sixty or seventy years, and were still apparently as fresh as that of the mutton-chop which he had just devoured for his breakfast,' and the grand view of the stout Collector, in his aged heroism, with the honors of Chippewa and Fort Erie on his brow, are all encircled with that visionary atmosphere which proves the humorist to be a poet, and indicates that his pictures are drawn from the images which observation has left on his imagination. The whole introduction, indeed, is worthy of a place among the essays of Addison and Charles Lamb.

With regard to *The Scarlet Letter,* the readers of Hawthorne might have expected an exquisitely written story, expansive in sentiment, and suggestive in characterization, but they will hardly be prepared for a novel of so much tragic interest and tragic power, so deep in thought and so condensed in style, as is here presented to them. It evinces equal genius in the region of great passions and elusive emotions, and bears on every page the evidence of a mind thoroughly alive, watching patiently the movements of morbid hearts when stirred by strange experiences, and piercing, by its imaginative power, directly through all the externals to the core of things. The fault of the book, if fault it have, is the almost morbid intensity with which the characters are realized, and the consequent lack of sufficient geniality in the delineation. A portion of the pain of the author's own heart is communicated to the reader, and although there is great pleasure received while reading the volume, the general impression left by it is not satisfying to the artistic sense. Beauty bends to power throughout the work, and therefore the power displayed is not always beautiful. There is a strange fascination to a

The house on Main Street in Salem where Hawthorne
wrote The Scarlet Letter

man of contemplative genius in the psychological details of a strange crime like that which forms the plot of *The Scarlet Letter,* and he is therefore apt to become, like Hawthorne, too painfully anatomical in his exhibition of them.

If there be, however, a comparative lack of relief to the painful emotions which the novel excites, owing to the intensity with which the author concentrates attention on the working of dark passions, it must be confessed that the moral purpose of the book is made more definite by this very deficiency. The most abandoned libertine could not read the volume without being thrilled into something like virtuous resolution, and the roué would find that the deep-seeing eye of the novelist had mastered the whole philosophy of that guilt of which practical roués are but childish disciples. To another class of readers, those who have theories of seduction and adultery modeled after the French school of novelists, and whom libertinism is of the brain, the volume may afford matter for very instructive and edifying contemplation; for, in truth, Hawthorne, in *The*

Scarlet Letter, has utterly undermined the whole philosophy on which the French novels rest, by seeing farther and deeper into the essence both of conventional and moral laws; and he has given the results of his insight, not in disquisitions and criticisms, but in representations more powerful even than those of Sue, Dumas, or George Sand. He has made his guilty parties end, not as his own fancy or his own benevolent sympathies might dictate, but as the spiritual laws, lying back of all persons, dictated to him. In this respect there is hardly a novel in English literature more purely objective.

As everybody will read *The Scarlet Letter,* it would be impertinent to give a synopsis of the plot. The principal characters, Dimmesdale, Chillingworth, Hester, and little Pearl, all indicate a firm grasp of individualities, although from the peculiar method of the story, they are developed more in the way of logical analysis than by events. The descriptive portions of the novel are in a high degree picturesque and vivid, bringing the scenes directly home to the heart and imagination, and indicating a clear vision of the life as well as forms of nature. Little Pearl is perhaps

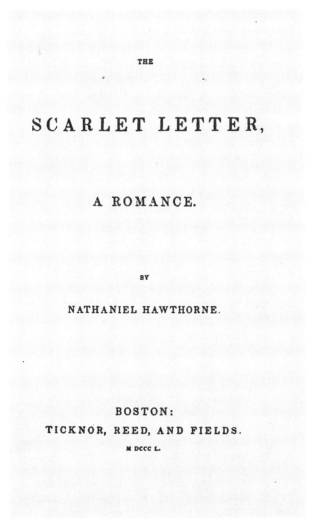

THE

SCARLET LETTER,

A ROMANCE.

BY

NATHANIEL HAWTHORNE.

BOSTON:
TICKNOR, REED, AND FIELDS.
M DCCC L.

*Title page for Hawthorne's second novel. When he read the conclusion
of the novel to his wife, he wrote to Horatio Bridge, "It broke her
heart and sent her to bed with a grievous headache—which I
look upon as triumphant success" (from C. E. Frazer
Clark Jr., Nathaniel Hawthorne: A
Descriptive Bibliography, 1978).*

Hawthorne's finest poetical creation, and is the very perfection of ideal impishness.

In common, we trust, with the rest of mankind, we regretted Hawthorne's dismissal from the Custom House, but if that event compels him to exert his genius in the production of such books as the present, we shall be inclined to class the Honorable Secretary of the Treasury among the great philanthropists. In his next work we hope to have a romance equal to *The Scarlet Letter* in pathos and power, but more relieved by touches of that beautiful and peculiar humor, so serene and so searching, in which he excels almost all living writers.

The Athenaeum, *a weekly periodical published in London, covered literature as well as fine arts, music, theater, politics, and popular science. Although book reviews were normally unsigned, most of the reviews in the magazine of Hawthorne's works have been identified as being written by the English novelist, playwright, poet, and critic Henry F. Chorley, who reviewed nearly 2,500 books between 1843 and 1869. Hawthorne and Chorley met in London in 1859, and Chorley wrote Hawthorne's obituary in the magazine. The reviewer for* The Scarlet Letter, *however, might have been David Masson, a professor of rhetoric and English literature at Edinburgh University, or his brother George Joseph Gustave Masson.*

Review of *The Scarlet Letter*
Athenaeum, 15 June 1850, p. 634

This is a most powerful but painful story. Mr. Hawthorne must be well known to our readers as a favourite with the *Athenaeum.* We rate him as among the most original and peculiar writers of American fiction. There is in his works a mixture of Puritan reserve and wild imagination, of passion and description, of the allegorical and the real, which some will fail to understand, and which others will positively reject,—but which, to ourselves, is fascinating, and which entitles him to be placed on a level with Brockden Brown and the author of Rip Van Winkle. *The Scarlet Letter* will increase his reputation with all who do not shrink from the invention of the tale; but this, as we have said, is more than ordinarily painful. When we have announced that the three characters are a guilty wife, openly punished for her guilt,—her tempter, whom she refuses to unmask, and who during the entire story carries a fair front and an unblemished name among his congregation,—and her husband, who, returning from a long absence at the moment of her sentence, sits himself down betwixt the two in the midst of a small and severe community to work out his slow vengeance on both under the pretext of magnanimous forgiveness,—when we have explained that The Scarlet Letter is the badge of Hester Prynne's shame, we ought to add that we recollect no tale dealing with crime so sad and revenge so subtly diabolical, that is at the same time so clear of fever and of prurient excitement. The misery of the woman is as present in every page as the heading which in the title of the romance symbolizes her punishment. Her terrors concerning her strange elvish child present retribution in a form which is new and natural:—her slow and painful purification through repentance is crowned by no perfect happiness, such as awaits the decline of those who have no dark and bitter past to remember. Then, the gradual corrosion of heart of Dimmesdale, the faithless priest, under the insidious care of the husband, (whose relationship to Hester is a secret known only to themselves), is appalling; and his final confession and expiation are merely a relief, not a reconciliation.—We are by no means satisfied that passions and tragedies like these are the legitimate subjects for fiction: we are satisfied that novels such as *Adam Blair* and plays such as *The Stranger* may be justly charged with attracting more persons than they warn by their excitement. But if Sin and Sorrow in their most fearful forms are to be presented in any work of art, they have rarely been treated with a loftier severity, purity, and sympathy than in Mr. Hawthorne's *Scarlet Letter*. The touch of the fantastic befitting a period of society in which ignorant and excitable human creatures conceived each other and themselves to be under the direct 'rule and governance' of the Wicked One, is most skilfully administered. The supernatural here never becomes grossly palpable:—the thrill is all the deeper for its action being indefinite, and its source vague and distant.

The daughter of a clergyman from Beverly, Massachusetts, Anne W. Abbott edited The Child's Friend and Family Magazine *from 1857 to 1858. She invented "The Mansion of Happiness, an Instructive Moral and Entertaining Amusement," a board game designed to teach morality to children, and created the card game "Dr. Busby." Both games were issued by W. and S. B. Ives in Salem and were popular in nineteenth-century America. In her review Abbott, who preferred Hawthorne's preface to his tale, praised the portrayal of Pearl, whom she called "the only genuine and consistent mortal in the book."*

Review of *The Scarlet Letter*
Anne W. Abbott
North American Review, 71 (July 1850): 135–148

That there is something not unpleasing to us in the misfortunes of our best friends, is a maxim we have always spurned, as a libel on human nature. But we must be allowed, in behalf of Mr Hawthorne's friend and gossip, the literary public, to rejoice in the event—a 'removal' from the office of Surveyor of the Customs for the port of Salem,—which has brought him back to our admiring, and, we modestly hope, congenial society, from associations and environments which have confessedly been detrimental to his genius, and to those qualities of heart, which, by an unconscious revelation through his style, like the involuntary betrayal of character in a man's face and manners, have won the affection of other than personal friends. We are truly grieved at the savage 'scratches' our phoenix has received from the claws of the national eagle, scratches gratuitous and unprovoked, whereby his plumage remains not a little

ruffled, if his breast be not very deeply lacerated. We hope we do not see tendencies to *self immolation* in the introductory chapter to this volume. It seems suicidal to a most enviable fame, to show the fine countenance of the sometime denizen of Concord Parsonage, once so serene and full of thought, and at the same time so attractively arch, now cloudy and peevish, or dressed in sardonic smiles, which would scare away the enthusiasm of less hearty admirers than those he 'holds by the button.' The pinnacle on which the 'conscience of the beautiful' has placed our author's graceful image is high enough, however, to make slight changes from the wear and tear of outdoor elements, highway dust, and political vandalism, little noticed by those accustomed to look lovingly up to it. Yet they cannot be expected to regret a 'removal,' which has saved those finer and more delicate traits, in which genius peculiarly manifests itself, from being worn away by rough contact, or obliterated by imperceptible degrees through the influence of the atmosphere.

Mr Hawthorne's serious apprehensions on this subject are thus candidly expressed:—

I began to grow melancholy and restless; continually prying into my mind, to discover which of its poor properties were gone, and what degree of detriment had already accrued to the remainder. I endeavored to calculate how much longer I could stay in the Custom House, and yet go forth a man. To confess the truth, it was my greatest apprehension,—as it would never be a measure of policy to turn out so quiet an individual as myself, and it being hardly in the nature of a public officer to resign,—it was my chief trouble, therefore, that I was likely to grow gray and decrepit in the Surveyorship, and become much such another animal as the old Inspector. Might it not, in the tedious lapse of official life that lay before me, finally be with me as it was with this venerable friend,—to make the dinner hour the nucleus of the day, and to spend the rest of it, as an old dog spends it, asleep in the sunshine or the shade? A dreary look-forward this, for a man who felt it to be the best definition of happiness to live throughout the whole range of his faculties and sensibilities! But, all this while, I was giving myself very unnecessary alarm. Providence had meditated better things for me than I could possibly imagine for myself.

A man who has so rare an individuality to lose may well shudder at the idea of becoming a soulless machine, a sort of official scarecrow, having only so much of manly semblance left as will suffice to warn plunderers from the property of 'Uncle Sam.' Haunted by the horror of mental annihilation, it is not wonderful that he should look askance at the drowsy row of officials, as they reclined uneasily in tilted chairs, and should measure their mental torpidity by the length of time they had been subjected to the soul-exhaling process in which he had not yet got beyond the conscious stage. It was in pure apprehension, let us charitably hope, and not in a satirical, and far less a malicious, mood, that he describes one of them as retaining barely enough of the moral and spiritual nature to keep him from going upon all fours, and possessing neither soul, heart, nor mind more worthy of immortality than the spirit of the beast, which 'goeth downward.' Judging his aged colleagues, thus, well might the young publican, as yet spiritually alive, stand aghast! A man may be excusable for starving his *intellect,* if Providence has thrown him into a situation where its dainty palate cannot be gratified. But for the well being of his *moral nature,* he is more strictly responsible, and has no right, under any circumstances, to remain in a position where, from causes beyond his control, his conscience is deprived of its supremacy over the will, and policy or expediency, whether public or selfish, placed upon its throne. 'Most men,' says our honest author, 'suffer moral detriment from this mode of life,' from causes which, (having just devoted four pages to a full-length caricature,) he had not space to hint at, except in the following pithy admonition to the aspirants after a place in the Blue Book.

> Uncle Sam's gold—meaning no disrespect to the worthy old gentleman—has, in this respect, a quality of enchantment, like that of the Devil's wages. Whoever touches it should look well to himself, or he may find the bargain to go hard against him, involving, if not his soul, yet many of his better attributes; its sturdy force, its courage and constancy, its truth, its self-reliance, and all that gives the emphasis to manly character.

It was great gain for a man like Mr Hawthorne to depart this truly unprofitable life; but we wish that his demise had been quiet and Christian, and not by violence. We regret that any of the bitterness of heart engendered by the political battle, and by his subsequent decapitation without being judged by his peers, should have come with him to a purer and higher state of existence. That a head should fall, and even receive 'an ignominious kick,' is but a common accident in a party struggle, and would be of no more consequence to the world in Mr Hawthorne's case than any other, (the metaphorical head not including brains,) provided the spirit had suffered no material injury in the encounter. Of that, however, we have no means of judging, except by comparing this book of recent production with his former writings. Of the 'stern and sombre' pictures of the world and human life, external and internal, found in *The Scarlet Letter,* we shall speak anon. The preface claims some farther notice.

One would conclude, that the mother on whose bosom the writer was cherished in his urchinhood had behaved herself like a very step-mother towards him, showing a vulgar preference of those sons who have gathered, and thrown into her lap, gifts more substantial than garlands and laurel wreaths. This appears from his reluctant and half ashamed confession of attachment to her, and his disrespectful remarks upon her homely and commonplace features, her chilly and unsocial disposition, and those marks of decay and premature age which needed not to be pointed out. The portrait is like, no doubt; but we cannot help imagining the ire of the ancient dame at the unfilial satire. Indeed, a faint echo of the voice of her indignation has arrived at our ears. She complains, that, in anatomizing the characters of his former associates for the entertainment of the public, he has used the scalpel on some subjects, who, though they could not defend themselves, might possibly wince; and that all who came under his hand, living or dead, had probably relatives among his readers, whose affections might be wounded.

Setting this consideration apart, we confess that, to our individual taste, this naughty chapter is more piquant than any thing in the book; the style is racy and pungent, not elaborately witty, but stimulating the reader's attention agreeably by original turns of expression, and unhackneyed combinations of words, falling naturally into their places, as if of their own accord, and not obtained by far seeking and impressment into the service. The sketch of General Miller is airily and lightly done; no other artist could have given so much character to each fine drawn line as to render the impression almost as distinct to the reader's fancy as a portrait drawn by rays of light is to the bodily vision. Another specimen of his word painting, the lonely parlor seen by the moonlight melting into the warmer glow of the fire, while it reminds us of Cowper's much quoted and admired verse, has truly a great deal more of genuine poetry in it. The delineations of wharf scenery, and of the Custom House, with their appropriate figures and personages, are worthy of the pen of Dickens; and really, so far as mere style is concerned, Mr Hawthorne has no reason to thank us for the compliment; he has the finer touch, if not more genial feeling, of the two. Indeed, if we except a few expressions which savor somewhat strongly of his late unpoetical associations, and the favorite metaphor of the guillotine, which, however apt, is not particularly agreeable to the imagination in such detail, we like the preface better than the tale.

No one who has taken up *The Scarlet Letter* will willingly lay it down till he has finished it; and he will do well not to pause, for he cannot resume the story where he left it. He should give himself up to the magic power of the style, without stopping to open wide the eyes of his good sense and judgment, and shake off the spell; or half the weird beauty' will disappear like a 'dissolving view.' To be sure, when he closes the book, he will feel very much like the giddy and bewildered patient who is just awakening from his first experiment of the effects of sulphuric ether. The soul has been floating or flying between earth and heaven, with dim ideas of pain and pleasure strangely mingled, and all things earthly swimming dizzily and dreamily, yet most beautiful, before the half shut eye. That the author himself felt this sort of intoxication as well as the willing subjects of his enchantment, we think, is evident in many pages of the last half of the volume. His imagination has sometimes taken him fairly off his feet, insomuch that he seems almost to doubt if there be any firm ground at all,–if we may so judge from such mist-born ideas as the following.

> But, to all these shadowy beings, so long our near acquaintances,–as well Roger Chillingworth as his companions,–we would fain be merciful. It is a curious subject of observation and inquiry, whether hatred and love be not the same thing at bottom. Each, in its utmost development, supposes a high degree of intimacy and heart-knowledge; each renders one individual dependent for the food of his affections and spiritual life upon another; each leaves the passionate lover, or the no less passionate hater, forlorn and desolate by the withdrawal of his object. Philosophically considered, therefore, the two passions seem essentially the same, except the one happens to be seen in a celestial radiance, and the other in a dusky and lurid glow. In the spiritual world, the old physician and the minister–mutual victims as they have been–may, unawares, have found their earthly stock of hatred and antipathy transmuted into golden love.

Thus devils and angels are alike beautiful, when seen through the magic glass; and they stand side by side in heaven, however the former may be supposed to have come there. As for Roger Chillingworth, he seems to have so little in common with man, he is such a gnome-like phantasm, such an unnatural personification of an abstract idea, that we should be puzzled to assign him a place among angels, men, or devils. He is no more a man than Mr Dombey, who sinks down a mere *caput mortuum,* as soon as pride, the only animating principle, is withdrawn. These same 'shadowy beings' are much like 'the changeling the fairies made o' a benweed.' Hester at first strongly excites our pity, for she suffers like an immortal being; and our interest in her continues only while we have hope for her soul, that its baptism of tears will reclaim it from the foul stain which has been cast upon it. We see her humble, meek, self-denying, charitable, and heart-wrung with anxiety for the moral welfare of her wayward child. But anon her humility catches a new tint, and we find it pride; and so a vague unreality steals by degrees over all her

most humanizing traits–we lose our confidence in all–and finally, like Undine, she disappoints us, and shows the dream-land origin and nature, when we were looking to behold a Christian.

There is rather more power, and better keeping, in the character of Dimmesdale. But here again we are cheated into a false regard and interest, partly perhaps by the associations thrown around him without the intention of the author, and possibly contrary to it, by our habitual respect for the sacred order, and by our faith in religion, where it has once been rooted in the heart. We are told repeatedly, that the Christian element yet pervades his character and guides his efforts; but it seems strangely wanting. 'High aspirations for the welfare of his race, warm love of souls, pure sentiments, natural piety, strengthened by thought and study, and illuminated by revelation–all of which invaluable gold was little better than rubbish' to Roger Chillingworth, are little better than rubbish at all, for any use to be made of them in the story. Mere suffering, aimless and without effect for purification or blessing to the soul, we do not find in God's moral world. The sting that follows crime is most severe in the purest conscience and the tenderest heart, in mercy, not in vengeance, surely; and we can conceive of any cause constantly exerting itself without its appropriate effects, as soon as of a seven years' agony without penitence. But here every pang is wasted. A most obstinate and unhuman passion, or a most unwearying conscience it must be, neither being worn out, or made worse or better, by such a prolonged application of the scourge. Penitence may indeed be life-long; but as for this, we are to understand that there is no penitence about it. We finally get to be quite of the author's mind, that 'the only truth that continued to give Mr Dimmesdale a real existence on this earth, was the anguish in his inmost soul, and the undissembled expression of it in his aspect. Had he once found power to smile, and wear an aspect of gayety, there had been no such man.' He duly exhales at the first gleam of hope, an uncertain and delusive beam, but fatal to his misty existence. From that time he is a fantasy, an opium dream, his faith a vapor, his reverence blasphemy, his charity mockery, his sanctity impurity, his love of souls a ludicrous impulse to teach little boys bad words; and nothing is left to bar the utterance of 'a volley of good, round, solid, satisfactory, heaven-defying oaths,' (a phrase which seems to smack its lips with a strange *goût!*) but good taste and the mere outward shell, 'the buckramed habit of clerical decorum.' The only conclusion is, that the shell never possessed any thing real,–never was the Rev. Arthur Dimmesdale, as we have foolishly endeavored to suppose; that he was but a changeling, or an imp in grave apparel, not an erring, and consequently suffering human being, with a heart still upright enough to find the burden of conscious unworthiness and undeserved praise more tolerable than open ignominy and shame, and refraining from relieving his withering conscience from its load of unwilling hypocrisy, if partly from fear, more from the wish to be yet an instrument of good to others, not an example of evil which should weaken their faith in religion. The closing scene, where the satanic phase of the character is again exchanged for the saintly, and the pillory platform is made the stage for a triumphant *coup de théatre,* seems to us more than a failure.

But Little Pearl—gem of the purest water—what shall we say of her? That if perfect truth to childish and human nature can make her a mortal, she is so; and immortal, if the highest creations of genius have any claim to immortality. Let the author throw what light he will upon her, from his magical prism, she retains her perfect and vivid human individuality. When he would have us call her elvish and imp-like, we persist in seeing only a capricious, roguish, untamed child, such as many a mother has looked upon with awe, and a feeling of helpless incapacity to rule. Every motion, every feature, every word and tiny shout, every naughty scream and wild laugh, come to us as if our very senses were conscious of them. The child is a true child, the only genuine and consistent mortal in the book; and wherever she crosses the dark and gloomy track of the story, she refreshes our spirit with pure truth and radiant beauty, and brings to grateful remembrance the like ministry of gladsome childhood, in some of the saddest scenes of actual life. We feel at once that the author must have a 'Little Pearl' of his own, whose portrait, consciously or unconsciously, his pen sketches out. Not that we would deny to Mr Hawthorne the power to call up any shape, angel or goblin, and present it before his readers in a striking and vivid light. But there is something more than imagination in the picture of 'Little Pearl.' The heart takes a part in it, and puts in certain inimitable touches of nature here and there, such as fancy never dreamed of, and only a long and loving observation of the ways of childhood could suggest. The most characteristic traits are so interwoven with the story, (on which we do not care to dwell,) that it is not easy to extract a paragraph which will convey much of the charming image to our readers. The most convenient passage for our purpose is the description of Little Pearl playing upon the sea-shore. We take in the figure of the old man as a dark background, or contrast, to heighten the effect.

In fine, Hester Prynne resolved to meet her former husband, and do what might be in her power for the rescue of the victim on whom he had so evidently set his gripe. The occasion was not long to seek. One after-

The Hawthornes' children, Julian and Una, circa 1850. Hawthorne used Una as a model for Pearl in The Scarlet Letter *(Boston Athenaeum).*

noon, walking with Pearl in a retired part of the peninsula, she beheld the old physician, with a basket on one arm, and a staff in the other hand, stooping along the ground, in quest of roots and herbs to concoct his medicines withal.

Hester bade Little Pearl run down to the margin of the water, and play with the shells and tangled seaweed, until she should have talked awhile with yonder gatherer of herbs. So the child flew away like a bird, and, making bare her small white feet, went pattering along the moist margin of the sea. Here and there, she came to a full stop, and peeped curiously into a pool, left by the retiring tide as a mirror for Pearl to see her face in. Forth peeped at her, out of the pool, with dark, glistening curls around her head, and an elf-smile in her eyes, the image of a little maid, whom Pearl, having no other playmate, invited to take her hand and run a race with her. But the visionary little maid, on her part, beckoned likewise, as if to say,—'This is a better place! Come thou into the pool!' And Pearl, stepping in, mid-leg deep, beheld her own white feet at the bottom; while, out of a still lower depth, came the gleam of a kind of fragmentary smile, floating to and fro in the agitated water.

Meanwhile, her mother had accosted the physician.

'I would speak a word with you,' said she,—'a word that concerns us much.'

Here follows a dialogue in the spirit of the idea that runs through the book,—that revenge may exist

Illustration for chapter 2 of The Scarlet Letter, *"The Market Place," by F. O. C. Darley in an 1879 edition of the novel.*
Felix Octavius Carr Darley (1821–1888) was the most highly regarded American illustrator of his time
(from Kenneth Cameron, Hawthorne among His Contemporaries, *1968).*

without any overt act of vengeance that could be called such, and that a man who refrains from avenging himself, may be more diabolical in his very forbearance than he who in his passionate rage inflicts what evil he may upon his enemy; the former having that spirit of cold hate which could goat for years, or forever, over the agonies of remorse and despair, over the anguish bodily and mental, and consequent death or madness, of a fellow man, and never relent– never for a moment be moved to pity. This master passion of hatred, swallowing up all that is undevilish and human in Roger Chillingworth, makes him a pure abstraction at last, a sort of mythical fury, a match for Alecto the Unceasing.

All this while, Hester had been looking steadily at the old man, and was shocked, as well as wonder-smitten, to discern what a change had been wrought upon him within the past seven years. It was not so much that he had grown older; for though the traces of advancing life were visible, he bore his age well, and seemed to retain a wiry vigor and alertness. But the former aspect of an intellectual and studious man, calm and quiet, which was what she best remembered in him, had altogether vanished, and been succeeded by an eager, searching, almost fierce, yet carefully guarded look. It seemed to be his wish and purpose to mask this expression with a smile; but the latter played him false, and flickered over his visage so derisively, that the spectator could see his blackness all the better for it. Ever and anon, too, there came a glare of red light out of his eyes; as if the old man's soul were on fire, and kept on smouldering duskily within his breast, until, by some casual puff of passion, it was blown into a momentary flame. This he repressed as speedily as possible, and strove to look as if nothing of the kind had happened.

In a word, old Roger Chillingworth was a striking evidence of man's faculty of transforming himself into a devil, if he will only, for a reasonable space of time, undertake a devil's office. This unhappy person had effected such a transformation by devoting himself, for seven years, to the constant analysis of a heart full of torture, and deriving his enjoyment thence, and adding fuel to those fiery tortures which he analyzed and gloated over.

The scarlet letter burned on Hester Prynne's bosom. Here was another ruin, the responsibility of which came partly home to her.

'What see you in my face,' asked the physician, 'that you look at it so earnestly?'

'Something that would make me weep, if there were any tears bitter enough for it,' answered she. 'But let it pass! It is of yonder miserable man that I would speak.'

So Roger Chillingworth—a deformed old figure, with a face that haunted men's memories longer than they liked—took leave of Hester Prynne, and went stooping away along the earth. He gathered here and there an herb, or grubbed up a root, and put it into the basket on his arm. His gray beard almost touched the ground, as he crept onward. Hester gazed after him a little while, looking with a half-fantastic curiosity to see whether the tender grass of early spring would not be blighted beneath him, and show the wavering track of his footsteps, sere and brown, across its cheerful verdure. She wondered what sort of herbs they were, which the old man was so sedulous to gather. Would not the earth, quickened to an evil purpose by the sympathy of his eye, greet him with poisonous shrubs, of species hitherto unknown, that would start up under his fingers? Or might it suffice him, that every wholesome growth should be converted into something deleterious and malignant at his touch? Did the sun, which shone so brightly everywhere else, really fall upon him? Or was there, as it rather seemed, a circle of ominous shadow moving along with his deformity, whichever way he turned himself? And whither was he now going? Would he not suddenly sink into the earth, leaving a barren and blasted spot, where, in due course of time, would be seen deadly nightshade, dogwood, henbane, and whatever else of vegetable wickedness the climate could produce, all flourishing with hideous luxuriance? Or would he spread bat's wings and flee away, looking so much the uglier, the higher he rose towards heaven?

'Be it sin or no,' said Hester Prynne bitterly, as she still gazed after him, 'I hate the man!'

She upbraided herself for the sentiment, but could not overcome or lessen it.

It is time to seek the exhilarating presence of 'Little Pearl,' whom we left on the sea-shore, making nature her playmate.

He being gone, she summoned back her child.

'Pearl! Little Pearl! Where are you?'

Pearl, whose activity of spirit never flagged, had been at no loss for amusement while her mother talked with the old gatherer of herbs. At first, as already told, she had flirted fancifully with her own image in a pool of water, beckoning the phantom forth, and—as it declined to venture—seeking a passage for herself into its sphere of impalpable earth and unattainable sky. Soon finding, however, that she or the image was unreal, she turned elsewhere for better pastime. She made little boats out of birch bark, and freighted them with snail-shells, and sent out more ventures on the mighty deep than any merchant in New England; but the larger part of them foundered near the shore. She

seized a live horseshoe by the tail, and made prize of several five-fingers, and laid out a jelly fish to melt in the warm sun. Then she took up the white foam, that streaked the line of the advancing tide, and threw it upon the breeze, scampering after it with winged footsteps, to catch the great snow-flakes ere they fell. Perceiving a flock of beach-birds, that fed and fluttered along the shore, the naughty child picked up her apron full of pebbles, and, creeping from rock to rock after these small sea-fowl, displayed remarkable dexterity in pelting them. One little gray bird, with a white breast, Pearl was almost sure, had been hit by a pebble, and fluttered away with a broken wing. But then the elf-child sighed, and gave up her sport; because it grieved her to have done harm to a little being that was as wild as the sea-breeze, or as wild as Pearl herself.

Her final employment was to gather sea-weed, of various kinds, and make herself a scarf, or mantle, and a head-dress, and thus assume the aspect of a little mermaid. She inherited her mother's gift for devising drapery and costume.

We know of no writer who better understands and combines the elements of the picturesque in writing than Mr Hawthorne. His style may be compared to a sheet of transparent water, reflecting from its surface blue skies, nodding woods, and the smallest spray or flower that peeps over its grassy margin; while in its clear yet mysterious depths we espy rarer and stranger things, which we must dive for, if we would examine. Whether they might prove gems or pebbles, when taken out of the fluctuating medium through which the sun-gleams reach them, is of no consequence to the effect. Every thing charms the eye and ear, and nothing looks like art and pains-taking. There is a naturalness and a continuous flow of expression in Mr Hawthorne's books, that makes them delightful to read, especially in this our day, when the fear of triteness drives some writers, (even those who might otherwise avoid that reproach,) to adopt an abrupt and dislocated style, administering to our jaded attention frequent thumps and twitches, by means of outlandish idioms and forced inversions, and now and then flinging at our heads an incomprehensible, break-jaw word, which uncivilized missile stuns us to a full stop, and an appeal to authority. No authority can be found, however, which affords any remedy or redress against determined outlaws. After bumping over 'rocks and ridges, and gridiron bridges,' in one of these prosaic latter-day omnibuses, how pleasant it is to move over flowery turf upon a spirited, but properly trained Pegasus, who occasionally uses his wings, and skims along a little above *terra firma,* but not with an alarming preference for cloudland or rarefied air. One cannot but wonder, by the way, that the master of such a wizard power over language as Mr Hawthorne manifests should not choose a less revolting subject than this of *The Scarlet Letter,* to which fine writing seems as inappropriate as

Illustrations by Darley for chapters 8, “The Elf-child and the Minister,” and 10, “The Leech and His Patient”

fine embroidery. The ugliness of pollution and vice is no more relieved by it than the gloom of the prison is by the rose tree at its door. There are some palliative expressions used, which cannot, even as a matter of taste, be approved.

Regarding the book simply as a picture of the olden time, we have no fault to find with costume or circumstance. All the particulars given us, (and he is not wearisomely anxious to multiply them to show his research,) are in good keeping and perspective, all in softened outlines and neutral tint, except the ever fresh and unworn image of childhood, which stands out from the canvas in the gorgeously attired 'Little Pearl.' He forbears to mention the ghastly gallows-tree, which stood hard by the pillory and whipping-post, at the city gates, and which one would think might have been banished with them from the precincts of Boston, and from the predilections of the community of whose opinions it is the focus. When a people have opened their eyes to the fact, that it is not the best way of discountenancing vice to harden it to exposure and shame, and make it brazen-faced, reckless, and impudent, they might also be convinced, it would seem, that respect for human life would not be promoted by publicly violating it, and making a spectacle, or a newspaper theme, of the mental agony and dying struggles of a human being, and of him least fit, in the common belief, to be thus hurried to his account. 'Blood for blood!' We are shocked at the revengeful custom among uncivilized tribes, when it bears the aspect of private revenge, because the executioners must be of the kindred of the slain. How much does the legal retribution in kind, which civilized man exacts, differ in reality from the custom of the savage? The law undertakes to avenge its own dignity, to use a popular phrase; that is, it regards the community as one great family, and constitutes itself the avenger of blood in its behalf. It is not punishment, but retaliation, which does not contemplate the reform of the offender as well as the prevention of crime; and where it wholly loses the remedial element, and cuts off the opportunity for repentance which God's mercy allows, it is worthy of a barbarous, not a Christian, social alliance. What sort of combination for mutual safety is it, too, when no man feels safe, because fortuitous circumstances, ingeniously bound into a chain, may so entangle. Truth that she cannot bestir herself to rescue us from the doom which the judgment of twelve fallible men pronounces, and our protector, the law, executes upon us?

But we are losing sight of Mr Hawthorne's book, and of the old Puritan settlers, as he portrays them with few, but clearly cut and expressive, lines. In these sketchy groupings, Governor Bellingham is the only prominent figure, with the Rev. John Wilson behind

him, 'his beard, white as a snowdrift, seen over the Governor's shoulder.'

Here, to witness the scene which we are describing, sat Governor Bellingham himself, with four sergeants about his chair, bearing halberds as a guard of honor. He wore a dark feather in his hat, a border of embroidery on his cloak, and a black velvet tunic beneath; a gentleman advanced in years, and with a hard experience written in his wrinkles. He was not ill-fitted to be the head and representative of a community, which owed its origin and progress, and its present state of development, not to the impulses of youth, but to the stern and tempered energies of manhood, and the sombre sagacity of age; accomplishing so much, precisely because it imagined and hoped so little.

With this portrait, we close our remarks on the book, which we should not have criticized at so great length, had we admired it less. We hope to be forgiven, if in any instance our strictures have approached the limits of what may be considered personal. We would not willingly trench upon the right which an individual may claim, in common courtesy, not to have his private qualities or personal features discussed to his face, with everybody looking on. But Mr Hawthorne's example in the preface, and the condescending familiarity of the attitude he assumes therein, are at once our occasion and our apology.

Theologian and transcendentalist philosopher Theodore Parker, who founded the Massachusetts Quarterly Review *(1847–1850) to continue the work of* The Dial *(1840–1844), asked George B. Loring to review* The Scarlet Letter. *Loring, who at the time was a surgeon at the Chelsea (Massachusetts) Marine Hospital, focuses on the theme of morality in* The Scarlet Letter, *observing that Hester Prynne learns "the power of love to sustain and guide and teach the soul," as the minister Arthur Dimmesdale does not.*

Review of *The Scarlet Letter*
George B. Loring
Massachusetts Quarterly Review,
3 (September 1850): 484–500

No author of our own country, and scarcely any author of our times, manages to keep himself clothed in such a cloak of mystery as Nathaniel Hawthorne. From the time when his *Twice-told Tales* went, in their first telling, floating through the periodicals of the day, up to the appearance of *The Scarlet Letter,* he has stood on the confines of society, as we see some sombre figure, in the dim light of the stage scenery, peering through that narrow space, when a slouched hat and a muffling cloak do not meet, upon the tragic events which are made conspicuous by the glare of the footlights. From nowhere in particular, from an old manse, and from the drowsy dilapidation of an old custom-house, he has spoken such oracular words, such searching thoughts, as sounded of old from the mystic God whose face was never seen even by the most worthy. It seems useless now to speak of his humor, subtile and delicate as Charles Lamb's; of his pathos, deep as Richter's; of his penetration into the human heart, clearer than that of Goldsmith or Crabbe; of his apt and telling words, which Pope might have envied; of his description, graphic as Scott's or Dickens's; of the delicious lanes he opens, on either hand, and leaves you alone to explore, masking his work with the fine *'faciebat'* which removes all limit from all high art, and gives every man scope to advance and develop. He seems never to trouble himself, either in writing or living, with the surroundings of life. He is no philosopher for the poor or the rich, for the ignorant or the learned, for the righteous or the wicked, for any special rank or condition in life, but for human nature as given by God into the hands of man. He calls us to be indignant witnesses of no particular social, religious, or political enormity. He asks no admiration for this or that individual or associated virtue. The face of society, with its manifold features, never comes before you, as you study the extraordinary experience of his men and women, except as a necessary setting for the picture. They might shine at tournaments, or grovel in cellars, or love, or fight, or meet with high adventure, or live the deepest and quietest life in unknown corners of the earth,—their actual all vanishes before the strange and shifting picture he gives of the motive heart of man. In no work of his is this characteristic more strikingly visible than in *The Scarlet Letter;* and in no work has he presented so clear and perfect an image of himself, as a speculative philosopher, an ethical thinker, a living man. Perhaps he verges strongly upon the supernatural, in the minds of those who would recognize nothing but the corporeal existence of human life. But man's nature is, by birth, *super*natural; and the deep mystery which lies beneath all his actions is far beyond the reach of any mystical vision that ever lent its airy shape to the creations of the most intense dreamer.

When he roamed at large, we cared not to attribute any of his wisdom to his mode of life. When he hailed from an old manse, 'living,' as he says,

for three years within the subtile influence of an intellect like Emerson's, indulging fantastic speculations beside the fire of fallen boughs with Ellery Channing, talking with Thoreau about pine trees and Indian relics,

in his hermitage at Walden, growing fastidious by sympathy with the classic refinement of Hillard's culture, becoming imbued with poetic sentiment at Longfellow's hearth-stone,

we seem ready to receive him as the fruit of such culture. When he *descended,* as he would have us believe, into the realms of the actual, and acted his part among practical men, we were not so ready as he was, himself, to submit to his burial, but waited for the next words which should fall from his lips. And we were obliged to wait until the breeze which bore his commission to his feet retired, and swept away the honors and emoluments to cast them before some other willing recipient. And now he comes before us, not only the deep and wonderful thinker, the man of intense life we have always known, but in the new attitude of an office-holder, and, in this guise, gives us his *dictum.*

One word upon this matter, contained in the 'Introduction' of the book. However singular he may be in other respects, his opinion of office-holding appears to be in common with that of the 'rest of mankind'—the possessors of place always excepted. The mental paralysis which attended his own experience in this mode of life,—which grows out of leaning on 'the mighty arm of the Republic,' which comes of feeding on the pap of government, and remains after the food is removed,—is, unquestionably, the disease which is peculiar to this locality of the business world. As pettifogging from law, quackery from medicine, bigotry and dogmatism from divinity, eagerness and avarice from the business of the counting-house and the market, uncompromising hate and bitterness from reform, callousness, in a word, from all the practical detail and manipulation of life,—so come subserviency and want of self-reliance from office-holding. No more, and no less. It is a painful fact that every way of life, whose tendency is to a practical result, becomes hard, bare, dusty, and ignoble from constant travel. Though many men resist this effect, all men feel it; and that power which makes a man an open-minded, sagacious jurist, a kind and honest physician, a liberal divine, a generous business-man, a gentle and charitable reformer, sustains some in the duties of office conferred by party, giving dignity and respectability to their place, and opportunity and experience to themselves. There is an energy which no circumstance can destroy, which belongs to that subtile and defiant essence called character. Life has two results—the development of the strong, and the destruction of the weak; and it is to the latter, alone, that the degradations of practical effort belong. If we run our eye over literary history, and see the intellectual fire which has been subjected to the quenching influences of patronage and place, from Chaucer to Hawthorne, we shall not condemn office-holding as wholly enervating. If we go from the custom-house into State Street, we shall find that office-holding is not the only mercenary sphere in the world. And if we wander out of the region of politics into the pulpit, we shall find that the former does not contain all the time-serving subserviency. To us who live under no rain of manna, the whole process of getting a living is hard enough at best. And he who can make this work secondary to the great life of thought, and a relaxation to his laboring mind, unites those powers which carry man to his highest development.

Of Hawthorne as a worker, especially as an office-holder, we would not think or speak more than is necessary. He has presented himself in this light, and of course demands notice, as every extraordinary man does, whatever be his sphere of action. And even here, condemn the position as he may, we are glad to admire his peculiar genius. From the height of that tall office-stool on which he sat, his survey of mankind around him was clear, just, and penetrating. There is not a life whose daily history, sincerely and earnestly presented, does not appeal to our sympathy and interest. And we are reminded of the strong human groups of Teniers and Poussin, as we read the graphic picture of those old custom-house attachés from the pen of Hawthorne. His appreciation of himself, and of each individual associate, whatever be his qualities, commands our unreserved assent. The general, the clerks, the inspectors, the 'father of the custom-house,' are real flesh and blood; and each acts his part in the drama with an interest and an effect which forbid his removal from the group. It is astonishing, how accurately he delineates the peculiar characteristics of his associates,— how delicately and how justly. While we sit and listen with the intensity of sympathetic interest to the effect which each foot-worn stone in the courtyard, each grass-grown corner of the old neglected wharf, each incursion of busy merchants, and 'sea-flushed' sailors, each rafter of that old building where the traditions were hung up to dry, each duty and interest has upon the mind and heart of this acute observer and delineator; we grow muscular, and peculiarly vital and stomachic, over the old evergreen inspector,—we are vitalized account-books with the accurate clerk; we are half asleep with the snoring old sea-dogs, who range along the passage; and we are firm, immovable, placid, patriotic, brave, when we read the tender and touching recognition of the peculiar reverence due the calm and silent night which rests upon the great quenched mass of forces contained in the hoary old collector himself. The humor here is inimitable too. The high stool sustains a keen and quaint surveyor, in one instance at least; and, although some might question the delicacy of the personal allusions, we are forced to admire the

twinkling good-nature, the honest confidence, the pathetic penetration, which play over that countenance as it takes its survey, and we know no such word as indelicacy as applicable to the result of that survey, for which we are as grateful as we are to Hogarth for his groups and faces. Although, to many minds, we doubt not a sense of spleen and vindictiveness may be imparted by the 'Introductory,' we should no sooner look for these passions from the high stool of the surveyor of the Salem custom-house, than from the desk of that clerk who carried, day after day for so many years, to his books in the India House, such wit and humor, such affection and touching devotion, such knowledge and gentleness, such purity of heart, and such elegant delicacy and power of mind.

But the office-holder is guillotined, his official head drops off—*presto*—and Hawthorne, resuming his literary cranium, marches out of the custom-house, with the manuscript and Scarlet Letter of old Surveyor Pue, in his pocket. The sale of the book has distributed the story—we would deal with its philosophy and merits. It is, as we had a right to expect, extraordinary, as a work of art, and as a vehicle of religion and ethics.

Surrounded by the stiff, formal dignitaries of our early New England Colony, and subjected to their severe laws, and severer social atmosphere, we have a picture of crime and passion. It would be hard to conceive of a greater outrage upon the freezing and self-denying doctrines of that day, than the sin for which Hester Prynne was damned by society, and for which Arthur Dimmesdale damned himself. For centuries, the devoted and superstitious Catholic had made it a part of his creed to cast disgrace upon the passions; and the cold and rigid Puritan, with less fervor, and consequently with less beauty, had driven them out of his paradise, as the parents of all sin. There was no recognition of the intention or meaning of that sensuous element of human nature which, gilding life like a burnishing sunset, lays the foundation of all that beauty which seeks its expression in poetry, and music, and art, and gives the highest apprehension of religious fervor. Zest of life was no part of the Puritan's belief. He scorned his own flesh and blood. His appetites were crimes. His cool head was always ready to temper the hot blood in its first tendency to come bounding from his heart. He had no sympathy, no tenderness, for any sinner, more especially for that hardened criminal who had failed to trample all his senses beneath his feet. Love, legalized, was a weakness in the mind of that mighty dogmatist, who, girt with the 'sword of the Lord and of Gideon,' subdued his enemies, and, with folios of texts and homilies, sustained and cheered his friends; and love, illegalized, was that burning, scarlet sin which had no forgiveness in these disciples of Him who said

Illustrations by Darley for chapters 15, "Hester and Pearl," and 19, "The Child and the Brookside"

to the woman, 'neither do I condemn thee.' The state of society which this grizzly form of humanity created, probably served as little to purify men as any court of voluptuousness; and, while we recognize with compressed lip that heroism which braved seas and unknown shores, for opinion's sake, we remember, with a warm glow, the elegances and intrepid courage and tropical luxuriance of the cavaliers whom they left behind them. Asceticism and voluptuarism on either hand, neither fruitful of the finer and truer virtues, were all that men had arrived at in the great work of sensuous life.

It was the former which fixed the scarlet letter to the breast of Hester Prynne, and which drove Arthur Dimmesdale into a life of cowardly and selfish meanness, that added tenfold disgrace and ignominy to his original crime. In any form of society hitherto known, the sanctity of the devoted relation between the sexes has constituted the most certain foundation of all purity and all social safety. Imperfect as this great law has been in most of its development, founded upon and founding the rights of property, instead of positively recognizing the delicacy of abstract virtue, and having become, of necessity, in the present organization, a bulwark of hereditary rights, and a bond for a deed of conveyance, it nevertheless appeals to the highest sense of virtue and honor which a man finds in his breast. In an age in which there is a tendency to liberalize these, as well as all obligations, in order to secure those which are more sacred and binding than any which have been born of the statute-book, we can hardly conceive of the consternation and disgust which overwhelmed our forefathers when the majesty of virtue, and the still mightier majesty of the law, were insulted. It was as heir of these virtues, and impressed with this education, that Arthur Dimmesdale, a clergyman, believing in and applying all the moral remedies of the times, found himself a criminal. We learn nothing of his experience during the seven long years in which his guilt was secretly gnawing at his breast, unless it be the experience of pain and remorse. He speaks no word of wisdom. He lurks and skulks behind the protection of his profession and his social position, neither growing wiser nor stronger, but, day after day, paler and paler, more and more abject. We do not find that, out of his sin, came any revelation of virtue. No doubt exists of his repentance,—of that repentance which is made up of sorrow for sin, and which grows out of fear of consequences; but we learn nowhere that his enlightened conscience, rising above the dogmas and catechistic creeds of the day, by dint of his own deep and solemn spiritual experiences, taught him what obligations had gathered around him, children of his crime, which he was bound to acknowledge before men, as they stood revealed to God. Why had

his religious wisdom brought him no more heroism? He loved Hester Prynne—he had bound himself to her by an indissoluble bond, and yet he had neither moral courage nor moral honesty, with all his impressive piety, to come forth and assert their sins and their mutual obligations. He was, evidently, a man of powerful nature. His delicate sensibility, his fervor, his influence upon those about him, and, above all, his sin, committed when the tides of his heart rushed in and swept away all the bulrush barriers he had heaped up against them, through years of studious self-discipline,— show what a spirit, what forces, he had. Against none of these forces had he sinned. And yet he was halting, and wavering, and becoming more and more perplexed and worn down with woe, because he had violated the dignity of his position, and had broken a law which his education had made more prominent than any law in his own soul. In this way, he presented the twofold nature which belongs to us as members of society;—a nature born from ourselves and our associations, and comprehending all the diversity and all the harmony of our individual and social duties. Violation of either destroys our fitness for both. And when we remember that, in this development, no truth comes except from harmony, no beauty except from a fit conjunction of the individual with society, and of society with the individual, can we wonder that the great elements of Arthur Dimmesdale's character should have been overbalanced by a detestable crowd of mean and grovelling qualities, warmed into life by the hot antagonism he felt radiating upon himself and all his fellow-men—from the society in which he moved, and from which he received his engrafted moral nature? He sinned in the arms of society, and fell almost beyond redemption; his companion in guilt became an outcast, and a flood of heroic qualities gathered around her. Was this the work of social influences?

Besides all this, we see in him the powerlessness of belief, alone, to furnish true justification through repentance. The dull and callous may be satisfied with the result of this machinery, in its operations upon their souls. But the sensitive and the clear-sighted require peace with themselves, growing out of a dignified and true position taken and held. It is not the unburthening relief afforded by the confessional, great as that relief may be, which brings self-poise and support under a weighty sense of sin, or the consciousness of actual crime; but it is faith in the power of a confident soul to stand upright before God, by means of that God-given strength which raises it above sin. And this every soul can do, until it is taught that it can not and must not. The spirit of the young clergyman struggled for this right, which his soul still recognized. He was a dogmatist by education alone, not by nature. His crime, rebuked by his theories, and by those religious rigors which destroyed all his cognizance of his soul's elements and rights, made him selfish and deceitful, while his heart rebelled against such a craven course, and demanded, with an importunity at last fatal to him, that he should become justified before man as he was before God, and longed to be before his own conscience, by the sincerity of his position. After imbibing unwonted strength from an interview with her whom worldly scorn had rendered resolute, he made an open avowal, which disarmed this wary enemy, and gave a calm and peaceful death to himself. In the same way might he have earned a peaceful life—and in no other. Not a human eye could look on him, and recognize the sinner. His secret was well locked and guarded. But all this safety was the poorest shame to him, whose nobility of nature demanded assertion.

In this matter of crime, as soon as he became involved, he appeared before himself no longer a clergyman, but a man—a human being. He answered society in the cowardly way we have seen. He answered himself in that way which every soul adopts, where crime does not penetrate. The physical facts of crime alone, with which society has to do, in reality constitute sin. Crimes are committed under protest of the soul, more or less decided, as the weary soul itself has been more or less besieged and broken. The war in the individual begins, and the result of the fierce struggle is the victory of the sensual over the spiritual, when the criminal act is committed. If there is no such war, there is no crime; let the deed be what it may, and be denominated what it may, by society. The soul never assents to sin, and weeps with the angels when the form in which it dwells violates the sacred obligations it imposes upon it. When this human form, with its passions and tendencies, commits the violation, and, at the same time, abuses society, it is answerable to this latter tribunal, where it receives its judgment; while the soul flees to her God, dismayed and crushed by the conflict, but not deprived of her divine inheritance. Between the individual and his God, there remains a spot, larger or smaller, as the soul has been kept unclouded, where no sin can enter, where no mediation can come, where all the discords of his life are resolved into the most delicious harmonies, and his whole existence becomes illuminated by a divine intelligence. Sorrow and sin reveal this spot to all men—as, through death, we are born to an immortal life. They reveal what beliefs and dogmas becloud and darken. They produce that intense consciousness, without which virtue can not rise above innocency. They are the toil and trial which give strength and wisdom, and which, like all other toil, produce weariness and fainting and death, if pursued beyond the limit where reaction and the invigorating process begin. We

can not think with too much awe upon the temptations and trials which beset the powerful. The solemn gloom which shuts down over a mighty nature, during the struggle, which it recognizes with vivid sense, between its demon and its divinity, is like that fearful night in which no star appears to relieve the murky darkness. And yet, from such a night as this, and from no other, the grandeur of virtue has risen to beautify and warm and bless the broad universe of human hearts, and to make the whole spiritual creation blossom like the rose. The Temptation and Gethsemane,—these are the miracles which have redeemed mankind.

Thus it stands with the individual and his soul. With himself and society come up other obligations, other influences, other laws. The tribunal before which he stands as a social being cannot be disregarded with impunity. The effects of education and of inheritance cling around us with the tenacity of living fibres of our own bodies, and they govern, with closest intimacy, the estimate of deeds which constitute the catalogue of vice and virtue, and which in their commission elevate or depress our spiritual condition.

We doubt if there is a stronger element in our natures than that which forbids our resisting with impunity surrounding social institutions. However much we may gain in the attempt, it is always attended with some loss. The reverence which enhanced so beautifully the purity and innocence of childhood, often receives its death-blow from that very wisdom out of which comes our mature virtue. Those abstractions whose foundation is the universe, and without an apprehension of which we may go handcuffed and fettered through life, may draw us away from the devotion which deepened and gilded the narrow world in which we were strong by belief alone. The institutions in which we were born controlled in a great degree the mental condition of our parents, as surrounding nature did their physical, and we owe to these two classes of internal and external operations the characters we inherit. An attack, therefore, upon these institutions, affects us to a certain degree as if we were warring against ourselves. Reason and conscience, and our sublimest sense of duty, may call us to the work of reform,—instinct resists. And the nervous energy called for in the struggle is felt through our whole frames with a convulsive influence, while our children seem to have been born with the spirit of unrest. That harmonious calm, out of which alone healthy creations can arise, appeals to all man's interests, even when the quiet sky he is admiring overhangs an ill-cultivated and sterile field. As he puts in his ploughshare for the upturning of the first furrow, he looks over the expanse which the rest of ages has sanctified, and sighs a farewell to the failure of the past, and a sad and sorrowful welcome to the toil and doubt and undeveloped promise of the future.

This law of our nature, which applies to the well-directed and honest efforts of good progressive intentions, applies also to misguided and sinful actions. The stormy life of the erring mother affords no rest for the healthy development of her embryonic child. It amounts to but little for her to say, with Hester Prynne, 'what we did had a consecration of its own,' unless that consecration produces a heavenly calm, as if all nature joined in harmony. Pearl, that wild and fiery little elf, born of love, was also born of conflict; and had the accountability of its parents extended no farther than the confines of this world, the prospective debt due this offspring involved fearful responsibilities. How vividly this little child typified all their startled instincts, their convulsive efforts in life and thought, their isolation, and their self-inflicted contest with and distrust of all mankind. Arthur Dimmesdale, shrinking from intimate contact and intercourse with his child, shrunk from a visible and tangible representation of the actual life which his guilty love had created for himself and Hester Prynne;—love, guilty, because, secured as it may have been to them, it drove them violently from the moral centre around which they resolved.

We have seen that this was most especially the case with the man who was bound and labelled the puritan clergyman; that he had raised a storm in his own heavens which he could not quell, and had cast the whirlwind over the life of his own child. How was it with Hester Prynne?

On this beautiful and luxuriant woman, we see the effect of open conviction of sin, and the continued galling punishment. The heroic traits awakened in her character by her position were the great self-sustaining properties of woman, which, in tribulation and perplexity, elevate her so far above man. The sullen defiance in her, was imparted to her by society. Without, she met only ignominy, scorn, banishment, a shameful brand. Within, the deep and sacred love for which she was suffering martyrdom,—for her crime was thus sanctified in her own apprehension,—was turned into a store of perplexity, distrust, and madness, which darkened all her heavens. Little Pearl was a token more scarlet than the scarlet letter of her guilt; for the child, with a birth presided over by the most intense conflict of love and fear in the mother's heart, nourished at a breast swelling with anguish, and surrounded with burning marks of its mother's shame in its daily life, developed day by day into a void little demon perched upon the most sacred horn of the mother's altar. Even this child, whose young, plastic nature caught the impress which surrounding circumstances most naturally gave, bewildered and maddened her. The pledge of love which God had given her, seemed perverted into an emblem of hate. And yet how patiently and courageously she labored on, bearing her burthen the more firmly, because, in its infliction, she recognized no higher hand than that of civil authority! In her earnest appeal to be allowed to retain her child, she swept away all external influences, and seems to have inspired the young clergyman, even now fainting with his own sense of meaner guilt, to speak words of truth, which in those days must have seemed born of heaven.

'There is truth in what she says,' began the minister, with a voice sweet, tremulous, but powerful, insomuch that the hall reëchoed, and the hollow armor rung with it, 'truth in what Hester says, and in the feeling which inspired her! God gave her the child, and gave her, too, an instinctive knowledge of its nature and requirements, both seemingly so peculiar, which no other mortal being can possess; and, moreover, is there not a quality of awful sacredness in the relation between this mother and this child?'

'Ay! how is that, good Master Dimmesdale?' interrupted the governor. 'Make that plain, I pray you!'

'It must be even so,' resumed the minister; 'for, if we deem it otherwise, do we not thereby say that the Heavenly Father, the Creator of all flesh, hath lightly recognized a deed of sin, and made of no account the distinction between unhallowed lust and holy love? The child of its father's guilt and its mother's shame hath come from the hand of God, to work in many ways upon her heart who pleads so earnestly, and with such bitterness of spirit, the right to keep her. It was meant for a blessing, for the one blessing of her life. It was meant doubtless, as the mother herself hath told us, for a retribution also, a torture to be felt at many an unthought-of moment; a pang, a sting, an ever-recurring agony, in the midst of troubled joy! Hath she not expressed this thought in the garb of the poor child, so forcibly reminding us of that red symbol which sears her bosom?'

'Well said, again,' cried good Mr Wilson. 'I feared the woman had no better thought than to make a mountebank of her child!'

'Oh, not so! not so!' continued Mr Dimmesdale. 'She recognizes, believe me, the solemn miracle which God hath wrought, in the existence of that child. And may she feel too, what methinks is very truth, that this boon was meant, above all things else, to keep the mother's soul alive, and to preserve her from blacker depths of sin, into which Satan might else have sought to plunge her! Therefore it is good for this poor, sinful woman that she hath an infant immortality, a being, capable of eternal joy or sorrow, confided to her care, to be trained up by her to righteousness, to remind her every moment of her fall, but yet to teach her, as it were by the Creator's sacred pledge, *that if she bring the child to heaven, the child also will bring its parent thither! Herein is the sinful mother happier than the sinful father. For Hester Prynne's sake, then, and no less for the poor child's sake, let us leave them as Providence hath seen fit to place them.'*

Illustrations by Darley for chapters 22, "The Procession," and 23, "The Revelation of the Scarlet Letter"

Her social ignominy forced her back upon the true basis of her life. She alone, of all the world, knew the length and breadth of her own secret. Her lawful husband no more pretended to hold a claim, which may always have been a pretence; the father of her child, her own relation to both, and the tragic life which was going on beneath that surface which all men saw, were known to her alone. How poor and miserable must have seemed the punishment which society had inflicted! The scarlet letter was a poor type of the awful truth which she carried within her heart. Without deceit before the world, she stands forth the most heroic person in all that drama. When, from the platform of shame, she bade farewell to that world, she retired to a holier, and sought for such peace as a soul cast out by men may always find. This was her right. No lie hung over her head. Society had heard her story, and had done its worst. And while Arthur Dimmesdale, cherished in the arms of that society which he had outraged, glossing his life with a false coloring which made it beautiful to all beholders, was dying of an inward anguish, Hester stood upon her true ground, denied by this world, and learning that true wisdom which comes through honesty and self-justification. In casting her out, the world had torn from her all the support of its dogmatic teachings, with which it sustains its disciples in their inevitable sufferings, and had compelled her to rely upon that great religious truth which flows instinctively around a life of agony, with its daring freedom. How far behind her in moral and religious excellence was the accredited religious teacher, who was her companion in guilt! Each day which bound her closer and closer to that heaven which was now her only home, drove him farther and farther from the spiritual world, whose glories he so fervently taught others.

It is no pleasant matter to contemplate what is called the guilt of this woman; but it may be instructive, nevertheless. We naturally shrink from any apparent violation of virtue and chastity, and are very ready to forget, in our eager condemnation, how much that is beautiful and holy may be involved in it. We forget that what society calls chastity is often far the reverse, and that a violation of this perverted virtue may be a sad, sorrowful, and tearful beauty, which we would silently and reverently contemplate,—silently, lest a harsh word of the law wound our hearts,—reverently, as we would listen to the fervent prayer. While we dread that moral hardness which would allow a human being to be wrecked in a storm of passion, let us not be unmindful of the holy love which may *long and pray for its development*. Man's heart recognizes this, whether society will or not. The struggle and the sacrifice which the latter calls a crime, the former receives as an exhilarating air of virtue. It is this recognition which taught the rude

and gentle humanity of John Browdie to offer such kind words to his loving, and, as he thought, erring Dot, all out of his great and natural heart. It is this recognition which brought forth the words, 'Neither do I condemn thee.' And it is only when we harden our hearts to a capacity for receiving the utmost rigor of the law, and render them cold, keen, and glittering, by the formularies of social virtue, that we are ready to cast out the sinner. Properly attuned, we look earnestly into his life, in search of that *hidden virtue, which his crime may stand pointing at.*

We would not condemn the vigilance and sensitiveness of society, were it really a tribute paid to the true sanctity of virtue. But is there no deeper sense, which wears out a life of martyrdom in obedience to the demands of the world? Is there no suffering which goes unrecognized, because it interferes with no avowed rights? Is there no violation of social law more radical and threatening than any wayward act of passion can be? It may be necessary, perhaps, that the safety of associated man demands all the compromises which the superficiality of social law creates, but the sorrow may be none the less acute because the evil is necessary. We see in the lives of Arthur Dimmesdale and Hester Prynne, that the severity of puritanic law and morals could not keep them from violation; and we see, too, that this very severity drove them both into a state of moral insanity. And does any benefit arise from such a sacrifice? Not a gentle word, or look, or thought, met those two erring mortals. Revenge embittered the heart of the old outraged usurper. Severity—blasting, and unforgiving, and sanctimonious—was the social atmosphere which surrounded them. We doubt not that, to many minds, this severity constitutes the saving virtue of the book. But it is always with a fearful sacrifice of all the gentler feelings of the breast, of all the most comprehensive humanity, of all the most delicate affections and appreciations, that we thus rudely shut out the wanderer from us; especially when the path of error leads through the land whence come our warmest and tenderest influences. We gain nothing by this hardness, except a capability to sin without remorse. The elements of character upon which vice and virtue hang are so nearly allied, that the rude attempts to destroy the one may result in a fatal wounding of the other; the harvest separates the tares from the wheat with the only safety. Who has not felt the forbidding aspect of that obtrusive and complacent virtue which never cherishes the thought of forgiveness? And who, that has recognized the deep and holy meaning of the human affections, has not been frozen into demanding a warm-hearted crime as a relief for the cold, false, vulgar, and cowardly asperity which is sometimes called chastity?

The father, the mother, and the child, in this picture,—the holy trinity of love,—what had the world done for them? And so they waited for the divine developments of an hereafter. Can this be a true and earnest assurance that we may hope for the best development there? This imaginary tale of wrong, is but a shadow of the realities which daily occur around us. The opportunities for opening our hearts to the gentle teachings of tender error and crushed virtue, lie all along our pathway, and we pass by on the other side. Not a significant deed, to which the purest virtues cling in clusters, has yet been committed, that society has not resisted with the ferocity of a tyrant. Not a word has been spoken for the captive, the wounded, the erring and the oppressed, that has not met with 'religious' opposition. Not the first line of that picture, which would represent error in its alliance with virtue, has yet been drawn, that has not been stigmatized as immoral.

To those who would gladly learn the confidence, and power, and patient endurance, and depth of hallowed fervor, which love can create in the human heart, we would present the life of this woman, in her long hours of suffering and loneliness, made sweeter than all the world beside, by the cause in which she suffered. We dare not call that a wicked perversity, which brought its possessor into that state of strong and fiery resolution and elevation, which enabled her to raise her lover from his craven sense of guilt, into a solemn devotion to his better nature. She guided him rightly, by her clear vision of what was in accordance with the holiest promptings of her true heart. Aided by this, she learned what all his theology had never taught him—the power of love to sustain and guide and teach the soul. This bore her through her trial; and this, at that glowing hour when both rose above the weight which bowed them down, tore the scarlet letter from her breast, and made her young and pure again.

The stigma gone, Hester heaved a long, deep sigh, in which the burden of shame and anguish departed from her spirit. O, exquisite relief! She had not known the weight, till she felt the freedom. By another impulse, she took off the formal cap that confined her hair, and down it fell upon her shoulders, dark and rich, with at once a shadow and a light, in its abundance, and imparting the charm of softness to her features. There played around her mouth, and beamed out of her eyes, a radiant and tender smile, that seemed gushing from the very heart of womanhood. A crimson flush was glowing on her cheek, that had long been so pale. Her sex, her youth, and the whole richness of her beauty, came back from what men call the irrevocable past, and clustered themselves, with her maiden hope, and a happiness before unknown, within the magic circle of this hour. And, as if the gloom of the earth and sky had been but the effluence of these two mortal

hearts, it vanished with their sorrow. All at once, as with a sudden smile of heaven, forth burst the sunshine, pouring a very flood into the obscure forest, gladdening each green leaf, transmuting the yellow fallen ones to gold, and gleaming adown the gray trunks of the solemn trees. The objects that had made a shadow hitherto, embodied the brightness now. The course of the little brook might be traced by its merry gleam afar into the wood's heart of mystery, which had become a mystery of joy.

The ecstasy of Murillo's conceptions, the calm, solemn maternity of Raphael's madonnas, the sterling wealth of beauty in Titian's Magdalens, and the appealing and teaching [?] heart of woman, in all these, come crowding before us, as we rise with Hester to this holy exaltation.

The wisdom and power which came to this woman from the scarlet letter, which society imprinted on her breast, may come to every one who will honestly affix this token to his own. As who of us may not? It is only an open confession of our weakness which brings us strength. The flattering self-assurance that we pursue virtue with conscientious diligence, never enables us to reach what we are striving for. We may perchance escape the dangers which beset our path, but never, through ignorance, shall we overcome the obstacles. There is no more fatal error than moral ignorance and hypocrisy. Bigotry, and superstition, and dogmatism may coil around the mind, until intellectual imperiousness springs up, more pitiful than the most abject ignorance, and the instincts of the heart will almost always be found to protest against them. Moral obliquity may misguide the senses, and the effect is temporary and superficial. Social influences may produce the grossest misconceptions, and, as the circle enlarges, the magic may vanish. But that cowardice which prompts to the denial of error to one's own soul; which refuses to receive the impression that all experience brings, with honesty and intelligence, and, intrenched behind good intentions, feels safe from attacks of sin, is the most hopeless of all mortal defects. There is a false delicacy which avoids the contemplation of evil, and which severe experience may destroy. There is a sweeping belief that vice stands at one pole and virtue at the other, which the deep trials of life may eradicate. There is a want of sympathy for the erring, and an ignorant closing of the heart against those whose entrance would enlarge and beautify and warm our souls, which the knowledge of our own temptations may remove. But no experience, no knowledge, no power, short of miracle, will bring the needed relief to that spirit which will not confess its guilt either to itself, or to its God. The heroic power which comes through avowal, is like the soft and vernal earth, giving life to a sweet and flowery growth of virtues. It gives self-knowledge, and the deepest and most startling wisdom, by which to test our fellow-men. But is it not most sad and most instructive that Love, the great parent of all power and virtue and wisdom and faith, the guardian of the tree of knowledge of good and evil, the effulgence of all that is rich and generous and luxuriant in nature, should rise up in society to be typified by the strange features of *The Scarlet Letter?*

Arthur C. Coxe

Arthur C. Coxe (1818–1896), an Episcopal priest who became the bishop of western New York in 1865, was a lyricist for hymns and an author whose books include An Apology for the Common English Bible *(1857) and* The Church and the Press *(1859). In his essay on Hawthorne's career Coxe claims a purpose "rather religious than literary." While criticizing the degree to which Hawthorne in his stories is affected by the "Bay School," a reference to fellow Massachusetts writers such as Ralph Waldo Emerson and Theodore Parker, Coxe chiefly focuses on the author's "delicately immoral" novel,* The Scarlet Letter. *Coxe's concern for the deleterious effect of the popular novel on the character of school-age girls is a recurring theme of American literary criticism, most famously articulated by the influential realist William Dean Howells in* Criticism and Fiction *(1891).*

The Writings of Hawthorne
Arthur C. Coxe
The Church Review, 3 (January 1851): 489–511

Current Literature, in America, has generally been forced to depend, for criticism, upon personal partiality or personal spleen. We have had very little reviewing on principle; almost none with the pure motive of building up a sound and healthful literature for our country, by cultivating merit, correcting erratic genius, abasing assumption and imposture, and insisting on the fundamental importance of certain great elements, without which no literature can be either beneficial or enduring. Our reviews have, accordingly, exercised very little influence over public taste. They have been rather tolerated than approved; and, for the most part, have led a very precarious existence, rather as attempts than as achievements; creditable make-believes; tolerable domestic imitations of the imported article; well enough in their way, but untrustworthy for opinion, and worthless for taste. Their reviewals of cotemporary authors have too commonly been a mere daubing of untempered mortar, or else a deliberate assault, with intent to kill. In either case the reviewer has betrayed himself, as writing, not for the public, but for the satisfaction or the irritation of the author; and the game of mock reviewing has become as notorious as that of mock auctions. The intelligent public hears the hammering and the outcry, but has got used to it, and passes by. Nobody's opinion of a book is the more or less favorable for anything that can be said in this or that periodical. If a reviewal appears, it is at once understood that some friendly Maecenas has elaborated three sheets of tender concern for the sale of Mr Plume's new Poem, and has bribed the Editor of *The Ephemeral* to print it, by placing it, gratuitously, at his service, and purchasing a number of copies; or that, by a similar arrangement, Mr Penn's particular enemy, an old college rival, has found vent for a long-fermenting heartfull of malice, in a criticism of Penn's maiden romance, which lacks nothing but a little imitative wit and pungency to make its borrowed formalisms a tolerable caricature of Jeffrey. Who cares for a volume of such mere puffs and invectives? The review comes quarterly, and is taken benevolently, and read skippingly, and paid for grumblingly; but it drags on from year to year without expiring, for several reasons; for, in the first place, everybody contributes to it, and wants to lay up his own trash in a convenient form; and then, everybody that do n't [*sic*] contribute has a friend that does, and would n't like to seem indifferent to a friend's lucubrations; and lastly, everybody else that subscribes, does it for the encouragement of American manufactures, or because he is aware that it looks respectable to have a review somewhere at hand, in his parlor. Ah! how differently an old subscriber takes to his *Blackwood,* or his *Edinburgh.* There is a welcome for the genuine article, which can no more be mistaken than the warm shake of the hand, and the illuminated stare, with which we make a time-honored friend at home in a minute. 'Here it comes, true to the day,' shouts the subscriber, as he wheels the great chair to the parlor grate, and snatches *Maga* from the grinning negro, who hands it in, with the air of a Pharisee doing a good action–'here's old Ebony! candles, Pompey! Mary, my dear, bring my paper-knife! now for Kit North! Why, no! buff and blue, after all–well, it's the *Edinburgh,* and we'll have something about France and Louis Napoleon; let's see how the world goes.' Who has not been actor, or spectator, in scenes like this? But now for a picture even more likely to be recognized. 'Who rung the door-bell, Pompey?' 'Nobody, sir, but a boy with a book; I left it in the entry, sir.' 'Left it in the entry–blockhead, why did n't ye bring it here!' 'La! papa,' says Miss Mary, ''t was nothing but the *National Review;* Pompey knows you never read it.' 'Oh, dear!' responds the old worthy–'well, child, let's have a game of chess.' American periodical literature is, verily, in a flourishing condition.

So it must be, however, till our periodicals become something more than repositories of sophomorical eulogy, or ribaldry, upon literary toys and trifles. Reviews are superfluous, except as they represent a want, which they undertake to supply, from competent resources, and in an earnest spirit of accomplishing an honorable purpose. We make no apology, therefore, for becoming reviewers, when we acknowledge our earnest hope, not only that we may do something to assist the literary and theological studies of Anglo-American Churchmen, but that we may make the voice of the Church more audible to the American public in general, and thus may exercise, for the benefit of popular authors, some salutary influence upon public taste. Our mission–to borrow a little cant from the times–is, indeed, rather religious than literary; yet, in an age when literature makes very free with religion, we must be pardoned for supposing that religion owes some attention to literature. We grant that we have little taste for popular criticism, and if anybody chooses to assert that we are not qualified critics, we concede it entirely. A critic of popular writers should undoubtedly be *totus in his,* and we confess ourselves, almost *totus in aliis.* A critic should have no sick folk to visit, no sad folk to comfort, no heavy-laden to minister unto; he should

have no babes to christen, no couples to marry, no sermons to prepare, no disciples to teach; above all, he should have no spasmodic door-bell, with its perpetual dingle-dingle communicating perpetual breaks, dashes, and disconnections to his pen; and to all such disqualifications, with others, we plead guilty, still devoutly hoping that we shall never be disposed to exchange the wear and tear of this kind of life for the fairest ideal of literary seclusion of which we ever dreamed. And yet we grant the critic's to be no ignoble, albeit an 'ungentle craft.' Our views of its importance are very high, and we consider the devotion of enthusiasm its just demand. Let him only be allowed a critic who can sit, like Pygmalion, studying beauty by the day's work, in lonely rapture, alike imperturbable and undisturbed; or give him the name, who can bend, as we once beheld an anatomist, over a putrid corpse, cutting and sawing with intense satisfaction, and wholly oblivious of his nose. A critic, we allow, must be, both actively and passively, an abstraction; he must be 'an honest chronicler, like Griffith,' if he would prove

A speaker of men's living actions,
And keep true honor from corruption;

and yet, in order thereto, he must first be like Burton, 'a mere spectator of other men's fortunes and adventures, and how they play their parts.' It is true that to most of these demands we are wanting; yet our apology for taking up a popular work, now and then, in a critical vein, shall be offered in pleading an abstraction of another kind. We are free, at least, from that literary contact which has infected American reviewers so generally, with the malady of which we complain, and which necessarily breeds selfish and personal feelings of affection or of hate. We know not the literary world, except from a distant view, and have nothing in common with its aims or its occupations; but we think it high time that the literary world should learn that Churchmen are, in a very large proportion, their readers and book-buyers, and that the tastes and principles of Churchmen have as good a right to be respected as those of Puritans and Socialists. It is in this relation to our subject that we have taken up the clever and popular writings of Hawthorne; and we propose to consider them, without any attempt to give them a formal review, just in the free and conversational manner which is permitted to table-talk or social intercourse; and if we can thus afford our author a candid exhibition of the impressions he is producing on a large, but quiet portion of the community, and prompt him to a future career more worthy of their entire regard, we shall feel that we have done the State, as well as the Church, some service; and no anxiety for our reputation as critics shall spoil our appetite for a smoking plum-pudding at Christmas.

In taking up Mr Hawthorne's volumes, we are happy to particularize our general professions of impartiality, and to describe ourselves as heartily his well-wishers, knowing nothing either of him or his works, beyond what is patent to all men, in his own published confessions, or in other publications of the popular character. True we must own to a little prejudice against him, as a conspicuous member of the Bay School, but, in counterpoise, we must put in a profession of a specific feeling in his favor, as at all events one of the best of them, the very Irving of Down-East. He is one of the few Bays whose freest egotism seldom moves our disgust, and whom we are, in truth, disposed to thank for gossiping at random about himself and friends, as if every one knew both him and them, and were anxiously watching them with telescopes and lorgnettes. In fact, we were particularly interested in his graphic description of that ancient seat of witchcraft in which he tells us he was born, for having had forefathers of our own among the broad-banded and steeple-crowned worthies of old Salem, we were glad to learn, more than geographies and gazetteers are wont to tell us, of its appearance and present condition. Nay, we began to feel a degree of cousinry with our author, in spite of ourselves, when, in an old family record of a marriage not very remotely connected with our own existence, we found the name of his ancestor, *Colonel Hathorn,* familiarly mentioned, with those of other Salemites who hasted to the wedding, in the year of Grace 1713, and were there gravely lectured, over their sack-posset, by godly Master Noyes, the Puritan parson. With such, and many other feelings in our author's favor, we take up his works. In fact, who can resist a pleasant influence in his behalf, exhaling from his very name, redolent as it is of guilelessness and springtide, and rich with associations derived from old ballads and madrigals that celebrate the garden-like agriculture of England? In faint suggestiveness too of 'Hawthornden,' it has a flavor of Scots poesy and the English drama; of Drummond and of Jonson; and if some patriot Pope or Gifford wants a name whose easy lubricity of pronunciation just suits a flowing line, who would not wish that Hawthorne's might be paired with Irving's, as indissolubly as Beaumont's with Fletcher's, and that the twain might be freely allowed to rank as the *lucida sidera* of our literary horizon? It is not for want of a predisposition to admire and praise our author and his performances, that we shall be obliged to say many things in a different humor.

Mr Hawthorne must be now in the middle-way of his life, and we are glad to learn, by a morning paper of the day on which we write this paragraph, that both he and Mr Longfellow have bought farms in Berskhire, Massachusetts, which will necessarily keep them, for a good part of the year, about as distant from Boston as the limits of the Bay State will allow. These two fine specimens of the Eastern School, in poetry and prose, seem to have been, in some degree, yoke-fellows, from the start. They are both set down, by Mr Griswold, as born in 1807, and they seem to have been classmates at Bowdoin College, in 1825. In more than one of his works, Mr Hawthorne has shown a disposition to make no secret of his intimate relations with Longfellow, and of his familiar visits to the poet's charming domestic circle; and we can easily conceive that it is with much of brotherly feeling that these distinguished gentlemen are now turning themselves into a pair of metaphorical farmers, among the turnips and pigs of Berkshire. As an author, Mr Hawthorne's name came before the public, for the first time, in 1837, when the first volume of his *Twice-told Tales* was collected from magazines and other periodicals, and given to the world under its very appropriate, and not infelicitous title. A second volume appeared in 1842; and he has since published *The Journal of an African cruiser,* and *Mosses from an old Manse.* His last production is *The Scarlet Letter,* which appears to have been commenced only as one tale of a series, similar to those of his former books, but which is expanded to a little book of itself, and comes forth as 'a romance,' with a more ambitious appearance than belongs to any of its predecessors. As its author has freely indulged in autobiography, we shall be pardoned for presenting our readers with a few particulars derived from that source, and from others of a similar kind. Mr Bancroft, it would seem, procured him the post of 'Surveyor of the port of Salem,' the duties of which are very amusingly described in his introduction to The '*Scarlet Letter.*' After three years of public employment, the change of Administration, in 1849, remitted him, in company with many other patriotic public servants, to 'the shades of private life,' and he appears to have resumed his literary occupations, in consequence of this alteration in his circumstances. At some former period, since his leaving college, he has managed to spend three years of his life in an old New England parsonage, which fell vacant by the demise of its more appropriate tenant, the last of a long succession of village pastors, which evidently began with a Calvinistic dynasty, and died out in a Socinian one. To this residence in a decayed mansion, we owe the *Mosses from an old Manse,* a very euphonious title certainly, although, to let the 'Mosses' alone, we are disposed to doubt whether the house from which they came was a 'Manse,' any more than its departed occupants would have professed themselves Scotch presbyterians. However, we wish our author had never found worse quarters; but the life of a Bay writer generally leads us somewhere into a mist, and we accordingly encounter an intimation that 'the Brook-farm community, at West Roxbury,' was once the wiser and richer for Mr Hawthorne's residence among them, as a practical disciple of Owen, Fourier, and St Simon! In his own volumes we find plaintive allusions to the fact; and, as Mr Griswold's biographical sketch does not pretend to make it a secret, we have only to congratulate our author upon the timely disbanding of the *phalansteries,* into which he had suffered himself to be enrolled. Like other 'Boston Notions,' the community at Brook-farm has had its day, and its former associates, as we learn, have passed into various phases of subsequent existence, most of them running the restless round of enthusiasm, and finding themselves at last, some Quakers and some Papists, some believing nothing at all, and some trying to believe everything. We bespeak indulgence, however, for our author, whom some will be inclined to censure unduly for the company he has kept. Our readers have probably no idea of the way in which such experiments are regarded at the seat of Mutual Admiration. There, where every man is a gospel unto himself, and where the necessity of a new revelation, suited to the age, is the only admitted doctrine of religion, a graduate of Brook-farm would be regarded with particular consideration, as an experimental philosopher; and we doubt not that he has accordingly made considerable figure in the charmed circle, and is the more looked up to for his acquaintance with the interior of a community, compared with which a madhouse should be regarded as a University. Mr Hawthorne has too much good taste to tell us of the degree of considerations to which he has been borne by his real talent and peculiar qualifications, among his literary friends; but he spares no encomium when he takes an opportunity to mention the names of Alcott, Thoreau, Lowell, Hillard, and a Mr Ellery Channing of Assabeth, whose classic refinement, subtile intellect, poetic sentiment and what not, are never sparingly attested, although it is impossible for us to conjecture what these respectable persons may have to do with either the *Old Manse* or *The Scarlet Letter,* to justify their being mentioned in one, or both, in a manner so unusual that we are led to suppose them heroes of the narrative, or else to lament our own ignorance of their possible celebrity. The only direct allusion to his own rank, into which our author is betrayed by the habits of his School, occurs, if we rightly recollect, in the introduction to his last work, where he *naively* confesses his surprise that the clerks and tide-waiters at the Custom-house evinced no sense of his literary importance when he came among them, and, as 'Surveyor of the port,' undertook to show them that 'a man of thought, fancy, and sensibility, may at any time be a man of

affairs.' To our homely ideas, it would be something to the purpose if Mr Hawthorne could show a dignified precedent for his life at Brook-farm; but, with an evident fear that his Custom-house life would be most likely to imperil his caste in 'the circle,' he goes on to remember that Burns was an exciseman, and Chaucer a comptroller of the wool-tax, and smuggles in the conclusion that 'they were each of them a Custom-house officer in his day, as well as himself.' After this consoling discovery of a literary warrant for his employment, it is pleasing to find that Mr Hawthorne allowed his name to be grossly marked on boxes of herrings, and bags of coffee, and quintals of codfish, in due course of trade, with a praiseworthy effort to maintain a sublime indifference to the fact that the same had been 'blazoned abroad on title-pages.' It will illustrate what we have heretofore said of the Trimontane horizon, if we proceed to quote our author's lament over the indifference with which Salem tax-gatherers daily accosted him, when compared with his experiences in Boston. 'It is a good lesson, though it may often be *a hard one,*' says he, 'for a man who has dreamed of literary fame, and of making for himself a rank among the world's *dignitaries* by such means, to step aside, out of the narrow *circle* in which his claims are recognized, and to find how utterly void of significance beyond that *circle,* is all that he achieves, and all he aims at!' We waive allusion to this use of the word *dignitaries,* which might alarm a Sidney Smith or a Milman, with fears that Mr Hawthorne was looking to a stall at their side, but we must be allowed a laugh at the downright Bostonian character of this whole extract. Who but one of the *circle* could ever have entered a Custom-house with so many thoughts of literature? Surely, had we been so fortunate in our lay experiences, as to have got that Surveyorship, and had we enjoyed twice the reputation that even the *Twice-told Tales* could give, it does seem to us there would have been no great hardship in entering at once upon our duties, without a thought of being saluted either as a Burns or a Chaucer in disguise. It strikes us, moreover, that we should have pushed in among the herrings, and scored our democratic name upon the gunny-bags, without any of our author's misgivings that we were throwing away valuable autographs. We are sure that nothing could have been harder to endure with gravity, than a *salaam* to our authorship from the deputy-surveyors and inspectors. Tare and trett should be the only literary associations with such officials, and red tape and sealing-wax the nearest approach to 'books and stationery' which we could wish from them. How it should be 'a hard lesson' to become a witness of their simple devotion to their business, and to find one's self not half so important to them as their next meal, we are at loss to conjecture. What should they have done to soothe

First page of Hawthorne's 15 September 1851 letter to George W. Childs, a Philadelphia publisher and bookseller, in which he comments on The Scarlet Letter. *After citing the historical basis of wearing such a mark of shame, Hawthorne speculates on the origin of the practice: "I cannot say whether this mode of ignominious punishment was brought from beyond the Atlantic; or originated with the New England Puritans. At any rate, the idea was so worthy of them that I am piously inclined to allow them all the credit of it" (from C. E. Frazer Clark Jr.,* Hawthorne at Auction, *1972).*

our author's feelings, or to acquit themselves of insensibility? We really can think of no ceremony that would have relieved him, short of that for making a Grand *Mamamouchi,* in Molière's *Bourgeois Gentilhomme.* The fact is, a Bay-writer is too commonly afflicted with a painful sense of literary consequence; he lives among imaginary Boswells; he feels that eating, drinking, sleeping and snoring with him are a virtual biography; and the tincture of this spirit which amuses us in Hawthorne, is merely a proof of the intensity with which it pervades the School to which he belongs.

Still another illustration of the School may be found in our author's elaborate remarks upon himself, under the ingenious paronyme of 'Mons. de l'Aubépine.' We think far more highly of Hawthorne than he does of himself, judging by the reflection which we find in his own mirror. 'He occupies,' says he,

> an unfortunate position, between the transcendentalists, (who, under one name or another, have their share in all the current literature of the world,) and the great body of pen-and-ink men, who address the intellect and sympathies of the multitude. If not *too refined,* at all events too remote, too shadowy and unsubstantial in his mode of development to suit the taste of the latter class, and yet too popular to satisfy the spiritual or metaphysical requisitions of the former, he must necessarily find himself without an audience, except here and there an individual, or *possibly an isolated clique.*

Pooh, pooh! Mr Hawthorne, are you in earnest, or are you not? If not–why, in the name of sense, stand whining about Mons. de l'Aubépine's unpopularity, when you know that Hawthorne's books are fairly thumbed to pieces by the readers of all circulating libraries, and that everybody is disposed to like them and to buy them; if you are, pray throw away your transcendentalism, and your sympathetic ink, your refinement and your remoteness, your circle and your clique, and come down to flesh and blood, and live, and act, and talk like other men, and we assure you, you have talents that will take care of themselves, yes, and give you returns in hard cash besides, to stock that Berkshire farm! Forgive the matter-of-fact suggestion; but we live in 'a bank-note world,' and must sometimes condescend to men whose 'talk is of bullocks.' In our opinion, a little less starch and cambric and a little more bone and sinew, would be the thing for many a clever fellow in the Bay metropolis who is always 'dying of a rose in aromatic pain;' and we never hear a really gifted man talking in this vein of Mons. de l'Aubépine, without longing to make so bold as to ask him to a bit of roast beef and a bottle of brown stout, in a plain, family way, with a benevolent idea of invigorating his constitution in time to prevent the process of evaporative dissolution.

We have done ourselves injustice, if, in our free-spoken attempts to expose the unhappy effects of the School upon Mr Hawthorne's originally fine powers, we have shown any lack of regard for his genius, in itself considered. Far more should we deprecate any appearance of personal disrespect; and we trust our good humored purpose in the banter we have indulged, will not be misinterpreted. We are sorry, and we own it, to see so really fine a mind, so much provincialized; and we speak the more earnestly, because we are sure that were he only a little less of a man than we think him to be, he could not but have become much more intensely so, and because we fear that this provincialism is, even now, likely to increase upon him. But to prove how exceedingly we were taken with him, at first sight, we must acknowledge that we were ignorant of the existence of so clever a writer, until we came across his 'Celestial Railroad,' in the columns of a newspaper. Such genuine grit, in so perishable a form, arrested our attention in no ordinary degree; and it was not until we had shown about our discovery among our friends, that we found we were merely admiring what everybody seemed to know. It is a humorous and satirical vision of a modern railway, erected on the route of Bunyan's Pilgrim. Was ever a happier thought, except the original? The story has all the humor of travesty, with nothing of its vulgar poverty of invention; and one is made to feel as if he were whisking in cars over the weary lengths which Christian once plodded on foot, and observing everywhere the effects of the nineteenth century, upon antiquated places and fashions. The *Pilgrim's Progress,* in spite of its doctrinal errors, is a prodigy of literature. It is the one instance which flings back the sneer–*ne sutor ultra crepidam*–let the tinker stick to his kettle. To ignore it as the work of an illiterate enthusiast, is no longer possible; it is a classic of the language; part of that great store of literary material, which has so inwrought itself with the productions of other men's minds, that it is the hypothesis of the entertainment to be derived from general reading. A chance-begotten thing it may be; such a progeny as morbid religion and erratic genius never procreated before, and can never by any luck, repeat; but here it is, not only living, but immortal. Hawthorne's 'Railroad' assumes that no one who reads the English language can be ignorant of the original, and so it is: nor can we say a better thing of the parody, than that it deserves to become a perpetual pendant to its archetype. We should imagine it the most natural production of our author's genius, which his books contain. It seems to have proceeded from the man himself, in a happy moment of oblivious indifference to his School, and his circle; for strange to say, it satirizes Ger-

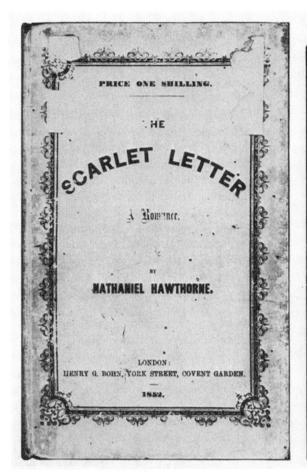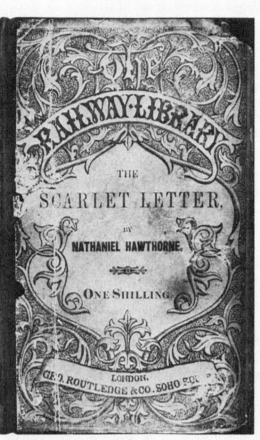

Covers for the first two English editions, both pirated (from C. E. Frazer Clark Jr.,
Nathaniel Hawthorne: A Descriptive Bibliography, *1978)*

man rationalism, transcendentalism, and all the varieties of dreamy irreligion, for habitual encouragement of which, the School are so notorious. It is one of the cleverest, best sustained, and most ingenious specimens of quiet satire to be found in our language.

To Hawthorne, if we judge him in his best mood, may justly be ascribed the merit of reflective powers habitually active, connected with a style that is taking, apparently unstudied, and generally perspicuous and expressive. He has been compared with Irving; but though in some respects he is not injured by the experiment, he must be considered, in others, as decidedly inferior. Irving is the better artist, and that not only in the choice of words; but in the arrangement of details, the production of effect, and the breadth and completeness of design; but had Hawthorne the taste and discrimination, and something more of the instinctive delicacy of Irving, we are not sure that the latter would long be left lonely in his preëminence. We are confirmed in these impressions by the opinions expressed in a very favorable critique of the *Mosses from an old*

Manse, which appeared a few years ago in a European Periodical [*Blackwood's Magazine,* November 1847]. The reviewer considers Hawthorne's style only occasionally comparable to that of Irving, but gives him credit for deeper thought. He is said to fail in character, and in verisimilitude; not that his incidents are particularly improbable, but that his leading ideas are extravagant, while he depends for effect upon a playful fancy and a charming control of language. If this criticism be just, it points out one very great fault; but from a Bay-writer we should naturally look for the *non ben trovato* precisely there, in personal character, because the ideal of character, after which the imagination of the School is perpetually straining, is essentially a false and unnatural one. Hence their humanities are the reverse of human. A bewitching 'Birth-mark' on the cheek of Aylmer's lovely wife–the print of some fairy's tiny fingers who touched the sweet babe with benediction–becomes a torment to the husband who has a chemical devil in his head, and must needs devote soul and body to the erasure of the brilliant blemish, which consumes him the more, because but for it, his Georgiana would be an angel. This is the basis of one of Hawthorne's unnatural stories, which the reviewer cites. With ordinary husbands such a blemish would become a beauty; even a mole becomes proverbially attractive to a devoted lover: but with one who dreams of reconstructing society, and who would have men and women live as if the Fall were not a reality, we must not marvel that an Aylmer is a very plausible sort of a person. There is a good moral, however, in the result, for he succeeds triumphantly—so triumphantly that the lady dies of chemistry in the moment when her husband is shouting his raptures over the splendid experiment. What would Transcendentalism be at, but a similar attempt to erase the outside birth-marks of humanity, which would end in destroying humanity itself! Then again, the reviewer cites the story entitled the 'Artist of the Beautiful,' in criticising which he labors under the same infelicitous ignorance of what a Bay-writer is thinking about. More than once he complains of an unintelligible sentence, without the least idea that he is censuring the vernacular of a School in which 'achieving the Beautiful,' is the daily effort of every disciple; and he seems equally surprised that the Promethean passion of the hero should exhaust itself in the creation of a mechanical butterfly, which might be the more becoming handiwork of a watchmaker and a Chinese painter of piths! But here again, as in the disappointing issue of the story, the spirit of the School is dominant over the genius of the author. He lives and breathes in an atmosphere where men and women are wont to expend a fever of inspiration in the creation of just such butterflies, and where life itself is wasted in chasing them to destruction.

We thank the Scottish critic for touching gently these faults in the tales of our clever countryman, while he goes on to commend his style as much better in the essays, and as not unworthy of Addison or Steele. Though he somewhat dilutes this high compliment, afterwards, it is with a common reference to all correct writers in America. He thinks our purists are too pure, or rather too artificially so; much the same, we suppose, as a dentist's teeth are more perfect than nature's, and become repulsive for lack of those very inequalities which are graceful and like-like. Poor Jonathan! We despair of his ever learning to write the language which he pronounces so ill; for if he exposes himself in the manner of Headley, its incurable vulgarity is cited as essential and instinctive; while the mannerism of Channing and Ware is equally laughed at, as the adoption of a schoolboy's accuracy, for want of the confident, but careless art of a well-bred man. It is curious to observe what minute blemishes, moreover, always strike an Englishman, in an American author. The *Blackwood* critic, whom we have cited, though far enough above

the spirit of picking motes out of Brother Jonathan's eye, furnishes us not a little amusement, when we discover that without mentioning the alteration, he has slyly changed a *baggage-car* into a *luggage-van,* for the benefit of English travelers in Mr Hawthorne's 'Celestial Railroad.'

Our readers must have felt that it is rather of our author's School, than of him, that we have been disposed to complain; for to it we have alike attributed the blemishes pointed out by ourselves and others. He is a writer, who, under other influences, might have contributed to our literature a variety of sterling and invaluable works, admitting of no dispute as to their merit, or who would have made even popular tales the vehicle of deep and earnest suggestion to the young, as well as of pure amusement to all classes. We would exhort him against becoming a trifler, as one who must give account for gifts that might be prolific of good to the world. If, even now, he would resolve to make his future career one of high moral principle, and to use his talents not so much for 'making himself a rank among the world's *dignitaries,*' as for doing good in his day and generation, we know of no one more likely to succeed in becoming one of the world's *benefactors,* and gaining quite enough of its empty admiration beside. Not that we would have him change his songs into sermons, or his tales and romances into moral essays. We are not of those who question the utility of fairy fiction as the costume of severe and homely truth. Parable and allegory have been the vehicle of wisdom, among all cultivated nations; yes, of inspired wisdom, too; of Nathan's rebuke, when he pointed the arrows of the Law at the sinner's conscience, and the love of JESUS CHRIST, when he opened to the sick and needy the healing waters of the Gospel. The principle thus established leaves nothing for the casuist to prescribe, but that stories should be always of moral benefit to those whole faculties of soul, and mind, and heart, with which GOD claims to be loved and served. Here is the standard, therefore, by which we are to estimate the tale-writer. In the one case, he may be justly regarded as a preceptor who has mastered the difficult art of imparting instruction, with impressions of pastime, and who has managed to make even the recreations of the mind, subservient to its most laborious exercises: in the other he is, in short, a nuisance in society, which it becomes the duty of good citizens to abate. Let the father snatch the pestilent romance from the hands of the maiden and the boy, and give it to be ignominiously destroyed by the scullion: let the school-master weed the filthy pages out of desks and pockets, and give the lads a laugh at the bonfire they will create; and let the press approve itself as an engine of moral, as well as of mental light, by such wise judicial censures, as shall fix all the ignominy of the scourge, the pillory, and the brand, upon the writer who panders to the brothel, and exhausts his powers in producing and sowing the seeds of incalculable evils to the souls of men and the structure of society.

But this principle of moral criticism bears harder upon our author than anything we have said before. As yet our literature, however humble, is undefiled, and as such is a just cause for national pride, nor, much as we long to see it elevated in style, would we thank the Boccaccio who should give it the classic stamp, at the expense of its purity. Of course we cannot expect to see it realize that splendid ideal which a thoughtful Churchman would sketch for it, as equally chaste in morals, lofty in sentiment, uncorrupt in diction, and in all points conformable to truth; but surely we may demand that it shall keep itself from becoming an offense to faith, and a scandal to virtue. Not that we expect the literary pimp to cease from his disgusting trade, but that we hope to keep writers of that class out of the pale of Letters, and to effect the forcible expulsion of any one of a higher class, who, gaining upon our confidence by dealing at first in a sterling article, afterwards debases his credit, by issuing with the same stamp a vile, but marketable, alloy. In a word, we protest against any toleration to a popular and gifted writer, when he perpetrates bad morals. Let this brokerage of lust be put down at the very beginning. Already, among the million, we have imitations enough of George Sand and Eugene Sue; and if as yet there be no reputable name, involved in the manufacture of a Brothel Library, we congratulate the country that we are yet in time to save such a reputation as that of Hawthorne. Let him stop where he has begun, lest we should be forced to select an epitaph from Hudibras, for his future memorial:

Quoth he—for many years he drove
A kind of broking trade in love,
Employed in all th' intrigues and trust
Of feeble, speculative lust;
Procurer to th' extravagancy
And crazy ribaldry of fancy.

It is chiefly, in hopes, to save our author from embarking largely into this business of Fescennine romance, that we enter upon a brief examination of his latest and most ambitious production, *The Scarlet Letter*.

The success which seems to have attended this bold advance of Hawthorne, and the encouragement which has been dealt out by some professed critics, to its worst symptoms of malice prepense, may very naturally lead, if unbalanced by a moderate dissent, to his further compromise of his literary character. We are glad, therefore, that *The Scarlet Letter* is, after all, little more than an experiment, and need not be regarded as a step necessarily fatal. It is an attempt to rise from the composition of petty tales, to the historical novel; and we use the expression *an attempt,* with no disparaging significance, for it is confessedly a trial of strength only just beyond some former efforts, and was designed as part of a series. It may properly be called a novel, because it has all the ground-work, and might have been very easily elaborated into the details, usually included in the term; and we call it *historical,* because its scene-painting is in a great degree true to a period of our Colonial history, which ought to be more fully delineated. We wish Mr Hawthorne would devote the powers which he only partly discloses in this book, to a large and truthful portraiture of that period, with the patriotic purpose of making us better acquainted with the stern old worthies, and all the *dramatis personae* of those times, with their yet surviving habits, recollections, and yearnings, derived from maternal England. Here is, in fact, a rich and even yet an unexplored field for historic imagination; and touches are given in *The Scarlet Letter,* to secret springs of romantic thought, which opened unexpected and delightful episodes to our fancy, as we were borne along by the tale. Here a maiden reminiscence, and here a grave ecclesiastical retrospection, clouding the brow of the Puritan colonists, as they still remembered home, in their wilderness of lasting exile! Now a lingering relic of Elizabethan fashion in dress, and now a turn of expression, betraying the deep traces of education under influences renounced and foresworn, but still instinctively prevalent!

Time has just enough mellowed the facts, and genealogical research has made them just enough familiar, for their employment as material for descriptive fiction; and the New England colonies might now be made as picturesquely real to our perception, as the Knickerbocker tales have made the Dutch settlements of the Hudson. This, however, can never be done by the polemical pen of a blind partisan of the Puritans; it demands Irving's humorously insinuating gravity, and all his benevolent satire, with a large share of honest sympathy for at least the earnestness of wrong-headed enthusiasm. We are stimulated to this suggestion by the very life-like and striking manner in which the days of Governor Winthrop are sketched in the book before us, by the beautiful picture the author has given us of the venerable old pastor Wilson, and by the outline portraits he has thrown in, of several of their contemporaries. We like him all the better for his tenderness of the less exceptionable features of the Puritan character; but we are hardly sure that we like his flings at their failings. If it should provoke a smile to find us sensitive in this matter, our consistency may be very briefly demonstrated. True, we have our own fun with the follies of the Puritans; it is our inseparable privilege as Church-

Bindings for nineteenth-century editions (from C. E. Frazer Clark Jr., Nathaniel Hawthorne: A Descriptive Bibliography, *1978)*

men, thus to compensate ourselves for many a scar which their frolics have left on our comeliness. But when a degenerate Puritan, whose Socinian conscience is but the skimmed-milk of their creamy fanaticism, allows such a conscience to curdle within him, in dyspeptic acidulation, and then belches forth derision at the sour piety of his forefathers—we snuff at him, with an honest scorn, knowing very well that he likes the Puritans for their worst enormities, and hates them only for their redeeming merits.

The Puritan rebelling against the wholesome discipline of that Ecclesiastical Law, which Hooker has demonstrated, with Newtonian evidence, to be but a moral system of central light with its dependent order and illumination; the Puritan with his rough heel and tough heart, mounted upon altars, and hacking down crosses, and sepulchres, and memorials of the dead; the Puritan with his axe on an Archbishop's neck, or holding up in his hand the bleeding head of a martyred king; the Puritan in all this guilt, has his warmest praise, and his prompt witness that he allows the deeds of his fathers, and is ready to fill up the measure of their iniquity; but the Puritans, with a blessed inconsistency, repeating liturgic doxologies to the triune GOD, or, by the domestic hearth, bowing down with momentary conformity, to invoke the name of Jesus, whom the

Church had taught him to adore as an atoning Saviour—these are the Puritans at whom the driveler wags his head, and shoots out his tongue! We would not laugh in that man's company. No—no! we heartily dislike the Puritans, so far as they were Puritan; but even in them we recognize many good old English virtues, which Puritanism could not kill. They were in part our ancestors, and though we would not accept the bequest of their enthusiasm, we are not ashamed of many things to which they clung, with principle quite as characteristic. We see no harm in a reverent joke now and then, at an abstract Puritan, in spite of our duty to our progenitors, and Hudibras shall still be our companion, when, at times, the mental bow requires fresh elasticity, and bids us relax its string. There is, after all, something of human kindness, in taking out an old grudge in the comfort of a hearty, side-shaking laugh, and we think we are never freer from bitterness of spirit, than when we contemplate the Banbury zealot hanging his cat on Monday, and reflect that Strafford and Montrose fell victims to the same mania that destroyed poor puss. But there is another view of the same Puritan, which even a Churchman may charitably allow himself to respect, and when precisely that view is chosen by his degenerate offspring for unfilial derision, we own to a sympathy for the grim old Genevan features, at which their seventh reproduction turns up a repugnant nose; for sure we are that the young Ham is gloating over his father's nakedness, with far less of sorrow for the ebriety of a parent, than of satisfaction in the degradation of an orthodox patriarch. Now without asserting that it is so, we are not quite so sure, as we would like to be, that our author is not venting something of this spirit against the Puritans, in his rich delineation of 'godly Master Dimmesdale,' and the sorely abused confidence of his flock. There is a provoking concealment of the author's motive, from the beginning to the end of the story; we wonder what he would be at; whether he is making fun of all religion, or only giving a fair hint of the essential sensualism of enthusiasm. But, in short, we are astonished at the kind of incident which he has selected for romance. It may be such incidents were too common, to be wholly out of the question, in a history of the times, but it seems to us that good taste might be pardoned for not giving them prominence in fiction. In deference to the assertions of a very acute analyst, who has written ably on the subject of colonialization, we are inclined to think, as we have said before, that barbarism was indeed 'the first danger' of the pilgrim settlers. Of a period nearly contemporary with that of Mr Hawthorne's narrative, an habitual eulogist has recorded that

> on going to its Church and court records, we discover mournful evidences of incontinence, even in the respectable families; as if, being cut off from the more refined pleasures of society, their baser passions had burnt away the restraints of delicacy, and their growing coarseness of manners had allowed them finally to seek, in these baser passions, the spring of their enjoyments.

We are sorry to be told so, by so unexceptionable a witness. We had supposed, with the Roman satirist, that purity might at least be credited to those primitive days, when a Saturnian simplicity was necessarily revived in primeval forests, by the New England colonists:

Quippe aliter tunc orbe novo, coeloque recenti
Vivebant homines:

but a Puritan doctor in divinity publishes the contrary, and a Salemite novelist selects the intrigue of an adulterous minister, as the groundwork of his ideal of those times! We may acknowledge, with reluctance, the historical fidelity of the picture, which retailers of fact and fiction thus concur in framing, but we cannot but wonder that a novelist should select, of all features of the period, that which reflects most discredit upon the cradle of his country, and which is in itself so revolting,

and so incapable of receiving decoration from narrative genius.

And this brings inquiry to its point. Why has our author selected such a theme? Why, amid all the suggestive incidents of life in a wilderness; of a retreat from civilization to which, in every individual case, a thousand circumstances must have concurred to reconcile human nature with estrangement from home and country; or amid the historical connections of our history with Jesuit adventure, savage invasion, regicide outlawry, and French aggression, should the taste of Mr Hawthorne have preferred as the proper material for romance, the nauseous amour of a Puritan pastor, with a frail creature of his charge, whose mind is represented as far more debauched than her body? Is it, in short, because a running undertide of filth has become as requisite to a romance, as death in the fifth act to a tragedy? Is the French era actually begun in our literature? And is the flesh, as well as the world and the devil, to be henceforth dished up in fashionable novels, and discussed at parties, by spinsters and their beaux, with as unconcealed a relish as they give to the vanilla in their ice cream? We would be slow to believe it, and we hope our author would not willingly have it so, yet we honestly believe that *The Scarlet Letter* has already done not a little to degrade our literature, and to encourage social licentiousness: it has started other pens on like enterprises, and has loosed the restraint of many tongues, that have made it an apology for 'the evil communications which corrupt good manners.' We are painfully tempted to believe that it is a book made for the market, and that the market has made it merchantable, as they do game, by letting everybody understand that the commodity is in high condition, and smells strongly of incipient putrefaction.

We shall entirely mislead our reader if we give him to suppose that *The Scarlet Letter* is coarse in its details, or indecent in its phraseology. This very article of our own, is far less suited to ears polite, than any page of the romance before us; and the reason is, we call things by their right names, while the romance never hints the shocking words that belong to its things, but, like Mephistophiles, insinuates that the arch-fiend himself is a very tolerable sort of person, if nobody would call him Mr Devil. We have heard of persons who could not bear the reading of some Old Testament Lessons in the service of the Church: such persons would be delighted with our author's story; and damsels who shrink at the reading of the Decalogue, would probably luxuriate in bathing their imagination in the crystal of its delicate sensuality. The language of our author, like patent blacking, 'would not soil the whitest linen,' and yet the composition itself, would suffice, if well laid on, to Ethiopize the snowiest conscience that ever sat like a swan upon that mirror of heaven, a Christian maiden's imagination. We are not sure we speak quite strong enough, when we say, that we would much rather listen to the coarsest scene of Goldsmith's *Vicar,* read aloud by a sister or daughter, than to hear from such lips, the perfectly chaste language of a scene in *The Scarlet Letter,* in which a married wife and her reverend paramour, with their unfortunate offspring, are introduced as the actors, and in which the whole tendency of the conversation is to suggest a sympathy for their sin, and an anxiety that they may be able to accomplish a successful escape beyond the seas, to some country where their shameful commerce may be perpetuated. Now, in Goldsmith's story there are very coarse words, but we do not remember anything that saps the foundations of the moral sense, or that goes to create unavoidable sympathy with unrepenting sorrow, and deliberate, premeditated sin. *The Vicar of Wakefield* is sometimes coarsely virtuous, but *The Scarlet Letter* is delicately immoral.

There is no better proof of the bad tendency of a work, than some unintentional betrayal on the part of a young female reader, of an instinctive consciousness against it, to which she has done violence, by reading it through. In a beautiful region of New England, where stagecoaches are not yet among things that were, we found ourselves, last summer, one of a traveling party, to which we were entirely a stranger, consisting of young ladies fresh from boarding-school, with the proverbial bread-and-butter look of innocence in their faces, and a nursery thickness about their tongues. Their benevolent uncle sat outside upon the driver's box, and ours was a seat next to a worshipful old dowager, who seemed to bear some matronly relation to the whole coach-load, with the single exception of ourselves. In such a situation it was ours to keep silence, and we soon relapsed into nothingness and a semi-slumberous doze. Meanwhile our young friends were animated and talkative, and as we were approaching the seat of a College, their literature soon began to expose itself. They were evidently familiar with the *Milliners' Magazines* in general, and even with *Graham's* and *Harper's.* They had read James, and they had read Dickens; and at last their criticisms rose to Irving and Walter Scott, whose various merits they discussed with an artless anxiety to settle forever the question whether the one was not 'a charming composer,' and the other 'a truly beautiful writer.' Poor girls! had they imagined how much harmless amusement they were furnishing to their drowsy, dusty, and very unentertaining fellow traveler, they might, quite possibly, have escaped both his praise and his censure! They came at last to Longfellow and Bryant, and rhythmically regaled us with the

'muffled drum' of the one, and the somewhat familiar opinion of the other, that

Truth crushed to earth will rise again.

And so they came to Hawthorne, of whose *Scarlet Letter* we then knew very little, and that little was favorable, as we had seen several high encomiums of its style. We expected a quotation from the 'Celestial Railroad,' for we were traveling at a rate which naturally raised the era of railroads in one's estimation, by rule of contrary; but no—the girls went straight to *The Scarlet Letter.* We soon discovered that one Hester Prynne was the heroine, and that she had been made to stand in the pillory, as, indeed, her surname might have led one to anticipate. We discovered that there was a mysterious little child in the question, that she was a sweet little darling, and that her 'sweet, pretty little name,' was 'Pearl.' We discovered that mother and child had a meeting, in a wood, with a very fascinating young preacher, and that there was a hateful creature named Chillingworth, who persecuted the said preacher, very perseveringly. Finally, it appeared that Hester Prynne was, in fact, Mrs Hester Chillingworth, and that the hateful old creature aforesaid had a very natural dislike to the degradation of his spouse, and quite as natural a hatred of the wolf in sheep's clothing who had wrought her ruin. All this leaked out in conversation, little by little, on the hypothesis of our protracted somnolency. There was a very gradual approximation to the point, till one inquired—'did n't you think, from the first, that he was the one?' A modest looking creature, who evidently had not read the story, artlessly inquired—'what one?'—and then there was a titter at the child's simplicity, in the midst of which we ventured to be quite awake, and to discover by the scarlet blush that began to circulate, that the young ladies were not unconscious to themselves that reading *The Scarlet Letter* was a thing to be ashamed of. These school-girls had, in fact, done injury to their young sense of delicacy, by devouring such a dirty story; and after talking about it before folk, inadvertently, they had enough of mother Eve in them, to know that they were ridiculous, and that shame was their best retreat.

Now it would not have been so if they had merely exhibited a familiarity with *The Heart of Mid-Lothian,* and yet there is more mention of the foul sin in its pages, than there is in *The Scarlet Letter.* Where then is the difference? It consists in this—that the holy innocence of Jeanie Deans, and not the shame of Effie, is the burthen of that story, and that neither Effie's fall is made to look like virtue, nor the truly honorable agony of her stern old father, in bewailing his daughter's ruin, made a joke, by the insinuation that it was quite gratuitous. But in Hawthorne's tale, the lady's frailty is philosophized into a natural and necessary result of the Scriptural law of marriage, which, by holding her irrevocably to her vows, as plighted to a dried up old book-worm, in her silly girlhood, is viewed as making her heart an easy victim to the adulterer. The sin of her seducer too, seems to be considered as lying not so much in the deed itself, as in his long concealment of it, and, in fact, the whole moral of the tale is given in the words—'Be true—be true,' as if sincerity in sin were virtue, and as if 'Be clean—be clean,' were not the more fitting conclusion. 'The untrue man' is, in short, the hang-dog of the narrative, and the unclean one is made a very interesting sort of person, and as the two qualities are united in the hero, their composition creates the interest of his character. Shelley himself never imagined a more dissolute conversation than that in which the polluted minister comforts himself with the thought, that the revenge of the injured husband is worse than his own sin in instigating it. 'Thou and I never did so, Hester'—he suggests: and she responds—'never, never! What we did had a *consecration of its own,* we felt it so—we said so to each other!' This is a little too much—it carries the Bay-theory a little too far for our stomach! 'Hush, Hester!' is the sickish rejoinder; and fie, Mr Hawthorne! is the weakest token of our disgust that we can utter. The poor bemired hero and heroine of the story should not have been seen wallowing in their filth, at such a rate as this.

We suppose this sort of sentiment must be charged to the doctrines enforced at 'Brook-farm,' although 'Brook-farm' itself could never have been Mr Hawthorne's home, had not other influences prepared him for such a Bedlam. At all events, this is no mere slip of the pen; it is the essential morality of the work. If types, and letters, and words can convey an author's idea, he has given us the key to the whole, in a very plain intimation that the Gospel has not set the relations of man and woman where they should be, and that a new Gospel is needed to supersede the seventh commandment, and the bond of Matrimony. Here it is, in full: our readers shall see what the world may expect from Hawthorne, if he is not stopped short, in such brothelry. Look at this conclusion:–

Women–in the continually recurring trials of wounded, wasted, wronged, misplaced, or erring and sinful passion, or with the dreary burden of a heart unyielded, because unvalued and unsought–came to Hester's cottage, demanding why they were so wretched, and what the remedy! Hester comforted and counseled them as best she might. She assured them too *of her firm belief,* that, at some brighter period, when

the world should have grown ripe for it, in Heaven's own time, *a new truth would be revealed, in order to establish the whole relation between man and woman on a surer ground of mutual happiness.*

This is intelligible English; but are Americans content that such should be the English of their literature? This is the question on which we have endeavored to deliver our own earnest convictions, and on which we hope to unite the suffrages of all virtuous persons, in sympathy with the abhorrence we so unhesitatingly express. To think of making such speculations the amusement of the daughters of America! The late Convention of females at Boston, to assert the 'rights of woman,' may show us that there are already some, who think the world is even now *ripe for it;* and safe as we may suppose our own fair relatives to be above such a low contagion, we must remember that to a woman, the very suggestion of a mode of life for her, as preferable to that which the Gospel has made the glorious sphere of her duties and her joys, is an insult and a degradation, to which no one that loves her would allow her to be exposed.

We assure Mr Hawthorne, in conclusion, that nothing less than an earnest wish that his future career may redeem this misstep, and prove a blessing to his country, has tempted us to enter upon a criticism so little suited to our tastes, as that of his late production. We commend to his attention the remarks of Mr Alison, on cotemporary popularity, to be found in the review of Bossuet. We would see him, too, rising to a place among those immortal authors who have 'clothed the lessons of religion in the burning words of genius,' and let him be assured, that, however great his momentary success, there is no lasting reputation for such an one as he is, except as it is founded on real worth, and fidelity to the morals of the Gospel. The time is past, when mere authorship provokes posthumous attention; there are too many who write with ease, and too many who publish books, in our times, for an author to be considered anything extraordinary. Poems perish in newspapers, now-a-days, which, at one time, would have made, at least, a name for biographical dictionaries; and stories lie dead in the pages of magazines, which would once have secured their author a mention with posterity. Hereafter those only will be thought of, who have enbalmed their writings in the hearts and lives of a few, at least, who learned from them to love truth and follow virtue. The age of 'mute inglorious Miltons,' is as dead as the age of chivalry. Everybody can write, and everybody can publish. But still, the wise are few; and it is only the wise, who can attain, in any worthy sense, to shine as the stars forever.

"Careering on the
Utmost Verge of a Precipitous Absurdity":
The House of the Seven Gables, *A Wonder-Book for Girls and Boys,* and *The Snow Image*

The House of the Seven Gables begins with this sentence: "Half-way down a by-street of one of our New England towns, stands a rusty wooden house, with seven acutely peaked gables facing towards various points of the compass, and a huge, clustered chimney in the midst." The town is Salem, where the house still stands. This location is significant because of the most famous episode in the history of the town, the 1692 witchcraft trials. In the novel, in order to claim land owned by Matthew Maule, Colonel Pyncheon helps convict Maule of witchcraft and sees him hanged. From the gallows Maule curses Pyncheon and his family; the novel details the effects of the curse.

While he was still working on the novel, Hawthorne wrote on 3 November 1850 to his publisher, James T. Fields:

I write diligently, but not so rapidly as I had hoped. I find the book requires more care and thought than the "Scarlet Letter";—also, I have to wait oftener for a mood. The Scarlet Letter being all in one tone, I had only to get my pitch, and could then go on interminably. Many passages of this book ought to be finished with the minuteness of a Dutch picture, in order to give them their proper effect. Sometimes, when tired of it, it strikes me that the whole is an absurdity, from begin-

The Salem house that is believed to be the model for the Pyncheon home in The House of the Seven Gables

Gallows Hill, believed to be the site where witches were executed in Salem

ning to end; but the fact is, in writing a romance, a man is always–or always ought to be–careering on the utmost verge of a precipitous absurdity, and the skill lies in coming as close as possible, without actually tumbling over. My prevailing idea is, that the book ought to succeed better than the Scarlet Letter; though I have no idea that it will.

Hawthorne concludes his romance by having Phœbe Pyncheon and Holgrave, descendants of the original conflicting families, marry, thus ending Maule's curse on the Pyncheons.

Some 1,690 copies (190 of them distributed to reviewers) of the first edition of The House of the Seven Gables *were published on 9 April 1851; within a year more than 6,700 copies were in print. The book sold for $1.00, and Hawthorne received a 15 percent royalty. Reviews were generally good. The absence of a sketch similar to "The Custom-House" led critics to consider* The House of the Seven Gables *as more unified than its predecessor.*

Publishing *The House of the Seven Gables*

In his memoir, publisher James T. Fields provides an account of the author during the period that his novel was going to press.

As I turn over his letters, the old days, delightful to recall, come back again with added interest.

"I sha'n't have the new story," he says in one of them, dated from Lenox on the 1st of October, 1850, "ready by November, for I am never good for anything in the literary way till after the first autumnal frost, which has somewhat such an effect on my imagination that it does on the foliage here about me,–multiplying and brightening its hues; though they are likely to be sober and shabby enough after all.

"I am beginning to puzzle myself about a title for the book. The scene of it is in one of those old projecting-storied houses, familiar to my eye in Salem; and the story, horrible to say, is a little less than two hundred years long; though all but thirty or forty pages of it refer to the present time. I think of such titles as 'The

House of the Seven Gables,' there being that number of gable-ends to the old shanty; or 'The Seven-Gabled House'; or simply 'The Seven Gables.' Tell me how these strike you. It appears to me that the latter is rather the best, and has the great advantage that it would puzzle the Devil to tell what it means."

A month afterwards he writes further with regard to "The House of the Seven Gables," concerning the title to which he was still in a quandary:–

"'The Old Pyncheon House: A Romance'; 'The Old Pyncheon Family; or the House of the Seven Gables: A Romance';–choose between them. I have rather a distaste to a double title? otherwise, I think I should prefer the second. Is it any matter under which title it is announced? If a better should occur hereafter, we can substitute. Of these two, on the whole, I judge the first to be the better."

. . . .

On the 9th of December he was still at work on the new romance, and writes:–

"My desire and prayer is to get through with the business in hand. I have been in a Slough of Despond for some days past, having written so fiercely that I came to a stand-still. There are points where a writer gets bewildered and cannot form any judgment of what he has done, or tell what to do next. In these cases it is best to keep quiet."

On the 12th of January, 1851, he is still busy over his new book, and writes: "My 'House of the Seven Gables' is, so to speak, finished; only I am hammering away a little on the roof, and doing up a few odd jobs, that were left incomplete.' At the end of the month the manuscript of his second great romance was put into the hands of the expressman at Lenox, by Hawthorne himself, to be delivered to me. On the 27th he writes:–

"If you do not soon receive it, you may conclude that it has miscarried; in which case, I shall not consent to the universe existing a moment longer. I have no copy of it, except the wildest scribble of a first draught, so that it could never be restored.

"It has met with extraordinary success from that portion of the public to whose judgment it has been submitted, viz. from my wife. I likewise prefer it to 'The Scarlet Letter'; but an author's opinion of his book just after completing it is worth little or nothing, he being then in the hot or cold fit of a fever, and certain to rate it too high or too low.

"It has undoubtedly one disadvantage in being brought so close to the present time; whereby its romantic improbabilities become more glaring.

"I deem it indispensable that the proof-sheets should be sent me for correction. It will cause some delay, no doubt, but probably not much more than if I lived in Salem. At all events, I don't see how it can be helped. My autography is sometimes villanously blind; and it is odd enough that whenever the printers do mistake a word, it is just the very jewel of a word, worth all the rest of the dictionary."

I well remember with what anxiety I awaited the arrival of the expressman with the precious parcel, and with what keen delight I read every word of the new story before I slept. Here is the original manuscript, just as it came that day, twenty years ago, fresh from the author's hand. The printers carefully preserved it for me; and Hawthorne once made a formal presentation of it, with great mock solemnity, in this very room where I am now sitting.

After the book came out he wrote:–

"I have by no means an inconvenient multitude of friends; but if they ever do appear a little too numerous, it is when I am making a list of those to whom presentation copies are to be sent. Please send one to General Pierce, Horatio Bridge, R. W. Emerson, W. E. Channing, Longfellow, Hillard, Sumner, Holmes, Lowell, and Thompson the artist. You will yourself give one to Whipple, whereby I shall make a saving. I presume you won't put the portrait into the book. It appears to me an improper accompaniment to a new work. Nevertheless, if it be ready, I should be glad to have each of these presentation copies accompanied by a copy of the engraving put loosely between the leaves. Good by. I must now trudge two miles to the village, through rain and mud knee-deep, after that accursed proof-sheet. The book reads very well in proofs, but I don't believe it will take like the former one. The preliminary chapter was what gave 'The Scarlet Letter' its vogue."

The engraving he refers to in this letter was made from a portrait by Mr. C. G. Thompson, and at that time, 1851, was an admirable likeness. On the 6th of March he writes:–

"The package, with my five heads, arrived yesterday afternoon, and we are truly obliged to you for putting so many at our disposal. They are admirably done. The children recognized their venerable sire with great delight. My wife complains somewhat of a want of cheerfulness in the face; and, to say the truth, it does appear to be afflicted with a bedeviled melancholy; but it will do all the better for the author of 'The Scarlet Letter.' In the expression there is a singular resemblance (which I do not remember in Thompson's picture) to a miniature of my father."

–*Yesterdays with Authors*, pp. 55–58

Reviews of *The House of the Seven Gables*

Evert A. Duyckinck was one of the major literary figures in New York during the middle of the nineteenth century. He and his brother, George Duyckinck, edited the influential weekly literary review The Literary World. *They also wrote* Cyclopaedia of American Literature *(1855), a still-valuable reference book.*

Review of *The House of the Seven Gables*
E. A. Duyckinck
The Literary World, 8 (26 April 1851): 334–336

In the preface to this work, the anxiously looked-for successor to *The Scarlet Letter,* Mr Hawthorne establishes a separation between the demands of the novel and the romance, and under the privilege of the latter, sets up his claim to a certain degree of license in the treatment of the characters and incidents of his coming story. This license, those acquainted with the writer's previous works will readily understand to be in the direction of the spiritualities of the piece, in favor of a process semi-allegorical, by which an acute analysis may be wrought out and the truth of feeling be minutely elaborated; an apology, in fact, for the preference of character to action, and of character for that which is allied to the darker elements of life–the dread blossoming of evil in the soul, and its fearful retributions. *The House of the Seven Gables,* one for each deadly sin, may be no unmeet adumbration of the corrupted soul of man. It is a ghostly, mouldy abode, built in some eclipse of the sun, and raftered with curses dark; founded on a grave, and sending its turrets heavenward, as the lightning rod transcends its summit, to invite the wrath supernal. Every darker shadow of human life lingers in and about its melancholy shelter. There all the passions allied to crime,–pride in its intensity, avarice with its steely gripe, and unrelenting conscience, are to be expiated in the house built on injustice. Wealth there withers, and the human heart grows cold: and thither are brought as accessories the chill glance of speculative philosophy, the descending hopes of the aged laborer, whose vision closes on the workhouse, the poor necessities of the humblest means of livelihood, the bodily and mental dilapidation of a wasted life.

A residence for woman, child, and man,
A dwelling place,–and yet no habitation;
A Home,–but under some prodigious ban
Of excommunication.
O'er all these hung a shadow and a fear;
A sense of mystery the spirit daunted,
And said, as plain as whisper in the ear,
The place is haunted!

Evert A. Duyckinck

Yet the sunshine casts its rays into the old building, as it must, were it only to show us the darkness.

In truth there is sunshine brought in among the inmates, and these wrinkled, cobwebbed spiritualities with gentle Phœbe,–but it is a playful, typical light of youth and goodness,–hardly crystallizing the vapory atmosphere of the romance into the palpable concretions of actual life.

Yet, withal, these scenes and vivid descriptions are dramatic and truthful; dramatic in the picturesque and in situation rather than in continuous and well developed action; true to the sentiment and inner reality, if not to the outer fact. The two death scenes of the founder of the family and of his descendant, Judge Pyncheon, possess dramatic effect of a remarkable character; and various other groupings, at the fountain and elsewhere, separate themselves in our recollection. The chief, perhaps, of the dramatis personae, is the house itself. From its turrets to its kitchen, in every nook and recess without and within, it is alive and vital, albeit of a dusty antiquity. We know it by sunlight and moonlight; by the elm which surmounts its roof, the mosses in its crevices, and its supernatural mist-swept blackness. Truly it is an actor in the scene. We move about

147

Page from the printer's copy for The House of the Seven Gables
(Houghton Library, Harvard University, MS Am 121.26)

tremblingly among its shadows,—the darkness of poverty and remorse dogging ruthlessly at our heels.

Verily this Hawthorne retains in him streaks of a Puritan ancestry. Some grave beater of pulpit cushions must lie among his ancestry; for of all laymen he will preach to you the closest sermons, probe deepest into the unescapable corruption, carry his lantern, like Belzoni among the mummies, into the most secret recesses of the heart; and he will do this with so vital a force in his propositions that they will transcend the individual example and find a precedent in every reader's heart. So true is it that when you once seize an actual thing you have in it a picture of universal life.

His Old Maid (Hepzibah) sacrificing pride to open her shop of small wares in one of the gables of the building, and her reluctant experiences of the first day, is not only a view of family pride in its shifts and reluctance, but covers all the doubts and irresolutions which beset a sensitive mind on the entrance upon any new sphere of duty in the great world.

These pictures are clear, distinct, full. The description is made out by repeated touches. There is no peculiar richness in the style: in some respects it is plain, but it flows on pellucid as a mountain rivulet, and you feel in its refreshing purity that it is fed by springs beneath.

You must be in the proper mood and time and place to read Hawthorne, if you would understand him. We think any one would be wrong to make the

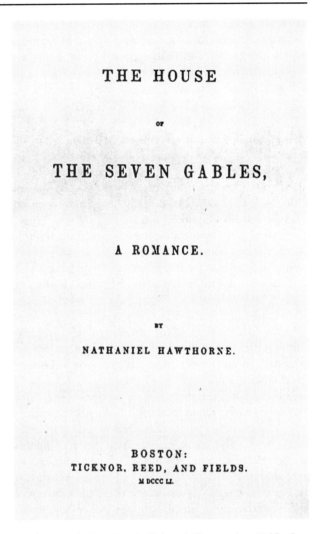

THE HOUSE

OF

THE SEVEN GABLES,

A ROMANCE.

BY

NATHANIEL HAWTHORNE.

BOSTON:
TICKNOR, REED, AND FIELDS.
M DCCC LI.

Title page for Hawthorne's third novel. He wrote in a 15 March 1851 letter to Horatio Bridge that he believed it was better than The Scarlet Letter *and "that portions of it are as good as anything that I can hope to write" (from C. E. Frazer Clark Jr.,* Nathaniel Hawthorne: A Descriptive Bibliography, 1978).

Defining *Romance*

At the beginning of his preface to The House of the Seven Gables *Hawthorne distinguishes between the novel and the romance.*

WHEN a writer calls his work a Romance, it need hardly be observed that he wishes to claim a certain latitude, both as to its fashion and material, which he would not have felt himself entitled to assume had he professed to be writing a Novel. The latter form of composition is presumed to aim at a very minute fidelity, not merely to the possible, but to the probable and ordinary course of man's experience. The former—while, as a work of art, it must rigidly subject itself to laws, and while it sins unpardonably so far as it may swerve aside from the truth of the human heart—has fairly a right to present that truth under circumstances, to a great extent, of the writer's own choosing or creation.

He concludes his preface with the assertion that he would be glad if his book were read "strictly as a Romance, having a great deal more to do with the clouds overhead than with any portion of the actual soil of the County of Essex."

---

attempt on a rail-car, or on board a steamboat. It is not a shilling novel that you are purchasing when you buy *The House of the Seven Gables,* but a book—a book with lights and shades, parts and diversities, upon which you may feed and pasture, not exhausting the whole field at an effort, but returning now and then to uncropped fairy rings and bits of herbage. You may read the book into the small hours beyond midnight, when no sound breaks the silence but the parting of an expiring ember, or the groan of restless mahogany, and you find that the candle burns a longer flame, and that the ghostly visions of the author's page take shape about you. Conscience sits supreme in her seat, the fountains of pity and terror are opened; you look into the depths of the soul, provoked at so painful a sight—but you are strengthened as you gaze; for of that pain comes peace at last, and these shadows you must master by virtuous magic. Nathaniel Hawthorne may be the Cornelius Agrippa to invoke them, but you are the mirror in which they are reflected.

The story of *The House of the Seven Gables* is a tale of retribution, of expiation extending over a period of two hundred years, it taking all that while to lay the ghost of the earliest victim, in the time of the Salem witchcraft; for, by the way, it is to Salem that this blackened old dwelling, mildewed with easterly scud, belongs. The yeoman who originally struck his spade into the spot, by the side of a crystal spring, was hanged for a wizard, under the afflictive dispensation of Cotton Mather. His land passed by force of law under cover of an old sweeping grant from the State, though not without hard words and thoughts and litigations, to the possession of the Ahab of the Vineyard, Colonel Pyncheon, the founder of the house, whose statuesque death scene was the first incident of the strongly ribbed tenement built on the ground thus suspiciously acquired. It was a prophecy of the old wizard on his execution at Gallows Hill, looking steadfastly at his rival, the Colonel, who was there, watching the scene on horseback, that 'God would give him blood to drink.' The sudden death of apoplexy was thereafter ministered to the great magnates of the Pyncheon family. After an introductory chapter detailing this early history of the house, we are introduced to its broken fortunes of the present day, in its decline. An Old Maid is its one tenant, left there with a life interest in the premises by the late owner, whose vast wealth passed into the hands of a cousin, who, immediately, touched by this talisman of property, was transformed from a youth of dissipation into a high, cold, and worldly state of respectability. His portrait is drawn in this volume with the repeated limnings and labor of a Titian, who, it is known, would expend several years upon a human head. We see him in every light, walk leisurely round the vast circle of that magical outline, his respectability just mentioned, till we close in upon the man, narrowing slowly to his centre of falsity and selfishness. For a thorough witch laugh over fallen hollow-heartedness and pretence, there is a terrible sardonic greeting in the roll-call of that man's uncompleted day's performances as he sits in the fatal chamber, death-cold, having drunk the blood of the ancient curse. But this is to anticipate. Other inmates gather round Old Maid Hepzibah. A remote gable is rented to a young artist, a daguerreotypist, and then comes upon the scene the brother of the Old Maid, Clifford Pyncheon, one day let out from life incarceration for—what circumstantial evidence had brought home to him—the murder of the late family head. Thirty years had obliterated most of this man's moral and intellectual nature,

save in a certain blending of the two with his physical instinct for the sensuous and beautiful. A rare character that for our spiritual limner to work upon! The agent he has provided, nature's ministrant to this feebleness and disease, to aid in the rebuilding of the man, is a sprig of unconscious, spontaneous girlhood—'a thing of beauty, and a joy for ever'—who enters the thick shades of the dwelling of disaster as a sunbeam, to purify and nourish its stagnant life. Very beautiful is this conception, and subtly wrought the chapters in which the relation is developed. Then we have the sacrifice of pride and solitary misanthropy in the petty retail shop Hepzibah opens for the increasing needs of the rusty mansion. This portion, as we have intimated, reaches the heart of the matter; and the moral here is as healthy as the emotion is keenly penetrated. What the tale-writer here says of his picture of the dilapidated figure of the Old Maid, applies to the poor and humble necessities of her position—

> If we look through all the heroic fortunes of mankind, we find an entanglement of something mean and trivial with whatever is noblest in joy or sorrow. Life is made up of marble and mud. What is called poetic insight is the gift of discerning, in this sphere of strangely-mingled elements, the beauty and the majesty which are compelled to assume a garb so sordid.

So, when gentility, and family decency, and the pride of life, seemed all to be sacrificed in the degradation and low vulgarities of the shop for boys and servant maids, a new ray of light breaks in upon the scene, quite unexpected and more noble than any form of magnificent selfishness. Note the crisis:

> The new shop-keeper dropped the first solid result of her commercial enterprise into the till. It was done! The sordid stain of that copper coin could never be washed away from her palm. The little schoolboy, aided by the impish figure of the negro dancer, had wrought an irreparable ruin. The structure of ancient aristocracy had been demolished by him, even as if his childish gripe had torn down the seven-gabled mansion! Now let Hepzibah turn the old Pyncheon portraits with their faces to the wall, and take the map of her eastern territory to kindle the kitchen fire, and blow up the flame with the empty breath of her ancestral traditions! What had she to do with ancestry? Nothing; no more than with posterity! No lady, now, but simply Hepzibah Pyncheon, a forlorn old maid, and keeper of a cent-shop! Nevertheless, even while she paraded these ideas somewhat ostentatiously through her mind, it is altogether surprising what a calmness had come over her. The anxiety and misgivings which had tormented her, whether asleep or in melancholy day-dreams, ever since her project began to take an aspect of solidity, had now vanished quite away. She felt the novelty of

her position, indeed, but no longer with disturbance or affright. Now and then, there came a thrill of almost youthful enjoyment. It was the invigorating breath of a fresh outward atmosphere, after the long torpor and monotonous seclusion of her life. So wholesome is effort! So miraculous the strength that we do not know of! The healthiest glow that Hepzibah had known for years had come now, in the dreaded crisis, when, for the first time, she had put forth her hand to help herself. The little circlet of the schoolboy's copper coin—dim and lustreless though it was, with the small services which it had been doing, here and there about the world—had proved a talisman, fragrant with good, and deserving to be set in gold and worn next her heart. It was as potent, and perhaps endowed with the same kind of efficacy, as a galvanic ring!

The scene passes on, while Hepzibah, her life bound up in the resuscitation of Clifford, supported by the salient life of the youthful womanhood of Phœbe, fulfils her destiny, the 'dukkeripens,' as that lay-divine,

the eminent Lavengro, has it in mystic, gipsy dialect, in the cent-shop—where, for a little sprinkling of pleasantry to this sombre tale, comes a voracious boy to devour the gingerbread Jim Crows, elephants, and other seductive fry of the quaintly-arranged window. His stuffed hide is a relief to the empty-waistcoated ghosts moving within. There is a humble fellow too, one Uncle Venner, a good-natured servitor at small chores—a poor devil in the eye of the world—of whom Hawthorne, with kindly eye, makes something by digging down under his tattered habiliments to his better-preserved human heart. He comes to the shop, and is a kind of out-of-door appendant to the fortunes of the house.

The Nemesis of the House is pressing for a new victim. Judge Pyncheon's thoughts are intent on an old hobby of the establishment, the procurement of a deed which was missing, and which was the evidence wanting to complete the title to a certain vast New Hamp-

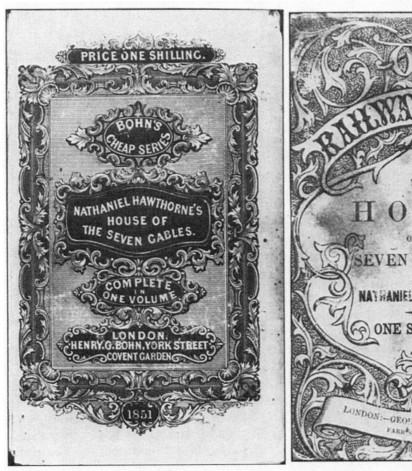 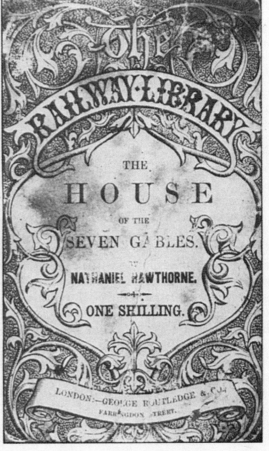

Covers for the first two English editions of Hawthorne's romance, both pirated (from C. E. Frazer Clark Jr., Nathaniel Hawthorne: A Descriptive Bibliography, 1978)

DLB 269

shire grant—a portentous and arch-deceiving ignis fatuus of the family. Clifford is supposed to know something of this matter; but, knowledge or not, the Judge is the one man in the world whom he will not meet. Every instinct of his nature rises within him, in self-protection of his weak, sensitive life, against the stern magnetic power of the coarse, granite judge. More than that lies underneath. Clifford had been unjustly convicted—by those suspicious death-marks of his suddenly deceased relative—and the Judge had suffered it, holding all the time the key which would have unlocked the mystery, besides some other shades of criminality. To escape an interview with this man, Clifford and Hepzibah leave the house in flight, while Judge Pyncheon sits in the apartment of his old ancestor, waiting for him. And how sits he there?—

Judge Pyncheon, while his two relatives have fled away with such ill-considered haste, still sits in the old parlor, keeping house, as the familiar phrase is, in the absence of its ordinary occupants . . . 'Up, therefore, Judge Pyncheon, up! You have lost a day. But to-morrow will be here anon. Will you rise, betimes, and make the most of it? To-morrow! To-morrow! To-morrow! We, that are alive, may rise betimes to-morrow. As for him that has died to-day, his morrow will be the resurrection morn.'

This, we conceive to be taking a pretty strong grip of Judge Pyncheon. It is a spiritual lashing of the old man, grievous as any material one Dickens ever inflicted in paying off an immitigable scoundrel at the close of a twenty months' cruise of sin and wickedness, in the last number of a long serial novel. The fortunes of the House, after this tremendous purgation, look more brightly for the future. The diverted patrimony of his ex-respectability—the Governor in posse of Massachusetts—returns to its true channel to irrigate the dry heart of the Old Maid, and furnish Clifford the luxuries of the Beautiful. The daguerreotypist, who turns out to be the descendant of the wizard,—the inventor of the curse—marries Phœbe, of course, and the parties have left the Old House, mouldering away in its by-street, for the summer realm of a country summer retreat.

Such is the material of Hawthorne's legend—with every 'coigne of vantage' for his procreant, melancholy fancy to work in, hanging his airy cobwebs about, not without a glitter on them of dew and sunshine. In tenderness and delicacy of sentiment, no writer of the present day can go beyond this book. This is Hawthorne's province of the world. In it his life is original, fanciful, creative.

George Ripley (1802–1880) was minister of the Boston Unitarian Church and edited the liberal Unitarian magazine Christian Register. *He also edited the influential* Specimens of Foreign Standard Literature *(1838–1845). In 1841 he retired from the ministry and helped found the transcendentalist magazine* The Dial *and Brook Farm. He served as director of the experimental community and edited its weekly journal,* The Harbinger. *He was an influential book reviewer for the* New-York Daily Tribune *from 1849 until his death.* Harper's New Monthly Magazine, *the forerunner of the* Harper's Magazine *of today, was then in its second year of existence.*

Review of *The House of the Seven Gables*
George Ripley
Harper's New Monthly Magazine, 2 (May 1851): 855–856

Ticknor, Reed, and Fields have issued *The House of the Seven Gables,* a Romance, by Nathaniel Hawthorne, which is strongly marked with the bold and unique characteristics that have given its author such a brilliant position among American novelists. The scene, which is laid in the old Puritanic town of Salem, extends from the period of the witchcraft excitement to the present time, connecting the legends of the ancient superstition with the recent marvels of animal magnetism, and affording full scope for the indulgence of the most weird and sombre fancies. Destitute of the high-wrought manifestations of passion which distinguished *The Scarlet Letter,* it is more terrific in its conception, and not less intense in its execution, but exquisitely relieved by charming portraitures of character, and quaint and comic descriptions of social eccentricities. A deep vein of reflection underlies the whole narrative, often rising naturally to the surface, and revealing the strength of the foundation on which the subtle, aerial inventions of the author are erected. His frequent dashes of humor gracefully blend with the monotone of the story, and soften the harsher colors in which he delights to clothe his portentous conceptions. In no former production of his pen, are his unrivalled powers of description displayed to better advantage. The rusty wooden house in Pyncheon-street, with its seven sharp-pointed gables, and its huge clustered chimney—the old elm tree before the door—the grassy yard seen through the lattice-fence, with its enormous fertility of burdocks—and the green moss on the slopes of the roof, with the flowers growing aloft in the air in the nook between two of the gables—present a picture to the eye as distinct as if our childhood had been passed in the shadow of the old weatherbeaten edifice. Nor are the characters of the story drawn with less sharp and vigorous perspective. They stand out from the canvas as living realities. In spite of the supernatural drapery in which they are enveloped, they have such a genuine expression of flesh and blood, that we can not doubt we have known them all our days. They have the air of old acquaintance–only we wonder how the artist got them to sit for their likenesses. The grouping of these persons is managed with admirable artistic skill. Old Maid Pyncheon, concealing under her verjuice scowl the unutterable tenderness of a sister–her woman-hearted brother, on whose sensitive nature had fallen such a strange blight–sweet and beautiful Phœbe, the noble village-maiden, whose presence is always like that of some shining angel–the dreamy, romantic descendant of the legendary wizard–the bold, bad man of the world, reproduced at intervals in the bloody Colonel, and the unscrupulous Judge–wise old Uncle Venner–and inappeasable Ned Higgins–are all made to occupy the place on the canvas which shows the lights and shades of their character in the most impressive contrast, and contributes to the wonderful vividness and harmony of the grand historical picture. On the whole, we regard *The House of the Seven Gables,* though it exhibits no single scenes that may not be matched in depth and pathos by some of Mr. Hawthorne's previous creations, as unsurpassed by any thing he has yet written, in exquisite beauty of finish, in the skillful blending of the tragic and comic, and in the singular life-like reality with which the wildest traditions of the Puritanic age are combined with the every-day incidents of modern society.

An Established Reputation

Hawthorne contributed twenty-three pieces to United States Magazine and Democratic Review *between its inception in October 1837 and April 1845, including such notable stories as "The Artist of the Beautiful" and "Rappaccini's Daughter." This monthly political and literary journal also published work by Edgar Allan Poe, Henry Wadsworth Longfellow, Walt Whitman, William Gilmore Simms, and William Cullen Bryant.*

The reputation of Mr. Hawthorne is sufficiently established and widely known, to procure for any stories of his production a large and eager circle of readers. His delineations of New-England manners, conversations and language, are governed by good taste in avoiding to adulterate the conversation of ordinary people with idioms and barbarisms, which rarely have existence in New-England. That the works of Mr. Hawthorne will go down to other generations, conveying a truthful picture of the manners of our times, there can be no doubt. He occupies the first rank among the imaginative writers of the day, and his productions are not excelled here or elsewhere.

–United States Magazine and Democratic Review,
28 (May 1851): 478

Henry T. Tuckerman's varied writings included literary criticism in books such as Thoughts on the Poets *(1846) and* Characteristics of Literature *(1849). Unlike the most famous critic associated with the* Southern Literary Messenger, *Edgar Allan Poe, who was famous for his vituperation, Tuckerman characteristically showed a sympathetic appreciation for the work he reviewed. In his overview of Hawthorne's career and comments on* The House of the Seven Gables, *he focuses on Hawthorne as a psychological author who combines "the philosophic tendency with the poetic instinct."*

Nathaniel Hawthorne
Henry T. Tuckerman
Southern Literary Messenger, 17 (June 1851): 344–349

I passed an hour lately in examining various substances through a powerful microscope, with a man of science at my elbow, to expound their use and relations. It was astonishing what revelations of wonder and beauty in common things were thus attained in a brief period. The eye aptly directed, the attention wisely given and the minute in nature enlarged and unfolded to the vision, a new sense of life and its marvels seemed created. What appeared but a slightly rough surface proved variegated iris-hued crystals: a dot on a leaf became a moth's nest with its symmetrical eggs and their hairy pent-house; the cold passive oyster displayed heart and lungs in vital activity; the unfolding wings grew visible upon the seed-vessels of the ferns; beetles looked like gorgeously emblazoned shields; and the internal economy of the nauseous cockroach, in its high and delicate organism, showed a remarkable affinity between insect and animal life. What the scientific use of lenses–the telescope and the microscope–does for us in relation to the external universe, the psychological writer achieves in regard to our own nature. He reveals its wonder and beauty, unfolds its complex laws and makes us suddenly aware of the mysteries within and around individual life. In the guise of attractive fiction and sometimes of the most airy sketches, Hawthorne thus deals with his reader. His appeal is to consciousness and he must, therefore, be met in a sympathetic relation; he shadows forth,–hints,–makes signs,–whispers,–muses aloud,–gives the keynote of melody–puts us on a track;–in a word, addresses us as nature does–that is unostentatiously, and with a significance not to be realized without reverent silence and gentle feeling–a sequestration from bustle and material care, and somewhat of the meditative insight and latent sensibility in which his themes are conceived and wrought out. Sometimes they are purely descriptive, bits of Flemish painting–so exact and arrayed in such mellow colors, that we unconsciously take them in as objects of sensitive rather than imaginative observation;

Henry T. Tuckerman

the 'Old Manse' and the 'Custom House'—those quaint portals to his fairy-land, as peculiar and rich in contrast in their way, as Boccaccio's sombre introduction to his gay stories—are memorable instances of this fidelity in the details of local and personal portraiture; and that chaste yet deep tone of colouring which secure an harmonious whole. Even in allegory, Hawthorne imparts this sympathetic unity to his conception; 'Fire Worship,' 'The Celestial Railroad,' 'Monsieur du Miroir,' 'Earth's Holocaust,' and others in the same vein, while they emphatically indicate great moral truth, have none of the abstract and cold grace of allegorical writing; besides the ingenuity they exhibit, and the charm they have for the fancy, a human interest warms and gives them meaning to the heart. On the other hand, the imaginative grace which they chiefly display, lends itself quite as aptly to redeem and glorify homely fact in the plastic hands of the author. 'Drowne's Wooden Image,' 'The Intelligence Office,' and other tales derived from common-place material, are thus moulded into artistic beauty and suggestiveness. Hawthorne, therefore, is a prose-poet. He brings together scattered beauties, evokes truth from apparent confusion, and embodies the tragic or humorous element of a tradition or an

event in lyric music—not, indeed, to be sung by the lips, but to live, like melodious echoes, in the memory. We are constantly struck with the felicity of his invention. What happy ideas are embodied in 'A Virtuoso's Collection,' and 'The Artist of the Beautiful'—independent of the grace of their execution! There is a certain uniformity in Hawthorne's style and manner, but a remarkable versatility in his subjects; and each as distinctly carries with it the monotone of a special feeling or fancy, as one of Miss Baillie's plays:—and this is the perfection of psychological art.

There are two distinct kinds of fiction, or narrative literature, which for want of more apt terms, we may call the melo-dramatic and the meditative; the former is in a great degree mechanical, and deals chiefly with incidents and adventure; a few types of character, an approved scenic material and what are called effective situations, make up the story; the other species, on the contrary, is modelled upon no external pattern, but seems evolved from the author's mind, and tinged with his idiosyncracy; the circumstances related are often of secondary interest—while the sentiment they unfold, the picturesque or poetic light in which they are placed, throw an enchantment over them. We feel the glow of individual consciousness even in the most technical description; we recognize a significance beyond the apparent, in each character; and the effect of the whole is that of life rather than history: we inhale an atmosphere as well as gaze upon a landscape; the picture offered to the mental vision has not outline and grouping, but color and expression, evincing an intimate and sympathetic relation between the moral experience of the author and his work, so that, as we read, not only scenes but sensations, not only fancies but experience seem borne in from the entrancing page.

There is a charm also essential to all works of genius which for want of a more definite term we are content to call the ineffable. It is a quality that seems to be infused through the design of the artist after its mechanical finish—as life entered the statue at the prayer of the Grecian sculptor. It is a secret, indescribable grace, a vital principle, a superhuman element imparting the distinctive and magnetic character to literature, art and society, which gives them individual life; it is what the soul is to the body, luminous vapour to the landscape, wind to sound, and light to color. No analysis explains the phenomenon; it is recognized by consciousness rather than through direct intellectual perception; and seems to appeal to a union of sensibility and insight which belongs, in the highest degree, only to appreciative minds. Its mysterious, endearing and conservative influence, hallows all works universally acknowledged as those of genius in the absolute significance of the word; and it gives to inanimate forms, the written page, the composer's harmony and the lyric or dramatic personation, a certain pervading interest which we instantly feel disarming criticism and attesting the presence of what is allied to our deepest instincts. It touches the heart with tender awe before a Madonna of Raphael; it thrilled the nerves and evoked the passions in the elocution of Kenn; it lives in the expression of the Apollo, in the characters of Shakespeare, and the atmospheres of Claude; and those once thus initiated by experience, know spontaneously the invisible line of demarkation which separates talent, skill and knowledge from genius by the affinity of impression invariably produced:—a distinction as clearly felt and as difficult to portray as that between the emotions of friendship and love. It would appear as if there was a provision in the minds of the highly gifted similar to that of nature in her latent resources; whereby they keep in reserve a world of passion, sentiment and ideas, unhackneyed by casual use and unprofaned by reckless display—which is secretly lavished upon their mental emanations:—hence their moral life, intense personality, and sympathetic charm. Such a process and result is obviously independent of will and intelligence; what they achieve is thus crowned with light and endowed with vitality by a grace above their sphere; the Ineffable, then, is a primary distinction and absolute token of genius; like the halo that marks a saintly head. Results like these are only derived from the union of keen observation with moral sensibility; they blend like form and color, perspective and outline, tone and composition in art. They differ from merely clever stories in what may be called flavor. There is a peculiar zest about them which proves a vital origin; and this is the distinction of Hawthorne's tales. They almost invariably possess the reality of tone which perpetuates imaginative literature;—the same that endears to all time De Foe, Bunyan, Goldsmith, and the old dramatists. We find in pictorial art that the conservative principle is either absolute fidelity to detail as in the Flemish, or earnest moral beauty as in the Italian school; the painters who yet live in human estimation were thoroughly loyal either to the real or the ideal—to perception or to feeling, to the eye or the heart. And, in literature, the same thing is evident. *Robinson Crusoe* is objectively, and *Pilgrim's Progress* spiritually, true to nature; *The Vicar of Wakefield* emanated from a mind overflowing with humanity; and it is the genuine reproduction of passion in the old English plays that makes them still awaken echoes in the soul.

It may be regarded as a proof of absolute genius to create a mood; to inform, amuse, or even interest is only the test of superficial powers sagaciously directed; but to infuse a new state of feeling, to change the frame of mind and, as it were, alter the consciousness—this is

the triumph of all art. It is that mysterious influence which beauty, wit, character, nature and peculiar senses and objects exert, which we call fascination, a charm, an inspiration or a glamour, according as it is good or evil. It may safely be asserted that by virtue of his individuality every author and artist of genius creates a peculiar mood, differing somewhat according to the character of the recipient, yet essentially the same. If we were obliged to designate that of Hawthorne in a single word, we should call it metaphysical, or perhaps soulful. He always takes us below the surface and beyond the material; his most inartificial stories are eminently suggestive; he makes us breathe the air of contemplation, and turns our eyes inward. It is as if we went forth, in a dream, into the stillness of an autumnal wood, or stood alone in a vast gallery of old pictures, or moved slowly, with muffled tread, over a wide plain, amid a gentle fall of snow, or mused on a ship's deck, at sea, by moonlight; the appeal is to the retrospective, the introspective to what is thoughtful and profoundly conscious in our nature and whereby it communes with the mysteries of life and the occult intimations of nature. And yet there is no painful extravagance, no transcendental vagaries in Hawthorne; his imagination is as human as his heart; if he touches the horizon of the infinite, it is with reverence; if he deals with the anomalies of sentiment, it is with intelligence and tenderness. His utterance too is singularly clear and simple; his style only rises above the colloquial in the sustained order of its flow; the terms are apt, natural and fitly chosen. Indeed, a careless reader is liable continually to lose sight of his meaning and beauty, from the entire absence of pretension in his style. It is requisite to bear in mind the universal truth, that all great and true things are remarkable for simplicity; the direct method is the pledge of sincerity, avoidance of the conventional, an instinct of richly-endowed minds; and the perfection of art never dazzles or overpowers, but gradually wins and warms us to an enduring and noble love. The style of Hawthorne is wholly inevasive; he resorts to no tricks of rhetoric or verbal ingenuity; language is to him a crystal medium through which to let us see the play of his humor, the glow of his sympathy, and the truth of his observation.

Although he seldom transcends the limited sphere in which he so efficiently concentrates his genius, the variety of tone, like different airs on the same instrument, gives him an imaginative scope rarely obtained in elaborate narrative. Thus he deals with the tragic element, wisely and with vivid originality, in such pieces as 'Roger Malvern's Burial' and 'Young Goodman Browne;' with the comic in 'Mr Higginbotham's Catastrophe,' 'A Select Party,' and 'Dr Heidegger's Experiment,' and with the purely fanciful in 'David Swan,'

First page of Hawthorne's 2 September 1851 letter to his friend William B. Pike, in which he comments on his hometown:
"As to Salem, I hope Providence has no intention of ever bringing me to reside within its limits again"
(Peabody Essex Museum)

'The Vision of the Fountain,' and 'Fancy's Show Box.' Nor is he less remarkable for sympathetic observation of nature than for profound interest in humanity; witness such limning as the sketches entitled 'Buds and Bird Voices,' and 'Snow-Flakes'—genuine descriptive poems, though not cast in the mould of verse, as graphic, true and feeling as the happiest scenes of Bryant or Crabbe. With equal tact and tenderness he approaches the dry record of the past, imparting life to its cold details, and reality to its abstract forms. The early history of New England has found no such genial and vivid illustration as his pages afford. Thus, at all points, his genius touches the interests of human life, now overflowing with a love of external nature, as gentle as that of Thomson, now intent upon the quaint or characteristic in life with a humor as zestful as that of Lamb, now developing the horrible or pathetic with something of Webster's dramatic terror, and again buoyant with a fantasy as aerial as Shelley's conceptions. And, in each instance, the staple of charming invention is adorned with the purest graces of style. This is Hawthorne's distinction. We have writers who possess in an eminent degree, each of these two great requisites of literary success, but no one who more impressively unites them; cheerfulness as if caught from the sea breeze or the green-fields, solemnity as if imbibed from the twilight, like colors on a palette, seem transferable at his will, to any legend or locality he chooses for a frame-work whereon to rear his artistic creation; and this he does with so dainty a touch and so fine a disposition of light and shade, that the result is like an immortal cabinet picture—the epitome of a phase of art and the miniature reflection of a glorious mind. Boccaccio in Italy, Marmontel in France, Hoffman and others in Germany, and Andersen in Denmark, have made the tale or brief story classical in their several countries; and Hawthorne has achieved the same triumph here. He has performed for New England life and manners the same high and sweet service which Wilson has for Scotland—caught and permanently embodied their 'lights and shadows.'

Brevity is as truly the soul of romance as of wit; the light that warms is always concentrated, and expression and finish, in literature as in painting, are not dependent upon space. Accordingly the choicest gems of writing are often the most terse; and as a perfect lyric or sonnet outweighs in value a mediocre epic or tragedy, so a carefully worked and richly conceived sketch, tale or essay is worth scores of diffuse novels and ponderous treatises. It is a characteristic of standard literature, both ancient and modern, thus to condense the elements of thought and style. Like the compact and well-knit frame, vivacity, efficiency and grace result from this bringing the rays of fancy and reflection to a

focus. It gives us the essence, the flower, the vital spirit of mental enterprise; it is a wise economy of resources and often secures permanent renown by distinctness of impression unattained in efforts of great range. We, therefore, deem one of Hawthorne's great merits a sententious habit, a concentrated style. He makes each picture complete and does not waste an inch of canvass. Indeed the unambitious length of his tales is apt to blind careless readers to their artistic unity and suggestiveness; he abjures quantity, while he refines upon quality.

A rare and most attractive quality of Hawthorne, as we have already suggested, is the artistic use of familiar materials. The imagination is a wayward faculty, and writers largely endowed with it, have acknowledged that they could expatiate with confidence only upon themes hallowed by distance. It seems to us less marvellous that Shakespeare peopled a newly discovered and half-traditional island with such new types of character as Ariel and Caliban; we can easily reconcile ourselves to the enchanting impossibilities of Arabian fiction; and the superstitious fantasies of northern romance have a dream-like reality to the natives of the temperate zone. To clothe a familiar scene with ideal interest, and exalt things to which our senses are daily accustomed, into the region of imaginative beauty and genuine sentiment, requires an extraordinary power of abstraction and concentrative thought. Authors in the old world have the benefits of antiquated memorials which give to the modern cities a mysterious though often disregarded charm; and the very names of Notre Dame, the Rialto, London Bridge, and other time-hallowed localities, take the reader's fancy captive and prepare him to accede to any grotesque or thrilling narrative that may be associated with them. It is otherwise in a new and entirely practical country; the immediate encroaches too steadily on our attention; we can scarcely obtain a perspective:

Life treads on life and heart on heart—
We press too close in church and mart,
To keep a dream or grave apart.

Yet with a calm gaze, a serenity and fixedness of musing that no outward bustle can disturb and no power of custom render hackneyed, Hawthorne takes his stand, like a foreign artist in one of the old Italian cities,—before a relic of the past or a picturesque glimpse of nature, and loses all consciousness of himself and the present, in transferring its features and atmosphere to canvass. In our view the most remarkable trait in his writings is this harmonious blending of the common and familiar in the outward world, with the mellow and vivid tints of his own imagination. It is with difficulty that his maturity of conception and his finish and geniality of style links itself, in our minds, with the streets of Boston and Salem, the Province House and even the White Mountains; and we congratulate every New Englander with a particle of romance, that in his native literature, 'a local habitation and a name,' has thus been given to historical incidents and localities;—that art has enshrined what of tradition hangs over her brief career—as characteristic and as desirable thus to consecrate, as any legend or spot, German or Scottish genius has redeemed from oblivion. The 'Wedding Knell,' the 'Gentle Boy,' the 'White Old Maid,' the 'Ambitious Guest,' the 'Shaker Bridal,' and other New England subjects, as embodied and glorified by the truthful, yet imaginative and graceful art of Hawthorne, adequately represent in literature, native traits, and this will ensure their ultimate appreciation. But the most elaborate effort of this kind, and the only one, in fact, which seems to have introduced Hawthorne to the whole range of American readers, is *The Scarlet Letter*. With all the care in point of style and authenticity which mark his lighter sketches, this genuine and unique romance, may be considered as an artistic exposition of Puritanism as modified by New England colonial life. In truth to costume, local manners and scenic features, *The Scarlet Letter* is as reliable as the best of Scott's novels; in the anatomy of human passion and consciousness it resembles the most effective of Balzac's illustrations of Parisian or provincial life, while in developing bravely and justly the sentiment of the life it depicts, it is as true to humanity as Dickens. Beneath its picturesque details and intense characterization, there lurks a profound satire. The want of soul, the absence of sweet humanity, the predominance of judgment over mercy, the tyranny of public opinion, the look [lack?] of genuine charity, the asceticism of the Puritan theology,—the absence of all recognition of natural laws, and the fanatic substitution of the letter for the spirit—which darken and harden the spirit of the pilgrims to the soul of a poet—are shadowed forth with a keen, stern and eloquent, yet indirect emphasis, that haunts us like 'the cry of the human.' Herein is evident and palpable the latent power which we have described as the most remarkable trait of Hawthorne's genius;—the impression grows more significant as we dwell upon the story; the states of mind of the poor clergymen. Hester, Chillingworth and Pearl, being as it were transferred to our bosoms through the intense sympathy their vivid delineation excites;—they seem to conflict, and glow and deepen and blend in our hearts, and finally work out a great moral problem. It is as if we were baptized into the consciousness of Puritan life, of New England character in its elemental state; and knew, by experience, all its frigidity, its gloom, its intellectual enthusiasm and its religious aspiration. *The House of the Seven Gables* is a more elaborate and harmonious realization of these characteristics. The scenery, tone and personages of the story are imbued with a local authenticity which is not, for an instant, impaired by the imaginative charm of romance. We seem to breathe, as we read, the air and be surrounded by the familiar objects of a New England town. The interior of the House, each article described within it, from the quaint table to the miniature by Malbòne;—every product of the old garden, the street-scenes that beguile the eyes of poor Clifford, as he looks out of the arched window, the noble elm and the gingerbread figures at the little shop window—all have the significance that belong to reality when seized upon by art. In these details we have the truth, simplicity and exact imitation of the Flemish painters. So life-like in the minutiæ and so picturesque in general effect are these sketches of still-life, that they are daguerreotyped in the reader's mind, and form a distinct and changeless background, the light and shade of which give admirable effect to the action of the story: occasional touches of humor, introduced with exquisite tact, relieve the grave undertone of the narrative and form vivacious and quaint images which might readily be transferred to canvass—so effectively are they drawn in words; take, for instance, the street-musician and the Pyncheon fowls, the judge balked of his kiss over the counter, Phœbe reading to Clifford in the garden, or the old maid, in her lonely chamber, gazing on the sweet lineaments of her unfortunate brother. Nor is Hawthorne less successful in those pictures that are drawn exclusively for the mind's eye and are obvious to sensation rather than the actual vision. Were New England Sunday, breakfast, old mansion, easterly storm, or the morning after it clears, ever so well described? The skill in atmosphere we have noted in his lighter sketches, is also as apparent: around and within the principal scene of this romance, there hovers an alternating melancholy and brightness which is born of genuine moral life; no contrasts can be imagined of this kind, more eloquent to a sympathetic mind, than that between the inward consciousness and external appearance of Hepzibah or Phœbe and Clifford, or the Judge. They respectively symbolize the poles of human existence; and are fine studies for the psychologist. Yet this attraction is subservient to fidelity to local characteristics. Clifford represents, though in its most tragic imaginable phase, the man of fine organization and true sentiments environed by the material realities of New England life; his plausible uncle is the type of New England selfishness, glorified by respectable conformity and wealth; Phœbe is the ideal of genuine, efficient, yet loving female character in the same latitude; Uncle Venner, we regard as one of the most fresh, yet familiar portraits in the book; all denizens of our eastern provincial towns must have known such a philosopher; and Holgrave embodies Yankee acuteness and hardihood redeemed by integrity and enthusiasm. The contact of these most judiciously selected and highly characteristic elements, brings out not only many beautiful revelations of nature, but elucidates interesting truth; magnetism and socialism are admirably introduced; family tyranny in its most revolting form, is powerfully exemplified; the distinction between a mental and a heartfelt interest in another, clearly unfolded; and the tenacious and hereditary nature of moral evil impressively shadowed forth. The natural refinements of the human heart, the holiness of a ministry of disinterested affection, the gracefulness of the homeliest services when irradiated by cheerfulness and benevolence, are illustrated with a singular beauty. 'He,' says our author, speaking of Clifford,

> had no right to be a martyr; and, beholding him so fit to be happy, and so feeble for all other purposes, a generous, strong and noble spirit would, methinks, have been ready to sacrifice what little enjoyment it might have planned for itself,—*it would have flung down the hopes so paltry in its regard—if thereby the wintry blasts of our rude sphere might come tempered to such a man:*

and elsewhere:

> Phœbe's presence made a home about her,—that very sphere which the outcast, the prisoner, the potentate, the wretch beneath mankind, the wretch aside from it, or the wretch above it, instinctively pines after—a home. She was real! Holding her hand, you felt something; a tender something; a substance and a warm one: *and so long as you could feel its grasp, soft as it was, you might be certain that your place was good in the whole sympathetic chain of human nature.* The world was no longer a delusion.

Thus narrowly, yet with reverence, does Hawthorne analyze the delicate traits of human sentiment and character; and open vistas into that beautiful and unexplored world of love and thought, that exists in every human being, though overshadowed by material circumstance and technical duty. This, as we have before said, is his great service; digressing every now and then, from the main drift of his story, he takes evident delight in expatiating on phases of character and general traits of life, or in bringing into strong relief the more latent facts of consciousness. Perhaps the union of the philosophic tendency with the poetic instinct is the great charm of his genius. It is common for American critics to estimate the interest of all writings by their comparative glow, vivacity and rapidity of action: somewhat of the restless temperament and enterprising life of the nation infects its taste: such terms as 'quiet,' 'gentle' and 'tasteful,' are equivocal when applied in this country, to a book; and yet they may envelope the rarest energy of thought and depth of insight as well as earnestness of feeling; these qualities, in reflective minds, are too real to find melo-dramatic development; they move as calmly as summer waves, or glow as noiselessly as the firmament; but not the less grand and mighty is

their essence; to realize it, the spirit of contemplation, and the recipient mood of sympathy, must be evoked, for it is not external but moral excitement that is proposed; and we deem one of Hawthorne's most felicitous merits—that of so patiently educing artistic beauty and moral interest from life and nature, without the least sacrifice of intellectual dignity.

The healthy spring of life is typified in Phœbe so freshly as to magnetize the feelings as well as engage the perceptions of the reader; its intellectual phase finds expression in Holgrave, while the state of Clifford, when relieved of the nightmare that oppressed his sensitive temperament, the author justly compares to an Indian-summer of the soul. Across the path of these beings of genuine flesh and blood, who constantly appeal to our most humane sympathies, or rather around their consciousness and history, flits the pale, mystic figure of Alice—whose invisible music and legendary fate overflow with a graceful and attractive superstition—yielding an Ariel-like melody to the more solemn and cheery strains of the whole composition. Among the apt though incidental touches of the picture, the idea of making the music-grinder's monkey an epitome of avarice, the daguerreotype a test of latent character, and the love of the reformer Holgrave for the genially practical Phœbe, win him to conservatism, strike us as remarkably natural yet quite as ingenuous and charming as philosophical. We may add that the same pure, even, unexaggerated and perspicuous style of diction that we have recognized in his previous writing, is maintained in this.

As earth and sky appear to blend at the horizon though we cannot define the point of contact, things seen and unseen, the actual and the spiritual, mind and matter, what is within and what is without our consciousness, have a line of union, and, like the colour of the iris, are lost in each other. About this equator of life the genius of Hawthorne delights to hover as its appropriate sphere; whether indulging a vein of Spenserian allegory, Hogarth sketching, Goldsmith domesticity, or Godwin metaphysics, it is around the boundary of the possible that he most freely expatiates; the realities and the mysteries of life to his vision are scarcely ever apart; they act and re-act as to yield dramatic hints or vistas of sentiment. Time broods with touching solemnity over his imagination; the function of conscience awes while it occupies his mind; the delicate and the profound in love, and the awful beauty of death transfuse his meditation; and these supernal he loves to link with terrestial influences—to hallow a graphic description by a sacred association or to brighten a commonplace occasion with the scintillations of humour—thus vivifying or chastening the 'light of common day.'

Hawthorne in 1851

Fields's memories of Hawthorne as he was coping with the response to The House of the Seven Gables *and working on* A Wonder-Book for Boys and Girls *led him to consider Hawthorne as a reader and a personality.*

His letters to me, during the summer of 1851, were frequent and sometimes quite long. "The House of the Seven Gables" was warmly welcomed, both at home and abroad. On the 23d of May he writes:–

"Whipple's notices have done more than pleased me, for they have helped me to see my book. Much of the censure I recognize as just; I wish I could feel the praise to be so fully deserved. Being better (which I insist it is) than 'The Scarlet Letter,' I have never expected it to be so popular (this steel pen makes me write awfully). —— Esq., of Boston, has written to me, complaining that I have made his grandfather infamous! It seems there was actually a Pyncheon (or Pynchon, as he spells it) family resident in Salem, and that their representative, at the period of the Revolution, was a certain Judge Pynchon, a Tory and a refugee. This was Mr. ——'s grandfather, and (at least, so he dutifully describes him) the most exemplary old gentleman in the world. There are several touches in my account of the Pyncheons which, he says, make it probable that I had this actual family in my eye, and he considers himself infinitely wronged and aggrieved, and thinks it monstrous that the 'virtuous dead' cannot be suffered to rest quietly in their graves. He further complains that I speak disrespectfully of the ——'s in Grandfather's Chair. He writes more in sorrow than in anger, though there is quite enough of the latter quality to give piquancy to his epistle. The joke of the matter is, that I never heard of his grandfather, nor knew that any Pyncheons had ever lived in Salem, but took the name because it suited the tone of my book, and was as much my property, for fictitious purposes, as that of Smith. I have pacified him by a very polite and gentlemanly letter, and if ever you publish any more of the Seven Gables, I should like to write a brief preface, expressive of my anguish for this unintentional wrong, and making the best reparation possible; else these wretched old Pyncheons will have no peace in the other world, nor in this. Furthermore, there is a Rev. Mr. ——, resident within four miles of me, and a cousin of Mr. ——, who states that he likewise is highly indignant. Who would have dreamed of claimants starting up for such an inheritance as the House of the Seven Gables!

"I mean to write, within six weeks or two months next ensuing, a book of stories made up of classical myths. The subjects are: The Story of Midas, with his Golden Touch, Pandora's Box, The Adventure of Hercules in quest of the Golden Apples, Bellerophon and the Chimera, Baucis and Philemon, Perseus and Medusa; these, I think, will be enough to make up a volume. As a framework, I shall have a young college student telling these stories to his cousins and brothers and sisters, during his vacations, sometimes at the fireside, sometimes in the woods and dells. Unless I greatly mistake, these old fictions will work up admirably for the purpose; and I shall aim at substituting a tone in some degree Gothic or romantic, or any such tone as may best please myself, instead of the classic coldness, which is as repellant as the touch of marble.

"I give you these hints of my plan, because you will perhaps think it advisable to employ Billings to prepare some illustrations. There is a good scope in the above subjects for fanciful designs. Bellerophon and the Chimera, for instance: the Chimera a fantastic monster with three heads, and Bellerophon fighting him, mounted on Pegasus; Pandora opening the box; Hercules talking with Atlas, an enormous giant who holds the sky on his shoulders, or sailing across the sea in an immense bowl; Perseus transforming a king and all his subjects to stone, by exhibiting the Gorgon's head. No particular accuracy in costume need be aimed at. My stories will bear out the artist in any liberties he may be inclined to take. Billings would do these things well enough, though his characteristics are grace and delicacy rather than wildness of fancy. The book, if it comes out of my mind as I see it now, ought to have pretty wide success amongst young people; and, of course, I shall purge out all the old heathen wickedness, and put in a moral wherever practicable. For a title how would this do: 'A Wonder-Book for Girls and Boys'; or, 'The Wonder-Book of Old Stories'? I prefer the former. Or 'Myths Modernized for my Children'; that won't do.

"I need a little change of scene, and meant to have come to Boston and elsewhere before writing this book; but I cannot leave home at present."

Throughout the summer Hawthorne was constantly worried by people who insisted that they, or their families in the present or past generations, had been deeply wronged in "The House of the Seven Gables." In a note, received from him on the 5th of June, he says:–

"I have just received a letter from still another claimant of the Pyncheon estate. I wonder if ever, and how soon, I shall get a just estimate of how many jackasses there are in this ridiculous world. My correspondent, by the way, estimates the number of these Pyncheon jackasses at about twenty; I am doubtless to be remonstrated with by each individual. After exchanging shots with all of them, I shall get you to publish the whole correspondence, in a style to match that of my other works, and I anticipate a great run for the volume.

"P.S. My last correspondent demands that another name be substituted, instead of that of the family; to which I assent, in case the publishers can be prevailed on to cancel the stereotype plates. Of course you will consent! Pray do!"

Praise now poured in upon him from all quarters. Hosts of critics, both in England and America, gallantly came forward to do him service, and his fame was assured. On the 15th of July he sends me a jubilant letter from Lenox, from which I will copy several passages:–

"Mrs. Kemble writes very good accounts from London of the reception my two romances have met with there. She says they have made a greater sensation than any book since 'Jane Eyre'; but probably she is a little or a good deal too emphatic in her representation of the matter. At any rate, she advises that the sheets of any future book be sent to Moxon, and such an arrangement made that a copyright may be secured in England as well as here. Could this be done with the Wonder-Book? And do you think it would be worth while? I must see the proof-sheets of this book. It is a cursed bore; for I want to be done with it from this moment. Can't you arrange it so that two or three or more sheets may be sent at once, on stated days, and so my journeys to the village be fewer?

"That review which you sent me is a remarkable production. There is praise enough to satisfy a greedier author than myself. I set it aside, as not being able to estimate how far it is deserved. I can better judge of the censure, much of which is undoubtedly just; and I shall profit by it if I can. But, after all, there would be no great use in attempting it. There are weeds enough in my mind, to be sure, and I might pluck them up by the handful; but in so doing I should root up the few flowers along with them. It is also to be considered, that what one man calls weeds another classifies among the choicest flowers in the garden. But this reviewer is certainly a man of sense, and sometimes tickles me under the fifth rib. I beg you to observe, however, that I do not acknowledge his justice in cutting and slashing among the characters of the two books at the rate he does; sparing nobody, I think, except Pearl and Phœbe. Yet I think he is right as to my tendency as respects individual character.

"I am going to begin to enjoy the summer now, and to read foolish novels, if I can get any, and smoke cigars, and think of nothing at all; which is equivalent to thinking of all manner of things."

The composition of the "Tanglewood Tales" gave him pleasant employment, and all his letters, during the period he was writing them, overflow with evidences of his felicitous mood. He requests that Billings should pay especial attention to the drawings, and is anxious that the porch of Tanglewood should be "well supplied with shrubbery." He seemed greatly pleased that Mary Russell Mitford had fallen in with his books and had written to me about them. "Her sketches," he said, "long ago as I read them, are as sweet in my memory as the scent of new hay." On the 18th of August he writes:–

"You are going to publish another thousand of the Seven Gables. I promised those Pyncheons a preface. What if you insert the following?

"(The author is pained to learn that, in selecting a name for the fictitious inhabitants of a castle in the air, he has wounded the feelings of more than one respectable descendant of an old Pyncheon family. He begs leave to say that he intended no reference to any individual of the name, now or heretofore extant; and further, that, at the time of writing his book, he was wholly unaware of the existence of such a family in New England for two hundred years back, and that whatever he may have since learned of them is altogether to their credit.)

"Insert it or not, as you like. I have done with the matter."

I advised him to let the Pyncheons rest as they were, and omit any addition, either as note or preface, to the romance.

Near the close of 1851 his health seemed unsettled, and he asked me to look over certain proofs "carefully," for he did not feel well enough to manage them himself. In one of his notes, written from Lenox at that time, he says:–

"Please God, I mean to look you in the face towards the end of next week; at all events, within ten days. I have stayed here too long and too constantly. To tell you a secret, I am sick to death of Berkshire, and hate to think of spending another winter here. But I must. The air and climate do not agree with my health at all; and, for the first time since I was a boy, I have felt languid and dispirited during almost my whole residence here. O that Providence would build me the merest little shanty, and mark me out a rood or two of garden-ground, near the sea-coast. I thank you for the two volumes of De Quincey. If it were not for your kindness in supplying me with books now and then, I should quite forget how to read."

Hawthorne was a hearty devourer of books, and in certain moods of mind it made very little difference what the volume before him happened to be. An old play or an old newspaper sometimes gave him wondrous great content, and he would ponder the sleepy, uninteresting sentences as if they contained immortal mental aliment. He once told me he found such delight in old advertisements in the newspaper files at the Boston Athenæum, that he had passed delicious hours among them. At other times he was very fastidious, and threw aside book after book until he found the right one. De Quincey was a special favorite with him, and the Sermons of Laurence Sterne he once commended to me as the best sermons ever written. In his library was an early copy of Sir Philip Sidney's "Arcadia," which had floated down to him from a remote ancestry, and which he had read so industriously for forty years that it was nearly worn out of its thick leathern cover. Hearing him say once that the old English State Trials were enchanting reading, and knowing that he did not possess a copy of those heavy folios, I picked up a set one day in a bookshop and sent them to him. He often told me that he spent more hours over them and got more delectation out of them than tongue could tell, and he said, if five lives were vouchsafed to him, he could employ them all in writing stories out of those books. He had sketched, in his mind, several romances founded on the remarkable trials reported in the ancient volumes; and one day, I remember, he made my blood tingle by relating some of the situations he intended, if his life was spared, to weave into future romances. Sir Walter Scott's novels he continued almost to worship, and was accustomed to read them aloud in his family. The novels of G. P. R. James, both the early and the later ones, he insisted were admirable stories, admirably told, and he had high praise to bestow on the works of Anthony Trollope. "Have you ever read these novels?" he wrote to me in a letter from England, some time before Trollope began to be much known in America. "They precisely suit my taste; solid and substantial, written on the strength of beef and through the inspiration of ale, and just as real as if some giant had hewn a great lump out of the earth and put it under a glass case, with all its inhabitants going about their daily business and not suspecting that they were made a show of. And these books are as English as a beefsteak. Have they ever been tried in America? It needs an English residence to make them thoroughly comprehensible; but still I should think that the human nature in them would give them success anywhere."

I have often been asked if all his moods were sombre, and if he was never jolly sometimes like other people. Indeed he was; and although the humorous side of Hawthorne was not easily or often discoverable, yet have I seen him marvellously moved to fun, and no man laughed more heartily in his way over a good story. Wise and witty H——, in whom wisdom and wit are so ingrained that age only increases his subtle spirit, and greatly enhances the power of his cheerful temperament, always had the talismanic faculty of breaking up that thoughtfully sad face into mirthful waves; and I remember how Hawthorne writhed with hilarious delight over Professor L——'s account of a butcher who remarked that "Idees had got afloat in the public mind with respect to sassingers." I once told him of a young woman who brought in a manuscript, and said, as she placed it in my hands, "I don't know what to do with myself sometimes, I'm so filled with *mammoth thoughts*." A series of convulsive efforts to suppress explosive laughter followed, which I remember to this day.

He had an inexhaustible store of amusing anecdotes to relate of people and things he had observed on the road. One day he described to me, in his inimitable and quietly ludicrous manner, being *watched,* while on a visit to a distant city, by a friend who called, and thought he needed a protector, his health being at that time not so good as usual. "He stuck by me," said Hawthorne, "as if he were afraid to leave me alone; he stayed past the dinner hour, and when I began to wonder if he never took meals himself, he departed and set another man to *watch* me till he should return. That man *watched* me so, in his unwearying kindness, that when I left the house I forgot half my luggage, and left behind, among other things, a beautiful pair of slippers. They *watched* me so, among them, I swear to you I forgot nearly everything I owned."

—*Yesterdays with Authors,* pp. 58–64

Hawthorne's novels elicited appreciative articles about his fiction generally. An early general assessment of Hawthorne's career is by Amory Dwight Mayo (1823–1907), at the time the pastor of the Independent Christian church in Gloucester, Massachusetts.

The Works of Nathaniel Hawthorne
Amory Dwight Mayo
Universalist Quarterly and General Review, 8 (July 1851): 272–293

If an essential qualification for a critic of an American novelist, be a thorough acquaintance with our national fictitious literature, we shall not claim the title. Whether it be a cause for congratulation or compassion we leave for more persevering readers than ourselves to decide; but we have only a limited knowledge of what native writers here achieved in this department. Yet we owe many pleasant days to the few it has been our privilege to read. One important recollection of our boyhood would be lost, should we forget the old circulating library in which were a few volumes of Sedgwick and Cooper. It is still pleasing to think of the vivacity of incident in *Redwood, Saratoga,* and *Hope Leslie,* although the individual personages of the story have faded from our remembrance—all but one; for Miss Sedgwick has done what no other writer of our acquaintance has accomplished, given a full-length and accurate portrait of a New-England 'Old Maid,' in *Aunt Deborah.* Cooper's Indians and stereotyped pair of heroines yet live dimly in our memory, with the revolutionary cocked

Amory Dwight Mayo (Unitarian Universalism Archives)

hat and warhorse, which has done so good service in his and other romances of our early history; while Leather Stocking must rejoice that he at last is relieved from the inconvenience of a yearly resurrection, to live again through two volumes of strange faces and scenes. Yet there is a charm of sensuous life in Cooper's pages, especially in his tales of the sea, which will preserve his books these many years.

We have always blessed the providence that sent us, at eighteen, to an academy in the valley of the Connecticut, and showed us the shelf on which reposed the long row of Irving's charming books. For surely Irving was made to write for those who have not yet lost their youth. A perpetual boy himself, he has lived and seen the world, only that he might gather wandering sunbeams and imprison them in his transparent pages; reproduce the manners of at least one original state of society, and coax us along sunny paths into the graver domain of History. The merit of Irving is, that he has told us how the life of the past and the present appear to a man of cheerful temperament and appreciating

taste. And in these days of analysis and overturn, who will not thank him that gives us the dear old world of our youth with all its mellow shades and gleaming distances, so perfect that we for a while forget that its right even to exist is fiercely debated in every village lyceum. We also acknowledge a debt of gratitude to the author of *Philothia,* and would ask how many American readers know there is such a book as *Monaldi,* written by the artist Allston,–a work of art, which will not suffer by comparison with his pictures. The *Paul Felton* of Dana, is a tale, in tragic power and spiritual insight, unrivalled in the literature of our land. Among the crowd of agreeable writers of later date, we only know Mr Judd, and Professor Longfellow. The author of *Margaret* and *Richard Edney,* possesses many admirable qualities for a novelist of New England life; a portion of *Margaret* being very true to its homliest [*sic*] aspects. But a lack of artistic power renders his vast accumulation of materials often a hindrance, while his philosophical theories drift him away into the apocryphal land of model churches and improved republics. Yet his books should be read by every body who can appreciate their thought, always subtle and often profound; their vivid portraiture of manners, and fine moral intuitions. We suppose the graceful stories of Mr Longfellow are only valuable, in his own eyes, for their gems of thought and sentiment. We admire the art which can expand a book of apothegms into a delightful summer-day's reading, carrying us along the path of narrative as by easy stages from one to another of these places of 'entertainment' for our best faculties and feelings. This writer has not only brought a religious philosophy of life from 'heaven to earth,' but made it an indispensable guest of the drawing room, and the most agreeable companion of our leisure hours.

But we must not linger over recollections, like these, while the name of Hawthorne stands at the head of our page. In the remarks we propose to make on this author, there are no pretensions to an exhaustive criticism. It is more than a spring-day's journey to walk around the boundaries, and explore all the paths of his remarkable mind; and he who would attempt to do it, may be compelled to reverse his decision by a deeper insight into his books, or a new manifestation of his power. We only say that we have faithfully read the half-dozen volumes by which he is known, and will try to convey the impression they leave upon our mind. The task of describing their contents and quoting fine passages, we leave to the newspapers. We write for those who have read, and, like ourselves, wish to talk an hour of 'things seen and heard' in this new world of genius.

The first thing which attracts our notice upon these pages, is the acuteness and extent of the writer's power of observation. His eye adjusts itself to objects beyond and within the ordinary circle of vision. Wherever he looks, he sees distinctly, and the sweep of his gaze comprehends a wide area. His perception of beauty in nature is singularly keen and comprehensive. He paints an object in the light as with sunbeams, while the shadow or the transition to it are transferred with equal fidelity. We think the works of few poets will present so accurate and extensive portraiture of nature as his; of living nature, for he sees the characteristic points in a landscape, and in a high degree possesses the Spenserian power of transforming, by one magic word, a lifeless pictured catalogue of natural objects, to an actual breathing and moving scene. Perhaps he dwells with more fondness upon the minute and evanescent, than the grand and substantial in nature. Yet he is not incompetent to interpret its noble appearances.

The same clearness of vision he carries into life. He has a vivid perception of historical events and periods, no less than of the actual existence of to-day. He pictures a street with such fidelity that we walk upon its pavements, elbow our way through its shadowy throngs, and raise our voices above the chatter of omnibus wheels, to shout into ghostly ears. Whether it be little Ned Higgins offering his cent to Hebzibah for the gingerbread Jim Crow–'the one that has not a broken foot,' or Peter Goldthwaite swinging his axe through the cloud of dust in his own attic, or Hester Prynne walking to the scene of public exposure, wearing the scarlet letter upon her bosom, or Judge Pyncheon sitting dead in the low-studded room, with the mouse at his foot, and grimalkin looking in at the window, and the fly walking across his naked eyeball, or the crowd of dancers in the hall of the old Province-House, and the shadowy procession of governors down its steps,–everywhere is the same wonderful daguerreotyping of the facts, and the same reproduction of the essential principle of life, which is the chief fact of the spectacle.

His eye does not fail, but increases in power, when directed to the world of thought and feeling. Mr Hawthorne's books are tables of spiritual statistics, embracing the natural history of the human mind in its ordinary, but oftener in its extraordinary conditions. One would think he had ransacked the experience of all the men, women and children in his neighborhood, been the chaplain of the state prison and madhouse, beside having telegraphic intelligence of the mental state of every out-of-the-way, queer creature in the land. He is a man to whom we would not care to talk an hour if we had any secrets, for as sure as we have a tongue, without invitation we should tell them all to him, even on the top of a mail coach, or in the Merchants' Exchange. If he ever seems to overlook common traits of character, or ordinary states of mind, it is

Brian Waller Procter (1787–1874) was a popular English writer who wrote under the name of Barry Cornwall; he was chiefly known as a writer of songs and lyrics. It is not known which of his books he sent Hawthorne.

LONDON, Nov. 6, 1851.

DEAR SIR,–I have ventured to send you a little book of mine, principally because it is a pleasure to me to do so, a little perhaps in the hope of pleasing *you*. Being desirous of drawing closer the acquaintance which I some time ago formed with you, through the medium of Mrs. Butler, afterwards through your books, I can hit upon no better method than this that I have adopted. It is a long way to send such a trifle; but I foresee that you have more than even the author's good-nature, and will accept graciously my little venture.

Your two last books have become very popular here. For my own part, I have read them with great pleasure; and you will not be displeased, I think, when I tell you that whilst I was reading your last book ("The House with the Seven Gables"), the turn of the thought or phrase often brought my old friend Charles Lamb to my recollection.

I entertain the old belief that one may know a good deal of an author (independently of his genius or capacity, I mean) from his works. And if you or Mr. Longfellow should assert that you are not the men that you really *are*, why, I shall turn a deaf ear to the averment, and put you both to the proof.

Farewell, my dear sir! I wish you all possible success in the world of letters, where you already look so long-lived and robust, and in all other worlds and circles where you desire to be held in affection or respect.

Believe me to be your very sincere

B. W. PROCTER.

–Hawthorne and his Wife, pp. 440–441

only from the absorbing interest attached to half developed germs of individuality, and flitting or profound spiritual appearances. Like all soul-gazers, he loves to walk along the dim labyrinthine passages of the mind, and poke his head into its cobwebbed closets, and clamber up stairways which are peculiarly unsafe. At all the critical moments of life–when a man is trying to choke down his confession of love, or holds his first child in his arms, or topples over into the gulf of some terrible sin, he is sure to be a spectator. Yet in moments of less intensity he loves to hear a child prattle, or the old gravestone-cutter of Martha's Vineyard gossip over his epitaphs, or the six vagabonds in the moving show-car retail their miscellaneous experience.

But he looks further than this. Nature, life, and the soul are only the foreground in his perspective, for beyond them he sees those spiritual laws, which sweep down ages of time, athwart the world, cross each other without confusion and almost annihilate human freedom by their fatal execution. All things are guarded by these relentless keepers, and if they ever escape for a moment, a million of eyes track the fugitives, and an unseen power compels them to walk of their own accord back through their open prison doors. We believe the faculty which perceives the invisible highways of God running up and down the universe, is the author's rarest gift,—more than any other, modifies the ordinary operations of his mind, and is the source of the chief characteristics in his method of delineation.

The human mind may be regarded from two points of observation. First, it may be contemplated as free, acting from volitions self-suggested or voluntarily adopted. It then assumes a definite individuality, and is not radically implicated with any other species of existence. It stands apart from nature, other souls, and the Deity, and by sheer will and energy creates a world of its own. Material agencies become its servants, life rearranges itself to form the scenery of its stage of action, the thoughts and purposes of other men receive a determined impress from its commanding influence, and even the progress of the spiritual world towards harmony may be accelerated or retarded by its conclusions. This view, consciously or unconsciously held, is the source of all human activity. No man acts truly and strongly who does not feel, at the time, that he is an individual; that he can make his mark upon nature, life, and other minds, and that his conduct does in some way affect the well being of the race. We are born with this innate and irreducible conviction, which in spite of the philosophers, has the same practical influence upon men to-day as upon the first man.

Yet this practical view of the human mind is not supported by the results of profound reasoning and observation. The eye trained to look beneath the outer shell of life, regards the soul as subject to influences which encompass it and insinuate themselves into its structure. The fatalist gathers up these influences into the idea of Destiny, the Christian, into the idea of Providence. The latter believes that God, in some way inexplicable to man, lives in his universe, and causes his will to be done through all modes and qualities of finite action. His regular appearances in the material and mental world are the laws of nature and life.

The more carefully and profoundly we examine the soul, with the aid of experience and history, the more does the conviction deepen that it exists amid this network of laws, from which it cannot free itself, which are perhaps the very outward conditions of its existence. These laws, of course, are very imperfectly understood. A few of the more obvious are perceived in their ordinary relations, others are seen only as the curve of a circle sweeping off into the darkness, and the existence of others is inferred by suggestions too subtle to be stated, but sufficiently weighty while held in the mind to command respect. In view of this method of Providential government, individuality has less distinctness of outline. The race is an organic body. Each man lives with the thought, affections, and will of all other men. Traits of character go down the line of families and generations, reappearing often enough to prove that this influence was never lost. The virtues of a man or nation, flower in the posterity of another century. The sin of a people or an individual, chases its descendants through ages of time.

This view of the soul and its relations to spiritual laws, gives a peculiar value to life and nature. The outward facts of history, and the ordinary appearances of life, depend, in an intimate and inexplicable manner, upon the operations of great Providential agencies. Outward existence becomes symbolical, and its changes correspond to motions of the life within. Its apparent fantastic and careless groups are the types of individual mental processes, and a thousand men in the street unconsciously act, in a regular drama, the most secret life of each human spirit. And nature also becomes symbolical of life. Its objects and appearances furnish man with language, its scenery changes a thousand times a day in obedience to his moods, as if the eye that saw him was related to a hand that reproduced on the canvas of the heaven, the ocean or the earth, with stars, foliage, waves, colors, perfumes and sounds, his perfect transcript.

But this view of the soul, though resting upon the most profound thoughts of the highest minds, is not the ordinary one. Yet an almost unconscious sense of the fact is the foundation both of religion and superstition. By the ordinary events of life, a reflecting man becomes convinced of the existence of forces and influences which circumscribe his activity and interfere with the assumption of his omnipotent individuality. If he accepts this fact cheerfully, and with obedient and faithful conformity to what it teaches, he arrives at the Christian idea of Providence, and although not competent to explain either the causes of his belief or the philosophy of divine and human agency, becomes, by an exercise of faith, a Christian. Otherwise his occasional glimpses of the tremendous operation of spiritual laws, appals him, distracts his mind, upsets his plans, and unsettles his faith. He becomes superstitious, and lives in a world filled with ghosts, demons, spiritual rappings, and vulgar and philosophic bugbears. For, a spiritual law, seen a moment through the fog which encircles such a man's mind, becomes a witch, a devil, or an angel.

There is a time in every man's life, and one sensitive spot in every man's nature, when this riddle of freedom and fate becomes painfully manifest. But the natural impulse is to get out of crises into the common way of life, and look away from that place in the soul where disorder has established its permanent rule. Indeed, the penalty of fixing the gaze upon either of these appearances is weakness, disease, and insanity. Now and then a man is born who can look straight down into the spirit without searing his eyeballs, witness this awful conflict of law and will, trace its results, know the impotence as well as the strength of man, and not lose his balance of mind, or health of affections. One poet alone looked through the length and breadth and depth of life, and unscared by the awful spectacle, with the ease and joy of a little child, wove a few of its groupings into dramas, by which all the poets in the world now swear. But this could not be until a greater than man had affirmed the paternity of God, and by the revelation of Christianity at once secured the welfare of the race, and widened to infinity the possibilities of art. Christianity alone made a Shakspeare possible, for no human creature without peril of insanity, could have looked so deeply into the very heart of existence, unless guarded by its love and faith, and arched over by is firmament of immortal hopes.

Among the few American writers who have the peculiarity of genius which consists of insight into this fact of the soul, Mr Hawthorne occupies a prominent position. We are convinced that the rarest quality of his mind is the power of tracing the relations of spiritual laws to character. He looks at the soul, life, and nature, from the stand-point of Providence. He follows the track of one of God's mental or moral laws. Every thing which appears along its borders is minutely investigated, though sometimes appreciated rather for its nearness to his path than its own value. If we mistake not, this is the clue to all his works. Even his lightest tale gains a peculiarity of treatment and depth of tone from it, though the tendency of his mind is better perceived in his more elaborate works. Wherever he goes, whoever he meets, or whatever may be the scenes amid which he mingles, this thought is uppermost:—How are these things related to each other, and to those great spiritual agencies which underlie and encompass them? Whatever else Mr Hawthorne may be, and we do not deny to him great versatility of powers, he is, more than any thing else, a seer.

His view of human nature determines his treatment of individuals. He can hardly be called a truthful delineator of character. His men and women have the elements of life, though not arranged in harmonious proportions. Our interest is concentrated upon the point, in the nature of each, where the battle is raging

between human will and spiritual laws. How far has the man obeyed or disobeyed these rules of life, by what process is he receiving reward or retribution, does he accept or resist it, and how are other men implicated in his fate,—are the chief objects of inquiry. A few remarkable exceptions to this mode of treatment will not disturb this assertion. His people either enlist our admiration by a single intense devotion to some high purpose, or compel our sympathies by their struggles to escape the ruin which their own sins or errors have invited. They are analyzed, rather than created, and we obtain from them the impression received from a crowd elated beyond measure by some absorbing enthusiasm, or writhing under the infliction of some terrible chastisement. An artist who should fill his gallery with portraits of inmates of lunatic asylums, disciples of Miller in their ascension robes, and orators at the top of their happiest climax, would hardly be regarded as a correct delineation of the human face, neither will consummate skill of analysis and execution redeem the ghostly family of our author's spiritual offspring from the charge of untruth to a healthy nature.

And his pictures of life are generally from the same point of view. He shows us a street, a domestic circle, a public assembly, or a whole village, describes them with wonderful fidelity, yet just as we think we have them securely located upon solid ground, by one magic sentence the whole is transmuted to a symbolic picture, and a witch element in the atmosphere makes us doubt whether we are not in dream-land. Even the beautiful introductions to the *Mosses from an old Manse,* and *The Scarlet Letter,* are tinged with this peculiarity. The concord there, is hardly the one that appears from the rail-track; and the Salem custom-house and its inmates, are judged from that point whence we all should put on a somewhat sorry aspect, whence the mercantile life of New England especially will not bear severe criticism. An observing reader will be struck by this tendency to symbolism on every page of these books.

So nature is regarded oftener by him in its relations to the human mind, and mental and moral laws, than as existing for any independent purpose. His exquisite pencilling of her beautiful scenes is generally illustrative of the person who is the central figure of the landscape. His winds howl a warning through open doors on the advent of some critical moment. 'Alice's Posies,' and 'The Pyncheon Elm,' the garden of *The House of the Seven Gables,* the wood where Hester and Dimmesdale talked, and the midnight sky, seen by the minister from the pillory, all prefigure in outline and detail the spiritual states of those who lived among them. No strange cat walks across a path, no mouse ventures out of the wainscot, no robin sings

Hawthorne's inscription to his children in A Wonder-Book *(American Art Association Anderson Galleries catalogue,* Richard C. Manning, *sale number 4296, 28–29 January 1937; reprinted in* Hawthorne at Auction, *p. 290)*

Frontispiece for A Wonder-Book for Girls and Boys, *an engraving by William J. Baker from a design by Hammatt Billings (Library of Congress)*

The Publication of *A Wonder-Book*

A Wonder-Book for Girls and Boys, *a series of linked stories, was published on 8 November 1851. None of the contents of the volume had previously appeared in magazines or other books: "Preface," "Tanglewood Porch, Introductory . . . ," "'The Gorgon's Head,' Tanglewood Porch, After . . . ," "Shadow Brook, Introductory . . . ," "The Golden Touch," "Shadow Brook, After . . . ," "Tanglewood Play-room, Introductory . . . ," "The Paradise of Children," "Tanglewood Play-room After . . . ," "Tanglewood Fireside, Introductory . . . ," "The Three Golden Apples," "Tanglewood Fireside, After . . . ," "The Hill-side, Introductory . . . ," "The Miraculous Pitcher," "The Hill-side, After . . . ," "Bald-summit, Introductory . . . ," "The Chimaera," and "Bald-summit, After the Story."*

upon the house-top, or bee dives into a squash blossom, which does not know its business and fulfil its destiny, in his drama.

This prominent tendency in Mr Hawthorne's mind, at times assumes the form of disease. Doubtless the most profound, and from an angel's point of view, the truest estimate of man, life and nature, is that in which they are woven into a spectacle illustrative of spiritual laws. God is indeed 'above all, through all, and in all,' yet this doctrine must be held in connection with all we have before said of man's consciousness of freedom, or it becomes a false statement of our relations to Providence. No man can reconcile this apparent contradiction, but any man knows that he must stand by himself, or go adrift to foolishness and ruin. Therefore this Providential view of life cannot legitimately occupy the foreground in a correct delineation of existence, but should rather be the mountain range, and the horizon line, and the forces beneath the surface; and he who ignores the more obvious relations of the spirit, to live always near its central blaze, must obtain and impart false impressions, and become an unfit medium for its complete interpretation. So is it to a degree with Mr Hawthorne. A tendency to disease in his nature, appears in the fearful intensity of his narratives. There is also a sort of unnaturalness in his world. It is seen not in the noon-day sun, so often as by moonbeams, and by auroral or volcanic lights. All he describes may and does actually happen, but something else happens, by the omission of which we fail sometimes to acknowledge the reality of his delineation. This tendency appears in many of the tales in the *Mosses from an Old Manse,* and reached its climax in *The Scarlet Letter.* In *The House of the Seven Gables,* we see the author struggling out of its grasp, with a vigor which we believe ensures a final recovery.

The constitution of Mr Hawthorne's mind, in other respects, is admirably calculated to fit him for his primary office of seer. For all danger of the godless or misanthropic spirit, which so often destroys men who know much of human nature, is averted by his great affections. He follows the track of a spiritual law into the darkest or wildest scene, without losing his faith in God, or his love for humanity. With an impressibility that makes him alive even to the buttons of his over-coat, with the quickest insight through motives, and the sophistry of sin, and an overpowering sense of the ludicrous, he never loses his human sympathies. He looks upon the spectacle of existence, with the same pensive smile always upon his face, changing only to a more touching gleam of joy and sadness. He is one whose eye we feel upon our souls, yet to whom we cheerfully confide their treasures. His humor, too, seems only a part of his great love, so innocently does it play over the surface of every thing he touches; it is beyond our power to analyze it, and were it not, we are sure we should hardly risk the loss of a tithe of the pleasure we receive from it, by the attempt. We know of no modern writer who holds us so completely at his will in this respect; not Emerson, or Lamb. Neither he, nor his readers, can ever be thrown into utter desperation, for thought of the very absurdity of the position.

In addition to these qualities, Mr Hawthorne is largely gifted with the higher forms of imagination. Were we a metaphysician, we might guess at its quality, and perhaps discover that the very spiritual insight of which we have been talking, is essentially imaginative. Be this as it may, he also possesses that form of the divine faculty which makes him alive in every corner of his soul, and that which gives him the power of vivid portraiture, also, to a considerable degree, the higher gift by which the poet weaves the deepest realities of life into an airy picture for artistic contemplation. A true poet is not ensnared in his own work, but has it at arm's length, and finally places it out of immediate contact with our sympathies, into the region of art. It is this which distinguishes the artist from the philanthropist. The latter gives us a picture of human happiness and wretchedness, which appeals only to our conscience and disturbs us sleeping and waking; the former uses the same materials, and creates the same groups, yet by a power of his own, forces it to appeal to our sense of beauty, and become a perpetual source of delight. There is no untruth in this. We do not ignore the moral relations of the work by thus acknowledging that God is both the all-good and the all-beautiful. We do not ascribe this power to Mr Hawthorne in the highest degree. Portions of his work are faultless, yet we have not in any case the sense, either of that completeness or entire beauty which declares a man a poet. Even in creative imagination, Mr Hawthorne is not deficient. Amid the throng of half human generalizations, we catch a glimpse occasionally of a true poetic creation. Phœbe is the only New England girl we ever met in a book, and Pearl is a new comer into the world of poetry. We yet hope to witness greater evidences of our author's power in this direction. We must also speak of his style, as a development of his imaginative life. It is truly original and admirable. We read page after page, till, satiated with its harmony and beauty, we lose all hold upon the narrative, and make it a substitute for a diorama or a concert.

Yet, though we hazard a little in saying it, it does seem to us that the final impression of these books is not poetical so decidedly as religious. The author sings, but sings oratorios and hymns. He paints, yet paints the 'spiritual body' and the world of souls. We regard him as a religious novelist, in a high and peculiar sense. He does not, like the tribe of disguised parsons who have broken into the realm of letters, write books and sew together men and women of paste-board, to illustrate artificial and arbitrary creeds, of rules of conduct. Neither like the able class which swears by Goethe, does he give a picture of actual life faithful in every particular, leaving the reader to find its law and morality; but he lays bare those spiritual laws of God to which we must conform, and with wonderful distinctness describes the soul's relations to them. His eye looks through reputation, cloth, and gold, even through an animal consciousness of sanctity, to the bottom of a man's soul, and with prophetic insight shows us retribution even in the act of wickedness. And this is done in no spirit of irreverence. A reverent atmosphere broods over his world, and everywhere we hear the footsteps and voice of God. Surely, faults of execution, or extravagances of statement, may be pardoned to one who can show Americans, in the nineteenth century, that the Deity is alive and in their midst. We shall have many an artist of the beautiful, many a poet and skilful writer of romance, before another seer, like Hawthorne, will come into the realm of polite literature, and overpower our admiration by awe and love, making us forget the beauty of the temple into which we are led, while we kneel in worship before the altar.

This estimate of Mr Hawthorne may not be a complete appreciation of his genius, yet it seems to us, verified by the most careful perusal we are able to give his books. These works display, from first to last, the same characteristic peculiarities, the difference between them being only that of progress; for lightly as the author appears to regard his earlier productions, we think a critical eye can see in them the prophecy of all, and more, than he has yet done.

There are few books in English literature more valuable as a pledge of eminence than the *Twice-told Tales*. The sketches are short, and often carelessly executed, yet display remarkable felicity of handling, delicacy of outlining, purity and flexibility of style, and insight into the working of spiritual laws and the dark corners of life and character. The ruling propensity of the writer here assumes the form of a love for the mysterious, and becomes almost an element of fatalism in his philosophy. Each of his shadowy personages is the slave of a destiny, and we see him only an instant at the point of its culmination. The whole book is written in that uncertain region between the most profound religion and a poetic superstition; too true to be put off among volumes of ghost stories, too highly colored to be valuable as an accurate description of life. Other qualities of mind, to which we have already referred, are here manifested or foreshadowed. Of the forty arti-

cles in these volumes, we have been most strongly impressed by 'The Minister's Black Veil,' 'The Gentle Boy,' 'The Prophetic Pictures,' the entire series of 'Legends of the Province House,' 'The Village Uncle,' 'The Seven Vagabonds,' and 'Peter Goldthwaite's Treasure.'

In the *Mosses from an old Manse,* the same mental characteristics appear in greater maturity of development. The tales of this series show a more decided treatment, more vivid and definite portrayal of character, and a deeper coloring than the writer's previous works. They are to the *Twice-told Tales,* what paintings in oils are to sketches in water colors. The introductory description of the *Old Manse* is not surpassed by any thing of its kind in English literature, and is the best part of the book. Perhaps the unhealthiness of the writer's mind is more prominently exhibited in a few of these stories, than elsewhere. 'The Birth-mark,' 'Rappaccini's Daughter,' and 'Roger Malvin's Burial,' are the nettles and mushrooms of Mr Hawthorne's mind, and certainly should not be tied up with a boquet of flowers for the public. Perhaps we hate these tales the more, that they are bound in the same covers with 'The Celestial Railroad,' and 'Drowne's Wooden Image,' the happiest efforts of the author in sketch writing.

We should be ungrateful for a day of the purest pleasure, did we overlook the next work in this series. Though written for children, the little volume bearing the title of *True Stories* is a book to be read by every body. Here the author has given a striking and connected view of the early history of New England, in a few simple tales related by a grandfather to a group of children. We admire, particularly, the manner in which the salient points of the historical period are seized, the skill of the grouping, the suggestive style of the narrative, the shy, sharp hits at popular vices and follies, and the profound, yet genial morality of the book.

Perhaps four years were never spent to better purpose, than those in Mr Hawthorne's life, between the publication of *Mosses from an old Manse,* and *The Scarlet Letter.* The only account we have of them, is in the sketch of the 'Custom House,' which introduces the latter work. Like most men of genius, our author is not disposed to do full justice to those influences which have powerfully contributed to the growth of his mind. Often when such men are receiving and appropriating most rapidly, they are tormented with a nervous suspicion of the decay of their power. But never was such want of faith more signally rebuked, than in the writer we are reviewing, for we suspect that 'spacious edifice of brick' has seldom been turned to so good use, as by this man who looked through its machinery and its occupants to the facts which they unconsciously represent. The portrait of this place is wonderfully vivid, and from the author's point of observation, doubtless true.

The story so gracefully introduced, is the most remarkable of Mr Hawthorne's works, whether we consider felicity of plot, sustained interest of development, analysis of character, or the witchery of a style which invests the whole with a strange, ethereal beauty. These qualities of the book are so evident, that we now desire to go beneath them to those which make it, in many respects, the most powerful imaginative work of the present era of English literature. No reader possessing the slightest portion of spiritual insight, can fail to perceive that the chief value of this romance is religious. It is an attempt to delineate the involved action of spiritual laws, and their effects upon individual character, with an occasional glimpse into the organization of society. Of course it has been a puzzle to the critics, and a pebble between the teeth of the divines, transcending the artificial rules of the former, and making sad work with the creeds and buckram moralities of the latter.

Standing as *The Scarlet Letter* does, at the junction of several moral highways, it is not easy to grasp the central idea around which it instinctively arranged itself in the author's mind. The most obvious fact upon its pages is, that the only safety for a human soul consists in appearing to be exactly what it is. If holy, it must not wrench itself out of its sphere to become a part in any satanic spectacle; if corrupt, it must heroically stand upon the low ground of its own sinfulness, and rise through penitence and righteousness.

This law of life is exhibited in the contrasted characters of Dimmesdale and Hester. Whatever errors of head or heart, or infelicity of circumstances, prevent Hester from fully realizing the Christian ideal of repentance, she sternly respects her moral relations to society. She embroiders the badge of her own infamy, and without complaint submits to isolation, the pity, scorn and indifference of the world, and the withering of her own nature under the blaze of a noonday exposure to the hot sun of social displeasure; she turns her face toward humanity, and begins the life-long task of beating up to virtue against the pitiless storm which overthrows so many an offender. If the impending fate of the minister forces her to catch at the sole hope of escaping from her penance, and the closing scenes of the drama are necessary to make her an angel of mercy to the very community she had outraged by the sin of her youth, we may in mercy impute her falterings to that infirmity of our nature, which its greatest interpreter has represented by the concession of Isabella to the artifice of Mariana, and the untruth of Desdemona. As far as human fidelity to a spiritual law can go, did Hester live out the fact of the correspondence of seeming and being. Not so with the less heroic partner of her guilt. We cannot deny that all the arguments which may be used to palliate insincerity apply to Dimmes-dale. The voluntary step he must take by confession, was from a more than mortal elevation to a more than human abasement. His constitutional weakness, too, is an excusing circumstance, and especially the genuineness of his repentance up to a certain point. Yet the radical vice of his soul was not submission to his passions, but cowardice; and the reflex action of this cowardice disarranged his whole life, placing him in false relations to the community and the woman he had wronged, and laying open his naked heart to the eye of the demon that was the appointed agent of his final ruin. Of the value of these two persons, considered as accurate delineations of character, nothing very flattering can be said. We see them in the midst of conflict, and in the strife of soul and law many wonderful revelations of human nature appear. Yet a strict fidelity to the engrossing object of the book, renders the author unfaithful to individual humanity. Dimmesdale and Hester are the incarnate action and reaction of the law of sincerity.

Another fact which appears in this book, is the downward tendency of sin; once let a soul be untrue, even though half in ignorance of its duty, and its world is disorganized, so that every step in its new path involves it in greater difficulties. The cardinal error, in this maze of guilt and wretchedness, is Hester's marriage with Chillingworth. She committed that sin which women are every day repeating, though never without retribution, as certain, if not as visible as hers, of giving her hand to a man she did not entirely love. There are souls great and good enough to stand firmly against the recoil of such an act, but Hester was not one of these. Her true husband at last came, and she could only give him a guilty love. By her fatal error she had cut herself off from the power to bless him by her affection as long as God should keep her in the bonds of a false marriage. The proclivity of her former error drove her on to sin again with more obvious consequences, if not with deeper guilt. And then came, in rapid succession, the ruin of Dimmesdale, the transformation of Chillingworth, the transmission of a diseased nature to her child, and the wide spread scandal of a whole community.

And growing out of this act, and its retribution, is the whole question of the relation of the sexes, and the organization of society. The author does not grapple with these intricate problems, though he knows as much of the falsity of what is called marriage, and the unnatural position of woman, as those who are more ready to undertake the cure of the world. And the hypocrisy of Dimmesdale, and the searing of heart in Hester, point to a social state in which purity will exist in connection with a mercy which shall throw no artificial obstacles in the way of a sinner's repentance.

Hawthorne's growing reputation reached into Germany, as is shown by this letter in which German translations of his works are proposed. Nothing came of the project, however.

DRESDEN, STRUVE ST., July 7, 1852.

DEAR SIR,–A countryman of yours, Mr. Motley, has given me your address so far that I hope this letter will reach you. Since the appearance of "The Scarlet Letter" in England, your name has become familiar even to Germany; two translations appeared of it, but written by people who write by the hour for their bread, and could not pay any attention to the style. The purport of this letter is to ask you whether you will kindly send us what you have written before "The Scarlet Letter." An author who will be one of us, we must know from the beginning of his career, to follow him step by step, and see the phases of his mind. You therefore would truly oblige me by collecting what you think will form in future times the complete edition of your works, and forward them to my publisher,–the Chevalier Dunker, in Berlin. And next to this, I should be glad to have the proof sheets of your next work, to prevent the professional translators from making a job of it. You write as if you wrote for Germany. The equality before the law–the moral law as well as the juridical–is the great wish of the women of my country; and you have illustrated this point with the skill of an artist, and a deep knowledge of man's secret motives and feelings. We know "The House of the Seven Gables," which is a lesson to family pride,–a frailty which must lie deep in human nature, since you have been able to trace it even in a free country. What it is with us, with our old aristocracy,–penniless beggars with long names,–you scarcely can imagine. Nevertheless, such a picture as you have drawn is a useful lesson, and will do good here if known in the right quarter. This is unfortunately not now the case, and it is the fault of the translators. Your passages are long, you do not write a racy style to carry on the reader, and in bad language it is impossible to get on with it. Instead of curtailing, they have spun out the matter, and made two volumes of one; and the consequence is that the second remains unread. We must prevent this for the future. Those who read English are enchanted with it; but their number is not large, and ladies are almost alone proficient in foreign languages, and at the same time ladies have no position in Germany.

Believe me that I truly appreciate your great talent, and sincerely wish that we might come to a sort of fusion, and longed-for Literature of the World.

With great regard,

AMELIE BÖTTA.

–Hawthorne and his Wife, pp. 442–443

Another fact more perplexing to a Christian moralist is here illustrated–that a certain experience in sin enlarges the spiritual energies and the power to move the souls of men to noble results. The effects of Dimmesdale's preaching are perfectly credible, and moral, although he stood in false relations to those he addressed. True, the limitation at last came in his public exposure, yet we had almost said he could not have left his mark so deep upon the conscience of that community, had he lived and died otherwise. And Hester's error was the downward step in the winding stair leading to a higher elevation. This feature of the work, so far from being a blemish, is only a proof of the writer's insight, and healthy moral philosophy. He has portrayed sin with all its terrible consequences, yet given the other side of a problem which must excite our wonder, rebuke our shallow theories, and direct us to an all-embracing, infinite love for its solution.

In the character of Chillingworth appears another law,–the danger of cherishing a merely intellectual interest in the human soul. The Leech, is a man of diseased mental acuteness, changed to a demon by yielding to an unholy curiosity. Seduced by the opportunity to know the nature of Dimmesdale, he is drawn to the discovery of the fatal secret,–a discovery which he is not strong enough to bear. His character and fate are an awful rebuke to that insatiable desire for soul-gazing, which is the besetting devil of many men. Our human nature is too sacred to be applied to such uses, and he who enters its guarded enclosure from the mere impulse for intellectual analysis, risks his own soul as surely as he outrages that of another.

Passing from these points of the book to its general moral tone, we find the author's delineation of spiritual laws equalled by his healthy and profound religious sentiment. In justice to human nature, he shows all the palliative circumstances to guilt, while he is sternly true to eternal facts of morality. It is not improper for a novelist to do the former, if he leave the latter uppermost in the mind of the reader. Throughout the work we have not once detected the writer in a concession to that sophistical philanthropy, which, from the vantage-ground of mercy, would pry up the foundation of all religious obligation. His book is a fine contrast to the volumes of a class of modern novelists, who with a large development of the humane sentiment, and an alarming briskness at catching the palliations of transgression, seem to have lost the sense of immutable moral distinctions. One side of Mr Hawthorne's mind would furnish the heads of several first class French romancers. It may be that some of his statements on the side of destiny are too strong, and that human will appears to have a play too limited in his world, yet we look upon such passages rather as exaggerations of his idea of the omnipotence of God's law, than as indications of an irreligious fatalism.

We have already noticed the tendency to a symbolical view of nature and life, in this author's genius. In *The Scarlet Letter,* it supplies the complete frame-work of the story—the age and social state in which the drama is cast being merely subsidiary to it. The gleam of the symbolical letter invests every object with a typical aspect. The lonely shores along which the minister walked, the wood in which he met Hester, the pillory and the street lit up by Mr Wilson's lantern, are seen in the mysterious relation to the characters and plot of the story. But all the symbolism of the tale concentrates in the witch-child, Pearl. She seems to absorb and render back, by each development of her versatile being, the secret nature of every thing with which she comes in contact. She is the microcosm of the whole history with its surroundings. As a poetical creation, we know not where to look for her equal in modern literature. She is the companion of Mignon and Little Nell, more original in conception than either, if not as strong in her hold upon our affections.

As a work of art, this book has great merits, shaded by a few conspicuous faults. We cannot too much admire the skill with which the tangled skein of counteracting law and character is unravelled, the compact arrangement and suggestive disposition of the parts. The analysis of character is also inimitable, and the style is a fit dress for the strange and terrible history it rehearses. Yet we shall be disappointed if we look for any remarkable delineation of character, or portraiture of historical manners. There is a certain ghastliness about the people and life of the book, which comes from its exclusively subjective character and absence of humor. The world it describes is untrue to actual existence; for, although such a tragedy may be acting itself in many a spot upon earth, yet it is hidden more deeply beneath the surface of existence than this, modified by a thousand trivialities, and joys, and humorous interludes of humanity. No puritan city ever held such a throng as stalks through *The Scarlet Letter;* even in a well conducted mad-house, life is not so lurid and intense. The author's love for symbolism occasionally amounts to a ridiculous melo-dramatic perversity, as when it fathers such things as the minister's hand over his heart, and the hideous disfigurement of his bosom, Dame Hibbins from Gov. Bellingham's window screeching after Hester to go into the forest and sign the black man's book, and the meteoric 'A' seen upon the sky during the mid-night vigil.

We must not linger over favorite pages of this remarkable book—a work as unique as powerful, and an addition of no mean value to the permanent literature of the language, but hasten on to a brief notice of the last of the author's romances.

The House of the Seven Gables, is inferior to *The Scarlet Letter* in artistic proportion, compactness and sustained power. It is not a jet of molten ore from a glowing furnace, but a work elaborated in thoughtful leisure, characterized by a more sober colouring, and less intensity of life than its predecessor. Yet whatever value the book may have lost by the absence of one class of peculiarities, is almost restored by the presence of another; for it cannot be denied, that as a whole, it is nearer actual life, and more comprehensively true to human nature, than any former work of its author.

Mr Hawthorne has here attempted to describe the operation of spiritual laws in the midst of the modern life in New England. The tale is the development of the providential retribution for gain unrighteously acquired, while the social problem of aristocracy and democracy naturally branches out from the main idea. *The House of the Seven Gables,* with its central solitudes, its shop door upon the street, and the room of the daguerreotypist in one corner, with the Pyncheon family, well represents the old order in the process of vexatious adjustment to the new. Hepzibah steps across the gulf that divides two social states, in her way from the parlor to the counter. The judge, the sister, and Clifford, each in their own way, represent the phases of a decaying order, while little Phœbe is its point of contact with the new incarnated in Holgrave. To illustrate, in this manner, a strictly moral and social fact, requires a delicacy of handling which might appal one less conscious of power than Mr Hawthorne, and we cannot say that he has done it perfectly. The separate portions are happily executed, but the welding of the parts is not always complete. The analysis of character and evaluation of spiritual forces are unexceptionable, and certainly we have never known such admirable rendering of American life as in many pages of the book; but we are occasionally at a loss to reconcile the two things, and a vague suspicion often haunts us that Pyncheon street is after all in dream-land. Had the romance been kept longer in the author's mind, it would probably not have provoked these strictures, but might have been more evidently a step forward than now.

The characters display the writer's usual habits of delineation. Judge Pyncheon, the type of respectability, with his wide extended influence, his popular philanthropy, his common-place philosophy and his rotten heart; Hepzibah,—ancient gentility gone to seed, toiling in vain to obey the dictates of a good heart and human necessities; and Holgrave, a rickety caricature of the 'good time coming,' are as valueless specimens of individual reality as any of their father's children, yet well enough adapted to be the spokesmen of laws and institutions. Upon the character of Clifford, Mr Hawthorne has evidently wreaked all his acuteness. The result is such a felicity of mental analysis as we never before witnessed. The manner in which this artist-soul, hovering alternately upon the verge of insanity and idiocy, is pictured with all its relations to nature and healthy and diseased mind, is truly amazing. The theory that Clifford is made to suggest, would doubtless be true if a purely artistic spirit ever did or could exist; but since every human being has a heart as well as an imagination, we suspect the moral law must hold yet, in place of its artistic substitute. But we forgive all the offence received from the ghostly family of our author, now that he has given us Phœbe. If he had picked her in pieces, we would have cursed him with all the heartiness of which an angry reader is capable. Thank Heaven, the beautiful creature comes out of the fire unsinged, the loveliest creation of American poetry, the truest delineation of American female character.

The author's propensity to symbolism, is here as strongly marked as elsewhere. The house and the garden, the elm, the street, the shop, Maule's well and Alice's posies, Mammon and Grimalkin, all do good service in the typical 'line.' The conception of the house and garden, is in this respect, one of the happiest in literature. Yet we are compelled occasionally to endure the old offence of melodramatic perversity in the dog-day smile of the Judge, the gurgle in the throat of the Pyncheons, and the ancestral race of hens. Grimalkin and Mammon, however, are genuine creatures. Nothing can be happier than the greediness of the little devil, and nothing out of Shakespeare more terrible than the cat looking through the window at the dead Judge.

In passages, this book is not inferior to any of the author's books. The picture of Maule's execution; the description of the house and garden; Hepzibah opening the shop; the crowd seen from the arched window; the analysis of Clifford; Phœbe waking, walking to church, and becoming conscious of her love in the moonlight arbor, and the death of Judge Pyncheon, present an ever-fresh claim upon our admiration. The style is every way worthy of the theme; and although in some respects inferior to *The Scarlet Letter,* the book has peculiar merits of its own, and is by far the most pleasing of the author's productions.

If in these pages we have done injustice to any of the qualities of Mr Hawthorne's genius, in our desire to present what seems to us its noblest characteristic, we regret the failure the less that it may be the more easily decided than if it were radical. With all the elements of ordinary success in novel-writing, he is the possessor of a higher gift than is often granted to a poet. That he should not yet have subdued his versatile endowments to perfect harmony of action is not strange;–that he has written *The Scarlet Letter,* and *The House of the Seven Gables,* is a new repetition of the perpetually recurring miracle of genius. And it is with a sense of gratitude for what we have received, too sincere for adulation, that we close by giving utterance to the hope of many readers, that yet other works are to come from the same source, in which justice shall be done to individual character, social life, and the eternal laws of Providence. All this in one book he can yet achieve, and on the day when that volume comes from the genial press of Messrs. Ticknor, Reed & Fields, Nathaniel Hawthorne will be the first writer, in the English tongue, of the highest order of romance.

Best known for her sketches of English country life collected as Our Village *(1832), Mary Russell Mitford also wrote poems and plays, such as* Rienzi *(1828). In* Recollections of a Literary Life *(1852) she begins her comments on Hawthorne by remarking on the American showing at the Great Exhibition held at the Crystal Palace in London in 1851.*

Nathaniel Hawthorne
Mary Russell Mitford
Recollections of a Literary Life, pp. 515–520, 525–526, 530–531

In spite of her apparent barrenness at the late Exhibition, a barrenness which probably resulted mainly from the actual riches of that vast country, its prodigious territory, and its still growing youth; in spite of our susceptibilities; and in spite of her own, America is a great nation, and the Americans are a great people; and if that Fair of the World had been a book fair, as at Leipsic, I suspect that we should have seen our kinsfolk over the water cutting a very good figure with their literary ware.

Certain it is, that when a people hardly seventy years old, who have still living among them men that remember when their republic was a province, can claim for themselves such a divine as Dr Channing, and my friend Professor Norton, the friend of Mrs Hemans; such an historian as Mr Prescott; and such an orator as Daniel Webster, they have good right to be proud of their sons of the soil.

To say nothing of these ornaments of our common language, or of the naturalists Wilson and Anderton–are they American? they are worth fighting for; or of the travelers, Dana, Stephens, and Willis, who are certainly transatlantic; or of the fair writers, Mrs Sigourney and

Portrait of Mary Russell Mitford by John Lucas (from
William James Roberts, Mary Russell Milford:
The Tragedy of a Blue Stocking, *1913)*

Miss Sedgwick, both my friends; or of the poor Margaret Fuller, drowned so deplorably only the other day, with her husband and her infant, on her own shores; her Italian husband said only the day before leaving Florence, that it had been predicted to him that he should die at sea; or of the great historian of Spanish literature, Mr Ticknor (another friend!); or of a class of writers in which New England is rich—orator-writers, whose eloquence, first addressed to large audiences, is at once diffused and preserved by the press—witness the orations of Mr Sumner, and the lectures of Mr Whipple and Mr Giles, to say nothing of these volumes, which will bear a competition with any of their class in the elder country, let us look at the living novelists, and see if they be of any ordinary stamp.

The author of the 'Sketch-book' is almost as much a classic with us as in his own country. That book, indeed, and one or two that succeeded it, were so purely English in style and feeling, that when their success—their immense and deserved success—induced the reprint of some drolleries which had for subject New York in its Dutch state, it was difficult to believe that they were by the same author. Since then, Mr Washington Irving, having happily for literature filled a diplomatic post in Spain, has put forth other works, half Spanish, half Moorish, equally full of local color and local history,

books as good as history, that almost make us live in the Alhambra, and increase our sympathy with the tasteful and chivalrous people who planned its halls and gardens. Then he returned home; and there he has done for the backwoods and the prairies what he before did for the manor-house of England and the palace of Granada. Few, very few, can show a long succession of volumes, so pure, so graceful, and so varied as Mr Irving. To my poor cottage, rich only in printed paper, people often come to borrow books for themselves or their children. Sometimes they make their own selection; sometimes, much against my will, they leave the choice to me; and in either case I know no works that are oftener lent than those that bear the pseudonym of Geoffrey Crayon.

Then Mr Cooper! original and natural as his own Pioneers; adventurous as Paul Jones; hardy as Long Tom; persevering and indomitable as the Leather-stocking whom he has conducted through fifteen volumes without once varying from the admirable portrait which he originally designed. They say that he does not value our praise—that he has no appreciation for his appreciators. But I do not choose to believe such a scandal. It can only be a 'they say.' He is too richly gifted to be wanting in sympathy even with his own admirers; and if he have an odd manner of showing that sympathy, why it must pass as 'Pretty Fanny's way.' Since these light words were written, I grieve to say that Mr Cooper is dead. I trust his gifted daughter will become his biographer. Few lives would be more interesting.

Next comes one with whom my saucy pen must take no freedom—one good and grave, and pure and holy—whose works, by their high aim and their fine execution, claim the respect of all. Little known by name, the excellently selected reprints of my friend Mr Chambers have made Mr Ware's letters from Palmyra and from Rome familiar to all, who seek to unite the excitement of an early Christian story, a tale of persecution and of martyrdom, with a style and detail so full of calm and sober learning, that they seem literally saturated with classical lore. So entire is the feeling of scholarship pervading these two books, in one of which Zenobia appears in her beautiful Palmyra a powerful Queen, in the other dragged through the streets of Rome a miserable captive, that we seem to be reading a translation from the Latin. There is not a trace of modern habits or modes of thinking; and if Mr Ware had been possessed by the monomania of Macpherson or of Chatterton, it would have rested with himself to produce these letters as a close and literal version of manuscripts of the third century.

Another talented romancer is Dr Bird, whose two works on the conquest of Mexico have great merit, although hidden behind the mask of most unpromising titles (one of them is called, I think, *Abdallah the Moor, or the*

Infidel's Doom). I never met with any one who had read them but myself, to whom that particular subject has an unfailing interest. His *Nick of the Woods,* a striking but very painful Indian novel, and his description of those wonderful American caves, in which truth leaves fiction far behind, are generally known and duly appreciated.

These excellent writers have been long before the public; but a new star has lately sprung into light in the Western horizon, who in a totally different manner—and nothing is more remarkable among all these American novelists than their utter difference from each other—will hardly fail to cast a bright illumination over both hemispheres. It is hardly two years since Mr Hawthorne, until then known only by one or two of those little volumes which the sagacious hold as promises of future excellence, put forth that singular book, *The Scarlet Letter; àpropos* to which, Dr Holmes, who so well knows the value of words, uses this significant expression:

I *snatch* the book along whose burning leaves
His scarlet web our wild romancer weaves.

And it is the very word. 'We do *snatch* the book;' and until we have got to the end, very few of us, I apprehend, have sufficient strength of will to lay it down.

The story is of the early days of New England; those days when, as Mr Whittier has shown in his clever mystification, called 'Margaret Smith's Journal,' the Pilgrim Fathers, just escaped from persecution in Europe, persecuted those who presumed to follow their example, and to exercise liberty of thought and worship in the new home of freedom. Lamentable inconsistency of human action! Nothing but the strongest historical evidence could make us believe that they who had cast away fortune and country, and every worldly good for conscience sake, should visit with fire and fagot the peaceful Quaker and poor demented creatures accused of witchcraft, and driven by the accusation into the confession, perhaps into a diseased craving for the power and the crime. But so it is. Oppression makes oppression; persecution propagates persecution. There is no end to the evil when once engendered.

The Scarlet Letter is not, however, a story of witch, or of Quaker, although an atmosphere of sorcery seems to pervade the air, but one of that strict and rigid morality peculiar to the Puritans, who loved to visit with legal penalties such sins as are kept in check by public opinion. Accordingly, our first sight of Hester, is exposed upon a scaffold, wearing upon her breast a scarlet A, glittering with gold embroidery, and carrying in her arms a female infant. She had been sent, without her husband, under the protection of some of the elders of the colony, and the punishment was not merely caused by the birth of this child of shame, but by her resolute concealment of the partner of her guilt. Step by step the reader becomes

acquainted with the secret. The participator of her frailty was a young and eloquent preacher, famed not only for learning and talent, but for severe sanctity. The husband arrives under a false character, recognized only by the erring wife, before whom, cruel, vindictive, hating and hateful, he appears as a visible conscience, and the sufferings of the proud and fiery Hester, suffering a daily martyrdom of shame and scorn, and of the seducer perishing under the terrible remorse of undeserved praise, respect, and honor, are among the finest and most original conceptions of tragic narrative. Detestable as the husband is, and with all the passionate truth that Mr Hawthorne has thrown into the long agony of the seducer, we never, in our pity for the sufferer, lose our abhorrence of the sin.

Scarcely a twelvemonth has passed, and another New England story, *The House of the Seven Gables* has come to redeem the pledge of excellence given by the first.

In this tale, Fate plays almost as great a part as in a Greek Trilogy. Two centuries ago, a certain wicked and powerful Colonel Pyncheon, was seized with a violent desire to possess himself of a certain bit of ground, on which to build the large and picturesque wooden mansion from which the story takes its title. Master Maule, the original possessor, obstinate and poor, refused all offers of money for his land; but being shortly afterward accused, no one very well knows why, of the fashionable sin of witchcraft, the poor man is tried, condemned, and burnt; the property forfeited and sold; and the rich man's house erected without let or pause. But the shadow of a great crime has passed over the place. A bubbling spring, famous for the purity and freshness of its waters, turns salt and bitter, and the rich man himself, the great, powerful, wicked Colonel Pyncheon is found dead in his own hall, stricken by some strange, sudden, mysterious death on the very day of his taking possession, and when he had invited half the province to his house-warming. Both proprietors, the poor old wizard, and the wealthy Colonel, leave one child, and during two succeeding centuries these races, always distant and peculiar, come at long intervals strangely across each other.

Nothing can exceed the skill with which this part of the book is managed. The story is not told; we find it out; we feel that there *is* a legend; that some strange destiny has hovered over the old house, and hovers there still. The slightness of the means by which this feeling is excited is wonderful. the mixture of the grotesque and the supernatural in Hoffman and the German School, seems coarse and vulgar blundering in the comparison; even the mighty magician of Udolpho, the Anne Radcliffe whom the French quote with so much unction, was a bungler at her trade, when compared with the vague, dim, vapory, impalpable ghastliness with which Mr Hawthorne has contrived to envelop his narrative.

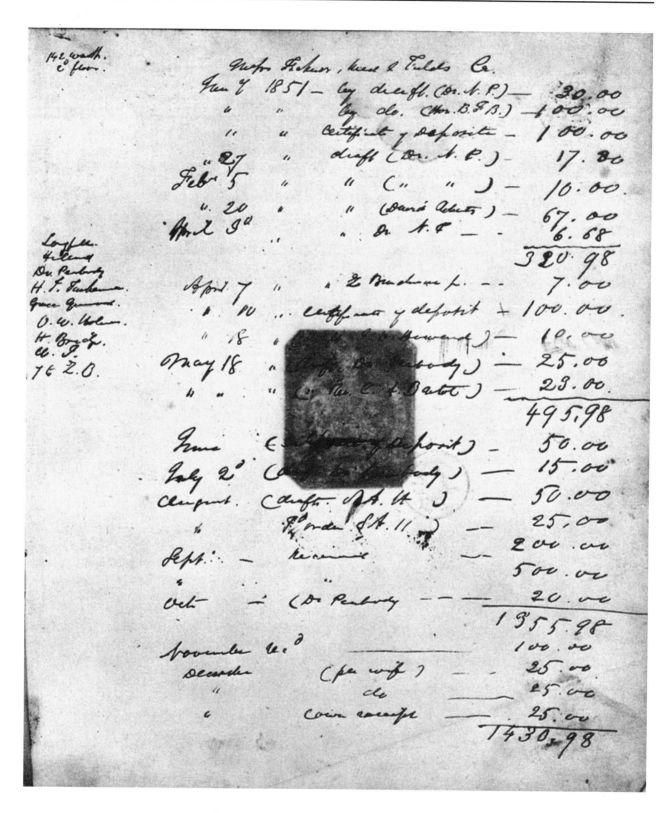

Page from one of Hawthorne's notebooks on which he records various payments made on his behalf by his publishers. The names listed to the left of the bookkeeping entries, beginning with Longfellow, were recipients of complimentary copies of his 1851 volume for children, A Wonder-Book *(MA577, Pierpont Morgan Library).*

Two hundred years have passed. The Maules have disappeared; and the Pyncheons are reduced by the mysterious death of the last proprietor to a poor old maid in extreme poverty, with little left but this decaying mansion; a brother whom she is expecting home after a long, mysterious imprisonment; a Judge, flourishing and prosperous, in whom we at once recognize a true descendant of the wicked Colonel; and a little New England girl, a country cousin, who is the veriest bit of life and light, the brightest beam of sunshine that has ever crossed the Atlantic. Monsier Eugène Sue had some such inspiration when, in his very happiest moment, he painted Rigolette; but this rose is fresher still. Her name (there is a great deal in names, let Juliet say what she will) is Phœbe. I am not going to tell the story of this book, but I must give one glimpse of Phœbe, although it will inadequately convey the charm that extends over the whole volume; and to make that understood, I must say that the poor old cousin Hepzibah, 'Old Maid Pyncheon,' as she is called by her townsfolk—(I wonder whether the Americans do actually bestow upon all their single women that expressive designation: one has some right to be curious as to the titles conferred upon one's order;)—'Old Maid Pyncheon' had that very day, for the purpose, as it afterward appeared, of supporting the liberated prisoner, opened in this aristocratic mansion a little shop;—N.B. I had once a fancy to set up a shop myself, not quite of the same kind; but there were other sorts of pride beside my own to be consulted, so beyond a jest, more than half-earnest, with a rich neighbor, who proposed himself as a partner, the fancy hardly came to words. Ah, I have a strong fellow-feeling for that poor Hepzibah—a decayed gentlewoman, elderly, ugly, awkward, near-sighted, cross! I have a deep sympathy with 'Old Maid Pyncheon' as she appears on the morning of this great trial.

> Forth she steps into the dusky time-darkened passage; a tall figure clad in black silk, with a long and shrunken waist, feeling her way toward the stairs, like a near-sighted person, as in truth she is . . . What is called poetic insight is the gift of discerning, in this sphere of strangely-minded elements, the beauty and the majesty which are compelled to assume a garb so sordid.

It would be difficult to deny the gift of 'poetic insight' to this mixture of admirable detail with something at once higher and deeper. Balzac, the great novelist of modern France, known only to those among us who thoroughly possess his language, for he is untranslated and untranslatable, has in certain romances of provincial life the same perfection of Dutch painting and of homely tragedy. But Mr Hawthorne is free from Balzac's scoff. The story of the first day behind the counter goes on with inimitable truth, minuteness and variety. The cracked bell tinkles, and the poor old lady totters nervously to her post. Her first customer is a friendly one; a young artist—an artist after a somewhat American fashion, a Daguerreotypist—who

inhabited one of the Seven Gables, and affords a capital specimen of the adventurous youth of the United States. Manly, comely, cheerful, kind, brimful of determined energy and common sense, he has already tried some half-score of careers—schoolmaster, editor, agent, engineer—and is sure to conquer fortune at last. Their conversation lets us into much of the story, and shows, besides, that poor Hepzibah will not make her fortune by her shop, for he comes to purchase biscuits, and she begs to be for one moment a gentlewoman, and not be forced into accepting money from her only friend. Then comes an old, humble, sauntering neighbor who again helps on the narrative; then a greedy boy, who finding the cent which he offered for the gingerbread Jim Crow refused from pure disgust, returns in half an hour and eats the elephant. Then the rich Judge passes; and Hepzibah trembles as his shadow darkens the window—and then the common crew.

> Customers came in as the forenoon advanced, but rather slowly; in some cases too, it must be owned, with little satisfaction either to themselves or Miss Hepzibah; nor, on the whole, with an aggregate of very rich emolument to the till . . . But whether it were the white roses, or whatever the subtile influence might be, a person of delicate instinct would have known at once that it was now a maiden's bedchamber, and had been purified of all former evil and sorrow by her sweet breath and happy thoughts.

There is a touch of Goethe's 'Margaret,' the Margaret of *Faust* in the last paragraph. But 'Phœbe' is a truly original conception. To quote her thousand prettinesses of thought and action, would be to copy half the volume. Suffice it that she stays with her good old cross cousin; and that, under her auspices, the shop flourishes, and the tottering mansion loses half its gloom.

P.S. I have just received an American reprint of Mr Hawthorne's earliest volumes, *Twice-told Tales* two or three of which are as fine as his larger efforts—one especially, in which a story is told by a succession of unspoken sounds as clearly as it could have been by pictures. It is one of Messrs. Ticknor, Reed and Field's beautiful editions, and the preface and portrait are most interesting. Nothing can exceed the modesty of that preface, and I am told that Mr Hawthorne is astonished at his own reputation, and thinks himself the most over-rated man in America. Then that portrait—what a head! and he is said to be of the height and build of Daniel Webster. So much the better. It is well that a fine intellect should be fitly lodged; harmony is among the rarest.

Mr Hawthorne is engaged on another tale, and on a work for young people, which, from such a man, will probably prove quite as acceptable to children of a larger growth as to those for whom it is ostensibly written.

Praise for a Children's Book

Hawthorne received a letter about A Wonder-Book *from Robert Carter, the editor of* The Pioneer, *which had published two of his stories—"The Hall of Fantasy" and "The Birthmark" in 1843.*

CAMBRIDGE, MASS., Feb. 10, 1853.

MY DEAR SIR,—At the time of publication, a copy of the "Wonder-Book" was sent to me as editor of the "Commonwealth." It got mislaid until last New Year's day, when I found it and took it home for my eldest child, a boy four years old, Master James Lowell Carter. Late in the evening, on lighting my cigar, I thought I would look into the book a little, and master the drift of at least one story, to be ready for my young inquisitor in the morning. A diligent reader of novels for at least a quarter of a century, I scarcely expected to find in a child's book a fresh fountain of new sensations and ideas. But the book threw me into a tumult of delight, almost equal to that of the first perusal of "Robinson Crusoe" or the "Arabian Nights." At two o'clock in the morning, my fire having entirely gone out, I laid down the book, every word read except "The Chimæra," which story I read aloud at breakfast to the immense delight of Master James, and the equal gratification of his mother, who pronounced it the finest poem she had heard for many a day, and thought, if the rest of the tales were as good, the book must be a wonder-book indeed.

Notwithstanding the beauty of many passages and descriptions in the tales and the framework, I do not so much admire the execution as the conception of

Washington Irving (from G. P. Putnam, Homes of American Authors, *1853)*

the book,—which seems to me exquisitely felicitous, developing as it does a new use for the apparently effete mythology of the ancients. It is, in fact, the most palpable hit that has been made in literature for many a day, and will mark an era in fiction, as did the translation of the "Arabian Nights." The Mahometan mythology does not excel the classic in romantic machinery, while it is far inferior to it in intellectual and moral interest, and in affinity with our current ideas and literature.

I observe with regret that in your preface you exhibit a doubtful, half-apologetic tone, as if you lacked confidence in your theme and its acceptance with critical readers,—the influence of which want of confidence seems to me perceptible in portions of the book, chiefly in leading you to adopt a lighter style now and then, which jars a little with the general effect,—as if, to forestall laughter, you desired to show that you were only in fun yourself. The intermediate parts—the framework—is exceedingly well written, with some fine Berkshire descriptions. But though the con-

---

Hawthorne apparently had sent Washington Irving, at the time the most acclaimed American author, a copy of A Wonder-Book.

MY DEAR SIR,—Accept my most cordial thanks for the little volume you have had the kindness to send me. I prize it as the right hand of fellowship extended to me by one whose friendship I am proud and happy to make, and whose writings I have regarded with admiration as among the very best that have ever issued from the American press.

Hoping that we may have many occasions hereafter of cultivating the friendly intercourse which you have so frankly commenced, I remain, with great regard,

Your truly obliged
WASHINGTON IRVING.

In a 16 July 1852 letter to Irving, Hawthorne explained, "I sent you 'The Wonder Book,' because, being meant for children, it seemed to reach a higher point, in its own way, than anything that I had written for grown people."

Robert Carter

Cover for the first English edition, which was scheduled for simultaneous publication with the American edition. Although the American edition was dated 1852 and the English edition 1851, it is believed that both were published in December 1851, with the American book preceding the English one by a few days (from C. E. Frazer Clark Jr., Nathaniel Hawthorne: A Descriptive Bibliography, *1978)*

trast is striking between the Old World tales and the fresh young life of America, I should have liked it better if you had given the tales a Greek setting, and thrown back Eustace Bright and his auditors a couple of thousand years, to a country-seat of Attica, Ionia, or Sicily. As it is, Mr. Pringle and his wife are decided excrescences, who ought to be condemned to the preface, and with them your friends the publisher and artist, who are now sadly out of place. I want to see nothing in the "Wonder-Book" that will not read harmoniously there a thousand years hence, or in any language of the world; for if you continue the book as well as you have begun it (and you ought to do it better), so that the value of quantity will be added to that of quality (for a book of tales must be pretty large to live), it will be read in the future as universally as the "Arabian Nights," and not only by children. An author has a strong temptation to introduce his friends into his pages, but it ought never to be done at a sacrifice of art. You doubtless remember that many of your friends and acquaintances who figured in "The Hall of Fantasy," as it appeared in the "Pioneer," have vanished from that structure in its present razeed condition.

Pardon me if I point out what seems to me another fault in the book. I observe that, for brevity,

Various bindings for editions of Hawthorne's works published in 1851 and 1852 (from C. E. Frazer Clark Jr.,
Nathaniel Hawthorne: A Descriptive Bibliography, *1978)*

or from some difficulty in the managing the stories, or from some cause which has not occurred to me, you have omitted to use some of the most striking portions of the myths you have dealt with. For instance, the adventures of Perseus on his return, his rescue of Andromeda, his petrifaction of Atlas, etc., would have added much to the incident of the story. And in "The Golden Touch," I do not understand why you have changed Bacchus into Mercury, or have omitted the capture of Silenus and his entertainment by Midas, which would have afforded fine material for pleasant and varied treatment. "The Three Golden Apples," likewise, ought not to exhaust the achievements of Hercules, which should rather be woven into a series rivalling those of "Sinbad the Sailor," in length and interest. But enough of fault-finding. My object in writing is merely to assure you that at least one of your readers is convinced that in the "Wonder-Book" you have hit upon the entrance to a golden mine, and that it is worth while to carry on the work with care and system, so as to get the full amount of the treasures; and not from haste or want of plan leave any part unworked or unexhausted.

    With high respect, I am very truly yours,
                                    ROBERT CARTER.

Literature and Politics:
The Blithedale Romance, Life of Franklin Pierce, and *Tanglewood Tales*

The Blithedale Romance *is Hawthorne's least celebrated novel, perhaps because it surprised readers and critics by differing considerably from* The Scarlet Letter *and* The House of the Seven Gables. *Instead of exploring moral issues arising from the Puritan past, Hawthorne in his fourth novel deals with his own recent past and with the problems associated with social reform. The setting for the novel is a thinly disguised Brook Farm, the experimental community where Hawthorne had lived in 1841, the year before marrying Sophia Peabody. In another departure for the author, the narrator is one of the characters involved in the action of the novel, Miles Coverdale. One of the main issues considered by reviewers of the novel is the appropriateness of patterning fictional characters on real people, as Hawthorne seemed to have done, especially with Zenobia, a strong-willed woman modeled in part on Margaret Fuller.*

On 14 July 1852, 5,090 copies of The Blithedale Romance *were published by Ticknor, Reed and Fields, with 90 copies being distributed to reviewers. An unknown number of copies of the English edition, set from proof sheets of the American typesetting, were actually printed before the American edition, around 7 July. The American edition sold for 75¢, and Hawthorne received a 15 percent royalty on the 5,000 copies. An additional 2,350 copies were printed on 12 August 1852, with the author receiving a 5¢ royalty per copy. Although more copies of* The Blithedale Romance *were printed within its first year than had been the case for either of the previous two novels, the initial interest in this novel was not sustained.*

In the same year that his third major romance saw print, Hawthorne also published a campaign biography, Life of Franklin Pierce, *for his former Bowdoin classmate who was elected the fourteenth president of the United States in November 1852, and began writing another collection for children,* Tanglewood Tales, *for Girls and Boys, which was published in August 1853.*

Publishing *The Blithedale Romance*

Publisher James T. Fields gives an account of Hawthorne's concerns as The Blithedale Romance *went to press, and the novelist prepared for life abroad.*

In 1852 I went to Europe, and while absent had frequent most welcome letters from the delightful dreamer. He had finished the "Blithedale Romance" during my wanderings, and I was fortunate enough to arrange for its publication in London simultaneously with its appearance in Boston. One of his letters (dated from his new residence in Concord, June 17, 1851) runs thus:–

"You have succeeded admirably in regard to the 'Blithedale Romance,' and have got £150 more than I expected to receive. It will come in good time, too; for my drafts have been pretty heavy of late, in consequence of buying an estate!!! and fitting up my house. What a truant you are from the Corner! I wish, before leaving London, you would obtain for me copies of any English editions of my writings not already in my possession. I have Routledge's edition of 'The Scarlet Letter,' the 'Mosses,' and 'Twice-Told Tales'; Bohn's editions of 'The House of the Seven Gables,' the 'Snow-Image' and the 'Wonder-Book,' and Bogue's edition of 'The Scarlet Letter';–these are all, and I should be glad of the rest. I meant to have written another 'Wonder-Book' this summer, but another task has unexpectedly intervened. General Pierce of New Hampshire, the Democratic nominee for the Presidency, was a college friend of mine, as you know, and we have been intimate through life. He wishes me to write his biography, and I have consented to do so; somewhat reluctantly, however, for Pierce has now reached that altitude when a man, careful of his personal dignity, will begin to think of cutting his acquaintance. But I seek nothing from him, and therefore need not be ashamed to tell the truth of an old friend. . . . . I have written to Barry Cornwall, and shall probably enclose the letter along with this. I don't more than half believe what you tell me of my reputation in England, and am only so

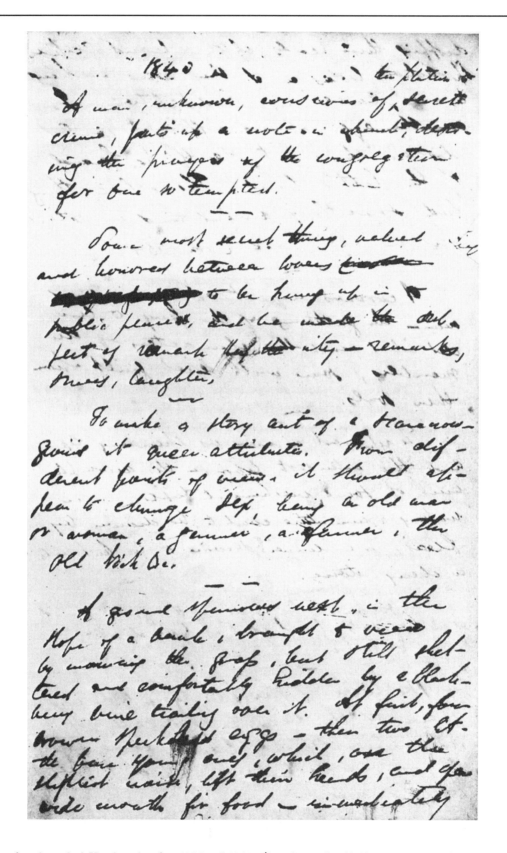

Page from the notebook Hawthorne kept from 1835 until 1841. The author acted on his idea to write a story about a scarecrow (third paragraph) in "Feathertop" (Pierpont Morgan Library).

Initial page of the manuscript for the story first published in the 1 February and 1 March 1852 numbers of International Monthly Magazine of Literature, Art, and Science. *It was collected in 1854 in the second American edition of* Mosses from an Old Manse *(Anderson Auction Company catalogue, George M. Williamson, sale number 274, 1 March 1904; reprinted in* Hawthorne at Auction, *p. 47).*

"The Wayside," Hawthorne's Concord home, where he lived from late May 1852 until he sailed for England on 6 July 1853 and again upon his return to the United States in late June 1860 until his death. Hawthorne bought the house from Bronson Alcott, who called it "Hillside," and land across from it from Samuel Sewell and Ralph Waldo Emerson.

far credulous on the strength of the £ 200, and shall have a somewhat stronger sense of this latter reality when I finger the cash. Do come home in season to preside over the publication of the Romance."

He had christened his estate The Wayside, and in a postscript to the above letter he begs me to consider the name and tell him how I like it.

Another letter, evidently foreshadowing a foreign appointment from the newly elected President, contains this passage:–

"Do make some inquiries about Portugal; as, for instance, in what part of the world it lies, and whether it is an empire, a kingdom, or a republic. Also, and more particularly, the expenses of living there, and whether the Minister would be likely to be much pestered with his own countrymen. Also, any other information about foreign countries would be acceptable to an inquiring mind."

Calling card of the Hawthornes for their Concord home (Peabody Essex Museum)

Passage from Hawthorne's 15 July 1852 letter to publisher George Palmer Putnam describing the "Old Manse." Hawthorne's residence was featured in Homes of American Authors, *published by G. P. Putnam & Co. for the 1852 Christmas season (from Kenneth Cameron,* Hawthorne among His Contemporaries, *1968).*

When I returned from abroad I found him getting matters in readiness to leave the country for a consulship in Liverpool. He seemed happy at the thought of flitting, but I wondered if he could possibly be as contented across the water as he was in Concord. I remember walking with him to the Old Manse, a mile or so distant from The Wayside, his new residence, and talking over England and his proposed absence of several years. We strolled round the house, where he spent the first years of his married life, and he pointed from the outside to the windows, out of which he had looked and seen supernatural and other visions. We walked up and down the avenue, the memory of which he has embalmed in the "Mosses," and he discoursed most pleasantly of all that had befallen him since he led a lonely, secluded life in Salem. It was a sleepy, warm afternoon, and he proposed that we should wander up the banks of the river and lie down and watch the clouds float above and in the quiet stream. I recall his lounging, easy air as he tolled me along until we came to a spot secluded, and ofttimes sacred to his wayward thoughts. He bade me lie down on the grass and hear the birds sing. As we steeped ourselves in the delicious idleness, he began to murmur some half-forgotten lines from Thomson's "Seasons," which he said had been favorites of his from boyhood. While we lay there, hidden in the grass, we heard approaching footsteps, and Hawthorne hurriedly whispered, "Duck! or we shall be interrupted by somebody." The solemnity of his manner, and the thought of the down-flat position in which we had both placed ourselves to avoid being seen, threw me into a foolish, semi-hysterical fit of laughter, and when he nudged me, and again whispered more lugubriously than ever, "Heaven help me, Mr. – is close upon us!" I felt convinced that if the thing went further, suffocation, in my case at least, must ensue.

–Yesterdays with Authors, pp. 71–73

A page from a draft of The Blithedale Romance *(left; the Ohio State Libraries) and the corresponding page from the fair-copy manuscript (right; Pierpont Morgan Library)*

35

... state of the corporeal system. The soul gets the better of the body, after wasting illness, or when a vegetable diet may have mingled too much ether in the blood. Vapors then rise up to the brain, and take shapes that often image falsehood, but sometimes truth. The spheres of our companions have, at such periods, a vastly greater influence upon our own, than when robust health gives us a repellent and self-defensive energy. Zenobia's sphere, I imagine, impressed itself powerfully on mine, and transformed me, during this period of my weakness, into something like a mesmerical clairvoyant.

Then, also, as anybody could observe, the freedom of her deportment (though, to some tastes, it might commend itself as the utmost perfection of manner, in a youthful widow, or a blooming matron) was not exactly maiden-like. What girl had ever laughed as Zenobia did! What girl had ever spoken in her mellow tones! Her unconstrained and inevitable manifestation, I said often to myself, was that of a woman to whom wedlock had thrown wide the gates of mystery. Yet, sometimes, I strove to be ashamed of these conjectures. I acknowledged it as a masculine grossness — a sin of wicked interpretation, of which man is often guilty towards the other sex — thus to mistake the sweet, liberal, but womanly frankness of a noble and generous disposition. Still, it was of no avail to reason with myself, nor to upbraid myself. Pertinaciously the thought — 'Zenobia is a wife! Zenobia has lived, and loved! There is no folded petal, no latent dew-drop, in this perfectly developed rose!' — irresistibly that thought drove out all other conclusions, as often as my mind reverted to the subject.

Zenobia was conscious of my observation, though not, I presume, of the point to which it led me.

"Mr. Coverdale!" said she, one day, as she saw me watching her, while she arranged my gruel on the table, "I have been exposed to a great deal of eye-shot in the few years of my mixing in the world, but never, I think, to precisely such glances as you are in the habit of favoring me with. I seem to interest you very much; and yet — or else a woman's instinct

THE

BLITHEDALE ROMANCE.

BY

NATHANIEL HAWTHORNE,

AUTHOR OF " THE SCARLET LETTER," " THE HOUSE OF THE SEVEN
GABLES," &c.

IN TWO VOLUMES.

VOL. I.

LONDON:
CHAPMAN AND HALL, 193, PICCADILLY.
1852.

THE

BLITHEDALE ROMANCE.

BY

NATHANIEL HAWTHORNE.

BOSTON:
TICKNOR, REED, AND FIELDS.
M DCCC LII.

Title pages for the English and American editions of Hawthorne's fourth novel. To protect English copyright, Ticknor and Fields delayed publication to allow Chapman and Hall to publish first (from C. E. Frazer Clark Jr., Nathaniel Hawthorne: A Descriptive Bibliography, *1978).*

Reaction to *The Blithedale Romance* and *The Life of Franklin Pierce*

A sometime journalist and Democratic politician, William B. Pike worked with Hawthorne at the customhouses in Salem and Boston. The intimacy of their friendship is evident in the closing of Hawthorne's 24 July 1851 letter to Pike: "You will never, I fear (you see that I take a friend's privilege to speak plainly), make the impression on the world that, in years gone by, I used to hope you would. It will not be your fault, however, but the fault of circumstances. Your flower was not destined to bloom in this world. I hope to see its glory in the next."

SALEM, July 18, 1852.

DEAR HAWTHORNE,—I want to come and see you, and shall tell no one that I am going, nor, when I return, that I have been. I have read your "Blithedale Romance." It is more like "The Scarlet Letter" than "The House of the Seven Gables." In this book, as in "The Scarlet Letter," you probe deeply,—you go down among the moody silences of the heart, and open those depths whence come motives that give complexion to actions, and make in men what are called states of mind; being conditions of mind which cannot be removed either by our own reasoning or by the reasonings of others. Almost all the novel-writers I have read, although truthful to nature, go through only some of the strata; but you are the only one who breaks through the hard-pan,—who accounts for that class of actions and manifestations in men so inexplicable as to call forth the exclamation, "How strangely that man acts! what a fool he is!" and the like. You explain, also, why the utterers of such exclamations, when circumstances have brought them to do the very things they once wondered at in others, feel that they themselves are acting rationally and consistently. Love is undoubtedly the deepest, profoundest, of the deep things of man, having its origin in the depths of depths,—the inmost of all the emotions that ever manifest themselves on the surface. Yet writers seldom penetrate very far below the outward appearance, or show its workings in a way to account for its strange phases and fancies. They say two young people fall in love, and then expend their whole talents in describing the disasters that attended them, and how many acts of heroism they performed before accomplishing a marriage union. My mother had a deep idea in her mind when, in talking of incongruous unions, she would say, "It requires deep thinking to account for fancy." In "Blithedale," as in "The Scarlet Letter," you show how such things take place, and open the silent, unseen, internal elements which first set the machinery in motion, which works out results so strange to those who penetrate only to a certain depth in the soul. And I intend this remark to apply not only to love, but to other subjects and persons described in these volumes. I sometimes wish I had the pen of some, for I should like to lay open to the world my idea of love, clear to my own mind, but difficult to communicate,—its profoundness, its elements; how 't is a part of every man and woman; how all other loves, affections, benevolences, aspirations, gratitudes, are from this same fountain; receiving its character, quality, and modification as it passes through the different avenues from the fountain to its object; and how the presence of each object calls forth through its proper channel the love appropriate to itself, as food in the stomach invites the gastric juices proper to itself; how men and women are not perfect without a true spiritual union with the opposite sexes; how the divine nature, ever seeking to come down in forms, cannot do so in making man alone or woman alone, but, whenever it ultimates itself in humanity, a man *and* a woman is made,—made to be one, and would, in an unperverted state, find each other and remain united forever. But this is not what I tended to write about,—'t was "Blithedale." In "Blithedale" you dig an Artesian well down among the questionings. I was reminded of an Artesian well opened by my neighbor, who, after boring through various strata of earth and several fresh springs, found clear, cold sea-water at the depth of two hundred feet, which came bubbling to the surface from beneath the whole. How little we on the upper crust imagined that, far in the depths, was a stream which received its origin, quality, and character from the mighty ocean,—or fancied that, ere the stream we saw pouring forth could be exhausted, the vast world of waters must be dried up! But so it is; and the motive powers, like pearls, shine far down in the deep waters, and we fail to see them. You show us that such depths exist, and how they operate through the different departments, till they reach the outward and become visible actions. Thus the strange acts of men are in perfect consistency with the individual self,—the profound self. How admirably you explore those lurking-places! I think "Blithedale" more profound in maxims than any work of yours. They will be quoted in the future as texts. You hit off the follies and errors of man with a quick humor, as no other man does. I cannot describe your humor, but I can feel and enjoy it. This peculiarity of your writings I always thought wonderful, but "Blithedale" I think excels the others in this particular. It is sudden, bright, but not flashy,—bright enough to make us feel our frailties and weaknesses, yet not so painfully that we hesitate to open our eyes and look again. You make us think the more and resolve the better, because the smart is not so sharp that we have to stop thinking to rub the wound. The best way I can describe it is to say that it opens and shuts just like heat lightning.

Tell your children that I have been thinking of them ever since I sat down to write.

Your friend truly,   WM. B. PIKE.

George Stillman Hillard (1808–1879) was a close friend to Hawthorne and served as his lawyer in his suit against Brook Farm and as the executor of his estate. Among his literary pursuits, he edited a five-volume edition of Edmund Spenser's works (1839).

BOSTON, July 27, 1852.

MY DEAR HAWTHORNE,—You have written another book full of beauty and power, which I read with great interest and vivid excitement. I hate the habit of comparing one work of an author with another, and never do so in my own mind. Many of your readers go off in this impertinent way, at the first, and insist upon drawing parallels between "The Blithedale Romance" and "The Scarlet Letter" or "The House of the Seven Gables." I do not walk in that way. It is enough for me that you have put another rose into your chaplet, and I will not ask whether it outblooms or outswells its sister flowers. Zenobia is a splendid creature, and I wish there were more such rich and ripe women about. I wish, too, you could have wound up your story without killing her, or that at least you had given her a drier and handsomer death. Priscilla is an exquisite sketch. I don't know whether you have quite explained Hollingsworth's power over two such diverse natures. Your views about reform and reformers and spiritual rappings are such as I heartily approve. Reformers need the enchantment of distance. Your sketches of things visible, detached observations, and style generally, are exquisite as ever. May you live a thousand years, and write a book every year!

Yours ever,   GEO. S. HILLARD.

Depiction of the steamboat disaster in which Hawthorne's sister Louisa died (New-York Historical Society)

Elizabeth Palmer Peabody, the mother of Hawthorne's wife, wrote in the wake of the death of the author's younger sister, Mary Louisa Hawthorne (1808–1852), who had died in a steamboat accident on 27 July 1852.

AUGUST 9, 1852.

MY BELOVED ONES,—Have your high and just views of the dealings of our Heavenly Father soothed the anguish nature must endure for a while under such a shock as you have received? Does Mr. Hawthorne mean to go to the seashore, or has this affliction changed his purpose? It would be best to go, if he can. His soul would then be filled with the glories of that Nature whose favored child he is. His perfect clearness of vision, his mildness, his calmness, his true strength and greatness, render him the ready recipient of *all* that magnificent scenery conveys to the soul. He is one of the few who can not only look at things, but into and through them. The world has great claims on one who can do so much towards raising the mind from stupid materialism to translucent wonder.

We are all reading "Blithedale." I am interested to see how differently it affects different minds. Some say (Mary, for one), "It is the greatest book Hawthorne has written." Another says, "I do not understand it;" another, "There is no interest in it to me;" another exclaims, "Was ever anything so exquisite!" I have not seen any review of it yet. I hope a reviewer will arise for the task who has soul; who can see the true philanthropist, the real reformer, piercing with a seer's eye all the vain efforts hitherto made to form associations that will really elevate the characters and better the worldly condition of men,—one who has power to realize why all such associations to ameliorate the condition of the laborer have hitherto failed. At Brook Farm, as elsewhere, they did not begin right. Many persons were huddled together there, with all their passions in full vigor; selfishness, covetousness, pride, love of dress, of approbation, of admiration, of flattery, operated on one and all. Petty jealousies rankled in hearts that ought to have throbbed only with love to God and man. How could such incongruous elements amalgamate and produce a genuine Brotherhood? Our associations carry in their very midst the causes of decay.

YOUR MOTHER.

Published in Boston, the Unitarian Christian Examiner, *whose motto was "Speaking the truth in love," supported the transcendental movement and was probably the most significant religious magazine of its time. Although the anonymous reviewer laments Hawthorne's habit of "confounding fact and fiction," he praises his abilities as a writer.*

Review of *The Blithedale Romance*
Christian Examiner, 53 (September 1852): 292–293

The preface to this captivating volume is by no means the least important part of it. And yet we would advise all readers who wish to peruse the work under an illusion which will add an intense interest to its pages, to postpone the preface till they have gone through the book. Certainly one has reason that believe that Mr Hawthorne is presenting in these pages a story, which, however it may depend for its decorative and fanciful details upon his rich imagination, is essentially a delineation of life and character as presented at 'Brook Farm.' It is well known that he was a member of that community of amiable men and women, who undertook there to realize their ideas of a better system of social relations. He fixes there the scene of his story, with frequent reference to the localities around, keeping up a close connection with the neighboring city of Boston; and the volume owes very much of its lifelike fidelity of representation to the reader's supposition that the characters are as real as the theory and the institution in which they have their parts. Yet in the preface Mr Hawthorne, with a charming frankness which neutralizes much of the charm of his story, repudiates altogether the matter-of-fact view so far as regards his associates at 'Brook Farm,' and pleads necessity as his reason for confounding fact and fiction.

We cannot but regard the license which Mr Hawthorne allows himself in this respect as open to grave objection. Seeing that many readers obtain all their knowledge of historical facts from the incidental implications of history which are involved in a well-drawn romance, we maintain that a novelist has no right to tamper with actual verities. His obligation to adhere strictly to historic truth is all the more to be exacted whenever the character and good repute of any real person are involved. Now Mr Hawthorne is a daring offender in this respect. It is the only drawback upon our high admiration of him. We trust he will take no offence at this our free expression of opinion, when, while offering to him a respectful and grateful homage for all the spiritual glow and all the human wisdom which we find on his pages, we venture to question his right to misrepresent the facts and characters of assured history. If he shaded and clouded his incidents somewhat more obscurely, if he removed them farther back

or farther off from the region of our actual sight and knowledge, he would be safer in using the privileges of the romancer. But he gives us such distinct and sharp boundary lines, and deals so boldly with matters and persons, the truth of whose prose life repels the poetry of his fiction, that we are induced to confide in him as a chronicler, rather than to indulge him as a romancer. Thus in his *Scarlet Letter* he assures us in his preface that he has historical papers which authenticate the story that follows. That story involves the gross and slanderous imputation that the colleague pastor of the First Church in Boston, who preached the Election Sermon the year after the death of Governor Winthrop, was a mean and hypocritical adulterer, and went from the pulpit to the pillory to confess to that character in presence of those who had just been hanging reverently upon his lips. how would this outrageous fiction, which is utterly without foundation, deceive a reader who had no exact knowledge of our history! We can pardon the anachronism, in the same work, by which the little children in Boston are represented as practising for the game of annoying Quakers half a score of years before such a thing as a Quaker had been heard of even in Old England. But we cannot admit the license of a novelist to go the length of a vile and infamous imputation upon a Boston minister of a spotless character. In his *Blithedale Romance,* Mr Hawthorne ventures upon a similar freedom, though by no means so gross a one, in confounding fact and fiction. So vividly does he present to us the scheme at Brook Farm, to which some of our acquaintance were parties, so sharply and accurately does he portray some of the incidents of life there, that we are irresistibly impelled to fix the real names of men and women to the characters of his book. We cannot help doing this. We pay a tribute to Mr Hawthorne's power when we confess that we cannot believe that he is drawing upon his imagination. We ask, Whom does he mean to describe as Zenobia? Is it Mrs –, or Miss –? Then, as we know that no one of the excellent women who formed the community at 'Brook Farm' was driven to suicide by disappointed love, we find ourselves constructing the whole character from a combination of some half a dozen of the women whose talents or peculiarities have made them prominent in this neighborhood. We can gather up in this way all the elements of his Zenobia, except the comparatively unimportant one of queenly beauty which he ascribes to her. We leave to the help-meet of the author to settle with him the issue that may arise from his description of himself as a bachelor.

Having thus relieved our minds of the disagreeable part of a critic's duty, we are the more free to express our delight and gratitude, after the perusal of the book before us. Mr Hawthorne is a writer of marvellous power, a most wise and genial philosopher, a true poet, and a skilful painter. We have gained instruction from his pages, of the most difficult kind to obtain, of the most valuable sort for use. The quiet humor, the good-tempered satire, which has no element of cynicism, the analysis of character, with the tracing of the deeper motives which fashion its outer workings and its inner growth, the clear vision for truth, and, above all, the sagacity which distinguishes between the really spiritual in thought and life and the morbid phenomena which so often propose themselves as spiritualities,– these are the tokens of a master-mind in our author. We thank him most heartily for this book, and gratefully acknowledge that it has offered to us wise and good lessons which ought to make us strong for faith and duty.

Orestes Augustus Brownson (1803–1876) began his career as a Presbyterian minister; as his religious beliefs evolved, he became successively a Universalist minister, a Unitarian minister, and a pastor of his own organization, the Society for Christian Union and Progress. In 1844 he converted to Roman Catholicism, a fact he alludes to in the following review. Brownson expressed his liberal and socialist ideas in journals he edited, such as The Boston Quarterly Review *(1838–1842) and* Brownson's Quarterly Review *(1844–1864, 1873–1875), and his writings were collected in twenty volumes (1882–1887). Because he had visited Brook Farm, Brownson was able to comment on the accuracy of Hawthorne's depiction of the experimental community.*

Review of *The Blithedale Romance*
Orestes Brownson
Brownson's Quarterly Review,
n.s. 6 (October 1852): 561–564

Mr Hawthorne has fully established his reputation as the first writer, in his favorite line, our American literature can boast, and we have nothing to do, when he publishes a new work, but to judge it without judging the general character, merits, or demerits of the author. We said of Mr Hawthorne in 1842, *apropos* of the publication of *Twice-told Tales,*–

> He is a genuine artist. His mind is creative; more so than that of any other American writer that has as yet appeared, with the exception, perhaps, of Washington Irving. He has wit, humor, pathos, in abundance; an eye for all that is wild, beautiful, or picturesque in nature; a generous sympathy with all forms of life, thought, and feeling, and warm, deep, unfailing love of his race. He has withal a vigorous intellect, and a serene and healthy spirit. He is gentle, but robust and

Orestes Augustus Brownson

manly; full of tenderness, but never maudlin. Through all his writings there runs a pure and living stream of manly thought and feeling . . . We have wished to enroll ourselves among those who regard Mr Hawthorne as fitted to stand at the head of American literature. We see the pledge of this in his modesty, in his simplicity, and in his sympathy with all that is young, fresh, childlike; and above all in his originality, and pure, deep feeling of nationality.

This judgment no doubt betrays the school to which we then belonged, or were laboring to found; but, extravagant as some thought it at the time, the reading public have ratified it, and abating a little as to vigor of intellect and healthiness of spirit, we are willing to abide by it. In the class of literature he has selected he has no superior amongst us, probably no equal, but we owe it to ourselves to say that the class is not the highest.

The Blithedale Romance we have read with a good deal of interest, for much in it is connected with some of our personal friends. Through them we had ourselves some share in it. The scene of the Romance is laid at Brook Farm in the neighboring town of West Roxbury, where one of the most intimate and dearest friends we ever had prior to our conversion founded an Institute of Agriculture with a half communitarian purpose. He himself avowed in it no general purpose of world reform, although he was moved by the socialistic spirit, which many of us at that time shared, and he probably hoped that Brook Farm in its developments would grow into a model community, and become the germ or nucleus of a new and better social organization. In this point of view we personally never had any faith in it, and from the first discouraged it; but as a practical Institute of Agriculture, where several persons of kindred sympathies might live together in a sort of community, enjoy the pleasures of a highly refined and cultivated society, and sustain themselves by labor in the field or garden and by the instruction of youth, which was all that its founder proposed, we thought not unfavorably of it. But the establishment was no sooner opened than it drew together a strange group of visionary projectors, of wild and lawless spirits of all sorts, weary of the restraints of society, and anxious chiefly to act out without reserve all their instincts, and to give free scope to all the impulses, passions, and whims of their undisciplined natures. It of course soon failed, and with it the hopes that it had excited. The men and women who had been collected together there for a brief period, expecting to find a new garden of Eden, were scattered again, most of them with saddened hearts, and some of them with an experience from which they have since derived a rich harvest of wisdom.

Mr Hawthorne was for a brief period one of the communitarians, attracted more, we apprehend, by the romance of the thing, than by any real belief in the principles of the establishment, or deep sympathy with its objects. Under the name of Miles Coverdale he sketches in this little volume his experiences during his brief residence at Brook Farm as one of the regenerators of society, mingled with various romantic instances which did, and many more which did not happen, but which might have happened. He has treated the institution and the characters of his associates with great delicacy and tenderness. He enjoys a quiet laugh and indulges in a little gentle satire now and then, and upon the whole makes the experiment appear, as it in reality was, a folly born of honest intentions and fervent zeal in behalf of society. But he brings none of the real actors in the comedy, or farce, or tragedy, whichever it may have been, upon the stage. We can recognize in the personages of his Romance individual traits of several real characters who were there, but no one has his or her whole counterpart in one who was actually a member of the community. There was no actual Zenobia, Hollingsworth, or Priscilla there, and no such catastrophe as described ever occurred there; yet none of these characters are purely imaginary. Hollingsworth, in relation to his one fixed purpose, had his counterpart there, and the author has given us in Miles Coverdale much that we dare affirm to have been true of himself. Still, there has been no encroachment on the sanctity of private character, and pain has been given, we presume, to no private feeling. The reader may collect from the Romance the general tone, sentiment, hopes, fears, and character of the establishment, but very little of the actual persons engaged in it, or of the actual goings-on at Brook Farm.

In the character of Hollingsworth the author has been exceedingly successful, as also in the sketch of Old Moody. They both stand out from his canvas lifelike, and impress us as real living and breathing men. Priscilla is too shadowy, and suffers by a comparison with the Alice and Fanny of Sir Edward Bulwer Lytton. It is a character which Hawthorne is too much of a man to delineate; he takes to it not naturally, and his likeness degenerates into a caricature. Zenobia stands in exact contrast to Priscilla, and is neither more complete nor truthful. Mr Hawthorne succeeds better with men and boys than with women and girls. He knows that vanity is a characteristic of women, and that every woman must have something to love, and that she will love the strong-minded and strong-willed man who speaks to her as a master, if also a man of deep feeling and strong passions, in preference to the man remarkable chiefly for personal beauty, gentle manners, kind feelings, and the readiness with which he devotes himself to her will and makes her pleasure his own. But this denotes no great insight into the female character. Love in its proper sense is no more a want of woman's heart than of man's, and she is in general less capable of love, and less steady in it, than man. All the pretty things said of woman's love in novels and romances are mere moonshine. Woman has a more impulsive and passionate nature than man, and love with her is an emotion. She craves not so much love as a strong emotion of some sort, it matters little to her of what sort, and hence she is already captivated by the man who gives her the most excitement, produces in her the strongest emotions, though nine tenths of the time they are emotions of anger or grief. Any woman would die for a Hollingsworth sooner than bestow a single smile on a Miles Coverdale. But Zenobia was not the woman to commit suicide because disappointed,—she who had been, as novelists say, 'in love' no one knows how many times, and whose heart had become as tough as sole-leather. No, if that had been all, she would have taken a cathartic, and found herself as well as ever. Women of her large experience and free principles never kill themselves for disappointed affection. Hollingsworth did not cause her to commit so rash an act by rejecting her for Priscilla. It was not the loss of her lover, but the

Electing Franklin Pierce

Hawthorne supported the presidential campaign of his former Bowdoin classmate and friend Pierce by writing Life of Franklin Pierce, *which was published in the United States on 11 September 1852, nearly two months before the election. Pierce became the fourteenth president of the United States and served one term.*

Portrait of Franklin Pierce by George P. A. Healy, 1852 (New Hampshire Historical Society)

Elizabeth Manning Hawthorne, who opposed her brother's involvement in politics, reported the reaction to Life of Franklin Pierce *in Salem, where she was visiting. The "Mr. Dike" referred to is John Dike, the husband of Pricilla Manning, Hawthorne's aunt.*

SALEM, Sept. 23, 1852.

DEAR BROTHER,—You will be surprised to see that this is dated at Salem; but I knew that I must come here again, though I was glad to get away for a little while. I wish to hear from you about the business that we spoke of. I wish to do everything that must be done, while I am here now, and I should be glad never to see the place again. In Beverly I can do exactly as I choose, and even appear to be what I am, in a great degree. They are sensible and liberal-minded people, though not much cultivated.

Mr. Dike has bought your Life of Pierce, but he will not be convinced that you have told the precise truth. I assure him that it is just what I have always heard you say. The "Puritan Recorder" eulogizes the book, for you are a favorite with the Orthodox, and especially with the clergy; and for that reason I think you should

judge more charitably of them. Vanity seems to me to be their besetting sin.

The "Gazette" calls the book "an honest biography," but says the subject of it "has never risen above respectable mediocrity." The "Register" calls it your "new Romance." People are talking about something that Mr. Pike is asserted to have said derogatory to General Pierce; perhaps you have heard of it. Uncle William thinks he was unguarded in some expressions in David Roberts's office, where he is in the habit of going, and that his words have been misinterpreted and misrepresented. I thought he was too experienced a politician to be guilty of any imprudence in speech.

Yours,   E. M. H.

I hope you and Una will come to Montserrat. I am sure she would enjoy it. Besides the variety of colors in the woods, the barberry bushes, of which you have none, are now more beautiful than vineyards, as I can testify, for I see abundance of grapes here. If you will send me the Life of Pierce, I could distribute some copies there, perhaps, with advantage.

—Hawthorne and his Wife, pp. 30–31

Hawthorne commented on writing Life of Franklin Pierce *in his 13 October 1852 letter to Horatio Bridge. The letter shows that Hawthorne was not surprised by his appointment as consul after Pierce's election.*

I did not send you the Life of Pierce, not considering it fairly one of my literary productions; but Sam Bridge tells me he transmitted one of the earliest copies. I was terribly reluctant to undertake this work, and tried to persuade Pierce, both by letter and viva voce, that I could not perform it so well as many others; but he thought differently, and of course, after a friendship of thirty years, it was impossible to refuse my best efforts in his behalf, at the great pinch of his life. It was a hard book to write; for the gist of the matter lay in explaining how it has happened that, with such extraordinary opportunities for eminent distinction, civil and military, as he has enjoyed, this crisis should have found him so obscure as he certainly was, in a national point of view. My heart absolutely sank, at the dearth of available material. However, I have done the business, greatly to

Frank's satisfaction; and, though I say it myself, it is judiciously done; and, without any sacrifice of truth, it puts him in as good a light as circumstances would admit. Other writers might have made larger claims for him, and have eulogized him more highly; but I doubt whether any other could have bestowed a better aspect of sincerity and reality on the narrative, and have secured all the credit possible for him, without spoiling all by asserting too much. And though the story is true, yet it took a romancer to do it.

Before undertaking it, I made an inward resolution that I would accept no office from him; but, to say the truth, I doubt whether it would not be rather folly than heroism to adhere to this purpose, in case he should offer me anything particularly good. We shall see. A foreign mission I could not afford to take;—the consulship at Liverpool, I might; and he could not do a better thing, either for me or the credit of his administration, than to make the appointment. . . .

—*Selected Letters of Nathaniel Hawthorne,* p. 106

Portrait of Hawthorne by George P. A. Healy, commissioned by Pierce for $1,000, 1852 (New Hampshire Historical Society)

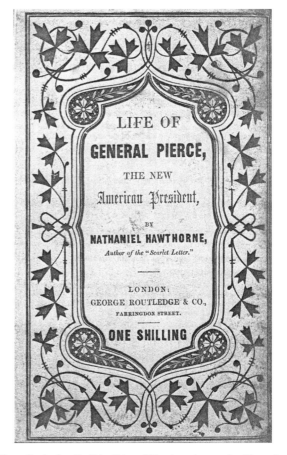

Cover for the first English edition of Hawthorne's campaign biography, which was published in December 1852, after Pierce's election (from C. E. Frazer Clark Jr., Nathaniel Hawthorne: A Descriptive Bibliography, *1978)*

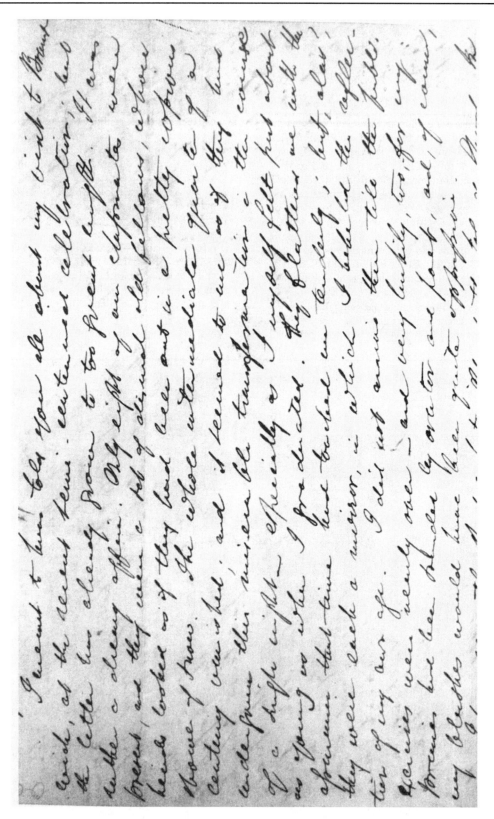

Passage from Hawthorne's 13 October 1852 letter to his former Bowdoin classmate Horatio Bridge in which he describes the semicentennial celebration at their college (Hawthorne-Longfellow Library, Bowdoin College)

loss of her estate, and with it the means of indulging her tastes of gratifying her vanity, though even that is to suppose her exceedingly unwomanly, as in fact she was. Indeed, her suicide was a blunder, and had, according to all that we have been able to observe of woman's nature, no *ratio sufficiens.* There was nothing in what we are told that would cause her to commit it, and we think bluff old Silas Foster was quite right when he refused to believe it, and declared it impossible. It is always an aesthetic no less than a moral defect for an author to make his heroes or heroines commit suicide. It is an exceeding bungling way of disposing of a character you do not know what to do with, and shows a poverty of invention as much as the common practice of novelists of making their lovers first-cousins. If the individual must die, why, give him a fever, the consumption, the plague, the cholera, the cholic; or if you can find no disease to carry him off, sure you can find a villain, a bravo, or an assassin kind enough to relieve you of your embarrassment. One of the best things Hawthorne says is, that, if Zenobia could have foreseen what a fright she would appear after having drowned herself, she would never have done so foolish a thing. Then, again, self-murder is too great a sin, and leaves too little possibility of contrition before the soul leaves the body, to be decked out with all the charms of romance and the choicest flowers of poetry. To introduce it in popular literature thus decked out is to conceal its horror, and to render the young, the passionate, the giddy, and the vain familiar with the thought of seeking repose by plunging themselves into hell, where there is no rest for ever. We do not charge Mr Hawthorne with approving suicide,–no, by no means; but he so manages the suicide of Zenobia that the shock we feel is not that of horror for her sin, but of indignation at the man who is assumed to have wronged her, and regret at the loss of so beautiful a woman.

Aside from the terrible catastrophe and a little too much tenderness for experiments like that of Brook Farm, *The Blithedale Romance* may be read by our Protestant community with great advantage, and perhaps nothing has been written among us better calculated to bring modern philanthropists into deserved disrepute, and to cure the young and enthusiastic of their socialistic tendencies and dreams of world reform. There is a quiet satire throughout the whole on all philanthropic and communitarian enterprises that will not fail to have a good effect on our community. In this point of view, we can commend *The Blithedale Romance,* not as unobjectionable, indeed, but as little so as we can expect any popular work to be that emanates from an uncatholic source.

The anonymous critic for The American Whig Review *not only reviews* The Blithedale Romance *but also comments on* The Scarlet Letter, The House of the Seven Gables, *and* Life of Franklin Pierce. *He faults* The Blithedale Romance *for its lack of tenderness and characterizes Hawthorne as an untrue author because of his failure to value human progress.* The American Whig Review *was founded in 1845 as* The American Review: A Whig Journal of Politics, Literature, Art and Science; *during its seven-year run it published literature of high quality, including works by Edgar Allan Poe and James Russell Lowell.*

Review of *The Blithedale Romance*
The American Whig Review, 16,
n.s. 10 (November 1852): 417–424

Every work which proposes to develop a new phase of human character, or philosophize upon an assumption of original responsibilities, derives a species of adventitious interest from the novelty of its subject, independent of any artistic ability by which it may be accompanied. When it was publicly understood that Mr Hawthorne was engaged in the composition of a romance, having for its origin, if not its subject, a community which once had a brief existence at Brook Farm, speculation was awakened, anticipations grew vivid, and the reading public awaited anxiously the issue of a book which it was hoped would combine in itself the palatable spices of novelty and personality. A portion of these expectations were doomed to disappointment. In the preface to *The Blithedale Romance,* Mr Hawthorne distinctly disavowed any intention of painting portraits. To his sojourn at Brook Farm he attributes his inspiration, but that is all. Blithedale is no caligraph of Brook Farm. Zenobia first sprang into actual existence from the printing press of Ticknor, Reed and Fields, and the quiet Priscilla is nothing more than one of those pretty phantoms with which Mr Hawthorne occasionally adorns his romances.

We believe that if Mr Hawthorne had intended to give a faithful portrait of Brook Farm and its inmates, he would have signally failed. He has no genius for realities, save in inanimate nature. Between his characters and the reader falls a gauze-like veil of imagination, on which their shadows flit and move, and play strange dramas replete with second-hand life. An air of unreality enshrouds all his creations. They are either dead, or have never lived, and when they pass away they leave behind them an oppressive and unwholesome chill.

This sluggish antiquity of style may suit some subjects admirably. When, as in *The Scarlet Letter,* the epoch of the story is so far removed from the present day as to invest all the events with little more than a reminiscent interest; when characters and customs were

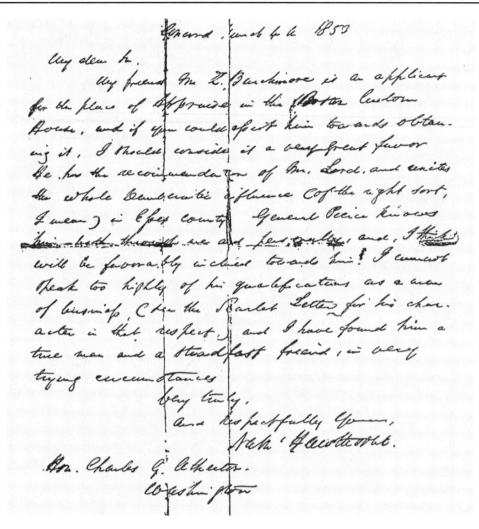

Hawthorne's 4 March 1853 letter to New Hampshire senator Charles G. Atherton in which he supports Zachariah Burchmore's application as an appraiser in the Boston Custom House by alluding to his portrayal in The Scarlet Letter *(Berg Collection, New York Public Library)*

The Custom-House in Himself

Hawthorne writes in "The Custom-House" of the moral and intellectual benefit of meeting individuals unlike oneself. He describes Zacharia Burchmore, unnamed in the sketch, as a man he learned to appreciate.

There was one man, especially, the observation of whose character gave me a new idea of talent. His gifts were emphatically those of a man of business; prompt, acute, clear-minded; with an eye that saw through all perplexities, and a faculty of arrangement that made them vanish, as by the waving of an enchanter's wand. Bred up from boyhood in the Cutom-House, it was his proper field of activity; and the many intricacies of business, so harassing to the interloper, presented themselves before him with the regularity of a perfectly comprehended system. In my contemplation, he stood as the ideal of his class. He was, indeed, the Custom-House in himself; or, at all events, the main-spring that kept its variously revolving wheels in motion; for, in an institution like this, where its officers are appointed to subserve their own profit and convenience, and seldom with a leading reference to their fitness for the duty to be performed, they must perforce seek elsewhere the dexterity which is not in them. Thus, by an inevitable necessity, as a magnet attracts steel-filings, so did our man of business draw to himself the difficulties which everybody met with. With an easy condescension, and kind forbearance towards our stupidity,–which, to his order of mind, must have seemed little short of crime,– would he forthwith, by the merest touch of his finger, make the incomprehensible as clear as daylight.

–*The Scarlet Letter,* The Centenary Edition, vol. 1, p. 24

so different to all circumstance that jostles us in the rude, quick life of today, and when we do not expect to meet, in the long corridors of Time down which the author leads us, any company beyond the pale, shadowy ancestry with whose names we are faintly familiar, but with whom we have no common sympathies. Mr Hawthorne's genius, if we may be permitted to use so extravagant a simile, reminds us forcibly of an old country mansion of the last century. It seems as if it had been built a very long time. It is but half inhabited, and throbs with only a moiety of life. The locks and bolts are rusty, and the doors creak harshly on their hinges. Huge twisted chimneys branch out of every gable, and in every chimney is lodged some capricious, eccentric old rook, who startles us unexpectedly with his presence. Great wings, and odd buttresses, jut out from all the corners, the phrenological bumps of architecture; while here and there, in warm sheltered nooks, sweet climbing flowers, dewy roses, and jessamine prodigal of its perfume, cling lovingly to the old moss-grown walls, and strive, but with ill success, to conceal the quaint deformity of the building.

In *The House of the Seven Gables* this dreary beauty is eminently prominent. The poetry of desolation, and the leaden vapors of solitude are wreathed around the scene. The doings of the characters awaken only a faint, dream-like interest in our hearts. We seem to hear the hollow echoes of their footsteps in the silence, and follow them with our fingers as if we expected them each moment to melt and mingle with the surrounding air. This sad and unsubstantial painting is no doubt excellently well achieved. Mr Hawthorne deals artistically with shadows. There is a strange, unearthly fascination about the fair spectres that throng his works, and we know no man who can distort nature, or idealize abortions more cleverly than the author of *The Scarlet Letter*. But we question much, if we strip Mr Hawthorne's works of a certain beauty and originality of style which they are always sure to possess, whether the path which he has chosen is a healthy one. To us it does not seem as if the fresh wind of morning blew across his track; we do not feel the strong pulse of nature throbbing beneath the turf he treads upon. When an author sits down to make a book, he should not alone consult the inclinations of his own genius regarding its purpose or its construction. If he should happen to be imbued with strange, saturnine doctrines, or be haunted by a morbid suspicion of human nature, in God's name let him not write one word. Better that all the beautiful, wild thoughts with which his brain is teeming should moulder for ever in neglect and darkness, than that one soul was overshadowed by stern, uncongenial dogmas, which should have died with their Puritan fathers. It is not alone necessary to produce a work of art. The soul of beauty is Truth, and Truth is ever progressive. The true artist therefore endeavors to make the world better. He does not look behind him, and dig out of the graves of past centuries skeletons to serve as models for his pictures; but looks onward for more perfect shapes, and though sometimes obliged to design from the defective forms around him, he infuses, as it were, some of the divine spirit of the future into them, and lo! we love them with all their faults. But Mr Hawthorne discards all idea of successful human progress. All his characters seem so weighed down with their own evilness of nature, that they can scarcely keep their balance, much less take their places in the universal march. Like the lord mentioned in Scripture, he issues an invitation to the halt, the blind, and the lame of soul, to gather around his board, and then asks us to feast at the same table. It is a pity that Mr Hawthorne should not have been originally imbued with more universal tenderness. It is a pity that he displays nature to us so shrouded and secluded, and that he should be afflicted with such a melancholy craving for human curiosities. His men are either vicious, crazed, or misanthropical, and his women are either unwomanly, unearthly, or unhappy. His books have no sunny side to them. They are unripe to the very core.

We are more struck with the want of this living tenderness in *The Blithedale Romance* than in any of Mr Hawthorn's previous novels. In *The Scarlet Letter* and *The House of the Seven Gables,* a certain gloominess of thought suited the antiquity of the subjects; but in his last performance, the date of the events, and the nature of the story, entitle us to expect something brighter and less unhealthy. The efforts of any set of hopeful, well-meaning people to shame society into better ways, are deserving of respect, as long as they do not attempt to interfere with those sacred foundation-stones of morality on which all society rests. It was a pure, fresh thought, that of flying from the turmoil of the city, and toiling in common upon the broad fields for bread. With all their fallacies, there is much that is good and noble about the American communists. It is a sad mistake to suppose them stern exponents of the gross and absurd system laid down by Fourier. They are not, at least as far as our knowledge goes, either dishonest or sensual. They do not mock at rational rights, or try to overturn the constitution of society. We believe their ruling idea to be that of isolating themselves from all that is corrupt in the congregations of mankind called cities, and seek in open country and healthy toil the sweets and triumphs of a purer life. One would imagine that dealing with a subject like this would in some degree counteract Mr Hawthorne's ascetic humor. One would have thought that, in narrating a course of events which, acted on as they were by the surrounding circumstances, must have been somewhat buoyant and fresh, he would have burst that icy chain of puritanical gloom, and for once made a holiday with Nature. No such thing! From the beginning to the end, *The Blithedale Romance* is a melancholy chronicle, less repulsive, it is true, than its predecessors, but still sad and inexpressibly mournful. Not that the author has intended it to be uniformly pathetic. It is very evident that he sat down with the intention of writing a strong, vigorous book, upon a strong, vigorous subject; but his own baneful spirit hovered over the pages, and turned the ink into bitterness and tears.

Let us review his characters, and see if we can find any thing genial among them. Hollingsworth in importance comes first. A rude fragment of a great man. Unyielding as granite in any matters on which he has decided, yet possessing a latent tenderness of nature that, if he had been the creature of other hands than Mr Hawthorne's, would have been his redemption. But our author is deeply read in human imperfection, and lets no opportunity slip of thrusting it before his readers. A horrid lump of unappeasable egotism is stuck between Hollingsworth's shoulders. He is depicted as a sort of human Maëlstrom, engulfing all natures that come within his range, and relentlessly absorbing them in his own vast necessities. He is selfish, dogmatic, and inhumanly proud, and all these frightful attributes are tacked on to a character that, in the hands of a Dickens or a Fielding, would have loomed out from the canvas with sufficient imperfection to make it human, but with enough of heart and goodness to compel us to love it.

Readers will perchance say that Mr Hawthorne has a right to deal with his characters according to his pleasure, and that we are not authorized to quarrel with the length of their noses, or the angularities of their natures. No doubt. But, on the other hand, Mr Hawthorne has no right to blacken and defame humanity, by animating his shadowy people with worse passions and more imperfect souls than we meet with in the world.

Miles Coverdale, the narrator of the tale, is to us a most repulsive being. A poet, but yet no poetry in his deeds. A sneering, suspicious, inquisitive, and disappointed man, who rejects Hollingsworth's advances because he fears that a connection between them may lead to some ulterior peril; who allows Zenobia to dominate over his nature, because she launches at him a few wild words, and who forsakes the rough, healthy life of Blithedale, because he pines for Turkey carpets and a sea-coal fire. Such is the man upon whose dictum Mr Hawthorne would endeavor covertly to show the futility of the enterprise in whose favour he was once enlisted.

Zenobia, the character on which he has probably bestowed the most pains, is no doubt true to nature. Women that thrust themselves out of their sphere must inevitably lose many of those graces which constitute their peculiar charm. Looked upon by their own sex with dismay, and by ours with certain mingled feelings of jealousy and pity, they voluntarily isolate themselves from the generality of the world, and fancy themselves martyrs. They are punished with contempt, and to reformers of their fiery nature, contempt is worse than death. They blaspheme God by stepping beyond the limits He has assigned to them through all ages, and seem to fancy that they can better laws which are eternal and immutable.

The Zenobia of our author does not command our interest. Her character, though poetically colored, is not sufficiently powerful for a woman that has so far outstridden the even pace of society. She has a certain amount of courage and passion, but no philosophy. Her impulses start off in the wrong direction, nor does she seem to possess the earnestness necessary to induce a woman to defy public opinion. She is a mere fierce, wild wind, blowing hither and thither, with no fixity of purpose, and making us shrink closer every moment from the contact.

In truth, with the exception of Priscilla, who is faint and shadowy, the dramatis personae at Blithedale are not to our taste. There is a bad purpose in every one of them—a purpose, too, which is neither finally redeemed nor condemned.

Notwithstanding the faults which we have alluded to, and which cling to Mr Hawthorne tenaciously in all his works, there is much to be admired in *The Blithedale Romance*. If our author takes a dark view of society, he takes a bright one of nature. He paints truthfully and poetically, and possesses a Herrick-like fashion of deducing morals from flowers, rocks, and herbage, or any other little feature in his visionary landscape. We cull a specimen of his powers in this respect:

> The pathway of that walk still runs along, with sunny freshness, through my memory . . . Nor why, amid all my sympathies and fears, there shot, at times, a wild exhilaration through my frame.

On the socialist theory Mr Hawthorne says little in *The Blithedale Romance*. That he is no longer a convert is evident, but he does not attempt to discuss the matter philosophically. Judging from many passages in the book, we should say that he had been sadly disappointed in the experiment made at Brook Farm, and sought thus covertly and incidentally to record his opinion. One of the most curious characteristics of the book is, that not one of the persons assembled at Blithedale treat the institution as if they were in earnest. Zenobia sneers at it–Coverdale grumbles at it–Hollingsworth condemns–Priscilla alone endures it. We know not if this is a feature drawn from realities. If it is not, Mr Hawthorne is immediately placed in the position of having created a group of fictitious hypocrites, not true to human nature, merely for the sake of placing them in a novel position and surrounding them with fresh scenery. The following account of the sensations of gentleman farmers is good:

> The peril of our new way of life was not lest we should fail in becoming practical agriculturists, but that we should probably cease to be anything else . . . The yeoman and the scholar–the yeoman and the man of finest moral culture, though not the man of sturdiest sense and integrity, are two distinct individuals, and can never be melted or welded into one substance.

With the last paragraph we cannot agree. The mind depends for healthy action upon the health and soundness of the flesh, and in no way can the physical constitution be developed better than by hard work; that is, work, not for hours, days or weeks, but constant, unremitting employment. Mr Hawthorne writes this passage very much like a man to whom labor was a new thing, and who, though he may have worked hard during the day, at night found himself from sheer exhaustion almost incapable of thought. But the man who habitually works feels no after lassitude. Were the laborer in the fields, or the blacksmith at the anvil, to be gifted with purer intellect or higher mental culture than is usually allotted to such men, they would not find their labor interfering with their inspiration. After working hours, such men do not experience any lassitude. They surrender themselves to a pleasing sensation of tranquillity, but would be as fit for any new physical or mental occupation as they ever were. But with the experimentalist in toil it is different. The muscles, that from their first maturity have been accustomed to lie at ease, are not so readily brought into play. The gentleman whose days have been spent in sedentary occupations, no matter how powerful his physical frame may be, will find that on his first initiation into the school of labor, he is unfit for any task save one. His nature is suddenly worked against the grain, and refuses to act beyond a certain time. But if these tasks were continued for any period, if day after day the gentleman were to go out into the fields and make fences or plough cornfields, the mental sluggishness complained of by Mr Hawthorne would wear off, and he would find that hardened muscles were not at all incompatible with the struggles of philosophic thought, or the play of imagination.

In Priscilla, Mr Hawthorne has essayed a delicate character, but in his portraiture he has availed himself of an ingenious expedient, which we know not whether to rank as intentional or accidental. In drawing a portrait, there are two ways of attaining delicacy of outline. One is by making the outline itself so faint and indistinct that it appears as it were to mingle with the surrounding shadow; the other and more difficult one is, to paint, and paint detail after detail, until the whole becomes so finished a work of art, so harmoniously colored, that one feature does not strike us more forcibly than another; so homogeneous in its aspect that outline, background and detail are all painted perfectly on our perceptions in a manner that defies analysis. Now, there is no question that the man who employs the first means has infinitely easier work than the last. He has nothing to do but conjure you up a pretty-looking ghost, and lo! the work is done. Mr Hawthorne is fond of these ghosts. Priscilla is a ghost; we do not realize her, even to the end. Her connection with Westervelt is shadowy and ill-defined. Zenobia's influence over her nature is only indistinctly intimated. Her own mental construction is left almost an open question; and even when, in the crowning of the drama, we find her the support, the crutch of the rugged Hollingsworth, there is no satisfactory happiness wreathed about her destiny. This is not artistic or wholesome. We all know that a certain fascination springs up in every breast when the undefined is presented. The love of spectral stories, and superhuman exhibitions, all have their root in this, and Mr Hawthorne appears to know well how to play upon this secret chord with his fantastic shadows. We do not look upon his treatment of character as fair. He does not give it to us in its entirety, but puts us off with a pleasant phantasmagoria. We should attribute this to inability in any other man, but we feel too well convinced of Mr Hawthorne's genius to doubt his capability for an instant to furnish us with a perfect picture. But we doubt his will. This sketchy painting is easy and rapid. A very few lines will indicate a spectre, when it would take an entire month to paint a woman; and Mr Hawthorne finds this unsubstantial picture-making suit his own dreamy and sometimes morbid fancy. For Heaven's sake, Mr Hawthorne, do not continue to give us shadows, even if they be as sweet and loveable as Priscilla! Recollect that you have earned a great name as a writer of romance, and will necessarily have many followers. Cease then, good sir; for if you continue to give us shadows, in another year your imitators will inundate their books with skeletons!

That Mr Hawthorne can paint vividly when he likes it, few who have read his novels can doubt. He

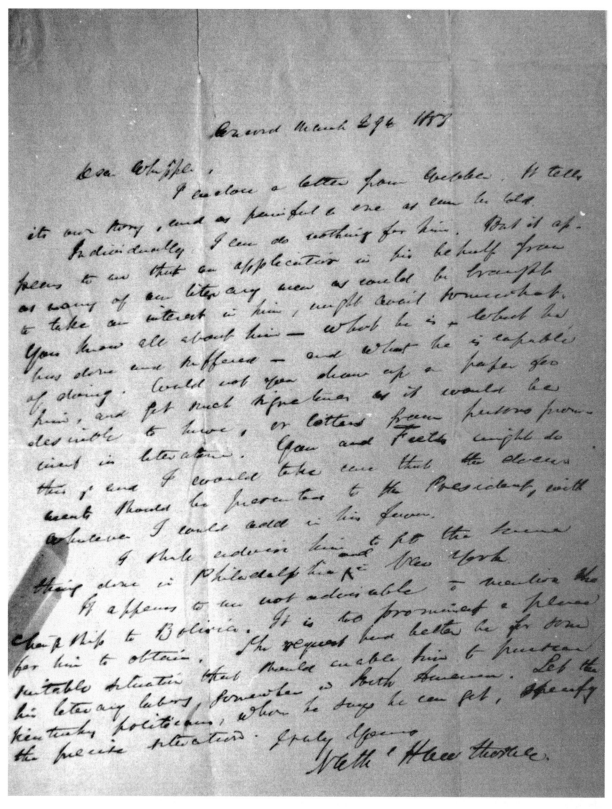

Hawthorne's 29 March 1853 letter to E. P. Whipple, who reviewed The Scarlet Letter, *concerning Charles Wilkins Webber,*
who was not appointed to the position in Bolivia that Hawthorne mentions (Peabody Essex Museum)

TANGLEWOOD TALES,

FOR

GIRLS AND BOYS:

Being a Second Wonder-Book.

BY

NATHANIEL HAWTHORNE.

WITH ILLUSTRATIONS.

LONDON:
CHAPMAN AND HALL, 193, PICCADILLY.
1853.

TANGLEWOOD TALES,

FOR

GIRLS AND BOYS;

BEING

A SECOND WONDER-BOOK.

BY

NATHANIEL HAWTHORNE.

WITH FINE ILLUSTRATIONS.

BOSTON:
TICKNOR, REED, AND FIELDS.
M DCCC LIII.

Title pages for the first English and American editions of the sequel to A Wonder-Book. *The collection was made up of seven tales:*
"The Wayside—Introductory," "The Minotaur," "The Pygmies," "The Dragon's Teeth," "Circe's Palace," "The Pomegranate Seeds,"
and "The Golden Fleece" (C. E. Frazer Clark Jr., Nathaniel Hawthorne: A Descriptive Bibliography, *1978).*

Illustration from "The Dragon's Teeth" in A Wonder Book *(Library of Congress)*

Bindings for Life of Pierce *and* Tanglewood Tales *published in 1852 and 1853 (from C. E. Frazer Clark Jr.,*
Nathaniel Hawthorne: A Descriptive Bibliography, *1978)*

possesses all the requisites for the task—power of language, felicity of collateral incident, and a certain subdued richness of style which is one of his greatest charms. The following description of the death of Zenobia is exquisitely managed. It is suspected that the proud woman has committed suicide, and Hollingsworth, Coverdale, and Silas Foster, the farm superintendent, set out to seek for the body:

> When our few preparations were completed, we hastened, by a shorter than the customary route, through fields and pastures, and across a portion of the meadows, to the particular spot on the river-bank which I had paused to contemplate in my afternoon's ramble . . .

> . . . By-and-by came three or four withered women and stood whispering around the corpse, or peering at it through their spectacles, holding up their skinny hands, shaking their night-capped heads, and taking counsel of one another's experience what was to be done.

With those tire-women we left Zenobia.

This is powerful—sadness and strength mingled into a most poetical and vivid death-scene. A thought crosses us, whether Mr Hawthorne would paint a wedding as well as a death; whether he could conjure as distinctly before our vision the bridal flowers, as he has done the black, damp weeds that waved around the grave of Zenobia. We fear not. His genius has a church-yard beauty about it, and revels amid graves, and executions, and all the sad leavings of mortality. We know no man whom we would sooner ask to write our epitaph. We feel assured that it would be poetical, and suitable in the highest degree.

Since the publication of his book, it grieved us to learn that a severe domestic affliction has overtaken Mr Hawthorne, through the terrible calamity that befell the *Henry Clay*. It was a sad coincidence that death by the waves should overtake a member of his family so soon after his fictitious tragedy of Zenobia. It was a bitter thing for the secluded author to be forced to entwine with his newly acquired laurel-wreaths so melancholy a leaf as that of cypress.

Since the publication of *The Blithedale Romance,* Mr Hawthorne has brought before the public a book which unquestionably will bring him neither fame nor credit. It is always hateful to see a man of genius degrading his pen into a party tool, and pressing genius, designed for better ends, into the service of every empty puppet that is thrust undeservedly into public notice. But still worse is it with Mr Hawthorne, who, it will be difficult to persuade the public, did not stir himself to the ungracious task of writing a man's life, whose life no one cares to know, without the vivid inspiration of some promised office. Mr Hawthorne was a place-holder once before, and we trust will be a place-holder again; for it is always pleasant to see the country dispensing its bounty to those whose genius had long been its boast and admiration. But there surely was no necessity that he should turn the biographer of so hitherto obscure a man as General Pierce. We grieve to see so distinguished a man of letters sullying his reputation by such mean and venal homage to ambitious mediocrity. The hateful days are gone by when the author required a patron, on whom, in return for his bounty, he lavished fulsome adulation. We no longer live in the time of Dryden and Johnson. The true literary man, thank Heaven, can be as free as the air which he inspires, and as unbending as the oak tree in the primeval forests of our giant land. He need not beg at great men's doors for favor or bread, nor exchange servile verses for current coin. He writes what he thinks, and thinks what he likes; and with industry, good conduct, and a fair amount of genius, he need not fear 'to look the whole world in the face,' nor 'owe to any man.' It is doubly disgusting, then, in an age of freedom to see a man of ability voluntarily prostitute his pen, for the paltry object of some governmental salary. There are 'hacks' enough, Heaven knows, infesting every city, who would be right glad and well fitted to perform such filthy work. Surrender, then, your degrading office to the Helots of literature, Mr Hawthorne! Live a quiet, pure and honest life upon your farm, and spurn with righteous indignation all those unscrupulous partisans who invite you to sacrifice your own fame and annihilate your own honesty. Give us such works as *The Scarlet Letter,* and *The Blithedale Romance*–works of art and beauty, with all their deformities–and let your rare genius soar for ever above the atmosphere of mushroom heroes and penny biographies.

Life Abroad and *The Marble Faun*

Hawthorne's pace of producing three significant novels in three years ended when President Franklin Pierce appointed him as the American consul to Liverpool, England, for official duties occupied his time. An extended stay in Italy following his consulate provided material for his longest and last completed novel, The Marble Faun, *published in early March 1860 in the United States. Within a year and a half the American edition required seven printings totaling 14,500 copies.*

Unlike his previous novels, The Marble Faun *(titled* Transformation *in England, where it was first published) is set not in America but in Italy. But while Hawthorne in his novel deals with art and gives the flavor of Italian, especially Roman, life, he explores such familiar themes as guilt (Miriam's and Donatello's) and Puritanism (Hilda's). As Hawthorne had reacted to reader response by writing a preface to the second edition of* The Scarlet Letter, *he did so again by composing a postscript to the second English printing of* Transformation, *though the evasive explanation of the novel's ambiguities doubtless frustrated readers who had wanted him to clarify its mysteries.*

Hawthorne Abroad

During Hawthorne's seven years abroad, James T. Fields often corresponded with him and sometimes visited the author.

He kept me constantly informed, after he went to Liverpool, of how he was passing his time; and his charming "English Note-Books" reveal the fact that he was never idle. There were touches, however, in his private letters which escaped daily record in his journal, and I remember how delightful it was, after he landed in Europe, to get his frequent missives. In one of the first he gives me an account of a dinner where he was obliged to make a speech. He says:–

"I tickled up John Bull's self-conceit (which is very easily done) with a few sentences of most outrageous flattery, and sat down in a general puddle of good feeling." In another he says: "I have taken a house in Rock Park, on the Cheshire side of the Mersey, and am as snug as a bug in a rug. Next year you must come and see how I live. Give my regards to everybody, and my love to half a dozen. . . . . I wish you would call on Mr.

Savage, the antiquarian, if you know him, and ask whether he can inform me what part of England the original William Hawthorne came from. He came over, I think, in 1634. . . . . It would really be a great obligation if he could answer the above query. Or, if the fact is not within his own knowledge, he might perhaps indicate some place where such information might be obtained here in England. I presume there are records still extant somewhere of all the passengers by those early ships, with their English localities annexed to their names. Of all things, I should like to find a gravestone in one of these old churchyards with my own name upon it, although, for myself, I should wish to be buried in America. The graves are too horribly damp here."

The hedgerows of England, the grassy meadows, and the picturesque old cottages delighted him, and he was never tired of writing to me about them. While wandering over the country, he was often deeply touched by meeting among the wild-flowers many of his old New England favorites,–bluebells, crocuses, primroses, foxglove, and other flowers which are cultivated in our gardens, and which had long been familiar to him in America.

I can imagine him, in his quiet, musing way, strolling through the daisied fields on a Sunday morning and hearing the distant church-bells chiming to service. His religion was deep and broad, but it was irksome for him to be fastened in by a pew-door, and I doubt if he often heard an English sermon. He very rarely described himself as *inside* a church, but he liked to wander among the graves in the churchyards and read the epitaphs on the moss-grown slabs. He liked better to meet and have a talk with the *sexton* than with the *rector*.

He was constantly demanding longer letters from home; and nothing gave him more pleasure than monthly news from "The Saturday Club," and detailed accounts of what was going forward in literature. One of his letters dated in January, 1854, starts off thus:–

"I wish your epistolary propensities were stronger than they are. All your letters to me since I left America might be squeezed into one. . . . . I send Ticknor a big cheese, which I long ago promised him, and my advice

DEPARTMENT OF STATE,
WASHINGTON, *April 17th 1853*.

Nathaniel Hawthorn, Esq,

Appointed Consul of the United States for *the Port of Liverpool England.*

SIR:

THE PRESIDENT, by and with the advice and consent of the Senate, having appointed you Consul of the United States for *the Port of Liverpool in England, to take effect from and after July 31st 1853.* I transmit to you a printed copy of the General Instructions to Consuls, to the 1st and 2d Chapters of which your immediate attention is called; a form of the Consular bond; and other documents for the use of your Consulate, of which a list is subjoined. Among them will be found a circular of July 30th, 1840, which contains a copy of an act of the 20th of that month, not embodied in the Instructions, and with the provisions of which it is important you should be fully acquainted.

Your Commission will be sent to the Legation of the United States at *London* with instructions to apply to the *British* Government for the usual Exequatur, which, when obtained, will be forwarded to you with the Commission.

You will communicate to the department the name of the State or Country in which you were born: and if you have ever resided *in Liverpool.*

I am, Sir,
Your obedient servant,

Wm. L. Marcy.

DOCUMENTS TRANSMITTED.

General Instructions, Blank bond, List of Ministers, Consuls, &c., Forms of Returns and Statement of Fees. Ink lines, ~~Circulars of~~

*Hawthorne's letter of appointment as a U.S. consul, signed by William L. Marcy, secretary of state
(from Bryan Homer,* An American Liaison, *1998)*

is, that he keep it in the shop, and daily, between eleven and one o'clock, distribute slices of it to your half-starved authors, together with crackers and something to drink. . . . . I thank you for the books you send me, and more especially for Mrs. Mowatt's Autobiography, which seems to me an admirable book. Of all things I delight in autobiographies; and I hardly ever read one that interested me so much. She must be a remarkable woman, and I cannot but lament my ill fortune in never having seen her on the stage or elsewhere. . . . . I count strongly upon your promise to be with us in May. Can't you bring Whipple with you?"

One of his favorite resorts in Liverpool was the boarding-house of good Mrs. Blodgett, in Duke Street, a house where many Americans have found delectable quarters, after being tossed on the stormy Atlantic. "I have never known a better woman," Hawthorne used to say, "and her motherly kindness to me and mine I can never forget." Hundreds of American travellers will bear witness to the excellence of that beautiful old lady, who presided with such dignity and sweetness over her hospitable mansion.

On the 13th of April, 1854, Hawthorne wrote to me this characteristic letter from the consular office in Liverpool:–

"I am very glad that the 'Mosses' have come into the hands of our firm; and I return the copy sent me, after a careful revision. When I wrote those dreamy sketches, I little thought that I should ever preface an edition for the press amidst the bustling life of a Liverpool consulate. Upon my honor, I am not quite sure that I entirely comprehend my own meaning, in some of these blasted allegories; but I remember that I always had a meaning, or at least thought I had. I am a good deal changed since those times; and, to tell you the truth, my past self is not very much to my taste, as I see myself in this book. Yet certainly there is more in it than the public generally gave me credit for at the time it was written.

"But I don't think myself worthy of very much more credit than I got. It has been a very disagreeable task to read the book. The story of 'Rappacini's Daughter' was published in the Democratic Review, about the year 1844, and it was prefaced by some remarks on the celebrated French author (a certain M. de l'Aubépine), from whose works it was translated. I left out this preface when the story was republished; but I wish you would turn to it in the Democratic, and see whether it is worth while to insert it in the new edition. I leave it altogether to your judgment.

"A young poet named — has called on me, and has sent me some copies of his works to be transmitted to America. It seems to me there is good in him; and he is recognized by Tennyson, by Carlyle, by Kingsley, and others of the best people here. He writes me that this edition of his poems is nearly exhausted, and that Routledge is going to publish another enlarged and in better style.

"Perhaps it might be well for you to take him up in America. At all events, try to bring him into notice; and some day or other you may be glad to have helped a famous poet in his obscurity. The poor fellow has left a good post in the customs to cultivate literature in London!

"We shall begin to look for you now by every steamer from Boston. You must make up your mind to spend a good while with us before going to see your London friends.

"Did you read the article on your friend De Quincey in the last Westminster? It was written by Mr. — of this city, who was in America a year or two ago. The article is pretty well, but does nothing like adequate justice to De Quincey; and in fact no Englishman cares a pin for him. We are ten times as good readers and critics as they.

"Is not Whipple coming here soon?"

Hawthorne's first visit to London afforded him great pleasure, but he kept out of the way of literary people as much as possible. He introduced himself to nobody, except Mr. —, whose assistance he needed, in order to be identified at the bank. He wrote to me from 24 George Street, Hanover Square, and told me he delighted in London, and wished he could spend a year there. He enjoyed floating about, in a sort of unknown way, among the rotund and rubicund figures made jolly with ale and port-wine. He was greatly amused at being told (his informants meaning to be complimentary) "that he would never be taken for anything but an Englishman." He called Tennyson's "Charge of the Light Brigade," just printed at that time, "a broken-kneed gallop of a poem." He writes:–

"John Bull is in high spirits just now at the taking of Sebastopol. What an absurd personage John is! I find that my liking for him grows stronger the more I see of him, but that my admiration and respect have constantly decreased."

One of his most intimate friends (a man unlike that individual of whom it was said that he was the friend of everybody that did not need a friend) was Francis Bennoch, a merchant of Wood Street, Cheapside, London, the gentleman to whom Mrs. Hawthorne dedicated the English Note-Books. Hawthorne's letters abounded in warm expressions of affection for the man whose noble hospitality and deep interest made his residence in England full of happiness. Bennoch was indeed like a brother to him, sympathizing warmly in all his literary projects, and giving him the benefit of his excellent judgment while he was sojourning among strangers. Bennoch's record may be found in Tom Taylor's admirable life of poor Haydon, the artist. All literary and artistic people who have had the good fortune to enjoy his friendship have loved him. I happen to know of his bountiful kindness to Miss Mitford and Hawthorne and poor old Jerdan, for these hospitalities happened in my time; but he began to befriend all who needed friendship long before I knew him. His name ought never to be omitted from the literary annals of England; nor that of his wife either, for she has always made her delightful fireside warm and comforting to her husband's friends.

Many and many a happy time Bennoch, Hawthorne, and myself have had together on British soil. I remember we went once to dine at a great house in the country, years ago, where it was understood there would be no dinner speeches. The banquet was in honor of some society,—I have quite forgotten what,—but it was a jocose and not a serious club. The gentleman who gave it, Sir ——, was a most kind and genial person, and gathered about him on this occasion some of the brightest and best from London. All the way down in the train Hawthorne was rejoicing that this was to be a dinner without speech-making; "for," said he, "nothing would tempt me to go if toasts and such confounded deviltry were to be the order of the day." So we rattled along, without a fear of any impending cloud of oratory. The entertainment was a most exquisite one, about twenty gentlemen sitting down at the beautifully ornamented table. Hawthorne was in uncommonly good spirits, and, having the seat of honor at the right of his host, was pretty keenly scrutinized by his British brethren of the quill. He had, of course, banished all thought of speech-making, and his knees never smote together once, as he told me afterwards. But it became evident to my mind that Hawthorne's health was to be proposed with all the honors. I glanced at him across the table, and saw that he was unsuspicious of any movement against his quiet serenity. Suddenly and without warning our host rapped the mahogany, and began a set speech of welcome to the "distinguished American romancer." It was a very honest and a very hearty speech, but I dared not look at Hawthorne. I expected every moment to see him glide out of the room, or sink down out of sight from his chair. The tortures I suffered on Hawthorne's account, on that occasion, I will not attempt to describe now. I knew nothing would have induced the shy man of letters to go down to Brighton, if he had known he was to be spoken at in that manner. I imagined his face a deep crimson, and his hands trembling with nervous horror; but judge of my surprise, when he rose to reply with so calm a voice and so composed a manner, that, in all my experience of dinner-speaking, I never witnessed such a case of apparent ease. (Easy-Chair C— himself, one of the best makers of after-dinner or any other

speeches of our day, according to Charles Dickens,—no inadequate judge, all will allow,—never surpassed in eloquent effect this speech by Hawthorne.) There was no hesitation, no sign of lack of preparation, but he went on for about ten minutes in such a masterly manner, that I declare it was one of the most successful efforts of the kind ever made. Everybody was delighted, and, when he sat down, a wild and unanimous shout of applause rattled the glasses on the table. The meaning of his singular composure on that occasion I could never get him satisfactorily to explain, and the only remark I ever heard him make, in any way connected with this marvellous exhibition of coolness, was simply, "What a confounded fool I was to go down to that speech-making dinner!"

During all those long years, while Hawthorne was absent in Europe, he was anything but an idle man. On the contrary, he was an eminently busy one, in the best sense of that term; and if his life had been prolonged, the public would have been a rich gainer for his residence abroad. His brain teemed with romances, and once I remember he told me he had no less than five stories, well thought out, any one of which he could finish and publish whenever he chose to. There was one subject for a work of imagination that seems to have haunted him for years, and he has mentioned it twice in his journal. This was the subsequent life of the young man whom Jesus, looking on, "loved," and whom he bade to sell all that he had and give to the poor, and take up his cross and follow him. "Something very deep and beautiful might be made out of this," Hawthorne said, "for the young man went away sorrowful, and is not recorded to have done what he was bidden to do."

One of the most difficult matters he had to manage while in England was the publication of Miss Bacon's singular book on Shakespeare. The poor lady, after he had agreed to see the work through the press, broke off all correspondence with him in a storm of wrath, accusing him of pusillanimity in not avowing full faith in her theory; so that, as he told me, so far as her good-will was concerned, he had not gained much by taking the responsibility of her book upon his shoulders. It was a heavy weight for him to bear in more senses than one, for he paid out of his own pocket the expenses of publication.

I find in his letters constant references to the kindness with which he was treated in London. He spoke of Mrs. S. C. Hall as "one of the best and warmest-hearted women in the world." Leigh Hunt, in his way, pleased and satisfied him more than almost any man he had seen in England. "As for other literary men," he says in one of his letters, "I doubt whether London can muster so good a dinner-party as that which assembles every month at the marble palace in School Street."

All sorts of adventures befell him during his stay in Europe, even to that of having his house robbed, and his causing the thieves to be tried and sentenced to transportation. In the summer-time he travelled about the country in England and pitched his tent wherever fancy prompted. One autumn afternoon in September he writes to me from Leamington:–

"I received your letter only this morning, at this cleanest and prettiest of English towns, where we are going to spend a week or two before taking our departure for Paris. We are acquainted with Leamington already, having resided here two summers ago; and the country round about is unadulterated England, rich in old castles, manor-houses, churches, and thatched cottages, and as green as Paradise itself. I only wish I had a house here, and that you could come and be my guest in it; but I am a poor wayside vagabond, and only find shelter for a night or so, and then trudge onward again. My wife and children and myself are familiar with all kinds of lodgement and modes of living, but we have forgotten what home is,–at least the children have, poor things! I doubt whether they will ever feel inclined to live long in one place. The worst of it is, I have outgrown my house in Concord, and feel no inclination to return to it.

"We spent seven weeks in Manchester, and went most diligently to the Art Exhibition; and I really begin to be sensible of the rudiments of a taste in pictures."

It was during one of his rambles with Alexander Ireland through the Manchester Exhibition rooms that Hawthorne saw Tennyson wandering about. I have always thought it unfortunate that these two men of genius could not have been introduced on that occasion. Hawthorne was too shy to seek an introduction, and Tennyson was not aware that the American author was present. Hawthorne records in his journal that he gazed at Tennyson with all his eyes, "and rejoiced more in him than in all the other wonders of the Exhibition." When I afterwards told Tennyson that the author whose "Twice-Told Tales" he happened to be then reading at Farringford had met him at Manchester, but did not make himself known, the Laureate said in his frank and hearty manner: "Why didn't he come up and let me shake hands with him? I am sure I should have been glad to meet a man like Hawthorne anywhere."

At the close of 1857 Hawthorne writes to me that he hears nothing of the appointment of his successor in the consulate, since he had sent in his resignation. "Somebody may turn up any day," he says, "with a new commission in his pocket." He was meanwhile getting ready for Italy, and he writes, "I expect shortly to be released from durance."

In his last letter before leaving England for the Continent he says:–

The Liverpool consulate, where Hawthorne had an office on the second floor (marked by an x; from J. O. Mays, Mr. Hawthorne Goes to England, *1983)*

"I made up a huge package the other day, consisting of seven closely written volumes of journal, kept by me since my arrival in England, and filled with sketches of places and men and manners, many of which would doubtless be very delightful to the public. I think I shall seal them up, with directions in my will to have them opened and published a century hence; and your firm shall have the refusal of them then.

"Remember me to everybody, for I love all my friends at least as well as ever."

Released from the cares of office, and having nothing to distract his attention, his life on the Continent opened full of delightful excitement. His pecuniary situation was such as to enable him to live very comfortably in a country where, at that time, prices were moderate.

In a letter dated from a villa near Florence on the 3d of September, 1858, he thus describes in a charming manner his way of life in Italy:–

"I am afraid I have stayed away too long, and am forgotten by everybody. You have piled up the dusty remnants of my editions, I suppose, in that chamber over the shop, where you once took me to smoke a cigar, and have crossed my name out of your list of

Consular Experiences.

The Consulate of the United States, in my day, was located in Washington Buildings, (a shabby and smoke-stained edifice of four stories high, thus illustriously named in honor of our national establishment,) at the lower corner of Brunswick-street, contiguous to the Goree Arcade, and in the neighborhood of some of the oldest docks. This was by no means a polite or elegant portion of England's great commercial city, nor were the apartments of the American official so splendid as to indicate the assumption of much consular pomp on his part. A narrow and ill-lighted staircase gave access to an equally narrow and ill-lighted passage-way on the first-floor, at the extremity of which, surmounting a door-frame, appeared an exceedingly stiff pictorial representation of the Goose and Gridiron, according to the English idea of those ever-to-be-honored symbols. The staircase and passage-way were often thronged, of a morning, with a set of beggarly and piratical-looking scoundrels, (I do no wrong to our own countrymen in styling them so, for not one in twenty was a genuine American,) purporting to belong to our mercantile marine, and chiefly composed of Liverpool Blackballers and the scum of every maritime nation on earth; such being the seamen by whose assistance we then disputed the navigation of the world with England. These specimens of a most unfortunate class of people were shipwrecked crews in quest of bridgeboard, and loathing invalids asking permits for the hospital; bruised and bloody wretches complaining of ill-treatment by their officers, drunkards, des-

First page of a revised manuscript for a sketch that first appeared in the October 1862 issue of the Atlantic Monthly *and was collected the following year in* Our Old Home: A Series of English Sketches *(Parke-Bernet. Drexel Institute, sale number 588, 17–18 October 1944; reprinted in* Hawthorne at Auction, *p. 331)*

authors, without so much as asking whether I am dead or alive. But I like it well enough, nevertheless. It is pleasant to feel at last that I am really away from America,—a satisfaction that I never enjoyed as long as I stayed in Liverpool, where it seemed to me that the quintessence of nasal and hand-shaking Yankeedom was continually filtered and sublimated through my consulate, on the way outward and homeward. I first got acquainted with my own countrymen there. At Rome, too, it was not much better. But here in Florence, and in the summer-time, and in this secluded villa, I have escaped out of all my old tracks, and am really remote.

"I like my present residence immensely. The house stands on a hill, overlooking Florence, and is big enough to quarter a regiment; insomuch that each member of the family, including servants, has a separate suite of apartments, and there are vast wildernesses of upper rooms into which we have never yet sent exploring expeditions.

"At one end of the house there is a moss-grown tower, haunted by owls and by the ghost of a monk, who was confined there in the thirteenth century, previous to being burned at the stake in the principal square of Florence. I hire this villa, tower and all, at twenty-eight dollars a month; but I mean to take it away bodily and clap it into a romance, which I have in my head ready to be written out.

"Speaking of romances I have planned two, one or both of which I could have ready for the press in a few months if I were either in England or America. But I find this Italian atmosphere not favorable to the close toil of composition, although it is a very good air to dream in. I must breathe the fogs of old England or the east-winds of Massachusetts, in order to put me into working trim. Nevertheless, I shall endeavor to be busy during the coming winter at Rome, but there will be so much to distract my thoughts that I have little hope of seriously accomplishing anything. It is a pity; for I have really a plethora of ideas, and should feel relieved by discharging some of them upon the public.

"We shall continue here till the end of this month, and shall then return to Rome, where I have already taken a house for six months. In the middle of April we intend to start for home by the way of Geneva and Paris; and, after spending a few weeks in England, shall embark for Boston in July or the beginning of August. After so long an absence (more than five years already, which will be six before you see me at the old Corner), it is not altogether delightful to think of returning. Everybody will be changed, and I myself, no doubt, as much as anybody. Ticknor and you, I suppose, were both upset in the late religious earthquake, and when I inquire for you the clerks will direct me to the 'Business Men's Conference.' It won't do. I shall be forced to come back again and take refuge in a London lodging. London is like the grave in one respect,—any man can make himself at home there; and whenever a man finds himself homeless elsewhere, he had better either die or go to London.

"Speaking of the grave reminds me of old age and other disagreeable matters; and I would remark that one grows old in Italy twice or three times as fast as in other countries. I have three gray hairs now for one that I brought from England, and I shall look venerable indeed by next summer, when I return.

"Remember me affectionately to all my friends. Whoever has a kindness for me may be assured that I have twice as much for him."

Hawthorne's second visit to Rome, in the winter of 1859, was not a fortunate one. His own health was excellent during his sojourn there, but several members of his family fell ill, and he became very nervous and longed to get away. In one of his letters he says:—

"I bitterly detest Rome, and shall rejoice to bid it farewell forever; and I fully acquiesce in all the mischief and ruin that has happened to it, from Nero's conflagration downward. In fact, I wish the very site had been obliterated before I ever saw it."

He found solace, however, during the series of domestic troubles (continued illness in his family) that befell, in writing memoranda for "The Marble Faun." He thus announces to me the beginning of the new romance:—

"I take some credit to myself for having sternly shut myself up for an hour or two almost every day, and come to close grips with a romance which I have been trying to tear out of my mind. As for my success, I can't say much; indeed, I don't know what to say at all. I only know that I have produced what seems to be a larger amount of scribble than either of my former romances, and that portions of it interested me a good deal while I was writing them; but I have had so many interruptions, from things to see and things to suffer, that the story has developed itself in a very imperfect way, and will have to be revised hereafter. I could finish it for the press in the time that I am to remain here (till the 15th of April), but my brain is tired of it just now; and, besides, there are many objects that I shall regret not seeing hereafter, though I care very little about seeing them now; so I shall throw aside the romance, and take it up against next August at The Wayside."

He decided to be back to England early in the summer, and to sail for home in July. He writes to me from Rome:—

"I shall go home, I fear, with a heavy heart, not expecting to be very well contented there. . . . . . If I were but a hundred times richer than I am, how very comfortable I could be! I consider it a great piece of good fortune that I have had experience of the discomforts and miseries of Italy, and I did not go directly home from England. Anything will seem like Paradise after a Roman winter.

"If I had but a house fit to live in, I should be greatly more reconciled to coming home; but I am really at a loss to imagine how we are to squeeze ourselves into that little old cottage of mine. We had outgrown it before we came away, and most of us are twice as big now as we were then.

"I have an attachment to the place, and should be sorry to give it up; but I shall half ruin myself if I try to enlarge the house, and quite if I build another. So what is to be done? Pray have some plan for me before I get back; not that I think you can possibly hit on anything that will suit me. . . . . I shall return by way of Venice and Geneva, spend two or three weeks or more in Paris, and sail for home, as I said, in July. It would be exceeding delight to me to meet your or Ticknor in England, or anywhere else. At any rate, it will cheer my heart to see you all and the old Corner itself, when I touch my dear native soil again."

I went abroad in 1859, and found Hawthorne back in England, working away diligently at "The Marble Faun." While traveling on the Continent, during the autumn I had constant letters from him, giving accounts of his progress on the new romance. He says: "I get along more slowly than I expected. . . . . If I mistake not, it will have some good chapters." Writing on the 10th of October he tells me:–

"The romance is almost finished, a great heap of manuscript being already accumulated, and only a few concluding chapters remaining behind. If hard pushed, I could have it ready for the press in a fortnight; but unless the publishers [Smith and Elder were to bring out the work in England] are in a hurry, I shall be somewhat longer about it. I have found far more work to do upon it than I anticipated. To confess the truth, I admire it exceedingly at intervals, but am liable to cold fits, during which I think it is the most infernal nonsense. You ask for the title. I have not yet fixed upon one, but here are some that have occurred to me; neither of them exactly meets my idea: 'Monte Beni; or, The Faun. A Romance.' 'The Romance of a Faun.' 'The Faun of Monte Beni.' 'Monte Beni: a Romance.' 'Miriam: a Romance.' 'Hilda: a Romance.' 'Donatello: a Romance.' 'The Faun: a Romance.' 'Marble and Man: a Romance.' When you have read the work (which I especially wish you to do before it goes to press), you will be able to select one of them, or imagine something better. There is an objection in my mind to an Italian name, though perhaps Monte Beni might do. Neither do I wish, if I can help it, to make the fantastic aspect of the book too prominent by putting the Faun into the title-page."

Hawthorne wrote so intensely on his new story, that he was quite worn down before he finished it. To recruit his strength he went to Redcar where the brac-

ing air of the German Ocean soon counteracted the ill effect of overwork. "The Marble Faun" was in the London printing-office in November, and he seemed very glad to have it off his hands. His letters to me at this time (I was still on the Continent) were jubilant with hope. He was living in Leamington, and was constantly writing to me that I should find the next two months more comfortable in England than anywhere else. On the 17th he writes:–

"The Italian spring commences in February, which is certainly an advantage, especially as from February to May is the most disagreeable portion of the English year. But it is always summer by a bright coal-fire. We find nothing to complain of in the climate of Leamington. To be sure, we cannot always see our hands before us for fog; but I like fog, and do not care about seeing my hand before me. We have thought of staying here till after Christmas and then going somewhere else,– perhaps to Bath, perhaps to Devonshire. But all this is uncertain. Leamington is not so desirable a residence in winter as in summer; its great charm consisting in the many delightful walks and drives, and in its neighborhood to interesting places. I have quite finished the book (some time ago) and have sent it to Smith and Elder, who tell me it is in the printer's hands, but I have received no proof-sheets. They wrote to request another title instead of the 'Romance of Monte Beni,' and I sent them their choice of a dozen. I don't know what they have chosen; neither do I understand their objection to the above. Perhaps they don't like the book at all; but I shall not torture myself about that, as long as they publish it and pay me my £ 600. For my part, I think it much my best romance; but I can see some points where it is open to assault. If it could have appeared first in America, it would have been a safe thing. . . .

"I mean to spend the rest of my abode in England in blessed idleness; and as for my journal, in the first place I have not got it here; secondly, there is nothing in it that will do to publish."

————

Hawthorne was, indeed, a consummate artist, and I do not remember a single slovenly passage in all his acknowledged writings. It was a privilege, and one that I can never sufficiently estimate, to have known him personally through so many years. He was unlike any other author I have met, and there were qualities in his nature so sweet and commendable, that, through all his shy reserve, they sometimes asserted themselves in a marked and conspicuous manner. I have known rude people, who were jostling him in a crowd, give way at the sound of his low and almost irresolute voice, so potent was the gentle spell of command that seemed born of his genius.

Although he was apt to keep aloof from his kind, and did not hesitate frequently to announce by his manner that

> "Solitude to him
> Was blithe society, who filled the air
> With gladness and involuntary songs,"

I ever found him, like Milton's Raphael, an "affable" angel, and inclined to converse on whatever was human and good in life.

Here are some more extracts from the letters he wrote to me while he was engaged on "The Marble Faun." On the 11th of February, 1860, he writes from Leamington in England (I was then in Italy):–

"I received your letter from Florence, and conclude that you are now in Rome, and probably enjoying the Carnival,–a tame description of which, by the by, I have introduced into my Romance.

"I thank you most heartily for your kind wishes in favor of the forthcoming work, and sincerely join my own prayers to yours in its behalf, but without much confidence of a good result. My own opinion is, that I am not really a popular writer, and that what popularity I have gained is chiefly accidental, and owing to other causes than my own kind or degree of merit. Possibly I may (or may not) deserve something better than popularity; but looking at all my productions, and especially this latter one, with a cold or critical eye, I can see that they do not make their appeal to the popular mind. It is odd enough, moreover, that my own individual taste is for quite another class of works than those which I myself am able to write. If I were to meet with such books as mine, by another writer, I don't believe I should be able to get through them.

.   .   .   .   .   .

"To return to my own moonshiny Romance; its fate will soon be settled, for Smith and Elder mean to publish on the 28th of this month. Poor Ticknor will have a tight scratch to get his edition out contemporaneously; they having sent him the third volume only a week ago. I think, however, there will be no danger of piracy in America. Perhaps nobody will think it worth stealing. Give my best regards to William Story, and look well at his Cleopatra, for you will meet her again in one of the chapters which I wrote with most pleasure. If he does not find himself famous henceforth, the fault will be none of mine. I, at least, have done my duty by him, whatever delinquency there may be on the part of other critics.

"Smith and Elder persist in calling the book 'Transformation,' which gives one the idea of Harlequin in a pantomime; but I have strictly enjoined upon Ticknor to call it 'The Marble Faun; a Romance of Monte Beni.'"

In one of his letters written at this period, referring to his design of going home, he says:–

The Hawthornes' home at 26 Rock Park in Rock Ferry, outside Liverpool, where the family resided from September 1853 to June 1855 (Liverpool City Libraries)

"I shall not have been absent seven years till the 5th of July next, and I scorn to touch Yankee soil sooner than that. . . . . As regards going home I alternate between a longing and a dread."

Returning to London from the Continent, in April, I found this letter, written from Bath, awaiting my arrival:–

"You are welcome back. I really began to fear that you had been assassinated among the Apennines or killed in that outbreak at Rome. I have taken passages for all of us in the steamer which sails the 16th of June. Your berths are Nos. 19 and 20. I engaged them with the understanding that you might go earlier or later, if you chose; but I would advise you to go on the 16th; in the first place, because the state-rooms for our party are the most eligible in the ship; secondly, because we shall otherwise mutually lose the pleasure of each other's company. Besides, I consider it my duty, towards Ticknor and towards Boston, and America at large, to take you into custody and bring you home; for I know you will never come except upon compulsion. Let me know at once whether I am to use force.

"The book (The Marble Faun) has done better than I thought it would; for you will have discovered, by this time, that it is an audacious attempt to impose a tissue of absurdities upon the public by the mere art of style of narrative. I hardly hoped that it would go down with John Bull; but then it is always my best point of writing, to undertake such a task, and I really put what strength I have into many parts of this book.

"The English critics generally (with two or three unimportant exceptions) have been sufficiently favorable, and the review in the Times awarded the highest praise of all. At home, too, the notices have been very kind, so far as they have come under my eye. Lowell had a good one in the Atlantic Monthly, and Hillard an excellent one in the Courier; and yesterday I received a sheet of the May number of the Atlantic containing a really keen and profound article by Whipple, in which he goes over all my works, and recognizes that element of unpopularity which (as anybody knows better than myself) pervades them all. I agree with almost all he says, except that I am conscious of not deserving nearly so much praise. When I get home, I will try to write a more genial book; but the Devil himself always seems to get into my inkstand, and I can only exorcise him by pensful at a time.

"I am coming to London very soon, and mean to spend a fortnight of next month there. I have been quite homesick through this past dreary winter. Did you ever spend a winter in England? If not, reserve your ultimate conclusion about the country until you have done so."

We met in London in early May, and, as our lodgings were not far apart, we were frequently together. I recall many pleasant dinners with him and mutual friends in various charming seaside and countryside places. We used to take a run down to Greenwich or Blackwall once or twice a week, and a trip to Richmond was always grateful to him. Bennoch was constantly planning a day's happiness for his friend, and the hours at that pleasant season of the year were not long enough for our delights. In London we strolled along the Strand, day after day, now diving into Bolt Court, in pursuit of Johnson's whereabouts, and now stumbling around the Temple, where Goldsmith at one time had his quarters. Hawthorne was never weary of standing on London Bridge, and watching the steamers plying up and down the Thames. I was much amused by his manner towards importunate and sometimes impudent beggars, some of whom would attack us even in the shortest walk. He had a mild way of making a severe and cutting remark, which used to remind me of a little incident which Charlotte Cushman once related to me. She said a man in the gallery of a theatre (I think she was on the stage at the time) made such a disturbance that the play could not proceed. Cries of "Throw

him over" arose from all parts of the house, and the noise became furious. All was tumultuous chaos until a sweet and gentle female voice was heard in the pit, exclaiming, "No! I pray you don't throw him over! I beg of you, dear friends, don't throw him over, but– *kill him where he is*."

One of our most royal times was at a parting dinner at the house of Barry Cornwall. Among the notables present were Kinglake and Leigh Hunt. Our kind-hearted host and his admirable wife greatly delighted in Hawthorne, and they made this occasion a most grateful one to him. I remember when we went up to the drawing-room to join the ladies after dinner, the two dear old poets, Leigh Hunt and Barry Cornwall, mounted the stairs with their arms round each other in a very tender and loving way. Hawthorne often referred to this scene as one he would not have missed for a great deal.

His renewed intercourse with Motley in England gave him peculiar pleasure, and his genius found an ardent admirer in the eminent historian. He did not go much into society at that time, but there were a few houses in London where he always seemed happy.

I met him one night at a great evening-party, looking on from a nook a little removed from the full glare of the *soirée*. Soon, however, it was whispered about that the famous American romance-writer was in the room, and an enthusiastic English lady, a genuine admirer and intelligent reader of his books, ran for her album and attacked him for "a few words and his name at the end." He looked dismally perplexed, and turning to me said imploringly in a whisper, "For pity's sake, what shall I write? I can't think of a word to add to my name. Help me to something." Thinking him partly in fun, I said, "Write an original couplet,– this one, for instance,–

'When this you see,
Remember me,'"

and to my amazement he stepped forward at once to the table, wrote the foolish little line I had suggested, and, shutting the book, handed it very contentedly to the happy lady.

We sailed from England together in the month of June, as we had previously arranged, and our voyage home was, to say the least, an unusual one. We had calm summer, moonlight weather, with no storms. Mrs. Stowe was on board, and in her own cheery and delightful way she enlivened the passage with some capital stories of her early life.

When we arrived at Queenstown, the captain announced to us that, as the ship would wait there six hours, we might go ashore and see something of our

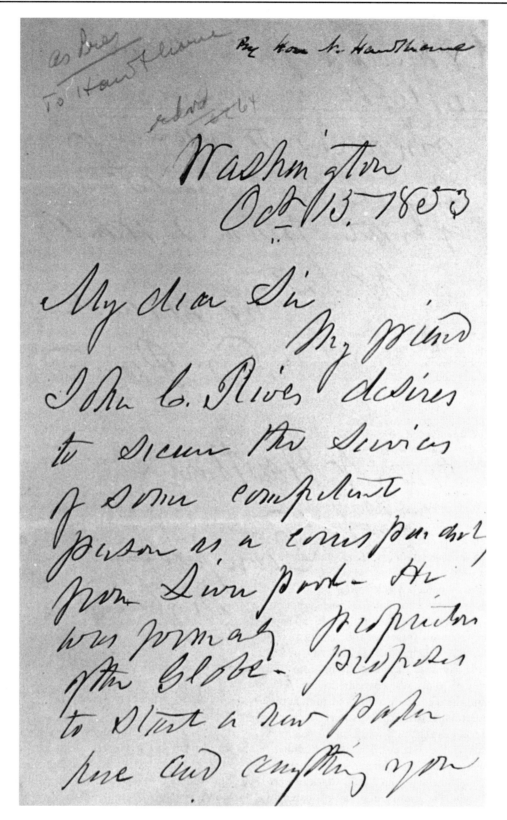

President Franklin Pierce's 15 October 1853 letter in which he requests assistance for John Rives
(House of the Seven Gables Historic Site)

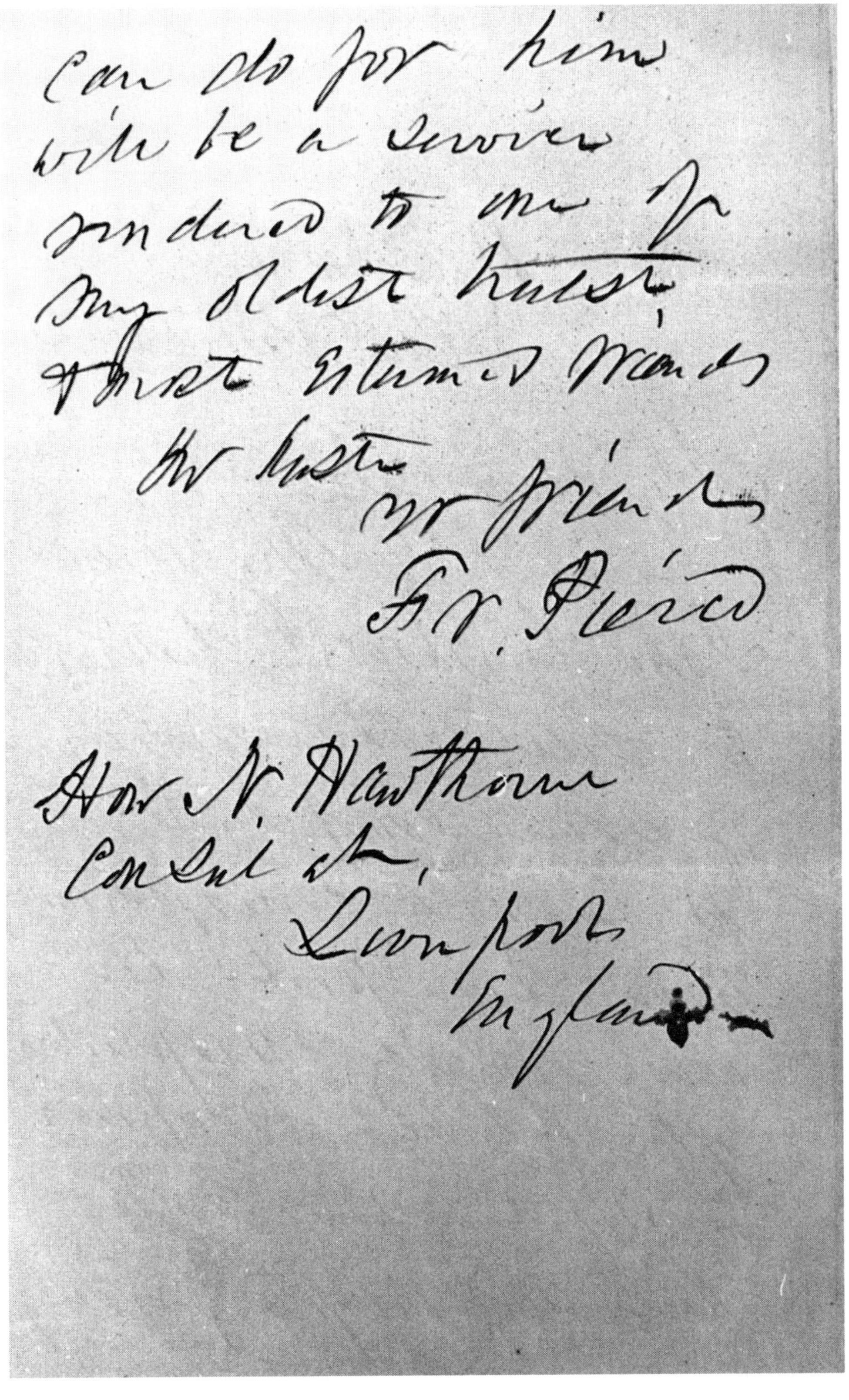

DLB 269

Life Abroad and *The Marble Faun*

Can do for him
will be a service
rendered to me by
my oldest truest
& most esteemed friends

Yr faithful
yr friend
Fr. Pierce

Hon N. Hawthorne
Consul &c,
Liverpool
England

Hawthorne's two closest friends in England: Henry Bright (left) and Francis Bennoch (right), both men of letters and businessmen who traveled with the Hawthornes during their stay abroad

Irish friends. So we chartered several jaunting-cars, after much tribulation and delay in arranging terms with the drivers thereof, and started off on a merry exploring expedition. I remember there was a good deal of racing up and down the hills of Queenstown, much shouting and laughing, and crowds of beggars howling after us for pence and beer. The Irish jaunting-car is a peculiar institution, and we all sat with our legs dangling over the road in a "dim and perilous way." Occasionally a horse would give out, for the animals were sad specimens, poorly fed and wofully driven. We were almost devoured by the ragamuffins that ran beside our wheels, and I remember the "sad civility" with which Hawthorne regarded their clamors. We had provided ourselves before starting with much small coin, which, however, gave out during our first mile. Hawthorne attempted to explain our inability further to supply their demands, having, as he said to them, nothing less than a sovereign in his pocket, when a voice from the crowd shouted, "Bedad, your honor, I can change that for ye"; and the knave actually did it on the spot.

Hawthorne's love for the sea amounted to a passionate worship; and while I (the worst sailor probably on this planet) was longing, spite of the good company on board, to reach land as soon as possible, Hawthorne was constantly saying in his quiet, earnest say, "I should like to sail on and on forever, and never touch the shore again." He liked to stand alone in the bows of the ship and see the sun go down, and he was never tired of walking the deck at midnight. I used to watch his dark, solitary figure under the stars, pacing up and down some unfrequented part of the vessel, musing and half melancholy. Sometimes he would lie down beside me and commiserate my unquiet condition. Seasickness, he declared, he could not understand, and was constantly recommending most extraordinary dishes and drinks, "all made out of the *artist's* brain," which he said were sovereign remedies for nautical illness. I remember to this day some of the preparations which, in his revelry of fancy, he would advise me to take, a farrago of good things almost rivalling "Oberon's Feast," spread out so daintily in Herrick's "Hesperides."

The corner in Henry Young's bookstore in Liverpool where Hawthorne often met Henry Bright

He thought, at first, if I could bear a few roc's eggs beaten up by a mermaid on a dolphin's back, I might be benefited. He decided that a gruel made form a sheaf of Robin Hood's arrows would be strengthening. When suffering pain, "a right gude willie-waught," or a stiff cup of hemlock of the Socrates brand, before retiring, he considered very good. He said he had heard recommended a dose of salts distilled from the tears of Niobe, but he did n't approve of that remedy. He observed that he had a high opinion of hearty food, such as potted owl with Minerva sauce, airy tongues of sirens, stewed ibis, livers of Roman Capitol geese, the wings of a Phoenix not too much done, love-lorn nightingales cooked briskly over Aladdin's lamp, chicken-pies made of fowls raised by Mrs. Carey, Nautilus chowder, and the like. Fruit, by all means, should always be taken by an uneasy victim at sea, especially Atalanta pippins and purple grapes raised by Bacchus & Co. Examining my garments one day as I lay on deck, he thought I was not warmly enough clad, and he recommended, before I took another voyage, that I should fit myself out in Liverpool with a good warm shirt from the shop of Nessus & Co. in Bold Street, where I could also find stout seven-league boots to keep out the damp. He knew another shop, he said, where I could buy raven-down stockings, and sable clouds with a silver lining, most warm and comfortable for a sea voyage.

His own appetite was excellent, and day after day he used to come on deck after dinner and describe to me what he had eaten. Of course his accounts were always exaggerations, for my amusement. I remember one night he gave me a running catalogue of what food he had partaken during the day, and the sum total was convulsing from its absurdity. Among the viands he had consumed, I remember he stated there were "several yards of steak," and a "whole warrenful of Welsh rabbits." The "divine spirit of Humor" was upon him during many of those days at sea, and he revelled in it like a careless child.

That was a voyage, indeed, long to be remembered, and I shall ever look back upon it as the most satisfactory "sea turn" I ever happened to experience. I have sailed many a weary, watery mile since then, but *Hawthorne* was not on board!

—*Yesterdays with Authors,* pp. 73–94

Hawthorne's 20 January 1855 letter to his Liverpool friend Henry Bright, in which he reports the death of his wife's father, Nathaniel Peabody (John Rylands Library, Manchester, England)

Reviews of *The Marble Faun*

At age thirty-eight, Henry Giles emigrated from Ireland to the United States, where he became a popular lecturer, especially about Shakespeare. In Boston, he belonged to the Town and Country Club, whose other members included Theodore Parker, W. H. Channing, Ralph Waldo Emerson, and Hawthorne. He wrote for various periodicals and published several books, including Lectures and Essays *(1850) and* Human Life in Shakespeare *(1868).*

Literature
Henry Giles
Boston Daily Courier, 72, no. 82 (5 April 1860), p. 1

Our delay in noticing this brilliant book, has not been occasioned by insensibility to its power. We were among the earliest of its readers, and the charm of its genius is yet fresh in our imagination. We had hoped that by waiting, the opportunity might be given us to do the work deliberate justice; but to our regret, we find that it is in literature as it is in life—the longer the procrastination, the greater at last is the hurry. We have accordingly not gained time, but lost it, and that which we did not desire to do rapidly in season,—we have to do still more rapidly out of season.

Indeed, reviewing a book of genuine merit is, in some sense an impertinence. The announcement which makes it known, is nearly all that it requires; it is then its own best recommendation; it has its truest eulogy in the thinking heads, and in the awakened hearts of a growing community of readers. Such eulogy has *The Marble Faun* by this time, from a public on both sides of the Atlantic, which hails it with ample and increasing sympathy.

The plot, the story, and the characters, are already so familiar to all who read romances, that we are saved the trouble of giving any account of them. Every one interested in fiction is now acquainted with Kenyon, the young American sculptor; with Hilda, the fair and ideal American girl, the enthusiast and copyist of the grand old masters; with Donatello, whose likeness to the ancient Marble Faun forms the central idea of the story; whose mythic origin and exceptional constitution, leads to its complications and catastrophe; with Miriam—the woman of mystery and genius, of passion, and who is the sovereign personage of the book.

In the remarks which we propose to make, we have to take for granted, not only that our readers have gone through this romance in particular, but that they are conversant with Hawthorne's writings in general.

Most of what we have to say will be confined to the illustrations of *one* impression which this work has made on us; and that is the singular subjectivity of

Henry Giles

Hawthorne's genius. More than any other of his writings, the present book reveals this characteristic; for it puts it into more distinct relief in contrast with the objectivity of circumstances and descriptions that are so prominent in the course of the narrative. It will be seen that these circumstances and descriptions are not vital and essential elements in his genius, but merely casual and accidental. They do not belong to the organic whole, but are externals to it; they are not there by necessity, but by design; and the tendency to deal with them is not involved in the innate and creative force out of which the organic whole arises.

We do not in the least, deny the author's acute as well as large apprehension of the outward in life and nature. We most heartily and sincerely admit his observant sensibility to all that is impressive in the universe, in humanity, and in art. Nor do we limit our admission, in this respect, merely to observant sensibility—the author is still more remarkable for observant thought. Both have been matured in him to the utmost, by culture and meditation; and of the fact here stated—*The Marble Faun* gives proof in every page. It would be hard to find a book in the literature of the time which shows more descriptive power, or more subtle aesthetic criticism; which shows more profound appreciation of grandeur or of beauty; which has so many passages distinguished by luxuriance of imagery and intensity of eloquence. Still—we maintain that all these qualities bear no comparison to the author's force of introspection, to his inwardness and individuality. How invincible the author is in this subjective personality, the present book—as we have intimated—makes all the plainer by its contrasts. We can hardly imagine a contrast more decided than that between Italy and New England; but none the less, the Hawthorne of New England is the Hawthorne of Italy. The influence of Italy is discernible on his senses, his feelings; it enlarges his experience; it has power on his emotion—mostly irritable, dreary, sad, and painful—but the essential action of his genius, it does not reach of even modify.

We select a few peculiarities in the action of Hawthorne's genius—as explanation of our idea—and we find them alike in *The Scarlet Letter* and *The Marble Faun*.

In whatever Hawthorne writes we always have the *mythic* and the *mysterious*. So it was in his earliest tales. So it has been in his latest. But, for the first time, these tendencies revealed themselves in *The Scarlet Letter* with an "imagination all compact." A queer peculiarity, however, about Hawthorne is that while other writers throw the mystic and mysterious into the obscure of history—he brings them boldly into its open light. No historical obscurity rests upon the time or the locality of *The Scarlet Letter*. The history of Boston is open to all who care to read it. The name of every minister who preached any Election Sermon is known to all the readers of such history; but you might as well expect to find Friar Tuck in the history of old England as to find the Rev. Mr. Dimmesdale in that of New England. In this tendency there is a strange contempt of facts—which only a very singular genius could overcome. The genius of Hawthorne *is* a singular one—and only a certain inspired witchery, which belongs to all that he writes, hinders us from thinking much that he writes unnatural and extravagant. But then, *there* is *that* witchery of genius, and genius is to literature, what charity is to life—it covers a multitude of sins.

In *The Marble Faun,* as in *The Scarlet Letter,* we have the same boldness of myth and mystery in still more open light. Such an instance is that of Hilda, with her tower and her taper. But this is simple, compared with the character of Donatello, with the legend of his family, and with all that belongs to his circumstances and his life. Boston two centuries ago is cast back into the darkest shadows of antiquity, as contrasted with the Rome of the present day; and New England of the olden time is mystery itself, when we think of Italy—as it is now, and long has been—the hacknied subject of bookmakers and tourists. The Boston of two centuries ago is now—except to those who have special interest in its history—almost as vague as the Troy of Homer; but Rome of the present day is the most exposed of cities. It is truly "the observed of all observers." And yet it is in this city that the author imagines a narrative of events which would really startle us in a story like to that of "Blue Beard."

More, however, in *character* than in time and place, we observe the tendency of Hawthorne to the mythic and the mysterious. Every character that he presents is seen in mist. None of his characters show themselves to us in a clear and a full horizon. We see each figure distinctly in itself, but we do not see it in a sky of circumambient sunshine. Always there is a haze about it, and our interest is the interest of uncertainty.

We note this in Dimmesdale, Hester Prynne, Chillingworth, and Pearl of *The Scarlet Letter;* so we likewise note it in Miriam, Kenyon, Hilda, Donatello, of *The Marble Faun*. Each is at once a myth and a mystery: a myth, in a certain dim actuality; a mystery, in certain exceptional elements of circumstance and character, which our knowledge of common human life can neither account for nor explain. In accordance with the tendency, every strongly-marked character which Hawthorne has created is always *in possession of a painful secret*. Any secret is necessarily painful, but the secret which Hawthorne clothes about with personality, is ever one which tortures the whole life. Hester Prynne has the secret of her love for Dimmesdale and of her hatred for Chillingworth. Chillingworth has the secret of his hatred for Hester Prynne—his unfaithful wife, and for Dimmesdale—the clerical partner of her crime—his sinful and saintly rival. To this he adds the secret contrivance of a direful revenge. Dimmesdale has the secret of his own deadly sin, made all the more terrible by his public success. The very success made the secret his damnation. He had genius—the genius of piety, but not its experience; the genius of eloquence, but not its truth; not only were his own keen thoughts "daggers" that stabbed him in the soul, but his brilliant words added poison to the sharpness of the daggers. When his audiences were most moved, he was most miserable, and the triumph of his eloquence brought him to the remorseful ruin of despair.

In *The Marble Faun,* Miriam not only *has* a secret, but *is* a secret. She is inscrutable in herself, or in her circumstances. We learn not whence she is, who she is, or to what she has come. By a look she is guilty of murder: this look creates guilt in the action of one individual, and wretchedness in the mind of another. Donatello,—the semi-animal, semi-human lover of Miriam,—catches murder from the look, and commits it on the person of her shadowy persecutor. Hilda, the enthusiastic admirer of Miriam, by accident, witness of the crime, obtains knowledge of a secret, which shocks, puzzles and tortures her. Donatello has the secret of a mythic genealogy, and in ears, always kept concealed, which in their hairy covering and their vine-leafed shape, might seem to give authority to this mystic superstition. He has, too, the secret of his having in hatred destroyed human life; in that he has his first sense of sin, and his first revelation of a conscience.

To trace the influences which *the feeling of sin* has upon the character, both as it arises within the mind, and as it is reflected from without, is another specialty of Hawthorne's genius. The dreadfulness of an interior contrition we read in the story of the youthful, impassioned and tragic Puritan pastor, Dimmesdale. The dreadful retribution from without, we have in the isolated misery of Hester Prynne. But the fearful contrition which, in *The Scarlet Letter,* hurries Dimmesdale to confession and despair, in *The Marble Faun* carries Donatello into rationality and thought. It is not a little curious that in these representations the characters which seem the strongest, those which seem to bear themselves most bravely against the sense of sin, are those of women. Hester Prynne wears her scarlet "A" defiantly; she almost seems to glory in it, and to be proud of it; but Dimmesdale cowers before even the possibility of a suspicion. In *The Marble Faun* the *sense of sin* which shocks Donatello into moral existence, by means of an awakened conscience, and through fear makes him despondent, excites the moral force of Miriam, and through sympathy makes her courageous. We could dwell long on this point, but we cannot within our space—ours is merely the space of a newspaper article, and the pressing demands on a daily journal are properly intolerant of extended disquisition.

In the fiction of Hawthorne we have passion more in its analysis than in its action. We do not see passion in its beginning and its growth, but in its issue and its catastrophe. In Hester Prynne, for instance, we do not see how her love for Dimmesdale began. We are not allowed to look into her heart, and note the pulsation and the throbbing of its earliest alarms. We hear not the first insidious whispers of temptations in their deceiving sweetness. We observe not the agonies and struggles between duty and inclination; the shame and fear, the weeping and the hesitancy, the ecstasy of wretchedness, the enthusiasm of despair, which always precede the fall of a yet uncorrupted woman, when she gives herself wholly, unreservedly, unconditionally to her lover. Nor do we in this case, either, behold the woman in the immediate terrors of her guilt; in her

rapture and remorse, and with the heavy sense of ruin, which her heart in its utmost delirium of excitement, in its wildest intoxication of devotion and delight, cannot possibly shake off. When we meet Hester Prynne her guilt has been completed, her punishment has begun; no more for her henceforth is the romance of transgression, but only its doleful retribution. In like manner, it is not until a murder has been committed that the force of passion in Miriam and Donatello is revealed, and they also then enter on their path of penalty. The intensity which Hawthorne gives to passion has often something in it that is Shakespearean.

The method, however, of Shakespeare is dramatic; that of Hawthorne is psychological; the one incarnates passion; the other dissects it; and a wonderful morbid anatomist, it must be confessed, Hawthorne is of man's moral nature. Taking the accomplished fact of sin or crime—he then traces it backward into its darkest sources, and onward into its most fatal consequences.

The romance is rich with suggestive thought on life, humanity, and art. Its best significance, its greatest value is not in the story or the characters, but in philosophy and criticism. In both the philosophy and criticism of the book, we have evidence of mature meditation, and of the insight of penetrating reason; we have, withal, through the whole book, exceeding wealth of beauty, poetry and eloquence.

Because of this very wealth in its diversity and its abundance, the book is one to which it is difficult in a hurried article to do justice. The style, as in all the writings of Hawthorne, has a condensed, masculine simplicity, and a certain wizard mannerism, which stamp the image and superscription of his genius on every sentence. Every sentence of his is like a Bank-of-England note: it defies forgery or imitation.

A book, written in Italy, and containing an Italian story, must, of necessity, include much criticism on Art. The criticism on Art in this book exhibits a good deal of shrewd as well as sympathetic discernment in reference to specific departments of Art, and on particular objects of it. But in our estimation, the value of the criticism consists mostly in its clear perception as to the unity of Art. For, the critic in apprehending the unit of Art, reaches to the very soul and spirit of Art. There is *one* spirit in Art; but diversity of ministration. The critic sees from this point of view that "*suggestiveness*" is a central function of Art. All arts are thus not only bound to our associations of instinct, of memory, of desire, of pleasure, and of pain; but they are also bound, throughout, each to the whole, and the whole to each. The critic sees, too, that though the spirit of art is immortal, certain forms of art die, and can never appear again but in the reproductions of traditional and mechanical imitation. Such, pre-eminently is the case with sculpture. We are not of those who say that the spirit of sculpture is dead. But we *do* say that until it gives up aping the classic, it is only a higher order of mimic mechanism. Costume, with ancient sculpture, was secondary; with modern sculpture it seems to be primary. Beauty and power with ancient sculpture were primary; in modern sculpture they seem to be secondary. Clothe a magnificent man, as the tailor of Proteus-fashion may, his presence in marble will ever be magnificent; and let a villainous milliner do her worst upon a lovely woman, the artist, even in copying the milliner, will miss nothing of the original loveliness. Nature ever vindicates herself; beauty and power shine by their own light, and are strong in their own strength. Humanity belongs to nature, and for all time, not to the milliner of any age or to its tailor. We think now ancient tailoring and millinery graceful, because ancient art made it splendid in the glory and glow of genius; let modern art cover modern life with such glory and such glow,—modern tailoring and millinery will, even in their worst deformities, throw no cloud upon its splendor. Classic art conquered the difficulties of ancient life; modern art must conquer the difficulties of modern life. When this conviction takes strong hold of genius—we have no fear even for sculpture. Marble is always under the surface, genius is always above it; and there is no place, no hour where and when genius may not have as much to give it worthy work as among the antiquated rabble of Olympian divinities. But, after all, Art is worthless for its own sake,—and Art has parted from genius, when it ceases to be the expression of reality, faith and nature. When conscious Art looks on unconscious Art, we have no analogy for such a condition of culture, but that of the ancient Augurs in the decline of ancient Rome, who had silent laughter in their look as they passed each other in the street.

Here it is time to close, and to make our last remark. In some criticisms of this book we find it asserted that a moody and melancholy temper overspreads it. We do not justify the assertion; but, within limits, a certain pathetic depth of feeling is what we should expect from the spirit of the author, and from the spirit of his subject. The author seems naturally driven to contemplate the dim, the dreary, and the troubled aspects of life; to look into the dreams and visions of wild and solitary imaginations; and to count the beatings of lonely and impassioned hearts. But a thinking and reflective man, however constitutionally cheerful, must write sadly of modern Italy. Suggestive contrast is, at once, the source of the comic and the tragic. The contrast in

Italy, more than in any other country, is suggestive only of the tragic—at all events, it is suggestive of pensiveness and pathos. In no other country does the transiency of man come so directly into contrast with the permanency of nature. We may be solitary, even affrighted with nature in the wilderness, but we are not humiliated or rebuked. It is where we see the institutions and monuments of man, dead or disappearing in the presence of immortal nature, that we despond,—that we cannot help but despond—and that often we despond all the more in the very consciousness of our infinite superiority to this very nature, which so shames us by its eternal stability. This contrast must, to a thoughtful man, be in Italy solemn—beyond expression. For there man has been in all his sublimest mutabilities,—and there nature still remains, unchanged—in all her glory and in all her beauty. Three men in modern times, more than any others, have, we think, comprehended the life of Italy; more than any others they grasped its knowledge, entered into its imagination, and became moved by its ideas and its passions. One is Niebuhr, who shows us ancient Italy, as a camp of arms,—another is Winkelmann, who describes modern Italy to us a Museum of Art; and the last is Lord Byron, who with the divine energy of song awakens voices of both ancient and modern Italy into music, which cannot die—while man can live. Yet all of these leave on us the sensation of depression—for none of them give us the hope of a new Italian greatness. We are not, therefore, to blame the novelist—if he, by the necessity of instinct and of art, cannot carry fiction beyond the influence of fact.

We are fond, in our American criticism, of comparisons. We sometimes call Emerson, the Yankee Plato: then might we call Hawthorne, the Yankee Æschylus. Perhaps we might, on such a plan, call Edgar A. Poe, the Yankee Mephistophiles; but to what purpose is any such method of comparison? What we have simply to say is, that the highest speculative and imaginative genius in America has not yet, except casually, been brought into contact with the present—the actual forces of American life, we might almost say human life. The most distinctive and original men of genius in America, are, in their best writings, subtle, sad, wild and strange. But American life, generally, is simple, cheerful, practical,—conventional. This contrast between the actual and the ideal in our American experience is worthy of examination; but we most willingly leave the task to philosophers and critics.

In the mid nineteenth century, under the editorship of John Thadeus Delane, The Times *(London) was the most influential newspaper in the English-speaking world, especially in foreign affairs. Hawthorne was pleased with the review of* Transformation *in* The Times, *going so far as to record his delight in letters from Bath, England, to his publishers.*

Review of *Transformation*
The Times, 7 April 1860, p. 5

It may be tempting to make sport of a poet's dream, and the occasion is here ready to our inclinations. Mr Hawthorne is a poet, and his *Transformation* is a dream, airy and illusory, enticing us to hot pursuit or leaving us to a sense of emptiness and ridicule. What is our proper province in a case like this? What have *we* to do with shadows or ethereal semblances? Even art has more solid materials for our investigation and opinion. We have, at all events, a shadow or rarefaction here, evoked by a poetical imagination from its contact with known facts. It may be tempting, as we have said, to keep within the domain of these facts, and to put a contemptuous commentary on the fancies which have sprung out of them. But it is a temptation which we shall wisely resist in the interests of a higher art than comes ordinarily to the reader's closet or the critic's tribunal. We will only state as a preliminary that this is an ideal romance, of which the dust of modern Rome is something more than the background, and in which its hoary monuments each play their part. The expectants of satire will understand our abstinence when we tell them that, among other transcendental processes, the Faun of Praxiteles walks down from its pedestal and becomes the most prominent of the *dramatis personæ*. On the other hand, those who welcome a work of pure phantasy will appreciate the ideal with reference to which it was moulded. A familiar marble statue is endued with a soul, and this soul is rigorously burdened with moral responsibilities beneath which it tends steadily to grow and develop itself. Strange as it

William D. Ticknor, Hawthorne's friend and publisher

Hawthorne wrote to William D. Ticknor in Boston on 19 April 1860 about the reception of his novel in England.

I am glad that the Romance has gone off so well. Here, it may also be called a successful affair; Smith & Elder having got out their third edition, and perhaps more by this time; for the good opinion of the "Times" has great weight with John Bull.

—Letters of Hawthorne to William D. Ticknor, p. 266

may sound, this conception is not altogether new. The principle of this Roman dream is an echo of other dreams, and the *Transformation* of Mr Hawthorne, thus freely effected, combines the feat of Pygmalion with the life ordeal of Undine.

We may wish to pass a balanced judgment on the artistic result, or at least to give the true *rationale* of the process. But when a work of imagination differs from the ordinary standard the task of the critic may be easy or it may be exceedingly difficult. It is easy to note and condemn certain deviations, which are unequivocal lapses, and the eccentricity, which is both an aberration and a weakness. The singularities of infirmity are the easiest blots to hit, for, like other blotches and distortions, they simply disfigure a type, and have nothing to commend their harsh departures from nature. But there are cases in which natural types have been and may be set aside for airy conceptions to which the world rightfully renders homage. Such conceptions belong to a truly ideal sphere, and their congruities of grace and proportion sufficiently vindicate their author's audacity. Criticism abdicates part of its functions, and accepts such conceptions as types, models—existences independent, and absolute. It allows a true creative capacity to be a law to itself, nor does it dream of insisting on the anomalies of tricksy Ariels or Pucks or the impossible combination of qualities in an Apollo Belvedere.

The art which attains this high impunity is so subtle that it defies analysis, and yet so definite in the manifestation that it admits of no dispute. In a book like this before us we at once admit its presence, perplexing and yet pleasing us, startling and leading us captive. As far as our knowledge of the world's present literature extends Mr Hawthorne possesses more of this rare capacity than any living writer. His art of expression is equal to the idealism of his conceptions, and his pure flexible English beguiles his readers into accepting them as among the sum of probable and natural things. But, none the less, they are pure transcendentalisms, impalpable to common sense and unamenable to law. Or rather, as we said, they are a law to themselves, beyond the convenanted rules and formulas of art, and externally independent of the critical scheme and dispensation.

If we conceive we are not entitled to assert our jurisdiction at their expense, we may nevertheless consider the *rationale* of their origin. There is a peculiar type of the American mind which is strongly in revolt against American utilities, and which is predisposed by the very monotony of its surroundings to hues of contrast and attitudes of antagonism. We have seen the manifestation of this revolt in American literature in Edgar Poe and even in Longfellow and Washington Irving. It is emphatically the desire of idealists like these and of Mr Hawthorne to escape from the 'iron rule' of their country and the 'social despotism' of their generation. They disdain to be parts of a complicated scheme of progress, which can only result in their arrival at a colder and drearier region than that they were born in, and they refuse to add to 'an accumulated pile of usefulness, of which the only use will be, to burden their posterity with even heavier thoughts and more inordinate labour than their own.' This impulse induces them to become vagrants in imagination and reality, tourists in the old world of Europe, dreamers and artificers in the older world of poetry and romance; and the contrast of that to which they attach themselves, as compared with that which they fly from, is more stimulating than early association with such influences is to us. We have, in truth, no parallel among ourselves to the freshness of their enthusiasm and no equivalent to its literary restlessness or *élan*. Send Mr

Thackeray to Rome, and he goes and comes with the average impressions of a man of the world, to whom art, history, and poetry are very passable *entrées,* in addition to the ordinary pabulum of a 'fogey' or 'fat contributor.' But the American artist finds himself in Rome with eyes full of innocent wonder, and a heart thumping against his breast like that of Aladdin in the cave. He comes, as he observes, from a country where 'there is no shadow, no antiquity, no mystery, no picturesque and gloomy wrong, nor anything but a commonplace prosperity, in broad and simple daylight;' and he stands in the centre of the ruins of the historic world till their very dust, as it floats in the air, intoxicates him like wine—till the ghosts of the Capitol dance before him in infinite confusion, like the night concourse of spectres which the magician of the Coliseum displayed to the excited gaze of Benvenuto Cellini. The statues and pictures take form and walk, as their subjects quicken; or at least they seem to the poet's eye to be struggling out of the tombs into which they are crushed by a vast heap of vague and ponderous remembrances.

We can easily conceive that Mr Hawthorne had no intention at the outset of working such impressions into a story or picture of his own constructing. In fact, from the extent to which he has introduced descriptions of various Italian objects, antique, pictorial, and statuesque, and, from the very miscellaneous nature of these items, we should rather infer that, in the first instance, he contemplated a work of descriptive criticism. Be this as it may, there is no work, even of this class, on Rome and its treasures which brings their details so closely and vividly before us. It is worth all the guide-books we ever met with, as regards the gems of Italian art, the characteristic features of Roman edifices, and the atmosphere of Roman life. In fact, we conceive it calculated, in many instances, to impart new views of objects with which travellers may have imagined themselves already too familiar. Thus we interpret its comments on the statuary by which Mr Hawthorne lingers, or the significance he attributes to the open *eye* of the Pantheon, or his expansion of that St Peter's, which is, at first sight, a gigantic casket, into the true metropolitan temple of the Catholic world. We obtain a fresh pleasure from our old favourites as their salient points and subtleties are presented to us anew through the medium of his clear discernment. We acknowledge that mystery of secret sorrow which he defines so sharply in the half averted gaze of Beatrice Cenci, or assent to his demand for a kid glove approbation which is alone due to the dainty triumph of Guido's Archangel. The grandeur and the moral atrophy, the gloom and languor, the carnality and nastiness of Rome, pervade his pictures and contrast with the sunlight which flashes through its many fountains. We renew our route by the tomb hillocks of the Appian way—solid and indestructible, as if each tomb were a single boulder of granite. We hear the Ilex trees of the Villa, Borghese whispering faint memories of their peril on the last occasion when the Gaul was at the gates; or we get a glimpse of a purer art in Perugia and Sienna, and a wave of purer air in the Umbrian valleys, or among the simple old world *oppida* of the Tuscan hills.

But, as we said, all these artistic and panoramic performances might have been easily turned to other account, and were probably sketched with another object, until Mr Hawthorne, standing within the gallery of the Capitol, conceived this pregnant theory of the Faun of Praxiteles:—

> The Faun is the marble image of a young man leaning his right arm on the trunk or stump of a tree; one hand hangs carelessly by his side; in the other he holds the fragment of a pipe, or some such sylvan instrument of music. . . . And, after all, the idea may have been no dream, but rather a poet's reminiscence of a period when man's affinity with nature was more strict, and his fellowship with every living thing more intimate and dear.

We conceive Mr Hawthorne's purpose as shaping itself out of this impression, and as exacting aid from his creative ingenuity in this wise. To embody the Faun for an experiment of the influences of mortal sin and sorrow on its Pagan nature, he transports us to the recesses of the Tuscan hills, where he supposes the existence of a noble race of immemorial antiquity and of hereditary peculiarities. A strange mystery surrounds the origin of this race, who are the Counts of Monte Beni. They have come down in a broad track through the middle ages, son after sire being distinctly visible in the gloom of the interval before chivalry put forth its flower; but they ascend above and beyond this through the Roman Imperial ages, and beyond these, again, into the epoch of kingly rule, until they reach an origin in the sylvan life of Etruria while Italy was yet guiltless of Rome—a vanishing point at such a venerable distance that heralds give up their lineage in despair. Imagination steps in where history falters and assigns them a local habitation and a name in retreats half Arcadian, amid uplands half reclaimed, when the myrtle and vine were new inventions, when goat's curds were a dainty diet, when the rustic mind had not yet risen from its community with nature to the artifices of Fescennine verses and Atellan plays. This race has its heirlooms in some cavernous tombs, a few bronzes,

and some quaintly wrought ornaments of gold, and in gems with mystical figures and inscriptions. The very foundations of their old tower were laid so long ago that one-half of its height is said to be sunken under the surface, and to hide subterranean chambers which once were cheerful with the olden sunshine.

But there is a story or a myth attached to this pre-historic race, and to which Mr Hawthorne gropes his way, until he finds it in the Golden Age itself. There was a time, as the trustful Lemprière declares, when deities and demigods appeared familiarly on earth, mingling with its inhabitants as friend with friend—when nymphs, satyrs, and the whole train of classic faith or fable hardly took pains to hide themselves in the primæval woods, and were neither awful nor shocking to the human imagination. At that dateless epoch, a sylvan creature, native among the woods, had loved a mortal maiden, and—possibly by kindness and the subtle courtesies which love might teach to his simplicity, or possibly by a ruder wooing—had won her to his haunts. Thence had sprung a vigorous progeny, that took its place unquestioned among human families, but which in that age and long afterwards showed the lineaments of its wild paternity. It was a pleasant and kindly race of men, but capable of savage fierceness, and never quite restrainable within the limits of social law. Yet, as centuries passed away, the Faun's wild blood had necessarily been attempered with constant intermixtures from the more ordinary streams of human life; while its original vigour kept it from extinction through the perils and emergencies of Roman wars, and its hardihood make it conformable to the exigencies of the feudal ages. Still its hereditary peculiarity, like a supernumerary finger or an anomalous shape of feature, like the Austrian lip, for example, was wont to show itself in the family after a wayward fashion. At intervals growing longer and longer this peculiarity had cropped out in some descendant of the Monte Benis, who bore nearly all the characteristics that were attributed to the original founder of the race. Some traditions even went so far as to enumerate the ears, covered with a delicate fur, and shaped like a pointed leaf, among the proofs of authentic descent which were seen in these favoured individuals. But it was indisputable that, once in a century or oftener, a son of Monte Beni gathered into himself the moral qualities of his race, and reproduced the character that had been assigned to it from immemorial times. Strong, kindly, sincere, with simple tastes and natural gifts, this personage had a power of associating himself with the wild creatures of the forests and hills, and could feel a sympathy even with the trees, among which it was his lot to dwell. On the

Sophia Hawthorne, circa 1855
(Peabody Essex Museum)

other hand, there were deficiencies both of intellect and heart, and especially, as it seemed in the development of the higher portion of man's nature, and these deficiencies showed themselves strongly with advancing age, when the animal spirits had subsided, and youthful impulses no longer beautified the original brute nature.

Around this *pedestal,* as it were, of his conception, Mr Hawthorne weaves a variety of suggestive legends and Arcadian fillets appropriate to the main figure; and his dream of a modern Faun in the person of Donatello, the last Count of Monte Beni, actually grows into a portrait by the marvellous skill and consistency with which it is elaborated. At a later period we have a picture of Donatello in his Tuscan home, with accessories such as Horace may have cherished at his Sabine farm, and with the same internal light of a calm rustic felicity. But the description of Donatello in the gardens of the Villa Borghese is a more quotable specimen of the ingenious art which sustains Mr Hawthorne in his extravagant audacity. The Faun has found his way to Rome, and

has attached himself to a young female artist, about whose antecedents and position there is a mystery of criminality. The pair meet in the glades of the Roman Eden, of which, as an appropriate background, this is part of the choice description:–

These wooded and flowery lawns are more beautiful than the finest of English park scenery, more touching, more impressive, through the neglect that leaves nature so much to her own ways and methods . . . But it could not, she decided for herself, be other than an innocent pastime, if they two–sure to be separated by their different paths in life tomorrow–were to gather up some of the little pleasures that chanced to grow about their feet, like the violets and wood-anemones, to-day.

The association of these two personages is the scaffolding by which Mr Hawthorne proceeds to the 'Transformation' of the Faun's nature on a theory which seems to pervade his works, that you may so change any nature by burdening it with heavy responsibilities. It is represented of Miriam that she has been equivocally involved in some awful catastrophe, on account of which she is living in retirement and isolation. A sort of half-mad priest is the depositary of her secret, and persecutes her incessantly in spite of warnings and prayers. Donatello is a witness to one of these interviews on the brink of the Tarpeian Rock, and at a signal of half assent from Miriam he murders the priest by throwing him headlong. Thenceforth he and Miriam are bound together by the consciousness of their common crime, while this consciousness subdues and shatters the nature of Donatello and leads up by degrees to his so-called 'Transformation.' The last steps of this process are not very happy, nor is their result clear, but the harmony of the conception is sustained even when its outlines are blurred and Donatello is losing his affinity to the wild creatures of the woods. An American artist, a friend of his and Miriam's, and who seeks him at his home, to which he has retired in a fit of remorse, is the means of their eliciting the fact that his natural virtue has gone out of him. Donatello is invited to try the fascination of his voice in the thicket, and the effect of his moral defilement is thus exquisitely indicated:–

'I doubt', said Donatello, 'whether they will remember my voice now. . .?' '. . . No innocent thing can come near me.'

From this point, which is midway in the second volume, Mr Hawthorne's purpose evidently falters, and there is comparatively a falling short of the intended result. The attentive reader cannot fail to perceive this miscarriage, and we suspect that Mr Hawthorne is not only conscious of it himself, but makes Kenyon, the artist, his spokesman in the difficulty:–

> He pointed to a bust of Donatello . . . It was the contemplation of this imperfect portrait of Donatello that originally interested us in his history, and impelled us to elicit from Kenyon what he knew of his friend's adventures.

Thus, as we infer, Mr Hawthorne has avowedly left us a vigorous sketch, instead of a finished work of art. His Transformation was too subtle a process for his skill to perfect in the range of pure mythological existences; or, possibly, he was conscious of a strain in contrasting such supernatural being with the common every-day life of the Rome around him. At all events, it is a startling effect to be got out of galleries and museums, from the hints and suggestions of classified, catalogued art. Our astonishment is moved by the near approach to a great composition under such conditions, and out of such rigid materials. We are more impressed by Mr Hawthorne's success up to a certain point than by the shortcomings which render this success imperfect; and, like the gazers on the sky in mythologic times, we are surprised that the wings of Icarus should bear him so far, instead of being amazed that they should dissolve so soon.

There is another female character, introduced as a foil to Miriam, and the happy issue of her intercourse with Kenyon is obviously designed as a contrast to the misery of the union which commences in crime. Otherwise Hilda is not worth much in our eyes, nor, we suspect, in Mr Hawthorne's. Nor is there any explanation of the mystery which surrounds Miriam herself which may or may not be considered a fault, at the option of the reader. Minor intricies we do not remark, and minor blemishes we are indifferent to. Our desire has been to arrive at the central principle of a work of exceptional aim and singular beauty, and to convey this idea definitely to our readers. We find here the nucleus of a clear conception, which is for the most part luminous, though in its outer diffusion it lapses into vapour. So we recognize the power of an artistic Prospero over the cloudy forms and hues of dreamland; while there is so much originality in the shapes into which he attempts to mould them that, though the effect is incomplete, the effort is a work of genius.

A dozen years after including Hawthorne in A Fable for Critics, *James Russell Lowell reviewed* The Marble Faun *in* Atlantic Monthly, *one of the major magazines of the time. It was owned by Hawthorne's publishers, William D. Ticknor and James T. Fields, and edited by Lowell, who was then a Harvard professor.*

Review of *The Marble Faun*
J. R. Lowell
Atlantic Monthly, 5 (April 1860): 509–510

It is, we believe, more than thirty years since Mr Hawthorne's first appearance as an author; it is twenty-three since he gave his first collection of "Twice-told Tales" to the world. His works have received that surest warranty of genius and originality in the widening of their appreciation downward from a small circle of refined admirers and critics, till it embraced the whole community of readers. With just enough encouragement to confirm his faith in his own powers, those powers had time to ripen and toughen themselves before the gales of popularity could twist them from the balance of a healthy and normal development. Happy the author whose earliest works are read and understood by the lustre thrown back upon them from his latest! for then we receive the impression of continuity and cumulation of power, of peculiarity deepening to individuality, of promise more than justified in the keeping: unhappy, whose autumn shows only the aftermath and rowen of an earlier harvest, whose would-be replenishments are but thin dilutions of his fame!

The nineteenth century has produced no more purely original writer than Mr. Hawthorne. A shallow criticism has sometimes fancied a resemblance between him and Poe. But it seems to us that the difference between them is the immeasurable one between talent carried to its ultimate, and genius,–between a masterly adaptation of the world of sense and appearance to the purposes of Art, and a so thorough conception of the world of moral realities that Art becomes the interpreter of something profounder than herself. In this respect it is not extravagant to say that Hawthorne has something of kindred with Shakspeare. But that breadth of nature which made Shakspeare incapable of alienation from common human nature and actual life is wanting to Hawthorne. He is rather a denizen than a citizen of what men call the world. We are conscious of a certain remoteness in his writings, as in those of Donne, but with such a difference that we should call the one super- and the other subter-sensual. Hawthorne is psychological and metaphysical. Had he been born without the poetic imagination, he would have written treatises on the Origin of Evil. He does not draw characters, but rather conceives them and then shows them acted upon by crime, passion, or circumstance, as if the element of Fate

James Russell Lowell

were as present to his imagination as that of a Greek dramatist. Helen we know, and Antigone, and Benedick, and Falstaff, and Miranda, and Parson Adams, and Major Pendennis,—these people have walked on pavements or looked out of club-room windows; but what are these idiosyncrasies into which Mr. Hawthorne has breathed a necromantic life, and which he has endowed with the forms and attributes of men? And yet, grant him his premises, that is, let him once get his morbid tendency, whether inherited or the result of special experience, either incarnated as a new man or usurping all the faculties of one already in the flesh, and it is marvellous how subtilely and with what truth to as much of human nature as is included in a diseased consciousness he traces all the finest nerves of impulse and motive, how he compels every trivial circumstance into an accomplice of his art, and makes the sky flame with foreboding or the landscape chill and darken with remorse. It is impossible to think of Hawthorne without at the same time thinking of the few great masters of imaginative composition; his works, only not abstract because he has the genius to make them ideal, belong not specially to our clime or generation; it is their moral purpose alone, and perhaps their sadness, that mark him as the son of New England and the Puritans.

It is commonly true of Hawthorne's romances that the interest centres in one roughly defined protagonist, to whom the other characters are accessory and subordinate,—perhaps we should rather say a ruling Idea, of which all the characters are fragmentary embodiments. They remind us of a symphony of Beethoven's, in which, though there be variety of parts, yet all are infused with the dominant motive, and heighten its impression by hints and far-away suggestions at the most unexpected moment. As in Rome the obelisks are placed at points toward which several streets converge, so in Mr Hawthorne's stories the actors and incidents seem but vistas through which we see the moral from different points of view,—a moral pointing skyward always, but inscribed with hieroglyphs mysteriously suggestive, whose incitement to conjecture, while they baffle it, we prefer to any prosaic solution.

Nothing could be more original or imaginative than the conception of the character of Donatello in Mr. Hawthorne's new romance. His likeness to the lovely statue of Praxiteles, his happy animal temperament, and the dim legend of his pedigree are combined with wonderful art to reconcile us to the notion of a Greek myth embodied in an Italian of the nineteenth century; and when at length a soul is created in this primeval pagan, this child of earth, this creature of mere instinct, awakened through sin to a conception of the necessity of atonement, we feel, that, while we looked to be entertained with the airiest of fictions, we were dealing with the most august truths of psychology, with the most pregnant facts of modern history, and studying a profound parable of the developments of the Christian Idea.

Everything suffers a sea-change in the depths of Mr. Hawthorne's mind, gets rimmed with an impalpable fringe of melancholy moss, and there is a tone of sadness in this book as in the rest, but it does not leave us sad. In a series of remarkable and characteristic works, it is perhaps the most remarkable and characteristic. If you had picked up and read a stray leaf of it anywhere, you would have exclaimed, 'Hawthorne!'

The book is steeped in Italian atmosphere. There are many landscapes in it full of breadth and power, and criticisms of pictures and statues always delicate, often profound. In the Preface, Mr. Hawthorne pays a well-deserved tribute of admiration to several of our sculptors, especially to Story and Akers. The hearty enthusiasm with which he elsewhere speaks of the former artist's "Cleopatra" is no surprise to Mr. Story's friends at home, though hardly less gratifying to them than it must be to the sculptor himself.

The Universal Review of Politics, Literature, and Social Science _was published in London by the firm of W. H. Allen. It lasted from March 1859 through May 1860. Typical articles include "Indian Finance," "The Homeless Poor," and "Literature and Life." Among the books it reviewed is Nicholas Trübner's_ Bibliographical Guide to American Literature.

Nathaniel Hawthorne

The Universal Review of Politics, Literature, and Social Science, 3 (May 1860): 742–771

American literature is always an interesting subject, not only because it is literature, but because it is one of the elements in the solution of a problem which is important in a greater or less degree to the whole world—the moral and intellectual influence of democratic government. Political philosophers have sometimes wished that the sphere of their data was not limited to the province of observation only, but was capable of including the results of experiment as well. They would be glad of the power of those Eastern despots who sometimes transplanted a whole nation, and who would doubtless have subjected it to any other mental or physical process if they had thought it worth while to do so. The resources of science have not hitherto been sufficient to compass a similar end for us; but, to compensate for this want, we have before our eyes a spectacle which, to an instructed vision, is scarcely less fraught with momentous lessons than the trials which such philosophers have imagined for us. We see a nation, one of the mightiest on the earth, in the yet early years of its existence, and undergoing the process of formation and self-development under influences scarcely less various than those which could have been invented for it by the most imaginative speculator. If we look at one aspect of the United States, we may see many things which constitute an admirable success, and which may make us emulous, if not envious, of the means by which results are achieved which, with us, seem as distant as they are confessedly desirable. If we look on another, we are reminded of a child who has possessed himself of a handful of powerful drugs, and perched himself out of reach of any one who can control him. We know that he will make experiments for himself much more extraordinary than any we should have courage to make on his constitution, and we await the issue with feelings in which sympathy and compassion are not without their alloy on scientific curiosity. Thus we are not forced, as in most instances of historic speculation, to search out, by more less imperfect means, the obscure and latent causes which have originated what we see before us. In almost all other cases we have to draw our conclusion from the results—to argue from effects to causes. We look upon the present state of old societies and nations as the geologist does upon a formation—and speculate on the forces which have upheaved it from its primæval bed,—which have studded it with innumerable fossils, telling some strange and unknown story of forgotten cataclysms—which have covered these ancient ruins with the alluvial soil, the trees, the grass, and the flowers, with which Nature delights to smooth over and efface former convulsions. But in America the traces of all that has contributed to form her state and shape her destiny, are patent to the view. It is like observing, beneath the surface of the ocean, the coral insects as they build up their reef—or like watching bees at work in their glass hive.

An imaginative mind—such as that of Mr Hawthorne himself, for instance—might discern in both the illustrations we have used, some analogy to the elements of national life. In the rocky or coralline strata of the earth—in the wavy structure, compacted with infinite though instinctive skill, by successive myriads of workers—he might trace the semblance of institutions and laws which are the matrix of the social development which forms their visible outgrowth. In the Flora and Fauna of the terrestrial surface—in the sweet contents of the hive—he might fancy a representation of the positive productions of physical and intellectual industry, and of the blossoms of Art, Poetry, and Literature; since it is these, as much as the stronger foundation which underlies them, that one generation leaves for a heritage to its successors. Whether, however, we look at the matter in this fanciful light or from a purely rational point of view, all would agree in thinking that the efflorescence of a nation's being which finds its expression in its literature is as well worthy of attention for what it points to, even if not for its own positive merit, as any other product of its institutions. And, especially at the present day, when social topics have become elevated, in the philosopher's consideration, to an equality with purely political ones, no view of a people could be considered complete which did not include some estimate of the manner in which they regarded such problems of life as are not directly connected with material interests, and the method they took of expressing it their solution of them.

In the case of America, the light which Art and Literature throw on the character of a nation has been to a great extent denied, because the country can hardly be said to possess in this respect anything peculiarly and distinctively its own. For, though it be a legitimate philosophic generalization to look at these things as natural results of general progress, it does not follow that their magnitude bears any proportion to the other constituents of a nation's being. The Roman literature, characteristic though it might be as far as it went, would have occupied but a meagre place in the literature of the

Hawthorne's 16 June 1856 warrant authorizing the transfer of a prisoner charged with murder to the custody of the United States (Peabody Essex Museum)

world but for the impulse and the material which is derived from Greece. And, if Rome had been from the earliest times of her history in as constant communication with the Hellenic mind as she was after her conquest of its country, it may be a question whether even that amount of purely Latin literature which we know to have existed would have sprung up at all. What the Greeks were to the Romans in a literary point of view, that the English are to the Americans. We have long supplied them with the greater part of what they require in this respect. Not that there is any deficiency of printed books in the United States, but the part which is not a reflection of something in the old country appears to be very small indeed. For almost every work of note which has been produced there, the mother nation can show a better counterpart. How can a national literature flourish when this is the case? It can scarcely do so, until the nation undergoes so great a change that the literature it imports no longer finds anything responsive to it in the national mind. By the time that such a result is accomplished, something also will have arisen which will find its appropriate literary vent. Till then, probably, the most distinctive feature of American literature will be that which has often been pointed out as its most remarkable feature now—the element of humour. Humour is universal enough in itself; but the manner of its expression is so dependent upon local peculiarities that it will hardly bear to travel. The best part of its aroma is lost, like that of tea, in crossing salt water. Hence every nation has had to make its humorous literature at home, if it required any. We do not require to remind the reader of the indigenous origin of Roman satire, Fescennine verses, ancient lays, and Atellane fables. It was not without a certain appropriateness that the witty authors of Bon Gaultier's *Ballads* chose for their American subjects to parody some of the verses in which Macaulay tried to set before us some notion of what ancient Roman poetry might have been. If we wished to preserve for posterity some idea of what the Americans are, and how they differ from us, we should choose not Irving or Longfellow, but Lowell and Sam Slick.

Are there, then, no signs of a national American literature in any department except that of Humour? It must be confessed that there are but few. If we exclude from consideration all who have not gained sufficient fame to be read beyond their own limits, the number of American writers who are anything more than Englishmen in America does not amount to much. Irving dealt with national traditions, and devoted himself to national subjects. But his whole cast of thought, and of the dress of his thought, was formed upon English models. Longfellow is equally indebted to Germany; and the poem in which he is sometimes said to be most

original is a homage to the traditions of the red man rather than of his own white brethren. About Emerson, indeed, there is something which ones does not think would have been written in Europe, but it is not his strongest part. Poe seems altogether incapable of being classified; and if his works (omitting the American phrases and positive local allusions) had been published as translations from the French, German, or Danish, we do not think any one would have disbelieved in their assumed origin. This is not quite the case with the writer before us. Mr Hawthorne is, we are inclined to think, the most national writer, of a serious kind, whom the country has yet produced in the department of fiction. He seems to us to reflect many of the characteristics of the American mind more exactly than any of his predecessors. He has evidently a warm as well as an enlightened love for his country. He likes to dwell on the picturesque part of its early struggles, just as we like to hover about the region of the civil war. The primitive habits of the first settlers—the stern Puritanic training of the infant states—the conflict of asceticism with the old jovial English spirit—the legends which cluster, like bats round a ruined tower, about the decaying period of the English rule—are all familiar denizens of his mind, and the channels through which many of his ideas spontaneously flow. He reflects more unconsciously, perhaps, some of the perhaps transitional, characteristics of the America that is; the contrasts which are always presenting themselves between the material and the moral side of civilization, and the singular combination of knowingness and superstition, which some at least of the present phases of American life offer to our notice.

Mr Hawthorne has written upwards of sixty stories and sketches, and four novels, all of various kinds and degrees of merit. There is no necessity for regarding the classification under which these appeared, which seems to have been accidental, and dependent on the fact that he found he had, at certain times, written enough to compose a volume. We may also disregard the fact of their being longer or shorter—of their being mere stories, or three-volume novels. It will, for our present purpose, be most convenient to divide them into three classes:—I. Studies of Historic Events, or of Everyday Characters. II. Scenes and Stories purely imaginative and fantastic. III. Allegories, and Moral Sketches or Narratives. The first of these classes, as far as the shorter pieces are concerned, is not that in which Mr Hawthorne's originality is most apparent. except for the delicacy of observation which distinguishes all he writes, there is little about them to separate them from such sketches as those of Washington Irving. One kind are pictures of events in American annals, which he has striven to reproduce with a certain imaginative

Hawthorne (far right) and his wife (far left) with friends in an Oxford garden in summer 1856. In the English Notebooks
Hawthorne commented on the photograph and the efficiency of photographer Philip Delamotte
(Bancroft Library, University of California, Berkeley).

An Oxford Portrait

Hawthorne and his wife traveled with their friend Francis Bennoch to Oxford for a six-day visit with Richard James Spiers, a former mayor of Oxford, who was a friend of Bennoch and of the Halls. On the last day of the visit Philip Henry Delamotte, a professor of drawing and photography, came to breakfast and then took a group portrait.

Afterwards, when we were all come, he arranged us under a tree, in the garden–Mr. & Mrs. Spiers, with their eldest son, Mr. and Mrs. Hall, Fanny, Mr. Addison, my wife and me–and stained the glass with our figures and faces, in the twinkling of an eye; not my wife's face, however, for she turned away, and left only a pattern of her bonnet and gown; and Mrs. Hall, too, refused to countenance the proceeding, otherwise than with her back. But all the rest of us were caught, to the life; and i was really a little startled at recognizing myself so apart from myself, and done so quickly too.

– *The English Notebooks, 1856–1860,*
The Centenary Edition, vol. 22, pp. 146–147

colouring, rather than as transcripts of what might actually have happened. There is no study of costume as costume; it is introduced for the purpose of heightening the impression rather than of completing the portrait. Indeed, we may say generally, though there is much about Mr Hawthorne's writings of what would usually be called 'the picturesque,' and though he has a strong feeling for the thing itself, he has not the gift–perhaps has not the desire–of setting a landscape or a scene before our eyes in its unity as well as its variety. He has a certain power of selection, but he uses it to deepen the feeling that he wishes to inspire, not to dash down those few strong touches which form a living whole. His effect is produced by an accumulation of details, all of which converge to a certain impression, but we do not carry away from them a mental photograph. The effect rather resembles the result of what addresses itself to the ear than the feelings which are left by exercising the sense of sight. After reading a story of this kind we feel more as if we had been at a concert than at a play. There is the same sense of vague harmony, touching chords of feeling which it requires some subtle hand to reach; the same sense of occasional incompleteness in an intellectual point of view, and the same sort of semi-physical gratification which is produced by listening to music, or inhaling perfume. In other respects these sketches have but slight value, and we shall offer no excuse for passing on to the more important ones.

Under the head of 'Imaginative and Fantastic' Sketches we should include all he has written which does not, on the one hand, represent any actual fact, external circumstance, or character, and, on the other, involves no distinct moral lesson. In stories of this kind we are as far as possible from anything realistic. There is nothing about them which bears any relation to life as we habitually know it. The people have no more substantiality than the personages of a fairy tale; and though the recital of their fate may thrill us with a transient horror, or their characters excite a tepid fondness, they seldom rouse any deeper sentiment than that of wonder. It is in these stories that Mr Hawthorne bears the greatest resemblance to Poe, because it is in these that he is least moral, though always far more so than that singular writer. In the 'New Adam and Eve,' for instance we observe a similar power of taking some odd idea and working out the suggested hypothesis into all possible consequences. The author, in that sketch, imagines the whole human race to be destroyed—obliterated from the face of the earth, leaving no actual form of man, woman, or child, even dead, behind it; but leaving all the traces of its existence—its public and private buildings, its furniture and utensils, its untasted food, its ornaments and clothes, its books and pictures—as if the whole world were turned into one vast Pompeii. Into this strange solitude are introduced the two new beings who are to repeople it, and who survey, with perplexity, the vestiges of their predecessors. The point of the sketch consists in the contrast between primæval simplicity and the multifarious appliances with which civilization surrounds us—not without a sigh of regret at the kind of heavy weight which the rolling ages of his hoary old world have left upon its brows. No other moral than this is perceptible, but one may fancy a sort of appropriateness in the picture to an inhabitant of a land which embraces all degrees of the world's progress within the circuit of its territories, and which can show us, as it were, fainter and fainter zones of civilization melting away by imperceptible degrees into the primitive wildness of nature. Such a fancy would hardly have occurred to a dweller in one of the old continents. In 'David Swan' we find an apologue such as Parnell might have versified, though without the ethical force which would have recommended it to him. A youth falls asleep at a fountain, and during his slumber, various persons approach him who each intend, for a brief moment, to do something which,

were it done, would entirely change the course of his destiny. A childless old couple observe him, and it crosses their minds to adopt him as a son. A man passes who thinks of taking him as a clerk. A girl notices him; but his eyes are shut, and answer with no electric flash to hers. Three men resolve to murder him, and are within an ace of accomplishing their purpose. At the end of an hour he wakes and goes on his way, of course unconscious what a number of pregnant clouds of fate, so to speak, have sailed past him, without discharging either the beneficent dew or the destroying thunderbolt. This story is only so far moral that it suggests on what trifles the course of our life may depend; but though the thought is a solemn one, and forcibly put, it gives us nothing more than this to carry away. No moralist can teach us to control fate. In 'The Prophetic Pictures' is illustrated the idea—which is a favourite one with our author—that an artist has the power of calling on to the canvas the latent capacities, for good or evil, of his sitter, and fixing him with the expression which he will wear when those capacities have developed themselves into habits. A pair of betrothed lovers are supposed to be sitting for their portraits, but their characteristics take such hold on the artist's mind, that he embodies the relation in which he thinks they naturally stand to one another, in a supplementary sketch, which he keeps for himself. This is not intended to be shown, but the lady accidentally sees it, and is filled with horror at the vision of the future which it suggests. About the portraits, too, there is something strange, which impresses beholders with an indefinable awe. Years pass on, and both husband and wife grow more and more like their respective pictures. At last, as they one day stand looking at them, the husband is seized with a sudden fury—he realizes in himself the demoniac expression of his resemblance on the canvas—the insanity, so long dormant, bursts forth, and he raises his hand to murder his companion. It is arrested by the artist, who, drawn on by an inextinguishable curiosity to know whether his sitters have followed out their appointed path, has returned to visit them, and is in time to check the catastrophe which his sketch had prefigured. The effect of the tale is wild and ghastly in the author's way of telling it, and reminds us of some parts of the writings both of Poe and Wilkie Collins, though it does not aim at the matter-of-fact air which stands for so much in the power of the two latter writers. 'The Ambitious Guest'—which describes the violent death of a whole family, together with a stranger, all of whom had been making plans for the future to the moment of their fate—by the sudden fall of part of a mountain—owes its telling character to a similar feeling—that of the irresistibleness of our destiny. The most ghastly of all the stories in this class, however, is 'The Hollow of the Three

Hawthorne's 15 August 1857 letter in which he asserts that the Chapman and Hall edition of The Blithedale Romance
is the only book of his published in England that is not a piracy (Peabody Essex Museum)

Hills.' An old witch descends at sunset into one of those weird and lonely spots which have always been the scene of unholy operations. She is joined by a beautiful, but faded, lady, who kneels down and places her head in her lap. The hag summons up three pictures relating to the guilty woman's life; her forsaken parents, in their solitary grief; her betrayed husband, telling the story of his dishonour to the associates of his mad-house; and, lastly, the burial which is awaiting herself amid the curses and revilings of her former friends. The story concludes:—'But when the old woman stirred the kneeling lady, she lifted not her head. "Here has been a sweet hour's sport!" said the withered crone, chuckling to herself'—'The Hall of Fantasy,' and 'P's Correspondence,' are sketches of a lighter character. The former describes a sort of limbo, people with the shapes of inventors, theorists, and reformers—the representatives of all the wasted intellect and ingenuity that has ever existed. The latter purports to be the description, by a half-madman, of all manner of celebrated people—a strange jumble of the dead and the living—Byron and Shelley grown old, fat, and converted to respectability; Napoleon I., a denizen of Pall Mall; Canning, a peer, and Keats in middle age, with a completed epic. The wit of this latter fantasy is merely that of cross-readings ingeniously enough worked out. 'The Select Party,' which is much of the same kind, introduces us to such entities as the Oldest Inhabitant, the Clerk of the Weather, Old Harry, Davy Jones, and Posterity. In this section we may also, perhaps, include 'The Celestial Railroad,' which is a kind of travestie of the *Pilgrim's Progress*. There, however, the moral element is more distinctively brought out—since the railroad which levels the Slough of Despond, puts all the pilgrims' burdens in the luggage-break, tunnels through the Hill of Difficulty, and has Apollyon utilized as its stoker, is, of course, not recommended as a mode of transit to the Heavenly City. The author's ingenuity is shown in such alterations as the replacing Pope and Pagan by 'Giant Transcendentalist,' and by the modern aspects he gives to the well-remembered booths of Vanity Fair. Over the remaining pieces of this kind there is no need to linger. They are all marked by ingenuity, cleverness, and Mr Hawthorne's grace of style and sentiment, but many of them are air-drawn shapes, which leave but little impression when we have closed the book. We pass on to the third class, which comprehends the author's most impressive and important productions.

Upon looking over them, in connexion, we have been struck with the fact that they almost all represent one or other of two ideas, which appear to have a remarkable prominence in the author's mind.

One of these ideas is the notion expressed to a certain extent by Persius in a line, which Kant took as a kind of motto to his great metaphysical work,—*Tecum habita, et nôris quam sit tibi curta supellex*—the warning (in a larger sense) against attempting to transcend in any way the conditions of our being. Hartley Coleridge has attempted to show that a phase of this idea is the basis of *Hamlet*. The Prince of Denmark, he tells us, stepped out of the limits of our proper nature by placing himself in connexion with the unseen world, and thereby immediately assumed a false relation towards actual life, and ultimately found his mind unable to support the weight of the new experience laid upon him in a region for which our faculties are too weak. Mr Hawthorne, in about half of the tales we should include under our third section, teaches either a similar lesson, or its corollary, viz. that, seeing we cannot pass the bounds which encircle this human system, we should make the best of it as it is. Thus in 'The Birthmark,' he describes a man of science whose wife is all perfection, except that her cheek is marked with the figure of a tiny hand. He is annoyed by this defect, and persuades the lady to allow him to eradicate it by resorting to subtle devices of chemistry. He succeeds; but the same potent elixir which destroys the eyesore that has vexed him, destroys life also, and the woman fades out of the existence which had just received what the presumptuous experimentalist thought its finishing touch. In 'Rappacini's Daughter' is described a beautiful girl, whose father puts her out of the pale of humanity by nourishing her on poisons till her whole nature is saturated with them, so that she inhales with pleasure the noxious odours, which kill animals that breathe them, and causes flowers to wither by holding them in her hand. The youth who wins her heart is in process of being endowed, by sympathy and contact, with the same mysterious power, but is persuaded by a physician, the rival of her father, to give her a potion to neutralize the effect of all the poison she has imbibed. It is, in fact, an efficacious antidote; but her physiological nature is so completely reversed that what would be a remedy to any one else, acts as a poison on her; she takes the draught, and falls dead in her lover's arms. 'Earth's Holocaust' describes,—somewhat after the manner of the Vision of Mirza—a bonfire in which mankind had determined to get rid of all the rubbish and worn-out 'properties' that had accumulated in the history of the world, so as to begin entirely afresh and 'turn over a new leaf.' But, we are told, in spite of everything having been burnt, all that is valuable will re-appear in the ashes the succeeding day, while, unless the human heart itself is thrown on to the pile, everything for the sake of which the fire was kindled will spring up again as luxuriantly as ever. In 'Dr Heidegger's Experiment' (which we fancy may have been suggested by a scene in Dumas' *Mémoires d'un Medecin*), we are taught that, if we could renew our youth by some Medean draught, we should, unless altered in other respects, commit the same follies as we have now to look back to. 'Peter Goldthwaite's Treasure'–where a man pulls down his whole house, to find a concealed board which turns out worthless on discovery,–and 'The Threefold Destiny,' where the hero, after roaming over the world to meet with a lot such as he conceives unsuitable for him, after returning unsuccessful, finds it on the spot whence he set out,–both convey the same moral as the old fable of the sons who dug over their land to find the money which its improved fertility was really to give them. Nearly a similar lesson is enforced in 'The Great Carbuncle,' which like the 'Jewel of Giamschid,' eludes all those who set out to search for it, except one who dies at the instant of discovery, and two, who become aware that they can do much better without it. 'The Celestial Railroad,' which we have already looked at as a mere work of fancy, may probably also be meant to imply that there are no short cuts in spiritual matters. 'Mrs Bullfrog' is a comic sketch (not our author's happiest vein), symbolizing the philosophy which teaches us to 'make the best of it,' in the case of matrimonial as well as other disappointments. 'Egotism, or the Bosom Serpent,' needs no explanation. All these stories have great variety in treatment, and it is not until we look over them with a view to establishing some kind of classification, that we see how very many of them express different *facets,* so to speak, of the same idea. It is not, perhaps a novel one–no moral ideas are–but, it is sound as far as it goes, and if, to apply an oft-quoted sentence, its author has not 'solved the mystery of the universe,' he has, nevertheless, taught us 'to keep within the limits of the knowable.'

The other leading notion to which we referred as pervading a great number, and among them the most important, of Mr Hawthorne's moral tales, is the idea of secret guilt. Though the former point in his philosophy might not, in its manifold diversities of presentation, at once strike a casual reader, we should imagine that everyone at all acquainted with his writings must have recognized the predominance of the one of which we now speak. It reappears so often as almost to make us fancy that he must have had at some time or other the office of a confessor, or have enjoyed some peculiar opportunity for studying this phase of morbid moral anatomy. We will mention some of the phases under which the idea is presented–the garments in which it is clothed in the various sketches, quoting at the same time some of the passages in which we may trace its development through the author's mind in its progress towards the proportions it has assumed in some of his later works. 'The Haunted Mind' is a study of the miscellaneous fancies which occur to us on waking in the middle of the night. Among these the following passage is remarkable, not only as being a good specimen of Mr Hawthorne's style, but as containing the germ of much which we find elsewhere hinted at or expressed in a concrete form. After experiencing and revelling in the sensation of warmth in bed–'that idea,' he continues, 'has brought a hideous one in its train:'–

> You think how the dead are lying in their cold shrouds and narrow coffins, through the drear winter of the grave, and cannot persuade your fancy that they neither shrink nor shiver when the snow is drifting over their little hillocks, and the bitter blast howls against the door of the tomb . . .
> . . . Sufficient without such guilt is this nightmare of the soul; this heavy, heavy sinking of the spirits; this wintry gloom about the heart; this indistinct horror of the mind, blending itself with the darkness of the chamber.

'Young Goodman Brown' describes a man setting out to attend a witches' Sabbath, leaving his young wife (Faith) behind. On his way he becomes conscious that the most respectable persons of his acquaintance are bound in the same direction. At his initiation into the unhallowed mysteries, he is confronted by his fair young spouse, who has come there on a similar errand; but before he is able to learn whether she has the stain of guilt which would entitle her to admission, the scene dissolves, and he is at home again–to become a cynic and a disbeliever in human virtue for the rest of his life. The following is from the speech of the arch-fiend to the intending proselytes:–

> 'There,' resumed the sable form, 'are all whom ye have reverenced from youth . . . Far more than this! *It shall be yours to penetrate, in every bosom, the deep mystery of sin, the fountain of all wicked arts,* and which inexhaustibly supplies more evil impulses than human power–than my power at its utmost!–can make manifest in deeds. And now, my children, look upon each other.

In 'The Procession of Life,' which is a sort of classification of mankind according to their real not their conventional value, by their intellectual gifts, their virtue, or their vice, the same idea is pursued:–

> Come, all ye guilty ones, and rank yourselves in accordance with the brotherhood of crime.
> . . . Oh no! it must be merely the impertinence of those unblushing hussies; and we can only wonder how such respectable ladies should have responded to a summons that was not meant for them.'

In 'Egotism,' which describes an unfortunate person who has swallowed a snake, which is constantly preying on his vitals, we are reminded, in a slightly dif-

Page from Hawthorne's notebook, written in spring 1858 when he was in Rome. At the bottom of the page he describes the "peculiar charm" of the faun of Praxiteles, a quality that in part inspired The Marble Faun *(American Art Association Anderson Galleries, sale number 4323, 22–23 April 1937; reprinted in* Hawthorne at Auction, *p. 295).*

ferent form, of the freemasonry which exists between one guilty being and another. The victim wanders about the streets as if to establish a species of brotherhood between himself and the world.

> With cankered ingenuity, he sought out his own disease in every breast. Whether insane or not, he showed so keen a perception of error, frailty, and vice, that many persons gave him credit for being possessed not merely with a serpent, but with an actual fiend, who imparted this evil faculty of recognizing whatever was ugliest in man's heart.

In 'The Christmas Banquet,' supposed to be a convivial gathering of the ten most miserable persons that could be found in the world at one time, is introduced a misanthrope who had been soured by the failure of his trust in mankind. He 'had for several years employed himself in accumulating motives, for hating and despising his race, such as murder, treachery, ingratitude . . . *hidden guilt in men of saint-like aspect,* and, in short, all manner of black realties that sought to decorate themselves with outward grace or glory.' In 'Fancy's Show-box' the idea is carried still farther, and Fancy, Memory, and Conscience, are represented as bringing before the mental vision of a man who has committed none but the most venial faults, throughout his life, a variety of sins which at one time or other he had a passing wish to perpetrate. 'Not a shadow of proof could have been adduced in an earthly court that he was guilty of the slightest of the sins which were then made to stare him in the face.' But at each picture called up Conscience strikes a dagger to his heart. The author pleads for his imaginary 'Mr Smith,' that there is no such thing as a settled and full resolve either for good or evil, except at the very moment of execution,' and therefore it may be hoped that all the consequences of sin will not be incurred unless the act have set its seal upon the thought. Still there remains the awful truth that 'man must not disclaim his brotherhood, even with the guiltiest, since, though his hand to be clean, his heart has surely been polluted by the flitting phantoms of iniquity.' 'The Minister's Black Veil' conveys a similar idea, and is a sort of foreshadowing of *The Scarlet Letter.* A clergyman of perfectly blameless reputation, chooses for some inscrutable reason, to wear, from the age of thirty till his death, a black veil, which is never lifted, and which makes him a terror and a mystery to all beholders—alienates his betrothed wife, and isolates him from mankind. The first sermon he preaches after assuming it, for it is worn in the pulpit as elsewhere, has 'reference to secret sin, and those sad mysteries which we hide from our nearest and dearest, and would fain conceal from our own consciousness, even forgetting that the Omniscient can detect them.' Each one of the

congregation seems to creep behind the veil and 'discover his hoarded iniquity of deed or thought.' He becomes, apparently by the aid of this mysterious emblem alone, 'a man of awful power over souls that were in agony for sin.' Its gloom 'enables him to sympathize with all dark affections.' On his death-bed he tells his wondering friends not to tremble at him, but at each other, for that he alone wears the symbol, while all have the reality, of an impassable barrier drawn between soul and soul. An English reader recognizes the feeling expressed in the lines of Keble:–

> *Why should we faint and fear to live alone,*
> *Since Heaven has willed it all alone must die,*
> *Nor even the dearest heart and near our own*
> *Knows half the reasons why we smile or sigh?*
>
> *Each in his hidden sphere of bliss or woe,*
> *Our hermit spirits dwell and range apart;*
> *Our eyes see all around in gloom or glow–*
> *Hues of their own, fresh borrow'd from the heart.*

'The Intelligence Office,' which is one of those fantastic sketches in which the allegory is made more quaint by being conveyed through a common and familiar channel, embodies much the same notion as that of 'Fancy's Show-box.' A man is supposed to be seated at a desk in some large city. To him enter all manner of customers, in order to hear of what they want. One requires a place—he has never been in his right place in the world. A young man wants to exchange a heart, and meets with a girl bound on a similar errand. Some hearts were so finely tempered, and curiously made, that none could be found to match them, and had to be left on commission. Another person comes to inquire after a lost article. It is the 'Pearl of great Price.' Others come for locks of hair, flowers, and other love tokens, which they have lost. Another comes to dispose of an ill-gotten estate, on condition only that the transferee shall take the incumbrance which has been incurred in its acquisition. Some people come to exchange vice for virtue; some *vice versâ;* others for wealth; one person for to-morrow, of which he has been in chase all his life; one for truth. To a home question of the latter applicant the keeper of the office confesses that his desks and counter and ledgers are a blind, and that he is simply the recording angel—all whose ostensible operations are really performed by the desires of men's own hearts.

By far the most powerful of Mr Hawthorne's shorter works in this class, however, is the one entitled 'Roger Malvin's Burial'—both for the picturesque power of the colouring and the ghastly vividness with which the central idea is presented. Reuben Bourne, and his intended father-in-law, Roger Malvin, have been wounded in a fight with the Indians, and are making their way home through the forest. The elder man's strength fails him, and it is evident he can never reach the settlement. It is doubtful whether even the younger can do so, if he remains much longer without medical aid and sufficient food. They sit down at the foot of a huge rock, shaped like a gigantic headstone. The elder feels the certain, but slow, approach of death, and exhorts his companion since he can do nothing really to help him, to make the best of his time, reach home before it is too late for him also, and console Malvin's daughter, Dorcas, to whom he is betrothed. The conflict in Reuben's mind is long doubtful; it seems selfish to leave the old man to die alone; yet if he stays, he sacrifices himself for an idea, and gives up the realities of remaining life which await his escape. He yields, however, but vows to return either to save his friend's life, or to lay him in the grave.

> An almost superstitious regard, arising, perhaps, from the customs of the Indians, whose war was with the dead, as well as the living, was paid by the frontier inhabitants to the rites of sepulture; and there are many instances of the sacrifice of life, in the attempt to bury those who had fallen by the 'sword of the wilderness.' . . .
>
> . . . But such must have been Reuben's own fate, had he tarried another sunset; and who shall impute blame to him, if he shrank from so useless a sacrifice. As he gave a parting look, a breeze waved the little banner upon the sapling-oak, and reminded Reuben of his vow.

Reuben, however, shrinks with moral cowardice from telling Dorcas of the true state of affairs, and evades the question, allowing her to suppose that he has really attended her father's last moments, and interred his remains. He is long ill, and experiences, on his recovery, 'the miserable and humiliating torture of unmerited praise,' for having been faithful unto death to his old friend. Two years having passed, Dorcas and Reuben are married.

> There was now in the breast of Reuben Bourne an incommunicable thought; something which he was to conceal more heedfully from her whom he most loved and trusted . . . His one secret thought became like a chain, binding down his spirit, and, like a serpent, gnawing into his heart; and he was transformed into a sad and downcast, yet irritable man.

We need not pursue the details of the story. Misfortunes come upon Reuben, and the family leave their home to seek a new habitation in the West. They are accompanied by their only son, a youth of fifteen, and already a skilful hunter. In one of their encampments, Reuben and the boy go out to hunt in opposite directions. The father, after wandering about in a circle, sees

Marble bust of Hawthorne (1858) by Louisa Lander. Hawthorne drew on his notebook descriptions of Lander in his portrayal of Hilda in The Marble Faun *(Concord Free Public Library).*

something moving among the bushes, and fires at it. He finds his victim at the base of a gigantic rock, almost covered with a dense growth of underwood. It is the spot where he had left Roger Malvin sitting eighteen years before. What he has slain in his own son.

The Scarlet Letter is, probably, the best known of Mr Hawthorne's works, and it is unnecessary to recount the plot, which turns on one of the singular punishments inflicted by the early Puritans on adultery—that of making the culprit wear a symbol of her guilt on some conspicuous part of her dress. Whether there is actual historical warrant for the fact is not important. The story is complicated by the refusal of the adulteress to reveal the name of her paramour, and by the determination of her husband, who has returned in disguise to the scene of his dishonour, to track him out. His suspicions direct him aright, and the most saintly person in the colony–an Abelard before his fall– is the man who ought to have stood in the pillory beside his guilty partner. The torturing hypocrisy and remorse of this young clergyman in the midst of his fame as a preacher and a Christian are described with a subtle power, and a depth of psychological insight which has nowhere been equaled in its own line. The manner in which the husband, having become his medical adviser and confidential friend, surprises his secret, and uses his knowledge to inflict daily tortures–to touch the secret sores as if with a chance hand, and while veiling his real knowledge of the facts, never to let his victim forget his crime–is placed before us with marvellous force and elaboration, embodying, too, the deep truth that such a diabolical revenge causes the injured and the injurer to change places, and forces us to withdraw the sentiment of pity from the man who was originally wronged. How the woman bears her penance and educates her child–who, by a suggestive symbolism, is made to typify in her nature the mixture of conflicting influences which her parents seem to have bestowed–the temptation to fly from the scene of his secret shame, which assails the young clergyman–his baffled attempt to carry out his scheme, and his desperate self-revelation in the extremity of his mental anguish, may be read in the tale itself. But it may be interesting to trace, in various passages, the developments of the same ideas which have been associated by the author in former works with this favourite phase of moral experience, for which they seem in such points to have been studies. In the following passage we recognize the moral enforced in 'Young Goodman Brown:'–

> Hester felt or fancied, then, that the scarlet letter had endowed her with a new sense . . . Be it accepted as a proof that all was not corrupt in this poor victim of her own frailty and man's hard law, that Hester Prynne yet struggled to believe that no fellow-mortal was guilty like herself.'

The erring minister has a similarly quickened sense: 'His intellectual gifts, his moral perceptions, his power of experiencing and communicating emotion, were kept in a state of preternatural activity by the prick and anguish of his daily life.'

He naturally belonged to the ethereal and saintly class, whose life is spent among their books–spiritual scholars–who, however, lack

> The gift that descended upon the chosen disciples at Pentecost, in tongues of flame; symbolizing, it would seem, not the power of speech in foreign and unknown languages, but that of addressing the whole human brotherhood in the heart's native language.

His sin kept him down on a level with the lowest; yet

> This very burden it was that gave him sympathies so intimate with the sinful brotherhood of mankind; so that his heart vibrated in unison with theirs, and received their pain into itself, and sent its own throb of pain through a thousand other hearts, in gushes of sad, persuasive eloquence.

The House of the Seven Gables is a little less impressive than the earlier work, but it makes up for this in its greater variety and more life-like and real character. In *The Scarlet Letter* the chief personages seem to be almost as far removed from us as the characters in some old Greek tragedy; there is a halo of romance thrown round them which, to a degree, isolates them from our entire sympathies, however forcibly the record of their doom may come home to our hearts.

The House of the Seven Gables is a story of contemporary life, and though we scarcely feel that we are in the everyday world, the people are such as might be met with there. While preserving the romantic cast of the narrative in all that pertains to its essentials, nothing can surpass the art with which the familiar figures of the street and the shop are embroidered, as it were, on this dusky background, which seems to throw them into more prominent relief. The character of Hepzibah, with her faded gentility, her warmth of affection, and her struggles in assuming her new life, are painted with extraordinary skill. Judge Pyncheon is not described at so much length as most of Mr Hawthorne's characters, but the touches which pictures him to us, though few, are strong, and seem to give the man's inner nature. Were we on the look-out for merely descriptive passages, we should probably choose this novel as the best specimen of its author's power. Nowhere has he written with so much force and with so little apparent effort. The eighteenth chapter of this novel, in which the author describes all the schemes of ambitious man cut short by his sudden death, is full of a grim irony such as we find nowhere so well sustained except in some of the best passages of Dickens. Mr Hawthorne falls far short of the rich variety and comic power of the latter writer, but he may occasionally compete with him in the intensity wherewith certain strong emotions or situations are kneaded into the reader's mind, so as to leave an indelible impression.

The basis of this story, too, is the idea of secret guilt–and working on a broader scale than elsewhere in the author's creations. The house is the result of a Naboth's-vineyard kind of transaction on the part of the ancestral Pyncheon, who caused its right owner to

A watercolor sketch of Hawthorne by his son. The thirteen-year-old Julian sketched his father five times in an album he shared with his mother during the family's residence in Italy, providing the first visual evidence of the mustache Hawthorne began growing in April 1859 (Bancroft Library, University of California, Berkeley).

be burnt for witchcraft that he might possess himself of the property. The curse clings to the posterity, and reappears in the persons of the two last owners, the former of whom dies by the hand of the latter, though the blame is shifted to other shoulders, and the man who should have borne it enjoys the inheritance. Outwardly fair-seeming and prosperous, his life is darkened by the shadow of undetected crime:–

> The judge, beyond all question, was a man of eminent respectability. The Church acknowledged it; the State acknowledged it . . .
>
> . . . And, beneath the show of a marble palace, that pool of stagnant water, foul with many impurities, and, perhaps, tinged with blood–that secret abomination, above which, possibly, he may say his prayers, without remembering it–is this man's miserable soul!

The following, too, is a piece of acute analysis:–

> To apply this train of remark somewhat more closely to Judge Pyncheon.–We might say (without in the least imputing crime to his eminent respectability) that there was enough of splendid rubbish in his life to cover up and paralyze a more active and subtle conscience than the judge was ever troubled with . . .

> . . . Sickness will not always help him to it; not always the death-hour!

With the above passages may be compared the italicised passage in our extract from 'The Procession of Life.'

In reading the story from which these extracts are taken, we are apt to be so fascinated by the narrative, as to be unconscious of a certain disproportionateness in its construction which forces itself on us after we lay it down. The *dénouement* seems to be overbalanced by the characters and descriptions, and to be a little hurried over. Not that it is otherwise than a perfectly allowable one in a romance of the kind. The descendant of the man who was burnt through the old Pyncheon's agency having been in the secret of the house all through the story, comes forward at last to marry the heiress and remove the spell. His part, however, is rather too much that of a spectator all through, and we have a sort of feeling that his agency ought to have been of a more active character as regards the Judge; though how this could have been effected we do not presume to suggest. There is, on the other hand, as regards the conduct of the narrative, a skill which we do not remember to have been noticed, in the manner in which the fortunes of the family between the time of the remote ancestor and the personages in whom we are now interested, are set before us, by means of the story which Holgrave tells Phœbe of his own mesmeric progenitor. Had this been introduced in its proper place it would have given the book too much of the aspect of a family chronicle.

Before we pass on to Mr Hawthorne's most recent work, a few words must be said about *The Blithedale Romance*–though we are inclined to think, that this is the book which, of all he has written, is least likely to contribute to his fame. It was the result, we believe, of its author's experience at Brook Farm, a kind of Utopian or Fourierist agricultural community, which came to grief after a short trial. It was natural enough that the characters, who had self-reliance and singularity enough to quit the world for such experiment, should have had many traits which an observer of human nature would be glad to study, and which a writer like Mr Hawthorne would feel almost irresistibly compelled to draw out in some consistent framework. If, however, as we suspect, it was the characters which suggested the story, this would be enough to account for its inferior success to that of the author's former novels. A work of fiction may start from the central idea, and work outwards by means of characters which the author looks for to embody it in; or it may work towards some idea from the outside, because a number of characters have presented themselves which look as if they ought to do something if brought together. The best novels are those in which idea, plot, and character, all spring up together in the mind, one knows not how, but mutually dependent, and incapable of expressing a being expressed in any other form. To this degree of excellence, however, few attain. Mr Hawthorne's successes, we think, have arisen from the fact that his genius is of the former class. An idea has possessed him, and he has striven to bring it out in the most appropriate and forcible way he could devise; if aërial and exceptional, by fantastic and merely imaginative machinery; if more substantial and more based on the facts of life, then by a more realistic and living narrative. To have elaborated the notion of the freemasonry of guilt, which is conveyed in 'Young Goodman Brown,' by a series of mundane characters would have resulted in a monstrous and impossible work. In its full breadth, the idea would only bear handling in some light and allegoric fashion. When, however, this dark consciousness is confined to a single individual's breast who reaches the hearts of others by a shuddering warmth of sympathy and not by the full blaze of a complete knowledge of their whole secret history, the conception assumes a more practical and credible form, and can be made the foundation of a book bearing some relation to positive experience. By judiciously employing one or other of these methods, according to the exigency of the subject, Mr Hawthorne's chief successes have been won. In *The Blithedale Romance* he appears, as we have said, to have pursued a different plan. The result is, that there is a want of point and unity in the story. We are sensible of the power of particular scenes, such as the night-search by the river for the missing heroine, and the force and delicacy with which her character, and that of her stern and rugged friend, are drawn. But we close the book with a certain feeling of dissatisfaction, only mitigated by that halo which a man of genius contrives to throw round any creation of his pen, and transfer us by means of it into the enchanted region of which he keeps the key.

Of the latest work for which we are indebted to Mr Hawthorne, we scarcely know whether we can give a more favourable account. It is full of graceful and beautiful thoughts, and its finish and ease of style are greater than any former writing of the author. But it is largely deficient in the vigour which has held us spellbound over many of his other pages. We question whether many persons have finished *Transformation* at a sitting, unless they really had nothing else to do. One might fancy that the Italian atmosphere which has lent colour and brilliancy to the book, had also imparted something of the enervating softness, with which it often affects those who breathe it not as their native air. The nervous American fibre with its remote under-strength of stalwart British organization, seems to have been relaxed, or led away from its former strivings after positive results. The effect appears in a sort of feebleness of purpose, which makes the book a compromise between an art novel and a psychological study, without a thoroughly complete working out of either, and without the attractiveness of narrative, structure, and pointed interest, which have distinguished the two best of the novels above described. The story moves between five personages, Miriam, a dark, Amazonian beauty of mysterious origin and fortunes, and full of such fascination as usually accompanies these characteristics; 'the model'–a strange being who exercises some unintelligible influence over her; Hilda, a delicate New England girl, tender and pure as a snowdrop, endowed with firmness of purpose and intellectual power, but with apparently little more relation than moonshine to any form of human passion; Kenyon, a countryman of Hilda's, clever as a sculptor, and full of sympathy, but in other respects not remarkable; and Donatello, a figure so original that nothing like him has ever before appeared in the range of fiction. He is a young Italian with a form of antique grace and beauty, which seemed, as if it might have furnished a model for the Faun of Praxiteles. His friends laughingly identify him with this well-known statue, not only on account of his outward appearance, but because, without showing anything like mental deficiency or vice, there is a singular want about him of the special human characteristics of moral feeling and self-consciousness; so that he is always looked upon as an exceptional being. The following extract will show Mr Hawthorne's refined artistic taste and insight, and will also serve to introduce another, in which the breathing counterpart of the marble image comes before us:–

> The Faun is the marble image of a young man, leaning his right arm on the trunk or stump of a tree; one hand hangs carelessly by his side; in the other he holds the fragment of a pipe or some such sylvan instrument of music . . .
>
> . . . It is possible, too, that the Faun might be educated through the medium of his emotions, so that the coarser animal portion of his nature might eventually be thrown into the background, though never utterly expelled.

Now for the semi-human being, to whom the banter of his friends has attributed furry ears like those of the Faun, and who has refused to lift his brown curls to verify the fact:–

> Donatello's refractoriness as regarded his ears had evidently cost him something, and he now came close to Miriam's side, gazing at her with an appealing air, as if to solicit forgiveness . . .
>
> . . . At all events, it appeared to afford Donatello exquisite pleasure; insomuch that he danced quite round the wooden railing that fences in the Dying Gladiator.

The key-note of Miriam's character appears in the following passage–in which, too, the reader will recognize some resemblance to many of those which we have quoted or referred to in the course of this article, and which point to the propensity which those who are overburdened with some fearful secret have for whispering it to any reed they find on their path. Donatello has come to visit her in her studio, and is looking over her sketches:–

> The first that he took up was a very impressive sketch, in which the artist had jotted down her rough ideas for a picture of Jael driving the nail through the temples of Sisera. It was dashed off with remarkable power, and showed a touch or two that were actually life-like and death-like, as if Miriam had been standing by when Jael gave the first stroke of her murderous hammer, or as if she herself were Jael, and felt irresistibly impelled to make her bloody confession in this guise.

* * * * *

Over and over again, there was the idea of woman, acting the part of a revengeful mischief towards man. It was, indeed, very singular to see how the artist's imagination seemed to run on these stories of bloodshed, in which woman's hand was crimsoned by the stain; and how, too–in one form or another, grotesque or sternly sad–she failed not to bring out the moral, that woman must strike through her own heart to reach a human life, whatever were the motive that impelled her.

She shows him her own portrait, in which he complains of the absence of a smile:–

> 'A forced smile is uglier than a frown,' said Miriam, a bright, natural smile breaking out over her face, even as she spoke . . .
>
> . . . 'You speak in vain,' replied the young man, with a deeper emphasis than she had ever before heard in his voice; 'shroud yourself in what gloom you will, I must needs follow you.'

Miriam is haunted by the strange figure we have mentioned, who passes for a model, and causes her an accession of gloom whenever he draws near. On a midnight visit to the Capitol, while Miriam and Donatello are looking over the edge of the Tarpeian rock, he approaches. Obeying a sudden impulse, and the lady's half-suggested menace, Donatello seizes him, and hurls him from the precipice. By this deed–at which Hilda, and she alone, accidentally makes a third–their two souls become linked together by that bond of guilt on which Mr Hawthorne loves to dwell:–

> 'They flung the past behind them, as she counselled, or else distilled from it a fiery intoxication, which sufficed to carry them triumphantly through those first moments of their doom . . .
>
> . . . And thus Miriam and her lover were not an insulated pair, but members of an innumerable confraternity of guilty ones, all shuddering at each other.

It is in this revelation of the moral law through the transgression that the 'Transformation' consists. Donatello is conceived as existing in a sort of Paradisiacal condition; he is neither moral nor the reverse, till roused to consciousness by the deed he has perpetrated. He goes back to his ancestral castle of Monte Beni, accompanied by Kenyon, to whom he recounts the old legend which hands down the tradition of his Faun-like nature from heroic times, when moral maidens might be wooed by denizens of the woods, and transmit a portion of that happy animal nature to their posterity. But the change which has somehow been wrought in him is evident to the sculptor's practised eye, though Donatello does not reveal its cause. At last, however, Miriam visits the castle, and has an interview with Kenyon, in which they arrive at the conclusion that her true place

The sculptor looked more attentively at the young man, and was surprised and alarmed to observe how entirely the fine, fresh glow of animal spirits had departed out of his face. Hitherto, moreover, even while he was standing perfectly still, there had been a kind of possible gambol indicated in his aspect. It was quite gone, now. All his youthful gaiety, and with it his simplicity of manner, was eclipsed, if not utterly extinct.

"You are surely ill, my dear fellow!" exclaimed Kenyon.

"Am I? Perhaps so," said Donatello indifferently. "I never have been ill, and know not what it may be."

"Do not make the poor lad fancy-sick," whispered Miriam, pulling the sculptor's sleeve. "He is of a nature to lie down and die, at once, if he finds himself drawing such melancholy breaths as we ordinary people are enforced to burthen our lungs withal. But we must get him away from this old, decayed, and dreary Rome, where nobody but himself ever thought of being gay. Its influences are too heavy to sustain the life of such a creature."

The above conversation had passed chiefly on the steps of the Cappuccini'; and, having said so much, Miriam lifted the leathern curtain that hangs before all church-doors, in Italy.

"Hilda has forgotten her appointment," she observed "or else her maiden slumbers are very sound, this morning. We will wait for her no longer."

They entered the nave. The interior of the church was of moderate compass, but of good architecture, with a vaulted roof over the nave, and a row of dusky chapels on either side of it, instead of the customary side-aisles. Each chapel had its saintly

der of the fatality that seems to [haunt your foot.   473
steps; and throws a shadow of crime about your path,
you being guiltless."
                                            225–52–Vol iii   721
    "There was such a fatality," said Miriam. "Yes;   Hopson
the shadow fell upon me, innocent, but I went astray in it,
and wandered — as Hilda would tell you — into crime."

    She went on to say, that, while yet a child, she
had lost her English mother. From a very early period of her life, there had been a contract of betrothal
between herself and a certain marchese, the representative of another branch of her paternal house;
a family arrangement, between two persons of disproportioned ages, and in which feeling went for nothing. Most
Italian girls of noble rank would have yielded themselves to such a marriage, as an affair of course. But
there was something in Miriam's blood, in her mixed
race, in her recollections of her mother — some characteristic, finally, in her own nature — which had given
her freedom of thought, and force of will, and made this
pre-arranged connection odious to her. Moreover,
the character of her destined husband would have been
a sufficient and insuperable objection; for it betrayed
traits so evil, so treacherous, so wild, and yet so strangely subtle, as would only be accounted for by the insanity
which often developes itself in old, close-kept races
of men, when long unmixed with newer blood. Reaching the age when the marriage-contract should have
been fulfilled, Miriam had utterly repudiated it.

    Sometime afterwards had occurred that terri-
ble event to which Miriam alluded, when she revealed
her name; an event, the frightful and mysterious cir-

is by the side of the man whom she has been the means of leading into crime, and who loves her still more intensely through his wakened nature.

We are given, doubtless, to understand that Miriam and her fellow-criminal are united, but whether they continue so, or whether the sacrifice of one is found compulsory–a point afterwards suggested by the sculptor–must be left in doubt, for Mr Hawthorne veils them henceforth in a deep obscurity. The remainder of the plot of the story, so far as it can be said to have any, is simple, yet not very intelligible. Kenyon goes back with a renewed hope that the shy and cool Hilda will become his wife. On his arrival at Rome, he finds that she has fled from the tower where she had kept the Virgin's lamp constantly alight, and fed the white doves, who seemed sisters and emblems of her purity. What really became of her is not told, but she reappears during the Carnival, and we are left to suppose that her abduction (as it seems to be) was the act of some religious body, and connected with her knowledge of the murder committed by Donatello. For their victim was a monk. The fate of Donatello and Miriam is left, as we have said, to perplex the reader. Hilda and Kenyon while one day in the Coliseum, observe a kneeling penitent whom they recognize as Miriam; and Hilda receives a valuable wedding gift, which she remembers as belonging to her friend; but of the two nothing more is known.

The moral of the story is summed up after the following fashion, though the conclusion, winding round as it does into an offer of marriage, leaves the theory very much to the reader's choice:–

> 'Was Donatello really a Faun?'
> 'If you had ever studied the pedigree of the far-descended heir of Monte Beni, as I did,' answered Kenyon, with an irrepressible smile, 'you would have retained few doubts on that point . . .'
> . . . 'Were you my guide, my counsellor, my inmost friend, with that white wisdom which clothes you as a celestial garment, all would go well. Oh, Hilda, guide me home!'

In our extracts from *Transformation* we have been obliged to confine ourselves to such passages as most clearly indicate the purpose of the book and the kind of view of human nature it embodies; and have consequently been unable to convey any idea of its brilliancy of style, the justness of its artistic criticisms, the force of particular scenes and passages, and the general elegance of thought and imagination by which it is pervaded. As a novel in the ordinary sense of the term it is undoubtedly defective. To those who read 'for the story' it will be found tedious, for there is but little action, and the mystery relating to the influence exercised by Miriam's

victim over her career, is left unsolved, except by vague hints which we are at liberty to fill up in any way we like. We think this a fault in art; for, the greatest writers, whatever might be the weight of the moral they meant to inculcate, or the significance of the problem they wished to discuss, have always seen the necessity of also condescending to a lower order of appreciation, and of making the vesture and outward presentation of the truth attractive in itself, and competent to satisfy, as a narrative of incident, the minds of those who would not be at first, or perhaps even at all, awake to its inner meanings. The audience who listened to the *Agamemnon* of Æschylus, were not all, we may be sure, able to fathom the depth of the reflections on the self-propagating force of ancestral guilt, which to the more thoughtful reader make the marrow and substance of the poem; but there can be no doubt that they were thrilled and absorbed by the incidents of the drama. Of this dramatic vigour Mr Hawthorne has in his former works shown himself so capable a master, that we must conclude that it is of set purpose and design that he has now constructed his story so loosely, and encumbered it with matter not directly germane to its primary conception. He seems to have been possessed with the idea, on the one hand, of embodying his Italian impressions in something like an 'art-novel'–a form of literature which has yet to become naturalized among us–an amphibious creation, to which nothing but some example of transcendent excellence will persuade us to be reconciled; and, on the other, to bring before us the suggestive idea, the theory of which is most fully presented in our last extract. With the fullest admiration for Mr Hawthorne's genius, and the entire recognition of the power with which this notion, in its concrete shape, is exhibited in the shifting aspects of the romance, we question, after all, the propriety of the form under which it has come to light. It seems more properly belonging to the class of ideas with which the author has dealt in his imaginative and fantastic tales. We seem to see the same incongruity in its present extensive and elaborate attire that there would have been in drawing out, for instance, the theme of 'Rappacini's Daughter' to a similar length. The conception, indeed, is one more fit for verse than prose. To tie it down to the limits and conditions of a three-volume novel is like imprisoning Ariel in the oak-tree. The matter-of-fact solidity which we require in a prose story might be dispensed with in a poem, and the vagueness to which we have objected, though it would not be a merit, would be far less of a defect than it is in the actual case; while the philosophic or ethical aspect of the question, which is now unavoidably postponed to the incidents, might have been developed in a manner more calculated to do it justice. We may say, in conclusion, that those who read *Transformation* for its interest as a

TRANSFORMATION:

OR, THE

ROMANCE OF MONTE BENI.

BY

NATHANIEL HAWTHORNE,

AUTHOR OF "THE SCARLET LETTER," ETC. ETC.

IN THREE VOLUMES.

VOL. I.

LONDON:
SMITH, ELDER AND CO., 65, CORNHILL.

M.DCCC.LX.

THE MARBLE FAUN:

OR, THE

ROMANCE OF MONTE BENI.

BY

NATHANIEL HAWTHORNE,

AUTHOR OF "THE SCARLET LETTER," ETC., ETC.

IN TWO VOLUMES.

VOL. I.

BOSTON:
TICKNOR AND FIELDS.

M DCCC LX.

Title pages for the English and American editions of Hawthorne's last published novel. Hawthorne inscribed this copy of
Transformation *to Captain E. M. Shaw of the London Fire Engine Establishment (from C. E. Frazer Clark Jr.,*
Nathaniel Hawthorne: A Descriptive Bibliography, *1978).*

romance, in the usual sense of the expression, will be disappointed. But, having got through it, those readers whose intelligent appreciation an author chiefly values, will return again and again to its pages for correct and striking thoughts on art expressed in the happiest language—for scenes of Arcadian beauty—and for glimpses into the moral *arcana* of our nature such as few novelists afford.

We have said, at the outset of this article, that we think Mr Hawthorne one of the most national writers that the United States have produced; and the tone and temper of mind which seem to us to have given birth to his latest work, if we are correct in our estimate of them, bear out a part of this opinion. Mr Hawthorne belongs to the historic side of American life by his patriotic feeling, by his vivid local colouring, by his choice of subjects, such as (except in the last instance) no English

writer would be competent to deal with, and by his freedom, so far as is possible consistently with his writing in the English language at all, from any restrictions through deference to European models. He has taken what material he could find in his own country, and, to a great extent, peculiar to it, has looked at it with an artist's imaginative eye, and has made as much of it probably as any one could do. That there are not the materials in American history for grand mediæval romances is not his fault. To breathe life into the dry bones of dusty chroniclers, to flash the ray of genius on historic problems, as Scott did in *Ivanhoe,* to summon into visible mixture of earth's mould the mythic phantoms which flit round a nation's cradle, is not given to the citizen of a land the pedigree of whose liberties is far younger than the time of legal memory, and whose annals are written, not in grass-grown entrenchments, mouldering castles, and half-effaced monuments, but in treaties and declarations and newspapers. To have produced so much from such materials is a triumph of which a much greater writer might well be proud.

If, as we have tried to show, Mr Hawthorne may be held to represent, with some faithfulness, the historic and picturesque side of the life of America, no less, we think, does he embody, much more unconsciously, perhaps, some of the peculiar characteristics of her mental condition. His writings, in the first place, are those of a recluse, and bring before us the cultivated tone of thought of the class which, in the United States, has usually kept aloof from politics. Acquainted with practical life, so far as it can be learnt in an official situation, he shows but little sympathy with anything but its artistic side. He seems essentially a man of letters; his humour is that of a spectator *ab extra*, and is of the school of Addison and Charles Lamb rather than of Sam Slick. Endowed with a genial sympathy, and the power as well as the disposition to penetrate into the feelings, and ideally assume the position of people quite different from himself, he has shown no tendency to make use of this faculty for anything like class representation of contemporary life in the way, for instance, which Mr Disraeli had done in *Sybil*. The spirit of his time comes out through him in quite a different manner. He represents the *youthfulness* of America—not in respect of its physical vigour and energy, but of its vague aspirations, in eager curiosity, its syncretism, its strainings after the perception of psychologic mysteries, its transitory phases of exhausted cynicism, its tendency to the grotesque in taste and character, and its unscrupulous handling of some of the deepest secrets of our nature. His philosophy, on its practical side, seems to combine a resignation to the pressure of the inevitable (when it is *really* Destiny which causes our failure), with a moral elasticity which teaches us to 'make the best of it' when a way of escape can be found, and which latter feeling connects him with that large class of his countrymen whom he has represented in his portrait of Holgrave, who have a sort of Protean faculty of turning their powers to account under all varieties of circumstances, and a prehensile instinct which breaks their fall, and furnishes a fresh starting-point for more hopeful enterprises. On its religious side it seems to be deeply tinged with that Puritan and Calvinistic element which has left such deep traces wherever it has had any root. The idea of remorse—of the hell which the soul may bear within itself, transfiguring all outward things with the shadows and lurid lights cast by its own internal flames, is the one which seems to have obtained the firmest hold on his mind, and to have inspired his strongest and best writing. No feeling, perhaps, in the range of those with which a writer of fiction may deal,

is more available for powerful effects, and for that accumulation of external detail mingled with deep psychological insight which has constituted the basis of Mr Hawthorne's fame. We would only take leave to warn him that such a theme holds out temptations to morbid treatment more than almost any other, and that a writer of his great acuteness and wide observation, ought not to be at a loss for future subjects, not necessarily of a more shallow, but, we may hope, of a more cheerful and varied tendency. And, as regards more particularly the novel which has suggested our survey of him, we suspect—even with a 'third edition' before us—that another, on such a plan, would be an experiment which it would not be safe for his popularity to repeat.

A Response to Critics

In an essay about her brother-in-law, published four years after his death, Peabody addresses readers who were dissatisfied with Hawthorne for "raising curiosities he does not gratify."

The Genius of Hawthorne
E. P. Peabody
Atlantic Monthly, 22 (September 1868): 359–374

To understand *The Marble Faun,* or, as the English publishers compelled Hawthorne to call their edition, *Transformation,* it should be read in the atmosphere of Rome. Everything in that moral, or rather entirely immoral, atmosphere serves to interpret the artistic work of an author in whom intellect and sensibility are one to a degree that scarcely can be predicated of any other; and whose power to express what he *felt with his mind,* and *thought with his heart* (we use these expressions advisedly), are unsurpassed, if not unsurpassable.

Every one, whether cultivated or uncultivated, acknowledges the charm of Hawthorne's style; but the most cultivated best appreciate the wonder of that power by which he wakes into clear consciousness shades of feeling and delicacies of thought, that perhaps have been experienced by us all, but were never embodied in words before.

We are not prepared to fully adopt the dogmatic statement of a recent critic, who declared prose composition a higher kind of expression than that which the world has hitherto united in calling poetry; but Hawthorne goes far to prove that language even without rhythm is an equal organ of that genius which, whether it speak in music, sculpture, painting, or measured words, is a still more ethereal image of the Infinite in the finite; an utterance of the divine by the human which may not always be understood at once,

The Faun of Praxiteles, *Hawthorne's source for*
Donatello in The Marble Faun

The House of the Seven Gables is a tragedy that takes rank by the side of the Trilogy of the *Agamemnon, Choephoroi,* and *Eumenides,* without the aid of the architecture, sculpture, verse, dancing, and music which Æschylus summoned to his aid to set forth the operation of the Fury of the house of Atrides that swept to destruction four generations of men. It takes two hundred years for the crime which the first Pyncheon perpetrated against the first Maule to work itself off,—or, we should rather say, for the forces of the general humanity to overcome the inevitable consequences of one rampant individuality, that undertook to wield the thunderbolts of Omnipotence against a fellow-mortal possessing gifts not understood, and therefore condemned. The peaceful solution of the problem of fate in the modern tragedy is undoubtedly due to the Christian light which the nobel heathen lacked; it is love, in every pure and unselfish form, that undoes the horrible spell which pride of possession and place and a pharisaic lust of rule laid upon the house of Pyncheon. As soon as the father of Phœbe freely followed out, in his own individual case, the genial impulse of nature, which consumed in its passionate glow the family pride that had proved so fatal, and thus admitted the general humanity into equality, or rather sued, as lovers wont, to be allied to it, even at the expense of all the external advantages of his birthright, the good providence of God accepted and justified the deed, by sending into the first real home that a Pyncheon had made for himself one of those 'angels that behold the face of the Father,' who, in process of time, goes back to the desolate old house to bless it, without consciousness of the high place she holds among ministering spirits, or what a mighty deed she does by simply being the innocent, sweet, loving creature she is; while the corresponding last Maule in the light of the science which the general progress of society has given him finds an explanation of the peculiar power which the exceptional organization of his lineage had made hereditary; and, exercising it in a common-sense way, and with simple good feeling, the curse of the first Maule upon the first Pyncheon is at last replaced by a marriage blessing and bond, laying to sleep the Fury of Retribution, attendant on the crime which is the key-note of the whole story, and which had reappeared through so many generations,—for it makes the two families one.

In *The Marble Faun* we have a picture of Rome, not only as it appears to the senses and to the memory, but also to the spiritual apprehension which penetrates the outward show. Genius in Hawthorne was limited, as that of all men must be, by his temperament, but less than that of most men by his will. To 'give his thought act' was not his impulse, but to represent it to other men. He was not, therefore, so much an effective power

but which creates understanding within us more and more forever.

Judging by this standard,—the power of creating understanding within those whom he addresses,—Hawthorne takes rank with the highest order of artists. For it is not the material in which a man works that determines his place as an artist, but the elevation and fineness of the truth his work communicates. Was ever a more enduring house built by architectural genius, or made more palpable to the senses of men, than The House of the Seven Gables? Or did any sculptor ever uncover a statue of marble that will last longer than the form of Judge Pyncheon, over whose eyeball the fly crawls as he sits dead? And what painted canvas or frescoed wall by any master of color has preserved a more living, breathing image of the most evanescent moods of sensibility and delicacies of action than are immortalized in the sketches of Alice and of Clifford, and the tender nursing of the latter after the arrival of Phœbe?

among other powers in the current life, as the quiet, open eye that gathers truth for other men to enact. His vocation was to set forth what he saw so clearly with such accuracy of outline, fulness of coloring, and in such dry light as would enable other men to interpret the phenomena about them as he did. He does not invent incidents, much less a dramatic narrative. He loved best to take some incident ready made to his hand, and to work out in thought the generation of it from eternal principles, or the consequences of it in the spiritual experience of those concerned in it, whether actively or passively. Most writers of fiction not only tell you what their heroes and heroines do, but why; dogmatically stating how they feel and what they think. Hawthorne seldom does this. He does not seem to know much more about his heroes and heroines than he represents them to know of each other; but, recognizing the fact that most outward action is from mixed motives, and admits of more than one interpretation, he is very apt to suggest two or three quite diverse views, and, as it were, consult with his readers upon which may be the true one; and not seldom he gives most prominence to some interpretation which we feel pretty sure is not his own.

This characteristic peculiarity is nowhere more conspicuous than in *The Marble Faun*. He does not seem to know whether Donatello has pointed and furry ears or not. He touches the story of Miriam which such delicacy that those readers who are more interested in the gossip of temporary life than in the eternal powers which underlie it, generating a spiritual being which is never to pass away, are angry with the author, and accuse him of trifling with their feelings by raising curiosities which he does not gratify, and exciting painful sympathies which he does not soothe; they even call it a malicious use of a power which he ought to consecrate to increasing the enjoyment of his readers.

But few authors are really so little guilty as Hawthorne of any wanton use of their power over other minds. A work of literary art he did not view as merely an instrument for giving pleasure, but as a means to discover truth, or, rather, to put his readers on the track of discovering it in company with himself. What he especially seeks for are those great laws of human thought, feeling, and action which are apt to be covered from self-consciousness by transient emotions, and the force of outward circumstances of habit and general custom. In *The Scarlet Letter,* for instance, he is plainly inquiring into the law of repentance, or the human being's sober second thought upon his own action, after it has become an irrevocable fact of nature; and he also asks what is the part that the social whole has to do, or does do, to make his sober second thought work the cure of the sinning soul and of wounded society. In one of the

Twice-told Tales ('Endicott and his Men') he brings before our eyes, by the magic of his art, a day of the Puritan life of New England which was historical; for the dry chronicles tell us of Endicott's cutting the Red Cross out of the English banner on the 'training-day,' when the news suddenly reached him from England of some untoward act of Charles I. As usual, Hawthorne gives a framework to this historical incident from the characteristic phenomena of Puritan life as it appeared at that period in New England. 'Training-day' was always the afternoon of 'lecture-day,' when all the people were required to assemble for a sermon, and the militia were in their uniforms. It was on this day that all the wrong-doers were punished. Among these he mentions a woman standing on the 'meeting-house' steps, with the letter A on her breast, which, he adds, she was condemned to wear all her life before her children and the townspeople. For our fathers, he observes (we quote from memory), thought it expedient to give publicity to crime as its proper punishment. And then he queries whether the modern mode of keeping certain kinds of crime out of sight were better, or even more merciful, to the criminal and society. A friend asked Hawthorne if for this particular punishment he had documentary evidence; and he replied that he had actually seen it mentioned in the town records of Boston, but with no attendant circumstances. This friend said to another at that time, 'We shall hear of that letter A again; for it evidently has made a profound impression on Hawthorne's mind.' And in eight or ten years afterwards appeared the romance of *The Scarlet Letter,* throwing its lurid glare upon the Puritan pharisaism and self-righteous pride, and engraved with spiritual fire on the naked breast of the *unsuspected* sinner.

If the musty chronicles of New England history could afford an artist material for such a sharp-cut high-relief of real life as excited him to a study of its meaning so earnest that it has drawn into sympathetic interest tens of thousands of readers, who feel as if they were living in the midst of that terribly bleak locality and day, we cannot wonder that Rome, whose very aspect is so picturesque, and whose history combines such varieties of human experience, should have awakened emotions and suggested questions of a kindred depth. Many such questions are certainly asked and answered, at least hypothetically, in *The Marble Faun*. It is rather remarkable that criticism has not yet attempted to analyze the power of this book, or even to pluck out the heart of Miriam's mystery,—the key to which, as we apprehend, is to be found in the conversation over the copy of Beatrice Cenci's portrait in Hilda's studio.

It is entirely characteristic of Hawthorne's genius to take up such a subject as the history of Beatrice Cenci, and to inquire what was her internal experience;

Portrait of Beatrice Cenci, attributed to Guido Reni, which is discussed in The Marble Faun
(Galleria Nazionale, Rome)

Hawthorne's Beatrice Cenci

The fate of Beatrice Cenci (1577–1599), a Roman noblewoman who was executed by Pope Clement VIII for her participation in the murder of her brutal father, has inspired works by many writers, including Percy Bysshe Shelley, Stendhal, and Alberto Moravia. In the following passage Hawthorne describes Hilda's copy of the famous portrait attributed to Guido Reni.

The picture represented simply a female head; a very youthful, girlish, perfectly beautiful face, enveloped in white drapery, from beneath which strayed a lock or two of what seemed a rich, though hidden luxuriance of auburn hair. The eyes were large and brown, and met those of the spectator, but evidently with a strange, ineffectual effort to escape. There was a little redness about the eyes, very slightly indicated, so that you would question whether or no the girl had been weeping. The whole face was quiet; there was no distortion or disturbance of any single feature; nor was it easy to see why the expression was not cheerful, or why a single touch of the artist's pencil should not brighten it into joyousness. But, in fact, it was the very saddest picture ever painted or conceived; it involved an unfathomable depth of sorrow, the sense of which came to the observer by a sort of intuition. It was a sorrow that removed this beautiful girl out of the sphere of humanity, and set her in a far-off region, the remoteness of which—while yet her face is so close before us—makes us shiver as at a spectre.

–*The Marble Faun,* The Centenary Edition,
vol. 4, p. 64

how a temperament so delicate and a spirit so innocent as Guido's portrait shows Beatrice's to have been stood before herself, whether as a victim or as a participator in the bloody deed for which she suffered death. Still more would he be apt to inquire what would be the spiritual result of the same outrage upon quite another temperament and cast of mind,–Miriam's, for instance. And again it was inevitable, as we have already intimated, that Rome should have suggested to his mind questions upon the efficacy or inefficacy of ritualistic confession and penance on the various degrees of criminal consciousness. Hilda says of Beatrice Cenci, that 'sorrow so black as hers oppresses very nearly as sin would,' for she was innocent in her own eyes until her misfortune had driven her into parricide; which, trusting to the fidelity of Guido's portrait of her remembered face, and comparing that with the portrait of the stepmother, may be believed to have been not the suggestion of her own mind, though 'that spotless flower of Paradise trailed over by a serpent,' as Beatrice has been well described, was too much bewildered by the incomprehensible woe in which she found herself involved, and her will was too much paralyzed to do other than obey the impulse given by the only less outraged wife. The same calamity met by the clearer reason and stronger character of Miriam would not only suggest means of escape, especially if she had, as is intimated, wealth, and other easily imagined favoring circumstances, but would give energy to accomplish a certain moral independence of her most unnatural enemy, and would excite her intellect and creative imagination, rather than 'oppress her whole being.' It would seem from the sketches which Donatello found in Miriam's portfolio, that her hideous circumstances had not failed to arouse thoughts of murderous revenge which had governed her artistic creativeness in the selection and treatment of subjects, but that she had not thought of any more harmful realization of the dark dreams that haunted her than upon canvas. Until the fatal 'look' passed from her eyes, which tempted Donatello to give free way to the impulse of hatred, with which his love for her had inspired him, towards one who was evidently her enemy,–and no common enemy,–the author plainly accounts her not only actually innocent, but a most humane person, and, like Beatrice, 'if a fallen angel, yet without sin.' Thus he speaks of her 'natural language, her generosity, kindliness, and native truth of character,' as banishing all suspicions, and even questions, from the minds of Hilda and Kenyon, to both of whom he ascribes the fine poetic instincts that intimate more truths concerning character than we can account for by phenomena. These traits insured to her their warm friendship and confidence, though her history was no less unknown and mysterious to them than to the public, who had speculated on it so wildly. They therefore acquiesced in the generally received opinion, that 'the spectre of the catacomb' was her model; nor ever asked why it was that he followed her so pertinaciously. Any relation between Miriam and him other than the most superficial and accidental one was effectually forbidden by their sense of her character, which also annulled in the mind of Kenyon the strange significance of the 'Spectre's' own words:–

> 'Inquire not what I am, nor wherefore I abide in the darkness,' said he, in a hoarse, harsh voice, as if a great deal of damp were clustering in this throat. 'Henceforth I am nothing but a shadow behind her footsteps. She came to me when I sought her not. She has called me forth, and must abide the consequences of my reappearance in the world.'

But the reflective reader, not being, like Kenyon, under the spell of Miriam's individuality, will hardly fail of detecting the relations between her and the so-called model, if he will compare this not unmeaning speech with the conversation in Hilda's study, to which we have already referred, when that inexperienced child pronounced the parricide an 'inexpiable crime':–

> 'O Hilda! your innocence is like a sharp steel sword,' exclaimed her friend. 'Your judgments are often terribly severe, though you seem all made up of gentleness and mercy. Beatrice's sin may not have been so great; perhaps it was no sin at all, *but the best virtue possible in the circumstances.* If she viewed it as a *sin,* it may have been because *her nature was too feeble for the fate imposed upon her.* Ah,' continued Miriam, passionately, 'if I could only get within *her consciousness!*–if I could only clasp Beatrice Cenci's ghost, and draw it into my self! I would *give up my life* to know whether she *thought herself innocent, or the one great criminal since time began.*' As Miriam gave utterance to these words, Hilda looked from the picture into her face, and was startled to observe that her friend's expression had become almost exactly that of the portrait, as if her passionate wish and struggle to penetrate poor Beatrice's mystery had been successful. 'O, for Heaven's sake, Miriam, do not look so!' she cried. 'What an actress you are! and I never guessed it before. Ah! now you are yourself again,' she added, kissing her. 'Leave Beatrice to me in future.'
> 'Cover up your magical picture then,' replied her friend, 'else I never can look away from it.'

And again, further on in the same chapter:–

> Hilda read the direction: it was to Signor Luca Barboni, at the Cenci Palace, third piano.
> 'I will deliver it with my own hand,' said she, 'precisely four months from today, unless you bid me to the contrary. Perhaps I shall meet the ghost of Beatrice in that grim old palace of her forefathers.'

'In that case,' rejoined Miriam, 'do not fail to speak to her, and win her confidence. Poor thing! she would be all the better for pouring her heart out freely, and would *be glad to do it if she were sure of sympathy.* It irks my brain and heart to think of her all *shut up within herself.*' She withdrew the cloth that Hilda had drawn over the picture, and took another long look at it. 'Poor sister Beatrice! for she was still a woman, Hilda,—still a sister, be her sins what they might.'

And still further on in the same chapter she says:—

'After all, if a woman had painted the original picture, there might have been something in it we miss now. I have a great mind to undertake a copy myself, and try to give it what it lacks.'

And again, having a touching manner alluded to Hilda's devout habits of mind, she says: 'When you pray next, dear friend, remember me.'

These significant sentences may be compared with others in Chapter XXIII. when Miriam, after the catastrophe of the Tarpeian rock, seeks Hilda; who, with the unconscious pharisaism of a child's innocence, repulses her because she knows her to have consented to a murder. Here the author makes Hilda appeal to Miriam for advice in her own uncertainty as to what she should do with her distressing knowledge, and adds: 'This *singular appeal* bore striking testimony to the impression Miriam's natural uprightness and impulsive generosity had made on the friend who *knew her best.*'

He also makes Miriam's answer justify Hilda's instinctive confidence:—

'If I deemed it for your peace of mind,' she said, 'to bear testimony against me for this deed, in the face of all the world, *no consideration of myself* should weigh with me an instant. But I believe that you would find no relief in such a course. What men call justice lies chiefly in outward formalities, and has never the close application and fitness that would be satisfactory to a soul like yours. *I cannot be fairly tried and judged before an earthly tribunal;* and of this, Hilda, you would perhaps become fatally conscious when it was too late. Roman justice, above all things, is a byword.'

It is certain that Hilda's narration of the scene of the murder had 'settled a doubt' in Miriam's mind. She took it, gladly perhaps, as collateral evidence that Donatello had not been mistaken when he said she had commanded his action with her eyes; for then she had all the responsibility of it. But how was it, then, that *she* was not crushed by remorse, seemed to feel no remorse? Was it not that she felt herself 'in the circumstances' that made the crime 'her best possible virtue'? The 'sorrow that was so black as to oppress (Beatrice)

Reni's painting of the archangel Michael slaying a demon. In The Marble Faun, *Hawthorne invents a preliminary sketch for the painting in which the demon's face is recognized by Hilda, Kenyon, and Donatello as that of Miriam's model (Chiesa dell'Immacollata Concezione, Rome).*

very much as sin would' (which was the limit of Hilda's view of her case) did actually, in Miriam's case, not only excite to artistic expression, but drove her further; and she was not 'too feeble for her fate,' as she proved in the Chapel of the Cappucini, when—

She went back, and gazed once more at the corpse. Yes, these were the features that Miriam *had known so well;* this was the visage that she remembered *from a far longer date than the most intimate of her friends suspected;* this form of clay had held the evil spirit which *blasted her sweet youth, and compelled her; as it were, to stain her womanhood with crime . . .* There had been nothing in his lifetime viler than this man; there was no other fact *within her consciousness* that she felt to be so *certain;* and yet, because her persecutor found himself safe and irrefutable in death, he frowned upon *his victim,* and threw back the blame on her. 'Is it thou indeed?' she murmured, under her breath. 'Then thou hast no right to scowl upon me so! But art thou real or a vision?'

She bent down over the dead monk till one of her rich curls brushed against his forehead. She touched one of his folded hands with her finger. 'It is he,' said Miriam, 'there is the scar which I know so well on his brow. And it is no vision, he is palpable to my touch. I will question the fact no longer, but deal with it as I best can.' It was wonderful to see how the crisis developed in Miriam its own proper strength and the faculty of sustaining the demand which it made on her fortitude. She ceased to tremble; the beautiful woman gazed sternly at her dead enemy, endeavoring to meet and quell the look of accusation that he threw from between his half-closed eyelids. 'No, thou shalt not scowl me down,' said she, 'neither now, nor when we stand together at the judgment-seat. *I fear not to meet thee there!* Farewell till that next encounter.'

Surely there is but one interpretation that can be put upon the power this vile wretch had over the noble Miriam, more than once bringing her to her knees:–

She must have had cause to dread some unspeakable evil from this strange persecutor, and to know that this was the very crisis of her calamity; for, as he drew near, such a cold, sick despair crept over her, that it impeded her natural promptitude of thought. Miriam seemed dreamily to remember falling on her knees; but in her whole recollection of that wild moment, she beheld herself in a dim show, and could not well distinguish what was done and suffered; no, not even whether she were really an actor and sufferer in the scene.

But Hilda had settled all doubts by her narration: 'He approached you, Miriam; you knelt to him.'

The hardly bestead, noble Miriam! Was there ever pictured a more tragic moment of human life than that brief one in which she knelt on the verge of the Tarpeian rock in spiritless deprecation? Only in Rome does natural innocence and virtue kneel in helplessness before personified vice, clad in the sacramental garments, and armed with the name and prestige of a Father!

And did not the genius of humanity hover over its priest when he gave that master-stroke to his picture,–making Miriam a symbol of Italy, beautiful in form, with the natural language of all nobleness; true to herself with all the unspent energies of her youth; and, in spite of outrage ineffable, reduced by the stress of her natural relationship to beg as a mercy, not the protection she has a right to demand, but mere immunity from its extreme opposite? Italy! outraged so beyond credibility that no one dares to tell the tale, lest humanity should be too much discouraged by the knowledge of the hideous moral disabilities her misfortunes involve; leaving her no path to purity and peace but through violence and civil war, which are apparently

her 'best possible virtue in the circumstances,' or certainly not to be accounted as sin.

An æsthetic critic must needs shrink from the work of elucidating the dark shadow which seems to be Miriam's evil fate; for the author himself seems to endeavor to hide its secret, as Hilda says Beatrice seemed to try 'to escape from (her) gaze.' There is a delicate moral sentiment in the author, which shrinks from giving definite outlines and name to a crime that is an unnatural horror. He says in Chapter XI,–

Of so much we are sure, that there seemed to be a sadly mysterious fascination in the influence of this ill-omened person over Miriam; it was such as beasts and reptiles of subtle and evil nature sometimes exercise upon their victims. Marvellous it was to see the hopelessness with which, being naturally of so courageous a spirit, she resigned herself to the thraldom in which he held her. That iron chain, of which some of the massive links were round her feminine waist and the others in his ruthless hand, or which perhaps bound the pair together by a bond equally torturing to each, must have been forged in some such unhallowed furnace as is only kindled by evil passions and fed by evil deeds.

Yet let us trust there may have been no crime in Miriam, but only one of those fatalities which are among the most insoluble riddles propounded to mortal comprehension; the fatal decree by which *every crime is made to be the agony of many innocent persons,* as well as of the single guilty one.

Again, when in pity for her tormentor, she suggests prayer and penance:–

In this man's memory there was something that made it awful for him to think of prayer, nor would any torture be more intolerable than to be reminded of such divine comfort and success as await pious souls merely for the asking. This torment was perhaps the token of a native temperament deeply susceptible of religious impressions, but which he had wronged, violated, and debased, until at length it was capable only of terror from the sources that were intended for our purest and loftiest consolation. He looked so fearfully at her, and with such intense pain struggling in his eyes, that Miriam felt pity. And now all at once it struck her that he might be mad. It was an idea that had never before seriously occurred to her mind, although, as soon as suggested, *it fitted marvellously into many circumstances that lay within her knowledge.* But alas! such was her evil fortune, that, whether mad or no, his power over her remained the same, and was likely to be used only the more tyrannously if exercised by a lunatic.

This chapter of 'fragmentary sentences' has suggested to some readers the idea that a mutual, or at least a shared crime, was 'the iron link that bound' these two

The Fountain of Trevi, the main setting of chapter 16 of The Marble Faun, *"A Moonlight Ramble"*

persons together. But a careful reading will find no proof of this in any word of the author or of Miriam; and the 'unmitigable will' which she tells him he mistook for an 'iron necessity' is quite sufficient to explain the identification which the possible madman insists on at that time, and intimates afterwards, by beckoning her to wash her hands in the fountain of Trevi when he did so himself.

To all those who ask if the author meant to represent Miriam, previous to the fatal night on the Tarpeian rock, as guilty of any *crime,* we commend a consideration of her words in her last conversation with Kenyon, when she tells him her history and name.

'You shudder at me, I perceive,' said Miriam, suddenly interrupting her narrative.

'No, you were innocent,' replied the sculptor. 'I shudder at the fatality that seems to haunt your footsteps, and throws a shadow of crime about your path, *you being guiltless.*'

'There was such a fatality,' said Miriam; 'yes, the shadow fell upon me innocent, but I went astray in it,– as Hilda could tell you,–into crime.'

What crime it was that *first* threw the shadow the author does not tell. It was unspeakable; and yet it is 'an open secret' to his readers, after all the indi-

cations that he has given. It took place 'some time after' she had repudiated the proposed marriage with a man 'so evil, so treacherous, so wild, and yet so strangely subtle, as could only be accounted for by the insanity which often develops itself in old close-kept races of men.'

Yet it is plain that this intended husband was not 'the spectre of the catacomb,' any more than that Miriam was an accomplice in the crime of which she was suspected. When she refers to this suspicion in her narrative:–

'But you know that I am innocent,' she cried, interrupting herself again, and looking Kenyon in the face.

'I know it by my deepest consciousness,' he answered, 'and I know it by Hilda's trust and entire affection, which you never could have won had you been capable of guilt.'

'That is sure ground, indeed, for pronouncing me innocent,' said Miriam, with the tears gushing into her eyes. 'Yet I have since become a horror to your saint-like Hilda by a crime which she herself saw me help to perpetrate.'

The fatal word which Miriam so dreaded was unquestionably that which would prove that she had *not* 'committed suicide,' and so expose her, like Beatrice

Cenci, to an ignominious death, notwithstanding her innocence.

> 'Looking back upon what had happened,' Miriam observed, she now considered him 'a madman.' Insanity must have been mixed up with his original composition, and *developed by those very arts of depravity* which it suggested, and still more intensified, by the remorse that ultimately followed them. Nothing was stranger in his dark career than the penitence which often seemed to go hand in hand with crime. Since his death she had ascertained that it finally led him to a convent, where his severe and self-inflicted penance had even acquired him the reputation of unusual sanctity, and had been the cause of his enjoying greater freedom than is commonly allowed to monks.
>
> 'Need I tell you more?' asked Miriam, after proceeding thus far. 'It is still a dim and dreary mystery, a gloomy twilight into which I guide you; but possibly you may catch a glimpse of much that I myself can explain only by conjecture. At all events, you can comprehend what my situation must have been after that fatal interview in the catacomb. My persecutor had gone thither for penance, but followed me forth *with fresh impulses to crime.*'

What a fine sarcasm it is to put this man, than whom, whether mad or not, 'nothing was viler,' into the brown frock and cowl of a Capuchin, and bury him in earth of the Holy Land in all the odor, such as it is, of Capuchin sanctity! Why not? He had said prayers at all the shrines of the Coliseum, going on his knees from one to another, until his devotions (?) were interrupted by Miriam's unexpected and unintentional appearance before his eyes, awakening in him 'fresh impulses' of the passion in which he was lost.

It is not unlikely, however, that Hawthorne, who, like Kenyon, 'was a devout man in his way,' was half unconscious of the sarcasm, in the deep religious earnestness with which he was treating those problems, inevitably presented to his mind in the place where he certainly first conceived the idea of this romance. As we have already intimated, how could such a man be in Rome, which pretends to be the centre of the spiritual universe, without having perpetually presented to his mind spiritual and moral problems deeper than all questions of ritualism without asking what is the nature of sin? what is its relation to crime? and for what were men put on the earth by God? Was it to outrage and lead each other astray; to dominate, and punish, and make each other suffer? or was it to 'honor all men,' to 'further one another' in worthy action, 'preferring one another in love'?

Or was it the Divine idea, that men should get into relation with God by becoming isolated from each other; denying the nearest relations in which they find themselves with each other as well as with outward nature? Is human existence a curse or a blessing? Is dying the business that God has given men to do? Is self-denial the substantial essence of human life, instead of the pruning of an exuberant tree, in order to its more beautiful growth? Where is the life of God to be seen?—in the exuberant sport of happy childhood; in the rush together of young hearts in love; in the subjection of stone and marble to beautiful forms that flow from the thinking mind; in the transfiguration of earths and minerals into the seven colors of light, to symbolize the glowing affections of the heart; in the heroic virtue, that, conscious of its own immortality and divinity, imperially gives away the lesser life of the senses, whenever it interferes with the larger life of the spirit? Is it, in short, in all manner of manifestation of the inner man to kindred men, in humble imitation, as it were, of God creating the outward universe to manifest himself to his rational and sensible creatures? Or is it in the asceticism of all these religious orders; in some of which the members make it their speciality *never to speak to each other,* much less do each other any service; who indulge in no natural sympathies; who, even when they actually do serve each other, eliminate all the spontaneity of love from the service, superseding it with a ritual by which they are earning a curtailment of the pangs of purgatory, or an immunity from everlasting suffering? This is not declamation. Vincent de St Paul, in his manual for the Sisters of Charity, tells them that if they do the deed of the good Samaritan from compassion for the poor man who has fallen among thieves, and bind up his wounds with an absorption of heart and mind in the relief of his suffering which shall make them forget themselves; if their outgushing sympathies for him cause a momentary oblivion of those church formulas to which are attached indulgences, and the *pater-nosters* and *ave Marias* are not consciously repeated as they do their charitable work,—their deed gains no indulgences, nor forms any part of their own divine life (which is the only meaning of being accepted of God).

The highest human activity, that which has a more spiritual quarry than marble, color, or whatever is the material of the so-called fine arts, is entirely unknown in Rome. Instead of a state which receives the coming generation as the father of a future age, leaving it free as a son to find 'the business which God has given it to do,' pondering all its expressed intuitions, and nurturing it with all means of development; giving it to eat of the fruit of all the trees of the Garden of Life, and only restraining it by the warning of love from the poisonous influence which will lead it into a lower plane of existence,—in short, instead of a state such as might be composed of men with the freedom to will, tender to nature, encouraging to spirit, cherishing infi-

The Catacomb of the Capuchins, which Hawthorne describes in chapter 21
of The Marble Faun, *"The Dead Capuchin"*

nite varieties of harmonizing and harmonized power, the Church gives this whited sepulchre of the Papacy, in which ghastly skeletons of humanity, or, what is worse, half-corrupted bodies, like those filthy Capuchins,—in their loathsome dresses (which they are compelled to wear three or four years without laying them off for the purposes of cleanliness), and hardly less disgusting Franciscans, doing nothing for the welfare of themselves and other men, but walking about idly, and begging,—alternate with magnificently arrayed ecclesiastical princes, expending upon their own pleasures and pompous environment whatever of wealth flows to this centre of Christendom from all parts of the world, over which it preposterously claims a dominion in the name of God, exacting taxes wrung from the fear of everlasting punishment, which it has made it its great business of fifteen centuries to exasperate to madness, until that base and selfish passion has well nigh swallowed up all the nobleness, as well as beauty, of human nature.

It was in this mockery of a Church and State that Hawthorne seized the idea of his *chef d'œuvre;* and the more we shall see into his multifarious meanings, the more we shall acknowledge that he has uttered no idle word from the beginning to the end. In the whole

sweep, from the nameless miscreant whose blackness makes the shadow of the picture, up through Miriam, Kenyon, Hilda, to Donatello, his imagination does not fail him in the effort to grasp and represent the common life, whose actions and reactions within itself kindle the fire that purifies, till, as the prophet says, the Refiner may see his own image in the furnace. Deeply as Hawthorne was impressed with 'what man has made of man' in Rome, his own exquisitely endowed organization opened every pore to the revelations of the nature in the midst of which Rome had grown up. Nothing is more wonderful than the power with which, in the whole delineation of Donatello, he withdraws himself from the present of Rome, heavy as it is with the ponderous ruins of time, and looks back to the original Italy, and even still further to the age of the world before this sin-shadowed human experience began. The innocence of Donatello is as far above the ordinary human experience as the evil of the so-called model is below it. If the latter is the nadir, the former is the zenith, of the natural universe; and yet we observe that the model is not treated as out of the pale of human sympathy, much as his own unnatural depravity has done to put him out. By a single stroke of genius, he is associated with 'the lost wretch' who betrayed the early Christians, but 'pined for the blessed sunshine and a companion to be miserable with him,' which, as Kenyon is made to playfully suggest, 'indicates something amiable in the poor fellow.' And when he is dead, the author says that

> A singular *sense of duty* . . . impelled (Miriam) to look at the final resting-place of the being whose fate had been so disastrously involved with her own, . . . and to put money into the sacristan's hand to an amount that made his eyes open wide and glisten, requesting that it might be expended in masses for the repose of Father Antonio's soul.

Besides the artistic balance of Donatello's innocence and joyousness with this monster's guilt and wretchedness, there is another fine contrast of his indescribable gaiety with Miriam's unutterable sorrow, all the more touching because we see that in her proper nature she has an equal gaiety. Her occasional self-abandonment to the pure elixir of mere existence,—witness the wild dance in the Borghese villa; the intellectual freedom that lifts her above her fate into creative genius,—witness her sporting with it in her pictures, her petulant criticisms on Guido's arch-angel, and the stories she invents to connect herself with the spectre of the catacomb; above all, the balm she finds for her wounded soul in Donatello's unqualified devotion to her, although for his sake she will not encourage, but even deprecates it,—all go to prove that her suffering has a source essentially out of herself, but yet so intimately connected with herself, that, as Hilda had said of Beatrice Cenci, 'She knows that she ought to be solitary forever, both for the world's sake and her own.'

In Chapter XXIII the author has said of the portrait:—

> Who can look at that mouth, with its lips half apart as innocent as a baby's that has been crying, and not pronounce Beatrice sinless? *It was the intimate consciousness of her father's sin* that threw its shadow over her, and frightened her into a remote and inaccessible region, where no sympathy could come.

Miriam had at one moment looked so like that picture 'of unutterable grief and mysterious shadow of guilt' that Hilda had exclaimed, 'What an actress you are!' (Chap. VIII.) But, for all the difference between Miriam's powerful and Beatrice's feebler temperament, she could only momentarily dwell in the mood of mind that would give that expression of face, and immediately afterwards feel that there was something missed in Guido's portrait which she could have given to it.

No one can say that Hawthorne does not appreciate 'the night side' of human nature. Many have maintained that he is morbid in the intensity of the shadows thrown over his delineations of character. So much the more, then, do we see and feel the inspiration of an insight which goes back beyond all historic memory, and sees men as they came forth from the creating breath, bound to one another by flesh and blood, instinct with kindly affections, and commanding all animated nature below him with a voice 'soft, attractive, persuasive, friendly'; and lying upon the universe like the smile of God which created it.

Donatello, like Undine, like Ariel, is a new creation of genius. As Hawthorne himself says, in the Postscript that his *philistine* English publishers compelled him to append to their second edition:—

> The idea of the modern Faun loses all the poetry and beauty which the author fancied in it, and becomes nothing better than a grotesque absurdity, if we bring it into the actual light of day. He had hoped to mystify this anomalous creature between the real and fantastic in such a manner that the reader's sympathies might be excited to a certain pleasurable degree, without impelling him to ask how Cuvier would have classified poor Donatello, or to insist upon being told, in so many words, whether he had furry ears or no. As respects all who ask such questions, the book is to that extent a failure.

But there are other questions which he intended his readers should ask, of a different nature, and whose answers are suggested in the representation of Donatello: What is or was man before he was acted upon from without by any moral circumstances,—a blank paper, an evil propensity, or the perfection of passive nature, everyone of whose parts, including the phenomenon man, are so many words of God's conversation with all men? Donatello first comes upon us in the passive form of his existence,—a healthy sensibility,—when, as Madame de Staël has said of the child, 'The Deity takes him by the hand, and lifts him lightly over the clouds of life.' His soul lives in the vision of natural beauty, and his whole expression is joy. He sympathizes with all harmless forms of animal life, and the innocent animal life, in its turn, recognizes his voice. Woman, the citadel and metropolis of beauty, so completely fulfils his conscious identity, that he seems to himself only to have lived since he knew Miriam, in whose 'bright natural smile' he was blest; but whose sadder moods disturbed him with a presentiment of pain he did not understand; and whose extremity of suffering inspired him with a 'fierce energy' to annihilate its manifest cause, that 'kindled him into a man.' For it is certain that his spiritual life began in the deed revealing to him that the law it broke came from a profounder and wider love than that which impelled him to its commission. If the reader asks then, with Hilda, 'Was Donatello really a faun?' he is referred for an answer to the words of Kenyon, in the original conversation in the Capitol, on the immortal marble of Praxiteles, where he says of

> That frisky thing . . . neither man nor animal, and yet no monster, but a being in whom both races meet on friendly ground. (Chap. II.) In some long past age he really must have existed. Nature needed, and still needs, this beautiful creature; standing betwixt man and animal, sympathizing with each, comprehending the speech of either race, and interpreting the whole existence of one to the other.

It was nothing less unsophisticated that could have served the author's purpose of simplifying the question of the origin of sin, which both etymologically and metaphysically means *separation,*—conscious separation from the principle of life. It was the perfected animal nature that revealed to his hitherto unreflecting mind, that an action which certainly originated in his 'loving much' was a crime. In one of his conversations with Kenyon he reveals this unawares. That 'long shriek wavering all the way down,' that 'thump against the stones,' that 'quiver through the crushed mass, and no more movement after that,' of a 'fellow-creature (but just before) living and breathing into (his) face,' awakened the idea in poor Donatello,—who himself clung to the life which he had felt to be 'so warm, so rich, so sunny,'—that there is a bond which antedates all the attractions of personal affinity, and whose violation takes the joy out of all narrower relations, however close they may be, startling the spirit into moral consciousness with the question *de profundis,* 'Am *I* my brother's keeper?'

It is true that for a moment the excitement of the action which took him so completely out of himself was felt both by him and Miriam to have 'cemented' their union 'with the blood of one worthless and wretched life,'—for that moment when they felt that neither of them could know any more loneliness; that they 'drew one breath' and 'lived one life.' But immediately afterwards they began to see that they had joined another mighty company, and 'melted into a vast mass of human crime' with a sense of being 'guilty of the whole'; and the next day, the sight of the corpse in the chapel of the Capuchins, and the sound of the chant for the dead, made Donatello's 'heart shiver,' and put 'a great weight' in his breast; and the love which he had felt to be his life was disenchanted! When Miriam saw that this was so, and, in spite of her warmly declared affection, which he had hitherto so passionately craved,

that he 'shuddered' at her touch, and confessed that 'nothing could ever comfort' him, 'with a generosity characteristic alike of herself and true love' she bade him leave and forget her:–

> 'Forget you, Miriam,' said Donatello, roused somewhat from his apathy of despair. 'If I could remember you and behold you apart from that frightful visage which stares at me over your shoulder, that were a consolation and a joy.'

But, as he could not do this, he reciprocated her farewell with apparent insensibility:–

> So soon after the semblance of such mighty love, and after it had been the impulse to so terrible a deed, they parted in all outward show as coldly as people part whose mutual intercourse has been encircled within an hour.

This parting, with all the reaction upon Donatello of what he had impulsively done, whether in the 'fiery intoxication which sufficed to carry them triumphantly through the first moments of their doom,' or in the blind gropings of his remorse, when he had returned to the old castle of Monte Beni, Hawthorne would evidently have us see, as in a pure mirror, that the fundamental principle of humanity, the brotherhood in which God created all souls, is affirmed in the law inscribed in our hearts, and handed down in all civilized tradition, which forbids an individual to assume over his fellows the office of judge and executioner; for that is the inherent prerogative of the social whole, which, and nothing less, is the image of God created to sit at his own right hand.

As long as Donatello fulfilled the law of impartial humanity by his geniality, easy persuadability, and glad abandonment of himself to friendship and love, though there might be 'no atom of martyr's stuff in him' considered as 'the power to sacrifice himself to an abstract idea,' yet there was no discord in all the echoes of his soul. As soon as he had made an exception to the universality of his good-will by executing on his sole responsibility a capital judgment on a fellow-pensioner of the Heavenly Father, he felt himself to be mysteriously and powerlessly drifting towards perdition, and his voice was no longer sterling in nature. Hawthorne is perhaps the only moral teacher of the modern time who has affirmed with power, that the origin of sin is in crime, and not *vice versa.* But it was affirmed of old by the most venerable scripture of the Hebrew Bible, in the statement that the first murderer was also the first who 'went out from the presence of the Lord,' and began the dark record of fallen humanity.

It was, therefore, an inconsiderate reader of *The Romance of Monte Beni* who said: 'But Donatello, with his unappeasable remorse, was no Italian; for, had he been one, he would at once have gone and confessed, received absolution, and thought never again of "the traitor who had met his just doom".' Hawthorne was not painting in Donatello an Italian such as the Church has made by centuries of a discipline so bewildering to the mind as to crush the natural conscience by substituting artificial for real duties, yet not restraining men, or itself refraining, from bursting into God's holy of holies, the destined temple of the Holy Spirit,—an Italian incapable of dreaming of anything holier than a passionate deprecation of that punishment for his crimes which he should crave as their expiation,—life for life. Donatello is an original inhabitant of Italy, as yet 'guiltless of Rome.'

In the genealogy of the counts of Monte Beni, *historic* vistas open up beyond recorded memory to 'A period when man's affinity with nature was more strict, and his fellowship with every living thing more intimate and dear.'

But of this the author himself may have been unconscious; for it was not historic facts, but the eternal truths they embody, on which his eye was fixed; and in the intimation that the Church ritual to which Donatello resorted to heal the wound of his soul, and which all his earnest sincerity of purpose found as ineffectual for that end as it had proved to the lost sinner whom the sight of the object of his vile passion had driven forth alike from the Catacombs he had sought as a penance and the shrines of the Coliseum which he was visiting on his knees, we have hints of an interpretation of Christianity more vital than has yet been symbolized by any ritual, or systematized by any ecclesiasticism. This is generally put into the mouth of Kenyon, who seems to be the keystone of the arch of characters in this story, combining in his own healthy affections and clear reason, and comprehending in his intelligent and discriminating sympathy all the others.

It is almost impossible to make extracts from the chapters describing the summer in the Apennines with his saddened friend, to whom he ministers with such unpretending wisdom and delicate tenderness. Quoting almost at random, his words seem to be oracles. For instance, in Chapter II. of the second volume:–

> 'What I am most inclined to murmur at is this death's head. It is absurdly monstrous, my dear friend, thus to fling the dead weight of our mortality upon our immortal hopes. While we live on earth, 't is true we must needs carry our skeletons about with us; but, for Heaven's sake, do not let us burden our spirits with them in our feeble efforts to soar upwards! Believe me, it will change the whole aspect of death, if you can once disconnect it in your idea with that corruption from which it disengages our higher part.'

And when Donatello subsequently says:–

> 'My forefathers being a cheerful race of men in their natural disposition found it needful to have the skull often before their eyes, because they dearly loved life and its enjoyments, and hated the very thought of death.' 'I am afraid,' said Kenyon, 'they liked it none the better for seeing its face under this abominable mask.'

Again, in Chapter III. of the same volume, Kenyon says:–

> 'Avoid the convent my dear friend, as you would shun the death of the soul. But for my own part, if I had an insupportable burden, if for any cause I were bent on sacrificing every earthly hope as a peace-offering towards heaven, I would make the wide earth my cell, and good deeds to mankind my prayer. Many penitent men have done this, and found peace in it.'
> 'Ah! but you are a heretic,' said the Count. Yet his face brightened beneath the stars, and, looking at it through the twilight, the sculptor's remembrance went back to that scene in the Capitol where both in features and expression Donatello had seemed identical with the Faun, and still there was a resemblance; for now, when first the idea was suggested of living for his fellow-creatures, the original beauty, which sorrow had partly effaced, came back, elevated and spiritualized. In the black depths the Faun had found a soul, and was struggling with it towards the light of heaven.

Afterwards, in Chapter IV. of the second volume, we find this wise advice:–

> 'Believe me,' said he, turning his eyes towards his friend, full of grave and tender sympathy, 'you know not what is requisite for your spiritual growth, seeking, as you do, to keep your soul perpetually in the unwholesome region of remorse. It was needful for you to pass through that dark valley, but it is infinitely dangerous to linger there too long; there is poison in the atmosphere when we sit down and brood in it, instead of girding up our loins to press onward. Not despondency, not slothful anguish, is what you require, but effort! Has there been an unutterable evil in your young life? Then crowd it out with good, or it will lie corrupting there forever, and cause your capacity for better things to partake its noisome corruption.'

It is an originality of the religious teaching of Hawthorne, that he really recognizes the inherent freedom of man, that is, his freedom to good as well as to evil. While he shows forth so powerfully that 'grief and pain' have developed in Donatello 'a more definite and nobler individuality,' he does not generalize the fact, as is so common, but recognizes that 'sometimes the instruction comes without the sorrow, and oftener the sorrow teaches no lesson that abides with us'; in fine, that love like Kenyon's and Hilda's reveals the same truth much more fully and certainly than did the crime which is made so cunningly to lie between Miriam and Donatello, that they become one by it in sorrow, as Hilda and Kenyon become one in joy ineffable, by their mutual recognition of each other's humility and purity.

Yet Hilda is not put above that 'common life' which is never to be lost sight of, being God's special dwelling-place, into any superhuman immunity from the 'ills that flesh is heir to.' She suffers, as well as Miriam, from 'the fatal decree by which every crime is made to be the agony of many innocent persons.' Hence we are told of

> That peculiar despair, that chill and heavy misery, *which only the innocent can experience,* although it possesses many of the gloomy characteristics of guilt. It was that heartsickness which, it is to be hoped, we may all of us have been pure enough to feel once in our lives, but the capacity for which is usually exhausted early, and perhaps with a single agony. It was that dismal certainty of the existence of evil in the world which, though we may fancy ourselves fully assured of the sad mystery long before, never becomes a portion of our practical belief until it takes substance and reality from the sin of some guide whom we have deeply trusted and revered, or some friend whom we have dearly loved.

And, besides, Hilda is indirectly developed into a larger sphere of duty and more comprehensive practical humanity, by the share she necessarily has in the misfortunes and sorrows of Miriam and Donatello.

Her conversation with Kenyon, after the relief experienced by her communication of the cause of her long-pent sorrow, leaves on her mind the painful doubt, whether in her struggle to keep 'the white robe' God had given her, 'and bade her wear it back to him as white as when she put it on,' 'a wrong had not been committed towards the friend so beloved'; 'Whether a close bond of friendship, in which we once voluntarily engage, ought to be severed on account of any unworthiness which we subsequently detect in our friend.'

Here we have Hawthorne's judgment upon a subject which is often an importunate practical problem in our daily conversation:–

> In these unions of hearts—call them marriage or whatever else—we take each other for better, for worse. Availing ourselves of our friend's intimate affection, we pledge our own as to be relied on in every emergency . . . Who need the tender succor of the innocent more than wretches stained with guilt? And must a selfish care for the spotlessness of our own garments keep us from pressing the guilty ones close to our hearts, wherein, for the very reason that we are innocent, lies their securest refuge from further ill . . . 'Miriam loved me

The last sculpted likeness of Hawthorne made during his lifetime, a bas-relief portrait by Edward J. Kuntze that he began in spring 1860 (New-York Historical Society)

well,' thought Hilda, remorsefully, 'and I failed her in her utmost need.'

This adjustment of the contending claims of the law of individuality and the law of our common nature frequently solicited Hawthorne's attention; and in *The Blithedale Romance* he has discussed it with earnestness. That Romance was intended to meet a peculiar and transient mood of mind in a special locality when there seemed to spread abroad a sudden doubt of those natural social unions growing out of the inevitable instincts and wants of human beings, which insure the organization of families. In *The House of the Seven Gables* he had shown how the tendency of families to isolation results, when unchecked by a liberal humanity, in physical deterioration, morbid affections, and malignant selfishness. In *The Blithedale Romance,* on the other hand, he teaches that by wilfully adopting schemes of social organization, based on abstractions of individual intellects,–however great and with whatever good motives,–we are liable ruthlessly, even if unconsciously, to immolate thereto living hearts that are attracted to us by profound affinities and generous imaginations. Zenobia,–was she not murdered by Hollingsworth as certainly, though not as obviously, as was Father Antonio by Donatello? No real philanthropy can grow out of social action that ignores the personal duties of parents, children, brothers, sisters, husbands, wives, friends, and lovers.

The last conversation between Hilda and Kenyon upon Donatello is one of those great touches of art by which Hawthorne is accustomed to lead his readers to a point of view from which they can see what the personages of his story, who seem to see and say all, certainly do not say, if they see:—

> 'Here comes my perplexity,' continued Kenyon. 'Sin has educated Donatello, and elevated him. Is sin, then, which we deem such a dreadful blackness in the universe,—is it like sorrow, merely an element of human education through which we struggle to a higher and purer state than we could otherwise have attained? Did Adam fall that we might ultimately rise to a far loftier paradise than his?'
>
> 'O, hush!' cried Hilda, shrinking from him with an expression of horror which wounded the poor speculative sculptor to the soul. 'This is terrible, and I could weep for you if you indeed believe it. Do not you perceive what a mockery your creed makes, not only of all religious sentiment, but of moral law, and how it annuls and obliterates whatever precepts of Heaven are written deepest within us? You have shocked me beyond words.'
>
> 'Forgive me, Hilda!' exclaimed the sculptor, startled by her agitation; 'I never did believe it! But the mind wanders wild and wide; and, so lonely as I live and work, I have neither polestar above, nor light of cottage window here below, to bring me home. Were you my guide, my counsellor, my inmost friend, with that white wisdom which clothes you as a celestial garment, all would go well. O Hilda, guide me home.'

We must bring this protracted article to a close, though we have by no means made an exhaustive analysis of *The Romance of Monte Beni*. The mere drama of it is wonderfully knit together, all its incidents growing directly out of the characters, and their interaction with universal laws. As Hilda's imprisonment is the direct consequence of her faithful execution of Miriam's commission, and complicated with her involuntary knowledge of Donatello's crime, so her deliverance is the immediate motive of the self-surrender of Donatello, which Miriam makes to bear this fruit of practical justice. He is no martyr, therefore, even at last, 'to an abstract idea,' but sacrifices himself for a substantially beneficent end. And it is left probable that the sacrifice proved by Divine Providence no immolation; for the last words of the original romance are, after asking, 'What was Miriam's life to be? and Where was Donatello? . . . Hilda had a hopeful soul, and saw sunlight on the mountain-tops.' Thus we are led to hope that 'the bond between them,' which Kenyon had pronounced to be 'for mutual support . . . for one another's final good, . . . for effort, for sacrifice,' and which they had accepted 'for mutual elevation and encouragement towards a severe and painful life,' 'but not for earthly happiness,' did at last

conciliate 'that shy, subtle thing' as 'a wayside flower springing along a path leading to higher ends.'

We shall have done quite as much as we had proposed to ourselves in this review, if we shall induce any of our readers to recur to the book and study it; for in it they will find earnestly treated the highest offices and aims, as well as the temptations and limitations, of art, in its well-discriminated and fairly appreciated varieties of mode; they will find there delicate criticisms on pictures and statues, ancient and modern, with original thoughts on nearly every subject of moral, intellectual, and æsthetic interest presenting itself to a sojourner in Italy, to whose richest meanings, whether sad or glad, the romance will prove the best of guide-books. But we must not close without observing that whatever short comings in theory or iniquities in practice the author hints at or exposes in the Roman Catholic Church and state, he exhibits no narrow Protestantism. In many time-honored customs, in 'the shrines it has erected at the waysides, as reminders of the eternal future imbosomed in the present'; and especially in the description of the 'world's cathedral' where he makes the suffering Hilda find relief, he does not fail to recognize whatever Romanism has appropriated of the methods of universal love.

But he puts the infallible priesthood to school, as it were, to the pure soul which has preserved by humble religious thought 'the white robe' of pristine innocence God had bid her 'wear back to him unstained,' and has faithfully *increased in the knowledge of God* by the study and reproduction of beauty, without making into stumbling-blocks, as the merely instinctive too generally do, the stepping-stones given for our advancement from the glory of the natural to the glory of the spiritual life.

Hilda's rebuke to the priest, who would narrow the sacred confidences of his office to orthodox ritualism and her confession, which she tells Kenyon would have been made to him if he had been at hand, express the idea that in the loneliness created by sin, not only in the guilty, but in the guiltless soul, it is at once inevitable and legitimate to claim *human* sympathy; also that 'it is not good for man to be alone,' because God created us in countless relations, which it is our salvation to discover and fulfil, as is revealed by the very etymology of the word *conscience*. In fine, may we not say that *The Marble Faun* takes a high place in that library of sacred literature of the modern time which is the prophetic intimation of the Free Catholic Christian Church, 'whose "far-off coming" shines,'—a Church whose *credo* is not abstract dogma, but the love of wisdom and the wisdom of love; whose cathedral is universal nature, and whose ritual is nothing short of virtue, truth, and charity, the organs of piety?

Last Years: *Our Old Home*

Hawthorne's four mature novels brought him fame and financial security. During the last four years of his life he continued to write, but because of poor health and anxieties about the Civil War he found it impossible to bring any of his fictional projects to completion. The only book he published was Our Old Home, *a collection of sketches in which he describes his experiences in England. At his death, Hawthorne was honored in tributes written on both sides of the Atlantic.*

Return to Concord

In his memoir Yesterdays with Authors, *James T. Fields gives an account of Hawthorne's life after his return to his Concord home in late June 1860 until his death on 18 May 1864.*

The summer after his arrival home he spent quietly in Concord, at the Wayside, and illness in his family made him at times unusually sad. In one of his notes to me he says:–

"I am continually reminded nowadays of a response which I once heard a drunken sailor make to a pious gentleman, who asked him how he felt, 'Pretty d—d miserable, thank God!' It very well expresses my thorough discomfort and forced acquiescence."

Occasionally he wrote requesting me to make a change, here and there, in the new edition of his works then passing through the press. On the 23d of September, 1860, he writes:–

"Please to append the following note to the foot of the page, at the commencement of the story called 'Dr. Heidegger's Experiment, in the 'Twice-Told Tales': 'In an English Review, not long since, I have been accused of plagiarizing the idea of this story from a chapter in one of the novels of Alexandre Dumas. There has undoubtedly been a plagiarism, on one side or the other; but as my story was written a good deal more than twenty years ago, and as the novel is of considerably more recent date, I take pleasure in thinking that M. Dumas has done me the honor to appropriate one of the fanciful conceptions of my earlier days. He is heartily welcome to it; nor is it the only instance, by many, in which the great French romancer has exercised the privilege of commanding genius by confiscating the intellectual property of less famous people to his own use and behoof.'"

Hawthorne was a diligent reader of the Bible, and when sometimes, in my ignorant way, I would question, in a proof-sheet, his use of a word, he would almost always refer me to the Bible as his authority. It was a great pleasure to hear him talk about the Book of Job, and his voice would be tremulous with feeling, as he sometimes quoted a touching passage from the New Testament. In one of his letters he says to me:–

"Did not I suggest to you, last summer, the publication of the Bible in ten or twelve 12mo volumes? I think it would have great success, and, at least (but, as a publisher, I suppose this is the very smallest of your cares), it would result in the salvation of a great many souls, who will never find their way to heaven, if left to learn it from the inconvenient editions of the Scriptures now in use. It is very singular that this form of publishing the Bible in a single bulky or closely printed volume should be so long continued. It was first adopted, I suppose, as being the universal mode of publication at the time when the Bible was translated. Shakespeare, and the other old dramatists and poets, were first published in the same form; but all of them have long since been broken into dozens and scores of portable and readable volumes; and why not the Bible?"

During this period, after his return from Europe, I saw him frequently at the Wayside, in Concord. He now seemed happy in the dwelling he had put in order for the calm and comfort of his middle and later life. He had added a tower to his house, in which he could be safe from intrusion, and where he could muse and write. Never was poet or romancer more fitly shrined. Drummond at Hawthornden, Scott at Abbotsford, Dickens at Gad's Hill, Irving at Sunnyside, were not more appropriately sheltered. Shut up in his tower, he could escape from the tumult of life, and be alone with only the birds and the bees in concert outside his casement. The view from this apartment, on every side, was

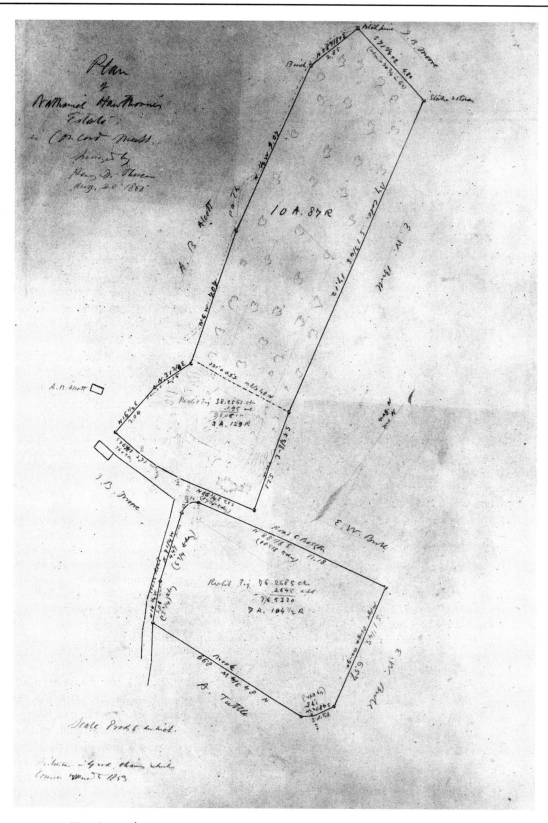

Henry David Thoreau's survey of Hawthorne's Concord property (The Concord Free Public Library)

lovely, and Hawthorne enjoyed the charming prospect as I have known few men to enjoy nature.

His favorite walk lay near his house,—indeed it was part of his own grounds,—a little hillside, where he had worn a foot-path, and where he might be found in good weather, when not employed in the tower. While walking to and fro on this bit of rising ground he meditated and composed innumerable romances that were never written, as well as some that were. Here he first announced to me his plan of "The Dolliver Romance," and, from what he told me of his design of the story as it existed in his mind, I thought it would have been the greatest of his books. An enchanting memory is left of that morning when he laid out the whole story before me as he intended to write it. The plot was a grand one, and I tried to tell him how much I was impressed by it. Very soon after our interview, he wrote to me:—

"In compliance with your exhortations, I have begun to think seriously of that story. not, as yet, with a pen in my hand, but trudging to and fro on my hilltop. . . . . I don't mean to let you see the first chapters till I have written the final sentence of the story. Indeed, the first chapters of a story ought always to be the last written. . . . . If you want me to write a good book, send me a good pen; not a gold one, for they seldom suit me; but a pen flexible and capacious of ink, and that will not grow stiff and rheumatic the moment I get attached to it. I never met with a good pen in my life."

Time went on, the war broke out, and he had not the heart to go on with his new Romance. During the month of April, 1862, he made a visit to Washington with his friend Ticknor, to whom he was greatly attached. While on this visit to the capital he sat to Leutze for a portrait. He took a special fancy to the artist, and, while he was sitting to him, wrote a long letter to me. Here is an extract from it:—

"I stay here only while Leutze finishes a portrait, which I think will be the best ever painted of the same unworthy subject. One charm it must needs have,—an aspect of immortal jollity and well-to-doness; for Leutze, when the sitting begins, gives me a first-rate cigar, and when he sees me getting tired, he brings out a bottle of splendid champagne; and we quaffed and smoked yesterday, in a blessed state of mutual good-will, for three hours and a half, during which the picture made a really miraculous progress. Leutze is the best of fellows."

In the same letter he thus describes the sinking of the Cumberland, and I know of nothing finer in its way:—

"I see in a newspaper that Holmes is going to write a song on the sinking of the Cumberland; and feeling it to be a subject of national importance, it occurs to me that he might like to know her present condition. She lies with her three masts sticking up out of the water, and careened over, the water being nearly on a level with her maintop,—I mean that first landing-place from the deck of the vessel, after climbing the shrouds. The rigging does not appear at all damaged. There is a tattered bit of a pennant, about a foot and a half long, fluttering from the tip-top of one of the masts; but the flag, the ensign of the ship (which never was struck, thank God), is under water, so as to be quite invisible, being attached to the gaff, I think they call it, of the mizzenmast; and though this bald description makes nothing of it, I never saw anything so gloriously forlorn as those three masts. I did not think it was in me to be so moved by any spectacle of the kind. Bodies still occasionally float up from it. The Secretary of the Navy says she shall lie there till she goes to pieces, but I suppose by and by they will sell her to some Yankee for the value of her old iron.

"P.S. My hair really is not so white as this photograph, which I enclose, makes me. The sun seems to take an infernal pleasure in making me venerable,—as if I were as old as himself."

Hawthorne has rested so long in the twilight of impersonality, that I hesitate sometimes to reveal the man even to his warmest admirers. This very day Sainte-Beuve has made me feel a fresh reluctance in unveiling my friend, and there seems almost a reproof in these words, from the eloquent French author:—

"We know nothing or nearly nothing of the life of La Bruyère, and this obscurity adds, it has been remarked, to the effect of his work, and, it may be said, to the piquant happiness of his destiny. If there was not a single line of his unique book, which from the first instant of its publication did not appear and remain in the clear light, so, on the other hand, there was not one individual detail regarding the author which was well known. Every ray of the century fell upon each page of the book and the face of the man who held it open in his hand was veiled from our sight."

Beautifully said, as usual with Sainte-Beuve, but I venture, notwithstanding such eloquent warning, to proceed.

After his return home from Washington Hawthorne sent to me, during the month of May, an article for the Atlantic Monthly, which he entitled "Chiefly about War-Matters." The paper, excellently well done throughout, of course, contained a personal description of President Lincoln, which I thought, considered as a portrait of a living man, and drawn by Hawthorne, it would not be wise or tasteful to print. The office of an editor is a disagreeable one sometimes, and the case of Hawthorne on Lincoln disturbed me not a little. After reading the manu-

Views of the path near The Wayside where Hawthorne frequently walked

script, I wrote to the author, and asked his permission to omit his description of the President's personal appearance. As usual–for he was the kindest and sweetest of contributors, the most good-natured and the most amenable man to advise I ever knew,–he consented to my proposal, and allowed me to print the article with the alterations. If any one will turn to the paper in the Atlantic Monthly (it is in the number for July, 1862), it will be observed there are several notes; all of these were written by Hawthorne himself. He complied with my request without a murmur, but he always thought I was wrong in my decision. He said the whole description of the interview and the President's personal appearance were, to his mind, the only parts of the article worth publishing. "What a terrible thing," he complained, "it is to try to let off a little bit of truth into this miserable humbug of a world!" President Lincoln is dead, and as Hawthorne once wrote to me, "Upon my honor, it seems to me the passage omitted has an historical value," I will copy here verbatim what I advised my friend, both on his own account and the President's, not to print nine years ago. Hawthorne and his party had

gone into the President's room, annexed, as he says, as supernumeraries to a deputation from a Massachusetts whip-factory, with a present of a splendid whip to the Chief Magistrate:–

> "By and by there was a little stir on the staircase and in the passage way, and in lounged a tall, loose-jointed figure, of an exaggerated Yankee port and demeanor, whom (as being about the homeliest man I ever saw, yet by no means repulsive or disagreeable) it was impossible not to recognize as Uncle Abe.
>
> "Unquestionably, Western man though he be, and Kentuckian by birth, President Lincoln is the essential representative of all Yankees, and the veritable specimen, physically, of what the world seems determined to regard as our characteristic qualities. It is the strangest and yet the fittest thing in the jumble of human vicissitudes, that he, out of so many millions, unlooked for, unselected by any intelligible process that could be based upon his genuine qualities, unknown to those who chose him, and unsuspected of what endowments may adapt him for his tremendous responsibility, should have found the way open for him to fling his lank personality into the chair of state,–where, I presume, it was his first impulse to throw his legs on the

Abraham Lincoln, whom Hawthorne met in 1862

council-table, and tell the Cabinet Ministers a story. There is no describing his lengthy awkwardness, nor the uncouthness of his movement; and yet it seemed as if I had been in the habit of seeing him daily, and had shaken hands with him a thousand times in some village street; so true was he to the aspect of the pattern American, though with a certain extravagance which, possibly, I exaggerated still further by the delighted eagerness with which I took it in. If put to guess his calling and livelihood, I should have taken him for a country schoolmaster as soon as anything else. He was dressed in a rusty black frock-coat and pantaloons, unbrushed, and worn so faithfully that the suit had adapted itself to the curves and angularities of his figure, and had grown to be an outer skin of the man. He had shabby slippers on his feet. His hair was black, still unmixed with gray, stiff, somewhat bushy, and had apparently been acquainted with neither brush nor comb that morning, after the disarrangement of the pillow; and as to a nightcap, Uncle Abe probably knows nothing of such effeminacies. His complexion is dark and sallow, betokening, I fear, an insalubrious atmosphere around the White House; he has thick black eyebrows and an impending brow; his nose is large, and the lines about his mouth are very strongly defined.

"The whole physiognomy is as coarse a one as you would meet anywhere in the length and breadth of the States; but, withal, it is redeemed, illuminated, softened, and brightened by a kindly though serious look out of his eyes, and an expression of homely sagacity, that seems weighted with rich results of village experience. A great deal of native sense; no bookish cultivation, no refinement; honest at heart, and thoroughly so, and yet, in some sort, sly,—at least, endowed with a sort of tact and wisdom that are akin to craft, and would impel him, I think, to take an antagonist in flank, rather than to make a bull-run at him right in front. But, on the whole, I liked this sallow, queer, sagacious visage, with the homely human sympathies that warmed it; and, for my small share in the matter, would as lief have Uncle Abe for a ruler as any man whom it would have been practicable to put in his place.

"Immediately on his entrance the President accosted our member of Congress, who had us in charge, and, with a comical twist of his face, made some jocular remark about the length of his breakfast. He then greeted us all round, not waiting for an introduction, but shaking and squeezing everybody's hand with the utmost cordiality, whether the individual's name was announced to him or not. His manner towards us was wholly without pretence, but yet had a kind of natural dignity, quite sufficient to keep the forwardest of us from clapping him on the shoulder and asking for a story. A mutual acquaintance being established, our leader took the whip out of its case, and began to read the address of presentation. The whip was an exceedingly long one, its handle wrought in ivory (by some artist in the Massachusetts State Prison, I believe), and ornamented with a medallion of the President, and other equally beautiful devices; and along its whole length there was a succession of golden bands and ferrules. The address was shorter than the whip, but equally well made, consisting chiefly of an explanatory description of these artistic designs, and closing with a hint that the gift was a suggestive and emblematic one, and that the President would recognize the use to which such an instrument should be put.

"This suggestion gave Uncle Abe rather a delicate task in his reply, because, slight as the matter seemed, it apparently called for some declaration, or intimation, or faint foreshadowing of policy in reference to the conduct of the war, and the final treatment of the Rebels. But the President's Yankee aptness and not-to-be-caughtness stood him in good stead, and he jerked or wiggled himself out of the dilemma with an uncouth dexterity that was entirely in character; although, without his gesticulation of eye and mouth,—and especially the flourish of the whip, with which he imagined himself touching up a pair of fat horses,—I doubt whether his words would be worth recording, even if I could remember them. The gist of the reply was, that he accepted the whip as an emblem of peace, not punishment; and, this great affair over, we retired out of the presence in high good-humor, only regretting that we could not have seen the President sit down and fold up his legs (which is said to be a

Hawthorne's family, 1861: left, Sophia; right, Una, Julian, and Rose (Collection of Barbara Bacheler)

most extraordinary spectacle), or have heard him tell one of those delectable stories for which he is so celebrated. A good many of them are afloat upon the common talk of Washington, and are certainly the aptest, pithiest, and funniest little things imaginable; though, to be sure, they smack of the frontier freedom, and would not always bear repetition in a drawing-room, or in the immaculate page of the Atlantic."

So runs the passage which caused some good-natured discussion nine years ago, between the contributor and the editor. Perhaps I was squeamish not to have been willing to print this matter at that time. Some persons, no doubt, will adopt that opinion, but as both President and author have long ago met on the other side of criticism and magazines, we will leave the subject to their decision, they being most interested in

the transaction. I did what seemed best in 1862. In 1871 "circumstances have changed" with both parties, and I venture to-day what I hardly dared then.

———

Whenever I look at Hawthorne's portrait, and that is pretty often, some new trait or anecdote or reminiscence comes up and clamors to be made known to those who feel an interest in it. But time and eternity call loudly for mortal gossip to be brief, and I must hasten to any last session over that child of genius, who first saw the light on the 4th of July, 1804.

One of his favorite books was Lockhart's Life of Sir Walter Scott, and in 1862 I dedicated to him the Household Edition of that work. When he received the first volume, he wrote to me a letter of which I am so proud that I keep it among my best treasures.

"I am exceedingly gratified by the dedication. I do not deserve so high an honor; but if you think me worthy, it is enough to make the compliment in the highest degree acceptable, no matter who may dispute my title to it. I care more for your good opinion than for that of a host of critics, and have an excellent reason for so doing; inasmuch as my literary success, whatever it has been or may be, is the result of my connection with you. Somehow or other you smote the rock of public sympathy on my behalf, and a stream gushed forth in sufficient quantity to quench my thirst though not to drown me. I think no author can ever have had publisher that he valued so much as I do mine."

He began in 1862 to send me some articles from his English Journal for the Atlantic magazine, which he afterwards collected into a volume and called "Our Old Home." On forwarding one for December of that year he says:–

"I hope you will like it, for the subject seemed interesting to me when I was on the spot, but I always feel a singular despondency and heaviness of heart in reopening those old journals now. However, if I can make readable sketches out of them, it is no matter."

In the same letter he tells me he has been rereading Scott's Life, and he suggests some additions to the concluding volume. He says:–

"If the last volume is not already printed and stereotyped, I think you ought to insert in it an explanation of all that is left mysterious in the former volumes,–the name and family of the lady he was in love with, etc. It is desirable, too, to know what have been the fortunes and final catastrophes of his family and intimate friends since his death, down to as recent a period as the death of Lockhart. All such matter would make your edition more valuable; and I see no reason why you should be bound by the deference to living connections of the family that may prevent the English publishers from inserting these particulars. We stand in the light of posterity to them, and have the privileges of posterity. . . . . I should be glad to know something of the personal character and life of his eldest son, and whether (as I have heard) he was ashamed of his father for being a literary man. In short, fifty pages devoted to such elucidation would make the edition unique. Do come and see us before the leaves fall."

While he was engaged in copying out and rewriting his papers on England for the magazine he was despondent about their reception by the public. Speaking of them, one day, to me, he said: "We must remember that there is a good deal of intellectual ice mingled with this wine of memory." He was sometimes so dispirited during the war that he was obliged to post-

pone his contributions for sheer lack of spirit to go on. Near the close of the year 1862 he writes:–

"I am delighted at what you tell me about the kind appreciation of my articles, for I feel rather gloomy about them myself. I am really much encouraged by what you say; not but what I am sensible that you mollify me with a good deal of soft soap, but it is skilfully applied and effects all you intend it should. . . . . I cannot come to Boston to spend more than a day, just at present. It would suit me better to come for a visit when the spring of next year is a little advanced, and if you renew your hospitable proposition then, I shall probably be glad to accept it; though I have now been a hermit so long, that the thought affects me somewhat as it would to invite a lobster or a crab to step out of his shell."

He continued, during the early months of 1863, to send now and then an article for the magazine from his English Note-Books. On the 22d of February he writes:–

"Here is another article. I wish it would not be so wretchedly long, but there are many things which I shall find no opportunity to say unless I say them now; so the article grows under my hand, and one part of it seems just about as well worth printing as another. Heaven sees fit to visit me with an unshakable conviction that all this series of articles is good for nothing; but that is none of my business, provided the public and you are of a different opinion. If you think any part of it can be left out with advantage, you are quite at liberty to do so. Probably I have not put Leigh Hunt quite high enough for your sentiments respecting him; but no more genuine characterization and criticism (so far as the writer's purpose to be true goes) was ever done. It is very slight. I might have made more of it, but should not have improved it.

"I mean to write two more of these articles, and then hold my hand. I intend to come to Boston before the end of this week, if the weather is good. It must be nearly or quite six months since I was there! I wonder how many people there are in the world who would keep their nerves in tolerably good order through such a length of nearly solitary imprisonment?"

I advised him to begin to put the series in order for a volume, and to preface the book with his "Consular Experiences." On the 18th of April he writes:–

"I don't think the public will bear any more of this sort of thing. . . . . I had a letter from —, the other day, in which he sends me the enclosed verses, and I think he would like to have them published in the Atlantic. Do it if you like, I pretend to no judgment in poetry. He also sent this epithalamium by Mrs. —, and I doubt not the good lady will be pleased to see it copied into one of our American newspapers with a few laudatory

OUR OLD HOME:

A SERIES OF ENGLISH SKETCHES.

BY

NATHANIEL HAWTHORNE.

BOSTON:
TICKNOR AND FIELDS.
1863.

OUR OLD HOME.

BY

NATHANIEL HAWTHORNE,

AUTHOR OF "TRANSFORMATION," "THE SCARLET LETTER,"
ETC. ETC.

IN TWO VOLUMES.
VOL. I.

LONDON:
SMITH, ELDER AND CO., 65, CORNHILL.

M.DCCC.LXIII.

Title pages for the first American and English editions of the last book Hawthorne completed. The books were published simultaneously on 19 September 1863 (from C. E. Frazer Clark Jr., Nathaniel Hawthorne: A Descriptive Bibliography, *1978).*

remarks. Can't you do it in the Transcript, and send her a copy? You cannot imagine how a little praise jollifies us poor authors to the marrow of our bones. Consider, if you had not been a publisher, you would certainly have been one of our wretched tribe, and therefore ought to have a fellow-feeling for us. Let Michael Angelo write the remarks, if you have not the time."

("Michael Angelo" was a clever little Irish-boy who had the care of my room. Hawthorne conceived a fancy for the lad, and liked to hear stories of his smart replies to persistent authors who called during my absence with unpromising-looking manuscripts.) On the 30th of April he writes:–

"I send the article with which the volume is to commence, and you can begin printing it whenever you

like. I can think of no better title than this, 'Our Old Home; a Series of English Sketches, by,' etc. I submit to your judgment whether it would not be well to print these 'Consular Experiences' in the volume without depriving them of any freshness they may have by previous publication in the magazine?

"The article has some of the features that attract the curiosity of the foolish public, being made up of personal narrative and gossip, with a few pungencies of personal satire, which will not be the less effective because the reader can scarcely find out who was the individual meant. I am not without hope of drawing down upon myself a good deal of critical severity on this score, and would gladly incur more of it if I could do so without seriously deserving censure.

"The story of the Doctor of Divinity, I think, will prove a good card in this way. It is every bit true (like the other anecdotes), only not told so darkly as it might have been for the reverend gentleman. I do not believe there is any danger of his identity being ascertained, and do not care whether it is or no, as it could only be done by the impertinent researches of other people. It seems to me quite essential to have some novelty in the collected volume, and, if possible, something that may excite a little discussion and remark. But decide for yourself and me; and if you conclude not to publish it in the magazine, I think I can concoct another article in season for the August number, if you wish. After the publication of the volume, it seems to me the public had better have no more of them.

"J— has been telling us a mythical story of your intending to walk with him from Cambridge to Concord. We should be delighted to see you, though more for our own sakes than yours, for our aspect here is still a little winterish. When you come, let it be on Saturday, and stay till Monday. I am hungry to talk with you."

I was enchanted, of course, with the "Consular Experiences," and find from his letters, written at that time, that he was made specially happy by the encomiums I could not help sending upon that inimitable sketch. When the "Old Home" was nearly all in type, he began to think about a dedication to the book. On the 3d of May he writes:—

"I am of three minds about dedicating the volume. First, it seems due to Frank Pierce (as he put me into the position where I made all those profound observations of English scenery, life, and character) to inscribe it to him with a few pages of friendly and explanatory talk, which also would be very gratifying to my own lifelong affection for him.

"Secondly, I want to say something to Bennoch to show him that I am thoroughly mindful of all his hospitality and kindness; and I suppose he might be pleased to see his name at the head of a book of mine.

"Thirdly, I am not convinced that it is worth while to inscribe it to anybody. We will see hereafter."

The book moved on slowly through the press, and he seemed more than commonly nervous about the proof-sheets. On the 28th of May he says in a note to me:—

"In a proof-sheet of 'Our Old Home,' which I sent you to-day (page 43, or 4, or 5 or thereabout) I corrected a line thus, 'possessing a happy faculty of seeing my own interest.' Now as the public interest was my sole and individual object while I held office, I think that as a matter of scanty justice to myself, the line ought to stand thus, 'possessing a happy faculty of seeing my own interest and the public's.' Even then, you see, I only give myself credit for half the disinterestedness I really felt. Pray, by all means, have it altered as above, even if the page is stereotyped; which it can't have been, as the proof is now in the Concord post-office, and you will have it at the same time with this.

"We are getting into full leaf here, and your walk with J— might come off any time."

An arrangement was made with the liberal house of Smith and Elder, of London, to bring out "Our Old Home" on the same day of its publication in Boston. On the 1st of July Hawthorne wrote to me from the Wayside as follows:—

"I am delighted with Smith and Elder, or rather with you; for it is you that squeeze the English sovereigns out of the poor devils. On my own behalf I never could have thought of asking more than £ 50, and should hardly have expected to get £ 10; I look upon the £ 180 as the only trustworthy funds I have, our own money being of such a gaseous consistency. By the time I can draw for it, I expect it will be worth at least fifteen hundred dollars.

"I shall think over the prefatory matter for 'Our Old Home' to-day, and will write it to-morrow. It requires some little thought and policy in order to say nothing amiss at this time; for I intend to dedicate the book to Frank Pierce, come what may. It shall reach you on Friday morning.

"We find — a comfortable and desirable guest to have in the house. My wife likes her hugely, and for my part, I had no idea that there was such a sensible woman of letters in the world. She is just as healthy-minded as if she had never touched a pen. I am glad she had a pleasant time, and hope she will come back.

"I mean to come to Boston whenever I can be sure of a cool day.

"What a prodigious length of time you stayed among the mountains!

"You ought not to assume such liberties of absence without the consent of your friends, which I hardly think you would get. I, at least, want you always within attainable distance, even though I never see you. Why can't you come and stay a day or two with us, and drink some spruce beer?"

Those were troublous days, full of war gloom and general despondency. The North was naturally suspicious of all public men, who did not bear a conspicuous part in helping to put down the Rebellion. General Pierce had been President of the United States, and was not identified, to say the least, with the great party which favored the vigorous prosecution of the war. Hawthorne proposed to dedicate his new book to a very dear friend, indeed, but in doing so he would draw public attention in a marked way to an unpopular name. Several of Hawthorne's friends, on learning that he intended to inscribe his book to Franklin Pierce, came to me and begged that I would, if possible, help Hawthorne to see that he ought not to do anything to jeopardize the currency of his new volume. Accordingly I wrote to him, just what many of his friends had said to

Pencil sketches of Hawthorne in 1861 by his family. The profiles are by Una, left, and Julian, right (Henry W. and Albert A. Berg Collection, The New York Public Library), and the study of his eye and nose is presumed to be by Sophia (Collection of Manning Hawthorne).

me, and this is his reply to my letter, which bears date the 18th of July, 1863:–

"I thank you for your note of the 15th instant, and have delayed my reply thus long in order to ponder deeply on your advice, smoke cigars over it, and see what it might be possible for me to do towards taking it. I find that it would be a piece of poltroonery in me to withdraw either the dedication or the dedicatory letter. My long and intimate personal relations with Pierce render the dedication altogether proper, especially as regards this book, which would have had no existence without his kindness; and if he is so exceedingly unpopular that his name is enough to sink the volume, there is so much the more need that an old friend should stand by him. I cannot, merely on account of pecuniary profit or literary reputation, go back from what I have deliberately felt and thought it right to do; and if I were to tear out the dedication, I should never look at the volume again without remorse and shame. As for the literary public, it must accept my book precisely as I think fit to give it, or let it alone.

"Nevertheless, I have no fancy for making myself a martyr when it is honorably and conscientiously possible to avoid it; and I always measure out my heroism very accurately according to the exigencies of the occasion, and should be the last man in the world to throw away a bit of it needlessly. So I have looked over the concluding paragraph and have amended it in such a way that, while doing what I know to be justice to my friend, it contains not a word that ought to be objectionable to any set of readers. If the public of the North see fit to ostracize me for this, I can only say that I would gladly sacrifice a thousand or two of dollars rather than retain the good-will of such a herd of dolts and mean-spirited scoundrels. I enclose the rewritten paragraph, and shall wish to see a proof of that and the whole dedication.

"I had a call from an Englishman yesterday, and kept him to dinner; not the threatened —, but a Mr. —, introduced by —. He says he knows you, and he seems to be a very good fellow. I have strong hopes that he will never come back here again, for J— took him on a walk of several miles, whereby they both caught a most tremendous ducking, and the poor Englishman was frightened half to death by the thunder. . . . . On the other page is the list of presentation people, and it amounts to twenty-four, which your liberality and kindness allow me. As likely as not I have forgotten two or three, and I held my pen suspended over one or two of the names, doubting whether they deserved of me so especial a favor as a portion of my heart and brain. I have few friends. Some authors, I should think, would require half the edition for private distribution."

"Our Old Home" was published in the autumn of 1863, and although it was everywhere welcomed, in England the strictures were applied with a liberal hand. On the 18th of October he writes to me:–

"You sent me the 'Reader' with a notice of the book, and I have received one or two others, one of them from Bennoch. The English critics seem to think me very bitter against their countrymen, and it is, perhaps, natural that they should, because their self-conceit can accept nothing short of indiscriminate adulation; but I really think that Americans have more cause than they to complain of me. Looking over the volume, I am rather surprised to find that whenever I draw a comparison between the two people, I almost invariably cast the balance against ourselves. It is not a good nor a weighty book, nor does it deserve any great amount either of praise or censure. I don't care about seeing any more notices of it."

Meantime the "Dolliver Romance," which had been laid aside on account of the exciting scenes through which we were then passing, and which unfitted him for the composition of a work of the imagination, made little progress. In a note written to me at this time he says:–

"I can't tell you when to expect an instalment of the Romance, if ever. There is something preternatural in my reluctance to begin. I linger at the threshold, and have a perception of very disagreeable phantasms to be encountered if I enter. I wish God had given me the faculty of writing a sunshiny book."

I invited him to come to Boston and have a cheerful week among his old friends, and threw in as an inducement a hint that he should hear the great organ in the Music Hall. I also suggested that we could talk over the new Romance together, if he would gladden us all by coming to the city. Instead of coming, he sent this reply:–

"I thank you for your kind invitation to hear the grand instrument; but it offers me no inducement additional to what I should always have for a visit to your abode. I have no ear for an organ or a jewsharp, nor for any instrument between the two; so you had better invite a worthier guest, and I will come another time

"I don't see much probability of my having the first chapter of the Romance ready so soon as you want it. There are two or three chapters ready to be written, but I am not yet robust enough to begin, and I feel as if I should never carry it through.

"Besides, I want to prefix a little sketch of Thoreau to it, because, from a tradition which he told me about this house of mine, I got the idea of a deathless man, which is now taking a shape very different from the original one. It seems the duty of a live literary man to perpetuate the memory of a dead one, when there is such fair opportunity as in this case; but how Thoreau would scorn me for thinking that *I* could perpetuate him! And I don't think so.

I had frequent accounts of his ill health and changed appearance, but I supposed he would rally again soon, and become hale and strong before the winter fairly set in. But the shadows even then were about his pathway, and Allan Cunningham's lines, which he once quoted to me, must often have occurred to him,–

"Cauld's the snaw at my head,
And cauld at my feet,
And the finger o' death 's at my een,
Closing them to sleep."

We had arranged together that the "Dolliver Romance" should be first published in the magazine, in monthly instalments, and we decided to begin in the January number of 1864. On the 8th of November came a long letter from him:–

"I foresee that there is little probability of my getting the first chapter ready by the 15th, although I have a resolute purpose to write it by the end of the month. It will be in time for the February number, if it turns out fit for publication at all. As to the title, we must defer settling that till the book is fully written, and meanwhile I see nothing better than to call the series of articles 'Fragments of a Romance.' This will leave me to exercise greater freedom as to the mechanism of the story than I otherwise can, and without which I shall probably get entangled in my own plot. When the work is completed in the magazine, I can fill up the gaps and make straight the crookedness, and christen it with a fresh title. In this untried experiment of a serial work I desire not to pledge myself, or promise the public more than I may confidently expect to achieve. As regards the sketch of Thoreau, I am not ready to write it yet, but will mix him up with the life of The Wayside, and produce an autobiographical preface for the finished Romance. If the public like that sort of stuff, I too find it pleasant and easy writing, and can supply a new chapter of it for every new volume, and that, moreover, without infringing upon my proper privacy. An old Quaker wrote me, the other day, that he had been reading my Introduction to the 'Mosses,' and the 'Scarlet Letter,' and felt as if he knew me better than his best friend; but I think he considerably overestimates the extent of his intimacy with me.

"I received several private letters and printed notices of 'Our Old Home' from England. It is laughable to see the innocent wonder with which they regard my criticisms, accounting for them by jaundice, insanity, jealousy, hatred, on my part, and never admitting the least suspicion that there may be a particle of truth in them. The monstrosity of their self-conceit is such that anything short of unlimited admiration impresses them as malicious caricature. But they do me great injustice in supposing that I hate them. I would as soon hate my own people.

"Tell Ticknor that I want a hundred dollars more, and I suppose I shall keep on wanting more and more till the end of my days. If I subside into the almshouse

Hawthorne (center) with his publishers, William Ticknor (left) and James T. Fields (right), circa 1862 (photograph by James Wallace Black)

"I can think of no title for the unborn Romance. Always heretofore I have waited till it was quite complete before attempting to name it, and I fear I shall have to do so now. I wish you or Mrs. Fields would suggest one. Perhaps you may snatch a title out of the infinite void that will miraculously suit the book, and give me a needful impetus to write it.

"I want a great deal of money. . . . . I wonder how people manage to live economically. I seem to spend little or nothing, and yet it will get very far beyond the second thousand, for the present year. . . . . If it were not for these troublesome necessities, I doubt whether you would ever see so much as the first chapter of the new Romance.

"Those verses entitled 'Weariness,' in the last magazine, seem to me profoundly touching. I too am weary, and begin to look ahead for the Wayside Inn."

Hawthorne's 3 April 1862 letter to Joseph Henry, the secretary of the Smithsonian Institution, in which he included a carte de visite
*photograph made from a negative produced in Mathew Brady's studio. He writes that his hair appears whiter than it is: "The sun
has an ill-natured pleasure, I believe, in making me look as old as himself" (F. L. Pleadwell Collection).*

before my intellectual faculties are quite extinguished, it strikes me that I would make a very pretty book out of it; and, seriously, if I alone were concerned, I should not have any great objection to winding up there."

On the 14th of November came a pleasant little note from him, which seemed to have been written in better spirits than he had shown of late. Photographs of himself always amused him greatly, and in the little note I refer to there is this pleasant passage:–

"Here is the photograph,–a grandfatherly old figure enough; and I suppose that is the reason why you select it.

"I am much in want of *cartes de visite* to distribute on my own account, and am tired and disgusted with all the undesirable likenesses as yet presented of me. Don't you think I might sell my head to some photographer who would be willing to return me the value in small change; that is to say, in a dozen or two of cards?"

The first part of Chapter I. of "The Dolliver Romance" came to me from the Wayside on the 1st of December. Hawthorne was very anxious to see it in type as soon as possible, in order that he might compose the rest in a similar strain, and so conclude the preliminary phase of Dr. Dolliver. He was constantly imploring me to send him a good pen, complaining all the while that everything had failed him in that line. In one of his notes begging me to hunt him up something that he could write with, he says:–

"Nobody ever suffered more from pens than I have, and I am glad that my labor with the abominable little tool is drawing to a close."

In the month of December Hawthorne attended the funeral of Mrs. Franklin Pierce, and, after the ceremony, came to stay with us. He seemed ill and more nervous than usual. He said he found General Pierce greatly needing his companionship, for he was overwhelmed with grief at the loss of his wife. I well remember the sadness of Hawthorne's face when he told us he felt obliged to look on the dead. "It was," said he, "like a carven image laid in its richly embossed enclosure, and there was a remote expression about it as if the whole had nothing to do with things present." He told us, as an instance of the ever-constant courtesy of his friend General Pierce, that while they were standing at the grave, the General, though completely overcome with his own sorrow, turned and drew up the collar of Hawthorne's coat to shield him from the bitter cold.

. . . .

On the 15th of December Hawthorne wrote to me:–

"I have not yet had courage to read the Dolliver proof-sheet, but will set about it soon, though with terrible reluctance, such as I never felt before. . . . . I am most grateful to you for protecting me from that visitation of the elephant and his cub. If you happen to see Mr. — or L—, a young man who was here last summer, pray tell him anything that your conscience will let you, to induce him to spare me another visit, which I know he intended. I really am not well and cannot be disturbed by strangers without more suffering than it is worth while to endure. I thank Mrs. F— and yourself for your kind hospitality, past and prospective. I never come to see you without feeling the better for it, but I must not test so precious a remedy too often."

The new year found him incapacitated from writing much on the Romance. On the 17th of January, 1864, he says:–

"I am not quite up to writing yet, but shall make an effort as soon as I see any hope of success. You ought to be thankful that (like most other broken-down authors) I do not pester you with decrepit pages, and insist upon your accepting them as full of the old spirit and vigor. That trouble, perhaps, still awaits you, after I shall have reached a further stage of decay. Seriously, my mind has, for the present, lost its temper and its fine edge, and I have an instinct that I had better keep quiet. Perhaps I shall have a new spirit of vigor, if I wait quietly for it; perhaps not."

The end of February found him in a mood which is best indicated in this letter, which he addressed to me on the 25th of the month:–

"I hardly know what to say to the public about this abortive Romance, though I know pretty well what the case will be. I shall never finish it. Yet it is not quite pleasant for an author to announce himself, or to be announced, as finally broken down as to his literary faculty. It is a pity that I let you put this work in your programme for the year, for I had always a presentiment that it would fail us at the pinch. Say to the public what you think best, and as little as possible; for example: 'We regret that Mr. Hawthorne's Romance, announced for this magazine some months ago, still lies upon the author's writing-table, he having been interrupted in his labor upon it by an impaired state of health'; or, 'We are sorry to hear (but know not whether the public will share our grief) that Mr. Hawthorne is out of health and is thereby prevented, for the present, from proceeding with another of the promised (or threatened) Romances, intended for this magazine'; or, 'Mr. Hawthorne's brain is addled at last, and, much to our satisfaction, he tells us that he cannot possibly go on with the Romance announced on the cover of the January magazine. We consider him finally shelved,

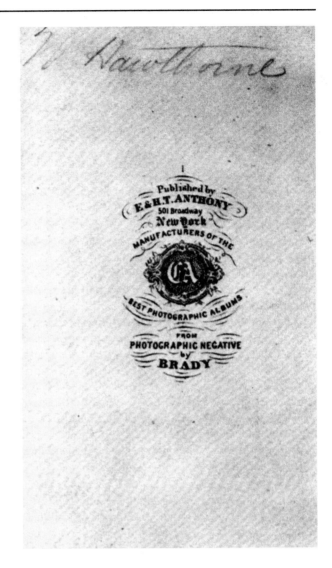

Front and back of a carte de visite *made from a photograph by Alexander Gardner for Mathew Brady*

and shall take early occasion to bury him under a heavy article, carefully summing up his merits (such as they were) and his demerits, what few of them can touched upon in our limited space'; or, 'We shall commence the publication of Mr. Hawthorne's Romance as soon as that gentleman chooses to forward it. We are quite at a loss how to account for this delay in the fulfilment of his contract; especially as he has already been most liberally paid for the first number.' Say anything you like, in short, though I really don't believe that the public will care what you say or whether you say anything. If you choose, you may publish the first chapter as an insulated fragment, and charge me with the overpayment. I cannot finish it unless a great change comes over me; and if I make too great an effort to do so, it will be my death; not that I should care much for that, if I could fight the battle through and win it, thus end-

ing a life of much smoulder and scanty fire in a blaze of glory. But I should smother myself in mud of my own making. I mean to come to Boston soon, not for a week but for a single day, and then I can talk about my sanitary prospects more freely than I choose to write. I am not low-spirited, nor fanciful, nor freakish, but look what seem to be realities in the face, and am ready to take whatever may come. If I could but go to England now, I think that the sea voyage and the 'Old Home' might set me all right.

"This letter is for your own eye, and I wish especially that no echo of it may come back in your notes to me.

"P.S. Give my kindest regards to Mrs. F—, and tell her that one of my choicest ideal places is her drawing-room, and therefore I seldom visit it."

On Monday, the 28th of March, Hawthorne came to town and made my house his first station on a journey to the South for health. I was greatly shocked at his invalid appearance, and he seemed quite deaf. The light in his eye was beautiful as ever, but his limbs seemed shrunken and his usual stalwart vigor utterly gone. He said to me with a pathetic voice, "Why does Nature treat us like little children! I think we could bear it all if we knew our fate; at least it would not make much difference to me now what became of me." Toward night he brightened up a little, and his delicious wit flashed out, at intervals, as of old; but he was evidently broken and dispirited about his health. Looking out on the bay that was sparkling in the moonlight, he said he thought the moon rather lost something of its charm for him as he grew older. He spoke with great delight of a little story, called "Pet Marjorie," and said he had read it carefully through twice, every word of it. He had much to say about England, and observed, among other things, that "the extent over which her dominions are spread leads her to fancy herself stronger than she really is; but she is not to-day a powerful empire; she is much like a squash-vine, which runs over a whole garden, but, if you cut it at the root, it is at once destroyed." At breakfast, next morning, he spoke of his kind neighbors in Concord, and said Alcott was one of the most excellent men he had ever known. "It is impossible to quarrel with him, for he would take all your harsh words like a saint."

He left us shortly after this for a journey to Washington, with his friend Mr. Ticknor. The travellers spent several days in New York, and then proceeded to Philadelphia. Hawthorne wrote to me from the Continental Hotel, dating his letter "Saturday evening," announcing the severe illness of his companion. He did not seem to anticipate a fatal result, but on Sunday morning the news came that Mr. Ticknor was dead. Hawthorne returned at once to Boston, and stayed here over night. He was in a very excited and nervous state, and talked incessantly of the sad scenes he had just been passing through. We sat late together, conversing of the friend we had lost, and I am sure he hardly closed his eyes that night. In the morning he went back to his own home in Concord.

His health, from that time, seemed to give way rapidly, and in the middle of May his friend, General Pierce, proposed that they should go among the New Hampshire hills together and meet the spring there.

The first letter we received from Mrs. Hawthorne after her husband's return to Concord in April gave us great anxiety. It was dated "Monday eve," and here are some extracts from it:—

> "I have just sent Mr. Hawthorne to bed, and so have a moment to speak to you. Generally it has been late and I have not liked to disturb him by sitting up after

him, and so I could not write since he returned, though I wished very much to tell you about him, ever since he came home. He came back unlooked for that day; and when I heard a step on the piazza, I was lying on a couch and feeling quite indisposed. But as soon as I saw him I was frightened out of all knowledge of myself,—so haggard, so white, so deeply scored with pain and fatigue was the face, so much more ill he looked than I ever saw him before. He had walked from the station because he saw no carriage there, and his brow was streaming with a perfect rain, so great had been the effort to walk so far. . . . . He needed much to get home to me, where he could fling off all care of himself and give way to his feelings, pent up and kept back for so long, especially since his watch and ward of most excellent, kind Mr. Ticknor. It relieved him somewhat to break down as he spoke of that scene. . . . . But he was so weak and weary he could not sit up much, and lay on the couch nearly all the time in a kind of uneasy somnolency, not wishing to be read to even, not able to attend or fix his thoughts at all. On Saturday he unfortunately took cold, and, after a most restless night, was seized early in the morning with a very bad stiff neck, which was acutely painful all Sunday. Sunday night, however, a compress of linen wrung in cold water cured him, with belladonna. But he slept almost most of this morning. . . . . He could as easily build London as go to the Shakespeare dinner. It tires him so much to get entirely through his toilet in the morning, that he has to lie down a long time after it. To-day he walked out on the grounds, and could not stay ten minutes, because I would not let him sit down in the wind, and he could not bear any longer exercise. He has more than lost all he gained by the journey, by the sad event. From being the nursed and cared for,—early to bed and late to rise,—led, as it were, by the ever-ready hand of kind Mr. Ticknor, to become the nurse and night-watcher with all the responsibilities, with his mighty power of sympathy and his vast apprehension of suffering in others, and to see death for the first time in a state so weak as his,—the death also of so valued a friend,—as Mr. Hawthorne says himself, 'it told upon him' fearfully. There are lines ploughed on his brow which never were there before. . . . . I have been up and alert ever since his return, but one day I was obliged, when he was busy, to run off and lie down for fear I should drop before his eyes. My head was in such an agony I could not endure it another moment. But I am well now. I have wrestled and won, and now I think I shall not fail again. Your most generous kindness of hospitality I heartily thank you for, but Mr. Hawthorne says he cannot leave home. He wants rest, and he says when the wind is *warm* he shall feel well. This cold wind ruins him. I wish he were in Cuba or on some isle in the Gulf Stream. But I must say I could not think him able to go anywhere, unless I could go with him. He is too weak to take care of himself. I do not like to have him go up and down stairs alone. I have read to him all the afternoon and evening and after he walked in the morning to-day. I do nothing but sit with him, ready to do or not to do, just as he wishes. The wheels

First page of Hawthorne's 8 January 1863 letter to Samuel M. Cleveland, the compiler of A Compendium of American
Literature *(1858). The author, who recalls burning his earliest tales, names "The Gentle Boy" and "Roger Malvin's
Burial" as his earliest surviving stories (Peabody Essex Museum).*

of my small *ménage* are all stopped. He is my world and all the business of it. He has not smiled since he came home till to-day, and I made him laugh with Thackeray's humor in reading to him; but a smile looks strange on a face that once shone like a thousand suns with smiles. The light for the time has gone out of his eyes, entirely. An infinite weariness films them quite. I thank Heaven that summer and not winter approaches."

On Friday evening of the same week Mrs. Hawthorne sent off another dispatch to us:–

"Mr. Hawthorne has been miserably ill for two or three days, so that I could not find a moment to speak to you. I am most anxious to have him leave Concord again, and General Pierce's plan is admirable, now that the General is well himself. I think the serene jog-trot in a private carriage into country places, by trout-streams and to old farm-houses, away from care and news, will be very restorative. The boy associations with the General will refresh him. They will fish, and muse, and rest, and saunter upon horses' feet, and be in the air all the time in fine weather. I am quite content, though I wish I could go for a few *petits soins*. But General Pierce has been a most tender, constant nurse for many years, and knows how to take care of the sick. And his love for Mr. Hawthorne is the strongest passion of his soul, now his wife is departed. They will go to the Isles of Shoals together probably, before their return.

"Mr. Hawthorne cannot walk ten minutes now without wishing to sit down, as I think I told you, so that he cannot take sufficient air except in a carriage. And his horror of hotels and rail-cars is immense, and human beings beset him in cities. He is indeed *very* weak. I hardly know what takes away his strength. I now am obliged to superintend my workman, who is arranging the grounds. Whenever my husband lies down (which is sadly often) I rush out of doors to see what the gardener is about.

"I cannot feel rested till Mr. Hawthorne is better, but I get along. I shall go to town when he is safe in the care of General Pierce."

On Saturday morning this communication from Mrs. Hawthorne reached us:–

"General Pierce wrote yesterday to say he wished to meet Mr. Hawthorne in Boston on Wednesday, and go from thence on their way.

"Mr. Hawthorne is much weaker, I find, than he has been before at any time, and I shall go down with him, having a great many things to do in Boston; but I am sure he is not fit to be left by himself, for his steps are so uncertain, and his eyes are very uncertain too. Dear Mr. Fields, I am very anxious about him, and I write now to say that he absolutely refuses to see a physician officially, and so I wish to know whether Dr. Holmes could not see him in some ingenious way on Wednesday as a friend; but with his experienced, acute obser-

vation, to look at him also as a physician, to note how he is and what he judges of him comparatively since he last saw him. It almost deprives me of my wits to see him growing weaker with no aid. He seems quite bilious, and has a restlessness that is infinite. His look is more distressed and harassed than before; and he has so little rest, that he is getting worn out. I hope immensely in regard of this sauntering journey with General Pierce.

"I feel as if I ought not to speak to you of anything when you are so busy and weary and bereaved. But yet in such a sad emergency as this, I am sure your generous, kind heart will not refuse me any help you can render. . . . . I wish Dr. Holmes would feel his pulse; I do not know how to judge of it, but it seems to me irregular."

. . . .

I saw Hawthorne alive, for the last time, the day he started on this his last mortal journey. His speech and his gait indicated severe illness, and I had great misgivings about the jaunt he was proposing to take so early in the season. His tones were more subdued than ever, and he scarcely spoke above a whisper. He was very affectionate in parting, and I followed him to the door, looking after him as he went up School Street. I noticed that he faltered from weakness, and I should have taken my hat and joined him to offer my arm, but I knew he did not wish to *seem* ill, and I feared he might be troubled at my anxiety. Fearing to disturb him, I followed him with my eyes only, and watched him till he turned the corner and passed out of sight.

On the morning of the 19th of May, 1864, a telegram, signed by Franklin Pierce, stunned us all. It announced the death of Hawthorne. In the afternoon of the same day came this letter to me:–

"PEMIGEWASSET HOUSE, PLYMOUTH, N. H.,
Thursday morning, 5 o'clock
"MY DEAR SIR,–The telegraph has communicated to you the fact of our dear friend Hawthorne's death. My friend Colonel Hibbard, who bears this note, was a friend of H—, and will tell you more than I am able to write.

"I enclose herewith a note which I commenced last evening to dear Mrs. Hawthorne. O, how will she bear this shock! Dear mother–dear children–

"When I met Hawthorne in Boston a week ago, it was apparent that he was much more feeble and more seriously diseased than I had supposed him to be. We came from Centre Harbor yesterday afternoon, and I thought he was on the whole brighter than he was the day before. Through the week he had been inclined to somnolency during the day, but restless at night. He retired last night soon after nine o'clock, and soon fell into a quiet slumber. In less than half an hour changed his position, but continued to sleep. I left the door open between his bedroom and mine,–our beds being opposite to each other,–and was asleep myself before eleven

To a Friend.

The first page of a four-page letter from Hawthorne to Franklin Pierce. Hawthorne included this letter at the beginning of Our Old Home *(1863), which he dedicated to Pierce (Henry E. Huntington Library, San Marino, California).*

Portrait of Hawthorne painted in 1862 by Emanuel G. Leutze, who was famous for his painting of George Washington crossing the Delaware. This portrait was the last oil painting for which the author sat (National Portrait Gallery, Washington, D.C.).

o'clock. The light continued to burn in my room. At two o'clock, I went to H—'s bedside; he was apparently in a sound sleep, and I did not place my hand upon him. At four o'clock I went into his room again, and, as his position was unchanged, I placed my hand upon him and found that life was extinct. I sent, however, immediately for a physician, and called Judge Bell and Colonel Hibbard, who occupied rooms upon the same floor and near me. He lies upon his side, his position so perfectly natural and easy, his eyes closed, that it is difficult to realize, while looking upon his noble face, that this is death. He must have passed from natural slumber to that from which there is no waking without the slightest movement.

"I cannot write to dear Mrs. Hawthorne, and you must exercise your judgment with regard to sending this and the unfinished note, enclosed, to her.

"Your friend,

"FRANKLIN PIERCE."

Hawthorne's lifelong desire that the end might be a sudden one was gratified. Often and often he has said to me, "What a blessing to go quickly!" So the same swift angel that came as a messenger to Allston, Irving, Prescott, Macaulay, Thackeray, and Dickens was commissioned to touch his forehead, also, and beckon him away.

The room in which death fell upon him,

"Like a shadow thrown
Softly and lightly from a passing cloud,"

The grave of Nathaniel Hawthorne in Sleepy Hollow Cemetery, Concord (photograph by Edwin Haviland Miller)

looks toward the east; and standing in it, as I have frequently done, since he passed out silently into the skies, it is easy to imagine the scene on that spring morning which President Pierce so feelingly describes in his letter.

On the 24th of May we carried Hawthorne through the blossoming orchards of Concord, and laid him down under a group of pines, on a hillside, overlooking historic fields. All the way from the village church to the grave the birds kept up a perpetual melody. The sun shone brightly, and the air was sweet and pleasant, as if death had never entered the world. Longfellow and Emerson, Channing and Hoar, Agassiz and Lowell, Greene and Whipple, Alcott and Clarke, Holmes and Hillard, and other friends whom he loved, walked slowly by his side that beautiful spring morning. The companion of his youth and his manhood, for whom he would willingly, at any time, have given up his own life, Franklin Pierce, was there among the rest, and scattered flowers into the grave. The unfinished Romance, which had cost him so much anxiety, the last literary work on which he had ever been engaged, was laid on his coffin.

> "Ah ! who shall lift that wand of magic power,
>   And the lost clew regain?
> The unfinished window in Aladdin's tower
>   Unfinished must remain."

Longfellow's beautiful poem will always be associated with the memory of Hawthorne, and most fitting was it that his fellow-student, whom he so loved and honored, should sing his requiem.

—Yesterdays with Authors, pp. 94–124

Henry Fothergill Chorley

Tributes

English reviewer Henry F. Chorley commented on Hawthorne's works often, and the two men met in England in 1859.

Nathaniel Hawthorne
Henry F. Chorley
Athenaeum, 1911 (11 June 1864): 808

An original mind, an original fancy, an original nature as regards social intercourse have gone from the world of poetical fiction in the person of the author of *The Scarlet Letter.* America has few, if any, such complete authors and complete artists left as Nathaniel Hawthorne, who died suddenly, though after a period of ill-health, at Plymouth, N.H., on the 19th of May.

The events of his life were these. He was born at Salem, Mass., in 1804; was educated at Bowden College,

in the same class as Prof. Longfellow; early began to write; after a period of narrow circumstances, received an appointment from the Boston Custom House, and subsequently one at the Port of Salem; breaking away for a while from official life to join the experimental Socialist colony at Brook Farm, and relinquishing it in 1849. After some years of literary toil, Hawthorne was nominated, by his old schoolfellow, Franklin Pierce, to the post of American Consul at Liverpool. There he remained for only a few years, being by this time married. On resigning what must have been, for one of his disposition, most uncongenial duties, he made a prolonged journey abroad and residence at Rome, to which we owe his last novel, *Transformation.* He returned home from his sojourn in 'the old country,' and when, again, in America, yielding to the bad and irritating temptations of the time, gave out his last collection of papers—his ill-natured Essays on England—to the sorrow of his admirers here.

We may well feel more than ordinary sadness in recording the departure of one so distinct, so national and yet so universal as Hawthorne from the world of poetical fiction; because it was this journal, if we do not mistake, which first drew attention to his genius. Some time before his *Twice-told Tales* were collectedly published, in the year 1837, the *Athenæum,* without the slightest clue to their authorship, had singled out one or two of the sketches which had figured in the American periodicals as something remarkable and precious, for their delicacy, quaintness and colour, which could only be attained by a Transatlantic author,–a colour, to boot, widely different from that of Irving's 'Knickerbocker' legends,–and still more finely apart from the tint of Brockden Brown's stories, which, American as they were, were modelled after the fashion of Godwin, even as Fenimore Cooper's were according to the pattern of the Scott romances. At first they attracted not much attention among the many, but sufficient to make their writer sought for by the managers of periodicals. They were presently followed by other miscellanies and books for children, and by four novels, two of which were *The Scarlet Letter* and *The House of the Seven Gables*. The publication of these drew the attention of Europe to Hawthorne, as one of the greatest and most individual masters of fiction living, and his tales were thenceforth eagerly sought for, and translated, as we know, into French, German, Russian, and probably other foreign languages. The terse vigour of their style, combined with a quaint and dreamy fancy,–the hold with which the stories of *The Scarlet Letter* and *The House of the Seven Gables* grasp the reader,–the vigorous and delicate markings of character, as in the erring minister, who tempted Hester Prynne to shame, and the poor brain-crazed creature in *The House,*–the exquisite power of description, witness the pictures of the Borghese garden at Rome, in *Monte Beni,* could not fail to arrest the sympathy of all who appreciate what is best in Art, and to be remembered. If ever there lived an imaginative writer, who had a manner of his own–not therefore a mannerism,–it was Nathaniel Hawthorne.

The man was, in every respect, singular. With a handsome presence, and no common powers of pleasing, when once a way was forced to them (the word is not too strong), he hid himself from his popularity and its privileges, with a shyness which might have been misread for affectation, had it not been persistent,–or for sullenness by those who never saw the bright candid smile, and never heard the genial talk in which he could indulge, when he could prevail on himself to break the spell. But this happened rarely. It may be questioned whether, during his years of residence in England, when hospitalities and offers of service, distinct from the vulgarities of lionism, were pressed on him by the best of his literary brethren, he made personal acquaintance with a dozen among them, though he knew and appreciated their works. Those whom he did meet, could not but be impressed favourably by his bearing and conversation. It may be added, as close to a hasty sketch of a subject singularly difficult and delicate to treat at a moment's warning, that Hawthorne was as fortunate as he was amiable in his domestic life. He leaves, we repeat, a wide and deep void in the rank of American authors.

Oliver Wendell Holmes

Oliver Wendell Holmes was a doctor as well as a literary man. His most celebrated work, The Autocrat of the Breakfast-Table *(1858), was composed of the imaginary table talk at a Boston boardinghouse and included such poems as "The Chambered Nautilus" and "The Deacon's Masterpiece." Holmes and Hawthorne, along with such writers as Ralph Waldo Emerson, Henry Wadsworth Longfellow, John Greenleaf Whittier, and James Russell Lowell, were members of* The Saturday Club.

Hawthorne
Oliver Wendell Holmes
Atlantic Monthly, 14 (July 1864): 98–101

It is with a sad pleasure that the readers of this magazine will see in its pages the first chapter of *The Dolliver Romance,* the latest record of Nathaniel Hawthorne meant for the public eye. The charm of his description and the sweet flow of his style will lead all who open upon it to read on to the closing paragraph. With its harmonious cadences the music of this quaint, mystic overture is suddenly hushed, and we seem to hear instead the tolling of a bell in the far distance. The procession of shadowy characters which was gathering in our imaginations about the ancient man and the little child who come so clearly before our sight seems to fade away, and in its place a slow-pacing train winds through the village-road and up the wooded hillside until it stops at a little opening among the tall trees. There the bed is made in which he whose dreams had peopled our common life with shapes and thoughts of beauty and wonder is to take his rest. This is the end of the first chapter we have been reading, and of that other first chapter in the life of an Immortal, whose folded pages will be opened, we trust, in the light of a brighter day.

It was my fortune to be among the last of the friends who looked upon Hawthorne's living face. Late in the afternoon of the day before he left Boston on his last journey I called upon him at the hotel where he was staying. He had gone out but a moment before. Looking along the street, I saw a figure at some distance in advance which could only be his,—but how changed

An interior view of the hotel founded in 1855 by Harvey D. Parker, where the members of The Saturday Club met

The Saturday Club

The Saturday Club met from 1855 on the fourth Saturday of each month, at the Parker House hotel, on Tremont Street, not far from The Old Corner Bookstore in Boston. The club began as a meeting of literary men concerned with the Atlantic Monthly *magazine, of which Oliver Wendell Holmes and James T. Fields were original editors. Fields recalls Hawthorne's participation in* Yesterdays with Authors: *"After he was chosen a member of the Saturday Club he came frequently to dinner with Felton, Longfellow, Holmes, and the rest of his friends, who assembled once a month to dine together. At the table, on these occasions, he was rather reticent than conversational, but when he chose to talk it was observed that the best things said that day came from him." Holmes's poem "At the Saturday Club" (1884) includes a reference to Hawthorne:*

But who is he whose massive frame belies
The maiden shyness of his downcast eyes?
Who broods in silence till, by questions pressed,
Some answer struggles from his laboring breast?
An artist Nature meant to dwell apart,
Locked in his studio with a human heart,
Tracking its caverned passions to their lair,
And all its throbbing mysteries laying bare.

Count it no marvel that he broods alone
Over the heart he studies,— 'tis his own;
So in his page, whatever shape it wear,
The Essex wizard's shadowed self is there,—
The great ROMANCER, hid beneath his veil
Like the stern preacher of his sombre tale;
Virile in strength, yet bashful as a girl,
Prouder than Hester, sensitive as Pearl.

from his former port and figure! There was no mistaking the long iron-gray locks, the carriage of the head, and the general look of the natural outlines and movement; but he seemed to have shrunken in all his dimensions, and faltered along with an uncertain, feeble step, as if every movement were an effort. I joined him, and we walked together half an hour, during which time I learned so much of his state of mind and body as could be got at without worrying him with suggestive questions,—my object being to form an opinion of his condition, as I had been requested to do, and to give him some hints that might be useful to him on his journey.

His aspect, medically considered, was very unfavorable. There were persistent local symptoms, referred especially to the stomach,—'boring pain,' distension, difficult digestion, with great wasting of flesh and strength. He was very gentle, very willing to answer questions, very docile to such counsel as I offered him, but evidently had no hope of recovering his health. He spoke as if his work were done, and he should write no more.

With all his obvious depression, there was no failing noticeable in his conversational powers. There was the same backwardness and hesitancy which in his best days it was hard for him to overcome, so that talking with him was almost like lovemaking, and his shy, beautiful soul had to be wooed from its bashful pudency like an unschooled maiden. The calm despondency with which he spoke about himself confirmed the unfavorable opinion suggested by his look and history.

The journey on which Mr Hawthorne was setting out, when I saw him, was undertaken for the benefit of his health. A few weeks earlier he had left Boston on a similar errand in company with Mr William D. Ticknor, who had kindly volunteered to be his companion in a trip which promised to be of some extent and duration, and from which this faithful friend, whose generous devotion deserves the most grateful remembrance, hoped to bring him back restored, or at least made stronger. Death joined the travellers, but it was not the invalid whom he selected as his victim. The strong man was taken, and the suffering valetudinarian found himself charged with those last duties which he was so soon to need at the hands of others. The fatigue of mind and body thus substituted for the recreation which he greatly needed must have hastened the course of his disease, or at least have weakened his powers of resistance to no small extent.

Once more, however, in company with his old college-friend and classmate, Ex-President Pierce, he made the attempt to recover his lost health by this second journey. My visit to him on the day before his departure was a somewhat peculiar one, partly of friendship, but partly also in compliance with the request I have referred to.

I asked only such questions as were like to afford practical hint as to the way in which he should manage himself on his journey. It was more important that he should go away as hopeful as might be than that a searching examination should point him to the precise part diseased, condemning him to a forlorn self-knowledge such as the masters of the art of diagnosis sometimes rashly substitute for the ignorance which is comparative happiness. Being supposed to remember something of the craft pleasantly satirized in the chapter before us, I volunteered, not 'an infallible panacea of my own distillation,' but some familiar palliatives which I hoped might relieve the symptoms of which he complained most. The history of his disease must, I suppose, remain unwritten, and perhaps it is just as well that it should be so. Men of sensibility and genius hate to have their infirmities dragged out of them by the

roots in exhaustive series of cross-questionings and harassing physical explorations, and he who has enlarged the domain of the human soul may perhaps be spared his contribution to the pathology of the human body. At least, I was thankful that it was not my duty to sound all the jarring chords of this sensitive organism, and that a few cheering words and the prescription of a not ungrateful sedative and cordial or two could not lay on me the reproach of having given him his 'final bitter taste of this world, perhaps doomed to be a recollected nauseousness in the next.'

There was nothing in Mr Hawthorne's aspect that gave warning of so sudden an end as that which startled us all. It seems probable that he died by the gentlest of all modes of release, fainting, without the trouble and confusion of coming back to life,—a way of ending liable to happen in any disease attended with much debility.

Mr Hawthorne died in the town of Plymouth, New Hampshire, on the nineteenth of May. The moment, and even the hour, could not be told, for he had passed away without giving any sign of suffering, such as might call the attention of the friend near him. On Monday, the twenty-third of May, his body was given back to earth in the place where he had long lived, and which he had helped to make widely known,—the ancient town of Concord.

The day of his burial will always live in the memory of all who shared in its solemn, grateful duties. All the fair sights and sweet sounds of the opening season mingled their enchantments as if in homage to the dead master, who, as a lover of Nature and a student of life, had given such wealth of poetry to our New-England home, and invested the stern outlines of Puritan character with the colors of romance. It was the bridal day of the season, perfect in light as if heaven were looking on, perfect in air as if Nature herself were sighing for our loss. The orchards were all in fresh flower,—

One boundless blush, one white-empurpled shower
Of mingled blossoms;—

the banks were literally blue with violets; the elms were putting out their tender leaves, just in that passing aspect which Raphael loved to pencil in the backgrounds of his holy pictures, not as yet printing deep shadows, but only mottling the sunshine at their feet. The birds were in full song; the pines were musical with the soft winds they sweetened. All was in faultless accord, and every heart was filled with the beauty that flooded the landscape.

The church where the funeral services were performed was luminous with the whitest blossoms of the luxuriant spring. A great throng of those who loved him, of those who honored his genius, of those who held him in kindly esteem as a neighbor and friend, filled the edifice. Most of those who were present wished to look once more at the features which they remembered with the lights and shadows of life's sunshine upon them. The cold moonbeam of death lay white on the noble forehead and still, placid features; but they never looked fuller of power than in his last aspect with which they met the eyes that were turned upon them.

In a patch of sunlight, flecked by the shade of tall, murmuring pines, at the summit of a gently swelling mound where the wild-flowers had climbed to find the light and the stirring of fresh breezes, the tired poet was laid beneath the green turf. Poet let us call him, though his chants were not modulated in the rhythm of verse. The element of poetry is air: we know the poet by his atmospheric effects, by the blue of his distances, by the softening of every hard outline he touches, by the silvery mist in which he veils deformity and clothes what is common so that it changes to awe-inspiring mystery, by the clouds of gold and purple which are the drapery of his dreams. And surely we have had but one prose-writer who could be compared with him in aerial perspective, if we may use the painter's term. If Irving is the Claude of our unrhymed poetry, Hawthorne is its Poussin.

This is not the occasion for the analysis and valuation of Hawthorne's genius. If the reader wishes to see a thoughtful and generous estimate of his powers, and a just recognition of the singular beauty of his style, he may turn to the number of this magazine published in May, 1860. The last effort of Hawthorne's creative mind is before him in the chapter here printed. The hand of the dead master shows itself in every line. The shapes and scenes he pictures slide at once into our consciousness, as if they belonged there as much as our own homes and relatives. That limpid flow of expression, never laboring, never shallow, never hurried nor uneven nor turbid, but moving on with tranquil force, clear to the depths of its profoundest thought, shows itself with all its consummate perfections. Our literature could ill spare the rich ripe autumn of such a life as Hawthorne's, but he has left enough to keep his name in remembrance as long as the language in which he shaped his deep imagination is spoken by human lips.

Edward Dicey (from Herbert Mitgang, ed.,
Spectator of America, *1989)*

Edward Dicey was an English journalist who wrote about the American Civil War and European wars for British periodicals.

Nathaniel Hawthorne
Edward Dicey
Macmillan's Magazine, 10, no. 57 (1864): 241–246

All persons, I fancy, who have lived for a period in America must, at times, feel a sort of strange doubt as to whether their recollections are not creations of their own fancy. My life in the United States often seems to me, on looking back, like a stray chapter interleaved by mistake into the book of my existence. I have lived longer in other foreign countries, but in them I was always a stranger, and knew that I should remain so to the end. In the Northern States, I was, for the time, at home. I lived the life of the people amongst whom I was thrown. I learnt to know their family histories, the details of their household existence, the little cares and pleasures which make up the sum of daily life all the world over. For a time I was a sharer in this life, and then, with the sailing of the packet from the shores of the New World, the whole of this existence came to an abrupt close. So I often catch myself thinking about some home far away in that distant country, and wondering whether it looks the same as when I saw it last; and then, when the recollection comes that time has gone by, and that the children are growing up and have forgotten me, doubtless, long ago, the whole scene becomes so confused and hazy that I begin to doubt whether I have ever seen it or only have dreamed it. It is so hard to realize that if I returned I should not find things exactly as I left them: that, for instance, if I went back I should no longer find a welcome in the house of Hawthorne. Let me write of him as I knew him. Let me say a few words in recollection of a man of genius, whom it was my fortune to know somewhat intimately.

My acquaintance with Hawthorne was not one of long duration. I first shook hands with him one Sunday evening, at a Washington party, in the month of March 1861. I shook hands with him for the last time in parting at the door of his own house, at Concord, some three months later. Circumstances, however, rendered this acquaintance of a more intimate character than that which usually springs up from a chance letter of introduction; and I fancy that the knowledge I thus gained enabled me to understand something of the true nature of a man little understood in this country, and much misunderstood in his own. I need hardly say that the winter of 1862 was the first of the great civil war. McClellan was then in his glory as the young Napoleon; the grand army of the Potomac was just leaving its winter-quarters to commence what was regarded as a triumphal progress, and Washington was filled with travellers of all classes and all nations, gathered to witness the aspects of this vast struggle. Amongst others, Hawthorne had come there, in company with the late Mr Ticknor, the well-known Boston publisher. It was at a reception of my kind friend, Mrs E——, a lady whom every English visitor at Washington has cause to feel grateful to, that I met Hawthorne. I fancy that I had once seen him before in Rome. At any rate, his face seemed strangely familiar to me. He was utterly un-American in look—unlike, that is, the normal Yankee type, as we picture it to ourselves. As I write, I can see him now, with that grand, broad forehead, fringed scantily by the loose worn wavy hair, passing from black to grey, with the deep-sunk flashing eyes—sometimes bright, sometimes sad, and always 'distrait'-looking—as if they saw something beyond what common eyes could see, and with the soft feminine mouth, which, at its master's bidding—or, rather, at the bidding of some thought over which its master had no control—could smile so wondrous pleasantly. It was not a weak face—far from it. A child, I think, might have cheated Hawthorne; but there were few men who could have cheated him with-

out his knowing that he was being cheated. He was not English-looking except in as far as he was not American. When you had once gazed at his face or heard him speak, the very idea that he ever could have gone a-head in any way, or ever talked bunkum of any kind seemed an absurdity in itself. How he ever came to have been born in that bustling New World became, from the first moment I knew him, an increasing mystery to me. If ever a man was out of his right element it was Hawthorne in America. He belonged, indeed, to that scattered Shandean family, who never are in their right places wherever they happen to be born—to that race of Hamlets, to whom the world is always out of joint anywhere. His keen poetic instinct taught him to appreciate the latent poetry lying hid dimly in the great present and the greater future of the country in which his lot was thrown; and, though keenly, almost morbidly, sensitive to the faults and absurdities of his countrymen, he appreciated their high sterling merit with that instinctive justice which was the most remarkable attribute of his mind. England itself suited him but little better than the States—more especially that part of England with which his travels had made him most familiar. To have been a happy man, he should, I think, have been born in some southern land, where life goes onwards without changing, where social problems are unknown, and what has been yesterday is to-day, and which will be to-morrow. Never was a man less fitted to buffet out the battle of life amidst our Anglo-Saxon race. He held his own, indeed, manfully, and kept his head above those waters which so many men of genius have sunk. But the struggle was too much for him, and left him worn-out and weary. Had, however, the conditions of his life been more suited to his nature, he would, I suspect, have dreamed the long years away—and what he gained the world would have lost.

Before I met him for the first time, I was warned not to be surprised at his extreme shyness. The caution was not unneeded. There was something almost painful in the nervous timidity of his manner when a stranger first addressed him. My impression was that he meant to say, The kindest thing you can do is not to speak to me at all; and so, after a few formal phrases, of which I can recall nothing, our conversation ended, and, as I thought, our acquaintance also. Circumstances, however, threw us gradually together. There were, at that time, in Washington, numerous expeditions to the different localities of the war, to which we both were invited. The list of my acquaintances was necessarily small, as I was a stranger; and it so happened that persons with whom I was most intimate were also old friends of Hawthorne. Moreover—I say this out of no personal feeling, but in order to illustrate

Hawthorne (fifth from left) in Washington Irving and His Literary Friends at Sunnyside *(second version, 1864), an oil painting by Christian Schussele that was based on F.O.C. Darley's composite india-ink drawing honoring Irving after his death. Gathered in the late author's study at his home are, left to right, Henry T. Tuckerman, Holmes, William Gilmore Simms, Fitz-Greene Halleck, Hawthorne, Henry Wadsworth Longfellow, Nathaniel Parker Willis, William H. Prescott, Irving, James Kirke Paulding, Ralph Waldo Emerson, William Cullen Bryant, John Pendleton Kennedy, James Fenimore Cooper, and George Bancroft (National Portrait Gallery, Washington, D.C.).*

the character of the man of whom I write—he felt himself more at his ease with me than with his own countrymen at that particular crisis. The American mind, being of our own nature, is not a many-sided one. It grasps one idea, or rather one side of an idea, and holds it with a sublime and implicit confidence in the justice of its views. That McClellan was a heaven-born general, that the army of the Potomac must take Richmond, that the rebellion was nearly crushed, that the rebels were, one and all, villains of the deepest dye, that the North was wholly and altogether in the right, and the South wholly and altogether in the wrong, were axioms held in Washington, during the spring of 1862, as confidently and as unhesitatingly as we held an analogous belief during our wars with the Great Napoleon. Now, it was impossible for a man like Hawthorne to be an enthusiastic partisan. When Goethe was attacked, because he took no part in the patriotic movement which led to the war of German independence, he replied, 'I love my country, but I cannot hate the French.' So Hawthorne, loving the North, but not hating the South, felt himself altogether out of harmony with the passion of the hour. If he spoke his own mind freely, he was thought by those around him to be wanting in attachment to his country. And therefore, seeing that, I—though sympathizing with the cause which at least was his cause also—could not look upon it after the fashion of Americans, he seemed to take a pleasure in talking to me about his views. Many are the conversations that I have had with him, both about the war and about slavery. To make his position intelligible, let me repeat an anecdote which was told me by a very near friend of his and mine, who had heard it from President Pierce himself. Frank Pierce had been, and was to the day of Hawthorne's death, one of the oldest of his friends. At the time of the Presidential election of 1856, Hawthorne, for once, took part in politics, wrote a pamphlet in favour of his friend, and took a most unusual interest in his success. When the result of the nomination was known, and Pierce was president-elect, Hawthorne was among the first to come and wish him joy. He sat down in the room moodily and silently, as was his wont when anything troubled him; then, without speaking a word, he shook Pierce warmly by the hand, and at last remarked, 'Ah, Frank, what a pity!' The moment the victory was won, that timid, hesitating mind saw the evils of the successful course—the advantages of the one which had not been followed. So it was always. Of two lines of action, he was perpetually in doubt which was the best; and so, between the two, he always inclined to letting things remain as they are. Nobody disliked slavery more cordially than he did; and yet the difficulty of what was to be done with the slaves weighed constantly upon his mind. He told me once, that, while he had been consul at Liverpool, a vessel arrived there with a number of negro sailors, who had been brought from the slave-states and would, of course, be enslaved again on their return. He fancied that he ought to inform the men of the fact, but then he was stopped by the reflection—who was to provide for them if they became free; and, as he said, with a sigh, 'while I was thinking the vessel sailed.' So I recollect, on the old battle-field of Manassas, in which I strolled in company with Hawthorne, meeting a batch of runaway slaves—weary, footsore, wretched, and helpless beyond conception; we gave them food and wine, some small sums of money, and got them a lift upon a train going Northwards; but not long afterwards, Hawthorne turned to me with the remark, 'I am not sure we were doing right after all. How can those poor beings find food and shelter away from home?' Thus this ingrained and inherent doubt incapacitated him from following any course vigorously. He thought, on the whole, that Wendell Philips and Lloyd Garrison and the Absolutionists were in the right, but then he was never quite certain that they were not in the wrong after all; so that his advocacy of their cause was of a very uncertain character. He saw the best, to alter slightly the famous Horatian line, but he never could quite make up his mind whether he altogether approved of its wisdom, and therefore followed it but falteringly;

> Better to bear those ills we have
> Than fly to others that we know not of,

expressed the philosophy to which Hawthorne was thus borne imperceptibly. Unjustly, but yet not unreasonably, he was looked upon as a pro-slavery man, and suspected of Southern sympathies. In politics he was always halting between two opinions; or, rather, holding one opinion, he could never summon up his courage to adhere to it and it only. Moreover, if I am to speak the truth, the whole nature of Hawthorne shrank from the rough wear and tear inseparable from great popular movements of any kind. His keen observant intellect served to show him the weaknesses and vanities and vulgarities of the whole class of reformers. He recognised that their work was good; he admired the thoroughness he could not imitate; but somehow the details of popular agitation were strangely offensive to him. On one occasion I was present with Hawthorne at a great picnic, where the chief celebrities of the then new Republican Congress were assembled. Many of them were men who had come raw from the Western States, with all the manners and customs of those half-civilized communities. There was a good deal of horse-play and rough joking and good-humoured vulgarity, sufficient to amuse, without annoying, any one who liked to observe eccentricity of character. But to Hawthorne the whole scene seemed inexpressively disagreeable and repulsive, and I shall never forget the expression of intense disgust with which he turned to me, after a leading senator had enlivened the day by telling a very broad story in front of a bar where we all were liquoring, and whispered, 'How would *you* like to see the Lord Chancellor of England making a fool of himself in a pot-house?' And so this fastidiousness often, I think, obscured the usual accuracy of his judgment. The impression, for instance, made upon him by the personal manner and behaviour of President Lincoln was so inconsistent with his own ideas of dignity, that he longed, as I know, to describe him as he really appeared, and only failed to do so, in his 'Sketches of the War,' in consequence of the representations of his friends. Still, I can recall how, after he had been describing to me the impression left upon him by his visit to the White House, an eminently characteristic doubt crossed his mind as to whether he was not in the wrong. 'Somehow,' he said, 'though why I could never discern, I have always observed that the popular instinct chooses the right man at the right time. But then,' he added, 'as you have seen Lincoln, I wish you could have seen Pierce too; you would have seen a real gentleman.'

Thus, about the whole question of the war, Hawthorne's mind was, I think, always hovering between two views. He sympathised with the war in principle; but its inevitable accessories—the bloodshed, the bustle, and, above all perhaps, the bunkum which accompanied it—were to him absolutely hateful. Never was a man more strangely misplaced by fate than Hawthorne in that revolutionary war-time. His clear powerful intellect dragged him one way, and his delicate sensitive taste the other. That he was not in harmony with the tone of his countrymen was to him a real trouble, and he envied keenly the undoubting faith in the justice of their cause, which was possessed by the brother men-of-letters among whom he lived. To any one who knew the man, the mere fact that Hawthorne should have been able to make up his mind to the righteousness and expediency of the war at all, is evidence of the strength of that popular passion which has driven the North into conflict with the South. It was curious to me at that time to see how universal this conviction of the justice of the war was amongst the American people. A man less like Hawthorne than his friend and companion Ticknor cannot well be conceived. A shrewd, kindly man of business, with little sentiment in his disposition, he valued, and was valued by, Hawthorne—exactly because each possessed the qualities in which the other was deficient. In a different way, and on different grounds, he was, perhaps, naturally more adverse to the war than even Hawthorne himself. Ticknor, as I knew him, always seemed to me a man who took life very pleasantly—eminently not a reformer; ready enough, after a kindly fashion, to think that everything was for the best in the best possible of worlds; and well inclined towards the Southerners, with whom he had had business and personal relations of old standing date. I remember, one night that I passed at his house, his telling me, as we sat alone upstairs smoking after the family were gone to bed, that often and often he could not get to sleep because he felt so wretched when he thought of the war then raging in the land he had known so peaceful and so prosperous. And yet he also had, as far as I could learn, no question whatever that the war he deplored so much was righteous and inevitable.

But I wish not to wander into politics. I am thinking now rather of the contrast between those two friends—one so shrewd, the other so simple—both so kind. Their relation was more like that of old school-boy friends than the ordinary one of author and publisher. Ticknor was so proud of Hawthorne and Hawthorne was so fond of Ticknor; and yet in a relationship of this kind there was absolutely no loss of dignity on either side. When I was in Boston, Hawthorne was going to write—or, rather, was thinking of writing—a novel, to be brought out in England simultaneously with its production in America; and it was arranged, at Hawthorne's request, that Ticknor was to accompany him over to England to make the arrangements for the sale of his copyright. I can recall now the plans we made for meeting and dining together in London, and how both the men, each after his own fashion, seemed to enjoy the prospect of coming over to the old country, which they loved so well. Here, in England, people accused Hawthorne, as I think, unfairly, for the criticisms contained in his last book upon our national habits and character. The abuse was exaggerated, after our wont; but I admit, freely, that there were things in the Old Home which I think its author would not have written if his mind had not been embittered by the harsh and unsparing attacks that, ever since the outbreak of the war, have been poured upon everything and everybody in the

North. With all his sensitiveness, and all his refinement, and all his world-culture, Hawthorne was still a Yankee in heart. He saw the defects of his own countrymen only too clearly; he was willing enough to speak of them unsparingly; but, when others abused his country, then the native New England blood was roused within that thoughtful nature. Possibly, if my own country were in trouble, and on the very verge of ruin, I should not be able to take so lightly the few bitter half-truths which Hawthorne wrote about England and its people. Happily, we are strong enough not to feel sarcasm; and even if it were not so, I, for one, should find it difficult to have anything but the kindliest memories of Nathaniel Hawthorne. The days that I spent in his house at Concord are recorded in my memory as among the pleasantest of a wandering life. Most of the family happened to be away from home, so that our company was a very small one. It was in the first blush of the early summer, and the little New England village was at the height of its quiet beauty. The house itself, lying beyond the village, at the front of a low hill, buried almost in trees, was a fitting home for the author of *The Scarlet Letter*. In his own home, the shyness which often rendered it difficult to get on with him seemed to fall away. To me, at least, he was the most courteous and kindly of hosts; and I think, before the end of my visit, he had overcome the nervous doubt which always oppressed him, whether it was possible for anybody not to get bored in his company. As I write, I recall, one by one, all the incidents of that visit—the strolls in the pine wood above the house, where the leaves fluttered to and fro, and the wind sighed fitfully; the lounges on the hot summer afternoons, on the banks of the torpid Concord stream, watching the fish dart in and out underneath the rushes; the row upon the little lake, with the visits to the neighbours' houses, in that genial, kindly community; and, above all, the long talks at night, when everybody else was asleep, and when over the cigars and whisky Hawthorne would chat on in that low musical voice I found such a charm in listening to. He was not a brilliant talker; there are not many sayings of his I can recollect, worth repeating in themselves as disjointed fragments. It is difficult to analyse the charm of anything which pleases you; but if I were obliged to try to explain the attraction of Hawthorne's talk, I should say it lay in the odd combination of clear, hard-headed sense and dreamy fancy. Cynical he was not; his mind was too large a one for anything small or mean; but he was tolerant of everything to a marvellous degree; catholic in all his judgments; sceptical because he saw any question from so many points of view. In truth, at the time I often fancied that Shakspeare's conversation in private life must have been akin to that I heard on those evenings spent in Hawthorne's study. On the last evening that I passed there I remember that our talk rambled, after many things, as men's talk

George William Curtis

A friend of Hawthorne, George W. Curtis wrote about his travels in such books as Nile Notes of a Howadji *(1851) and* The Howadji in Syria *(1852).*

The Works of Nathaniel Hawthorne
George W. Curtis
North American Review, 99 (October 1864): 539–557

The traveller by the Eastern Railroad, from Boston, reaches in less than an hour the old town of Salem, Massachusetts. It is chiefly composed of plain wooden houses, but it has a quaint air of provincial grandeur, and has indeed been an important commercial town. The first American ship for Calcutta and China sailed from this port; and Salem ships opened our trade with New Holland and the South Seas. But its glory has long since departed, with that of its stately and respectable neighbors, Newburyport and Portsmouth. There is still, however, a custom-house in Salem, there are wharves, and chandlers' shops, and a faint show of shipping, and an air of marine capacity which no apparent result justifies. It sits upon the shore like an antiquated sea-captain, grave and silent, in tarpaulin and duck trousers, idly watching the ocean upon which he will never sail again.

But this touching aspect of age and lost prosperity merely serves to deepen the peculiar impression of the old city, which is not derived from its former commercial importance, but from other associations. Salem village was a famous place in the Puritan annuals. The tragedy of the witchcraft tortures and murders has cast upon it a ghostly spell, from which it seems never to have escaped; and even the sojourner of to-day, as he loiters along the shore in the sunniest morning of June, will sometimes feel an icy breath in the air, chilling the very marrow of his bones. Nor is he consoled by being told that it is only the east wind; for he cannot help believing that an invisible host of Puritan spectres have breathed upon him, revengeful, as he poached upon their ancient haunts.

The Puritan spirit was neither gracious nor lovely, but nothing softer than its iron hand could have done its necessary work. The Puritan character was narrow, intolerant, and exasperating. The forefathers were very 'sour' in the estimation of Morton and his merry company at Mount Wollaston. But for all that, Bradstreet and Carver and Winthrop were better forefathers than the gay Morton, and the Puritan spirit is doubtless the moral influence of modern civilization, both in Old and New England. By the fruit let the seed be judged. The State to whose rough coast the *Mayflower* came, and in which the Pilgrim spirit has been most active, is to-day the chief of all human societies, politically, morally, and socially. It is the community in

often will, to the question of what was to happen to us when life is over. We were speaking of the spiritualist creed, that existence recommences under another form, the moment after death. 'Ah,' said Hawthorne, half laughing, half seriously, 'I hope there will be a break. A couple of thousand years or so of sleep is the least that I can do with before I begin life again.'

These few words which I have written I have written frankly, knowing, or at any rate believing, that Hawthorne himself would prefer to be so written of. I think he knew and judged himself with the same measure as he judged others. I recollect, as we shook hands for the last time, at the door of his house, he said to me, in parting, 'I am glad for once to have met an Englishman who can see there are two sides to every question.' The compliment was undeserved enough, but I have sought to merit it in saying something of him who made it. And those who knew him best, and therefore loved him best, will not, I think, be angry with me for so doing.

which the average of well-being is higher than in any state we know in history. Puritan though it be, it is more truly liberal and free than any large community in the world. But it had bleak beginnings. The icy shore, the sombre pines, the stealthy savages, the hard soil, the unbending religious austerity, the Scriptural severity, the arrogant virtues, the angry intolerance of contradiction,–they all made a narrow strip of sad civilization between the pitiless sea and the remorseless forests. The moral and physical tenacity which is wrestling with the Rebellion was toughened among these flinty and forbidding rocks. The fig, the pomegranate, and the almond would not grow there, nor the nightingale sing; but nobler men than its children the sun never shone upon, nor has the heart of man heard sweeter music than the voices of James Otis and Samuel Adams. Think of Plymouth in 1620, and of Massachusetts to-day! Out of strength came forth sweetness.

With some of the darkest passages in Puritan history the old town of Salem, which dozes apparently with the most peaceful conscience in the world, is identified, and while its Fourth of July bells were joyfully ringing sixty years ago Nathaniel Hathorne was born. He subsequently chose to write the name Hawthorne, because he thought he had discovered that it was the original spelling. In the Introduction to *The Scarlet Letter,* Hawthorne speaks of his ancestors as coming from Europe in the seventeenth century, and establishing themselves in Salem, where they served the state and propitiated Heaven by joining in the persecution of Quakers and witches. The house known as the Witch House is still standing on the corner of Summer and Essex Streets. It was built in 1642 by Captain George Corwin, and here in 1692 many of the unfortunates who were palpably guilty of age and ugliness were examined by the Honorable Jonathan Curwin, Major Gedney, Captain John Higginson, and John Hathorn, Esquire.

The name of this last worthy occurs in one of the first and most famous of the witch trials,–that of 'Goodwife Cory,' in March, 1692, only a month after the beginning of the delusion at the house of the minister Parris. Goodwife Cory was accused by ten children, of whom Elizabeth Parris was one; they declared that they were pinched by her, and strangled, and that she brought them a book to sign. 'Mr. Hathorn, a magistrate of Salem,' says Robert Calef, in *More Wonders of the Invisible World,'*

> asked her why she afflicted these children. She said she did not afflict them. He asked her who did then. She said, I do not know, how should I know? She said they were poor, distracted creatures, and no heed ought to be given to what they said. Mr Hathorn and Mr Noyes

> replied, that it was the judgment of all that were there present that they were bewitched, and only she (the accused) said they were distracted. She was accused by them that the *black man* whispered to her in her ear now (while she was upon examination), and that she had a yellow bird that did use to suck between her fingers, and that the said bird did suck now in the assembly.

John Hathorn and Jonathan Curwin were 'the Assistants' of Salem village, and held most of the examinations and issued the warrants. Justice Hathorn was very swift in judgment, holding every accused person guilty in every particular. When poor Jonathan Cary of Charlestown attended his wife charged with witchcraft before Justice Hathorn, he requested that he might hold one of her hands,

> but it was denied me. Then she desired me to wipe the tears from her eyes and the sweat from her face, which I did; then she desired that she might lean herself on me, saying she would faint. Justice Hathorn replied, she had strength enough to torment these persons, and she should have strength enough to stand. I speaking something against their cruel proceedings, they commanded me to be silent, or else I should be turned out of the room.

What a piteous picture of the awful Colonial Inquisition and the village Torquemada! What a grim portrait of an ancestor to hang in your memory, and to trace your kindred to!

Hawthorne's description of his ancestors in the Introduction to *The Scarlet Letter* is very delightful. As their representative, he declares that he takes shame to himself for their sake, on account of these relentless persecutions; but he thinks them earnest and energetic.

> From father to son, for above a hundred years, they followed the sea; a gray-headed ship-master, in each generation, retiring from the quarter-deck to the homestead, while a boy of fourteen took the hereditary place before the mast, confronting the salt spray and the gale, which had blustered against his sire and grandsire. The boy also, in due time, passed from the forecastle to the cabin, spent a tempestuous manhood, and returned from his world-wanderings, to grow old, and die, and mingle his dust with the natal earth.

Not all, however, for the last of the line of sailors, Captain Nathaniel Hathorne, who married Elizabeth Clarke Manning, died at Calcutta after the birth of three children, a boy and two girls. The house in which the boy was born is still standing upon Union Street, which leads to the Long Wharf, the chief seat of the old foreign trade of Salem. The next house, with a back entrance on Union Street, is the Manning house, where many years of the young Hawthorne's life were spent in the care of his Uncle Robert Manning. He lived often upon an estate belonging to his mother's family, in the town of Raymond, near Sebago Lake, in Maine. The huge house there was called Manning's Folly, and is now said to be used as a meeting-house. His uncle sent Hawthorne to Bowdoin College, where he graduated in 1825. A correspondent of the Boston Daily Advertiser, writing from Bowdoin at the late Commencement, says that he had recently found 'in an old drawer' some papers which proved to be the manuscript 'parts' of the students at the Junior exhibition of 1824; among them was Hawthorne's 'De Patribus Conscriptis Romanorum.' 'It is quite brief,' writes the correspondent,

> but is really curious as perhaps the only college exercise in existence of the great tragic writer of our day (has there been a greater since Shakespeare?). The last sentence is as follows; note the words which I put in italics: 'Augustus equidem antiquam magnificentiam patribus reddidit, *sed fulgor tantum fuit sine fervore.* Nunquam in republica senatoribus potestas recuperata, postremum species etiam amissa est.' On the same occasion Longfellow had the salutatory oration in Latin,—'Oratio Latina;—Anglici Poetæ.'

Hawthorne has given us a charming glimpse of himself as a college boy in the letter to his fellow-student, Horatio Bridge of the Navy, whose *Journal of an African Cruiser* he afterward edited.

> I know not whence your faith came; but while we were lads together at a country college,—gathering blueberries, in study-hours, under those tall academic pines; or watching the great logs, as they tumbled along the current of the Androscoggin; or shooting pigeons and gray-squirrels in the woods; or bat-fowling in the summer twilight; or catching trouts in that shadowy little stream which, I suppose, is still wandering riverward through the forest—though you and I will never cast a line in it again,—two idle lads, in short (as we need not fear to acknowledge now), doing a hundred things that the Faculty never heard of, or else it had been the worse for us,—still it was your prognostic of your friend's destiny, that he was to be a writer of fiction.

From this sylvan university Hawthorne came home to Salem; 'as if,' he wrote later, 'Salem were for me the inevitable centre of the universe.'

The old witch-hanging city had no weirder product than this dark-haired son. He has certainly given it an interest which it must otherwise have lacked; but he speaks of it with small affection, considering that his family had lived there for two centuries. 'An unjoyous attachment,' he calls it. And, to tell the truth, there was evidently little love lost between the little city and its

most famous citizen. Stories still float in the social gossip of the town, which represent the shy author as inaccessible to all invitations to dinner and tea; and while the pleasant circle awaited his coming in the drawing-room, the impracticable man was—at least so runs the tale—quietly hobnobbing with companions to whom his fame was unknown. Those who coveted him as a phoenix could never get him, while he gave himself freely to those who saw in him only a placid barn-door fowl. The sensitive youth was a recluse, upon whose imagination had fallen the gloomy mystery of Puritan life and character. Salem was the inevitable centre of his universe more truly than he thought. The mind of Justice Hathorn's descendant was bewitched by the fascination of a certain devilish subtlety working under the comeliest aspects in human affairs. It overcame him with strange sympathy. It colored and controlled his intellectual life.

Devoted all day to lonely reverie and musing upon the obscurer spiritual passages of the life whose monuments he constantly encountered, that musing became inevitably morbid. With the creative instinct of the artist, he wrote the wild fancies into form as stories, many of which, when written, he threw into the fire. Then, after nightfall, stealing out from his room into the silent streets of Salem, and shadowy as the ghosts with which to his susceptible imagination the dusky town was thronged, he glided beneath the house in which the witch-trials were held, or across the moonlight hill upon which the witches were hung, until the spell was complete. Nor can we help fancying that, after the murder of old Mr White in Salem, which happened within a few years after his return from college, which drew from Mr Webster his most famous criminal plea, and filled a shadowy corner of every museum in New England, as every shivering little man of that time remembers, with an awful reproduction of the scene in wax-figures, with real sheets on the bed, and the murderer in a glazed cap stooping over to deal the fatal blow,—we cannot help fancying that the young recluse who walked by night, the wizard whom as yet none knew, hovered about the house, gazing at the windows of the fatal chamber, and listening in horror for the faint whistle of the confederate in another street.

Three years after he graduated, in 1828, he published anonymously a slight romance with the motto from Southey, 'Wilt thou go with me?' Hawthorne never acknowledged the book, and it is now seldom found; but it shows plainly the natural bent of his mind. It is a dim, dreamy tale, such as a Byron-struck youth of the time might have written, except for that startling self-possession of style and cold analysis of passion, rather than sympathy with it, which showed no imitation, but remarkable original power. The same lurid glow overhangs it that shadows all his works. It is uncanny; the figures of the romance are not persons, they are passions, emotions, spiritual speculations. So the *Twice-told Tales,* that seem at first but the pleasant fancies of a mild recluse, gradually hold the mind with a Lamia-like fascination; and the author says truly of them, in the Preface of 1851, 'Even in what purport to be pictures of actual life, we have allegory not always so warmly dressed in its habiliments of flesh and blood as to be taken into the reader's mind without a shiver.' There are sunny gleams upon the pages, but a strange, melancholy chill pervades the book. In 'The Wedding Knell,' 'The Minister's Black Veil,' 'The Gentle Boy,' 'Wakefield,' 'The Prophetic Pictures,' 'The Hollow of the Three Hills,' 'Dr Heidegger's Experiment,' 'The Ambitious Guest,' 'The White Old Maid,' 'Edward Fane's Rose-bud,' 'The Lily's Quest,'—or in the 'Legends of the Province House,' where the courtly provincial state of governors and ladies glitters across the small, sad New England world, whose very baldness jeers it to scorn—there is the same fateful atmosphere in which Goody Cloyse might at any moment whisk by upon her broomstick, and in which the startled heart stands still with unspeakable terror.

The spell of mysterious horror which kindled Hawthorne's imagination was a test of the character of his genius. The mind of this child of witch-haunted Salem loved to hover between the natural and the supernatural, and sought to tread the almost imperceptible and doubtful line of contact. He instinctively sketched the phantoms that have the figures of men, but are not human; the elusive, shadowy scenery which, like that of Gustave Doré's pictures, is Nature sympathizing in her forms and aspects with the emotions of terror or awe which the tale excites. His genius broods entranced over the evanescent phantasmagoria of the vague debatable land in which the realities of experience blend with ghostly doubts and wonders.

But from its poisonous flowers what a wondrous perfume he distilled! Through his magic reed, into what penetrating melody he blew that deathly air! His relentless fancy seemed to seek a sin that was hopeless, a cruel despair that no faith could throw off. Yet his naive and well-poised genius hung over the gulf of blackness, and peered into the pit with the steady nerve and simple face of a boy. The mind of the reader follows him with an aching wonder and admiration, as the bewildered old mother forester watched Undine's gambols. As Hawthorne describes Miriam in *The Marble Faun,* so may the character of his genius be most truly indicated. Miriam, the reader will remember, turns to Hilda and Kenyon for sympathy.

Title page for a pirated edition of a fragment that appeared in the July 1864 issue of The Atlantic Monthly *(from C. E. Frazer Clark Jr.,* Nathaniel Hawthorne: A Descriptive Bibliography, *1978)*

Yet it was to little purpose that she approached the edge of the voiceless gulf between herself and them. Standing on the utmost verge of that dark chasm, she might stretch out her hand and never clasp a hand of theirs; she might strive to call out, 'Help, friends! help!' but, as with dreamers when they shout, her voice would perish inaudibly in the remoteness that seemed such a little way. This perception of an infinite, shivering solitude, amid which we cannot come close enough to human beings to be warmed by them, and where they turn to cold, chilly shapes of mist, is one of the most forlorn results of any accident, misfortune, crime, or peculiarity of character, that puts an individual ajar with the world.

Thus it was because the early New England life made so much larger account of the supernatural element than any other modern civilized society, that the man whose blood had run in its veins instinctively turned to it. But beyond this alluring spell of its darker and obscurer individual experience, it seems neither to have touched his imagination nor even to have aroused his interest. To Walter Scott the romance of feudalism was precious, for the sake of feudalism itself, in which he believed with all his soul, and for that of the heroic old feudal figures which he honored. He was a Tory in every particle of his frame, and his genius made him the poet of Toryism. But Hawthorne had apparently no especial political, religious, or patriotic affinity with the spirit which inspired him. It was solely a fascination of the intellect. And although he is distinctively the poet of the Puritans, although it is to his genius that we shall always owe that image of them which the power of *The Scarlet Letter* has imprinted upon literature, and doubtless henceforth upon historical interpretation, yet what an imperfect picture of that life it is! All its stern and melancholy romance is there,—its picturesque gloom and intense passion; but upon those quivering pages, as in every passage of his stories drawn from that spirit, there seems to be wanting a deep, complete, sympathetic appreciation of the fine moral heroism, the spiritual grandeur, which overhung that gloomy life, as a delicate purple mist suffuses in summer twilights the bald crags of the crystal hills. It is the glare of the Scarlet Letter itself, and all that it luridly reveals and weirdly implies, which produced the tale. It was not beauty in itself, nor deformity, not virtue nor vice, which engaged the author's deepest sympathy. It was the occult relation between the two. Thus while the Puritans were of all men pious, it was the instinct of Hawthorne's genius to search out and trace with terrible tenacity the dark and devious thread of sin in their lives.

Human life and character, whether in New England two hundred years ago or in Italy to-day, interested him only as they were touched by this glamour of sombre spiritual mystery; and the attraction pursued him in every form in which it appeared. It is as apparent in the most perfect of his smaller tales, 'Rappaccini's Daughter,' as in *The Scarlet Letter, The Blithedale Romance, The House of the Seven Gables,* and *The Marble Faun.* You may open almost at random, and you are as sure to find it, as to hear the ripple in Mozart's music, or the pathetic minor in a Neapolitan melody. Take, for instance, 'The Birth-Mark,' which we might call the best of the smaller stories, if we had not just said the same thing of 'Rappaccini's Daughter,'—for so even and complete is Hawthorne's power, that, with few exceptions, each work of his, like Benvenuto's, seems the most characteristic and felicitous. In this story, a scholar marries a beautiful woman, upon whose face is a mark which has hitherto seemed to be only a greater charm. Yet in one so lovely the husband declares that, although it is the slightest possible defect, it is yet the mark of earthly imperfection, and he proceeds to lavish all the resources of science to procure its removal. But it will not disappear; and at last he tells her that the crimson

hand 'has clutched its grasp' into her very being, and that there is mortal danger in trying the only means of removal that remains. She insists that it shall be tried. It succeeds, but it removes the stain and her life together. So in 'Rappaccini's Daughter.' The old philosopher nourishes his beautiful child upon the poisonous breath of a flower. She loves, and her lover is likewise bewitched. In trying to break the spell, she drinks an antidote which kills her. The point of interest in both stories is the subtle connection, in the first, between the beauty of Georgiana and the taint of the birth-mark; and, in the second, the loveliness of Beatrice and the poison of the blossom.

This, also, is the key of his last romance, *The Marble Faun,* one of the most perfect works of art in literature, whose marvellous spell begins with the very opening words: 'Four individuals, in whose fortunes we should be glad to interest the reader, happened to be standing in one of the saloons of the sculpture-gallery in the Capitol at Rome.' When these words are read, the mind familiar with Hawthorne is already enthralled. What a journey is beginning, not a step of which is trodden, and yet the heart palpitates with apprehension! Through what delicate, rosy lights of love, and soft, shimmering humor, and hopes and doubts and vanishing delights, that journey will proceed, on and on into utter gloom. And it does so, although 'Hilda had a hopeful soul, and saw sunlight on the mountain-tops.' It does so, because Miriam and Donatello are the figures which interest us most profoundly, and they are both lost in the shadow. Donatello, indeed, is the true centre of interest, as he is one of the most striking creations of genius. But the perplexing charm of Donatello, what is it but the doubt that does not dare to breathe itself, the appalled wonder whether, if the breeze should lift those clustering locks a little higher, he would prove to be faun or man? It never does lift them; the doubt is never solved, but it is always suggested. The mystery of a partial humanity, morally irresponsible but humanly conscious, haunts the entrancing page. It draws us irresistibly on. But as the cloud closes around the lithe figure of Donatello, we hear again from its hidden folds the words of 'The Birth-Mark': 'Thus ever does the gross fatality of earth result in its invariable triumph over the immortal essence, which, in this dim sphere of half-development, demands the completeness of a higher state.' Or still more sadly, the mysterious youth, half vanishing from our sympathy, seems to murmur, with Beatrice Rappaccini, 'And still as she spoke, she kept her hand upon her heart,—"Wherefore didst thou inflict this miserable doom upon thy child?"'

We have left the story of Hawthorne's life sadly behind. But his life had no more remarkable events than holding office in the Boston Custom-House under

Mr Bancroft as Collector; working for some time with the Brook Farmers, from whom he soon separated, not altogether amicably; marrying and living in the old manse at Concord; returning to the Custom-House in Salem as Surveyor; then going to Lenox, in Berkshire, where he lived in what he called 'the ugliest little old red farm-house that you ever saw,' and where the story is told of his shyness, that, if he saw anybody coming along the road whom he must probably pass, he would jump over the wall into the pasture, and so give the stranger a wide berth; back again to Concord; then to Liverpool as Consul; travelling in Europe afterward, and home at last and forever, to 'The Wayside' under the Concord hill. 'The hillside,' he wrote to a friend in 1852,

> is covered chiefly with locust-trees, which come into luxurious blossom in the month of June, and look and smell very sweetly, intermixed with a few young elms and some white-pines and infant oaks, the whole forming rather a thicket than a wood. Nevertheless, there is some very good shade to be found there. I spend delectable hours there in the hottest parts of the day, stretched out at my lazy length with a book in my hand or an unwritten book in my thoughts. There is almost always a breeze stirring along the side or brow of the hill.

It is not strange, certainly, that a man such as has been described, of a morbid shyness, the path of whose genius diverged always out of the sun into the darkest shade, and to whom human beings were merely psychological phenomena, should have been accounted ungenial, and sometimes even hard, cold, and perverse. From the bent of his intellectual temperament it happens that in his simplest and sweetest passages he still seems to be studying and curiously observing, rather than sympathizing. You cannot help feeling constantly that the author is looking askance both at his characters and you, the reader; and many a young and fresh mind is troubled strangely by his books, as if it were aware of a half-Mephistophelean smile upon the page. Nor is this impression altogether removed by the remarkable familiarity of his personal disclosures. There was never a man more shrinkingly retiring, yet surely never was an author more naively frank. He is willing that you should know all that a man may fairly reveal of himself. The great interior story he does not tell, of course, but the introduction to the *Mosses from an Old Manse,* the opening chapter of *The Scarlet Letter,* and the 'Consular Experiences', with much of the rest of *Our Old Home,* are as intimate and explicit chapters of autobiography as can be found. Nor would it be easy to find anywhere a more perfect idyl than that introductory chapter of the *Mosses.* Its charm is perennial and undescribable; and

why should it not be, since it was written at a time in which, as he says, 'I was happy'? It is, perhaps, the most softly-hued and exquisite work of his pen. So the sketch of 'The Custom-House,' although prefatory to that most tragically powerful of romances, *The Scarlet Letter,* is an incessant play of the shyest and most airy humor. It is like the warbling of bobolinks before a thunder-burst. How many other men, however unreserved with the pen, would be likely to dare to paint, with the fidelity of Teniers and the simplicity of Fra Angelico, a picture of the office and the companions in which and with whom they did their daily work? The Surveyor of Customs in the port of Salem treated the town of Salem, in which he lived and discharged his daily task, as if it had been, with all its people, as vague and remote a spot as the town of which he was about to treat in the story. He commented upon the place and the people as modern travellers in Pompeii discuss the ancient town. It made a great scandal. He was accused of depicting with unpardonable severity worthy folks, whose friends were sorely pained and indignant. But he wrote such sketches as he wrote his stories. He treated his companions as he treated himself and all the personages in history or experience with which he dealt, merely as phenomena to be analyzed and described, with no more private malice or personal emotion than the sun, which would have photographed them, warts and all.

Thus it was that the great currents of human sympathy never swept him away. The character of his genius isolated him, and he stood aloof from the common interests. Intent upon studying men in certain aspects, he cared little for man; and the high tides of collective emotion among his fellows left him dry and untouched. So he beholds and describes the generous impulse of humanity with sceptical courtesy rather than with hopeful cordiality.

He does not chide you if you spend effort and life itself in the ardent van of progress, but he asks simply, 'Is six so much better than half a dozen?' He will not quarrel with you if you expect the millennium to-morrow. He only says, with that glimmering smile, 'So soon?' Yet in all this there was no shadow of spiritual pride. Nay, so far from this, that the tranquil and pervasive sadness of all Hawthorne's writings, the kind of heart-ache that they leave behind, to spring from the fact that his nature was related to the moral world, as his own Donatello was to the human. 'So alert, so alluring, so noble,' muses the heart as we climb the Apennines toward the tower of Monte Beni;—'alas! is he human?' it whispers, with a pang of doubt.

How this directed his choice of subjects, and affected his treatment of them, when drawn from early history, we have already seen. It is not, therefore, sur-

Bindings for books posthumously published from Hawthorne's writing: three unfinished romances–Septimius Felton *(1872),* The Dolliver
Romance *(1876), and* Doctor Grimshawe's Secret *(1883); two books of correspondence*–Love Letters of Nathaniel
Hawthorne *(1907) and* Letters of Hawthorne to William D. Ticknor *(1907); and one book he edited*–
The Yarn of a Yankee Privateer, *published in 1926 (from C. E. Frazer Clark Jr.,*
Nathaniel Hawthorne: A Descriptive Bibliography, *1978)*

prising, that the history into which he was born interested him only in the same way.

When he went to Europe as Consul, *Uncle Tom's Cabin* was already published, and the country shook with the fierce debate which involved its life. Yet eight years later Hawthorne wrote with calm ennui, 'No author, without a trial, can conceive of the difficulty of writing a romance about a country where there is no shadow, no antiquity, no mystery, no picturesque and gloomy wrong, nor anything but a commonplace prosperity, in broad and simple daylight, as is happily the case with my dear native land.' Is crime never romantic, then, until distance ennobles it? Or were the tragedies of Puritan life so terrible that the imagination could not help kindling, while the pangs of the plantation are superficial and common-place? Charlotte Brontë, Dickens, and Thackeray were able to find a shadow even in 'merrie England.' But our great romancer looked at the

American life of his time with these marvellous eyes, and could see only monotonous sunshine. That the Devil, in the form of an elderly man clad in grave and decent attire, should lead astray the saints of Salem village, two centuries ago, and confuse right and wrong in the mind of Goodman Brown, was something that excited his imagination, and produced one of his weirdest stories. But that the same Devil, clad in a sombre sophism, was confusing the sentiment of right and wrong in the mind of his own countrymen he did not even guess. The monotonous sunshine disappeared in the blackest storm. The commonplace prosperity ended in tremendous war. What other man of equal power, who was not intellectually constituted precisely as Hawthorne was, could have stood merely perplexed and bewildered, harassed by the inability of positive sympathy, in the vast conflict which tosses us all in its terrible vortex?

In political theories and in an abstract view of war men may differ. But this war is not to be dismissed as a political difference. Here is an attempt to destroy the government of a country, not because it oppressed any man, but because its evident tendency was to secure universal justice under law. It is therefore a conspiracy against human nature. Civilization itself is at stake; and the warm blood of the noblest youth is everywhere flowing in as sacred a cause as history records,—flowing not merely to maintain a certain form of government, but to vindicate the rights of human nature. Shall there not be sorrow and pain, if a friend is merely impatient or confounded by it,—if he sees in it only danger or doubt, and not hope for the right,—or if he seem to insinuate that it would have been better if the war had been avoided, even at that countless cost to human welfare by which alone the avoidance was possible?

Yet, if the view of Hawthorne's mental constitution which has been suggested be correct, this attitude of his, however deeply it may be regretted, can hardly deserve moral condemnation. He knew perfectly well that, if a man has no ear for music, he had better not try to sing. But the danger with such men is, that they are apt to doubt if music itself be not a vain delusion. This danger Hawthorne escaped. There is none of the shallow persiflage of the sceptic in his tone, not any affectation of cosmopolitan superiority. Mr Edward Dicey, in his interesting reminiscences of Hawthorne, published in *Macmillan's Magazine,* illustrates this very happily:

. . . .

The truth is, that his own times and their people and their affairs were just as shadowy to him as those of any of his stories, and his mind held the same curious, half-wistful poise among all the conflicts of principle and passion around him, as among those of which he read and mused. If you ask why this was so,—how it was that the tragedy of an old Italian garden, or the sin of a lonely Puritan parish, or the crime of a provincial judge, should so stimulate his imagination with romantic appeals and harrowing allegories, while either it did not see a Carolina slave-pen, or found in it only a tame prosperity,—you must take your answer in the other question, why he did not weave into any of his stories the black and bloody thread of the Inquisition. His genius obeyed its law. When he wrote like a disembodied intelligence of events with which his neighbors' hearts were quivering,—when the same half-smile flutters upon his lips in the essay 'About War Matters,' sketched as it were upon the battlefield, as in that upon 'Fire Worship,' written in the

rural seclusion of the mossy Manse,—ah me! it is Donatello, in his tower of Monte Beni, contemplating with doubtful interest the field upon which the flower of men are dying for an idea. Do you wonder, as you see him and hear him, that your heart, bewildered, asks and asks again, 'Is he human? Is he a man?'

Now that Hawthorne sleeps by the tranquil Concord, upon whose shores the old Manse was his bridal bower, those who knew him chiefly there revert beyond the angry hour to those peaceful days. How dear the old Manse was to him, he has himself recorded; and in the opening of the *Tanglewood Tales* he pays tribute to that placid landscape, which will always be recalled with pensive tenderness by those who, like him, became familiar with it in happy hours. 'To me,' he writes,

> there is a peculiar, quiet charm in these broad meadows and gentle eminences. They are better than mountains, because they do not stamp and stereotype themselves into the brain, and thus grow wearisome with the same strong impression, repeated day after day. A few summer weeks among mountains, a lifetime among green meadows and placid slopes, with outlines forever new, because continually fading out of the memory,—such would be my sober choice.

He used to say, in those days,—when, as he was fond of insisting, he was the obscurest author in the world, because, although he had told his tales twice, nobody cared to listen,—that he never knew exactly how he contrived to live. But he was then married, and the dullest eye could not fail to detect the feminine grace and taste that ordered the dwelling, and perceive the tender sagacity that made all things possible.

Such was his simplicity and frugality, that, when he was left alone for a little time in his Arcadia, he would dismiss 'the help,' and, with some friend of other days who came to share his loneliness, he cooked the easy meal, and washed up the dishes. No picture is clearer in the memory of a certain writer than that of the magician, in whose presence he almost lost his breath, looking at him over a dinner-plate which he was gravely wiping in the kitchen, while the handy friend, who had been a Western settler, scoured the kettle at the door. Blithedale, where their acquaintance had begun, had not allowed either of them to forget how to help himself. It was amusing to one who knew this native independence of Hawthorne, to hear, some years afterward, that he wrote the 'campaign' *Life of Franklin Pierce* for the sake of getting an office. That such a man should do such a work was possibly incomprehensible, to those who did not know him, upon any other supposition, until the fact was known that Mr Pierce was an old and constant friend. Then it was explained. Hawthorne asked simply how he could help his friend; and he did the only thing he could do for that purpose. But although he passed some years in public office, he had neither taste nor talent for political life. He owed his offices to works quite other than political. His first and second appointments were virtually made by his friend Mr Bancroft, and the third by his friend Mr Pierce. His claims were perceptible enough to friendship, but would hardly have been so to a caucus.

In this brief essay we have aimed only to indicate the general character of the genius of Hawthorne, and to suggest a key to his peculiar relation to his time. The reader will at once see that it is rather the man than the author who has been described; but this has been designedly done, for we confess a personal solicitude, shared, we are very sure, by many friends of Nathaniel Hawthorne, that there shall not be wanting to the future student of his works such light as acquaintance with the man may throw upon them, as well as some picture of the impression his personality made upon his contemporaries.

Strongly formed, of dark, poetic gravity of aspect, lighted by the deep, gleaming eye that recoiled with girlish coyness from contact with your gaze; of rare courtesy and kindliness in personal intercourse, yet so sensitive that his look and manner can be suggested by the word glimmering; giving you a sense of restrained impatience to be away; mostly silent in society, and speaking always with an appearance of effort, but with a lambient light of delicate humor playing over all he said in the confidence of familiarity, and firm self-possession under all, as if the glimmering manner were only the tremulous surface of the sea,—Hawthorne was personally known to few, and intimately to very few. But no one knew him without loving him, or saw him without remembering him; and the name Nathaniel Hawthorne, which, when it was first written, was supposed to be fictitious, is now one of the most enduring facts of English literature.

Remembering and Assessing Hawthorne

This concluding section documents the posthumous reputation of Hawthorne through the 1904 centennial celebration of his birth. Along with such authors as Edgar Allan Poe, Walt Whitman, his friend Herman Melville, and neighbors Ralph Waldo Emerson and Henry David Thoreau, Hawthorne was a major literary figure in the American romantic period. When this era concluded during the Civil War, new cultural realities emerged. The realism (then naturalism) that dominated American letters for the remainder of the century did not keep critics from appreciating Hawthorne's accomplishment. One of the writers who most admired Hawthorne was Henry James, the master realist who wrote a book about him, Hawthorne (1879), and who in his novels addressed international themes, as Hawthorne had done in* The Marble Faun. *While critics found aesthetic delights in Hawthorne, publishers appreciated him for commercial reasons: following the publication of* The Scarlet Letter, *he has never been out of print.*

An 1861 photograph of Hawthorne (Collection of C. E. Frazer Clark Jr.), one of his wife's favorites, and a crayon portrait based on it by Samuel W. Rowse (photographic copy, Longfellow National Historic Trust)

Rowse Portrait

In his memoir of Hawthorne, James T. Fields begins by admiring Samuel W. Rowse's portrait of the author.

I am sitting today opposite the likeness of the rarest genius America has given to literature,–a man who lately adjourned in this busy world of ours, but during many years of his life

"Wandered lonely as a cloud,"–

a man who had, so to speak, a physical affinity with solitude. The writings of this author have never soiled the public mind with one unlovely image. His men and women have a magic of their own, and we shall wait a long time before another arises among us to take his place. Indeed, it seems probable no one will ever walk precisely the same round of fiction which he traversed with so free and firm a step.

The portrait I am looking at was made by Rowse (an exquisite drawing), and is a very truthful representation of the head of Nathaniel Hawthorne. He was several times painted and photographed, but it was impossible for art to give the light and beauty of his wonderful eyes. I remember to have heard, in the literary circles of Great Britain, that, since Burns, no author had appeared there with a finer face than Hawthorne's. Old Mrs. Basil Montagu told me, many years ago, that she sat next to Burns at dinner, when he appeared in society in the first flush of his fame, after the Edinburgh edition of his poems had been published. She said, among other things, that, although the company consisted of some of the best bred men of England, Burns seemed to her the most perfect gentleman among them. She noticed, particularly, his genuine grace and deferential manner toward women, and I was interested to hear Mrs. Montagu's brilliant daughter, when speaking of Hawthorne's advent in English society, describe in almost the same terms as I had heard her mother, years before, describe the Scottish poet. I happened to be in London with Hawthorne during his consular residence in England, and was always greatly delighted at the rustle of admiration his personal appearance excited when he entered a room. His bearing was modestly grand, and his voice touched the ear like a melody.

Here is a golden curl which adorned the head of Nathaniel Hawthorne when he lay a little child in his cradle. It was given to me many years ago by one near and dear to him. I have two other similar "blossoms," which I keep pressed in the same book of remembrance. One is from the head of John Keats, and was given to me by Charles Cowden Clarke, and the other graced the head of Mary Mitford, and was sent to me after her death by her friendly physician, who watched over her last hours. Leigh Hunt says with a fine poetic emphasis,

"There seems a love in hair, though it be dead.
It is the gentlest, yet the strongest thread
Of our frail plant,–a blossom from the tree
Surviving the proud trunk;–as though it said,
Patience and Gentleness is Power. In me
Behold affectionate eternity."

– *Yesterdays with Authors,* pp. 41–42

Amos Bronson Alcott

A Concord Memory

Amos Bronson Alcott, the father of Louisa May Alcott, writes about Hawthorne in his book Concord Days. *Hawthorne bought the Concord residence he renamed* The Wayside *from Alcott in 1852. In the 1830s Alcott operated a school for children and was assisted by Hawthorne's future sister-in-law Elizabeth Peabody. Alcott's recollection of Hawthorne's being particularly disturbed by news of "the New-York mob" is a reference to the draft riots that took place in the city on 11–13 July 1863.*

Hawthorne
Amos Bronson Alcott
Concord Days (Philadelphia: Albert Saifer, 1872),
pp. 193–197

Hawthorne was of the darker temperament and tendencies. His sensitiveness and sadness were native, and he cultivated them apparently alike by solitude, the pursuits and studies in which he indulged, till he became almost fated to know gayer hours only by stealth. By disposition friendly, he seemed the victim of his temperament, as if he sought distance, if not his pen, to put himself in communication, and possible sympathy with others,—with his nearest friends, even. His reserve and imprisonment were more distant and close, while the desire for conversation was livelier, than any one I have known. There was something of strangeness even in his cherished intimacies, as if he set himself afar from all and from himself with the rest; the most diffident of men, as coy as a maiden, he could only be won by some cunning artifice, his reserve was so habitual, his isolation so entire, the solitude so vast. How distant people were from him, the world they lived in, how he came to know so much about them, by what stratagem he got into his own house or left it, was a marvel. Fancy fixed, he was not to be jostled from himself for a moment, his mood was so persistent. There he was in the twilight, there he stayed. Was he some damsel imprisoned in that manly form pleading always for release, sighing for the freedom and companionships denied her? Or was he some Assyrian ill at ease afar from the olives and the East? Had he strayed over with William the Conqueror, and true to his Norman nature, was the baron still in republican America, secure in his castle, secure in his tower, whence he could defy all invasion of curious eyes? What neighbor of his ever caught him on the highway, or ventured to approach his threshold?

> His bolted Castle gates, what man should ope,
>   Unless the Lord did will
>   To prove his skill,
> And tempt the fates hid in his horoscope?

Yet if by chance admitted, welcome in a voice that a woman might own for its hesitancy and tenderness; his eyes telling the rest.

> For such the noble language of his eye,
> That when of words his lips were destitute,
> Kind eyebeams spake while yet his tongue was mute.

Your intrusion was worth the courage it cost; it emboldened to future assaults to carry this fort of bashfulness. During all the time he lived near me, our estates being separated only by a gate and shaded avenue, I seldom caught sight of him; and when I did it was but to lose it the moment he suspected he was visible; oftenest seen on his hill-top screened behind the shrubbery and disappearing like a hare into the bush when surprised. I remember of his being in my house but twice, and then he was so ill at ease that he found excuse for leaving politely

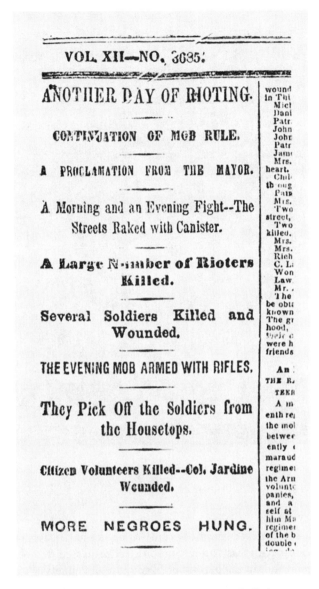

Headline in the New York Evening Post Bulletin
reporting the draft riots that disturbed Hawthorne

forthwith,—'the stove was so hot,' 'the clock ticked so loud.' Yet he once complained to me of his wish to meet oftener, and dwelt on the delights of fellowship, regretting he had so little. I think he seldom dined from home; nor did he often entertain any one,—once, an Englishman, when I was also his guest; but he preserved his shrinking taciturnity, and left to us the conversation. Another time I dined with a Southern guest at his table. The conversation turning on the war after dinner, he hid himself in the corner, as if a distant spectator, and fearing there was danger even there. It was due to his guest to hear the human side of the question of slavery, since she had heard only the best the South had to plead in its favor.

Bindings for the first edition of Hawthorne's collected works (1865–1876; 23 volumes), the "Tinted Edition"
(from C. E. Frazer Clark Jr., Nathaniel Hawthorne: A Descriptive Bibliography, *1978)*

I never deemed Hawthorne an advocate of Southern ideas and institutions. He professed democracy, not in the party, but large sense of equality. Perhaps he loved England too well to be quite just to his native land,–was more the Old Englishman than the New. He seemed to regret the transplanting, as if reluctant to fix his roots in our soil. His book on England, entitled *Our Old Home,* intimates his filial affection for that and its institutions. If his themes were American, his treatment of them was foreign, rather. He stood apart as having no stake in home affairs. While calling himself a democrat, he sympathized apparently with the absolutism of the old countries. He had not full faith in the people; perhaps feared republicanism because it had. Of our literary men, he least sympathized with the North, and was tremulously disturbed, I remember, at the time of the New-York mob. It is doubtful if he ever attended a political meeting or voted on any occasion throughout the long struggle with slavery. He stood aloof,

hesitating to take a responsible part, true to his convictions, doubtless, strictly honest, if not patriotic.

He strove by disposition to be sunny and genial, traits not native to him. Constitutionally shy, recluse, melancholy, only by shafts of wit and flow of humor could he deliver himself. There was a soft sadness in his smile, a reserve in his glance, telling how isolate he was. Was he ever one of his company while in it? There was an aloofness, a *besides,* that refused to affiliate himself with himself, even. His readers must feel this, while unable to account for it, perhaps, or express it adequately. A believer in transmitted traits needs but read his pedigree to find the genesis of what characterized him distinctly, and made him and his writings their inevitable sequel. Everywhere you will find persons of his type and complexion similar in cast of character and opinions. His associates mostly confirm the observation.

Assessments

The following essay is valuable because the anonymous writer identifies what he considers to be Hawthorne's weaknesses. The magazine in which it appeared, The Southern Review, *the second American journal so named, was founded in 1867 in Baltimore by Albert Taylor Bledsoe, a lawyer, Episcopal minister, and professor of mathematics.*

Writings of Nathaniel Hawthorne

Southern Review, 7 (April 1870): 328–354

New England has produced one satirist, in the person of James Russell Lowell, whose trenchant powers of biting sarcasm and wit make us continually regret that a faculty so large should be balked by a temper so unjust, so ungracious, so inconsequent. She has produced one genuine poet, John Greenleaf Whittier; a Quaker Tyrtaeus, to be sure, and something too nasal in his twang, but a Tyrtaeus still, and oftentimes, in happy moments, far better than a Tyrtaeus–the sweetest plaintive player upon the homely pastoral pipe, in fact, that has delighted the world since Burns. She has produced a comfortable number of second-rate singers, parodists in rhythm, dainty echoes, who warble, not without melody, albeit at second hand, and in the buckram fashion that proceeds out of a plethora of self-consciousness. But she has produced only one artist to her manner born and indigenous to her soil–we mean, of course, Nathaniel Hawthorne.

Hawthorne is in many respects the legitimate successor of Washington Irving. He has not Irving's sunny enjoyment of life, nor his cheery, buoyant humor, but he has all his grace, and much more than all his power. Irving represents a generation that is past and gone, and a tone of thought now quite archaic. Hawthorne belongs to a generation that is living and present, and antiquity is to him but a medium through which he catches the multiform lights and shadows of modern life. His hectic morbidness, his subtle allegory, his weird fancy, and the plaintive minor tones that play fitfully among the exquisitely modulated cadences of his incomparable style, are proof enough that his paper bark, which he would fain launch upon the broad ocean of the absolute and infinite, to wander whither it lists, is ever grating harshly upon the narrow and inadequate shores of the present, anchored, but not at rest. As in some degree a typical writer of these times, as a novelist of unusual powers, as one of the few American authors who have cultivated art for art's sake, and have studied to express themselves worthily rather than ostentatiously, it has seemed eminently proper to us that his merits should be canvassed in the pages of the *Southern Review.*

No estimate of Hawthorne's genius can go for much unless it takes into the account the fact that he was born and nurtured in New England,–as ambergris is engendered in the spleen of the dyspeptic whale. No statement of the force of the creative impulse within him can be more emphatic than the mere fact that it made him an artist even in Salem, which is as if one should say a Camoens had come out of Iceland, or a Correggio had survived the spiritual blockade of Spitzbergen. The soul that gives its days and nights to the cultivation of the amenities and the worship of beauty, finds no where so rude a reception, nor anywhere, surroundings more ungracious than in New England, and particularly that part of New England upon which the East wind, gathered in by the long scrawny arm of Cape Cod, thick with fog and megrims, is dashed like that *bufera infernal* of Dante, which never rests, but,

> *'Mena gli spirti con la sua rapina,*
> *Voltando e percotendo li molesta.'[1]*

The soil, the climate, the religion, if not the genius, of the people, are peculiarly hostile to artistic impulses. There never was a country, perhaps, since the automatic republic of Lycurgus, that was more steadily intolerant of all those free and sportive tendencies and influences which are essential to the development and naturalization of aesthetic culture. From the earliest settlement at Plymouth until within a generation or two its people have made it at once their moral duty and their spiritual pride to frown upon playfulness, and to thrust the beautiful out of doors. They have consistently inculcated and persistently practiced the suppression, nay, the crucifixion, of taste, as a thing that led to unuseful manners, to latitudinarian views, and was therefore an abomination to the Lord, and to be dealt with by the Tithingman. Even now, this same illiberal spirit is ingrained in their hearts. Only two years since, in a series of Thanksgiving sermons fresh from the press, we found the following paragraph, strikingly illustrative of those dregs of Puritanism that yet linger in the New England temper. 'Thanksgiving Day has a history attached to it,' remarks the author, an eminent preacher.[2] 'Like the latin word '*virtus,*' it is a history which runs through the entire life of a people. We cannot afford to lose reverence for ancestral memories. It is to be regretted that Mr Irving, our American Goldsmith, has expended so much time and labor in the prolix exaggeration of the peculiar habits of the early Dutch colonists.' And Mr Ward Beecher, in his late so-called novel,[3] has said still more plainly: 'New England has always been economical of holi-

Page from Hawthorne's American notebook with passages deleted by Sophia Hawthorne
(MA569, Pierpont Morgan Library)

days. Christmas she threw away with indignant emphasis, as stained and spattered with papal superstition. The only two festivals were Thanksgiving Day and Fast Day–the last to put in the seed with, and the former to celebrate the year's harvest. New England never made provision for amusements . . . The old Puritans, regarding games and amusements as poisonous flowers, whose odors bewitched the senses and stupified manhood, abhorred them . . . It was the practical philosophy of New England that a free and intelligent people, thrifty in business, managing their own matters, and zealously occupied in building up the commonwealth, had excitement enough and variety of interest enough in their normal affairs, and that earnest men, did not need, like children, to be fed on frolic and amusement.' 'This view,' Mr Beecher magnanimously admits, 'was carried to an extreme. But it was a reaction from a use of amusement which was degrading to manhood and inconsistent with the freedom of the commonwealth.'

This dogmatism and intolerance have banished from the soil of New England nearly all the best and most generous spirits who have had the misfortune to be born there. The experience of Morton of Merry Mount, Endicott's contemporary, has been the experience of all the free souls who have come after him. 'This harmless mirth,' he says,[4] describing the May-pole revels at Ma-re Mount,

> made by young men . . . was much distasted by the precise Separatists: that kept much ado, about the tithe of mint and cummin, troubling their brains more than reason would require about things that are indifferent; and from that time sought occasion against my honest Host of Ma-re Mount to overthrow his undertakings, and to destroy his plantation quite and clear.

The moral grip of society has been as severe, as unrelenting, as cruel, as the actual grip of John Endicott was upon his sword hilt, when he hewed away at the May-pole, and sent the revellers to be scourged at the cart-tail. There was no alternative but submission or banishment, both for Morton, and for his successors. Franklin, who superadded a most un-yankee liberality of sentiment to a thoroughly Yankee thrift in practice, fled away to Philadelphia, and abode there. Nathaniel Greene, the Quaker warrior of Rhode Island, took his peaceful retirement and his Penates to Georgia. Webster preferred even the thirsty summers and arid atmosphere of Washington to those granite hills of New Hampshire, from which–at a distance–his imagination received such succor. Beecher's Plymouth Church abides at Brooklyn, and the Vermonter, Greeley, goes any whither rather than east of the East River. The same causes drove Herman Melville to the South Seas, made a prophet of Brigham Young in Utah, a fighting lawyer of Sergeant S. Prentiss at Vicksburg, a fighting editor of George D. Prentice at Louisville, and a fighting poet of Albert Pike in Arkansas. Of those who have stayed at home and dared to think for themselves, nine-tenths have effloresced into that peculiar insanity of ideas which has made New England a hot-bed for every ism that the diseased imagination of man ever spawned, and for all the loathsomeness that the cold and the corrupt fancy ever engendered.

We must seek the philosophy of all this state of things in the characteristics of the people, their system of administration, their habits of thought, and manner of life. They are a community who are what they are, by reason, in a very great measure, of domestic government. The Puritans who first landed founded what was a purely hierocratic state, and essentially such it has continued ever since. It was a community that rested upon a dark and repulsive system of worship, made terrible with superstition, administered without respect to the character of individuals, and enforced with inquisitorial appliances and inconceivable severity. It was a government inexorable as the iron rule of Philip of Spain, and meddlesome as the petticoat surveillance of a sewing-circle. Such a repressive force, brooding over a sunless land, over a cold and unfruitful soil, in a raw and unwholesome climate, could not fail to develop many unlovely propensities in a people naturally hard-faced and atrabilious, ingenious, thrifty, but close, and given to trick and make-shift. And the warmest admirers of New England admit that such were the effects of the system. Says Mr Beecher:[5]

> 'Perhaps nowhere in the world can be found more unlovely wickedness–a malignant, tenacious, bitter hatred of good–than in New England. The good are very good, and the bad are very bad. The high moral tone of public sentiment, in many New England towns, and its penetrating and almost inquisitorial character, either powerfully determines men to good, or chafes and embitters them. This is especially true when, in certain cases, good men are so thoroughly bent upon public morality that the private individual has scarcely any choice left. Under such a pressure, some men act in open wickedness out of spite, and some secretly; and the bottom of society wages clandestine war with the top.'

This system, while it encouraged rigidity in the rigid, and ranked 'cuteness' among the high virtues, fostered also a disposition to discordant enthusiasm, and opened the way to a fanatical habit of life that was an indescribable mixture

PASSAGES

FROM THE

AMERICAN NOTE-BOOKS

OF

NATHANIEL HAWTHORNE.

VOL. I.

BOSTON:
TICKNOR AND FIELDS.
1868.

Title page for the first volume that Hawthorne's wife prepared for publication from the author's notebooks (from C. E. Frazer Clark Jr., Nathaniel Hawthorne: A Descriptive Bibliography, *1978)*

Sophia's Editing

Sophia Hawthorne was initially reluctant to publish her husband's notebooks, but eventually acceded to the arguments of James T. Fields and took up the task of editing. All references to Hawthorne's drinking were deleted as well as any of his language that she considered indelicate. James R. Mellow summarizes and judges the effect of Sophia's work as an editor in Nathaniel Hawthorne in His Times *(1980): "The result was that the picture of Hawthorne as a man who could be down-to-earth in his private moments was considerably altered. In very direct fashion, Sophia tempered the blunter forms of Hawthorne's vocabulary: 'pimp' was replaced by 'agent'; 'whores' was translated as 'women.' Later critics might complain of editorial tampering, but it was clearly the standard of the age. It was the same standard Hawthorne himself had applied when transcribing his notes into fiction or editing the sometimes saltier versions of his anonymously published stories for book publication" (p. 584).*

---

of piety and Pharisaism. It blunted the social instincts, subdued the kindly impulses that flow like virgin waters from the unsophisticated heart, and pampered into unnatural growth a tendency, in those who were its victims, to timidity, falsehood, and meanness in all the private and interior relations of life. Everything that was kindly, genial, sportive, went down under the relentless chariot-wheels of this iron-clad despotism, until even the sense of the comfortable embraced nothing more than a wretched patchwork of expedients; and as for the sense of the beautiful, it was literally starved to death.

This constitution of the State and of society made life in that atmosphere peculiarly oppressive to the liberal and the sensitive spirit. The petty cruelty and cowardice of the people, their harsh and narrow rule of being, their selfish hypocrisy and 'inverterate curiosity,' made association with them a torture for the poet, the dreamer, the enthusiast, who sought an unhampered communion with nature or his own thoughts. For such it was truly a witch-haunted region, about whose befogged and sunless valleys hung a blasting miasm[a] that chilled him to the soul. In the early and enthusiastic days of the colonies, when the fanaticism was real, and the enthusiasm genuine, this despotism was still endurable, as Hawthorne has himself remarked. 'All was well,' says he, 'so long as their lamps were freshly kindled at the heavenly flame. After a while, however, whether in their time or their children's, those lamps began to burn more dimly, or with a less genuine lustre; and then it might be seen how hard, cold, and confined was their system,–how like an iron cage was that which they called Liberty.'[6] And he adds, with a fervor that is scarcely in his style:

> Happy are we, if for nothing else, yet because we did not live in those days . . . Its daily life must have trudged onward with hardly anything to diversify and enliven it, while also its rigidity could not fail to cause miserable distortions of the moral nature. Such a life was sinister to the intellect and sinister to the heart . . . It was impossible for the succeeding race to grow up, in heaven's freedom, beneath the discipline which their gloomy energy of character had established; nor, it may be, have we even yet thrown off all the unfavorable influences which, among many good ones, were bequeathed to us by our Puritan forefathers. Let us thank God for having given us such ancestors; and let each successive generation thank him, not less fervently, for being one step further from them in the march of ages.

But Hawthorne felt this influence of New England upon the development of his genius much more poignantly than most of his contemporaries did, and much more keenly than the above paragraph would seem to indicate. His works abound in internal evidence to this fact, and, in regard to these works, we must remember that, while positively disclaiming the imputation that he had infused too much of his personality into his prefaces and introductions, he admits that the 'essential traits' of his character are to be discerned[7] nevertheless, in his main writings, the *ensemble* of which, at any rate, indirectly reflects the color of his actual thought. Now the especial personality which is revealed to us in Hawthorne's works, is that of a genius subdued into a melancholy that is only too nigh akin to morbidness; and so subdued by the chilling, the bewildering, the prostrating consciousness of having to live a life necessarily 'at variance with his country and his time.' 'To persons whose pursuits are insulated from the common business of life,' says our author in one of his most elaborate tales,[8] 'who are either in advance of mankind, or apart from it,—there often comes a sensation of moral cold, that makes the spirit shiver, as if it had reached the frozen latitude around the pole.' In this story, indeed, under the characters of Robert Danforth and Peter Hovenden, he has portrayed the opposite poles of the New England nature; hard, uncouth materialism, and a narrow, grovelling, sneering selfishness, showing the crushing influence of such a contact to the lover of beauty. 'He would drive me mad, were I to meet him often,' says the sensitive artist of the blacksmith. 'His hard, brute force darkens and confuses the spiritual element within me . . . You are my Evil Spirit,' he cries; 'you and the hard, coarse world! The leaden thoughts and the despondency that ye fling upon me, are my clogs!' So, likewise, in that profound and saddest of allegories, 'Young Goodman Brown,' our author bodies forth his writhing and impotent consciousness of the secret hollowness and Pharisaic iniquity of New England life. 'When the minister spoke from the pulpit, with power and fervid eloquence, and with his hand upon the open Bible, of the sacred truths of our religion, and of saint-like lives and triumphant deaths, and of future bliss or misery unutterable, then did Goodman Brown turn pale, dreading lest the roof should thunder down upon the grey blasphemer and his hearers.' In the same way he gives the key-note to the melancholy that predominates over the tone of his sketches.[9] 'These scenes, you think, are all too sombre,' says the complaisant showman; 'so, indeed, they are; but the blame must rest on the sombre spirit of our forefathers, who wove their web of life with hardly a single thread of rose color or gold, and not on me, who have a tropic love of sunshine, and would gladly gild all the world with it.'

But this is still not all. We must contemplate this gentle spirit, cast adrift in this uncongenial atmosphere as it is, and feebly struggling against the hard and sour austerities of the surrounding life that clash so rudely with its artistic aspirations, and weigh so gloomily upon its brooding melancholy—we most contemplate this timid and shrinking spirit brought face to face with the consciousness of a retribution which it must *personally* pay, and from the penalties of which it can in no wise escape. There is no article of faith in all his creed that Hawthorne has dwelt upon so often, so earnestly, so painfully, as that which he styles emphatically 'the truth,

A drawing of a scene from "Young Goodman Brown" by W. B. Brown Jr. (Autograph Edition, Houghton, Mifflin, 1900; Thomas Cooper Library, University of South Carolina)

that the wrong-doing of one generation lives into the successive ones, and divesting itself of every temporary advantage, becomes a pure and uncontrollable mischief.' He repeats this idea more often than any other in his tales; he allegorizes it elaborately and under a hundred protean shapes, and he has made it the key-note to this two most extensive books, *The House of the Seven Gables,* and *The Romance of Monte Beni.* Not only this; he seems to brood over the notion with a subtle dread, and a sense of doom, that most resembles the fatal fascination with which the subject of hereditary insanity watches for, and prognosticates, the accursed symptoms, until—truly *veniente occurrens morbo*—his very horror itself has attained the proportions of the disease he would give his life to avert. For an instance of this feeling, remark this: 'To the thoughtful mind, there will be no tinge of superstition in what we figuratively express, by affirming that the ghost of a dead progenitor—perhaps as a portion of his own punishment—is often doomed to become the Evil Genius of his family.' Again, observe how, in the *Old Manse,* he speaks of the boy who killed the wounded soldier upon the battle-field of Concord:

The story comes home to me like truth. Often-times, as an intellectual and moral exercise, I have sought to follow that poor youth through his subsequent career, and observe how his soul was tortured by the blood-stain, contracted, as it had been, before the long custom of war had robbed human life of its sanctity, and while it still seemed murderous to slay a brother man. *This one circumstance has borne more fruit for me than all that history tells us of the fight.*

Compare, likewise, the intense morbidness of 'Roger Malvin's Burial,' and then, having gotten an idea of his way of thought upon the subject, you will find a significance that is almost appalling in the description he has given of the scourging of the Quakeress in Salem streets by his own ancestor:

A strong-armed fellow is that constable; and each time he flourishes his lash in the air, you see a frown wrinkling and twisting his brow, and, at the same time, a smile upon his lips. He loves his business, faithful officer that he is, and puts his soul into every stroke, zealous to fulfil the injunction of Major Hawthorne's warrant, in the spirit and to the letter. There came down a stroke that has drawn blood! Ten such stripes are to be given in Salem, ten in Boston, and ten in Dedham; and with those thirty stripes of blood upon her, she is to be driven into the forest. The crimson trail goes wavering along the Main street; but Heaven grant that, as the rain of so many years has wept upon it, time after time, and washed it all away, so there may have been a dew of mercy to cleanse this cruel blood-stain out of the record of the persecutor's life!

Such, then, is Hawthorne's relation to New England. That such a man, in such evil case, with nerves so delicately strung, a Democrat among high-dry Federalists, a fainéant among busy-bodies, a beauty-worshipper in the Paradise of the Main-Chance, shy as a cuckoo, recluse as a Trappist, and poor as a Carthusian—that such a man, so circumstanced, should have made himself a great artist, argues, we repeat, genius of a very transcendent kind.

It is as an artist that Hawthorne must be studied most. Whatever the limitations of this genius—and these limitations are many—he was emphatically an artist, whose materials are always subdued to, and plastic in, his hand. His sphere is a narrow one, and remote, but within it he is completely sovereign. His material is achromatic, and somewhat thin, but he assimilates it thoroughly, and weaves it smoothly and easily into the texture of his thought. He is exigent with himself, also; his standard is very high: he waits for the moment of invention, and, like Leonardo da Vinci, cannot be driven to work until

the happy inspiration is upon him. Thus, his idea is always completely wrought, as far as it goes, and we find in him nothing fragmentary, nothing of guess-work, nothing tentative and premonitory of things to come. The peculiarly artistic impression that his works create, is furthered by his instinctive ideality, his constructive skill, and the careful finish he gives to everything he touches. He has the most poignantly acute susceptibility to every form of mystic sentiment and weird consciousness—a susceptibility that enables him to fling his peculiar glamour of ethereal but pensive fancy about the most trivial circumstances and pettiest incidents of life. He conjoins to this delicate receptivity the power of transmuting his most aerial thought into an image of speech that preserves all its fragile tenderness, and all its minute perfection of contour and of tone. His execution is indeed incomparable, luminous by a firm hand and a clear purpose, and is in itself a living witness to *pictor ignotus* Blake's aphorism, that 'Execution is the chariot of Genius.' In perfect concurrence and intelligence betwixt means and ends, and in that rare simplicity of uses which goes most efficiently, most directly, to the purpose, and which is the last and most difficult attainment in art, Hawthorne has very few superiors. His *Note-Book* reveals to us what the quality of his performance would have constrained us to infer: his deep, thorough, patient study, his zealous and elaborate preparation, and the fidelity with which he worked out each hint, each detail, until, touch by touch, he wrought each little tale and sketch into a cabinet piece of exquisite finish, as conscientiously done as an illuminated mind of the eleventh century, as effectively done as a picture of Meissonier or Gerome. This series of studies, indeed, suggests to us what we are told of those books of drawings left us—precious heritage!—by Leonardo da Vinci, of whom Hawthorne often reminds us. Like that greatest of all the artists—greatest not in what he has done, but in what he showed power to do—we see our author continually feeling his way towards perfection 'through a series of disgusts.' Like Leonardo again,

he plunged into the study of nature . . . He brooded over the hidden virtues of plants and crystals, the lines traced by the stars as they moved in the sky, over the correspondencies which exist between the different orders of living things, through which, to eyes opened, they interpret each other; and for years he seemed to those about him as one listening to a voice silent for other men.[10]

It is in this susceptible conscientiousness, this wearisome desire to overlay each thought with perfection, this utter impatience of all half-way processes, that we must seek for the cause of the limitation of Hawthorne's powers; for limited they are, and upon many sides. His invention is sobered continually, and his quickening fancy held in reins, by the fastidiousness of his conception, and by the ingrained reserve and timidity of his disposition. His observation is minute, but his judgment is indeterminate. He never quite makes up his mind upon which side of an idea to place himself, and often fails in his picture through his reluctance to present its central thought in a decisive light. You cannot make yourself sure in regard to any of his atmospheres, he has such a propensity to neutralize every effect with the contrary one, to temper lurid glare with pallid moonlight, and make it uncertain whether they be veritable witches that chase Tam o' Shanter and Kirk Alloway Brig, or only shadows of the night manipulated by an apprehensive fancy. He has none of Tieck's robustness of faith in the supernatural, nor any of Fouqué's simple and implicit spirituality, nor of Hoffmann's shuddering horror lest the figments of his too active brain should really be standing there behind him, looking over his shoulder. So, these writers are able always to excel him in breadth of effect. His self-consciousness likewise costs him much, for it leads constantly in his case to the query so fatal to the orator, 'Pleads he in earnest?' In the same way, as was early remarked by Edgar Poe, he overwhelms the most of his subjects in a strain of allegory which destroys everything like dramatic effect. But, indeed, there is nothing dramatic in Hawthorne. In 'The Snow Image,' which is imitated from Goethe's *Erl-King,* and is the most dramatic of his pieces, one cannot help being irritated the whole time he is reading it, to see so many opportunities for forcible effect let slip, as if his grasp had no nervousness whatsoever in it. He approaches most of his subjects by intimation and suggestion, not directly; he is never dogmatic, but constantly informs you he has no decided convictions in the premises, and is prepared to abandon those he has—glimmering speculations as they are—if you make strenuous demand upon him. There is nothing of the Vesalius in his fashion of probing into the phenomena of consciousness; on the contrary, he seems to tremble in the presence of his own creations, lest they should assume the voice and re-enact the passions of actual men. There is no rush, no flow, in his narrative, nor in his description. He gives you the impression of a timid student, of a pensive, minute, observant habit, seeking, like Jacques, the shade of forest-glades and the company of their dappled citizens; harkening with ears as acute and susceptible as those of Donatello, to the slightest whispers of Nature, which he interprets in every instance with the vibrating delicacy and unerring fidelity of an electrometer; yet so shy of speech, and so abstemious in opinion, that you had rather go to Touchstone and Audrey than to this halting scholar, who tantalizes you with half-words, revealing continually a power that he as continually refuses to exercise. You are drawn to him, however, irresistibly; and you seek from him something that will suffice to soften 'the iron facts of life;' in lieu thereof, with a faint, half pensive, half ironic smile, he flings over you a tissue of shadows and a veil of unrealities, hiding himself the while. You are uncertain whether to weep or not; you are very certain not to laugh. There is nothing so genuine as a hearty laugh in all his writings. Withal, he impresses you irresistibly with the consciousness of immense forces held in reserve—forces never brought up, never shown, never heard from, yet whose existence you predicate with mathematical certainty. The oracle is dumb, yet the invisible presence of the god descends about you like an odor, and, although the miracle is never wrought, you have a perfect and abiding faith. The oak is at the root, although the blossoms are merely anemones, faint, delicate, shrinking wind-flowers.[11]

The *Note-Book* more than bears out the impression of exuberant fertility of thought and imagination which lies perdu in the authorized works, behind the veil of his subdued, reticent, and timid manner; but at the same time, it confirms the final estimate to which every student of Hawthorne's art must come: That he did not depict, nor attempt to depict, nor even conceive of, men and women as such, but only certain attributes, which he clad in the garb of shadowy but fascinating form. His characters are essentially phantasmagoria, and he looks upon them as such, and developes them as such; nay, more, he transforms to suit his mood even the real people whom he puts into his magic lantern, so that the instrument shows you only their shadows, definitely outlined, it is true, but thin and unsubstantial. He was an ideologistic chemist,—not an analyst nor synthesist like Lavoisier or Dalton, eager to evoke systematic philosophy or practical results,—but one of those fanciful creative chemists of the seventeenth century, who did not seek even the philosopher's stone, nor the Paracelsian panacea; but, haunted by dreams, shadowy, unreal dreams of beauty and strangeness, experimented all their days upon symbolisms, transmutations, coincidences and signatures—inventing *arbores Dianae,* sporting with the mystic significances of the Rosy Cross, pondering over the beautiful wonders of metamorphosis

Bindings for the first American and English editions of Our Old Home *and* Passages from the American Notebooks
(from C. E. Frazer Clark Jr., Nathaniel Hawthorne: A Descriptive Bibliography, *1978)*

and palingenesis, and losing themselves in the fascinating company of the visions that perplex the twilight dawn of philosophy. What a contrast between Hawthorne and Charles Reade! How elastic and robust the one, what a shrinking sensitive plant the other. How hope unconquerable, and joy, and life, bound even out of the very depth of misery, beneath Reade's sanguine touch. How a dark strand of gloom runs through the tenderest flights of Hawthorne's fancy, until

> —*medio de fonte leporum*
> *Surgit amari aliquid.*

Part of this shadowy, unreal, and dejected texture of all that he writes is due to the causes of which we have already spoken; part is due to that 'unconquerable reserve' to which he himself pleads guilty; part must be explained by the chilling influences of the neglect with which his earlier writings were received by an unappreciative public. It is quite apparent that much of Hawthorne's shyness and timidity of statement is constitutional. Curtis, in the *Homes of American Authors,* has told us that during his three years' residence at the 'Old Manse' in Concord, Hawthorne was not seen by a dozen people of the place altogether; and he himself, speaking of the apparently confidential character of his prefaces, says: 'I have been especially careful to make no disclosures respecting myself which the most indifferent observer might not have been acquainted with, and which I was not perfectly willing my worst enemy should know.' He adds, in another place, 'So far as I am a man of really individual attributes, I

veil my face; nor am I, nor have I ever been, one of those supremely hospitable people, who serve up their own hearts delicately fried, with brain sauce, as a tidbit for their beloved public.' In the same preface, he has, not incorrectly, characterized his own writings, and has perhaps indicated one great cause of the long and wearisome halt he had to make in the wilderness of unrecognition. 'They [the tales] have the pale tint of flowers that blossomed in too retired a shade—the coolness of a meditative habit, which diffuses itself through the feeling and observation of every sketch . . . Whether from lack of power, or an unconquerable reserve, the author's touches have often an effect of tameness.' The author, he continues, 'on the internal evidence of his sketches, came to be regarded as a mild, shy, gentle, melancholic, exceedingly sensitive, and not very forcible man . . . He is by no means certain, that some of his subsequent productions have not been influenced and modified by a natural desire to fill up so amiable an outline, and to act in consonance with the character assigned him.'[12] In this hint we undoubtedly have an explanation of the unsatisfactory portrait of that not very commendable hero, Miles Coverdale, in *Blithesdale,* as well as of the tameness and lack of sinew so much complained of in *The Marble Faun.* It is unfortunate that our author should have come to take this view of things. Charlotte Brontë has indeed very strikingly said, that 'the pensiveness of reserve is the best phase for some minds,' and Hawthorne seems to work freest behind a veil. But he purchases this freedom too dear, when he shadows himself thus completely.

That something of life and fire was pressed out of Hawthorne by the dead weight of a blind and unapprehensive public, is very certain. No spirit as sensitive as his could preserve its perfect health under such a burthen of obscurity as he had to endure. He says:

> The author of *Twice-told Tales* has a claim to one distinction, which, as none of his literary brethren will care about disputing it with him, he need not be afraid to mention. He was, for a good many years, the obscurest man of letters in America. These stories were published in magazines and annuals, extending over a period of ten or twelve years, and comprising the whole of the writer's young manhood, without making (so far as he has ever been aware) the slightest impression on the public . . . Throughout the time above specified, he had no incitement to literary effort in a reasonable prospect of reputation or profit; nothing but the pleasure itself of composition–an enjoyment not at all amiss in its way, and perhaps essential to the merit of the work in hand, but which, in the long run, will hardly keep the chill out of a writer's heart, or the numbness out of his fingers.

And, in another place, he complains still more audibly:

> Was there ever such a weary delay in obtaining the slightest recognition from the public, as in my case? I sat down by the way-side of life, like a man under enchantment, and a shrubbery sprung up around me, and the bushes grew to be saplings, and the saplings became trees, until no exit appeared possible, through the entangling depths of my obscurity.

The philosophy of popularity has yet to be written, but it is not difficult to see why Hawthorne was so slow in being recognized. Crates, the philosopher, once compiled a statement of the wages awarded by his contemporaries to the different trades and professions, from which it appears that while a cook received hundreds of dollars, a physician was thought to be paid with a shilling; the toad-eater got his thousands, the courtezan counted her wages upon the fourth finger, but the philosopher received only a sixpence, and the moral adviser was paid in–smoke. Hawthorne, while principally an artist, was still a good deal of a moralist, and something of a philosopher. Much of his best art is 'caviare to the general.' It is a harmonious and beautiful art, to be sure; but it is not spontaneous, and so misses something of the impulsive charm of naturalness and directness. No premeditated art, no matter how cunning, can simulate that which gushes by the first intention, warm and fluid, from the heart. Neither taste nor culture can supply the place of that glowing power of nature, which seizes upon the soul by the mere force of sympathy. Taste and culture, in

fact, the outgrowths of educated thought, are drawbacks to popularity, so far forth at least as they tend to add angles reflective and refractive to the media through which people see works of art. The law is, the more transparent the medium, the more instinctive the recognition. Mrs Jameson has remarked it as a curious fact that, just in proportion as the schools of art in Italy refined and elevated the type of beauty under which the Madonna was presented, did the popular reverence and the popular worship fall back to the rude pictures of the old Byzantine type, pictures in which sanctity and venerableness seemed to preclude the necessity for design and perspective.[13] Why was this so? Because art, refining too much, yielding itself too much to the guidance of cultivated taste, unconsciously elevated itself to a point *above* the popular comprehension, always crass, and clamorous for broad effects only. *In hâc nuce* lies the whole distinction between popular and unpopular art; and it is only the greatest minds that are able to break down this distinction–it is only the very highest genius that, employing the simplest symbols and the most universal language, is able to stretch its golden chain of fascination from the highest mountain peaks to the lowliest valleys. Genius constrained to work at a lower level, genius that, like Hawthorne's seeks to be recognized not by sympathy but through appreciation, can never hope to attain this sort of popularity. The distinction that subsists in the moral world between the worldly and the unworldly, says De Quincey,[14] subsists equally in the literary world. 'From qualities, for instance, of childlike simplicity, of shy profundity, or of inspired self-communion, the world does and must turn away its face towards grosser, bolder, more determined, or more intelligible expressions of character and intellect.' In any such classification, our author would not fail to win a place high up in the list of the unworldly brethren.

A shallower spirit than Hawthorne would have changed his style, gone into more sensational walks, or sought eclat in some shape or other of simulated *hysterica passio*. A more dishonest spirit might have stooped still lower, even to the mud and mire, as we have seen a contemporary do, who, to revive a notoriety waning for lack of sustenance, violated the sanctity of the grave, and battened her prurient fancy in nauseous libels of the helpless dead. But Hawthorne upheld his art with unblenching fidelity, patiently waiting for the only kind of popularity that is worth having:–'that popularity which follows, not that which is run after; that popularity which, sooner or later, never fails to do justice to the pursuit of noble ends by noble means.'[15] And Hawthorne was right, for there is much that is of greater worth to the

NOTES

IN

ENGLAND AND ITALY.

By MRS. HAWTHORNE.

NEW YORK:
G. P. PUTNAM & SON.
1869.

Title page for Sophia Hawthorne's only book. She chose not to publish with Fields because she believed the royalty payment for Passages from the American Note-Books *was too low (from C. E. Frazer Clark Jr.,* Nathaniel Hawthorne: A Descriptive Bibliography, *1978)*

artist than popularity can be. The youth will not be able to see this, but, as a man grows in years, and perforce in wisdom,—since wisdom consists chiefly in revised opinions and more methodic, because wiser, experience,—the pertinacious itch for merely literary fame must be sensibly mitigated in the presence of superior indwelling forces, of later, but higher, growth. Of course, no man is willing to hide his light under a bushel, nor simply to leave it there, if it be so hidden; he wants to go abroad and be known, as much in maturity as in youth. But the impelling motive is different, if one's self-culture have been of the right sort. Instead of seeking to be known for himself, to publish abroad all the great and glorious gifts he fancies himself to possess, he wishes to be known through the excellence of his work of art, or the efficacy of his work of doctrine.

He demands recognition through that which he has to impart, and only values his conspicuousness in that it is a proof that his teaching prevails, and his doctrine is acceptable. Of course, moreover, a person who adopts literature as a profession, and as the business of his life, expects to make a living by it, and has as much the right to demand, and to try to secure, a high price for his labors, as the clerk, the mechanic, or the professional man. But he is only a poor mercenary dog indeed, who will sacrifice his art to his greed; who will prostitute his talents, or keep his sincere impulses hidden away and undeveloped for lack of a good market. The true man desires wealth quite as much as the rogue; he desires it more perhaps, because wealth will do so much for him; and his dreams of riches,—with the comforts thus to be obtained, the conveniences, the luxuries and refinements, the aids to study and culture, the material encouragement to happiness,—are tantalizing indeed. But not for money nor for fame will the true man sell his art; not for hire will he set out his talents to grin or dance the rope in the market place; not for miserable pelf and plaudit will he forego his studies, his convictions, and the deep-rooted sentiments of scrupulous probity at the bottom of the unsullied artistic conscience. What he writes must be his own, not the populace's; if it do not suit them, he cannot help it, but will go on, trusting to create an audience on whom his appeal will finally have its effect; if it bring name, fame, fortune, so much the better for him. To write as some modern fiction-mongers have written, and with their avowed purposes, to proclaim one's self court-fool and *ex-officio* jester to King Vulgus,—this is an ignoble occupation, and a position the true man will not have, even if he can seize it, like a ripe pear, by merely stretching out his hand. The truly great writers have never done so. They may have changed their style, to attract attention, but they have always remained true to their art and their instincts,—they have always preserved the heart of Socrates behind the mask of Silenus. Through all the rugosities of *Sartor Resartus,* it is quite apparent that Teufelsdrockh is Carlyle still. Thackeray from the heights of his early *Pendennis* aspirations, condescended to *Titmarsh* and to *Jeemes de la Pluche,* but the Thackeray of *Frazer* and of *Punch,* so far forth as moral purpose goes, and so far forth as fidelity to art goes, is the same noble friend who has blessed the world with Henry Esmond, and George Warrington, and Ethel Newcome, and with the dear old Colonel, the most incomparable figure in fiction since Don Quixote.

Hawthorne did not even modify his vehicle of expression, deeming that he had no business to swerve from what he regarded the most appropriate form for his art, which was at once a worthy art in itself, and the best he could do in the premises. It is probable that he felt about this matter as Charles Dickens felt, when he said:[16] 'It has always been my observation of human nature, that a man who has any good reason to believe in himself never flourishes himself before the face of other people, in order that they may believe in him.' And it is quite likely also that, in spite of his shyness, his reserve, and a naturally despondent temper, he had yet sufficient confidence in his art to believe, with De Quincy,[17] that 'all merit which is founded in truth, and is strong enough, reaches by sweet exhalations in the end a higher sensory; reaches higher organs of discernment, lodged in a selecter audience.' So that we may say, without paradox, that, if Hawthorne's obscurity injured the tone of his genius, by quenching in some degree the fire of his temper, it at the same time enabled him to approve the strength of his fidelity to art, and contributed, besides, sensibly to *purify* it. If he is fastidious to an extreme, he is yet perfect in his class; if he confines himself within too restrictive limits, within those limits each performance of his is a gem almost flawless. And possibly, if his had been a success of the first blush, he would have over-written himself, as so many promising young authors do, eager to catch the whole tide of applause upon its crest: or, (which is more probable, taking into consideration his constitutional timidity and fastidiousness,) would have found a stumbling block to future achievement in the career of his first work. It was not without reason that Garrick feared for Sheridan's second play, on account of his too powerful *Rivals:* nor was Karl von Weber deploring an unusual event when, in speaking of the too rapid culmination of his lyric fame, he exclaimed: 'That young rascal *Der Freyschutz* has shot his poor sister *Euryanthe* dead.'

The excellence of Hawthorne's genius are as marked and peculiar as its limitations. There is not a book nor a tale from his pen but completely fills the niche he assigns to it in his gallery of art:—there is not a page, a paragraph, a line of his, against which the too frequent reproach can be urged that it was

Merely writ at first for filling,
To raise the volume's price a shilling.

His refined taste, his competent scholarship, his practised constructiveness, are always available, always apparent, never obtrusive. He fences ever with a foil, and in gloves, like an amateur, but each parry and thrust suggest to you the sinewy wrist, the consummate exercise, and a reserved strength capable of wielding the broadsword as dexterously as the rapier. He holds fast to his ideal always, with adroit facility, and always presents it to you in its worthiest phase and most charming colors. His aerial fancy, his placid and equable grace, never desert him for a single moment, nor does he ever relinquish his easy mastery of the refined harmonies so predominantly characteristic of his thought and his style.

He is much more frank in his intercourse with the unintelligent world that he is with man, and his companionship with Nature in her best moods is one of his sincerest and most pleasant traits. Neither Thoreau, nor Emerson, nor Channing, who were his teachers in the study of Nature, have been able to surpass him in close and beautiful observation of her multitudinous aspects. He is *nemorum studiosus;* the sky and the waters speak to him in intelligible and affectionate language; and even the yellow squashes in the gardens yield up to him their thought, and enrich his fancy with new analogies. The gnarled and blasted trees in an old orchard invite him to intimacy with them; a river slumbering betwixt shade and sunshine imparts to him pregnant lessons from the spiritual world; and as for the pond-lily that grows by its banks, it bequeaths to him a whole treatise in ethical philosophy. 'It is a marvel,' he says,

> whence this perfect flower derives its loveliness and perfume, springing, as it does, from the black mud over which the river sleeps, and where lurk the slimy eel, and speckled frog, and the mud-turtles, whom continual washing cannot cleanse. It is the very same black mud out of which the yellow lily sucks its obscene life and noisome odor. Thus we see, too, in the world, that some persons assimilate only what is ugly and evil from the same moral circumstances which supply good and beautiful results—the fragrance of celestial flowers—to the daily life of others.

Isaac Walton's contemplativeness was not more marked than that of Hawthorne, though the latter's is made more pensive, and, we must add, less cheerful, by his introvertive and darker mood. His sunshine wears often an Indian summer hue to veil its brightness, and sometimes a cloud of morbidness comes over it with an effect unpleasantly chilling; but generally, even his most pensive reveries are pervaded with a sweet serenity that cannot be compared to anything so nearly as to the notes of the Hermit Thrush, heard in the deep silent noontides of June woods, remote, long-drawn, clear as a silver bell,—the summer-time anthem of a blissful voice, chanting its happiness in 'full-throated' ease.

Not less remarkable than our author's constructive skill is his deep and sagacious scrutiny of the human heart, his subtle perception of moral analogies,

PASSAGES

FROM THE

ENGLISH NOTE-BOOKS

OF

NATHANIEL HAWTHORNE.

VOL. I.

BOSTON:
FIELDS, OSGOOD, & CO.
1870.

PASSAGES

FROM THE

FRENCH AND ITALIAN
NOTE-BOOKS

OF

NATHANIEL HAWTHORNE.

VOL. I.

BOSTON:
JAMES R. OSGOOD AND COMPANY,
Late Ticknor & Fields, and Fields, Osgood, & Co.
1872.

Title pages and bindings for the first American and English editions of Passages from the English Note-Books *and* Passages
from the French and Italian Note-Books of Nathaniel Hawthorne, *published in 1870 and 1871*
(from C. E. Frazer Clark Jr., Nathaniel Hawthorne: A Descriptive Bibliography, *1978)*

and his wondrous insight, that gives him such mastery of knowledge in the remoter and more intricate phenomena of psychology. Never were the spiritual weaknesses and infirmities of human nature interrogated so curiously, nor made to respond in such strange fashion, as when Hawthorne pursued them to their dark recesses with his shy but incessant and acute research. His scalpel, delicately, almost timidly, handled, has a searching persistence that cuts through tissue, and nerve, and fibre, and organ, never content until it has touched the quivering fountain of life within. He adjusts his moral stethoscope to every breast, and fails not to find the hidden disease, the secret shame, the cherished selfishness, the unguessed hypertrophy, the encysted but malignant ulcer.

All nature is thus full of significance to him, and not the less suggestive is his own consciousness. But his perceptions and conceptions, high-strung until they have grown morbidly acute, lend a certain sombre sense of inadequacy, corruption, and decay to all that significance. He is too many-sided in feeling to give himself up to a pure enjoyment of any phase of thought. Even when he longs to soar on the wings of the lark to the blue elysium above us, his sensitive soul halts apprehensively, and shivers at the 'cold and solitary thought.' He cannot even contemplate the bright visions of enthusiastic youth without dwelling upon the thought that those visions must be 'realized in chillness, obscurity, and tears.'[18] He cannot present to his mind even the simple image of a decayed old maid reading aloud, without imparting to it the morbid tints of his too alert apprehension.

> This sister's voice, too, naturally harsh, had, in the course of her sorrowful life-time, contracted a kind of croak, which, when it once gets into the human throat, is as ineradicable as sin. In both sexes, occasionally, this life-long croak—accompanying each word of joy or sorrow, is one of the symptoms of a settled melancholy; and whenever it occurs, the whole history of misfortunes is conveyed in its slightest accent. The effect is as if the voice had been dyed black; or,—if we must use a more moderate simile,—this miserable croak, running through all the variations of the voice, is like a black silken thread, on which the crystal beads of speech are strung, and whence they take their hue. Such voices have put on mourning for dead hopes; and they ought to die and be buried along with them.

Still more perfect than his analysis, still more subtle, and far more beautiful from the artistic point of view, as well as more grateful to the general reader, is our author's synthetic skill. The character of Clifford, in *The House of the Seven Gables,* a character built up touch by touch, as we may imagine Titian to have elaborated his most perfect works, is perhaps the most unique specimen of that delicate and evanescent handicraft in the entire range of fiction. The art is so ethereal, the touches are so light, so discriminative, yet so cogent, and keeping and color are so wonderfully well apportioned, that in this character, for the first and last time in Hawthorne's writings, you seem to recognize a photograph fresh from Nature's laboratory, and cannot convince yourself that it is simply a cameo mosaic like all the rest, only more happily conceived, and more matchlessly inwrought.

Hawthorne's effort is so easy and unapparent, his manner is so reticent, so subdued, so demure, so tranquil, and the flow of his thought glides along with such an unboisterous motion, that you must study him if you would discover at once how deep he is, and how original. In the same way, his humor, which is never more than a half smile, is so fine, so delicate, so acute, that the best part of it is always lost to him who reads as he runs. This humor never stammers into a sudden bewilderment of laughter amid tears, like the humor of Charles Lamb, nor does it ever flush and throb, like Jean Paul's sunset rhythm, with the warm, glowing, and ever varying colors of an effusive and melting pathos. Indeed, Hawthorne is not a master of the pathetic, and seldom exerts himself in that way. He is too discursive, too analytic, too coolly contemplative, to know how, by one of those direct, soul-wringing touches of the old objective masters, to make you gush out in a moment with the sudden sense of tears. It is in the essential, immanent, habitual tenderness of his thought and his fancy that we seem to find his strongest vein. This tenderness lingers about and dwells tenderly within all his impulses, as the scent of lavender lingers about a grandmother's drawer. It is the secret charm of all his sweetest moods, and the happy incentive to all his most delicate conceptions. He clothes all his scenery in this mellow, luminous twilight; he lifts it like an aureole above the brows of his favorite characters, until it seems to glorify poor Hepzibah's scowl, dignifies Uncle Venner's patches, makes the little Yankee girl loveable as Madonna, and transfigures the poor shattered wreck that remains of Clifford, into the sacred semblance of a martyr, crowned and triumphant. It is this same ingrained sympathetic tenderness which comes like a shower in June to humanize and freshen up his sombre and arid morality, until, under its transmuting influence, even the sternest deserts of the human heart blossom and rejoice.

Hawthorne's style is the fit and competent organ for his thought and his fancy. This style is so clear, so accurate, so pliant, that you are almost startled to find into what intricacies of thought, what dark recesses of feeling, it can glide at will. Its calm, unvarying repose, and the gracious evenness of its flow and movement, scarcely permit you to suspect its innate force, and the weird powers it continually holds in reserve. It is not until you have looked

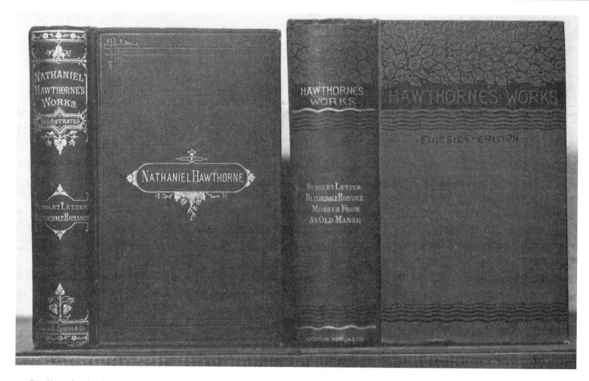

Bindings for the third volume in the Illustrated Library Edition (1871–1882), published by Osgood, and the second volume in the
"New" Fireside Edition (1886), published by Houghton, Mifflin (from C. E. Frazer Clark Jr.,
Nathaniel Hawthorne: A Descriptive Bibliography, *1978)*

back at one of his smooth, easy sentences, and have analyzed it, that you become aware of the magic spells it is
weaving, and the recondite spiritual forces it is bringing
into play. What very easy writing, apparently, is this paragraph about the rain; and yet what a dreary monotone
runs through it, all fraught with kindred associations, and
dropping quietly from its movement, as the round drops
fall down from the eaves. 'Nature,' he says,

> has no kindness—no hospitality—during a rain. In the fierc-
> est heat of sunny days, she retains a secret mercy, and
> welcomes the wayfarer to shady nooks of the woods,
> whither the sun cannot penetrate. But she provides no
> shelter against her storms. It makes us shiver to think of
> those deep, umbrageous recesses—those overshadowing
> banks—where we found such enjoyment during the sultry
> afternoons. Not a twig of foliage there but would dash a
> little shower into our faces. Looking reproachfully
> towards the impenetrable sky—if sky there be, above that
> dismal uniformity of cloud—we are apt to murmur against
> the whole system of the universe; since it involves the
> extinction of so many summer days, in so short a life, by
> the hissing and spluttering rain. In such spells of weather—
> and it is to be supposed such weather came—Eve's bower
> in Paradise must have been but a cheerless and aguish
> kind of shelter; no wise comparable to the old parsonage,
> which had resources of its own to beguile the week's
> imprisonment. The idea of sleeping on a couch of wet
> roses![19]

The limpid simplicity of Hawthorne's style, its most
apparent merit, is conjoined to an almost infinite scope of
expression, by which the most recondite imaginings are
adequately bodied forth in the simplest and most musical
terms. He can utter as deep a thought quite as poignantly
as Carlyle, without any of that distortion, that strain of his
strength, which the Chelsean philosophers find necessary.
In every page from our author's pen, the critic will discover proofs of consummate taste, profound study, and
elaborate practice, to the end of a perfect fluency and consistency of language. In the very repose of his style slumbers a rare power of bringing together and reconciling
analogies, far-fetched from all the abounding storehouse of
Nature. The slightest object thus becomes fraught with an
incomparably deep significance. Describing the avenue
which led in to his residence at Concord, *the old Manse,* he
says: 'The glimmering shadows that lay half asleep
between the door of the house and the public highway,
were a kind of spiritual medium, seen through which, the
edifice had not quite the aspect of belonging to the material world.'

   We cannot better close our notice of Hawthorne
than with the following example of his graceful, tender,
suggestive manner, taken from the introductory chapter to
the *Mosses from an Old Manse,* a work in which all the powers and witchery of his style seem to have culminated.[20]

How early in the summer the prophecy of autumn comes!–earlier in some years than in others,–sometimes even in the first weeks of July.

. . . This sunshine is the golden pledge thereof. It beams through the gates of Paradise, and shows us glimpses far inward.

Notes

1 *Divina Commedia.*–L'Inferno. v. 32.

2 Rev. W. Adams, D. D.–*Thanksgiving Memoirs and Habits.*

3 *Norwood.*

4 *New English Canaan.* By Thomas Morton, of Clifford's Inne, Gent.

5 *Norwood; or Village Life in New England.*

6 *Twice-told Tales,*–'Main Street.'

7 As for egotism, a person who has been burrowing, to his utmost ability, into the depths of our common nature, for the purposes of psychological romance,–and who pursues his researches in that dusky region, as he needs must, as well by the tact of sympathy as by the light of observation,–will smile at incurring such an imputation in virtue of a little preliminary talk about his external habits, his abode, his casual associates, and other matters entirely upon the surface. These things hide the man, instead of displaying him. You must make quite another kind of inquest, and look through the whole range of his fictitious characters, good and evil, in order to detect any of his essential traits.– *Twice-told Tales.* Second Series,–Prefatory Letter.

8 *Mosses from an Old Manse.*–'The Artist of the Beautiful.'

9 'Main Street'.

10 *Fortnightly Review,* November, 1869.–'Notes on Leonardo da Vinci.'

11 *'Tis as if a rough oak that for ages had stood,*
With his gnarled bony branches like ribs of the wood,
Should bloom, after cycles of struggle and scathe,
With a single anemone trembly and rathe.

Lowell.–'*A Fable for Critics*.'

12 *Twice-told Tales.*–Preface.

13 *Legends of the Madonna.*

14 'Essay on Charles Lamb'.

15 Lord Mansfield.

16 *David Copperfield.*

17 'Essay on Charles Lamb'.

18 'Sights from a Steeple.'

19 *Mosses from an Old Manse.*

20 We quote from the edition of Putnam, published in 1850, pp. 23–4.

Nineteen years after reviewing The House of the Seven Gables *in* Southern Literary Messenger, *Henry T. Tuckerman reflected on Hawthorne's life and career.* Lippincott's Magazine *was the major Philadelphia magazine of the time.*

Nathaniel Hawthorne

Henry T. Tuckerman

Lippincott's Magazine, 5 (May 1870): 498–507

Half a decade has elapsed since Hawthorne died, and in the retrospect we find his literary example emphasized by a survey of our limited native field of artistic development in letters; for he eminently possessed the patience of the true artist; he obeyed the laws of intellectual achievement; he subdued that vivacity of temperament which is only content with immediate and obvious results; he turned resolutely aside from the thoroughfare and the arena, and in solitude wrought out his conceptions with conscientious skill and calm reflection; and therefore it is they still appeal to us, still conserve for us not only his name, but his nature–not his fancies merely, but his life; therefore it is they are a permanent trophy, and not a casual memorial, and, amid so much that is incomplete and ephemeral, retain intact their graceful individuality and normal interest. Nor is this an accidental result. It was assured by the earliest as it was confirmed by the latest of his productions; for both are alike distinguished by pure taste in expression, high finish, distinct aim and artistic fidelity–the conservative elements of literature. Years ago, when Hawthorne's name was scarcely known beyond his native region, we wrote of him in an old diary thus:

> I have passed this long, balmy forenoon delightfully–reading Hawthorne. How considerate in B–to send these winsome volumes to refresh my exile!
> . . . He certainly has done much to obviate the reproach which a philosophical writer, not without reason, has cast upon our authors, when he asserts their object to be to astonish rather than please.

Although Hawthorne, the man, was comparatively so little known in his lifetime in that social way that affords such available material for gossip and criticism in the case of so many contemporary authors, yet in another sense few writers of the time are more thoroughly revealed in their inmost personality to such as mediate his record; for this is essentially the history of his mind–the revelation of his consciousness; and as if to complete and confirm it, copious extracts from his note-books and letters have been published since his decease. A leading English critical journal sneered at these data of observation and experience as too unimportant to be interesting; but to the student of literature and the analyst of character they are eminently so, for thereby we learn the process of his authorship, the fidelity of his observation, and his manner of regarding the most familiar elements of life. Taken in connection with his finished works, in these notes we trace his development and his career step by step: we see the details of his daily experience, and realize how he garnered and arranged them for purposes of art. That these are often the reverse of extraordinary, that they are such as thousands are familiar with, and to an unreflecting and unobservant mind they convey no romantic hints, ethical truths or infinite possibilities, only render their statement more suggestive of the latent significance of the most common lot and surroundings when noted by patient intelligence or meditated by an earnest soul. To such, Nature is an ever-new and inspiring picture, sentiment and sensation a conscious relation to the universe and to destiny, and life itself a wonderful drama. From old Salem to Brook Farm, thence to Berkshire valleys and a Massachusetts village, or across the ocean; at an English seaport and in the heart of Italy; as an officer of the customs, a Socialistic novice, a consul, farmer, author; in an old manse of New England or lone villa in Tuscany; wandering in his native fields, along the green lanes of old England or beside moonlit Roman fountains,—we follow his thoughtful step and his dreamy eye, and feel anew the mysterious process through which life is interpreted, Nature described and Art illustrated by Experience. What strikes us in these desultory notes is the variety of his observation, the facility of his psychological sympathies. Not only secluded dell and radiant sunset, historic scenes and the trophies of genius, but the homeliest details and least inspiring facts of daily life find mention—a wharf and a bar-room not less than a wood or a lake; the weather, a garden, an orchard, a roadside encounter with vagrants, the talk of the gifted, a solitary ramble, the advent of apple blossoms or the ripening of a gourd—whatever the eye beholds or the heart responds to yields food for speculation or a glimpse into the philosophy of life. Open the casual record at hazard and you light on a glimpse that hints a picture, a humorous sketch or idea, an anecdote that may be expanded into a tale, a fantasy which is the germ of an allegory, a trait of human character to be wrought into dramatic interest. Slight as are the incidents, familiar as are the scenes, we can imagine that to such a mind they have a meaning and a use, and learn to appreciate the great truth that 'a man's best things are nearest him—lie close about his feet.' Hawthorne noted moods of mind as well as external facts: he elicited with zest the ideas of diverse human beings, to compare and contrast them; and found suggestive alike the talk of critic and vagabond, sailor and farmer, politician and bigot. The Notch in the White Hills, the limited view from a city window, and the sights and sounds of a lunatic asylum, were each and all to him sources of curious knowledge and avenues of truth. How simple the habits, intent the observation and patient the record of the reticent man thus humbly yet profoundly occupied in the study of life; which, to most of his fellows, was and is a whirlpool absorbing consciousness and whelming individuality! 'I bathed in the cave o'erhung with maples and walnuts—the water cool and thrilling;' 'what a beautiful afternoon this has been!' 'men of cold passions have quick eyes;' 'the natural tastes of man for the original Adam's occupation is fast developing in me: I find I am a good deal interested in our garden;' 'O perfect day! It opens the gates of heaven, and gives us glimpses far inward;' 'I found one cracker in the tureen, and exulted over it as if it had been gold;' 'I take an interest in all the nooks and crannies and every development of cities;' 'a morning mist fills up the whole length and breadth of the valley between my house and Monument Mountain;' 'the wind-turn—the lightning-catch—a child's phrases for weathercock and lightning-rod;' 'a walk with the children: we went through the wood: they found Houstonias there more than a week ago;' 'one thing, if no more, I have gained by my custom-house experience—to know a politician. It is a knowledge which no previous thought or power of sympathy could have taught me, because the animal, or the machine rather, is not in Nature.'

There is one remarkable passage in these note-books which tells the whole story of Hawthorne's authorship, and tells it from his inmost heart: there is a great lesson to be thence learned, and a singular pathos and power involved therein. On one of his visits to the home of his childhood, just as prosperity began faintly to dawn upon his long and sequestered life-work, local associations, always strong in their appeal to his nature, seem to have inspired him to unwonted self-revelation; and he thus recorded his baffled zeal and self-reliant loyalty, so unconsciously indicative of rare natural gifts and an intensely reflective character:

'*Salem, Oct.* 4, 1840–*Union St Family Mansion.* If ever I should have a biographer, he ought to mention this chamber in my memoirs . . . We are not endowed with real life, and all that seems real about us is but the thinnest substance of a dream till the heart be troubled: that touch creates us; then we begin to be; thenceforth we are beings of reality and inheritors of eternity.

This last conviction lies at the basis of all genuine productiveness in Art—verbal, plastic and pictorial—and fidelity thereto is a test of the integrity of genius. De Quincey has well defined the two great divisions of literature—that of power and that of knowledge; the

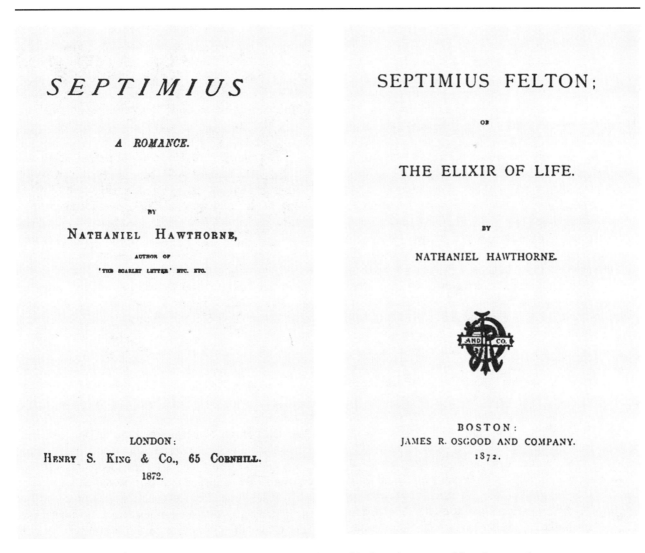

Title pages for the first English and American editions of the first volume prepared from the manuscripts Hawthorne left unfinished at his death (from C. E. Frazer Clark Jr., Nathaniel Hawthorne: A Descriptive Bibliography, *1978)*

former, being in its essence creative, implies an absolute inward experience as the condition and inspiration of original and genuine work: all earnest natures recognize the law, and are not to be lured into factitious labor or ingenious imitation as a substitute for what must be born of personal emotion and imperative consciousness. These were the traits which made Charlotte Brontë's few novels memorable; and her biographer tells us that 'she thought every serious delineation of life ought to be the product of personal experience and observation—experience naturally occurring, and observation of a normal kind.' 'I have not accumulated since I published *Shirley*,' she said. 'What makes it needful for me to speak again? and till I do so, may God give me grace to be dumb.' There are special temptations for an American author to evade this ethical condition—the

demands of the immediate are so pertinacious, while vanity and gain conspire to compromise both fame and faculty. It is a rare distinction of Hawthorne that he was so true to himself in this regard.

He alludes to the number of stories which he burned as unsatisfactory to his mind: those he published at first appeared in a casual form: they came out successively in periodicals—some of the earliest in a literary annual, then a favorite mode of dispensing the best obtainable prose and verse. In 1837 these were collected in a volume under the name of *Twice-told Tales:* his old classmate, Longfellow, praised them in the *North American Review;* and long before their descriptive merit, 'glancing wit, tender satire and subtle analysis' had been recognized by a few, another fellow-collegian, the Rev. Dr Cheever, had also written of their 'darkly passionate and weird' inspiration. They were more finished in style than any writings of the kind since the appearance of the *Sketch Book* and *The Idle Man,* yet they made their way slowly; and their author, from sheer necessity, had to have recourse to less artistic and more temporary expedients, such as a political brochure—the *Life of Pierce,* when he became the Democratic candidate for the Presidency—and the *Journal of an African Cruiser,* which he edited for his friend Bridges. It was on the appearance of this latter volume that I received from Hawthorne a letter which evidently cost him no small effort to write to one then comparatively a stranger. The book appeared in New York, and he wrote that, having learned I took an interest in his writings, he wished I would call attention to this new venture in the journals of that city, stating, by way of apology for the request, that he understood such advertisement of New England products was essential to their sale beyond the limits of the Eastern States, and that this was now to him of vital importance, inasmuch as for twenty years he had been writing with little pecuniary remuneration, and had a family to maintain by his pen. This consideration it evidently was that induced him to overcome his pride and reserve and endeavor to enlist external aid. The letter was singularly modest and courteous. Fortunately, his wishes had been anticipated: before the gentle and dignified appeal was made I had sent an article to a leading magazine, wherein the claims of his genius were inadequately but sincerely affirmed. Soon after, *The Scarlet Letter* was published, and its success revived the fortunes of his previous work: he had also proved apt and inventive in juvenile literature. Although still restricted and secluded, he did not work in vain, 'I live,' he wrote me in June, 1851, from his humble home among the Berkshire hills—

> I live in the very ugliest little bit of an old red farm-house you ever saw, but with a beautiful view before, or rather behind, it. In the vicinity there is every sort of walk—mountain walks, and wood walks, and walks by the lake shore; but sometimes, I must own, I sigh for walks on a pavement. For more than a year past I have not been ten miles from Lenox: thus far, since the summer began, I have been busy with a book of stories for children.

Thenceforth his literary activity, alternating with periods of official duty, kept him prosperously occupied; his actual life and environment always forming the vestibule of his romance—as in the introductory picture of the 'old manse' in the *Mosses* therefrom, of the Salem custom-house in *The House of the Seven Gables,* and of the consular experiences in *Our Old Home.* Whether a weigher and gauger (like Burns) in Boston, where it appears he was a favorite with sailors, or a volunteer

delver and mower at Brook Farm, an experiment embalmed so subtly in his *Blithedale Romance;* in the old parsonage at Concord (with Thoreau and Emerson for neighbors), 'from whose windows the old clergyman watched the fight between his parishioners and the British in the Revolution;' at his busy post in Liverpool, where he gave away no small amount of his salary to impoverished countrymen—whence he made charming excursions into the rural interior of England, and where he had such formidable encounters with 'civic banquets'—all forming delightful chapters of his English sketch-book; in his walks and talks in old Rome, so vividly embodied in *The Marble Faun;* and the brief interval of competence and repose on his return from his long exile to his new house in Concord—shadowed and saddened by the war for the Union, which seemed to cast down his soul in unutterable protest and pity,—his authorship and experience kept pace together, with graceful emphasis and progressive significance—at once the fruit and flower of that loyalty to his high vocation which had sustained his long and lonely novitiate.

Thoroughly American, and of the genuine Eastern type, were the antecedents of Hawthorne: his nature and surroundings were fitted to deepen the traditional idiosyncrasies of his birth-place, and endow him to become their most characteristic interpreter. Born in the old New England town whose colonial history is so tragically memorable, on the fourth of July, 1804, his progenitors had emigrated from England and participated in the persecution of the Quakers so pathetically illustrated by their descendant in his first successful sketch as a verbal artist—'The Gentle Boy.' On the father's side his ancestors were seafaring men—'a gray-haired shipmaster, in each generation, returning from the quarter-deck to the homestead, while a boy of fourteen took the hereditary place before the mast.' Here we have the origin of the adventurous and observant vein in the future author, over whose young soul a domestic bereavement cast no transitory shadow, when, in 1810, his father died of yellow fever at Havana, and made his mother a sorrowful recluse for life. She is described as beautiful, and this widowed loyalty proves her rare sensibility, which her son inherited. She sent him, when ten years old, to a farm belonging to the family on Sebago Lake, in Maine, to regain his health: he returned invigorated, and completed his studies in a year, so as to enter Bowdoin College in that State in 1825, with Longfellow, Cheever and Franklin Pierce. After graduating, Hawthorne lived retired in his native town—a hermit, a dreamer and a thinker—'passing the day alone in his room, writing wild tales, most of which he destroyed; and walking out at night.' In 1832 he published an anonymous romance, which he never claimed, and the public could not identify. Such a youth is exceptional in America, where the struggle for life's prizes begins at its threshold, and the exigencies of the hour usually launch the collegian into the world prematurely to work for bread and fame. The inestimable benefit of an interval of rest–for the mind to lie fallow and the faculties to strengthen–in our busy land, between academic education and the career of manhood, is obvious, especially in the instance of such refined aspirations as those of Hawthorne. This episode, so unusual then and there, has been described as a 'wandering uncertain and mostly unnoticed life;' but that it was auspicious to the author's development and conservative of the man's best nature, he, as we have seen, long after recorded as his grateful conviction. After his contributions to the *Token* and the *Democratic Review* had made manifest his rare gifts, he received an appointment from the Boston collector, but lost it on Harrison's inauguration in 1841: then passed a few months in a co-operative community in West Roxbury, Massachusetts, which furnished him with several types of character–

> the self-conceited philanthropist; the high-spirited woman bruising herself against the narrow limitations of her sex; the weakly maiden whose trembling nerves endowed her with Sibylline attributes; the minor poet beginning life with strenuous aspirations which die out with his youthful fervor.

In 1843 he married and settled at Concord, where he lived for three years, when a change in the political world made him surveyor of the port of Salem, where, for another three years, he was the chief executive officer of 'the decayed old custom-house.' When, in 1850, the Whigs were once more in the ascendant, Hawthorne lost his office and retired to Lenox, Massachusetts, to dwell on the borders of the lake called the Stockbridge Bowl, and resume, with new zest and success, his literary pursuits. In 1852 he returned to Concord, and on the election of Franklin Pierce as President of the United States was appointed United States consul at Liverpool, where he remained eight years; and after visiting the Continent and passing a winter in Rome and a summer in Tuscany, returned to his native land, crowned with fame in literature, and so far prosperous in circumstances as, for the first time, to feel himself independent. A long and happy evening to his days was anticipated by all who knew and honored him; but his pleasure in being once more at home was embittered by the sanguinary, and, as he long thought, hopeless, struggle that convulsed the nation. Still, in the serene exercise of his rare powers, in the congenial retrospect of his foreign experience, and the comfort and cheer of assured success as the reward of past waiting and vicissitude–in domestic happiness and social recognition and genial activity–benign were the closing years of Hawthorne; but their close none the less seemed sadly premature. A future for him and for us had shaped itself nobly from the firm and faithful basis of past achievement, and to the natural grief for the departure of a gifted spirit and an illustrious countryman, was added the pang which attends the abrupt ending of a happy dream.

Introspective authors, known intimately as such, excite singular personal interest, and we eagerly desire to be admitted to their consciousness when the crises of life occur or the shadow of death is upon them. All who followed Hawthorne with sympathetic insight as a man through the discipline and self-distrust of hope deferred, and as an author in his psychological and picturesque delineations of life, character and their environments, felt a tender and reverent curiosity, when his own existence on earth closed, to realize his feelings and faith in those waning hours which had become too sacred for the familiar record he used to keep in more vital and observant days. Such knowledge is only obtainable through the confidence of intimate friends. Reticent as Hawthorne was by nature and habit, and few as were his associates, we have sought not in vain to follow his patient and faltering steps as he descended into the dark valley. The friend of his youth was alone the witness of his departure. It has been thought and said that Hawthorne's friendships were unaccountable: it has created surprise that he found apparent congeniality in men of totally diverse tastes and temperaments from his own. This, however, is explicable if we consider that men of genius, especially of the kind which distinguished him, are feminine in this–that they find solace and satisfaction in 'variety of the accustomed.' Constitutional shyness makes the process of intimacy and confidence long and often irksome with them. They may enjoy, to the full, intercourse with kindred minds, and appreciate the regard and fellowship of those devoted to the same pursuits, but they shrink from self-revelation to such: they reserve their 'abandon' for those with whom old and early habit has made them perfectly at home. In college, as we know, Hawthorne and Franklin Pierce grew into the most intimate relations–first, through constant association, and then by virtue of the very diversity of their natures. This kind of fellowship, if it survives youth, is rarely superseded by later ties; and it is therefore quite natural that the friend Hawthorne chose to be near him in the days of his decline, and who felt himself drawn specially to that sad ministry, should be he who learned to love the reserved student, and, when politically successful, sought and secured prosperity for the gifted author.

Many remember the surprise created by the nomination of Franklin Pierce for President of the United States–one of those partisan exigencies which have again and again thwarted the plans of the sagacious and disappointed the most prominent and probable candidates. The astonishment was shared, in this case, by the candidate himself: he heard of his nomination while sojourning at a Boston hotel, which was immediately

besieged by office-seekers and politicians, who, for some hours, were refused admittance by the bewildered nominee. When, however, Hawthorne's card was handed him, he was glad to see the friend of his youth at such a time. The latter's first greeting was, 'Frank, I pity you;' to which the candidate replied, 'I pity myself.' All lovers of genius and of literary integrity, of whatever party, rejoiced that Hawthorne's friend had it in his power to honorably provide for a man who had so bravely endured privation and so modestly awaited the ordeal of public appreciation. He had the fortitude and pride, as well as the sensitiveness and delicacy, of true and high genius. Not even his nearest country neighbors knew aught of his meagre larder or brave economies: he never complained, even when editors were dilatory in their remuneration and friends forgetful of their promises. When the poor author had the money he would buy a beefsteak for dinner: when he had not, he would make a meal of chestnuts and potatoes. He had the self-control and the probity to fulfill that essential condition of self-respect alike for those who subsist by brain-work and those who inherit fortunes–he always lived within his income; and it was only by a

kind of pious fraud that a trio of his oldest friends occasionally managed to pay his rent.

For many months it had been evident that the vital forces of Hawthorne were declining. He grew easily fatigued; his step was less certain; he became more and more silent; he was often sad. Like all men of intense mental activity and sensitive temperament, when overworked or discouraged his chief resource was a ramble or a journey. In the spring of 1864 he accompanied one of his publishers to Philadelphia, escaping a while the bleak atmosphere of that season in New England. His relations to this his best financial friend were peculiar; through him his first literary success was secured; he received and invested the surplus earnings of the absentee author when American consul at Liverpool, and had obtained from Hawthorne a promise, on the eve of his departure for his post, that he would faithfully keep a journal of his observations and experiences, and that he would send him all he could spare from his official income, to be carefully nursed into a competence for his family. Never was better advice given or wiser service performed by publisher to author. The investments, pecuniary and intellectual, thus made, became the means of comfort and genial as well as lucrative occupation to the returned writer in the maturity of his years and his fame.

They started on this brief excursion–Hawthorne an invalid and Ticknor in health; but the latter was stricken down and died at the hotel in Philadelphia, and the former, as he afterward expressed it, 'saw him through;' an anxious and terrible vigil for one in his enfeebled condition and with his delicate sympathies. The care and the shock precipitated his own death. When, after his return home, his strength continued obviously to decline, he and his old friend proposed a little jaunt, such as in days of health Hawthorne specially enjoyed–a drive in their own vehicle, and as convenience or caprice might dictate, amid the hills and valleys of New England, just as May was bringing out the early wild flowers, tinging the maples with red buds, and making the woods pure and fresh with the blossoms of the dogwood and the star-like anemones on the moss below. Hawthorne, probably owing to his nervous condition, felt better in a carriage than when sitting still or lying down: the movement soothed him. At times his old pedestrian habits revived, and he walked miles through the snow late in the winter. They left Concord, Massachusetts, and drove to Centre Harbor. A continuous rain had kept them in doors, but when it cleared, next day, and Hawthorne declared himself better, his friend was encouraged, and they started for Plymouth, New Hampshire.

Before leaving home, he was much depressed, and wrote in a memorandum-book what seemed like the intention of a will–commencing, 'In the name of God, amen. I, N. H., being in danger of sudden death,' etc.; but it was simply a request to his wife to give a certain sum to his sister, living at Beverly, to whom he was tenderly attached. It was afterward a not unnatural surmise of his companion that, with his curious introspection and affectionate nature, he may have gone on this journey with a presentiment that it was his last, and undertaken it for the express purpose of avoiding the painful parting with his family; like Sterne preferring to die at an inn. As they proceeded, Hawthorne seemed to revive, but he had no appetite and little strength; and when they reached the Warner House at Plymouth, where they were to pass the night, he declined dinner. On the way he asked his friend if he saw Thackeray when in this country–that author's death had recently occurred–and Mr Pierce, wishing to beguile the invalid into a literary or personal discussion which would divert his attention from himself, replied to the inquiry, 'Yes, I saw him, and he said an extraordinary thing to me–viz.: that your *Blithedale Romance* was your best.'

Instead of dwelling upon this opinion of the famous satirist, however, Hawthorne's mind was evidently intent upon Thackeray's recent departure, and he replied, 'But there is another thing: we must all go.' 'Yes,'

acquiesced his friend, 'but not yet, I hope,' and tried to engage him in cheerful talk until their arrival at the inn; but his mind was evidently occupied with the idea of his approaching dissolution, although there was no apparent cause for immediate apprehension. 'We must all go,' he continued, 'and if we could go without the agony and the consciousness, what a blessing!' Toward evening he was tempted to a slight repast, which he seemed to relish, and then lay down upon a sofa and fell asleep. In two hours his faithful companion awoke him and said, 'You will be more comfortable in bed.' 'I think so,' he said, cheerfully. Assisted to undress, he was soon in a tranquil sleep again. It was the 19th of May, 1864, at three o'clock in the morning, when his friend looked into the room, which adjoined and communicated with his own, and noticed that Hawthorne had not moved from the posture assumed when he first retired. Alarmed at this immobility, he went and leaned over him and found he had ceased to breathe: neither temple nor heart responded to his touch. The gifted thinker, the weird dreamer, the baffled aspirant, the patient artist, to whom life had been so deep a mystery, so long a struggle, so pure a triumph–Hawthorne was no more: his spirit had passed quietly, unconsciously, peacefully, as he had, a few hours before, prayed that it might.

In one of his early sketches, 'The Haunted Mind,' there is a prophetic hint, as it were, of his own calm and mysterious departure from earth: her alludes to the vague line of demarkation between sleeping and waking as akin to that which divides present conscious being and 'that undiscovered country from whose bourne no traveler returns:'

> With an involuntary start, you seize hold on consciousness, and prove yourself but half awake by running a doubtful parallel between human life and the hour which has now elapsed. In both you emerge from mystery, pass through a vicissitude that you can but imperfectly control, and are borne onward to another mystery. Now comes the peal of the distant clock, with fainter and fainter strokes as you plunge farther into the wilderness of sleep. It is the knell of a temporary death. Your spirit has departed, and strays like a free citizen among the people of a shadowy world, beholding strange sights, yet without wonder or dismay. So calm, perhaps, will be the final change–so undisturbed, as if among familiar things, the entrance of the soul to its eternal home!

Irving was buried on so beautiful an Indian-summer day in December that its tranquil and misty glow is associated in the minds of those present with the last scene of his life and the memorable landscape his fancy and fondness had peopled with legend and lore, as if Nature had sympathized with the sad rites of his funeral day. A like charm, though of spring-time, hallowed the obsequies of Hawthorne, and is commemorated by one of the gifted group who assembled around his bier. It was one of those days of sudden transition from an easterly rain-storm to tempered sunshine, when the air is fragrant with the odor of fruit blossoms wafted on a light southern breeze: it was too subtle in its loveliness to be called a 'crystal day;' an afternoon of brooding elemental life, the calm mystery whereof seemed analogous to the psychological suggestiveness of him whom sudden and quiet flitting awed while it melted the mourners—a mingled and overpowering sentiment truly expressed by Longfellow:

> Across the meadows, by the gray old manse,
>   The historic river flowed:
> I was as one who wanders in a trance,
>   Unconscious of his road.
>
> The faces of familiar friends seemed strange:
>   Their voices I could hear;
> And yet the words they uttered seemed to change
>   Their meaning to the ear.
>
> For the one face I looked for was not there,
>   The one low voice was mute:
> Only an unseen presence filled the air,
>   And baffled my pursuit.

Athlete, mathematician, clergyman, Cambridge don, and political activist, Englishman Leslie Stephen is best known for his contributions to literature and for his interest in philosophy. He wrote for several literary periodicals, including Cornhill Magazine. *As its editor, he encouraged young writers and became friends with some of them, including Robert Louis Stevenson, Thomas Hardy, and Henry James. For the series "English Men of Letters" he wrote books about Samuel Johnson, Alexander Pope, Jonathan Swift, George Eliot, and Thomas Hobbes. He was the initial editor of* Dictionary of National Biography. *He summarized his study of philosophy in "Science of Ethics" (1882). In the course of his several visits to the United States, Stephen became a friend of James Russell Lowell, Charles Eliot Norton, and Oliver Wendell Holmes.*

Nathaniel Hawthorne
Leslie Stephen
Cornhill Magazine, 26 (July–December 1872): 717–734

I have always sympathized with the famous senior-wrangler who, on being invited to admire *Paradise Lost*, inquired, 'What does it prove?' To the theory, indeed, on which his question is generally supposed to be based, that any human composition is worthless which does not end with the magical letters Q.E.D., I

can by no means yield an unqualified assent. I fully share the ordinary prejudice against stories with a moral. No poem or novel should be conspicuously branded with a well-worn aphorism, and declare to the whole listening universe that honesty is the best policy. The tracts which in the days of our childhood went to prove that little boys who didn't go to church would be drowned in a millrace or gored by a bull, and the more pretentious allegories where abstract qualities are set masquerading in frigid forms of flesh and blood, moved, like the figures on a barrel-organ, not by passions but by a logical machinery grinding out syllogisms below the surface, are equally vexatious. And yet I fancy that the senior-wrangler had a dim perception of a more tenable theory. Some central truth should be embodied in every work of fiction, which cannot indeed be compressed into a definite formula, but which acts as the animating and informing principle, determining the main lines of the structure and affecting even its most trivial details. Critics who try to extract it as a formal moral, present us with nothing but an outside husk of dogma. The lesson itself is the living seed which, cast into a thousand minds, will bear fruit in a thousand different forms. The senior-wrangler was therefore unreasonable if he expected to have *Para-*

Leslie Stephen

dise Lost packed for him into a single portable formula. The true answer to him would have been, 'Read and see. The world will be changed for you when you have assimilated the master's thought, though you have gone through no definite process of linking x and y with a and b. Though the poem proves nothing, it will persuade you of much. It is not a demonstration, but an education.'

These remarks, certainly obvious enough, are but a clumsy comment on part of Hawthorne's preface to *The House of the Seven Gables;* they roughly express, therefore, Hawthorne's theory of his own art; and they are preparatory to the question, so far as it is a rational question, what do his romances prove? Abandoning the absurdity of answering that question as one would answer a hostile barrister or a Civil Service examiner, one may still attempt to indicate what is for some persons the most conspicuous tendency of writings in which the finest, if not the most powerful genius of America has embodied itself. Compressing the answer to its narrowest limits, one may say that Hawthorne has shown what elements of romance are discoverable amongst the harsh prose of this prosaic age. And his teaching is of importance, because it is just what is most needed at the present day. How is the novelist who, by the inevitable conditions of his style, is bound to come into the closest possible contact with facts, who has to give us the details of his hero's clothes, to tell us what he had for breakfast, and what is the state of the balance at his banker's—how is he to introduce the ideal element which must, in some degree, be present in all genuine art? A mere photographic reproduction of this muddy, money-making, bread-and-butter-eating world would be intolerable. At the very lowest, some effort must be made at least to select the most promising materials, and to strain out the coarse or the simply prosaic ingredients. Various attempts have been made to solve the problem since Defoe founded the modern school of English novelists by giving us what is in one sense a servile imitation of genuine narrative, but which is redeemed from prose by the unique force of the situation. Defoe painting mere every-day pots and pans is as dull as a modern blue-book; but when his pots and pans are the resource by which a human being struggles out of the most appalling conceivable 'slough of despond,' they become more poetical than the vessels from which the gods drink nectar in epic poems. Since he wrote novelists have made many voyages of discovery, with varying success, though they have seldom had the fortune to touch upon so marvellous an island as that still sacred to the immortal Crusoe. They have ventured far into cloudland, and returning to *terra firma,* they have plunged into the trackless and savage-haunted regions which are girdled by the Metropolitan

Railway. They have watched the magic coruscations of some strange *Aurora Borealis* of dim romance, or been content with the domestic gas-light of London streets. Amongst the most celebrated of all such adventurers were the band which obeyed the impulse of Sir Walter Scott. For a time it seemed that we had reached a genuine Eldorado of novelists, where solid gold was to be had for the asking, and visions of more than earthly beauty rewarded the labours of the explorer. Now, alas! our opinion is a good deal changed; the fairy treasures which Scott brought back from his voyages have turned into dead leaves according to custom; and the curiosities, upon which he set so extravagant a price, savour more of Wardour Street than of the genuine mediæval artists. Nay, there are scoffers, though I am not of them, who think that the tittle-tattle which Miss Austen gathered at the country-houses of our grandfathers is worth more than the showy but rather flimsy eloquence of the 'Ariosto of the North.' Scott endeavoured at least, if with indifferent success, to invest his scenes with something of—

> *The light that never was on sea or land,*
> *The consecration and the poet's dream.*

If he too often indulged in mere theatrical devices and mistook the glare of the footlights for the sacred glow of the imagination, he professed, at least, to introduce us to an ideal world. Later novelists have generally abandoned the attempt, and are content to reflect our work-a-day life with almost servile fidelity. They are not to be blamed; and doubtless the very greatest writers are those who can bring their ideal world into the closest possible contact with our sympathies, and show us heroic figures in modern frock-coats and Parisian fashions. The art of story-telling is manifold, and its charm depends greatly upon the infinite variety of its applications. And yet, for that very reason, there are moods in which one wishes that the modern story-teller would more frequently lead us away from the commonplace region of newspapers and railways to regions where the imagination can have fair play. Hawthorne is one of the few eminent writers to whose guidance we may in such moods most safely entrust ourselves; and it is tempting to ask what was the secret of his success. The effort, indeed, to investigate the materials from which some rare literary flavour is extracted is seldom satisfactory. After cataloguing all the constituents, the analytical chemist is often bound to admit that the one all-important element is too fine to be grasped by his clumsy instruments. We are reminded of the automaton chess-player who excited the wonder of the last generation. The showman, like the critic, laid bare his inside, and displayed all the cunning wheels and cogs and cranks by which his motions were supposed to be regulated. Yet, after all, the true secret was that there was a man inside the machine. Some such impression is often made by the most elaborate demonstrations of literary anatomists. We have been mystified, not really entrusted with any revelation. And yet, with this warning as to the probable success of our examination, let us try to determine some of the peculiarities to which Hawthorne owes this strange power of bringing poetry out of the most unpromising materials.

In the first place, then, he had the good fortune to be born in the most prosaic of all countries–the most prosaic, that is, in external appearance, and even in the superficial character of its inhabitants. Hawthorne himself reckoned this as an advantage, though in a very different sense from that in which we are speaking. It was as a patriot, and not as an artist, that he congratulated himself on his American origin. There is a humorous struggle between his sense of the rawness and ugliness of his native land and the dogged patriotism befitting a descendant of the genuine New England Puritans. Hawthorne the novelist writhes at the discords which torture his delicate sensibilities at every step; but instantly Hawthorne the Yankee protests that the very faults are symptomatic of excellence. He is like a sensitive mother, unable to deny that her awkward hobblede-hoy of a son offends against the proprieties, but tacitly resolved to see proofs of virtues present or to come even in his clumsiest tricks. He forces his apologies to sound like boasting. 'No author,' he says, 'can conceive of the difficulty of writing a romance about a country where there is no shadow, no antiquity, no mystery, no picturesque and gloomy wrong, nor anything but a commonplace prosperity, as is happily' (it must and shall be happily) 'the case with my dear native land. It will be very long, I trust, before romance-writers may find congenial and easily-handled themes either in the annals of our stalwart republic, or in any characteristic and probable events of our individual lives. Romance and poetry, ivy, lichens and wallflowers need ruins to make them grow.' If, that is, I am forced to confess that poetry and romance are absent, I will resolutely stick to it that poetry and romance are bad things, even though the love of them is the strongest propensity of my nature. To my thinking, there is something almost pathetic in this loyal self deception; and therefore I have never been offended by certain passages in *Our Old Home* which appear to have caused some irritation in touchy Englishmen. There is something, he

says by way of apology, which causes an American in England to take up an attitude of antagonism. 'These people think so loftily of themselves, and so contemptuously of everybody else, that it requires more generosity than I possess to keep always in perfectly good-humour with them.' That may be true; for, indeed, I believe that deep down in the bosom of every Briton, beneath all superficial roots of cosmopolitan philanthropy, there lies an ineradicable conviction that no foreigner is his equal; and to a man of Hawthorne's delicate perceptions, the presence of that sentiment would reveal itself through the most careful disguises. But that which really caused him to cherish his antagonism was, I suspect, something else: he was afraid of loving us too well; he feared to be tempted into a denial of some point of his patriotic creed; he is always clasping it, as it were, to his bosom, and vowing and protesting that he does not surrender a single jot or tittle of it. Hawthorne in England was like a plant suddenly removed to a rich soil from a dry and thirsty land. He drinks in at every pore the delightful influences of which he has had so scanty a supply. An old cottage, an ivy-grown wall, a country churchyard with its quaint epitaphs, things that are commonplace to most Englishmen and which are hateful to the sanitary inspector, are refreshing to every fibre of his soul. He tries in vain to take the sanitary inspector's view. In spite of himself he is always falling into the romantic tone, though a sense that he ought to be sternly philosophical just gives a humorous tinge to his enthusiasm. Charles Lamb could not have improved his description of the old hospital at Leicester, where the twelve brethren still wear the badge of the Bear and Ragged Staff. He lingers round it, and gossips with the brethren, and peeps into the garden, and sits by the cavernous archway of the kitchen fireplace, where the very atmosphere seems to be redolent with aphorisms first uttered by ancient monks, and jokes derived from Master Slender's note-book, and gossip about the wrecks of the Spanish Armada. No connoisseur could pore more lovingly over an ancient black-letter volume or the mellow hues of some old painter's masterpiece. He feels the charm of our historical continuity, where the immemorial past blends indistinguishably with the present, to the remotest recesses of his imagination. But then the Yankee nature within him must put in a sharp word or two; he has to jerk the bridle for fear that his enthusiasm should fairly run away with him. 'The trees and other objects of an English landscape,' he remarks, or, perhaps we should say, he complains, 'take hold of one by numberless minute tendrils as it were, which, look as closely as we choose, we never find in

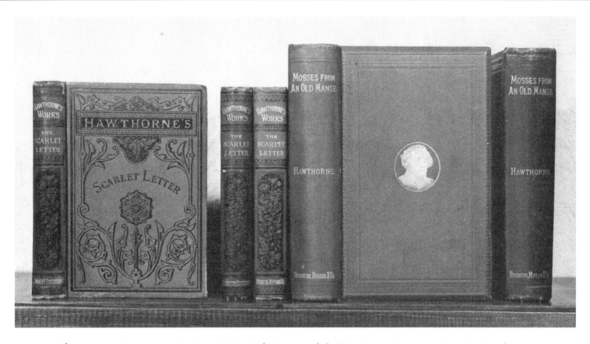

Three bindings from the "Little Classic Edition" (1875–1883) for The Scarlet Letter *and two bindings from the "Fireside Edition" (1879–1882) for* Mosses from an Old Manse *(from C. E. Frazer Clark Jr.,* Nathaniel Hawthorne: A Descriptive Bibliography, *1978)*

an American scene;' but he inserts a qualifying clause, just by way of protest, that an American tree would be more picturesque if it had an equal chance; and the native oak of which we are so proud is summarily condemned for 'John Bullism'—a mysterious offence common to many things in England. Charlecote Hall, he presently admits, 'is a most delightful place.' Even an American is tempted to believe that real homes can only be produced by 'the slow ingenuity and labour of many successive generations,' when he sees the elaborate beauty and perfection of a well-ordered English abode. And yet he persuades himself that even here he is the victim of some delusion. The impression is due to the old man which still lurks even in the polished American, and forces him to look through his ancestors' spectacles. The true theory, it appears, is that which Holgrave expresses for him in the *Seven Gables,* namely, that we should free ourselves of the material slavery imposed upon us by the brick-and-mortar of past generations, and learn to change our houses as early as our coats. We ought to feel—only we unfortunately can't feel—that a tent or a wigwam is as good as a house. The mode in which Hawthorne regards the Englishman himself is a quaint illustration of the same theory. An Englishwoman, he admits reluctantly and after many protestations, has some few beauties not possessed by her American sisters. A maiden in her teens has 'a certain charm of half blossom and delicately-folded

leaves, and tender womanhood shielded by maidenly reserves, with which, somehow or other, our American girls often fail to adorn themselves during an appreciable moment.' But he revenges himself for this concession by an almost savage onslaught upon the full-blown British matron with her 'awful ponderosity of frame . . . massive with solid beef and streaky tallow,' and apparently composed 'of steaks and sirloins.' He laments that the English violet should develop into such an overblown peony, and speculates upon the whimsical problem, whether a middle-aged husband should be considered as legally married to all the accretions which have overgrown the slenderness of his bride. Should not the matrimonial bond be held to exclude the three-fourths of the wife that had no existence when the ceremony was performed? A question not to be put without a shudder. The fact is, that Hawthorne had succeeded only too well in misleading himself by a common fallacy. That pestilent personage, John Bull, has assumed so concrete a form in our imaginations, with his top-boots and his broad shoulders and vast circumference, and the emblematic bull-dog at his heels, that for most observers he completely hides the Englishman of real life. Hawthorne had decided that an Englishman must and should be a mere mass of transformed beef and beer. No observation could shake his preconceived impression. At Greenwich Hospital he encountered the mighty shade of the concentrated essence of our strongest national qualities; no truer Englishman ever lived than Nelson. But Nelson was certainly not the conventional John Bull, and, therefore, Hawthorne roundly asserts that he was not an Englishman. 'More than any other Englishman he won the love and admiration of his country, but won them through the efficacy of qualities that are not English.' Nelson was of the same breed as Cromwell, though his shoulders were not so broad; but Hawthorne insists that the broad shoulders, and not the fiery soul, are the essence of John Bull. He proceeds with amusing unconsciousness to generalize this ingenious theory, and declares that all extraordinary Englishmen are sick men, and, therefore, deviations from the type. When he meets another remarkable Englishman in the flesh, he applies the same method. Of Leigh Hunt, whom he describes with warm enthusiasm, he dogmatically declares, 'there was not an English trait in him from head to foot, morally, intellectually, or physically.' And the reason is admirable. 'Beef, ale, or stout, brandy or port-wine, entered not at all into his constitution.' All Englishmen are made of those ingredients, and if not, why, then, they are not Englishmen. By the same method it is easy to show that all Englishmen are drunkards, or that they are all teetotallers; you have only to exclude as irrelevant every case that contradicts your theory. Hawthorne, unluckily, is by no means solitary in his mode of reasoning. The ideal John Bull has hidden us from ourselves as well as from our neighbours, and the race which is distinguished above all others for the magnificent wealth of its imaginative literature, is daily told—and, what is more, tells itself—that it is a mere lump of prosaic flesh and blood, with scarcely soul enough to keep it from stagnation. If we were sensible we should burn that ridiculous caricature of ourselves along with Guy Fawkes; but meanwhile we can hardly complain if foreigners are deceived by our own misrepresentations.

Against Hawthorne, as I have said, I feel no grudge, though a certain regret that his sympathy with that deep vein of poetical imagination which underlies all our 'steaks and sirloins' should have been intercepted by this detestable lay figure. The poetical humorist must be allowed a certain licence in dealing with facts; and poor Hawthorne, in the uncongenial atmosphere of the Liverpool Custom-house, had, doubtless, much to suffer from a thick-skinned generation. His characteristic shyness made it a hard task for him to penetrate through our outer rind—which, to say the truth, is often elephantine enough—to the central core of heat; and we must not complain if he was too apt to deny the existence of what to him was unattainable. But the problem recurs—for everybody likes to ask utterly unanswerable questions—whether Hawthorne would not have developed into a still greater artist if he had been more richly supplied with the diet so dear to his inmost soul? Was it not a thing to weep over, that a man so keenly alive to every picturesque influence, so anxious to invest his work with the enchanted haze of romantic association, should be confined till middle age amongst the bleak granite rocks and the half-baked civilization of New England? 'Among ourselves,' he laments, 'there is no fairy land for the romancer.' What if he had been brought up in the native home of the fairies—if there had been thrown open to him the gates through which Shakespeare and Spencer caught their visions of ideal beauty? Might we not have had an appendix to the *Midsummer Night's Dream,* and might not a modern *Faerie Queen* have brightened the prosaic wilderness of this nineteenth century? The question, as I have said, is rigidly unanswerable. We have not yet learnt how to breed poets, though we have made some progress in regard to pigs. Nobody can tell, and perhaps, therefore, it is as well that nobody should guess, what would have been the effect of transplanting Shakespeare to modern Stratford, or of exiling him to the United States. And yet—for it is impossible to resist entirely the pleasure of fruitless speculation—we may guess that there are some reasons why there should be a risk in transplanting so delicate a growth as the genius of Hawthorne. There are more ways, so wise men tell us, of killing a cat than choking it with cream; but it is a very good way. Over-feeding produces atrophy of some of the vital functions in higher animals than cats, and the imagination may be enfeebled rather than strengthened by an over-supply of materials. Hawthorne, if his life had passed where the plough may turn up an antiquity in every furrow, and the whole face of the country is enamelled with ancient culture, might have wrought more gorgeous hues into his tissues, but he might have succumbed to the temptation of producing mere upholstery. The fairy land for which he longed is full of dangerous enchantments, and there are many who have lost in it the vigour which comes from breathing the keen air of every-day life. From that risk Hawthorne was effectually preserved in his New England home. Having to abandon the poetry which is manufactured out of mere external circumstances, he was forced to draw it from deeper sources. With easier means at hand of enriching his pages, he might have left the mine unworked. It is often good for us to have to make bricks without straw. Hawthorne, who was conscious of the extreme difficulty of the prob-

NATHANIEL HAWTHORNE'S WORKS.

NEW ILLUSTRATED LIBRARY EDITION.

Eleven vols. 12mo. Price, per vol. $2.00

Twice-Told Tales.	English Note-Books.
Mosses from an Old Manse.	American Note-Books.
The Scarlet Letter, and The Blithedale Romance.	French and Italian Note-Books.
The House of the Seven Gables, and the Snow Image.	Our Old Home, and Septimius Felton.
The Marble Faun.	The Wonder Book, etc.
	Tanglewood Tales, etc.

HOUSEHOLD EDITION.

Complete, 23 vols., on Tinted Paper, in Box....................$34.50

SEPARATE WORKS.

OUR OLD HOME. 16mo...................................... $1.50

THE MARBLE FAUN. 2 vols. 16mo...................... 3.00

THE SCARLET LETTER. 16mo........................... 1.50

THE HOUSE OF THE SEVEN GABLES. 16mo........ 1.50

TWICE-TOLD TALES. With Portrait. 2 vols. 16mo...... 3.00

THE SNOW-IMAGE, and Other Twice-Told Tales.......... 1.50

THE BLITHEDALE ROMANCE. 16mo 1.50

MOSSES FROM AN OLD MANSE. 2 vols. 16mo........ 3.00

AMERICAN NOTE-BOOKS. 2 vols. 16mo............... 3.00

ENGLISH NOTE-BOOKS. 2 vols. 16mo................... 3.00

FRENCH AND ITALIAN NOTE-BOOKS. 2 vols. 16mo.. 3.00

SEPTIMIUS FELTON; or, The Elixir of Life. 16mo...... 1.50

FANSHAWE, and Other Pieces. 16mo. 1.50

THE DOLLIVER ROMANCE, and Other Pieces. 16mo.... 1.50

TWICE-TOLD TALES. With Portrait. Blue and Gold. 2 vols. 32mo 2.50

JUVENILES.

TRUE STORIES FROM HISTORY AND BIOGRAPHY. Illustrated. 16mo... 1.50

THE WONDER-BOOK. Illustrated. 16mo............. 1.50

TANGLEWOOD TALES. Illustrated. 16mo............. 1.50

. For sale by all Booksellers. Sent, post-paid, on receipt of price by the Publishers, **JAMES R. OSGOOD & CO., Boston.**

Advertisement included in an 1876 edition of Fanshawe *(Thomas Cooper Library, University of South Carolina)*

lem, and but partially conscious of the success of his solution of it, naturally complained of the severe discipline to which he owed his strength. We who enjoy the results may feel how much he owed to the very sternness of his education and the niggard hand with which his imaginative sustenance was dealt out to him. The observation may sound paradoxical at the first moment, and yet it is supported by analogy. Are not the best cooks produced just where the raw material is the worst, and precisely because it is there worst? Now, cookery is the art by which man is most easily distinguished from beasts, and it requires little ingenuity to transfer its lessons to literature. At the same time it may be admitted that some closer

inquiry is necessary in order to make the hypothesis probable, and I will endeavour from this point of view to examine some of Hawthorne's exquisite workmanship.

The story which perhaps generally passes for his masterpiece is *Transformation*, for most readers assume that a writer's longest book must necessarily be his best. In the present case, I think that this method, which has its conveniences, has not led to a perfectly just conclusion. In *Transformation*, Hawthorne has for once the advantage of placing his characters in a land where 'a sort of poetic or fairy precinct,' as he calls it, is naturally provided for them. The very stones of the streets are full of romance, and he cannot mention a name that has not a musical ring. Hawthorne, moreover, shows his usual tact in confining his aims to the possible. He does not attempt to paint Italian life and manners; his actors belong by birth, or by a kind of naturalization, to the colony of the American artists in Rome; and he therefore does not labour under the difficulty of being in imperfect sympathy with his creatures. Rome is a mere background, and surely a most felicitous background, to the little group of persons who are effectually detached from all such vulgarizing associations with the mechanism of daily life in less poetical countries. The centre of the group, too, who embodies one of Hawthorne's most delicate fancies, could have breathed no atmosphere less richly perfumed with old romance. In New York he would certainly have been in danger of a Barnum's museum, beside Washington's nurse and the woolly horse. It is a triumph of art that a being whose nature trembles on the very verge of the grotesque should walk through Hawthorne's pages with such undeviating grace. Let him show but the extremest tip of one of his furry ears—or were they not furry?—and he would be irretrievably lost. Mr Darwin or Barnum would claim him as their own, and he would pass from the world of poetry into the dissecting-room or the showman's booth. In the Roman dreamland he is in little danger of such prying curiosity, though even there he can only be kept out of harm's way by the admirable skill of his creator. Perhaps it may be thought by some severe critics that, with all his merits, Donatello stands on the very outside verge of the province permitted to the romancer. But without cavilling at what is indisputably charming, and without dwelling upon certain defects of construction which slightly mar the general beauty of the story, it has another weakness which it is impossible quite to overlook. Hawthorne himself remarks that he was surprised, in rewriting his story, to see the extent to which he had introduced descriptions of various Italian subjects. 'Yet these things,' he adds, 'fill the mind everywhere in Italy, and especially in Rome, and cannot be kept from flowing out upon the page when one writes freely and with self-enjoyment.' The associations which they called up in England were so pleasant, that he could not find it in his heart to cancel. Doubtless that is the precise truth, and yet it is equally true that they are artistically out of place. There are, to put it bluntly, passages which strike us like masses of undigested guide-book. To take one instance—and, certainly, it is about the worst—the whole party is going to the Coliseum, where a very striking scene takes place. On the way, they pass a baker's shop.

'The baker is drawing his loaves out of the oven,' remarked Kenyon. 'Do you smell how sour they are? I should fancy that Minerva (in revenge for the desecration of her temple) had slyly poured vinegar into the batch, if I did not know that the modern Romans prefer their bread in the acetous fermentation.'

The instance is trivial, but it is characteristic. Hawthorne had vivid recollection of some stroll in Rome; for, of all our senses, the smell is the most powerful in awakening associations. But then what do we who read him care about the Roman taste for bread 'in acetous fermentation?' When the high-spirited girl is on the way to meet her tormentor, and to receive the provocation which leads to his murder, why should we be worried by a gratuitous remark about Roman baking? It somehow jars upon our taste, and we are certain that, in describing a New England village, Hawthorne would never have admitted a touch which has no conceivable bearing upon the situation. There is almost a super-abundance of minute local colour in his American romances, as, for example, in *The House of the Seven Gables;* but still, every touch, however minute, is steeped in the sentiment and contributes to the general effect. In Rome the smell of a loaf is sacred to his imagination, and intrudes itself upon its own merits, and, so far as we can discover, without reference to the central purpose. If a baker's shop impresses him unduly because it is Roman, the influence of ancient ruins and glorious works of art is of course still more distracting. The mysterious Donatello, and the strange psychological problem which he is destined to illustrate, are put aside for an interval, whilst we are called upon to listen to descriptions and meditations, always graceful, and often of great beauty in themselves, but yet, in a strict sense, irrelevant. Hawthorne's want of familiarity with the scenery is of course responsible for part of this failing. Had he been a native Roman, he would not have been so pre-occupied with the wonders of Rome. But it seems that for a romance bearing upon a spiritual problem, the scenery, however tempting, is not really so serviceable as the less prepossessing surroundings of America. The objects have too great an intrinsic interest. A counter-attraction distorts the symmetry of the system. In the shadow of the Coliseum and St Peter's you cannot pay much attention to the troubles of a young lady whose existence is painfully ephemeral. Those mighty objects will not be relegated to the background, and condescend to act as mere scenery. They are, in fact, too romantic for a romance. The fountain of Trevi, with all its allegorical marbles, may be a very picturesque object to describe, but for Hawthorne's purposes it is really not equal to the town pump at Salem; and Hilda's poetical tower, with the perpetual light before the Virgin's image, and the doves floating up to her from the street, and the column of Antoninus looking at her from the heart of the city, somehow appeals less to our sympathies than the quaint garret in the House of the Seven Gables, from which Phœbe Pyncheon watched the singular idiosyncracies of the superannuated breed of fowls in the garden. The garret and the pump are designed in strict subordination to the human figures: the tower and the fountain have a distinctive purpose of their own. Hawthorne, at any rate, seems to have been mastered by his too powerful auxiliaries. A human soul, even in America, is more interesting to us than all the churches and picture-galleries in the world; and, therefore, it is as well that Hawthorne should not be tempted to the too easy method of putting fine description in place of sentiment.

But how was the task to be performed? How was the imaginative glow to be shed over the American scenery, so provokingly raw and deficient in harmony? A similar problem was successfully solved by a writer whose development, in proportion to her means of cultivation, is about the most remarkable of recent literary phenomena. Miss Brontë's bleak Yorkshire moors, with their uncompromising stone walls, and the valleys invaded by factories, are at first sight as little suited to romance as New England itself, to which, indeed, both the inhabitants and the country have a decided family resemblance. Now that she has discovered for us the fountains of poetic interest, we can all see that the region is not a mere stony wilderness; but it is well worth while to make a pilgrimage to Haworth, if only to discover how little the country corresponds to our preconceived impressions, or, in other words, how much depends upon the eye which sees it, and how little upon its intrinsic merits. Miss Brontë's marvellous effects are obtained by the process which enables an 'intense and glowing mind' to see everything through its own atmosphere. The ugliest and most trivial objects seem, like objects heated by the sun, to radiate back the glow of passion with which she has regarded them. Perhaps, this singular power is still more conspicuous in *Villette,* where she had even less of the raw material of poetry. An odd parallel may be found between one of the most striking passages in *Villette* and one in *Transformation.* Lucy Snowe in one novel, and Hilda in the other, are left to pass a summer vacation, the one in Brussels and the other in pestiferous Rome. Miss Snowe has no external cause of suffering but the natural effect of solitude upon a homeless and helpless governess. Hilda has to bear about with her the weight of a terrible secret, affecting, it may be, even the life of her dearest friend. Each of them wanders into a Roman Catholic church, and each, though they have both been brought up in a Protestant home, seeks

relief at the confessional. So far the cases are alike, though Hilda, one might have fancied, has by far the strongest cause for emotion. And yet, after reading the two descriptions–both excellent in their way–one might fancy that the two young ladies had exchanged burdens. Lucy Snowe is as tragic as the innocent confidante of a murderess; Hilda's feelings never seem to rise above that weary sense of melancholy isolation which besieges us in a deserted city. It is needless to ask which is the best bit of work artistically considered. Hawthorne's style is more graceful and flexible; his descriptions of the Roman Catholic ceremonial and its influence upon an imaginative mind in distress are far more sympathetic, and imply a wider range of intellect. But Hilda does not touch and almost overawe us like Lucy. There is too much delicate artistic description of picture-galleries and of the glories of St Peter's to allow the poor little American girl to come prominently to the surface. We have been indulging with her in some sad but charming speculations, and not witnessing the tragedy of a deserted soul. Lucy Snowe has very inferior materials at her command; but somehow we are moved by a sympathetic thrill: we taste the bitterness of the awful cup of despair which, as she tells us, is forced to her lips in the night-watches; and are not startled when so prosaic an object as the row of beds in the dormitory of a French school suggest to her images worthy rather of stately tombs in the aisles of a vast cathedral, and recall dead dreams of an elder world and mightier race long frozen in death. Comparisons of this kind are almost inevitably unfair; but the difference between the two illustrates one characteristic–we need not regard it as a defect–of Hawthorne. His idealism does not consist in conferring grandeur upon vulgar objects by tinging them with the reflection of deep emotion. He rather shrinks than otherwise from describing the strongest passions, or shows their working by indirect touches and under a side-light. An excellent example of his peculiar method occurs in what is in some respects the most perfect of his works, *The Scarlet Letter.* There, again, we have the spectacle of a man tortured by a life-long repentance. The Puritan clergyman, reverenced as a saint by all his flock, conscious of a sin which, once revealed, will crush him to the earth, watched with a malignant purpose by the husband whom he has injured, unable to summon up the moral courage to tear off the veil, and make the only atonement in his power, is undoubtedly a striking figure, powerfully conceived and most delicately described. He yields under terrible pressure to the temptation of escaping from the scene of his prolonged torture with the partner of his guilt. And then, as he is returning homewards after yielding a reluctant consent to the flight, we are invited to contemplate the agony of

THE

DOLLIVER ROMANCE

AND

OTHER PIECES.

BY

NATHANIEL HAWTHORNE.

BOSTON:
JAMES R. OSGOOD AND COMPANY.
1876.

Title page for a collection that includes a previously unpublished fragment of one of Hawthorne's unfinished romances (from C. E. Frazer Clark Jr., Nathaniel Hawthorne: A Descriptive Bibliography, 1978)

his soul. The form which it takes is curiously characteristic. No vehement pangs of remorse, or desperate hopes of escape, overpower his faculties in any simple and straightforward fashion. The poor minister is seized with a strange hallucination. He meets a venerable deacon, and can scarcely restrain himself from uttering blasphemies about the communion-supper. Next appears an aged widow, and he longs to assail her with what appears to him to be an unanswerable argument against the immortality of the soul. Then follows an impulse to whisper impure suggestions to a fair young maiden, whom he has recently converted. And, finally, he longs to greet a rough sailor with a 'volley of good round, solid, satisfactory, and heaven-defying oaths.' The minister, in short, is in that state of mind

which gives birth in its victim to a belief in diabolical possession; and the meaning is pointed by an encounter with an old lady, who, in the popular belief, was one of Satan's miserable slaves and dupes, the witches, and is said—for Hawthorne never introduces the supernatural without toning it down by a supposed legendary transmission—to have invited him to meet her at the blasphemous sabbath in the forest. The sin of endeavouring to escape from the punishment of his sins had brought him into sympathy with wicked mortals and perverted spirits.

This mode of setting forth the agony of a pure mind, tainted by one irremovable blot, is undoubtedly impressive to the imagination in a high degree; far more impressive, we may safely say, than any quantity of such rant as very inferior writers could have poured out with the utmost facility on such an occasion. Yet I am inclined to think that a poet of the highest order would have produced the effect by more direct means. Remorse overpowering and absorbing does not embody itself in these recondite and, one may almost say, over-ingenious fancies. Hawthorne does not give us so much the pure passion as some of its collateral effects. He is still more interested in the curious psychological problem than moved by sympathy with the torture of the soul. We pity poor Mr Dimmesdale profoundly, but we are also interested in him as the subject of an experiment in analytical psychology. We do not care so much for his emotions as for the strange phantoms which are raised in his intellect by the disturbance of his natural functions. The man is placed upon the rack, but our compassion is aroused, not by feeling our own nerves and sinews twitching in sympathy, but by remarking the strange confusion of ideas produced in his mind, the singularly distorted aspect of things in general introduced by such an experience, and hence, if we please, inferring the keenness of the pangs which have produced them. This turn of thought explains the real meaning of Hawthorne's antipathy to poor John Bull. That worthy gentleman, we will admit, is in a sense more gross and beefy than his American cousin. His nerves are stronger, for we need not decide whether they should be called coarser or less morbid. He is not, in any proper sense of the word, less imaginative, for a vigorous grasp of realities is rather a proof of a powerful than a defective imagination. But he is less accessible to those delicate impulses which are to the ordinary passions as electricity to heat. His imagination is more intense and less mobile. The devils which haunt the two races partake of the national characteristics. John Bunyan, Dimmesdale's contemporary, suffered under the pangs of a remorse equally acute, though with apparently far less cause. The devils who tormented him whispered blasphemies in his ears; they pulled at his clothes; they persuaded him that he had committed the unpardonable sin. They caused the very stones in the streets and tiles on the houses, as he says, to band themselves together against him. But they had not the refined and humorous ingenuity of the American fiends. They tempted him, as their fellows tempted Dimmesdale, to sell his soul; but they were too much in earnest to insist upon queer breaches of decorum. They did not indulge in their quaint play of fancy which tempts us to believe that the devils in New England had seduced the 'tricksy spirit,' Ariel, to indulge in practical jokes at the expense of a nobler victim than Stephano or Caliban. They were too terribly diabolical to care whether Bunyan blasphemed in solitude or in the presence of human respectabilities. Bunyan's sufferings were as poetical, but less conducive to refined speculation. His were the fiends that haunt the valley of the shadow of death; whereas Hawthorne's are to be encountered in the dim regions of twilight, where realities blend inextricably with mere phantoms, and the mind confers only a kind of provisional existence upon the 'airy nothings' of its creation. Apollyon does not appear armed to the teeth and throwing fiery darts, but comes as an unsubstantial shadow threatening vague and undefined dangers, and only half detaching himself from the background of darkness. He is as intangible as Milton's Death, not the vivid reality which presented itself to mediæval imaginations.

This special aptitude of mind is probably easier to the American than to the English imagination. The craving for something substantial, whether in cookery or in poetry, was that which induced Hawthorne to keep John Bull rather at arm's length. We may trace the working of similar tendencies in other American peculiarities. Spiritualism and its attendant superstitions are the gross and vulgar form of the same phase of thought as it occurs in men of highly-strung nerves but defective cultivation. Hawthorne always speaks of these modern goblins with the contempt they deserve, for they shocked his imagination as much as his reason; but he likes to play with fancies which are not altogether dissimilar, though his refined taste warns him that they become disgusting when grossly translated into tangible symbols. Mesmerism, for example, plays an important part in *The Blithedale Romance* and *The House of the Seven Gables,* though judiciously softened and kept in the background. An example of the danger of such tendencies may be found in his countryman, Edgar Poe, who, with all his eccentricities, had a most unmistakable vein of genius. Poe is a kind of Hawthorne and *delirium tremens.* What is exquisitely fanciful and airy in the genuine artist is replaced in his rival by an attempt to overpower us by dabblings in the charnel-house and prurient appeals to our fears of the horribly revolting.

After reading some of Poe's stories one feels a kind of shock to one's modesty. We require some kind of spiritual ablution to cleanse our minds of his disgusting images; whereas Hawthorne's pure and delightful fancies, though at times they may have led us too far from the healthy contact of every-day interests, never leave a stain upon the imagination, and generally succeed in throwing a harmonious colouring upon some objects in which we had previously failed to recognize the beautiful. To perform that duty effectually is perhaps the highest of artistic merits; and though we may complain of Hawthorne's colouring as too evanescent, its charm grows upon us the more we study it.

Hawthorne seems to have been slow in discovering the secret of his own power. The *Twice-told Tales,* he tells us, are only a fragmentary selection from a great number which had an ephemeral existence in long-forgotten magazines, and were sentenced to extinction by their author. Though many of the survivors are very striking, no wise reader will regret that sentence. It could be wished that other authors were as ready to bury their innocents, and that injudicious admirers might always abstain from acting as resurrection-men. The fragments which remain, with all their merits, are chiefly interesting as illustrating the intellectual developments of their author. Hawthorne, in his preface to the collected edition (all Hawthorne's prefaces are remarkably instructive) tells us what to think of them. The book, he says, 'requires to be read in the clear brown twilight atmosphere in which it was written; if opened in the sunshine it is apt to look exceedingly like a volume of blank pages.' The remark, with deductions on the score of modesty, is more or less applicable to all his writings. But he explains, and with perfect truth, that though written in solitude, the book has not the abstruse lore which marks the written communications of a solitary mind with itself. The reason is that the sketches 'are not the talk of a secluded man with his own mind and heart, but his attempts . . . to open an intercourse with the world.' They may, in fact, be compared to Brummell's failures; and, though they do not display the perfect grace and fitness which would justify him in presenting himself to society, they were well worth taking up to illustrate the skill of the master's manipulation. We see him trying various experiments to hit off that delicate mean between the fanciful and the prosaic which shall satisfy his taste and be intelligible to the outside world. Sometimes he gives us a fragment of historical romance, as in the story of the stern old regicide who suddenly appears from the woods to head the colonists of Massachusetts in a critical emergency; then he tries his hand at a bit of allegory, and describes the search for the mythical carbuncle which blazes by its inherent splendour on the face of a mysterious cliff in the depths of the untrodden wilderness, and lures old and young, the worldly and the romantic, to waste their lives in the vain effort to discover it–for the carbuncle is the ideal which mocks our pursuit, and may be our curse or our blessing. Then perhaps we have a domestic piece,–a quiet description of a New England country scene–touched with a grace which reminds us of the creators of Sir Roger de Coverley or the Vicar of Wakefield. Occasionally there is a fragment of pure *diablerie*, as in the story of the lady who consults the witch in the hollow of the three hills; and more frequently he tries to work out one of those strange psychological problems which he afterwards treated with more fulness of power. The minister, who for an unexplained reason, puts on a black veil one morning in his youth and wears it until he is laid with it in his grave–a kind of symbolical prophecy of Dimmesdale; the eccentric Wakefield (whose original, if I remember rightly, is to be found in *King's Anecdotes*), who leaves his house one morning for no particular reason, and though living in the next street, does not reveal his existence to his wife for twenty years; and the hero of the 'Wedding Knell', the elderly bridegroom whose early love has jilted him, but agrees to marry him when she is an elderly widow and he an old bachelor, and who appals the marriage-party by coming to the church in his shroud, with the bell tolling as for a funeral,–all these bear the unmistakable stamp of Hawthorne's mint, and each is a study of his favourite subject, the borderland between reason and insanity. In many of these stories appears the element of interest, to which Hawthorne clung the more closely both from early associations and because it is the one undeniably poetical element in the American character. Shallow-minded people fancy Puritanism to be prosaic, because the laces and ruffles of the Cavaliers are a more picturesque costume at a masked ball than the dress of the Roundheads. The Puritan has become a grim and ugly scarecrow, on whom every buffoon may break his jest. But the genuine old Puritan spirit ceases to be picturesque only because of its sublimity: its poetry is sublimed into religion. The great poet of the Puritans fails, so far as he fails, when he tries to transcend the limits of mortal imagination–

The living throne, the sapphire blaze,
Where angels tremble as they gaze,
He saw; but blasted with excess of light,
Closed his eyes in endless night.

To represent the Puritan from within was not, indeed, a task suitable to Hawthorne's powers. Mr Carlyle has done that for us with more congenial sentiment than could have been well felt by the gentle romancer. Hawthorne fancies the grey shadow of a

stern old forefather wondering at his degenerate son. 'A writer of story-books! What kind of business in life, what mode of glorifying God, or being serviceable to mankind in his day and generation may that be? Why, the degenerate fellow might as well have been a fiddler!' And yet the old strain remains, though strangely modified by time and circumstance. Every pure Yankee represents one or both of two types–the descendant of the Puritans and the shrewd peddler; one was embodied in the last century in Jonathan Edwards, and the other in Benjamin Franklin; and we may still trace both in literature and politics the blended currents of feeling. It is an equal mistake–as various people have had to discover before now–to neglect the existence of the old fanaticism or enthusiasm–whichever you please to call it–in the modern Yankee, or to fancy that a fanatic is a bad hand at a bargain. In Hawthorne it would seem that the peddling element had been reduced to its lowest point; the more spiritual element had been refined till it is probable enough that the ancestral shadow would have refused to recognize the connection. The old dogmatical framework to which he attached such vast importance had dropped out of his descendant's mind, and had been replaced by dreamy speculation, obeying no laws save those imposed by its own sense of artistic propriety. But we may often recognize, even where we cannot express in words, the strange family likeness which exists in characteristics which are superficially antagonistic. The man of action may be bound by subtle ties to the speculative metaphysician; and Hawthorne's mind, amidst the most obvious differences, had still an affinity to his remote forefathers. Their bugbears had become his playthings; but the witches, though they have no reality, have still a fascination for him. The interest which he feels in them, even in their now shadowy state, is a proof that he would have believed in them in good earnest a century and a half earlier. The imagination, working in a different intellectual atmosphere, is unable to project its images upon the external world; but it still forms them in the old shape. His solitary musings necessarily employ a modern dialect, but they often turn on the same topics which occurred to Jonathan Edwards in the woods of Connecticut. Instead of the old Puritan speculations about predestination and freewill, he dwells upon the transmission by natural laws of an hereditary curse, and upon the strange blending of good and evil, which may cause sin to be an awakening impulse in a human soul. The change which takes place in Donatello in consequence of his crime is a modern symbol of the fall of man and the eating the fruit of the knowledge of good and evil. As an artist he gives concrete images instead of abstract theories;

but his thoughts evidently delight to dwell in the same regions where the daring speculations of his theological ancestors took their origin. Septimius, the rather disagreeable hero of his last romance, is a peculiar example of a similar change. Brought up under the strict discipline of New England, he has retained the love of musing upon insoluble mysteries, though he has abandoned the old dogmatic guide-posts. When such a man finds that the orthodox scheme of the universe provided by his official pastors has somehow broken down with him, he forms some audacious theory of his own, and is perhaps plunged into an unhallowed revolt against the Divine order. Septimius, under such circumstances, develops into a kind of morbid and sullen Hawthorne. He considers—as other people have done—that death is a disagreeable fact, but refuses to admit that it is inevitable. The romance tends to show that such a state of mind is unhealthy and dangerous, and Septimius is contrasted unfavourably with the vigorous natures who preserve their moral balance by plunging into the stream of practical life. Yet Hawthorne necessarily sympathizes with the abnormal being whom he creates. Septimius illustrates the dangers of the musing temperament, but the dangers are produced by a combination of an essentially selfish nature with the meditative tendency. Hawthorne, like his hero, sought refuge from the hard facts of commonplace life by retiring into a visionary world. He delights in propounding much the same questions as those which tormented poor Septimius, though, for obvious reasons, he did not try to compound an elixir of life by means of a recipe handed down from Indian ancestors. The strange mysteries in which the world and our nature are shrouded are always present to his imagination; he catches dim glimpses of the laws which bring out strange harmonies, but on the whole, tend rather to deepen than to clear the mysteries. He loves the marvellous, not in the vulgar sense of the word, but as a symbol of the perplexity which encounters every thoughtful man in his journey through life. Similar tenets at an earlier period might, with almost equal probability, have led him to the stake as a dabbler in forbidden sciences, or have caused him to be revered as one to whom a deep spiritual instinct had been granted.

Meanwhile, as it was his calling to tell stories to readers of the English language in the nineteenth century, his power is exercised in a different sphere. No modern writer has the same skill in so using the marvellous as to interest without unduly exciting our incredulity. He makes, indeed, no positive demands on our credulity. The strange influences which are suggested rather than obtruded upon us, are kept in the background so as not to invite, nor, indeed, to

Septimius Felton brooding in his study (illustration by A. I. Keller; Autograph Edition, Houghton, Mifflin, 1900; Thomas Cooper Library, University of South Carolina)

render possible the application of scientific tests. We may compare him once more to Miss Brontë, who shows us, in *Villette,* a haunted garden. She shows us a ghost who is for a moment a very terrible spectre indeed, and then, rather to our annoyance, rationalizes him into a flesh and blood lover. Hawthorne would neither have allowed the ghost to intrude so forcibly, nor have expelled him so decisively. The garden in his hands would have been haunted by a shadowy terror of which we could render no precise account to ourselves. It would have refrained from actual contact with professors and governesses; and as it would never have taken bodily form, it would never have been quite dispelled. His ghosts are confined to their proper sphere, the twilight of the mind, and never venture into the broad glare of daylight. We can see them so long as we do not gaze directly at them; when we turn to examine them they are gone, and we are left in doubt whether they were realities or an ocular delusion generated in our fancy by some accidental collocation of half-seen objects. So in *The*

House of the Seven Gables we may hold what opinion we please as to the reality of the curse which hangs over the family of the Pyncheons and the strange connection between them and their hereditary antagonists; in *The Scarlet Letter* we may, if we like, hold that there was really more truth in the witch legends which colour the imaginations of the actors than we are apt to dream of in our philosophy; and in *Transformation* we are left finally in doubt as to the great question of Donatello's ears, and the mysterious influence which he retains over the animal world so long as he is unstained by bloodshed. In *Septimius* alone, it seems to me that the supernatural is left in rather too obtrusive a shape in spite of the final explanations; though it might possibly have been toned down had the story received the last touches of the author. The artifice, if so it may be called, by which this is effected, and the romance is just sufficiently dipped in the shadow of the marvellous to be heightened without becoming offensive, sounds, like other things, tolerably easy when it is explained: and yet the difficulty is enormous, as may appear on reflection as well as from the extreme rarity of any satisfactory work in the same style by other artists. With the exception of a touch or two in Scott's stories, such as the impressive Bodach Glas in *Waverley* and the apparition in the exquisite *Bride of Lammermoor,* it would be difficult to discover any parallel.

In fact Hawthorne was able to tread in that magic circle only by an exquisite refinement of taste, and by a delicate sense of humour, which is the best preservative against all extravagance. Both qualities combine in that tender delineation of character which is, after all, one of his greatest charms. His Puritan blood shows itself in sympathy, not with the stern side of the ancestral creed, but with the feebler characters upon whom it weighed as an oppressive terror. He resembles, in some degree, poor Clifford Pyncheon, whose love of the beautiful makes him suffer under the stronger will of his relatives and the prim stiffness of their home. He exhibits the suffering of such a character all the more effectively because, with his kindly compassion, there is mixed a delicate flavour of irony. The more tragic scenes affect us, perhaps, with less sense of power; the playful, though melancholy, fancy seems to be less at home when the more powerful emotions are to be excited; and yet once, at least, he draws one of those pictures which engrave themselves instantaneously on the memory. The grimmest or most passionate of writers could hardly have improved the scene where the body of the magnificent Zenobia is discovered in the river. Every touch goes straight to the mark. The narrator of the story, accompanied by the man whose coolness has caused the suicide, and the shrewd, unimaginative Yankee farmer, who interprets with coarse, down-right language the suspicions which they fear to confess to themselves, are sounding the depths of the river by night in a leaky punt with a long pole. Silas Foster interprets the brutal, commonplace comments of the outside world, which jar so terribly on the more sensitive and closely interested actors in the tragedy. 'Heigho!' he soliloquizes, with offensive loudness, 'life and death together make sad work for us all. Then I was a boy, bobbing for fish; and now I'm getting to be an old fellow, and here I be, groping for a dead body! I tell you what, lads, if I thought anything had really happened to Zenobia, I should feel kind o' sorrowful.' That is the kind of sympathy one gets from the Silas Fosters of this world, who insist upon forcing their discordant chorus upon us, like the gravediggers in *Hamlet.* At length the body is found, and poor Zenobia is brought to the shore with her knees still bent in the attitude of prayer, and her hands clenched in immitigable defiance. Foster tries in vain to straighten the dead limbs. As the teller of the story gazes at her, the grimly ludicrous reflection occurs to him that if Zenobia had foreseen all 'the ugly circumstances of death—how ill it would become her, the altogether unseemly aspect which she must put on, and especially old Silas Foster's efforts to improve the matter—she would no more have committed the dreadful act than have exhibited herself to a public assembly in a badly-fitting garment.'

That is a true touch of genius; and here probably it is as well to close an attempt at the analysis of an almost unique writer. Such attempts, as I admitted at starting, are not very profitable, however tempting. Nor do I flatter myself that I have thrown any new light on the question of why we should feel what every one feels. Be that as it may, Hawthorne is specially interesting because one fancies that, in spite of the marked idiosyncracies which forbid one to see in him the founder of a school—as, indeed, any rivalry would be dangerous—he is, in some sense, a characteristic embodiment of true national tendencies. If so, we may hope that, though America may never produce another Hawthorne, yet other American writers may arise who will apply some of his principles of art, and develop the fineness of observation and delicate sense of artistic propriety for which he was so conspicuous. On that matter, at least, we can have no jealousies; and if our cousins raise more Hawthornes, we may possibly feel more grateful than for some of their other productions.

Henry James's 1879 study of Hawthorne constitutes the first book about an indisputably great American novelist by another one. The fifth chapter, reproduced here, focuses on Hawthorne's three mature American novels: The Scarlet Letter, The House of the Seven Gables, *and* The Blithedale Romance. *Probably the most important American critic of the entire century, James, who spent much of his life in Europe, viewed American culture as uncongenial to creativity and devoid of subject matter for serious artistic expression; one of his major themes concerns simple Americans in complex Europe.*

The Three American Novels
Henry James
Hawthorne (1879)

The prospect of official station and emolument which Hawthorne mentions in one of those paragraphs from his Journals which I have just quoted, as having offered itself and then passed away, was at last, in the event, confirmed by his receiving from the administration of President Polk the gift of a place in the Custom-house of his native town. The office was a modest one, and 'official station' may perhaps appear a magniloquent formula for the functions sketched in the admirable Introduction to *The Scarlet Letter*. Hawthorne's duties were those of Surveyor of the port of Salem, and they had a salary attached, which was the important part; as his biographer tells us that he had received almost nothing for the contributions to the *Democratic Review*. He bade farewell to his ex-parsonage, and went back to Salem in 1846, and the immediate effect of his ameliorated fortune was to make him stop writing. None of his Journals of the period, from his going to Salem to 1850, have been published; from which I infer that he even ceased to journalise. *The Scarlet Letter* was not written till 1849. In the delightful prologue to that work, entitled 'The Custom-house,' he embodies some of the impressions gathered during these years of comparative leisure (I say of leisure, because he does not intimate in this sketch of his occupations that his duties were onerous). He intimates, however, that they were not interesting, and that it was a very good thing for him, mentally and morally, when his term of service expired—or rather when he was removed from office by the operation of that wonderful 'rotatory' system which his countrymen had invented for the administration of their affairs. This sketch of the Custom-house is, as simple writing, one of the most perfect of Hawthorne's compositions, and one of the most gracefully and humorously autobiographic. It would be interesting to examine it in detail, but I prefer to use my space

Henry James

for making some remarks upon the work which was the ultimate result of this period of Hawthorne's residence in his native town; and I shall, for convenience' sake, say directly afterwards what I have to say about the two companions of *The Scarlet Letter*—*The House of the Seven Gables* and *The Blithedale Romance*. I quoted some passages from the prologue to the first of these novels in the early pages of this essay. There is another passage, however, which bears particularly upon this phase of Hawthorne's career, and which is so happily expressed as to make it a pleasure to transcribe it—the passage in which he says that

for myself, during the whole of my Custom-house experience, moonlight and sunshine, and the glow of the firelight, were just alike in my regard, and neither of them was of one whit more avail than the twinkle of a tallow-candle. An entire class of susceptibilities, and a gift connected with them—of no great richness or value, but the best I had—was gone from me.

Illustration of the scene in chapter 6 of The House of the Seven Gables *in which Phoebe Pyncheon meets the daguerreotypist Holgrave (from the Nottingham Society edition of Hawthorne's works; Thomas Cooper Library, University of South Carolina)*

He goes on to say that he believes that he might have done something if he could have made up his mind to convert the very substance of the commonplace that surrounded him into matter of literature.

> I might, for instance, have contented myself with writing out the narratives of a veteran shipmaster, one of the inspectors, whom I should be most ungrateful not to mention; since scarcely a day passed that he did not stir me to laughter and admiration by his marvellous gift as a story-teller . . . But, nevertheless, it is anything but agreeable to be haunted by a suspicion that one's intellect is dwindling away, or exhaling, without your consciousness, like ether out of phial; so that at every glance you find a smaller and less volatile residuum.

As, however, it was with what was left of his intellect after three years' evaporation, that Hawthorne wrote

The Scarlet Letter, there is little reason to complain of the injury he suffered in his Surveyorship.

His publisher, Mr Fields, in a volume entitled *Yesterdays with Authors,* has related the circumstances in which Hawthorne's masterpiece came into the world.

> In the winter of 1849, after he had been ejected from the Custom-house, I went down to Salem to see him and inquire after his health, for we heard he had been suffering from illness. He was then living in a modest wooden house . . . I found him alone in a chamber over the sitting-room of the dwelling, and as the day was cold he was hovering near a stove. We fell into talk about his future prospects, and he was, as I feared I should find him, in a very desponding mood.

His visitor urged him to bethink himself of publishing something, and Hawthorne replied by calling his attention to the small popularity his published productions had yet acquired, and declaring he had done nothing, and had no spirit for doing anything. The narrator of the incident urged upon him the necessity of a more hopeful view of his situation, and proceeded to take leave. He had not reached the street, however, when Hawthorne hurried to overtake him, and, placing a roll of MS. in his hand, bade him take it to Boston, read it, and pronounce upon it. 'It is either very good or very bad,' said the author; 'I don't know which.' 'On my way back to Boston,' says Mr Fields,

> I read the germ of *The Scarlet Letter;* before I slept that night I wrote him a note all aglow with admiration of the marvellous story he had put into my hands, and told him that I would come again to Salem the next day and arrange for its publication. I went on in such an amazing state of excitement, when we met again in the little house, that he would not believe I was really in earnest. He seemed to think I was beside myself, and laughed sadly at my enthusiasm.

Hawthorne, however, went on with the book and finished it, but it appeared only a year later. His biographer quotes a passage from a letter which he wrote in February, 1850, to his friend Horatio Bridge.

> I finished my book only yesterday; one end being in the press at Boston, while the other was in my head here at Salem; so that, as you see, my story is at least fourteen miles long . . . My book, the publisher tells me, will not be out before April. He speaks of it in tremendous terms of approbation; so does Mrs Hawthorne, to whom I read the conclusion last night. It broke her heart, and sent her to bed with a grievous headache—which I look upon as a triumphant success. Judging from the effect upon her and the publisher, I may calculate on what bowlers call a ten-strike. But I don't make any such calculation.

And Mr Lathrop calls attention, in regard to this passage, to an allusion in the *English Note-Books* (September 14, 1855).

> Speaking of Thackeray, I cannot but wonder at his coolness in respect to his own pathos, and compare it to my own emotions when I read the last scene of *The Scarlet Letter* to my wife, just after writing it—tried to read it, rather, for my voice swelled and heaved as if I were tossed up and down on an ocean as it subsides after a storm. But I was in a very nervous state then, having gone through a great diversity of emotion while writing it, for many months.

The work has the tone of the circumstances in which it was produced. If Hawthorne was in a sombre mood, and if his future were painfully vague, *The Scarlet Letter* contains little enough of gaiety or of hopefulness. It is densely dark, with a single spot of vivid colour in it; and it will probably long remain the most consistently gloomy of English novels of the first order. But I just now called it the author's masterpiece, and I imagine it will continue to be, for other generations than ours, his most substantial title to fame. The subject had probably lain a long time in his mind, as his subjects were apt to do; so that he appears completely to possess it, to know it and feel it. It is simpler and more complete than his other novels; it achieves more perfectly what it attempts, and it has about it that charm, very hard to express, which we find in an artist's work the first time he has touched his highest mark—a sort of straightness and naturalness of execution, an unconsciousness of his public, and freshness of interest in his theme. It was a great success, and he immediately found himself famous. The writer of these lines, who was a child at the time, remembers dimly the sensation the book produced, and the little shudder with which people alluded to it, as if a peculiar horror were mixed with its attractions. He was too young to read it himself; but its title, upon which he fixed his eyes as the book lay upon the table, had a mysterious charm. He had a vague belief, indeed, that the 'letter' in question was one of the documents that come by the post, and it was a source of perpetual wonderment to him that it should be of such an unaccustomed hue. Of course it was difficult to explain to a child the significance of poor Hester Prynne's blood-coloured *A*. But the mystery was at last partly dispelled by his being taken to see a collection of pictures (the annual exhibition of the National Academy), where he encountered a representation of a pale, handsome woman, in a quaint black dress and a white coif, holding between her knees an elfish-looking little girl, fantastically dressed, and crowned with flowers. Embroidered on the woman's breast was a great crimson *A,* over which the child's fin-

gers, as she glanced strangely out of the picture, were maliciously playing. I was told that this was Hester Prynne and little Pearl, and that when I grew older I might read their interesting history. But the picture remained vividly imprinted on my mind; I had been vaguely frightened and made uneasy by it; and, when, years afterwards, I first read the novel, I seemed to myself to have read it before, and to be familiar with its two strange heroines. I mention this incident simply as an indication of the degree to which the success of *The Scarlet Letter* had made the book what is called an actuality. Hawthorne himself was very modest about it; he wrote to his publisher, when there was a question of his undertaking another novel, that what had given the history of Hester Prynne its 'vogue' was simply the introductory chapter. In fact, the publication of *The Scarlet Letter* was in the United States a literary event of the first importance. The book was the finest piece of imaginative writing yet put forth in the country. There was a consciousness of this in the welcome that was given it—a satisfaction in the idea of America having produced a novel that belonged to literature, and to the forefront of it. Something might at last be sent to Europe as exquisite in quality as anything that had been received, and the best of it was that the thing was absolutely American; it belonged to the soil, to the air; it came out of the very heart of New England.

It is beautiful, admirable, extraordinary; it has in the highest degree that merit which I have spoken of as the mark of Hawthorne's best things—an indefinable purity and lightness of conception, a quality which in a work of art affects one in the same way as the absence of grossness does in a human being. His fancy, as I just now said, has evidently brooded over the subject for a long time; the situation to be represented had disclosed itself to him in all its phases. When I say in all its phases, the sentence demands modification; for it is to be remembered that if Hawthorne laid his hand upon the well-worn theme, upon the familiar combination of the wife, the lover, and the husband, it was, after all, but to one period of the history of these three persons that he attached himself. The situation is the situation after the woman's fault has been committed, and the current of expiation and repentance has set in. In spite of the relation between Hester Prynne and Arthur Dimmesdale, no story of love was surely ever less of a 'love-story.' To Hawthorne's imagination the fact that these two persons had loved each other too well was of an interest comparatively vulgar; what appealed to him was the idea of their moral situation in the long years that were to follow. The story, indeed, is in a secondary degree that of Hester Prynne; she becomes, really, after the first scene, an accessory figure; it is not upon her the *dénoûment* depends. It is upon her guilty lover that the author projects most frequently the cold, thin rays of his fitfully-moving lantern, which makes here and there a little luminous circle, on the edge of which hovers the livid and sinister figure of the injured and retributive husband. The story goes on, for the most part, between the lover and the husband—the tormented young Puritan minister, who carries the secret of his own lapse from pastoral purity locked up beneath an exterior that commends itself to the reverence of his flock, while he sees the softer partner of his guilt standing in the full glare of exposure and humbling herself to the misery of atonement—between this more wretched and pitiable culprit, to whom dishonour would come as a comfort and the pillory as a relief, and the older, keener, wiser man, who, to obtain satisfaction for the wrong he has suffered, devises the infernally ingenious plan of conjoining himself with his wronger, living with him, living upon him; and while he pretends to minister to his hidden ailment and to sympathise with his pain, revels in his unsuspected knowledge of these things, and stimulates them by malignant arts. The attitude of Roger Chillingworth, and the means he takes to compensate himself—these are the highly original elements in the situation that Hawthorne so ingeniously treats. None of his works are so impregnated with that after-sense of the old Puritan consciousness of life to which allusion has so often been made. If, as M. Montégut says, the qualities of his ancestors *filtered* down through generations into his composition, *The Scarlet Letter* was, as it were, the vessel that gathered up the last of the precious drops. And I say this not because the story happens to be of so-called historical cast, to be told of the early days of Massachusetts, and of people in steeple-crowned hats and sad-coloured garments. The historical colouring is rather weak than otherwise; there is little elaboration of detail, of the modern realism of research; and the author has made no great point of causing his figures to speak the English of their period. Nevertheless, the book is full of the moral presence of the race that invented Hester's penance—diluted and complicated with other things, but still perfectly recognisable. Puritanism, in a word, is there, not only objectively, as Hawthorne tried to place it there, but subjectively as well. Not, I mean, in his judgment of his characters in any harshness of prejudice, or in the obtrusion of a moral lesson; but in the very quality of his own vision, in the tone of the picture, in a certain coldness and exclusiveness of treatment.

The faults of the book are, to my sense, a want of reality and an abuse of the fanciful element—of a certain superficial symbolism. The people strike me not as characters, but as representatives, very picturesquely arranged, of a single state of mind; and the interest of the story lies, not in them, but in the situation, which is insistently kept before us, with little progression, though with a great deal, as I have said, of a certain stable variation; and to which they, out of their reality, contribute little that helps it to live and move. I was made to feel this want of reality, this over-ingenuity, of *The Scarlet Letter,* by chancing not long since upon a novel which was read fifty years ago much more than to-day, but which is still worth reading—the story of *Adam Blair,* by John Gibson Lockhart. This interesting and powerful little tale has a great deal of analogy with Hawthorne's novel—quite enough, at least, to suggest a comparison between them; and the comparison is a very interesting one to make, for it speedily leads us to larger considerations than simple resemblances and divergences of plot.

Adam Blair, like Arthur Dimmesdale, is a Calvinistic minister who becomes the lover of a married woman, is overwhelmed with remorse at his misdeed, and makes a public confession of it; then expiates it by resigning his pastoral office and becoming a humble tiller of the soil, as his father had been. The two stories are of about the same length, and each is the masterpiece (putting aside, of course, as far as Lockhart is concerned, the *Life of Scott*) of the author. They deal alike with the manners of a rigidly theological society, and even in certain details they correspond. In each of them, between the guilty pair, there is a charming little girl; though I hasten to say that Sarah Blair (who is not the daughter of the heroine, but the legitimate offspring of the hero, a widower) is far from being as brilliant and graceful an apparition as the admirable little Pearl of *The Scarlet Letter.* The main difference between the two tales is the fact that in the American story the husband plays an all-important part, and in the Scottish plays almost none at all. *Adam Blair* is the history of the passion, and *The Scarlet Letter* the history of its sequel; but nevertheless, if one has read the two books at a short interval, it is impossible to avoid confronting them. I confess that a large portion of the interest of *Adam Blair,* to my mind, when once I had perceived that it would repeat in a great measure the situation of *The Scarlet Letter,* lay in noting its difference of tone. It threw into relief the passionless quality of Hawthorne's novel, its element of cold and ingenious fantasy, its elaborate imaginative delicacy. These things do not precisely constitute a weakness in *The Scarlet Letter;* indeed, in a certain way they constitute a great strength; but the absence of a certain something warm and straightforward, a trifle more grossly human and vulgarly natural, which one finds in *Adam Blair,* will always make Hawthorne's tale less touching to a large number of even very intelligent readers, than a love-story told with the robust, synthetic pathos which served Lockhart so well. His novel is not of the first rank (I should call it an

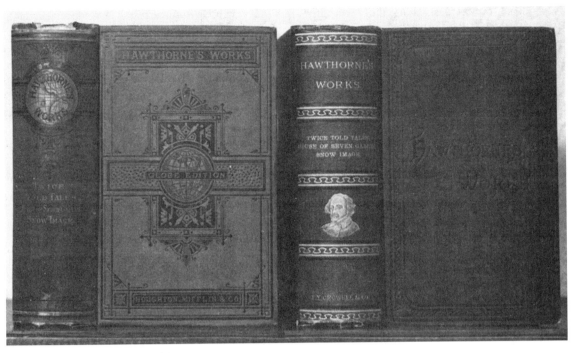

Bindings for the 1880 "Globe Edition" of Hawthorne's works, published in six volumes (from C. E. Frazer Clark Jr.,
Nathaniel Hawthorne: A Descriptive Bibliography, *1978)*

excellent second-rate one), but it borrows a charm from the fact that his vigorous, but not strongly imaginative, mind was impregnated with the reality of his subject. He did not always succeed in rendering this reality; the expression is sometimes awkward and poor. But the reader feels that his vision was clear, and his feeling about the matter very strong and rich. Hawthorne's imagination, on the other hand, plays with his theme so incessantly, leads it such a dance through the moonlighted air of his intellect, that the thing cools off, as it were, hardens and stiffens, and, producing effects much more exquisite, leaves the reader with a sense of having handled a splendid piece of silversmith's work. Lockhart, by means much more vulgar, produces at moments a greater illusion, and satisfies our inevitable desire for something, in the people in whom it is sought to interest us, that shall be the same pitch and the same continuity with ourselves. Above all, it is interesting to see how the same subject appears to two men of a thoroughly different cast of mind and of a different race. Lockhart was struck with the warmth of the subject that offered itself to him, and Hawthorne with its coldness; the one with its glow, its sentimental interest–the other with its shadow, its moral interest. Lockhart's story is as decent, as severely draped, as *The Scarlet Letter;* but the author has a more vivid sense than appears to have imposed itself upon Hawthorne, of some of the incidents of the situation he describes; his tempted man and tempting woman are more actual and personal; his

heroine in especial, though not in the least a delicate or a subtle conception, has a sort of credible, visible, palpable property, a vulgar roundness and relief, which are lacking to the dim and chastened image of Hester Prynne. But I am going too far; I am comparing simplicity with subtlety, the usual with the refined. Each man wrote as his turn of mind impelled him, but each expressed something more than himself. Lockhart was a dense, substantial Briton, with a taste for the concrete, and Hawthorne was a thin New Englander, with a miasmatic conscience.

In *The Scarlet Letter* there is a great deal of symbolism; there is, I think, too much. It is overdone at times, and becomes mechanical; it ceases to be impressive, and grazes triviality. The idea of the mystic *A* which the young minister finds imprinted upon his breast and eating into his flesh, in sympathy with the embroidered badge that Hester is condemned to wear, appears to me to be a case in point. This suggestion should, I think, have been just made and dropped; to insist upon it and return to it, is to exaggerate the weak side of the subject. Hawthorne returns to it constantly, plays with it, and seems charmed by it; until at last the reader feels tempted to declare that his enjoyment of it is puerile. In the admirable scene, so superbly conceived and beautifully executed, in which Mr Dimmesdale, in the stillness of the night, in the middle of the sleeping town, feels impelled to go and stand upon the scaffold where his mistress had formerly enacted her dreadful penance, and then, seeing Hester pass along the street, from watching at a sick-bed, with little Pearl at her side, calls them both to come and stand there beside him—in this masterly episode the effect is almost spoiled by the introduction of one of these superficial conceits. What leads up to it is very fine—so fine that I cannot do better than quote it as a specimen of one of the striking pages of the book.

> But before Mr Dimmesdale had done speaking, a light gleamed far and wide over all the muffled sky . . . They stood in the noon of the strange and solemn splendour, as if it were the light that is to reveal all secrets, and the daybreak that shall unite all that belong to one another.

That is imaginative, impressive, poetic; but when, almost immediately afterwards, the author goes on to say that 'the minister looking upward to the zenith, beheld there the appearance of an immense letter—the letter *A*—marked out in lines of dull red light,' we feel that he goes too far, and is in danger of crossing the line that separates the sublime from its intimate neighbour. We are tempted to say that this is not moral tragedy, but physical comedy. In the same way, too much is made of the intimation that Hester's badge had a scorching property, and that if one touched it one would immediately withdraw one's hand. Hawthorne is perpetually looking for images which shall place themselves in picturesque correspondence with the spiritual facts with which he is concerned, and of course the search is of the very essence of poetry. But in such a process discretion is everything, and when the image becomes importunate it is in danger of seeming to stand for nothing more serious than itself. When Hester meets the minister by appointment in the forest, and sits talking with him while little Pearl wanders away and plays by the edge of the brook, the child is represented as at last making her way over to the other side of the woodland stream, and disporting herself there in a manner which makes her mother feel herself,

> in some indistinct and tantalising manner, estranged from Pearl; as if the child, in her lonely ramble through the forest, had strayed out of the sphere in which she and her mother dwelt together, and was now vainly seeking to return to it.

And Hawthorne devotes a chapter to this idea of the child's having, by putting the brook between Hester and herself, established a kind of spiritual gulf, on the verge of which her little fantastic person innocently mocks at her mother's sense of bereavement. This conception belongs, one would say, quite to the lighter order of a story-teller's devices, and the reader hardly

goes with Hawthorne in the large development he gives to it. He hardly goes with him either, I think, in his extreme predilection for a small number of vague ideas which are represented by such terms as 'sphere' and 'sympathies.' Hawthorne makes too liberal a use of these two substantives; it is the solitary defect of his style; and it counts as a defect partly because the words in question are a sort of specialty with certain writers immeasurably inferior to himself.

I had not meant, however, to expatiate upon his defects, which are of the slenderest and most venial kind. *The Scarlet Letter* has the beauty and harmony of all original and complete conceptions, and its weaker spots, whatever they are, are not of its essence; they are mere light flaws and inequalities of surface. One can often return to it; it supports familiarity, and has the inexhaustible charm and mystery of great works of art. It is admirably written. Hawthorne afterwards polished his style to a still higher degree; but in his later productions—it is almost always the case in a writer's later productions—there is a touch of mannerism. In *The Scarlet Letter* there is a high degree of polish, and at the same time a charming freshness; his phrase is less conscious of itself. His biographer very justly calls attention to the fact that his style was excellent from the beginning; that he appeared to have passed through no phase of learning how to write, but was in possession of his means, from the first, of his handling a pen. His early tales, perhaps, were not of a character to subject his faculty of expression to a very severe test; but a man who had not Hawthorne's natural sense of language would certainly have contrived to write them less well. This natural sense of language—this turn for saying things lightly and yet touchingly, picturesquely yet simply, and for infusing a gently colloquial tone into matter of the most unfamiliar import—he had evidently cultivated with great assiduity. I have spoken of the anomalous character of his *Note-Books*—of his going to such pains often to make a record of incidents which either were not worth remembering, or could be easily remembered without its aid. But it helps us to understand the *Note-Books* if we regard them as a literary exercise. They were compositions, as schoolboys say, in which the subject was only the pretext, and the main point was to write a certain amount of excellent English. Hawthorne must at least have written a great many of these things for practice, and he must often have said to himself that it was better practice to write about trifles, because it was a greater tax upon one's skill to make them interesting. And his theory was just, for he has almost always made his trifles interesting. In his novels his art of saying things well is very positively tested; for here he treats of those matters among which it is very easy for a blundering writer to go wrong—the subtleties and mysteries of life, the moral and spiritual maze. In such a passage as one I have marked for quotation from *The Scarlet Letter,* there is the stamp of the genius of style:–

> Hester Prynne, gazing steadfastly at the clergyman, felt a dreary influence come over her, but wherefore or whence she knew not, unless that he seemed so remote from her own sphere and utterly beyond her reach . . . And thus much of woman there was in Hester, that she could scarcely forgive him–least of all now, when the heavy footstep of their approaching fate might be heard, nearer, nearer, nearer!–for being able to withdraw himself so completely from their mutual world; while she groped darkly, and stretched forth her cold hands, and found him not!

The House of the Seven Gables was written at Lenox, among the mountains of Massachusetts, a village nestling, rather loosely, in one of the loveliest corners of New England, to which Hawthorne had betaken himself after the success of *The Scarlet Letter* became conspicuous, in the summer of 1850, and where he occupied for two years an uncomfortable little red house, which is now pointed out to the inquiring stranger. The inquiring stranger is now a frequent figure at Lenox, for the place has suffered the process of lionisation. It has become a prosperous watering-place, or at least (as there are no waters), as they say in America, a summerresort. It is a brilliant and generous landscape, and thirty years ago a man of fancy, desiring to apply himself, might have found both inspiration and tranquillity there. Hawthorne found so much of both that he wrote more during his two years of residence at Lenox than at any period of his career. He began with *The House of the Seven Gables,* which was finished in the early part of 1851. This is the longest of his three American novels; it is the most elaborate, and in the judgment of some persons it is the finest. It is a rich, delightful, imaginative work, larger and more various than its companions, and full of all sorts of deep intentions, of interwoven threads of suggestion. But it is not so rounded and complete as *The Scarlet Letter;* it has always seemed to me more like a prologue to a great novel than a great novel itself. I think this is partly owing to the fact that the subject, the *donnée,* as the French say, of the story, does not quite fill it out, and that we get at the same time an impression of certain complicated purposes on the author's part, which seem to reach beyond it. I call it larger and more various than its companions, and it has, indeed, a greater richness of tone and density of detail. The colour, so to speak, of *The House of the Seven Gables* is admirable. But the story has a sort of expansive quality which never wholly fructifies, and as I lately laid it down, after reading it for the third time, I had a sense of having interested myself in a magnificent

fragment. Yet the book has a great fascination; and of all of those of its author's productions which I have read over while writing this sketch, it is perhaps the one that has gained most by reperusal. If it be true of the others that the pure, natural quality of the imaginative strain is their great merit, this is at least as true of *The House of the Seven Gables,* the charm of which is in a peculiar degree of the kind that we fail to reduce to its grounds–like that of the sweetness of a piece of music, or the softness of fine September weather. It is vague, indefinable, ineffable; but it is the sort of thing we must always point to in justification of the high claim that we make for Hawthorne. In this case, of course, its vagueness is a drawback, for it is difficult to point to ethereal beauties; and if the reader whom we have wished to inoculate with our admiration inform us, after looking awhile, that he perceives nothing in particular, we can only reply that, in effect, the object is a delicate one.

The House of the Seven Gables comes nearer being a picture of contemporary American life than either of its companions; but on this ground it would be a mistake to make a large claim for it. It cannot be too often repeated that Hawthorne was not a realist. He had a high sense of reality–his *Note-Books* superabundantly testify to it; and fond as he was of jotting down the items that make it up, he never attempted to render exactly or closely the actual facts of the society that surrounded him. I have said–I began by saying–that his pages were full of its spirit, and of a certain reflected light that springs from it; but I was careful to add that the reader must look for his local and national qualities between the lines of his writing and in the *indirect* testimony of his tone, his accent, his temper, of his very omissions and suppressions. *The House of the Seven Gables* has, however, more literal actuality than the others, and if it were not too fanciful an account of it, I should say that it renders, to an initiated reader, the impression of a summer afternoon in an elm-shadowed New England town. It leaves upon the mind a vague correspondence to some such reminiscence, and in stirring up the association it renders it delightful. The comparison is to the honour of the New England town, which gains in it more than it bestows. The shadows of the elms, in *The House of the Seven Gables,* are exceptionally dense and cool; the summer afternoon is peculiarly still and beautiful; the atmosphere has a delicious warmth, and the long daylight seems to pause and rest. But the mild provincial quality is there, the mixture of shabbiness and freshness, the paucity of ingredients. The end of an old race–this is the situation that Hawthorne has depicted, and he has been admirably inspired in the choice of the figures in whom he seeks to interest us. They are all figures rather than characters–they are all pictures rather than persons. But if their reality is light and vague, it is

Bindings for editions of Hawthorne's collected works published between 1883 and 1903 (from C. E. Frazer Clark Jr.,
Nathaniel Hawthorne: A Descriptive Bibliography, *1978)*

sufficient, and it is in harmony with the low relief and dimness of outline of the objects that surrounded them. They are all types, to the author's mind, of something general, of something that is bound up with the history, at large, of families and individuals, and each of them is the centre of a cluster of those ingenious and meditative musings, rather melancholy, as a general thing, than joyous, which melt into the current and texture of the story and give it a kind of moral richness. A grotesque old spinster, simple, childish, penniless, very humble at heart, but rigidly conscious of her pedigree; an amiable bachelor, of an epicurean temperament and an enfeebled intellect, who has passed twenty years of his life in penal confinement for a crime of which he was unjustly pronounced guilty; a sweet-natured and bright-faced young girl from the country, a poor relation of these two ancient decrepitudes, with whose moral mustiness her modern freshness and soundness are contrasted; a young man still more modern, holding the latest opinions, who has sought his fortune up and down the world, and, though he has not found it, takes a genial and enthusiastic view of the future: these, with two or three remarkable accessory figures, are the persons concerned in the little drama. The drama is a small one, but as Hawthorne does not put it before us for its own superficial sake, for the dry facts of the case, but for something in it which he holds to be symbolic and of large application, something that points a moral and that it behoves us to remember, the scenes in the rusty wooden house whose gables give its name to the story,

have something of the dignity both of history and of tragedy. Miss Hephzibah Pyncheon, dragging out a disappointed life in her paternal dwelling, finds herself obliged in her old age to open a little shop for the sale of penny toys and gingerbread. This is the central incident of the tale, and, as Hawthorne relates it, it is an incident of the most impressive magnitude and most touching interest. Her dishonoured and vague-minded brother is released from prison at the same moment, and returns to the ancestral roof to deepen her perplexities. But, on the other hand, to alleviate them, and to introduce a breath of the air of the outer world into this long unventilated interior, the little country cousin also arrives, and proves the good angel of the feebly distracted household. All this episode is exquisite—admirably conceived and executed, with a kind of humorous tenderness, an equal sense of everything in it that is picturesque, touching, ridiculous, worthy of the highest praise. Hephzibah Pyncheon, with her near-sighted scowl, her rusty joints, her antique turban, her map of a great territory to the eastward which ought to have belonged to her family, her vain terrors, and scruples, and resentments, the inaptitude and repugnance of an ancient gentlewoman to the vulgar little commerce which a cruel fate has compelled her to engage in—Hephzibah Pyncheon is a masterly picture. I repeat that she is a picture, as her companions are pictures; she is a charming piece of descriptive writing, rather than a dramatic exhibition. But she is described, like her companions, too, so subtly and lovingly that we enter into her virginal old heart and stand with her behind her abominable little counter. Clifford Pyncheon is a still more remarkable conception, though he is, perhaps, not so vividly depicted. It was a figure needing a much more subtle touch, however, and it was of the essence of his character to be vague and unemphasised. Nothing can be more charming than the manner in which the soft, bright, active presence of Phoebe Pyncheon is indicated, or than the account of her relations with the poor, dimly sentient kinsman for whom her light-handed sisterly offices, in the evening of a melancholy life, are a revelation of lost possibilities of happiness. 'In her aspect,' Hawthorne says of the young girl,

> there was a familiar gladness, and a holiness that you could play with, and yet reverence it as much as ever. She was like a prayer offered up in the homeliest beauty of one's mother-tongue. Fresh was Phoebe, moreover, and airy, and sweet in her apparel; as if nothing that she wore—neither her gown, nor her small straw bonnet, nor her little kerchief, any more than her snowy stockings—had ever been put on before; or, if worn, were all the fresher for it, and with a fragrance as if they had lain among the rose-buds.

Of the influence of her maidenly salubrity upon poor Clifford, Hawthorne gives the prettiest description, and then, breaking off suddenly, renounces the attempt in language which, while pleading its inadequacy, conveys an exquisite satisfaction to the reader. I quote the passage for the sake of its extreme felicity, and of the charming image with which it concludes.

> But we strive in vain to put the idea into words. No adequate expression of the beauty and profound pathos with which it impresses us is attainable . . . With his native susceptibility of happy influences, he inhales the slight ethereal rapture into his soul, and expires!

I have not mentioned the personage in *The House of the Seven Gables* upon whom Hawthorne evidently bestowed most pains, and whose portrait is the most elaborate in the book; partly because he is, in spite of the space he occupies, an accessory figure, and partly because, even more than the others, he is what I have called a picture rather than a character. Judge Pyncheon is an ironical portrait, very richly and broadly executed, very sagaciously composed and rendered—the portrait of a superb, full-blown hypocrite, a large-based, full-nurtured Pharisee, bland, urbane, impressive, diffusing about him a 'sultry' warmth of benevolence, as the author calls it again and again, and basking in the noontide of prosperity and the consideration of society; but in reality hard, gross, and ignoble. Judge Pyncheon is an elaborate piece of description, made up of a hundred admirable touches, in which satire is always

winged with fancy, and fancy is linked with a deep sense of reality. It is difficult to say whether Hawthorne followed a model in describing Judge Pyncheon; but it is tolerably obvious that the picture is an impression—a copious impression—of an individual. It has evidently a definite starting-point in fact, and the author is able to draw, freely and confidently, after the image established in his mind. Holgrave, the modern young man, who has been a Jack-of-all-trades, and is at the period of the story a daguerreotypist, is an attempt to render a kind of national type—that of the young citizen of the United States whose fortune is simply in his lively intelligence, and who stands naked, as it were, unbiased and unencumbered alike, in the centre of the far-stretching level of American life. Holgrave is intended as a contrast; his lack of traditions, his democratic stamp, his condensed experience, are opposed to the desiccated prejudices and exhausted vitality of the race of which poor feebly-scowling, rusty-jointed Hephzibah is the most heroic representative. It is, perhaps, a pity that Hawthorne should not have proposed to himself to give the old Pyncheon qualities some embodiment which would help them to balance more fairly with the elastic properties of the young daguerreotypist—should not have painted a lusty conservative to match his strenuous radical. As it is, the mustiness and mouldiness of the tenants of the House of the Seven Gables crumble away rather too easily. Evidently, however, what Hawthorne designed to represent was not the struggle between an old society and a new, for in this case he would have given the old one a better chance; but simply, as I have said, the shrinkage and extinction of a family. This appealed to his imagination; and the idea of long perpetuation and survival always appears to have filled him with a kind of horror and disapproval. Conservative, in a certain degree, as he was himself, and fond of retrospect and quietude and the mellowing influences of time, it is singular how often one encounters in his writings some expression of mistrust of old houses, old institutions, long lines of descent. He was disposed, apparently, to allow a very moderate measure in these respects, and he condemns the dwelling of the Pyncheons to disappear from the face of the earth because it has been standing a couple of hundred years. In this he was an American of Americans; or, rather, he was more American than many of his countrymen, who, though they are accustomed to work for the short run rather than the long, have often a lurking esteem for things that show the marks of having lasted. I will add that Holgrave is one of the few figures, among those which Hawthorne created, with regard to which the absence of the realistic mode of treatment is felt as a loss. Holgrave is not sharply enough characterised; he lacks features; he is not an individual, but a type. But

too palpable an influence upon literature. Hawthorne's stories are the old Greek myths, made more vivid to the childish imagination by an infusion of details which both deepen and explain their marvels. I have been careful not to read them over, for I should be very sorry to risk disturbing in any degree a recollection of them that has been at rest since the appreciative period of life to which they are addressed. They seem at that period enchanting, and the ideal of happiness of many American children is to lie upon the carpet and lose themselves in *The Wonder-Book*. It is in its pages that they first make the acquaintance of the heroes and heroines of the antique mythology, and something of the nursery fairy-tale quality of interest which Hawthorne imparts to them always remains.

I have said that Lenox was a very pretty place, and that he was able to work there Hawthorne proved by composing *The House of the Seven Gables* with a good deal of rapidity. But, at the close of the year in which this novel was published, he wrote to a friend (Mr Fields, his publisher) that,

to tell you a secret, I am sick to death of Berkshire, and hate to think of spending another winter here . . . The air and climate do not agree with my health at all, and for the first time since I was a boy I have felt languid and dispirited . . . O that Providence would build me the merest little shanty, and mark me out a rood or two of garden ground, near the sea-coast!

He was at this time for a while out of health; and it is proper to remember that though the Massachusetts Berkshire, with its mountains and lakes, was charming during the ardent American summer, there was a reverse to the medal, consisting of December snows prolonged into April and May. Providence failed to provide him with a cottage by the sea; but he betook himself for the winter of 1852 to the little town of West Newton, near Boston, where he brought into the world *The Blithedale Romance*.

This work, as I have said, would not have been written if Hawthorne had not spent a year at Brook Farm, and though it is in no sense of the word an account of the manners or the inmates of that establishment, it will preserve the memory of the ingenious community at West Roxbury for a generation unconscious of other reminders. I hardly know what to say about it, save that it is very charming; this vague, unanalytic epithet is the first that comes to one's pen in treating of Hawthorne's novels, for their extreme amenity of form invariably suggests it; but if, on the one hand, it claims to be uttered, on the other it frankly confesses its inconclusiveness. Perhaps, however, in this case it fills out the measure of appreciation more completely than in others, for *The Blithedale Romance* is the lightest, the brightest, the liveliest, of this company of unhumorous fictions.

Illustration by J. Watson Davis for a scene in chapter 8 of The Blithedale Romance *in which Miles Coverdale comments on the impossibility of combining the yeoman and the scholar in one man: "Pausing in the field to let the wind exhale the moisture from our foreheads, we were to look upward and catch glimpses into the far-off soul of truth" (from the Nottingham Society edition of Hawthorne's Works; Thomas Cooper Library, University of South Carolina).*

my last word about this admirable novel must not be a restrictive one. It is a large and generous production, pervaded with that vague hum, that indefinable echo, of the whole multitudinous life of man, which is the real sign of a great work of fiction.

After the publication of *The House of the Seven Gables*, which brought him great honour, and, I believe, a tolerable share of a more ponderable substance, he composed a couple of little volumes for children—*The Wonder-Book,* and a small collection of stories entitled *Tanglewood Tales*. They are not among his most serious literary titles, but if I may trust my own early impression of them, they are among the most charming literary services that have been rendered to children in an age (and especially in a country) in which the exactions of the infant mind have exerted much

The story is told from a more joyous point of view—from a point of view comparatively humorous—and a number of objects and incidents touched with the light of the profane world—the vulgar, many-coloured world of actuality, as distinguished from the crepuscular realm of the writer's own reveries—are mingled with its course. The book, indeed, is a mixture of elements, and it leaves in the memory an impression analogous to that of an April day—an alternation of brightness and shadow, of broken sun-patches and sprinkling clouds. Its *dénoûment* is tragical—there is, indeed, nothing so tragical in all Hawthorne, unless it be the murder of Miriam's persecutor by Donatello, in *Transformation,* as the suicide of Zenobia; and yet, on the whole, the effect of the novel is to make one think more agreeably of life. The standpoint of the narrator has the advantage of being a concrete one; he is no longer, as in the preceding tales, a disembodied spirit, imprisoned in the haunted chamber of his own contemplations, but a particular man, with a certain human grossness.

Of Miles Coverdale I have already spoken, and of its being natural to assume that, in so far as we may measure this lightly indicated identity of his, it has a great deal in common with that of his creator. Coverdale is a picture of the contemplative, observant, analytic nature, nursing its fancies, and yet, thanks to an element of strong good sense, not bringing them up to be spoiled children; having little at stake in life, at any given moment, and yet indulging, in imagination, in a good many adventures; a portrait of a man, in a word, whose passions are slender, whose imagination is active, and whose happiness lies, not in doing, but in perceiving—half a poet, half a critic, and all a spectator. He is contrasted excellently with the figure of Hollingsworth, the heavily treading Reformer, whose attitude with regard to the world is that of the hammer to the anvil, and who has no patience with his friend's indifferences and neutralities. Coverdale is a gentle sceptic, a mild cynic; he would agree that life is a little worth living—or worth living a little; but would remark that, unfortunately, to live little enough, we have to live a great deal. He confesses to a want of earnestness, but in reality he is evidently an excellent fellow, to whom one might look, not for any personal performance on a great scale, but for a good deal of generosity of detail. 'As Hollingsworth once told me, I lack a purpose,' he writes, at the close of his story.

> How strange! He was ruined, morally, by an overplus of the same ingredient the want of which, I occasionally suspect, has rendered my own life all an emptiness. I by no means wish to die . . . Further than that I should be loth to pledge myself.

The finest thing in *The Blithedale Romance* is the character of Zenobia, which I have said elsewhere strikes me as the nearest approach that Hawthorne has made to the complete creation of a *person.* She is more concrete than Hester or Miriam, or Hilda or Phoebe; she is a more definite image, produced by a greater multiplicity of touches. It is idle to inquire too closely whether Hawthorne had Margaret Fuller in his mind in constructing the figure of this brilliant specimen of the strong-minded class, and endowing her with the genius of conversation; or, on the assumption that such was the case, to compare the image at all strictly with the model. There is no strictness in the representation by novelists of persons who have struck them in life, and there can in the nature of things be none. From the moment the imagination takes a hand in the game, the inevitable tendency is to divergence, to following what may be called new scents. The original gives hints, but the writer does what he likes with them, and imports new elements into the picture. If there is this amount of reason for referring the wayward heroine of Blithedale to Hawthorne's impression of the most distinguished woman of her day in Boston; that Margaret Fuller was the only literary lady of eminence whom there is any sign of his having known; that she was proud, passionate, and eloquent; that she was much connected with the little world of Transcendentalism out of which the experiment of Brook Farm sprung; and that she had a miserable end and a watery grave—if these are facts to be noted on one side, I say; on the other, the beautiful and sumptuous Zenobia, with her rich and picturesque temperament and physical aspects, offers many points of divergence from the plain and strenuous invalid who represented feminine culture in the suburbs of the New England metropolis. This picturesqueness of Zenobia is very happily indicated and maintained; she is a woman in all the force of the term, and there is something very vivid and powerful in her large expression of womanly gifts and weaknesses. Hollingsworth is, I think, less successful, though there is much reality in the conception of the type to which he belongs—the strong-willed, narrow-hearted apostle of a special form of redemption for society. There is nothing better in all Hawthorne than the scene between him and Coverdale, when the two men are at work together in the field (piling stones on a dyke), and he gives it to his companion to choose whether he will be with him or against him. It is a pity, perhaps, to have represented him as having begun life as a blacksmith, for one grudges him the advantage of so logical a reason for his roughness and hardness.

> Hollingsworth scarcely said a word, unless when repeatedly and pertinaciously addressed . . . He ought to have commenced his investigation of the subject by

DOCTOR GRIMSHAWE'S SECRET

𝔄 Romance

BY

NATHANIEL HAWTHORNE

EDITED, WITH PREFACE AND NOTES

BY

JULIAN HAWTHORNE

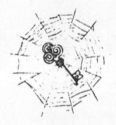

BOSTON

JAMES R. OSGOOD AND COMPANY

1883

Title page for a romance Hawthorne left at his death that was edited by his son (from C. E. Frazer Clark Jr., Nathaniel Hawthorne: A Descriptive Bibliography, *1978)*

committing some huge sin in his proper person, and examining the condition of his higher instincts afterwards.

The most touching element in the novel is the history of the grasp that this barbarous fanatic has laid upon the fastidious and high-tempered Zenobia, who, disliking him and shrinking from him at a hundred points, is drawn into the gulf of his omnivorous egotism. The portion of the story that strikes me as least felicitous is that which deals with Priscilla, and with her mysterious relation to Zenobia—with her mesmeric gifts, her clairvoyance, her identity with the Veiled Lady, her divided subjection to Hollingsworth and Westervelt, and her numerous other graceful but fantastic properties—her Sibylline attributes, as the author calls them. Hawthorne is rather too fond of Sibylline attributes—a taste of the same order as his disposition,

to which I have already alluded, to talk about spheres and sympathies. As the action advances, in *The Blithedale Romance,* we get too much out of reality, and cease to feel beneath our feet the firm ground of an appeal to our own vision of the world—our observation. I should have liked to see the story concern itself more with the little community in which its earlier scenes are laid, and avail itself of so excellent an opportunity for describing unhackneyed specimens of human nature. I have already spoken of the absence of satire in the novel, of its not aiming in the least at satire, and of its offering no grounds for complaint as an invidious picture. Indeed, the brethren of Brook Farm should have held themselves slighted rather than misrepresented, and have regretted that the admirable genius who for a while was numbered among them should have treated their institution mainly as a perch for starting upon an imaginative flight. But when all is said about a certain want of substance and cohesion in the latter portions of *The Blithedale Romance,* the book is still a delightful and beautiful one. Zenobia and Hollingsworth live in the memory; and even Priscilla and Coverdale, who linger there less importunately, have a great deal that touches us and that we believe in. I said just now that Priscilla was infelicitous; but immediately afterwards I open the volume at a page in which the author describes some of the out-of-door amusements at Blithedale, and speaks of a foot-race across the grass, in which some of the slim young girls of the society joined.

> Priscilla's peculiar charm in a foot-race was the weakness and irregularity with which she ran . . . Priscilla's life, as I beheld it, was full of trifles that affected me in just this way.

That seems to me exquisite, and the book is full of touches as deep and delicate.

After writing it, Hawthorne went back to live in Concord, where he had bought a small house, in which, apparently, he expected to spend a large portion of his future. This was, in fact, the dwelling in which he passed that part of the rest of his days that he spent in his own country. He established himself there before going to Europe, in 1853, and he returned to the Wayside, as he called his house, on coming back to the United States seven years later. Though he actually occupied the place no long time, he had made it his property, and it was more his own home than any of his numerous provisional abodes. I may, therefore, quote a little account of the house which he wrote to a distinguished friend, Mr George William Curtis.

> As for my old house, you will understand it better after spending a day or two in it . . . I know nothing of the history of the house except Thoreau's telling me

that it was inhabited, a century or two ago, by a man who believed he should never die. I believe, however, he is dead; at least, I hope so; else he may probably reappear and dispute my title to his residence.

As Mr Lathrop points out, this allusion to a man who believed he should never die is 'the first intimation of the story of *Septimius Felton*.' The scenery of that romance, he adds, 'was evidently taken from the Wayside and its hill.' Septimus Felton is, in fact, a young man who, at the time of the war of the Revolution, lives in the village of Concord, on the Boston road, at the base of a woody hill which rises abruptly behind his house, and of which the level summit supplies him with a promenade continually mentioned in the course of the tale. Hawthorne used to exercise himself upon this picturesque eminence, and, as he conceived the brooding Septimus to have done before him, to betake himself thither when he found the limits of his dwelling too narrow. But he had an advantage which his imaginary hero lacked; he erected a tower as an adjunct to the house, and it was a jocular tradition among his neighbours, in allusion to his attributive tendency to evade rather than hasten the coming guest, that he used to ascend this structure and scan the road for provocations to retreat.

In so far, however, as Hawthorne suffered the penalties of celebrity at the hands of intrusive fellow-citizens, he was soon to escape from this honourable incommodity. On the 4th of March, 1853, his old college-mate and intimate friend, Franklin Pierce, was installed as President of the United States. He had been the candidate of the Democratic party, and all good Democrats, accordingly, in conformity to the beautiful and rational system under which the affairs of the great Republic were carried on, began to open their windows to the golden sunshine of Presidential patronage. When General Pierce was put forward by the Democrats, Hawthorne felt a perfectly loyal and natural desire that his good friend should be exalted to so brilliant a position, and he did what was in him to further the good cause, by writing a little book about its hero. His *Life of Franklin Pierce* belongs to that class of literature which is known as the 'campaign biography,' and which consists of an attempt, more or less successful, to persuade the many-headed monster of universal suffrage that the gentleman on whose behalf it is addressed is a paragon of wisdom and virtue. Of Hawthorne's little book there is nothing particular to say, save that it is in very good taste, that he is a very fairly ingenious advocate, and that if he claimed for the future President qualities which rather faded in the bright light of a high office, this defect of proportion was essential to his undertaking. He dwelt chiefly upon General Pierce's exploits in the war with Mexico (before that, his record, as they say in America, had been mainly that of a suc-

cessful country lawyer), and exercised his descriptive powers, so far as was possible, in describing the advance of the United States troops from Vera Cruz to the city of the Montezumas. The mouthpieces of the Whig party spared him, I believe, no reprobation for 'prostituting' his exquisite genius; but I fail to see anything reprehensible in Hawthorne's lending his old friend the assistance of his graceful quill. He wished him to be President—he held afterwards that he filled the office with admirable dignity and wisdom—and as the only thing he could do was to write, he fell to work and wrote for him. Hawthorne was a good lover and a very sufficient partisan, and I suspect that if Franklin Pierce had been made even less of the stuff of a statesman, he would still have found in the force of old associations an injunction to hail him as a ruler. Our hero was an American of the earlier and simpler type—the type of which it is doubtless premature to say that it has wholly passed away, but of which it may at least be said that the circumstances that produced it have been greatly modified. The generation to which he belonged, that generation which grew up with the century, witnessed during a period of fifty years the immense, uninterrupted material development of the young Republic; and when one thinks of the scale on which it took place, of the prosperity that walked in its train and waited on its course, of the hopes it fostered and the blessings it conferred—of the broad morning sunshine, in a word, in which it all went forward—there seems to be little room for surprise that it should have implanted a kind of superstitious faith in the grandeur of the country, its duration, its immunity from the usual troubles of earthly empires. This faith was a simple and uncritical one, enlivened with an element of genial optimism, in the light of which it appeared that the great American state was not as other human institutions are, that a special Providence watched over it, that it would go on joyously forever, and that a country whose vast and blooming bosom offered a refuge to the strugglers and seekers of all the rest of the world, must come off easily, in the battle of the ages. From this conception of the American future the sense of its having problems to solve was blissfully absent; there were no difficulties in the programme, no looming complications, no rocks ahead. The indefinite multiplication of the population, and its enjoyment of the benefits of the common-school education and of unusual facilities for making an income—this was the form in which, on the whole, the future most vividly presented itself, and in which the greatness of the country was to be recognised of men. There was, indeed, a faint shadow in the picture—the shadow projected by the 'peculiar institution' of the Southern States; but it was far from sufficient to darken the rosy vision of most good Americans, and, above all, of most good Democrats. Hawthorne alludes to it in a passage of his life of Pierce, which I will quote, not only as a hint of the trouble that was in store for a cheerful race of men, but as an example of his own easy-going political attitude.

> It was while in the Lower House of Congress that Franklin Pierce took that stand on the Slavery question from which he has never since swerved by a hair's breadth . . . Nor did he ever shun the obloquy that sometimes threatened to pursue the Northern man who dared to love that great and sacred reality—his whole united country—better than the mistiness of a philanthropic theory.

This last invidious allusion is to the disposition, not infrequent at the North, but by no means general, to set a decisive limit to further legislation in favour of the cherished idiosyncrasy of the other half of the country. Hawthorne takes the license of a sympathetic biographer in speaking of his hero's having incurred obloquy by his conservative attitude on the question of Slavery. The only class in the American world that suffered in the smallest degree, at this time, from social persecution, was the little band of Northern Abolitionists, who were as unfashionable as they were indiscreet—which is saying much. Like most of his fellow-countrymen, Hawthorne had no idea that the respectable institution which he contemplated in impressive contrast to humanitarian 'mistiness,' was presently to cost the nation four long years of bloodshed and misery, and a social revolution as complete as any the world has seen. When this event occurred, he was, therefore, proportionately horrified and depressed by it; it cut from beneath his feet the familiar ground which had long felt so firm, substituting a heaving and quaking medium in which his spirit found no rest. Such was the bewildered sensation of that earlier and simpler generation of which I have spoken; their illusions were rudely dispelled, and they saw the best of all possible republics given over to fratricidal carnage. This affair had no place in their scheme, and nothing was left for them but to hang their heads and close their eyes. The subsidence of that great convulsion has left a different tone from the tone it found, and one may say that the Civil War marks an era in the history of the American mind. It introduced into the national consciousness a certain sense of proportion and relation, of the world being a more complicated place than it had hitherto seemed, the future more treacherous, success more difficult. At the rate at which things are going, it is obvious that good Americans will be more numerous than ever; but the good American, in days to come, will be a more critical person than his complacent and confident grandfather. He has eaten of the tree of knowledge. He will not, I think, be a sceptic, and still less, of course, a cynic; but he will be, without discredit to his well-known capacity for

action, an observer. He will remember that the ways of the Lord are inscrutable, and that this is a world in which everything happens; and eventualities, as the late Emperor of the French used to say, will not find him intellectually unprepared. The good American of which Hawthorne was so admirable a specimen was not critical, and it was perhaps for this reason that Franklin Pierce seemed to him a very proper President.

The least that General Pierce could do in exchange for so liberal a confidence was to offer his old friend one of the numerous places in his gift. Hawthorne had a great desire to go abroad and see something of the world, so that a consulate seemed the proper thing. He never stirred in the matter himself, but his friends strongly urged that something should be done; and when he accepted the post of consul at Liverpool there was not a word of reasonable criticism to be offered on the matter. If General Pierce, who was before all things good-natured and obliging, had been guilty of no greater indiscretion than to confer this modest distinction upon the most honourable and discreet of men of letters, he would have made a more brilliant mark in the annals of American statesmanship. Liverpool had not been immediately selected, and Hawthorne had written to his friend and publisher, Mr Fields, with some humorous vagueness of allusion to his probable expatriation.

> Do make some inquiries about Portugal; as, for instance, in what part of the world it lies, and whether it is an empire, a kingdom, or a republic. Also, and more particularly, the expenses of living there, and whether the Minister would be likely to be much pestered with his own countrymen. Also, any other information about foreign countries would be acceptable to an inquiring mind.

It would seem from this that there had been a question of offering him a small diplomatic post; but the emoluments of the place were justly taken into account, and it is to be supposed that those of the consulate at Liverpool were at least as great as the salary of the American representative at Lisbon. Unfortunately, just after Hawthorne had taken possession of the former post, the salary attached to it was reduced by Congress, in an economical hour, to less than half the sum enjoyed by his predecessors. It was fixed at $7,500 (£1,500); but the consular fees, which were often copious, were an added resource. At midsummer then, in 1853, Hawthorne was established in England.

The only son of Nathaniel and Sophia Peabody Haw-thorne, Julian Hawthorne spent many of his formative years abroad, in England and Italy. He wrote stories and novels and worked as a journalist for newspapers in the United States and England. His most lasting achievement is Nathaniel Haw-thorne and His Wife *(1884), which details the life of his parents. He also wrote* Nathaniel Hawthorne and His Circle *(1903).*

Hawthorne's Philosophy
Julian Hawthorne
Century Magazine, 32 (May 1886): 83–93

The profession of literature in America is not even now irresistibly inviting; reputation and profit are still to be obtained at less cost of time and labor in other ways. But if we go back sixty years, and imagine our-selves to be young people of twenty-two or three, with only a collegiate experience of life and the world, and living in a third-rate New England town, with no rail-ways and no society, the prospects of a literary career would probably seem nothing less than meager.

Hawthorne, at the outset of his life, before he had accomplished anything, had not the humility which characterized him afterwards. His mother and sisters admired him, none of his companions and peers were his intellectual superiors, and he was inwardly conscious of power and ability. The only thing that could temper his good opinion of himself was books. They showed him that there had been men in the world better than any he had met—Homer, Caesar, Shakespere, Napoleon, Goethe; but he could reflect that these giants had also once been young fel-lows like himself, with perhaps no better grounds for ambitious dreams than he had. Who could tell whether, if he had the faith to try, he might not rival the renown even of such names as these?

'The secret of the young man's character,' as he himself autobiographically observes in 'The Ambitious Guest,'

was a high and abstracted ambition. He could have borne to live an undistinguished life, but not to be for-gotten in the grave. Obscurely as he journeyed now, a glory was to beam on all his pathway—though not, per-haps, while he was treading it. But posterity should confess that a gifted one had passed from the cradle to the tomb with none to recognize him.

Allowing for artistic emphasis, this expresses Haw-thorne's early view of his own aspirations. He did not covet a quick and cheap success—stares and shouts and greasy night-caps tossed in the air; but he wished to be so spiritually great that only after he was gone should the world awake to a comprehension of his greatness.

Julian Hawthorne

He wanted to win the prize in the night, as it were, and be off before anybody was up to congratulate him. He did not wish his struggles, his anxieties, the sweat of his brow, to be visible. Let it be said only that a spirit once visited the earth, and worked wonders there, and van-ished before any were aware of him.

This was visionary and impractical enough, the dream of inexperienced youth, and not devoid of an element of selfishness; but it was lofty and refined, and agreeably in contrast with average ambition. It could not be realized, for no man has become great without first being made to confess his abject brotherhood with and dependence upon the race; but it was worth feeling for a time. Illusions are soon cured, but not every one is so fortunate as to experience a noble illusion. Mean-while, it was Hawthorne's concern to put himself to the proof. There never seems to have been any doubt in his mind as to the path in which he should seek renown. 'While we were lads together at a country college,' he writes to Bridge, 'doing a hundred things that the faculty never heard of,—or else it had been the worse for us,—still it was your prognostic of your friend's destiny that he was to be a writer of fiction. And a fiction-monger, in due season, he became.' Even before he went to college he remarks, in a letter to his mother, that none of the ordinary professions are to his taste, but that to be an author—! And yet, under the circumstances, he could scarcely have fixed upon a less promising pursuit.

Not only were the chances of success all against him, but the mere fact of his adopting such a calling would bring him into disrepute. 'There is a grossness,' he says,

> in the conceptions of my countrymen; they will not be convinced that any good thing may consist with what they call idleness. The principle is excellent in its general influence, but most miserable in its effects on the few who violate it. I had a quick sensitiveness to public opinion, and felt as if it ranked me with the tavern-haunters and town-paupers—with the drunken poet who hawked his own Fourth of July odes, and the broken soldier who had been good for nothing since last war.

The life of New England was a practical, material life, and the only standard for a man was what he could do in open, active competition with other men: the more he could add to the physical wealth of the country, the better man was he. The tavern-haunter and the town-pauper, having no ambition and no pride or sensitiveness, were serene under opprobrium; but for Hawthorne a good deal of courage and self-confidence was needed to defy the popular prejudice.

Courage in abundance, and self-confidence also, he no doubt had; but he was too young and not phlegmatic enough to maintain an absolute composure. His attitude was rather, as he intimates, a species of 'light-hearted desperation.' Not having any immediate means available for proving public opinion to be in the wrong, he took refuge in defiance. He made no effort to conciliate his unsympathetic neighbors, but withdrew himself from their society,—perhaps in a 'you'll-be-sorry-some-day' kind of spirit,—and settled himself as best he could to show that he was the best judge of what was good for him. The world—even his own little world—adjusted itself without difficulty to this order of things, and never once troubled itself to ask or to conjecture how the ambitious author was getting along. Nor is this extraordinary; for the author took unnecessary pains to cover such light traces as he made. Whatever he wrote was either signed with fictitious names or not signed at all; and during the first eight or ten years, probably not half a dozen human beings were aware

that he had written anything. He was indulging his 'abstracted ambition' to the top of its bent. He was resolved not to declare himself until the curiosity and enthusiasm aroused by his anonymous writings had reached such a pitch as to render concealment no longer possible. But he seemed likely to remain undisturbed a long time. Critical insight, literary appreciation, were not the strong point of our ancestors; and the channels through which literature could reach them were correspondingly scanty. Had Hawthorne begun with a *Scarlet Letter,* he might possibly have found some recognition; but, even supposing his genius to have been as yet equal to such an achievement, other scarcely less indispensable requisites were wanting. 'I have another great difficulty,' he wrote at the time the *Twice-told Tales* appeared, 'in the lack of materials; for I have seen so little of the world that I have nothing but thin air to concoct my stories of.' And again: 'I used to think that I could imagine all passions, all feelings and states of the heart and mind; but how little did I know!' Moreover, the vein and style of his writing not only was not popular, but never has become so; and the number of his readers to-day is very much less than the most moderate outside estimate would be likely to make it. Widely as his name is now known, not one in a thousand of those who are familiar with it have ever read a line of his inditing. A page of sound criticism here and there, and the avowed admiration and homage of the best contemporary intellects, have given him whatever popular vogue he can claim.

Neither can he be acquitted of having voluntarily deepened his own obscurity. The consciousness of being at odds with the spirit of his time and surroundings had the effect of making him build the wall of separation still higher. Naturally reserved, the dread of unsympathetic eyes rendered him an actual recluse. What passed for society in Salem was, indeed, as destitute of attraction as society can be, and an intelligent man, with thoughts and a soul of his own, might well shun contact with it; yet Hawthorne, while his reserve was still balanced by his youth and innate sociability,—for the last is by no means incompatible with the first,—might easily have accommodated himself to the situation. But, having once admitted the repellent chill, he was never afterwards to recover from its effects. His predicament bore some resemblance to that of his own Wakefield, who, having left his wife one night for a joke, found himself prevented by some nameless and intangible perversity from returning to her for twenty years. 'An influence beyond our control lays its strong hand on every deed which we do, and weaves its consequences into an iron tissue of necessity.' And again he remarks that 'amid the seeming confusion of our mysterious world, individuals are so nicely adjusted to a system, and systems to one another and to a whole, that, by stepping aside for a moment, a man exposes himself to a fearful risk of losing his place forever.' Unlike Wakefield, however, Hawthorne spent his period of self-banishment in something else besides speculating as to what Mrs Wakefield thought of his absence; and, whether he gained or lost by his solitary vigil, the literature of his country unquestionably gained. Hawthorne himself, when he was thirty-six years old, began to perceive that a Providential wisdom may have overruled his imprisonment, in order that, living in solitude till the fullness of time was come, he might still keep the dew of his youth and the freshness of his heart. In point of fact, this whole episode of his career is extraordinary, both intrinsically and in its results. It is as picturesque and emblematic as anything in his own tales. From the obscurest, he was destined to become perhaps the foremost man of letters in America, and to secure that end he must be kept apart from the rush of civilization for a space. The knights-errant of old watched their armor previous to embarking on their enterprise; the young Indian chiefs were made to undergo a period of solitude and fasting before being admitted to full standing; Bunyan wrote his book in Bedford jail; and Hawthorne, in Salem, withdrew himself from the face of man, and meditated for twelve lonely years upon humanity. He came forth a great original writer. But the example is by no means one to be followed. Hardly one man in a thousand would escape being ruined by such an experience, let alone deriving any advantage from it. Upon Hawthorne—apart from its influence upon his literary quality—it produced an ineffaceable impression. He constantly recurs to it, both in his tales and elsewhere. 'Was there ever such a weary delay in obtaining the slightest recognition from the public,' he asks, 'as in my case? I sat down by the wayside of life like a man under enchantment.' 'Trouble,' he says in another place, 'is the next best thing to enjoyment; and there is no fate in the world so horrible as to have no share in either its joys or sorrows. For the last ten years I have not lived, but only dreamed of living.' And again he alludes to 'my heavy youth, which has been wasted in sluggishness for lack of hope and impulse, or equally thrown away in toil that had no wise motive, and has accomplished no good end.' But the goodness of the end became apparent afterwards.

The truth seems to be that Hawthorne—who, in addition to his 'genius,' which is always indefinable, was a man of wide sympathies, and penetrating insight—got more benefit from his own society than he could have derived from any other society open to him. Providence, according to its custom, had in view not so much the individual's happiness or preferences as his possible uses to mankind. He was des-

tined to do a certain work, and to that end were needed, not only his native abilities, but an exceptional initiation, or forty days in the wilderness. He must meditate upon life abstractly—without either the confirmation or the bias afforded by actual experience. By this means would gradually be created within him an intuitive touchstone or standard of truth, unadulterated and indestructible, by which he might investigate and analyze, without danger or confusion, the problems and perplexities of the human heart. When once this standard had been established, the spell of seclusion might safely be broken, and the neophyte be suffered to go forth among men and prove his prowess. The effect was much the same as if Hawthorne had been born full-grown, with all the spiritual wisdom and reserved power that may come from half a lifetime's patience and meditation. He might be compared to his own Ernest in 'The Great Stone Face':

Ernest gazing at the noble face he perceives in a rock cliff in "The Great Stone Face" (by Amma Whelan Betts; Autograph Edition, Houghton, Mifflin, 1900; Thomas Cooper Library, University of South Carolina)

Angels seemed to have sat with him by the fireside; and, dwelling with angels as friend with friends, he had imbibed the sublimity of their ideas, and imbued it with the sweet and lowly charm of household words. . . . His words had power, because they accorded with his thoughts; and his thoughts had reality, because they harmonized with the life that he had always lived.

The organization of a man who could endure such a vigil must, of course, have been exceptionally thorough, and his nature unusually wholesome; and such we know to have been the case with Hawthorne. But perhaps as valuable a trait as any was his delectable leisureliness—his imperial refusal to be in a hurry. This was apparent very early, and indeed youth is apt to fancy that time is practically inexhaustible; but that leads to laziness, and between laziness and leisureliness there is a great difference. Hawthorne's space was not within the limits of the day or the year, but within himself. He had an instinctive persuasion that the garden of his mind had been well sown with all necessary seeds, and that they would grow up in their due season. At all events, he would not pull them up to see how they were getting on. He took his harvests as they came, and was inclined rather to delay than to hasten their ripening. The need for him to be patient was not more strong than his power to be so. In the second place, he had humor; not facetiousness or buffoonery,—a forced or imported brilliance,—but innate humor, that plays about the subject like the lambent flames of incandescent coal; following in this the system of his entire development, which was endogenous. He had gravity, but not solemnity; there were no arid spots in him; his perception of the vastness of the creative plan kept him from becoming lugubrious over any partial revelation of it. This deep and subtle smile does not, however, appear in his earliest writings, when he was trying his 'prentice hand, and was more anxious about the treatment than about the matter. The humorous passages of *Fanshawe* are not spontaneous and the papers referring to 'Oberon,' republished after Hawthorne's death, have a positively morbid strain in them. Another valuable quality, and one not often allied to a genius so refined as his, was his imperturbable common sense, which preserves even his most imaginative flights from extravagance. Even when we enter the 'Hall of Fantasy,' or are among the guests at 'A Select Party,' or try the virtues of 'Dr. Heidigger's Experiment,' still we feel that the 'great, round, solid earth' of which Hawthorne speaks so affectionately is beneath our feet. He does not float vaguely in mid-air, but takes his stand somewhere near the center of things, and always knows what he is about. Tracing back his fanciful vagaries, we invariably find them originating in some settled and constant middle ground of belief, from which they are measured, and which renders them comprehensible and significant.

Such being the man, and such the circumstances, let us see how they acted upon one another. We know, on his own confession, that his beginnings were by no means free from difficulties. He had to learn how to write, like other people. 'Hitherto,' he says in 'Passages from a Relinquished Work,' from which quotations have already been made—

Hitherto I had immensely underrated the difficulties of my idle trade; but now I recognized that it demanded nothing short of my whole powers, cultivated to the utmost and exerted with prodigality. No talents or attainments would come amiss: wide observation, varied knowledge, deep thoughts, and sparkling ones; pathos, levity, and a mixture of both; lofty imagination, veiling itself in the garb of common life; and the practiced art which alone could render such gifts available. Knowing the impossibility of satisfying myself, even should the world be satisfied, I did my best, investigated the causes of every defect, and strove with patient stubbornness to remove them in the next attempt. It is one of my few sources of pride that I followed 'my object' up with the firmness and energy of a man.

When a young man first attempts authorship, especially if he have selected the vein of fiction, he is apt to be misled by some traditional and artificial conception of 'literature.' Literature, he fancies, must be something quite distinct and different from life, and demands a new code of manners and cast of thought. It is only later that he discovers—if he makes the discovery at all—that the best literature is the simplest and most translucent expression of the mind that produces it; that much as there is to be learnt, there is yet more to unlearn. The redundancy and uncertainty of ordinary speech must be reformed, but its naturalness and spontaneity must be preserved. Hawthorne, as we know, burnt more than he published of his earlier writings, and we are therefore debarred from following the steps of his self-emancipation; but there is one little tale, 'The Antique Ring,' which he did not include in his republications, and which probably is as good an example of all that he wished to avoid as could now be found. With the exception, indeed, of an occasional allusion to the 'dusky glow' of the gem, there is nothing in either the conception or the treatment of the story that recalls the Hawthorne that we know. The precise date of the composition can only be conjectured; but conjecture would place it very far back indeed.

Hawthorne's boyish contributions to literature took the form of sentimental little poems of no originality or value; and 'The Antique Ring' would seem to be scarcely one remove above them. Between it and 'The

Great Carbuncle,' for example, the gulf is immense. A better vein was probably struck in the 'Seven Tales of my Native Land,' which had witchcraft for their theme, and which his sister, to whom Hawthorne showed them, and who was an excellent judge, has commended. At all events, every allusion to witches that survives in his published work is effective and characteristic; and the point of view from which he regards those picturesque beings is entirely peculiar to himself; in no other one direction is his indefinable genius more apparent. As regards the 'Seven Tales,' however, he is said to have remarked that they were 'not true'; and we may infer that the witches were allowed to have too much their own way in them—that their broomstick flights left the 'great, round, solid earth' too far behind. For the human nature in Hawthorne's witches—those that have been preserved to us—is at least as prominent as their supernatural attributes, and, indeed, is what gives these attributes their best effect. If, in the 'Seven Tales,' the author allowed himself to be subjectively dominated by his own witches, no wonder he was carried beyond the limits which his reflection could justify. The horror would be too fantastic and unmitigated, and devoid of that element upon which he uniformly insists so strongly—a 'moral.' There is one story among the *Twice-told Tales* which might almost be numbered in the discarded category, 'The Hollow of Three Hills.' But it was well worth retaining, for once in a way.

But if Hawthorne's improvement was very great, it seems also to have been very rapid. Some of the earliest published pieces, collected in the *Twice-told Tales* and *The Snow Image,* show, in a modified form, many of the excellences belonging to the later productions. He partly accounts for this by the remark that

> in youth men are apt to write more wisely than they really know or feel; and the remainder of life may not be idly spent in realizing and convincing themselves of the wisdom which they uttered long ago. The truth that was only in the fancy then may have since become a substance of the mind and heart.

Disraeli has a similar observation in his preface to *Vivian Grey*. But it is also to be remembered that the forty-five sketches, or thereabouts, republished in the two volumes above mentioned, are all that survive of the labor of a dozen years; which, considering that he was always a diligent worker, leaves a very large number to be accounted for. It was these, no doubt, that Hawthorne informs us he burnt, 'without mercy or remorse, and moreover without any subsequent regret'; and it is in them that we should have traced the development of his thought and style. Nevertheless, all allowances being made, the fact remains that he

schooled himself with unusual promptness and severity; a fact the more remarkable, inasmuch as he had not the benefit of outside criticism, which we of a later age enjoy in such profusion. He was his own critic, and plied his office with a truly Puritanic harshness. He was perhaps aided in this by the curious duality of his nature,—his imaginative and his matter-of-fact selves, which were always keeping each other in check. Most men in whom the imagination is highly developed are prone to be seduced by its allurements; but the spirit of Hawthorne's stern and square-visaged ancestors was strong within him, and, while it restrained him from excess, enabled him with rare impunity to career narrowly upon the verge of absurdity without ever tumbling off. In other words, his self-poise was such as to make it possible for him to do what no one else has done before or since—to write Hawthornesque romance. He invented a new definition of romance, and his proprietary rights in the domain he discovered have never been infringed upon. Hawthorne was neither afraid of his imagination nor in subjection to it; like Prospero, he wielded easily his magic wand, and smiled at the terrors of the storm he created. Through the black frown of the clouds he saw the smiling sunshine and the peaceful blue; and deeper than the roar and tumult of thunder and tempest he heard the quiet chirp of birds and the homely murmur of daily life.

We may conclude, then, that Hawthorne's apprenticeship practically came to an end at about his twenty-seventh year; the two or three surviving pieces (including *Fanshawe*) known to have been produced before that date being not only inferior to his later work, but different from it in aim and significance. He was now able to say whatever he wished, and was beginning to find out what he wished to say. The latter accomplishment might seem, in view of the writer's peculiar surroundings, the more difficult feat of the two. But Hawthorne was still too fresh to the business to admit discouragement on this score. 'The flow of fancy,' he says, 'soon came on me so abundantly, that its indulgence was its own reward—though the hope of praise also became a powerful incitement.' Indeed, no passage in a writer's career is so agreeable as this first enjoyment of the faculty of expression; every passing hour suggests a new theme, and the wealth of material opening out before him seems inexhaustible. Everything being untried, he feels an impulse to try everything; nothing is common or unclean, because the point of view from which he looks upon it is his own.

As was remarked just now, Hawthorne had no hesitation about making literature his profession; but there is nothing to show that he originally anticipated devoting himself exclusively, or mainly, to fiction. As a matter of fact, however, though many of his pieces are explicitly historical, and many others what might be termed essays, he inevitably threw about them all the glamour of a fictitious atmosphere. He saw things picturesquely, or even pictorially; and his reflections, upon whatever subject, assumed a figurative form. He has been called, in complimentary phraseology, a poet; but the remark is truer than most such compliments are. He is a poet, inasmuch as his mind tends instinctively to humanize everything—to impose upon every object of thought or sensation a human figure or order. His view is comprehensive and classifying, sensitive to analogies, and analytic because it has first been constructive. He admits nothing unrelated, but recognizes the central love and energy organizing all things. All these are poetic gifts, enabling their possessor to sum up and re-create the seeming chaos of phenomena, and to give it novel and enlightening utterance. But Hawthorne, however well fitted inwardly or spiritually to be a poet, was preserved therefrom by such comparatively external and accidental obstacles as an unmusical ear and an aversion to the trammels of rhythmical expression. I say 'preserved' in no invidious sense, for, generally speaking, nothing can be better than a poet. But extraordinary emergencies require exceptional prescriptions; and America's aesthetic want at that period seemed to demand precisely Hawthorne and nothing else. The voice was Jacob's, but the hands were Esau's. Poetry is essentially a perception of the spiritual reason and relation of things; but the American genius, which is not primitive and childlike, cannot give a full account of itself in measured feet and rhymes; it must speak at times with the directness and artlessness of homely conversation and be poetical in its influence rather than in its aspect. In neglecting the poetic form, therefore, Hawthorne proved himself in accord with the tendency of the age, which ignores form just in proportion as it insists upon the spirit.

Art, subjectively considered, is the means adopted by the artist to tell what is in him; and Hawthorne, up to the epoch of *The Scarlet Letter,* was moved to utter himself upon three classes of subjects—philosophy, history, and that derivative and sublimation of the two which is called Story. But so strong in him was the instinct of Story that it colored and shaped his treatment of the former topics. His essays take the form of allegories, and his historical pieces assume the aspect less of narratives than of pictures. He cannot be satisfied with simply telling us what happened; he must bring us to look upon the scene as transacted in his imagination. Man is his game—the living human being; nor will he consent even to follow the familiar metaphysical device, and, in his philosophical speculations, separate the subject perceiving from the object perceived. To do so was, in his opinon, a mere logical analysis of a living experience—an attempt to resuscitate the body of knowledge after its soul has fled. He blended the artificial scientific distinction of subject and object in the living life or consciousness which miraculously knows. Therefore his philosophy always expresses itself in allegory at least, if not in actual examples of human experience. Abstractions will not suit him; practical illustrations are his only wear. And if he will not divorce philosophy from man, neither, on the other hand, will he divorce man from philosophy. In other words, he will not be a mere painter of external life, of manners, of appearance; he must penetrate the secret of his characters, and know, and demonstrate either explicitly or implicitly, not so much the how as the wherefore of their actions and conditions. Thus it happens that all his stories have their moral. 'Thought,' he says, 'has always its efficacy, and every striking incident its moral.' To be at a loss for a moral would be tantamount to not knowing what he had been writing about; to understand a thing is to moralize it. Taking a comprehensive view, we might put the matter in a phrase by saying that he turns his philosophy into human beings, and his human beings into philosophy. But the older he grew, the more did he incline to the latter process in preference to the former. He relinquished the allegories and the allegorical essays, and found all the stage he needed for them and for his historical material in the imaginative circumstances of romance.

We need not suppose that Hawthorne made these discriminations deliberately, or even consciously. Like most wholesome and well-poised natures, he evinced great spontaneity of thought and action; and among the four maxims which he recorded for his use in his thirty-second year is 'to do nothing against one's genius.' He was probably led to romance as the fittest vehicle of his thoughts by sheer love of art—of beauty in its most highly organized form. In his investigations into the human mind and heart, he never acts the part of the surgeon or dissector; the living and breathing creature stands before us, and Hawthorne seems to endow us with a power to see through its fleshy walls into the workings beneath. But the fleshly walls are always there; there is nothing of the French or of the modern American analyst in our romancer. He clothes and veils his conceptions; he never strips or disembowels them; there is always reverence and delicacy in his attitude, though there is always, too, unswerving insistence upon the truth. This talk about 'cold-blooded dissection' is quite beside the mark. Hawthorne comprehends the personages of his dramas, and he is tender to them precisely because he comprehends them. He has assumed their trials and infirmities, and has looked out of their eyes before he investigates them with his own. 'If there be a faculty which I possess more perfectly than most men,' he says, 'it is that of throwing myself mentally into situations foreign to my own, and detecting the circumstances of each.' 'Cold-blooded dissection,' under such circumstances, would be a kind of imaginative suicide. He loved humanity; and no one who reads his books in an intelligent spirit can avoid feeling stimulated on the humane side.

But the profound and unsensational character of Hawthorne's work—the artistic beauty and repose of its form—lays it open to a singular objection. It makes us wish to discover its author in it; and at the same time, and for the same cause, it baffles that desire. Everything is so smoothly finished that we can with difficulty find the workman in his production. Nevertheless, he is there, and with due attention he may be discerned. In alluding to the objections taken by 'some of the more crabbed' of his critics to the personal tone of his introductions and prefaces, Hawthorne remarks that if he has touched upon facts which relate to himself, it is only because they chanced to be nearest at hand, and were likewise his own property. But 'these things,' he adds, 'hide the man instead of displaying him. You must make quite another kind of inquest, and look through the range of his fictitious characters, in order to detect any of his essential traits.' This was written in 1851, and of course refers to the pieces (except *The Scarlet Letter*) produced previous to that date—that is to say, to the *Twice-told Tales,* the *Mosses from an Old Manse,* and *The Snow Image* collection. In these volumes, then, we are to look for a reflection of the character and development of Hawthorne's mind. Here we shall find the materials—the germs—from which his creations were evolved. In several of the essays, especially, the blending of substance and form is not so complete as to render disintegration an abstruse matter. In the least guarded of them, however, the reader is curiously bamboozled, so to speak, as to the real point at issue. He is amused with a superficial phantasmagory of figures and scenery, and does not realize that the tune which sets these puppets dancing is the true gist of the whole matter. And yet this bamboozling seems to be almost involuntary on Hawthorne's part; one would say that he was deceived himself, and that the philosophical remarks and conclusions which he makes were but the fruit of a chance suggestion arising out of the concrete topic. Indeed, it is evident that his disquisitions aim not so much at establishing his claim to be an original thinker, as to ally himself in thought and belief with the mass of his fellow-men. The sketches, he tells us, 'are not the talk of a secluded man with his own heart and mind, but his attempts to open an intercourse with the world.' His seclusion was an accidental and external matter only; he wished to merge himself in the general human nature, and to prove his right to be assimilated with it.

Hawthorne's study in his tower at The Wayside
(photograph by Herbert W. Gleason)

Truth, not singularity, was the garment that Hawthorne coveted; for truth, while it gives its possessor the freedom of all societies, is also the real cloak of invisibility. The more closely we envelop ourselves in it, the less obtrusive become our impertinent personal lineaments. Who can see Shakspere in his plays, or Pheidias in his statues?

And the truth which Hawthorne perceived perhaps more profoundly than any other was that of the brotherhood of man. By inheritance and training he tended towards exclusiveness; but both his heart and his intellect showed him the shallowness of such a scheme of existence. So far back as 1835 we find him canvassing the idea of

some common quality or circumstance that should bring together people the most unlike in other respects, and make a brotherhood and sisterhood of them—the rich and the proud finding themselves in the same category with the mean and the despised.

In the following year he defines his conception more minutely. He will class mankind, first, by their sorrows; for instance, whenever there are any, whether in fair mansion or hovel, who are mourning for the loss of relatives or friends, and who wear black, whether the cloth be coarse or superfine, they are to make one class. Secondly, all who have the same maladies, whether they lie under damask canopies, or on straw pallets, or in the wards of hospitals, they are to form one class. Thirdly, all who are guilty of the same sins, whether the world knows them or not, whether they languish in prison, looking forward to the gallows, or walk honored among men, they also form a class. Then proceed to generalize and classify all the world together, as none can claim utter exemption from either sorrow, sin, or disease; and, if they could, yet death, like a great parent, comes and sweeps them all through one darksome portal–all his children.

In elaborating the scheme in the 'Procession of Life,' he finds, however, that Sin and Death are the broadest badges of humanity. Diseases are 'as proper subjects of human pride as any relations of human rank that man can fix upon. Disease is the natural aristocrat.' He is not satisfied, either, with the idea of forming a separate class of mankind on the basis of high intellectual power. 'It is but a higher development of innate gifts common to all,' and it may be doubted whether the peculiar relation of intellectual persons to one another 'may not vanish as soon as the procession shall have passed beyond the circle of the present world.' Even grief is not an invariable bond of alliance, for if the influence of the world's false distinctions remain in the heart, then sorrow lacks the earnestness that makes it holy and reverend; 'if the mourner have anything dearer than his grief, he must seek his true position elsewhere.' When, however, the trumpet sounds for the guilty to assemble,

> even the purest may be sensible of some faint responding echo in his breast; many, however, will be astonished at the fatal impulse that drags them thitherward. Nothing is more remarkable than the various deceptions by which guilt conceals itself from the perpetrator's conscience.

This idea of the catholicity of guilt runs through all Hawthorne's productions. 'Man,' he says (in 'Fancy's Show-Box'), 'must not disclaim his brotherhood even with the guiltiest, since, though his hand be clean, his heart has surely been polluted by the flitting phantoms of iniquity.' Again, the story of 'Young Goodman Brown'–perhaps the most remarkable piece of imaginative writing in the whole list of Hawthorne's works–inculcates the same appalling lesson of fraternity in sin. 'Evil is the nature of mankind!' exclaims the fallen angel. 'When the friend shows his inmost heart to his friend,' cries the dying Father Hooper,

the lover to his best beloved; when man does not vainly shrink from the eye of his Creator, loathsomely treasuring up the secret of his sin, then deem me a monster, for the symbol beneath which I have lived and die! I look around me, and, lo! on every visage a Black Veil!

But though he thus insisted upon the darker aspects of human association, Hawthorne was far from neglecting the other side. Speaking of the reformers and theorizers, in 'The Hall of Fantasy,'–'representatives of an unquiet period, when mankind is seeking to cast off the whole tissue of ancient custom like a tattered garment,'–and noting the apparent incompatibility of their various notions, he nevertheless perceives the underlying bond of union. 'Far down beyond the fathom of the intellect,' he says, 'the soul acknowledges that all these varying and conflicting developments of humanity were united in one sentiment–the struggle of the race after a better and purer life than had yet been realized on earth.' Or, once more, alluding to the religious sectarians, he observes that truth has an intoxicating quality when imbibed by any save a powerful intellect, and often impels the quaffer to quarrel in his cups; so that each sect surrounds its own righteousness with a hedge of thorns, and though their hearts be large, their minds are often exclusively filled with one idea. Nevertheless, though 'their own view may be bounded by country, creed, profession, the diversities of individual character, above them all is the breadth of Providence!'

Another of Hawthorne's strongest perceptions was of the artificiality of our present civilization, and of the superfluities and absurdities to which custom has insensibly blinded us. 'Earth's Holocaust' is the symbolic clearing out of these abuses. Rank, government, property, literature, and the gallows are consumed one after the other; and then the radicals would do away with marriage, theology, and even with the Bible. But Hawthorne will not allow the radicals to carry him off his feet; and though he is ready to admit that nature is better than any book, and the human heart deeper than any system of philosophy, yet he puts his finger unerringly upon the weak spot in all reformations; and though the observation is put into the mouth of a personage whose 'complexion was indeed fearfully dark, and his eyes glowed with a redder light than that of the bonfire,' it is none the less unanswerable. 'Be not so cast down, my good friends,' says this lurid individual; 'you shall see good days yet. There is one thing that these wiseacres have forgotten to throw into the fire, and without which all the rest of the conflagration is just nothing at all; yes, though they had burned the earth itself to a cinder.'

'And what may that be?' eagerly demanded the last murderer.

'What but the human heart itself?' said the dark-visaged stranger with a portentous grin.

'Purify that inward sphere,' adds Hawthorne,

> and the shapes of evil that now seem almost our only realities, will turn to shadowy phantoms and vanish of their own accord; but if we go no deeper than the intellect, and strive, with merely that feeble instrument, to discern and rectify what is wrong, our whole accomplishment will be a dream.

On the other hand, if reform be not always beneficial, it can do no lasting harm: 'not a truth is destroyed; only what is evil can feel the action of the fire.' The Titan of innovation, in short, is double in his nature, partaking of both angelic and diabolic elements; but Providence still stands behind, and overrules all to its own ends.

But he took more pleasure in imagining the condition of the world after all mistakes and irrationalities were done away with or forgotten. 'We who are born into the world's artificial system,' he says ('New Adam and Eve'),

> can never adequately know how little in our present state and circumstances is natural, and how much is merely the interpolation of the perverted mind and heart of man. It is only through the medium of the imagination that we can loosen these iron fetters which we call truth and reality, and make ourselves even partially sensible what prisoners we are.

And then he carries his newly created pair through a day's wandering about Boston, on that day when everything physical that can give evidence of man's present position remains untouched by the hand of destiny; but no breath of a creative being, save themselves, disturbs this earthly atmosphere. The satire is gracefully and delicately managed. 'Such a pair would at once distinguish between art and nature. Their instincts and intuitions would at once recognize the wisdom and simplicity of the latter; while the former, with its elaborate perversities, would offer them a continued succession of puzzles.' They behold each other without astonishment; but 'perhaps no other stride so vast remains to be taken as when they first turn from the reality of their mutual glance to the dreams and shadows that perplex them everywhere else.' They approach a church, attracted by its spire, pointing upwards to the sky, whither they have already yearned to climb; as they enter the portal, Time, who has survived his former progeny, speaks with the iron tongue that men gave him to his two grandchildren. 'They listen, but understand him not; nature would measure time by the

succession of thoughts and acts which constitute real life, and not by hours of emptiness.' They dimly feel some religious influence in the place, but are troubled by the roof between them and the sky. They go out and kneel at the threshold, and 'give way to the spirit's natural instinct of adoration towards a beneficent Father. But, in truth, their life thus far has been a continual prayer; purity and simplicity hold converse at every moment with their Creator.' Passing onward, they come to that 'hospital' whose patients 'were sick—and so were the purest of their brethren—with the plague of sin.' Every remedy had been tried for its extirpation except the single one, 'the flower that grew in Heaven and was sovereign for all the miseries of earth—man never had attempted to cure sin by Love!' His system had been one of 'fear and vengeance, never successful, yet followed to the last.' Escaping thence, they enter a private mansion, most of the contents of which are a puzzle to them. The pictures, for example, do not interest them, for 'there is something radically artificial and deceptive in painting.' This recalls Heine's apothegm—'Painting is nothing but a flat falsehood.' The statue of a little child, however, impresses them more agreeably. 'Sculpture in its highest excellence is more genuine than painting, and might seem to be evolved from some natural germ by the same law as a leaf or a flower.' They next enter a bank, where is hoarded 'the mainspring, the life, the very essence of the system that had wrought itself into the vitals of mankind and choked their original nature in its deadly gripe.' As Hawthorne elsewhere remarks, however, 'the desire for wealth is the natural yearning for that life in the midst of which we find ourselves.' Be that as it may, to Adam and Eve all the bullion in the bank is no better than 'heaps of rubbish.' A further discovery is that of a library, which excites Adam's curiosity; but Eve draws him forth again in good time, else

> all the perversions, and sophistries, and false wisdom so aptly mimicking the true,—all the narrow truth, so partial that it becomes more deceptive than falsehood,— all the wrong principles and worse practice, the pernicious examples and mistaken rules of life,—all the specious theories which turn earth into cloudland, and men into shadows,—all the sad experience which it took mankind so many ages to accumulate, and from which they never drew a moral for their future guidance,—the whole heap of this disastrous lore would have tumbled at once upon Adam's head.

Surely this view of literature is a radical one for even an American author to hold.

Hawthorne's religious faith was of an almost childlike simplicity, though it was as deeply rooted as his life itself. It was not his cue to insist upon the rational explanation of all mysteries; and if he had felt the longing for 'some master-thought to guide me through this labyrinth of life, teaching me wherefore I was born, and how to do my task on earth, and what is death,' yet he recognized the vanity of attempting to 'unveil the mysteries which Divine Intelligence has revealed so far as is needful to our guidance, and hit the rest.' What is essential is intuitive; and he remarks that 'a blind man might as reasonably contend that a reflection in a mirror does not exist, as we, because the Creator has hitherto withheld the spiritual perception, can therefore contend that there is no spiritual world.' Nor is that world a 'dark realm of nothingness'; it fulfills all the wants of the human soul; nor need we even doubt that 'man's disembodied spirit may re-create time and the world for itself, with all their peculiar enjoyments, should there still be human yearnings amid life eternal and infinite.' The riddle of the Sphinx does not keep him awake o' nights; perhaps he thinks, the reason of our existence 'may be revealed to us after the fall of the curtain; or, not impossibly, the whole drama, in which we are involuntary actors, may have been performed for the instruction of another set of spectators.' This last, however, is a fanciful theory, not a sober belief; and for a man who has become wedded to a theory there remains, in his opinion, little hope.

> There is no surer method of arriving at the Hall of Fantasy than to throw one's self into the current of a theory; for, whatever landmarks of fact may be set up along the stream, there is a law of nature that impels it thither. And let it be so; for what is good and true becomes gradually hardened into fact, while error melts away and vanishes.

'Therefore,' he adds, 'may none who believe and rejoice in the progress of mankind be angry with me because I recognized their apostles and leaders amid the fantastic radiance of those pictured windows. I love and honor such men as well as they.'

These are the words of an optimist, though not of an extreme one; but it is noticeable that the deeper the level at which Hawthorne moves, the more optimistic does he become. He is not an advocate; he holds the scales impartially; but his most momentous conclusions are also his most hopeful ones. A humorous or saturnine eccentricity might have attracted more curiosity; but, once more, he wished 'to open an intercourse with the world,' and eccentricity is a porcupine's coat. He aimed not to startle or to titillate his hearers, but to say only what the unprejudiced judgment of mankind must agree to. To do this without once descending to commonplace is the feat of the highest genius; yet so well has Hawthorne accomplished it, that one has to ponder his utterances more than once to realize how revolutionary many of them are.

He seldom indulges in satire; but when he does so, it is to good purpose. 'The Celestial Railroad' is a most felicitous conception, and is touched with a masterly hand. It exposes the modern tendency to postpone the warnings of conscience, to glide over and round the grim realities of life, and to skim comfortably forward from the cradle to the grave, outwardly respectable, but inwardly stained with every indulgence. Christian's old friend Evangelist presides at the ticket-office—though 'some malicious persons' deny his identity, 'and even pretend to bring competent evidence of an imposture.' Among the fashionable folk at the railway station there was much pleasant conversation on indifferent topics; 'while religion, though indubitably the main thing at heart, was thrown tastefully into the background. Even an infidel would have heard little or nothing to shock his sensibility.' The Valley of the Shadow of Death is artificially lighted, and there is a stopping-place at the mouth of Tophet, where, according to Mr Smooth-it-away, 'the directors had caused forges to be set up for the manufacture of railroad iron.' The giants Pope and Pagan are dead; but their cavern is occupied by an amorphous monster of German extraction, Giant Transcendentalist by name, who 'shouted after us, but in so strange a phraseology that we knew not what he meant, nor whether to be encouraged or affrighted.' At Vanity Fair everything proceeds swimmingly until the old-fashioned pilgrims make their appearance, when 'there were these two worthy simpletons, making the scene look wild and monstrous, merely by their sturdy repudiation of all part in its business or pleasures.' Another station was 'formerly the castle of the redoubted Giant Despair; but since his death Mr Flimsy-Faith has repaired it (in a modern and airy style of architecture), and keeps an excellent house of entertainment there.' And so they rattle along, 'at the tail of a thunderbolt,' with Apollyon for engineer, until they arrive at the river, where 'a steam ferry-boat, the last improvement on this important route,' stands ready to receive them. 'But the wheels, as they began their revolution, threw a dash of spray over me so cold—so deadly cold, with the chill that will never leave those waters until Death be drowned in his own river—that, with a shiver and a heartquake, I awoke. Thank heaven, it was a Dream!' Some people object to allegories; but, deftly managed, they give wings to satire. The historian of 'The Celestial Railroad' is at any rate chargeable with the same indiscretion that is ascribed to Elliston in 'The Bosom Serpent'—that of 'breaking through the tacit compact by which the world has done its best to secure repose without relinquishing evil.'

It might be objected to an analysis such as has been indicated (rather than made) in the foregoing

Melville's "Monody"

Melville, whose relationship with Hawthorne did not endure, may have written this poem soon after visiting Hawthorne's grave in the winter of 1864–1865. It was not published until 1891, the year of his own death.

To have known him, to have loved him
After loneness long;
And then to be estranged in life,
And neither in the wrong;
And now for death to set his seal–
Ease me, a little ease, my song!

By wintry hills his hermit-mound
The sheeted snow-drifts drape,
And houseless there the snow-bird flits
Beneath the fir-trees' crape:
Glazed now with ice the cloistral vine
That hid the shyest grape.

pages, that Hawthorne is substantially a romancer,–a teller of tales,–and that, therefore, his excursions into other regions are of little practical significance. But the story was never the chief object in Hawthorne's writings; the skeleton having once been designed, he immediately forgot all about it, and devoted all his energies to the flesh-and-blood of the composition. And this flesh-and-blood is no mere appendage; it is wrought out of the author's very life. In order that the outward beauty of the completed work may be adequately appreciated, it is, therefore, necessary to understand something of its inner organization and secret genesis. It is alive, and has the inexhaustible fascination of life–the depth beyond depth. It is illuminated by imagination and graced by art; but imagination only renders the informing truth more conspicuous, and art is the form which symmetrical truth inevitably assumes. In short, save as regards the merest externals, nothing in Hawthorne's fictions is fictitious. And therefore we lose what is best in them, unless we learn how to read between the lines– how to detect the writer's own lineaments beneath the multifarious marks wherewith he veils them. These shorter sketches, covering a wider area of thought than the complete romances, are consequently more transparent; and they show us how *The Scarlet Letter* and *The Marble Faun* came to be born. They show us, too, the value of his early seclusion, which caused him to begin with meditation instead of with observation, and thus to produce things with souls in them, instead of hollow shells painted to resemble life. However we may probe or test his writings, we shall find no vacuum in them; the material

envelope is sometimes imperfect, the spiritual reality is always there.

Hawthorne himself perceived his defects much more keenly than his excellences, and his effort to improve is constantly visible. He endeavors to balance his rare faculty of insight by the comparatively common faculty of outsight; and the volumes of his note-books are the patent records of this study. His aim, therefore, was the perfection which only Shakspere has attained; but Hawthorne was the bud of Shakspere's full-blown rose. He widened every year; his roots were nourished by the Shaksperian soil; and his perfume had a purity and potency which will, perhaps, cause it to linger in the memory as long as that of the mighty Elizabethan.

Thomas Bradfield was a minor English poet who published two volume of verse: Hermione *(1871) and* Deignton Farm *(1872). He argues that* The Transformation *is the least satisfactory of Hawthorne's major novels.*

The Romances of Nathaniel Hawthorne
Thomas Bradfield
Westminster Review, 142 (1894): 203–214

The principal source of fascination in the stories of Nathaniel Hawthorne proceeds from an exquisite sympathy with the spiritually mysterious and appalling in our nature. His delineation of the peculiar phases of mental experience upon which he loves to dwell is usually accompanied by a vivid romanticism of situation and incident singularly original; and his descriptive pencil is never more at home than when it lingers over what is weird, unreal, or ghostly. In addition, Hawthorne's romances belong to a region of fancy which allows of them being informed by a unique power of subtle introspection. This power, in union with his fine insight, suggests that the novelist's imagination was of the phase which, according to Mr Ruskin's classification, is in part analytical penetration and in part contemplative.[1] His genius, in its peculiar treatment of the idiosyncracies of his characters, may be said to resemble the whirlpool in its power of drawing all within its influence to one centre, although his artistic skill and sympathy enable him to dignify his conceptions with distinct if somewhat exclusive individualities. Our first experience of his works is one of mingled surprise and delight, to be succeeded by awe, not to say terror, as we grow more and more impressed with what is haunting and gruesome in his pages. Then it is we recognise how much of Hawthorne's power lies in the profound interest he evinces towards individuals in exceptionally ideal

CATALOGUE OF

THE UNIQUE COLLECTION

MADE BY

CHARLES B. FOOTE, ESQ.

OF THIS CITY

OF

FIRST EDITIONS
OF THE FOLLOWING AMERICAN AUTHORS

R. W. EMERSON,	HENRY W. LONGFELLOW,
NATH'L. HAWTHORNE,	JAS. RUSSELL LOWELL,
OLIVER WENDELL HOLMES,	EDGAR ALLAN POE,

and JOHN G. WHITTIER

TO BE SOLD AT AUCTION

FRIDAY, NOVEMBER 23, 1894

AT 3 P. M.

BY

BANGS & CO. 739 & 741 BROADWAY NEW YORK

☞ Bids executed by the Auctioneers for buyers unable to be present

---

155.00 32.   HAWTHORNE (NATHANIEL). FANSHAWE; a Tale. 12mo, full crushed levant morocco extra, *uncut*, by MATTHEWS. In slip case.   Boston, 1828

> * The last copy advertised by a book-seller in this city was bought by the British Museum.
> This is Hawthorne's first work, written while a student at Bowdoin College. A few copies only were sold and the remainder destroyed, hence its great rarity.

11.00 33.   HAWTHORNE (NATH'L). AMERICAN MAGAZINE. Vol. II. *Illustrations on wood, Portrait inserted.* Large 8vo, half morocco, by STIKEMAN.   Boston, 1836

> * This volume covers the period of Hawthorne's Editorship, from March, 1836, to September, 1836. The whole preparation of the volume devolved upon Hawthorne, and he contributed many articles from month to month. On last page of volume is an "Editorial Notice" to the effect that his Editorship ceased with the publication of the August number.

17.00 34.   HAWTHORNE (NATH'L). PETER PARLEY'S UNIVERSAL HISTORY. *Maps and engravings.* 2 vols. square 12mo, half morocco, by MATTHEWS.   Boston, 1837

> * This work was prepared by Hawthorne for S. G. Goodrich (Peter Parley), the compensation being $300.
> But very few Hawthorne collectors have been able to secure this work in the first edition. It was the last one to be secured by the present owner and came to him from San Francisco, Cal., after a two years' search in the East.

20.00 35.   HAWTHORNE (NATH'L). TWICE-TOLD TALES. *Portrait inserted.* Tall 12mo, full crushed levant morocco, *uncut*, by MATTHEWS.   Boston, 1837

> * Autograph Letter inserted.

Cover for the catalogue of the first significant collection of Hawthorne material offered at auction and a page from the catalogue showing prices paid for four items (from C. E. Frazer Clark, Hawthorne at Auction, 1972)

---

situations is—situations which he is able to present to the reader, by the magic of his rare genius, with unique and thrilling intensity.

The contemplative element in his imagination may have led the romancer, for the selection of his subjects, to those set types of humanity to be found not so long ago among the ancestral descendants of the early village folk of New England; just as for his incidents he loved to explore the traditions of these earliest settlers of America. But, beyond suggestive touches of local and historical interest—fresh and attractive of themselves—there is always an original charm proceeding from the author's simple, direct, penetrating insight into enduring phases of thought and feeling in connection with his personages. Into the fanciful semblance of his favourite types of humanity he breathes the warm spirit of an existence which, to borrow the romancer's own language, renders his conceptions, if not actually human, yet so like humanity that they must be preternatural. The subtle and cultured art of Hawthorne's genius in no way shows its fine quality more distinctly than in the

manner in which these delineations, although not of this world, are invested with a verisimilitude so natural, and in some instances so winning, as to draw us towards them in spite of their imaginative exclusiveness. Their affinity to humanity is unmistakable, sicklied o'er, though they be, with the pale cast of unreality. Another drawback to our sympathising to the full with Hawthorne's characters arises from the peculiarity of these not evolving the scenes of pathos and power which are the mainstays of his stories; on the contrary, the scenes are presented so as to illustrate by the force of their accumulated impressions the leading emotion or interest of the conception.

This brings us to another peculiarity of Hawthorne's artistic treatment. The special feature of his subject which he wishes to bring prominently out is illustrated by his powerful and painstaking fancy in so marked a manner as to make the spiritual lineaments of the character appear exaggeration if not deformity. No inapt illustration of this exceptional treatment may be found in that description of perspective drawing known as an anamorphosis, where a portrait or figure is in one special point of view a distorted representation. Hawthorne's characters, in the point of view of the absorbing idea he is desirous of emphasising, lose that harmony and consistency essential to an exact representation of human nature. It is characteristic that the eccentricity is generally most strikingly displayed in connection with some profoundly significant ethical position. In *The Scarlet Letter,* for instance, the great and absorbing point of interest springs from the inevitable result of the sin of adultery as it affects two otherwise beautiful and noble characters. In *Transformation* it may be said that Hawthorne lavishes all the riches of his cultured imaginative subtlety upon foreshadowing the after-effect of a murder, committed under an impulse, in which the two chief characters of the romance are concerned in as exquisitely delicate a manner as their guilty deed will allow. To take two dissimilar but very suggestive instances from the shorter pieces: in 'Roger Malvin's Burial' we have the picture of a sensitive-minded man, who had been induced to leave a companion to die while he himself escaped, passing through all the terrible experiences of one who had been guilty of some dastardly iniquity, and who finds no respite from the avenging recollection until by accident he has killed his son—has 'shed blood dearer to him than his own'; in 'Mr Higginbotham's Catastrophe' we have a happier but equally fatalistic accumulation of incidents, only in this instance the event is allowed to cast its shadow before, and in the end the tragic result is averted. But perhaps the most striking and intense illustration of the strange distorted manner in which Hawthorne's characters appear under the effect of a fixed or absorbing idea is to be found in 'Egotism, or the Bosom Serpent', an allegory which, when viewed in any other light than the fantastic one in which the story-teller presents it, loses its powerful meaning. Again, the character of the man who goes in search of the unpardonable sin, Etham Brand, a powerful and grotesque study, is only saved from becoming repulsive by that element of intense gloom and solitariness in his life which inevitably draws the victim to his doom, and finally leads him to plunge into the burning furnace. The vivid intensity of Hawthorne's genius when concentrated upon any particular feature of his conception, whether of incident or character, may be likened to the glare of fierce light which smote upon the face and figure of Ethan Brand in this story, when the iron door of the lime-kiln was thrown open before him. As Turner in his pictures by 'distinctness of shadow expresses vividness of light,' so in the representations of the American novelist, amid the gloomy fatalistic consequences of their actions, hovers a shining tenderness, ever ready, like a sanctifying peace, to descend when the destinies are satisfied.

Among the loveliest features of Hawthorne's works is the subtle and consummate manner in which he diffuses an etherealised atmosphere over his descriptions of natural scenery and imparts an idealised effect to the various situations in which his characters are placed. As Roger Malvin's burial—the novelist himself tells us—was 'one of the few incidents of Indian warfare susceptible of the moonlight of romance,' so most of the subjects Hawthorne's fancy delighted to elaborate, if we may judge of them as they appear now, were susceptible of an influence with a similar enchantment. Hawthorne's power in this respect sprang from the subtle informing charm of his genius, by which he was able to infuse something new and strange and wonderful into his work. Sensitive critic of himself as he was, Hawthorne, however, slighted the rare magic of his own powers when he dwelt so repeatedly upon the necessity of having an atmosphere as of 'clear, brown twilight' in which to read his stories. There may be, as he says in the Preface to *Transformation,* great difficulty in writing a romance 'about a country where there is no shadow, no antiquity, no mystery, no picturesque and gloomy wrong'; but the essential fascination of his genius transcended considerations of surroundings and created for itself the atmosphere best suited for its appreciation. That the beautiful tendrils of his fancy instinctively entwined themselves around what was congenial and vitalising, and gained strength from these accessories to the romantic and imaginative, is true enough. But it is pressing their assistance too far to regard them as indispensable. It would be easy, as it were, to confront the novelist from his own pages with instances which show how his genius itself creates the atmosphere of romance without need of antiquity or far-off lands. Hawthorne seems in this respect to resemble Ralph Cranfield, in his beautiful story 'The Threefold Destiny', who went a weary world-search for mysterious treasures which he found after all lay at his own door.

To illustrate briefly what we have stated, we will glance for a moment at some of the more remarkable of Hawthorne's short stories to be found in *Twice-told Tales* (First Series, 1837; Second Series, 1842); *Mosses from an Old Manse* (1846); and *The Snow Image and Other Tales* (1851). The subtlety, variety, and originality of the author's conceptions are what impress the mind most when we first become acquainted with these fascinating volumes. When, as in numerous instances, the novelist's characters are exhibited in connection with fears and forebodings which assail the human mind, as the result of some inherited tendency or of sin committed, the weird and gruesome element of Hawthorne's genius is predominant. This striking feature, and others referred to in Edgar Poe's succinct estimate of the romancer's powers—his possession of the 'purest style, the finest taste, the most available scholarship, the most delicate humour, the most touching pathos,'–indicate some of the exceptional attractions which are to be found in the early stories. Special mention may be made of three graceful fantasies, worked out with peculiar happiness and vigour–'David Swan,' 'The Great Carbuncle', and 'The Great Stone Face.' In a different manner, we have realistic sketches marked by careful finish and pathetic interest, such as 'The Old Apple Dealer,' 'The Toll Gatherer's Day,' and 'The Village Pump'; elaborate allegorical fancies with profound meaning underlying the quaint, even grim humour with which they are accompanied as 'The Christmas Banquet, The Devil in Manuscript' and 'Chippings with a Chisel'–this last having about it a flavour of Addison's famous paper on Westminster Abbey; studies full of delicate insight and a vein of original thought, pursued with graceful exuberance through a succession of delightful pictures, as in 'Sights from a Steeple,' 'The Maypole of Merry Mount,' or 'The Vision of the Fountain'; tender or fantastic apologues, through which runs a vein of refined irony, as in 'The Celestial Railroad,' 'A Select Party', and 'Earth's Holocaust'; and fairy legends of beauty–quaint, pathetic, or sentimental–like 'The Threefold Destiny,' 'Edward Fane's Rosebud,' or 'The Lily's Quest.' To give one or two instances of the higher and more radiant flight of the romancer's imaginative conceptions, as well as of his finished and fascinating descriptive powers, we may mention 'The Prophetic Pictures,' 'The Birth-Mark,' 'Dr Heidegger's Experiments,' 'Roger Malvin's Burial,' and 'Rappacini's Daughter,' all of which are elaborated with rare psychological insight and invested with that weird glamour, that haunting fascination, which, if we dare coin a word, we might term Hawthornesque. In many of the short stories the gaily-dressed fantasies turn to ghostly and sepulchral images of themselves–the intensely thrilling, even harrowing effect, however, generally issues in a clear, artistically ordered work, which at its close is irradiated with some lovely thought, which seems to spring out of it as naturally as fragrance from the leaves of a flower. The short stories of these volumes also instance the ease, variety, and finish of Hawthorne's admirable style–a style graceful, vigorous, and flowing, into which the freshness of morning no less than the repose and beauty of summer woodlands seems at times to steal; a style giving life and buoyancy and fascination to whatever it describes, changing like a prism with metaphor and trope; easy, natural, varied, as it grows warm with feeling, vivid with landscape, or eloquent with human misery and wrong.

The rare attraction and subtle spiritual insight of Hawthorne's short stories are seen with elaborated distinctness in the four extended romances to which he owes his more solid reputation. *The Blithedale Romance,* as the outcome of experiences earlier than the production of *The Scarlet Letter,* or *The House of the Seven Gables,* although written after these, may be referred to first of all as the most realistic of his works. The story deals with actual circumstances in the light of an enthusiasm which sought to carry out an impracticable experiment in Socialism. This 'transcendental picnic,' as the scheme of the Brook Farm Community was called, cost Hawthorne his last thousand dollars, and gave the world a fresh and delightful book. The place and incidents of the Socialist settlement were chosen by Hawthorne for the background of his story, ostensibly, as he tells us, because he required 'a theatre a little removed from the highways of ordinary travel, where the creatures of his brain may play their phantasmagorical antics without exposing them to too close a comparison with the actual events of real life.' Yet, with all the interest it may derive from its exceptional setting, the story disappoints on account of the vagueness of its purpose and incompleteness of design. The aspiration stirring the enamored Socialists is the enduring charm of the romance, which required no imaginative touches or beauty of surrounding to make lovelier than when it sprang radiant from the hearts of the little band of colonists. Hawthorne's genius could do for their noble ideal what the members of the community themselves failed to accomplish. It could give reality to a vision, and by associating vivid personalities with the futile attempt bestow upon posterity a living memorial of a lofty but ineffectual enthusiasm.

We now pass to *The Scarlet Letter,* a work of far grander aim and profounder intensity of genius than any other of Hawthorne's romances–a work, indeed, which, if not the most artistic outcome of his powers, is supremely beautiful, daring, and original in conception, and finished in workmanship. The little group of figures–a group worthy to have been portrayed by the powerful and discerning art of Rembrandt–in whom the interest of the story centres, are conceived with consummate vigour, delicacy, and imaginative suggestiveness. Hester Prynne, Arthur Dimmesdale, and the child Pearl, are wrought into the recollection, not only by the artist's minute and repeated touches, but by intense interest, sympathy, and regret. The restrained tenderness and pathos throughout–like springs of living water held in by stern granite rock–are all the more impressive on account of the forlorn nature of the position of Hester and the minister. The burning consciousness of her guilt, typified by the scarlet letter worn upon the fallen woman's breast, so that it is seen of all, is less hard to bear than the consciousness of the same wrong hidden in an otherwise pure and unsullied mind. Hester Prynne living a life of iron-minded resignation in her lonely cottage, until the symbol of her shame becomes idealised with another meaning, even to those who had imposed it upon her; and the Rev. Arthur Dimmesdale, preaching the Word of God with the sublimest fervour and eloquence to his all-confiding people, yet with the secret consciousness of his own unworthiness shrivelling away his life, until driven to brand himself with the same stigma as that so long borne publicly by his fellow-sinner—are conceptions which reveal the human spirit in two transcendentally remarkable phases of its convulsions with the result of sin. Idealistically more daring and marvellous is the inspiration of the elf-child Pearl, with her Protaean variety of moods and diversions, and the fanciful manner in which she, as it were, plays with the secret of her mother's shame, and unwittingly performs the part of a Nemesis towards both parents. There is no need to dwell upon the scenes of masterly power and refinement of insight by which the work is characterised, but one most exquisite feature of rare poetic subtlety lies in the manner with which the natural world around is portrayed in harmony with the peculiar feelings and positions of the two principal characters, as if a spiritual pencil had felt the influence of the guilt between them, and had passed with etherealised touch over the scenes amid which they move. If the agonising chapter descriptive of the minister's vigil is the most dramatic in the book, assuredly the meeting between Hester and Arthur in the forest is the loveliest and most touching. Hawthorne's vision in presenting vividly and sympathetically the influence of the overshadowing guilt at the heart of the story, so that it is never allowed to escape, raises the work to a very high level, inspiring it at times with something of the daring, although its execution is deficient in the restraint and unity of a Greek tragedy; a work, however, worthy of the new world, with a strength and freshness as of the pine forest, and a vitality and intensity belonging to youthful blood—its depths of moral purpose imparting splendour to the desolation which, as the inevitable consequence of sin, pervades the story throughout.

Although *The House of the Seven Gables* may not possess the intensity and interest of *The Scarlet Letter,* it is to us a lovelier and more fascinating story, and belongs to a higher region of imaginative art. From the first we seem spirited into another world—the characters and their surroundings possessing that indefinable charm which belongs to ideal scenes and personages. These are of the simplest and most attractive description. A sister, the elaborately delineated, delightfully aristocratic old maiden, Hepzibah Pyncheon, who is tenderly attached to her brother Clifford—the most exquisitely inspired and finely delineated of all Hawthorne's characters—but from

whom she has long been separated by the falsity of a relative, the Judge Pyncheon of the story; a bright, nimble-minded, joyous-hearted maiden, Phoebe, brought by stress of circumstances into the circle; and an intelligent, interesting, if somewhat moody artist, Holgrave. These are the suggestive characters to which the ancient and picturesque domicile of the Pyncheon family, the House of the Seven Gables, forms an artistic and appropriate background. Slowly, leisurely, but always beautifully, the story unfolds itself, like one of the legendary flowers in the quaint old garden behind the memorable house—with, too, a fragrance all its own. Everything in connection with the little group of characters is old-world, lovely, attractive, with an awe and interest owing to a mysterious shadow hovering round the inmates of the grotesque mansion. After the most startling event in the story—the sudden death of Judge Pyncheon—the shadow vanishes, and the romance closes in light and joyance. The feature of Hawthorne's genius which here stands out with more than usual refinement and charm is the art by which the exquisite group of characters, brought together by the simplest device of interest, are portrayed as forming parts of a harmonious whole. Among the pictures left upon the memory when we have closed the story, that of the dreamy, idealistic Clifford, with his refined, fanciful sensibilities, and tender, lovable admiration of what is beautiful and pleasing, so that his very existence seems to depend upon sunshine, is the most original and striking. One leading trait of this aesthetic dreamer is nowhere more finely illustrated than in his intercourse with Phoebe, who to his sensitive epicurean nature is as the light and fragrance of a spiritual bloom. Further, in no other of his stories does Hawthorne's humour play with such genuine and spontaneous effect. Its bright and glancing flashes usually linger on the surface, as if they had no power to penetrate deeply or warm through and through. His humour, as a rule, does not spring from the heart, or call forth irresistible mirth. Like his pathos, it is generally reserved, almost steeled, as if shy of showing itself. But through this story ever and again there are indications of a freer and heartier impulse, as in the inimitable description of Hepzibah's experience on the first morning of her opening her little shop, with the references to the boy who devoured a whole caravan of gingerbread animals; and in such touches as those describing Holgrave's friends, who 'ate no solid food, but lived on the scents of other people's cookery, and turned up their noses at that.' But it is as a whole that the work impresses one with its irresistible beauty. It is not often that the flower of romance

Beatrix Hawthorne, the daughter of Julian Hawthorne, unveiling a tablet commemorating her grandfather at the centenary celebration (photograph by Herbert W. Gleason)

blossoms so luxuriantly, or, when it does, bears such refreshing as well as ennobling fruit.

Transformation is the most unsatisfactory although in some parts the most richly descriptive of the longer stories. The author's method of elaborating his conception is so transparently revealed as to create impatience, and in the end disappointment, notwithstanding the fascination of individual parts. This conflicting experience arises from the contradiction between the chief incident of the story—one peculiarly suitable to Hawthorne's genius—and the surroundings he introduces of no special affinity to its essential interest. This essential interest culminates in a crime of an extraordinarily subtle and impulsive nature. The peculiar power of Hawthorne's imagination is here finely illustrated, and his delineation of the result of the crime upon the two personages concerned in it one of curious psychological discrimination. The story has no conventional ending, and perhaps fails to please some on that account; but from the peculiar nature of the leading incident such

an ending is impossible; and, so far as the Hawthornesque element is concerned, *Transformation* might suitably have formed another twice-told tale with a haunting interest running through it, like Roger Malvin. On other grounds—those, for instance, which made the book such a favourite with Dean Stanley, who had read it, he tells us himself, seven times—*Transformation* is a most enthralling work. Its descriptive powers are of the highest order; its art appreciation delicate and original; its autobiographical touches of supreme and engrossing interest; its literary charm of style and thought in every way worthy of the author's lofty and cultured powers. With regard to one point of autobiographical interest, the touching and beautiful impression which lingers in the memory of one of the characters, Hilda—as pure and ethereal a conception as ever floated before a poet's mind—becomes transfigured, when we remember that Hilda is an idealised picture of the novelist's daughter Una, whom those who knew have enshrined by their references as a woman of the tenderest sensibility and grace. Una's great trial from early years was physical delicacy, and as a sequel to this we may add that, after having at thirty-three sustained the irreparable loss of her betrothed, her golden hair turned grey, and while devoting herself to religious duties she died in an English convent in 1877.

These admirable romances, with the short tales already referred to, constitute Hawthorne's noblest contribution to the imaginative literature of his country. The incomplete stories published after his death hardly increase our 'rich surprise' at his fertile ingenuity. It is doubtful, had he been able, as he longed to do in the closing months of his life, 'to write a sunshiny book,' whether this would have materially added to the lustre of his reputation. For other and fresh illustrations of his original mind, we may turn to his various *Note-books,* and from these derive more intellectual wealth, as well as closer friendship with his richly-endowed faculties. Vivid flashes of mental and spiritual insight, imaginative suggestions of exquisite subtlety, incisive criticism upon natural and artistic subjects, incidental references to his own tastes and pursuits, make up the charm of writings which afford more and more delight on each re-perusal, and bring us face to face with the man in a most delightful and natural manner.

But it is as a writer of romance that Hawthorne principally concerns us now, with regard to whose special if limited imaginative powers, whose beautiful though peculiar inspiration of weird and ghostly rather than flesh-and-blood interest, we may add a few general considerations. Hawthorne's conceptions, for the most part, are deficient in human sympathy; his stories, long as well as short, are constructed without scaffolding of incidents or motives to sustain them; and beyond some absorbing idea as the central influence through the whole, independent of the usual accessories of the novel. If we turn in thought to one or two of our finest works of fiction—*Tom Jones* or *Waverly, Vanity Fair* or *Pickwick, Shirley* or *Adam Bede*—and compare these with *The Scarlet Letter* or *The House of the Seven Gables,* we are at once conscious of the vast difference both in design and effect, although there is a similar spirit at work throughout all, conducing to artistic harmony. But in the works we have mentioned in contrast to those of Hawthorne, the human interest is predominant and illustrated by rare delineation of character, in connection with stirring and varying incidents which go to make up life; and these, moreover, are presented with a distinct aim, as regards essential points in the narrative and to the final artistic result. But with Hawthorne, human interest, the impulse and diversion of action, the conflicts of feeling, the ambitions, fascinations, meannesses and vices of the world are not the keys upon which his skilled fingers loved to play. His harmonies are drawn from other sources, and although the ideas to which his fancy is most attracted are to its touch as strings of an Aeolian harp, owing to the peculiar nature of these, the music which he calls forth is at times strange, unearthly, even harrowing. Hawthorne painted souls more than bodies, moods and impressions at those significant moments which affect the current of the after-life, rather than the ambitions and energies called forth by action and stimulated by contact with the world. Referring again to the morbidly intricate and repellent in his works, we must not forget that accompanying these there is generally a touch of light which leads the mind to some higher consideration beyond the tangled and gloomy web. Masked under the modest reserve of a story-teller the noblest spirit is at work, and a beautiful and impressive lesson is found enclosed within the fancy. If Ruskin's assertion is sound, that the 'perfect function of the imagination is the intuitive perception of ultimate truth,' we have here one source of that noble feature of Hawthorne's stories by which through the contemplation of things lovely he rose to the appreciation of what is true. In his search for the beautiful, he too found more truth than philosophers in seeking the true, and through his divinations we are able to share in lofty and radiant secrets.

Hawthorne's method as a novelist—the process by which he arrived at the material for his stories—was very different from that of most gifted writers who have attained eminence in the same field. The American romancer's times of deepest inspiration were in those self-withdrawing moments when 'the visible scene would enter unaware into his mind,' and be carried 'far into his heart.' It was then that natural objects with which his spirit had affinity found recognition, to be presented to the world again in the light of his exquisite genius. But this affinity was essential before these could arrest his attention and become fused with his transcendental witchery. He himself felt the want of something substantial for his fancy to unite with. If he has a realistic background, such as that of *The Blithedale Romance,* we perceive how this enables him to present his scenes and characters more firmly and impressively; but if he abandons himself entirely to his own mental conjuring, as in *Transformation,* we have as the result a story hanging together as loosely as gossamer threads—hazy, beautiful, incomplete—and notwithstanding the light streaming over it from its vivid pictures of fascinating scenery, a confusing failure. The true cohesion of Hawthorne's stories lies in the subtle interest he is able to evoke by means of that penetrative imagination which is the rarest feature of his genius.

From his various *Note-books* we are able to form a very clear picture of the novelist's singularly pure, noble, and disinterested character. To the sterling qualities of the man, to his singleness of heart and mind, to his profound tenderness in his family circle, to the loyalty of his attachment to his friends as well as relatives, the testimony from all sides is exceptionally cordial and harmonious. A quiet, retiring, vision-loving, beauty-haunted spirit, Hawthorne recalls Joubert's assertion that 'poets are great-souled, heavenly-minded children.' The American romancer was a great-souled, heavenly-minded child in many respects. The world never lost for him its robe of wonder; to the last, as in his earliest years, it was to him a dream of mystic beauty—perhaps the more so as he grew old. This visionary gift revealed much to his inward eye unperceived by others, and was the source whence he derived many of his indefinable mental treasures. When we picture a congenially-suitable home for his unique spirit, we recall the Old Manse, where he lived in 1843, and which is associated with the collection of stories that may be said to have first diffused a new fragrance of genius beyond his own country. Hawthorne, living in this beautiful and secluded place, might well feel that those early writings were 'attempts to open an intercourse with the world.' 'Like his own Hilda in *Transformation,*' to quote the sympathetic words of an admirer, 'he was spiritually compelled to descend from his aërial hermitage, and unburden his heart in the world's confessional.' One characteristic feature of the man, no less than the writer, is here indicated–his imaginative solitariness. The natural tendency of Hawthorne's mind turned towards the companionship of his own thoughts, and, as with others of the world's visionaries, he found a welcome asylum in dreams and experiences beyond the visible things around him. Something of the same spirit in the instance of Keats led that poet to entwine his fancies round the mythic images of Greece, and banished into regions of unsatisfied splendour the longings and aspirations of Shelley; it craved for some new sensation or experience with Byron, and made its home in a world of sensuous refinement with De Musset; while it developed an accompaniment of cynical melancholy to the wild mysticism of Heine. With Hawthorne the exquisitely-wrought sensitiveness of his being took an even rarer, more ethereal direction, and he lived in the actual, so that no dream of his mind seems more imaginary than parts of his own life. It was not so much from his genius as from his temperament–if we may distinguish the two–that this proceeded–from that habit in his early life to which he alluded when he wrote: 'I lived in Maine like a bird of the air, so perfect was the freedom I enjoyed. But it was there I got my cursed habit of solitude.' But the natural tendency of his mind was towards solitude, and scenes and times most congenial to inward communing. Mr Conway suggests that Hawthorne might have been a fit emblem of twilight for Buonarotti to have carved over the gates of the New World; but Hawthorne's nature, like the subjects which were most suitable to the play of his genius, required the 'moonlight of romance' for its profoundest moments. The quiet, almost shy, manner of Miles Coverdale in *The Blithedale Romance,* his delicate observation, his open and natural tastes, his love for some lonely spot where he may meditate unobserved, and indulge his fancies without check, are also exquisitely true of Hawthorne, who has sometimes been identified with the character.

Hawthorne was a romancer, and the cycle of troubadour minstrelsy had long closed. Belonging to the region of true vision as his conceptions do, some of them, however, suggest that their author had not altogether escaped the intense quivering of his day. In some of his works ideas and experiences are reflected which indicate that his rapt gaze was not always fixed upon the azure. But, regarding Hawthorne's life as that of a singularly high-minded, disinterested man, gifted with a profound spiritual insight as the source of his sympathy with the beautiful and good, we may not inappropriately imagine gathering round his massive forehead a shining light,

similar to that which his own fancy has pictured flowing over the sweet, thoughtful countenance of him who resembled the Great Stone Face. With this impression in our mind, as we leave the 'high pavilion of his thoughts,' comes also the recollection of many hours of delightful intercourse with his fresh and original pages–with his idealisation of innumerable scenes and characters full of weird, grotesque, fascinating interest–with his visions of tender, lofty, and ennobling beauty, as well as of ineffable charm and witchery.

Note

[1] *Modern Painters,* Vol. i.: 'Imagination.'

The Hawthorne Centenary

In July 1904 a celebration of the hundredth anniversary of Hawthorne's birth was held at The Wayside in Concord. Among the speakers were Thomas Wentworth Higginson (minister, soldier, author, and reformer), Charles T. Copeland (Harvard professor), and Julia Ward Howe (poet, reformer, and author of "The Battle Hymn of the Republic").

Address of Thomas Wentworth Higginson
The Hawthorne Centenary Celebration, pp. 5–11

Perhaps it always appears to men, as they grow older, that there was rather more of positive force and vitality in their own generation and among their immediate predecessors than among those left on the stage. I do not know when I have been more surprised, for instance, than on being once asked whether Hawthorne was not physically very small. It seemed at the moment utterly inconceivable that he should have been anything less than the sombre and commanding personage he was. Ellery Channing well describes him as

"Tall, compacted figure, ably strung,
  To urge the Indian chase or point the way."

One can imagine any amount of visible energy–that of Napoleon Bonaparte, for instance–as included within a small physical frame. But the self-contained purpose of Hawthorne, the large resources, the waiting power,–these seem to the imagination to imply an ample basis of physical life; and certainly his stately and noble port is inseparable in my memory from these characteristics.

The actual Hawthorne was five feet ten and one half inches high, broad, but of light athletic build, weighing one hundred and fifty pounds. His eyes were large, dark, and brilliant, as his son tells us. Bayard Taylor said that they were the only ones he had seen that really flashed fire. Charles Reade said he never saw such in human head. People in London compared him to Burns, while in college an old gypsy woman asked him, "Are you a man or an angel?"

Vivid as this impression is, I yet saw him but twice, and never spoke to him. I first met him on a summer morning in Concord, as he was walking along the road near the Old Manse, with his wife by his side, and a noble-looking baby-boy in a little wagon which the father was pushing. I remember him as tall, firm, and strong in bearing; his wife looked pensive and dreamy, as she indeed was, then and always; the child Julian, then known among the neighbors as "the Prince." When I passed, Hawthorne lifted upon me his great gray eyes, with a look too keen to seem indifferent, too shy to be sympathetic—and that was all. But it comes back to memory like that one glimpse of Shelley which Browning describes, and which he likens to the day when he found an eagle's feather.

Again I met Hawthorne at one of the sessions of a short-lived literary club; and I recall the imperturbable dignity and patience with which he sat through a vexatious discussion, whose details seemed as much dwarfed by his presence as if he had been a statue of Olympian Zeus. After his death I had a brief but intimate acquaintance with that rare person, Mrs. Hawthorne; and with one still more finely organized, and born to a destiny of sadness,— their elder daughter. I have stayed at "The Wayside," occupying a room in the small tower built by Hawthorne, and containing his lofty and then deserted study, which still bore upon its wall the Tennysonian motto, "There is no joy but calm,"—this having been inscribed, however, not by himself, but by his son. But I do not want to dwell upon these things. Hawthorne had what Emerson once described as "the still living merit of the oldest New-England families;" he had, moreover, the unexhausted wealth of the Puritan traditions,—a wealth to which only he and Whittier have as yet done any justice. The value of the material to be found in contemporary American life he did not always recognize; but he was the first person to see that we truly have, for romantic purposes, a past; those hundred years being really quite enough to constitute antiquity. This was what his "environment" gave him, and this was much.

But, after all, his artistic standard was his own; there was nobody except Irving to teach him anything in that way; and Irving's work lay rather on the surface, and could be no model for Hawthorne's. Yet from the time when the latter began to write for "The Token," at twenty-three, his powers of execu-

THE

HAWTHORNE CENTENARY

CELEBRATION

AT

THE WAYSIDE

CONCORD, MASSACHUSETTS

JULY 4–7, 1904

BOSTON AND NEW YORK
HOUGHTON, MIFFLIN AND COMPANY
The Riverside Press, Cambridge
1905

Title page for the book published to commemorate the one hundredth anniversary of Hawthorne's birth (Thomas Cooper Library, University of South Carolina)

tion, as of thought, appear to have been full grown. The quiet ease is there, the pellucid language, the haunting quality: these gifts were born in him; we cannot trace them back to any period of formation. And when we consider the degree to which they were developed, how utterly unfilled remains his peculiar throne; how powerless would be the accumulated literary forces of London, for instance, at this day, to produce a single page that could possibly be taken for Hawthorne's;—we see that there must, after all, be such a thing as literary art, and that he must represent one of the very highest types of artist.

Through Hawthorne's journals we trace the mental impulses by which he first obtained his themes. Then in his unfinished "Septimius Felton"— fortunately unfinished for this purpose—we see his plastic imagination at work in shaping the romance; we watch him trying one mode of treatment, then modifying it by another; always aiming at the main point, but sometimes pausing to elaborate the details,

what finally became of Miriam and her lover. He will gladly share with you any information he possesses (nothing mean about him! he would not keep back anything for the world!), and, indeed, he has several valuable hints to offer; but that is all. The result is, that you place yourself by his side to look with him at his characters, and gradually share with him the conviction that they must be real. Then, when he has you thus in possession, he calls your attention to the profound ethics involved in the tale, and yet does it so gently that you never think of the moral as being obtrusive.

All this involved a trait which was always supreme in him,—a marvelous self-control. He had by nature that gift which the musical composer Jomelli went to a teacher to seek,—"the art of not being embarrassed by his own ideas." Mrs. Hawthorne told me that her husband grappled alone all winter with "The Scarlet Letter," and came daily from his study with a knot in his forehead; and yet his self-mastery was so complete that every sentence would seem to have crystallized in an atmosphere of perfect calm. We see the value of this element in his literary execution, when we turn from it to that of an author so great as Lowell, for instance, and see him often entangled and weighed down by his own rich thoughts, his style being overcrowded by the very wealth it bears. Hawthorne never needed italic letters to distribute his emphasis, never a footnote for assistance. There was no conception so daring that he shrank from attempting it; and none that he could not so master as to state it, if he pleased, in terms of monosyllables.

Having so much, why should we ask for more? An immediate popularity might possibly have added a little more sunshine to his thought, a few drops of redder blood to his style; thus averting the only criticism that can ever be justly made on either. Yet this very privation has made him a nobler and tenderer figure in literary history; and a source of more tonic influence for young writers, through all coming time. The popular impression of Hawthorne as a shy and lonely man gives but a part of the truth. When we think of him as reading "The Scarlet Letter" to his sympathetic wife, until she pressed her hands to her ears, and could bear no more; or when we imagine him as playing with his children so gayly that his elder daughter told me "there never was such a playmate in all the world,"—we may feel that he had, after all, the very best that earth can give, and all our regrets seem only an honest impertinence.

Thomas Wentworth Higginson, who wrote biographies of Margaret Fuller (1884), James Greenleaf Whittier (1902), and Henry Wadsworth Longfellow (1902)

and at other times dismissing them to be worked out at leisure. There hangs before me, in my study, a photograph of one of Raphael's rough sketches, drawn on the back of a letter: there is a group of heads, then another group drawn on a very different scale; you follow the shifting mood of the artist's mind; and so it is in reading "Septimius Felton." But in all Hawthorne's completed works, the penciling is rubbed out, and every trace of the preliminary labor has disappeared.

One of the most characteristic of Hawthorne's literary methods is his habitual use of guarded under-statements and veiled hints. It is not a sign of weakness, but of conscious strength, when he surrounds each delineation with a sort of penumbra, takes you into his counsels, offers hypotheses, as, "May it not have been?" or, "Shall we not rather say?" and sometimes, like a conjurer, urges particularly upon you the card he does not intend you to accept. He seems not quite to know whether Arthur Dimmesdale really had a fiery scar on his breast, or

Address of Charles T. Copeland
The Hawthorne Centenary Celebration, pp. 16–21

If, in this spare summary of a part of Hawthorne's career, which–by the way–might be called, "From Concord to Concord in Hawthorne's Life," the student of biography misses much of what seems to him important, it is because my sole endeavor has been to point the relation between the author's experience and his work. In the case of this particular author, the difficulty of seeing the man is only less than that of seeing the artist. Yet from the little really known of this New Englander of genius, a few illuminating facts easily disengage themselves. No one now thinks of the apparent connection between the campaign life of Pierce and the Liverpool consulship as leaving the slightest stain upon Hawthorne's unblemished honor and manliness. He wrote the book without thought of the consulship, to do his best for his friend. And it is due to Pierce–although not one of the most disinterested persons in history–to say that he would have done his best for Hawthorne if the book had never been written. A few words in the "Italian Note-Books," more touching than dithyrambs for print or from a more self-expressing man, sufficiently exhibit the tenderness of Hawthorne's life-long affection for Pierce.

A devoted son, he was the most admirable of fathers, and the rare sort of husband who remains a lover. Democratic, though conservative, he was far enough from the thorough-paced reformer, who too often takes for his motto that whatever is, is wrong. And this ingrained habit of mind conspired with loyalty to early training to keep a son of the Puritans from ranging himself with all other American writers of note, "on the side of the angels," in the burning question of his later years. Hawthorne's way of sticking to a political position, in which it is hard to visualize a Northern man of his intellect, is subtly explained, it may be, by Emerson's constant impression of a strong feminine element in his friend, and by Curtis's word that talking to Hawthorne was like talking to a woman. Neither–it says itself–doubted for a day his essential manliness: both, we may hazard, perceived some mingled trait of mind and temperament on which Francisque Sarcey has since put his finger in the delphic saying, "Every artist is a woman." But being an artist did not keep Hawthorne from being an exemplar of his own fine remark, apropos of Burns and Scottish scenery, that "a man is better than a mountain." People made way in a crowd for the gentle Titan, without his lifting hand or voice. Fields, a genius among publishers, and an especially good genius to Hawthorne, tells of him: "I happened to be in London with Hawthorne during his consular residence in England, and was always greatly delighted at the rustle of admiration his personal appearance excited when he entered a room. His bearing was modestly grand, and his voice touched the ear like a mel-

ody." Charles Reade said of him, using almost exactly Sir Walter's words about Burns, that he had never seen such an eye in any human head. And here is an anecdote communicated to Mr. Conway by Dr. Loring: "Placid, peaceful, calm, and retiring as he was in all the ordinary events of life, he was tempestuous and irresistible when aroused. An attempt on the part of a rough and overbearing sea captain to interfere with his business as an inspector of customs in charge of his ship, was met with such a terrific uprising of spiritual and physical wrath, that the dismayed captain fled up the wharf and took refuge in the office, inquiring, 'What in God's name have you sent on board my ship as an inspector?'"

In truth, neither as a servant of the public nor as master of himself, did Hawthorne know the name of fear. He loved beauty everywhere in Nature only less than he loved it in fair women. He loved books–in youth, particularly Spenser and Bunyan, the English masters of allegory; the Bible throughout his life. He was a lover of flowers, pets, the sea, friends, family; yet, whatever else he loved, with the stern probity of all his forbears he loved honor more. Churches, parsons, dinner parties, literary men (as a class), and his "equals" (as a rule) appear not to have pleased him; but he was at his ease with sea captains, cabin boys, longshoremen, children, and other beings who come to close quarters with Nature or deal with her at first hand. Most persons who encountered Hawthorne had poor Mr. Howells's "half hour of silence" with him. With a friend or two, however,–especially with a sole friend, he talked beguilingly and much. When public speaking was forced upon him, he could, though often shy unto death before no more than three fellow creatures, wring triumph from the occasion; and there are memorable records extant of these successes in talk with the few and in speech to the many. What Hawthorne got from his life may be known from what he wrote in the last year of it to Mr. R. H. Stoddard, on receipt of that writer's verses, entitled "The King's Bell:" "I sincerely thank you for your beautiful poem, which I have read with a great deal of pleasure. It is such as the public had a right to expect from what you gave us in years gone by; only I wish the idea had not been so sad. I think Felix might have rung the bell once in his lifetime, and again at the moment of death. Yet you may be right. I have been a happy man, and yet I do not remember any one moment of such happy conspiring circumstances that I could have rung a joy-bell for it."

Here is a fairly complete description. Let any painter who is skilled at deriving likenesses from passports evoke a speaking likeness of the person designated. Or let some magician who has what the stage calls a "practicable" cauldron, set it over the fire of his imagination, stir together in it these diverse elements of identity, and bid an apparition rise. The shadow is as likely to be Banquo as to be Hawthorne, and however good the charm, will be no more keenly limned than the remembrance of a dream of one whom we have never known. Hawthorne unconsciously mystified all but a very few of those who thought they understood him best; and even in the case of those few—such were his honest evasions, so undesignedly elusive was he—we cannot be sure that they perceived more than a certain phasis of the man who charmed them, or that they really knew more of him than Kenyon knew of Donatello. He had the strangest and, on the whole, I think, the most original imagination of his day, in any language. That the possessor—or the possessed—of such an imagination could harness himself to his heavy load in custom house and consulate, is only a heightening of the recurrent miracle which binds artist and man in one body. It would have been a more wonderful miracle than ever yet was worked, if Hawthorne's creating mind had not often strayed, even from those close at hand and heart, to the phantoms that "startle and waylay" his readers. Like every rare being that walks this earth awhile, he seemed to keep step to a march very different indeed from the treadmill measure that sets the pace for poor humanity. And when the baser rhythm broke in upon the airy music to which his feet kept time, he lost the beat, and, perforce, fell out. *Consule Hawthorne,* there were no romances.

Julia Ward Howe, who wrote a biography of Margaret Fuller (1883)

Address of Julia Ward Howe
The Hawthorne Centenary Celebration, pp. 30–40

I will say what I can to-day about the world in which Hawthorne lived. I shall ask permission to remain seated.

Much has been written, and mostly mis-written, regarding Hawthorne's social surroundings. Mr. Henry James, who supposed Salem to have been for such a man "the abomination of desolation," was evidently not well versed in the history of the ancient town, the town of the Devereux and Crowninshields, Silsbees and Peabodys, very prosperous before the day when Old Billy Gray quarreled with its selectmen, and carried its business to Boston.

Captain Hathorne, the father of the great romancer, died of fever in a foreign land. His widow, unable to withstand the weight of her sorrow, secluded herself even from her family, and ate her bread in the solitude of her own room. Her home then afforded but a sombre background for the life picture of her young son and daughters. It is said that Hawthorne once, speaking of himself and his sister, said, "We have been frozen together."

The Salem of that time had society enough of the usual sort, youths and maidens, lordly seniors and stately dames. But it was not among this goodly company that Nathaniel Hawthorne lived and moved. In a weird atmosphere of his own, his imagination shaped and draped the companions of his early manhood.

In the heart of Boston he erects a pillory, whereon, in the blazing heat of the summer afternoon, stands Hester Prynne, with her babe on her arm, a living monument of shame and disgrace. There, at a corner of the street, suddenly appears her husband, spellbound with horror, a prey to heat more fierce than that of the summer sun. Hidden on the breast of the saintly young minister burns the red letter which matches that fastened upon the partner of his offense.

How palpitating with life are the personages of this romance! Even the young minister's youthful catechumen, who, encountering him in a moment of unconcealed discomfort, fancies that she has done him some offense, her conscience being, like her workbag, full of harmless little articles. Even the ancient dame who openly cherishes her familiar spirits, and dreams of whirling in the dance with a wizard from Lapland. It all hangs together, is a region of imagination all compact, and those who people it walk logically to the crisis of their fate; the head criminal to agonized confession, the innocent child to a calm and happy career, the discredited mother to who shall say what lonely and unconsoling penitence?

And out of all Salem's stately mansions he shows the one he can best fill with the nebulous luminous atmosphere which seemed to be his true element. Here crime and cruelty have the upper hand, but the weird touch also is present. Alice's posies blossom on the housetop, while she, the hapless maiden, comes and goes in unwilling obedience to a force which she cannot understand, the compelling will of the man whose suit she has rejected and who thenceforth hunts her after this fashion.

"*Coelum non animum mutant qui trans mare currunt.*" Hawthorne goes to Italy, and sojourns there long enough to become penetrated with the charm of that lovely land. But even there he is so far master of the situation as to make the sculptor of ancient Greece his tributary, and endue the fame of Praxiteles with a life of his own.

Art criticism is not his *forte*. He contemns Crawford and admires without stint Miss Hosmer and Mr. Story. But what a throne does his fancy build for us! Fair Hilda with her doves is his ideal of maiden innocence. Miriam is the glorious guilty woman of passion and impulse who also belongs to his artistic family. Here, as elsewhere, crime goes to its bitter end. From this Hawthorne saw no escape. But what a wonderful light has he thrown upon the details of the eternal city! The grim, gloomy catacombs, the Capuchin Convent, the magnificent church itself, a world wonder, all come into position at his bidding, and form a life picture never to be forgotten.

Undoubtedly, the time in which Hawthorne produced his most important works was one of deep moral and religious questioning. The cast-iron Puritan rule involved so much that was not in accordance with man's noblest nature, that a rebellion and readjustment of moral values was imperatively called for. With the doubt of religious dogma came to many minds doubts regarding the true interpretation of the moral law. With the polemic controversies of the hour Hawthorne gave himself little concern. Were there not Parker, Phillips, Garrison to fight the real battle of ethics? Yet our friend in his opaline mirror made show of the evils which could lurk beneath the cloak of outward sanctity, of the dire temptation which could even assail a man of saintly disposition. The deep pathos and instruction of this portrayal are beyond words.

The bud of the new order did indeed have a bitter taste. The tides in opposition ran high, and wrecked much casual fellowship, perhaps some friendships which had been accounted real. Brother lifted up his voice against brother. The fathers of the church were unfatherly to its younger sons. Parker was Anathema Maranatha; the same bitterness may have been felt when Hawthorne wrote a life of Frank Pierce. But the bud had to unfold. I think that it fulfilled Cowper's prophecy,

"The bud may have a bitter taste,

But sweet will be the flower."

I remember my own first knowledge of this great author. I was not out of my teens when an admiring elder read me the strange story of the minister's black veil. Although I honored the fine reserve of the lady who declined to withdraw the veil from the face after death, I could not help wishing that she had withdrawn it, so strong is curiosity in the daughters of Eve. In those days I heard that a Miss Peabody had made a drawing illustrating Hawthorne's story of the Gentle Boy. When, years afterwards, I heard that Hawthorne had married this same Miss Peabody, it did not seem strange.

Allow me one more glimpse of the Hawthorne family. On a Fourth of July in the late forties, I had gone with Dr. Howe and a lady friend to see the display of fireworks on Boston Common. The lady friend fainted, and Dr. Howe carried her into the historic West Street house where the Peabodys still abode. The grandmother received us, holding in her arms a beautiful boy baby, perhaps eighteen months of age. He was struggling and crying vociferously. The grandame explained that the young people had gone to see the fireworks, and that she was doing her best to quiet their son. And this baby was Julian Hawthorne.

Hawthorne does much to redeem our literature from the charge brought against it in recent days, namely, that it mostly follows the trend of old world culture, and contributes to the world's knowledge little which may be called distinctively American. Our critics on the other side perhaps forget that the great inheritance of the English tongue naturally brings with it many of the traditions handed down in its literature. And yet, methinks, the criticism just cited has little foundation. To go as far back as Washington Irving's Knickerbocker, we have a work which could hardly have been produced elsewhere than in New York. His tales of Rip Van Winkle and Sleepy Hollow are full of the atmosphere of the region to which they are assigned. Time would fail me to follow this vein further, but I cannot but remember Tom Appleton's saying that in Mr. Emerson's pages you have the music of the pines. Cooper has preserved for us the romance of the early hunters and pioneers, Bret Harte has given to us pictures of California life which will live. But Hawthorne in his writings shows himself above all a child of the new world. The thrill of the tales that fascinated his childhood follows him in his mature manhood. He makes us believe what he himself believed in his nursery.

In my own youth I was well acquainted with one who called Hawthorne friend. This was John Lewis O'Sullivan, a figure well known in the New York of his time. The two men were akin in politics in so far as Hawthorne had any. O'Sullivan was a man of partly Irish descent, of much, over much sentiment, and an ardent humanitarian. Some sixty years ago he took up the topic of capital punishment, and published an arraignment of it which called forth bitter condemnation from orthodox divines. These personages then held that the sentence "Whoso sheddeth man's blood, by man shall his blood be shed," was a divine sentence, binding for all time.

O'Sullivan once called upon me after visiting Hawthorne at Brook Farm. He brought back the impression that the ways of the rural community were little to the liking of his friend. O'Sullivan was at the time editor of the "Democratic Review," for which Hawthorne had already written several stories. He seems to have relied somewhat upon his engagement with this magazine for lasting employment. But the periodical, if I remember rightly, turned out to be little more than a campaign document, and its immediate end being accomplished, it ceased to appear.

Some personal remembrance must add whatever it can to this very fragmentary tribute. More than fifty years ago, Dr. Howe and I drove out to Concord to visit Horace Mann and his wife, who had found a summer boarding place next door to the Manse, where the Hawthornes were installed. We brought with us our little daughter of about the same age as Una Hawthorne. In the course of the day, we found our way into the Hawthorne residence, where Mrs. Hawthorne received us very graciously. She promised that we should see her husband. Just then a male figure descended the stairs. "My husband," she cried, "here are Dr. and Mrs. Howe." What we did see was a broad hat pulled down over a hidden face, and a figure that quickly vanished through an opposite door.

I think that Mrs. Hawthorne made some excuse about an appointment which called her husband to go upon the river with Thoreau.

The Mann couple had a son of the age of Una and my Julia. The three little creatures prattled and played together under the trees in front of the house, while Mrs. Hawthorne kindly showed me the bedroom furniture which she had adorned with pen and ink outline. At the head and foot of her bedstead were Thorwaldsen's Night and Morning. On the washstand was outlined Venus rising from the Sea, from Flaxman's Illustrations of Homer.

Those three dear children, Una, Horace, and Julia, all lived to attain maturity, and all left the world too soon. The memory of the one last named binds me ever to Concord with a debt of gratitude, for she, my dearest child, fed upon its philosophy, and grew radiant in its atmosphere.

So, the first time that I saw Hawthorne, I did not see him, but I was yet to have that pleasure. Years after the time already named, Mrs. Mann, who was residing in Concord, invited me to spend a day or two with her, and also invited some friends for the evening. Among these were the Hawthornes, who were at that time domiciled at Wayside. After a while, Mrs. Mann told me that she wished to make me acquainted with Mr. Hawthorne. I replied, "Oh, no! I know too well how he hates to meet strangers." She insisted, saying that since his residence abroad he had changed much in this respect. Accordingly, we met, and I encountered the beauty of those eyes, which I could compare to nothing but tremulous sapphires. The next day I had his company on the train, returning to Boston. We talked a little of "Blithedale Romance," and I said, "Mr. Hawthorne, you were cruel to say that Zenobia would never have drowned herself if she had known how unsightly her appearance would have been when found."

"Was it not true?" he asked, with some mischief in his look, presently adding, "I had to go out in my boat to look for her."

We met once again at a familiar dinner at James T. Fields's house, where Anthony Trollope, Edwin Whipple were, with myself, the other guests. Of this occasion I can only remember that it was most delightful, and that Hawthorne seemed at ease and well pleased.

Hawthorne's use of the supernatural in his tales has truly a historic value. It preserves for us the fantastic melancholy of the Puritan imagination. Those forbears of ours everywhere perceived the influence of the bodily devil. He was as real to them as flesh and blood are to us. Their belief in witchcraft and demoniac possession was the logical outcome of their merciless theory of religion. Theirs was the terrible Jehovah of the Hebrews; to the Christian revelation of a God of love and pity, they had not attained.

The works which show most of this element were written in the author's unsocial days. We must deem the isolation fortunate in which these seeds of terror ripened into blossoms of power and beauty. Would Hawthorne have accomplished things more marvelous if he had had the run of the London clubs, or the *entrée* into the fashionable world of the world's metropolis? Truly, he needed them not.

What, then, was Hawthorne's world? I answer that he lived in a palatial region all his own. No occasion had he for page or butler, for tricksy spirits, fine as Ariel, served him at will. With a magician's power, he stood at the entrance of his airy abode, where all who entered must see and believe as he willed. He was not of Salem, nor of Boston, nor even of Concord:

"Instead of any upon earth,

The civic heavens receive him."

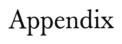

Appendix

C. E. Frazer Clark Jr. and Hawthorne Bibliography

C. E. Frazer Clark Jr. built the most comprehensive Nathaniel Hawthorne research collection; he produced nineteen volumes about his author; and he founded the Nathaniel Hawthorne Journal. *He did these things for the pleasure they gave him: not for professional advancement. Literary research excited him, and he enjoyed sharing his discoveries. Fraze did his scholarship while maintaining a demanding career as a marketing consultant. He supported his research with his own money. There were no grants, fellowships, or sabbaticals to support him; but he generated more scholarship than a department full of tenured loafers collecting from half a dozen charities.*

Frazer Clark raised the level of Hawthorne bibliography through the force of his energy, courage, and determination. He enriched all of us who are serious about the study of American literature.

–M. J. B.

C. E. Frazer Clark Jr. in his library, Bloomfield Hills, Michigan

C. E. Frazer Clark Jr. (1925–2001) made lasting contributions to Hawthorne studies. A businessman and not an academic, he accumulated the greatest private Hawthorne collection, which he sold to the Peabody Essex Museum and the House of the Seven Gables, both in Salem. Clark shared his collection eagerly with people interested in his favorite author. Yet, he was its most important user: it was the source for the majority of the entries in his supreme achievement, *Nathaniel Hawthorne: A Descriptive Bibliography* (1978).

Clark began collecting Hawthorne in 1951, the year he graduated from Kenyon College. Upon examining a copy of the first edition of *The Scarlet Letter* in the Detroit bookstore of Charles S. Boesen, where he worked part-time while a graduate student, Clark noticed that the free endpaper was signed "Nath Hawthorne." This signature had not previously been detected. After having the signature authenticated, Boesen generously let Clark buy the book for the price marked at the time Clark made his discovery. This book was the foundation of his collection, and it demonstrated the importance of one of his maxims: pay attention.

Clark worked for marketing firms in Detroit before establishing his own business, Paramarketing. Although his company was successful, he did not find it as rewarding as collecting Hawthorne. Paramarketing was essentially a means to the end of feeding his real passion, which he nourished lavishly. He invested his money in everything he could find relating to Hawthorne, and he spent much time hunting for items he did not have. But the collection itself was a means to an end: research. He wanted his books used as a basis for understanding Hawthorne and his work. He also wanted students to see what could result from pursuing a literary passion. In the early 1970s I twice took classes from the University of Michigan to his home in Bloomfield Hills, outside Detroit, where he dazzled us with rarity after rarity, explaining the publishing history of various items, illustrating their connection to Hawthorne's life, and gen-

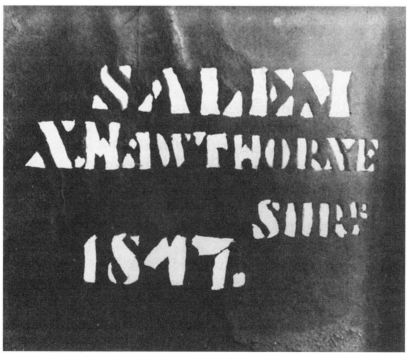

*Hawthorne's dispatch case, which he used during his years as a U.S. consul, and the stencil used by Hawthorne
when he was surveyor in the Salem Custom House, Clark's most prized Hawthorne item
(Peabody Essex Museum).*

erally indicating his serious commitment to the author who had inspired him two decades earlier. On the rides back to Ann Arbor, students talked nonstop about what they had just experienced. The passion in their subsequent papers for class was obvious, thanks to these evenings at the home of this masterful collector who had generously let us see and hold rare Hawthorne items, some of which could not be found elsewhere.

Clark was a Hawthorne completist, which means that he owned many rarities, including unique items. Among his most uncommon titles were the pirated first Irish edition of *Twice-Told Tales* (1850) and the pirated first English printing of *Mosses from an Old Manse* (1851). The collection that began with a signed first edition of *The Scarlet Letter* contained notable copies of this novel. Among them were the pirated first (1851) and second (1852) printings of the first English edition and the pirated first printing of the second edition (1851), including a copy in the Routledge Railway Library Series and another in the Routledge Standard Novels Series. He probably accumulated the best collection anywhere of English editions of Hawthorne titles in Bohn's Cheap Series and the Routledge Railway Library, books that demonstrate Hawthorne's popularity with the general English reading public in the 1850s.

The only Hawthorne first printings Clark lacked were those of the newspaper carriers' addresses *Time's Portraiture* and *The Sister Years*. He had two copies of *Fanshawe*, one of the rarest books by a major American author. One of them was a signed Manning family copy. (Hawthorne's mother was Elizabeth Clarke Manning Hathorne.) He was most proud of owning the stencil Hawthorne used at the Salem Custom House and that bears the name of N. Hawthorne. The author wrote about this stencil in the sketch prefatory to *The Scarlet Letter:*

> No longer seeking nor caring that my name should be blazoned abroad on title-pages, I smiled to think that it had now another kind of vogue. The Custom-House marker imprinted it, with a stencil and black paint, on pepper-bags, and baskets of anatto, and cigar-boxes, and bales of all kinds of dutiable merchandise, in testimony that these commodities had paid the impost, and gone regularly through the office. Borne on such queer vehicle of fame, a knowledge of my existence, so far as a name conveys it, was carried where it had never been before, and, I hope, will never go again.

When Clark bought the dispatch case Hawthorne used while American consul in Liverpool, the stencil was in it. Such a find resulted from his desire to own every possible Hawthorne item, even if pursuing his dream depleted his resources, as it did. One example illustrates his commitment. Upon learning that 15,000 old newspapers from the greater Boston area were for sale, he bought them all (they filled a room in his house), hoping some of them would include information about Hawthorne. They did. As a result of this purchase, he identified previously unknown printings of Hawthorne's early works, as well as unrecorded reviews of Hawthorne's books and information about the Hawthorne and Manning families. He traded or gave away the newspapers that included nothing relating to Hawthorne.

In time, Clark's collection grew to approximately 30,000 items. These included more than 900 first printings of Hawthorne's books, 5,000 reprints, more than 100 association items, 350 photographs and graphic items, 400 magazines, 1,500 dealer auction and auction catalogues, 2,500 reference works, 400 clippings, and more than 400 manuscripts, letters, and documents.

Though rightly best known as a scholar for his Hawthorne bibliography—the greatest result of his collection—Clark's other scholarly work provides insight into aspects of Hawthorne's life and career. He first investigated Hawthorne in "Nathaniel Hawthorne the Artist, A Self-Portrait," his master's thesis at Wayne State University (1957). He produced most of his Hawthorne scholarship from 1967 through 1972, though his Hawthorne bibliography falls outside this period. In 1967 he wrote an introduction to a reprint of Evangeline M. O'Connor's *An Analytical Index to the Works of Nathaniel Hawthorne*. He compiled *The Merrill Checklist of Nathaniel Hawthorne* (1970), which provides more information about Hawthorne's publications than anything of similar size. He edited *Hawthorne at Auction, 1894–1971* (1972), which includes facsimile catalogues of major Hawthorne auctions, some containing a record of the bidding. He was responsible for the publication of the reprint editions of *Love Letters of Nathaniel Hawthorne, 1839–1863* and *Letters of Hawthorne to William D. Ticknor, 1851–1864* (both 1972), for which he wrote forewords, thereby making available primary material about Hawthorne's relationship with two people of great importance to the author: his wife and his publisher.

Although he specialized in returning to circulation important documents relating to Hawthorne, Clark also wrote about him. Among his essays, of particular note is "Posthumous Papers of a Decapitated Surveyor: *The Scarlet Letter* in the Salem Press," which appeared in *Studies in the Novel* in 1970. Here, he demonstrates that material by and about Hawthorne published in the Salem press from 1825 until 1849 helped establish his reputation before the publication of *The Scarlet Letter*. He also proves that the extensive coverage of Hawthorne's dismissal from the Salem Custom House helped guarantee the success of *The Scarlet Letter,* where, in the prefatory sketch, the author describes

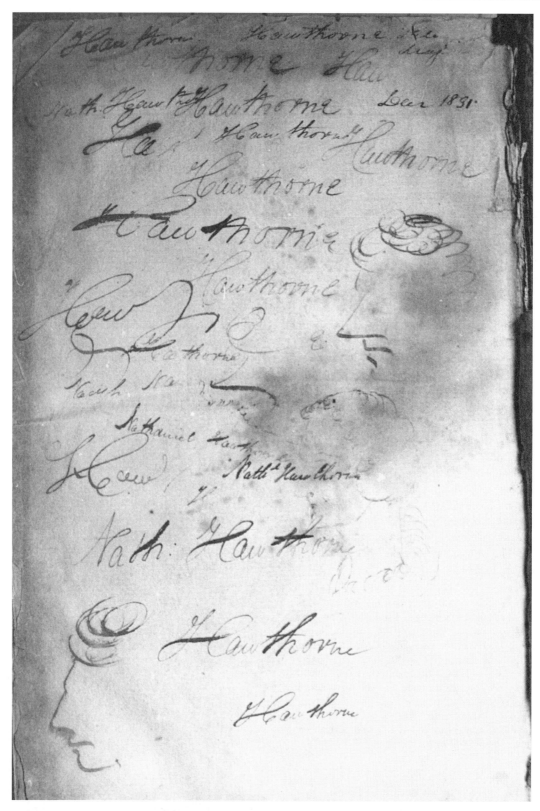

Rear flyleaf from Hawthorne's copy of A New Critical Pronouncing Dictionary of the English Language, *on which he experimented signing his name, sketched three portraits, and wrote the date "Dec. 1831." Clark acquired this item at the auction of the Charles E. Feinberg Library in 1968 (Peabody Essex Museum, Salem, Massachusetts).*

his life in the customhouse. Clark continued his examination of Hawthorne in American periodicals in "Origins of the American Renaissance: A Front-Page Story" in *Studies in the American Renaissance* (1977). In "Hawthorne and the Pirates," published in *Proof* (1971), Clark shows that because Hawthorne's works were pirated in England for seventeen years before the 1852 publication of *The Blithedale Romance* by Chapman and Hall, he made no money from these publications; yet, Hawthorne benefited from the piracies because they established his name in England.

To promote Hawthorne scholarship, in 1971 Clark established *The Nathaniel Hawthorne Journal,* a hardbound annual of approximately 300 pages that he edited through 1978. He was one of its major contributors. Of special importance are his "'The Interrupted Nuptials,'– A Question of Attribution" (1971), "In Quest of a Southern Admirer of Nathaniel Hawthorne" (1971), "Unexplored Areas of Hawthorne Bibliography" (1972), "New Light on the Editing of the 1842 Edition of *Twice-Told Tales*" (1972), "Hawthorne's 'Moonlight': A Lost Manuscript" (with Arthur Monke, 1973), "Distinguishing the First Printing of *The Blithedale Romance*" (1973), and "Census of Nathaniel Hawthorne Letters, 1850–1864" (1973). During the time he was editing *The Nathaniel Hawthorne Journal,* he cofounded the Nathaniel Hawthorne Society (1974); its newsletter, which evolved into the *Nathaniel Hawthorne Review,* provided another outlet for Hawthorne scholarship.

Clark took his collection on the road, sharing highlights with people who would not ordinarily have access to his Hawthorne books. He mounted exhibitions at various locations, including the Ohio State University Library (1964), the American Consulate in Liverpool, England (1971), the Grolier Club in New York City (1973), the William L. Clements Library at the University of Michigan (1974–1975), and the Kent State University Library (1975). Recognizing Clark's importance, the Clements Library made him a member of its Associates Board of Governors. He also served libraries and the world of books as president of the Friends of the Detroit Public Library, cofounder of the Book Club of Detroit, and managing editor of *First Printings of American Authors* (1977–1979) and the *Dictionary of Literary Biography* (1978–1988). He was a founding partner in Bruccoli Clark publishers (later Bruccoli Clark Layman). He also made substantial contributions to Ernest Hemingway studies.

Few people have advanced the cause of scholarship in any area more than Clark did with Hawthorne. All Hawthorne scholars are indebted to him. He bought and he bought and he bought, ultimately exhausting whatever wealth he had accumulated, in order to benefit anyone who wished to consult as

Title page for the standard bibliography that was largely based on Clark's extensive collection

complete a collection of Hawthorne's works as could be assembled.

Because of his accomplishments, encouragement, unfailing generosity, and the example he set, I dedicate this book to the memory of C. E. Frazer Clark Jr.

—Benjamin Franklin V

The Publications of C. E. Frazer Clark Jr.

An Exhibition of Books, Manuscripts, and Letters Nathaniel Hawthorne. Columbus: Ohio State University Library, 1964. Compiler with Bruccoli.

Longfellow, Hawthorne and Evangeline: A letter from Henry Wadsworth Longfellow, November 29, 1847, to Nathaniel Hawthorne, with an introductory Note by C. E. Frazer Clark, Jr. Brunswick, Maine: Bowdoin College, 1966.

An Analytical Index to the Works of Nathaniel Hawthorne with a Sketch of her Life by Evangeline M. O'Connor. Detroit: Gale Research, 1967. Reprinted with an introduction by Clark.

"Bulls, Bears & Books," *Among Friends,* 52–54 (Fall–Winter 1968; Spring 1969): 5–8.

Fitzgerald / Hemingway Annual, 1969–1979. Founding co-editor.

"Hemingway at Auction," *Fitzgerald / Hemingway Annual 1969*, 105–124.

"The Beginning of Dealer Interest in Hemingway," *Fitzgerald / Hemingway Annual 1970*, 191–194.

"Hawthorne's First Appearance in England," *CEAA Newsletter*, #3 (June 1970): 10–11.

The Merrill Checklist of Nathaniel Hawthorne. Columbus, Ohio: Merrill, 1970.

"Posthumous Papers of a Decapitated Surveyor: *The Scarlet Letter* in the Salem Press," *Studies in the Novel*, II (Winter 1970): 395–419.

"'Buying Commission Would Cut Out Waste': A Newly Discovered Hemingway Contribution to the *Toronto Daily Star*," *Fitzgerald / Hemingway Annual 1971*, 209–211.

"Census of Nathaniel Hawthorne Letters 1813–1849," *Nathaniel Hawthorne Journal 1971*, 257–282.

"The Crosby Copy of *In Our Time*," *Fitzgerald /Hemingway Annual 1971*, 237–238.

"Hawthorne and the Pirates," *Proof*, I (1971): 90–121.

"In Quest of a Southern Admirer of Nathaniel Hawthorne," *Nathaniel Hawthorne Journal 1971*, 209–212.

"'The Interrupted Nuptials,'–A Question of Attribution," *Nathaniel Hawthorne Journal 1971*, 49–66.

"'La Vie Est Beau Avec Papa,'" *Fitzgerald / Hemingway Annual 1971*, 190–194.

Nathaniel Hawthorne, Counsul of the United States of America, Liverpool, England, 1853–1857: An Exhibition. Liverpool: *Nathaniel Hawthorne Journal*, 1971. Compiler.

The Nathaniel Hawthorne Journal, 1971–1978. Founding editor.

"An Exhibition Commemorating Nathaniel Hawthorne in England," *Nathaniel Hawthorne Journal 1972*, 203–218.

F. Scott Fitzgerald and Ernest M. Hemingway in Paris An Exhibition. . . . Bloomfield Hills & Columbia: Bruccoli Clark, 1972. Compiler with Bruccoli.

"Having a Wonderful Time in Paris, Wish Scott and Papa Were Here," *Detroit [Detroit Free Press]*, 27 August 1972, 11–14.

Hawthorne at Auction, 1894–1971. Detroit: Bruccoli Clark / Gale Research, 1972. Editor.

"Hemingway in Advance," *Fitzgerald / Hemingway Annual 1972*, 195–206.

Love Letters of Nathaniel Hawthorne, 1839–1863. Washington, D.C.: NCR Microcard Editions, 1972. Reprinted with a foreword by Clark.

"*The Nathaniel Hawthorne Journal* at MLA," *Nathaniel Hawthorne Journal 1972*, 41–42.

"New Light on the Editing of the 1842 Edition of *Twice-Told Tales*," *Nathaniel Hawthorne Journal 1972*, 91–140.

"Unexplored Areas of Hawthorne Bibliography," *Nathaniel Hawthorne Journal 1972*, 47–52.

"Census of Nathaniel Hawthorne Letters, 1850–1864," *Nathaniel Hawthorne Journal 1973*, 202–254.

"Distinguishing the First Printing of *The Blithedale Romance*," *Nathaniel Hawthorne Journal 1973*, 172–176.

Hawthorne's Hand An Exhibition from the Collection of C.E. Frazer Clark, Jr. 31 October Through 8 December at the Grolier Club New York 1973. Compiler.

"Hawthorne's 'Moonlight': A Lost Manuscript," *Nathaniel Hawthorne Journal 1973*, 27–34. With Arthur Monke.

Hemingway at Auction 1930–1973. Detroit: Bruccoli Clark / Gale Research, 1973. Compiler with Bruccoli.

"House-Hunting with Hawthorne. Hawthorne to William B. Pike," *Nathaniel Hawthorne Journal 1973*, 3–8.

"Recent Hemingway at Auction," *Fitzgerald / Hemingway Annual 1973*, 295–298.

"American Red Cross Reports on the Wounding of Lt. Ernest M. Hemingway–1918," *Fitzgerald / Hemingway Annual 1974*, 131–136.

Nathaniel Hawthorne The America Experience An Exhibition from The Collection of C. E. Frazer Clark, Jr. 25 November 1974–17 January 1975. William L. Clements Library, The University of Michigan, Ann Arbor, Michigan. Compiler.

Nathaniel Hawthorne The College Experience from The Collection of C. E. Frazer Clark, Jr. . . . Kent State University Libraries . . . 1974.

"Nathaniel Hawthorne–The College Experience," *Among Friends*, 68 (Winter 1975).

"Primary Bibliography," *The Nathaniel Hawthorne Society*, I (Spring 1975): 1.

"The Scarlett Letter–A 'Fourteen-Mile-Long-Story,'" *Nathaniel Hawthorne Journal 1975*, 3–4.

"A Lost Miniature of Hawthorne," *Nathaniel Hawthorne Journal 1976*, 81–86.

"Norman Holmes Pearson," *Nathaniel Hawthorne Journal 1976*, 6–7.

Pages: The World of Books, Writers, and Writing. Detroit: Gale Research, 1976. Managing editor.

First Printings of American Authors, vols. 1–4. Detroit: Bruccoli Clark / Gale Research, 1977–1979. Managing Editor.

"John Gardner," *Conversations with Writers I*. Detroit: Bruccoli Clark / Gale Research, 1977, pp. 82–103.

"Origins of the American Renaissance: A Front-Page Story," *Studies in the American Renaissance 1977*, 155–164.

Dictionary of Literary Biography Volume One. Detroit: Bruccoli Clark / Gale Research, 1978. Managing editor, 1978–1988.

Nathaniel Hawthorne: A Descriptive Bibliography. Pittsburgh: University of Pittsburgh Press, 1978.

Checklist of Further Reading

LETTERS

Ellis, Bill, ed. *The Consular Letters, 1853–1855*. The Centenary Edition of the Works of Nathaniel Hawthorne. Volume 19. Columbus: Ohio State University Press, 1988.

Ellis, ed. *The Consular Letters, 1856–1857*. The Centenary Edition of the Works of Nathaniel Hawthorne. Volume 20. Columbus: Ohio State University Press, 1988.

Letters of Hawthorne to William D. Ticknor, 1851–1864. 2 volumes. Newark: Carteret Book Club, 1910.

Love Letters of Nathaniel Hawthorne, 1839–1863. 2 volumes. Chicago: Society of the Dofobs, 1907.

Woodson, Thomas, L. Neal Smith, and Norman Holmes Pearson, eds. *The Letters, 1813–1843*. The Centenary Edition of the Works of Nathaniel Hawthorne. Volume 15. Columbus: Ohio State University Press, 1984.

Woodson, Smith, and Pearson, eds. *The Letters, 1843–1853*. The Centenary Edition of the Works of Nathaniel Hawthorne. Volume 16. Columbus: Ohio State University Press, 1985.

Woodson, Smith, and Pearson, eds. *The Letters, 1853–1856*. The Centenary Edition of the Works of Nathaniel Hawthorne. Volume 17. Columbus: Ohio State University Press, 1987.

Woodson, Smith, and Pearson, eds. *The Letters, 1857–1864*. The Centenary Edition of the Works of Nathaniel Hawthorne. Volume 18. Columbus: Ohio State University Press, 1987.

BIBLIOGRAPHIES

Atkinson, Jennifer E. "Recent Hawthorne Scholarship, 1967–1970: A Checklist," *Nathaniel Hawthorne Journal* (1971): 295–305.

Clark Jr., C. E. Frazer. *Nathaniel Hawthorne: A Descriptive Bibliography*. Pittsburgh: University of Pittsburgh Press, 1978.

Francis, Gloria A. "Recent Hawthorne Scholarship, 1970–1971," *Nathaniel Hawthorne Journal* (1972): 273–278.

Francis. "Recent Hawthorne Scholarship, 1971–1972," *Nathaniel Hawthorne Journal* (1973): 269–277.

Jones, Buford. *A Checklist of Hawthorne Criticism, 1951–1966*. Hartford: Transcendental Books, 1967.

Jones, Wayne Allen. "A Checklist of Recent Hawthorne Scholarship," *Nathaniel Hawthorne Journal* (1977): 373–389.

Jones. "Recent Hawthorne Scholarship, 1973–1974, with Supplementary Entries from Other Years Added," *Nathaniel Hawthorne Journal* (1975): 281–316.

Ricks, Beatrice, and others. *Nathaniel Hawthorne: A Reference Bibliography, 1900–1971, with Selected Nineteenth Century Materials*. Boston: Hall, 1972.

Scharnhorst, Gary. *Nathaniel Hawthorne: An Annotated Bibliography of Comment and Criticism before 1900.* Metuchen, N.J.: Scarecrow Press, 1988.

Annual checklists or bibliographies of books and articles about Hawthorne appear in *The Nathaniel Hawthorne Society Newsletter* and *The Nathaniel Hawthorne Review* (except in volumes 18, 20, and 26; volume 27 has two such lists).

SELECTED BIOGRAPHIES

Bridge, Horatio. *Personal Recollections of Nathaniel Hawthorne.* New York: Harper, 1893.

Hawthorne, Julian. *Hawthorne and His Circle.* New York & London: Harper, 1903.

Hawthorne. *Nathaniel Hawthorne and His Wife: A Biography.* 2 volumes. Cambridge: Cambridge University Press, 1884.

Hoeltje, Hubert H. *Inward Sky: The Mind and Heart of Nathaniel Hawthorne.* Durham: Duke University Press, 1962.

Homer, Bryan. *An American Liaison: Leamington Spa and the Hawthornes, 1855–1864.* Madison & Teaneck: Fairleigh Dickinson University Press / London: Associated University Presses, 1998.

Lathrop, Rose Hawthorne. *Memories of Hawthorne.* Boston & New York: Houghton, Mifflin, 1897.

Mays, James O'Donald. *Mr. Hawthorne Goes to England: The Adventures of a Reluctant Consul.* Burley, Ringwood & Hampshire, U.K.: New Forest Leaves, 1983.

Mellow, James R. *Nathaniel Hawthorne in His Times.* Boston: Houghton Mifflin, 1980.

Miller, Edwin Haviland. *Salem Is My Dwelling Place: A Life of Nathaniel Hawthorne.* Iowa City: University of Iowa Press, 1991.

Moore, Margaret B. *The Salem World of Nathaniel Hawthorne.* Columbia & London: University of Missouri Press, 1998.

Stewart, Randall. *Nathaniel Hawthorne: A Biography.* New Haven: Yale University Press, 1948.

Ticknor, Caroline. *Hawthorne and His Publisher.* Boston & New York: Houghton Mifflin, 1913.

Turner, Arlin. *Nathaniel Hawthorne: A Biography.* New York & Oxford: Oxford University Press, 1980.

CONCORDANCE

Byers Jr., John R. and James J. Owen, *A Concordance to the Five Novels of Nathaniel Hawthorne.* 2 volumes. New York & London: Garland, 1979.

SELECTED BOOKS ON HAWTHORNE'S LIFE AND WORKS

Baym, Nina. *The Shape of Hawthorne's Career.* Ithaca & London: Cornell University Press, 1976.

Bell, Millicent, ed. *New Essays on Hawthorne's Major Tales.* Cambridge: Cambridge University Press, 1993.

Bunge, Nancy. *Nathaniel Hawthorne: A Study of the Short Fiction.* New York: Twayne, 1993.

Colacurcio, Michael J. *The Province of Piety: Moral History in Hawthorne's Early Tales.* Cambridge & London: Harvard University Press, 1984.

Crews, Frederick. *The Sins of the Fathers: Hawthorne's Psychological Themes,* enlarged edition. Berkeley & Los Angeles: University of California Press, 1989.

Dauber, Kenneth. *Rediscovering Hawthorne.* Princeton: Princeton University Press, 1977.

Davidson, Edward H. *Hawthorne's Last Phase.* New Haven: Yale University Press, 1949.

Donohue, Agnes McNeill. *Hawthorne: Calvin's Ironic Stepchild.* Kent: Kent State University Press, 1985.

Dunne, Michael. *Hawthorne's Narrative Strategies.* Jackson: University Press of Mississippi, 1995.

Easton, Alison. *The Making of the Hawthorne Subject.* Columbia & London: University of Missouri Press, 1996.

Erlich, Gloria C. *Family Themes and Hawthorne's Fiction: The Tenacious Web.* New Brunswick, N.J.: Rutgers University Press, 1984.

Faust, Bertha. *Hawthorne's Contemporaneous Reputation.* Philadelphia: University of Pennsylvania, 1939.

Fogle, Richard Harter. *Hawthorne's Fiction: The Light and the Dark,* revised edition. Norman: University of Oklahoma Press, 1964.

Gale, Robert L. *A Nathaniel Hawthorne Encyclopedia.* New York: Greenwood Press, 1991.

Gollin, Rita K. *Nathaniel Hawthorne and the Truth of Dreams.* Baton Rouge & London: Louisiana State University Press, 1979.

Gollin. *Portraits of Nathaniel Hawthorne: An Iconography.* De Kalb: Northern Illinois University Press, 1983.

Harding, Brian, ed. *Nathaniel Hawthorne: Critical Assessments.* 4 volumes. Mountfield, U.K.: Helm, 1995.

Hutner, Gordon. *Secrets and Sympathy: Forms of Disclosure in Hawthorne's Novels.* Athens & London: University of Georgia Press, 1988.

Idol Jr., John L. and Buford Jones, eds. *Nathaniel Hawthorne: The Contemporary Reviews.* Cambridge: Cambridge University Press, 1994.

James, Henry. *Hawthorne.* New York: Harper, 1879.

Kesselring, Marion L. *Hawthorne's Reading, 1828–1850: A Transcription and Identification of Titles Recorded in the Charge-Books of the Salem Athenaeum.* New York: New York Public Library, 1949.

Male, Roy R. *Hawthorne's Tragic Vision.* Austin: University of Texas Press, 1957.

Millington, Richard H. *Practicing Romance: Narrative Form and Cultural Engagement in Hawthorne's Fiction.* Princeton: Princeton University Press, 1992.

Moore, Thomas R. *A Thick and Darksome Veil: The Rhetoric of Hawthorne's Sketches, Prefaces, and Essays.* Boston: Northeastern University Press, 1994.

Pearce, Roy Harvey, ed. *Hawthorne Centenary Essays.* Columbus: Ohio State University Press, 1964.

Pfister, Joel. *The Production of Personal Life: Class, Gender, and the Psychological in Hawthorne's Fiction.* Stanford: Stanford University Press, 1991.

Ponder, Melinda M. *Hawthorne's Early Narrative Art*. Lewiston: Mellen, 1990.

Swann, Charles. *Nathaniel Hawthorne: Tradition and Revolution*. Cambridge: Cambridge University Press, 1991.

Thompson, G. R. *The Art of Authorial Presence: Hawthorne's Provincial Tales*. Durham & London: Duke University Press, 1993.

Turner, Arlin. *Nathaniel Hawthorne: An Introduction and Interpretation*. New York: Barnes & Noble, 1961.

Waggoner, Hyatt H. *Hawthorne: A Critical Study,* revised edition. Cambridge: Belknap Press of Harvard University Press, 1963.

JOURNALS DEVOTED TO HAWTHORNE

Nathaniel Hawthorne Journal (1971–1978).

Nathaniel Hawthorne Review (Spring 1986–   ).

Nathaniel Hawthorne Society Newsletter (Spring 1975–Fall 1985).

Cumulative Index

Dictionary of Literary Biography, Volumes 1-269
Dictionary of Literary Biography Yearbook, 1980-2001
Dictionary of Literary Biography Documentary Series, Volumes 1-19
Concise Dictionary of American Literary Biography, Volumes 1-7
Concise Dictionary of British Literary Biography, Volumes 1-8
Concise Dictionary of World Literary Biography, Volumes 1-4

Cumulative Index

DLB before number: *Dictionary of Literary Biography,* Volumes 1-269
Y before number: *Dictionary of Literary Biography Yearbook,* 1980-2001
DS before number: *Dictionary of Literary Biography Documentary Series,* Volumes 1-19
CDALB before number: *Concise Dictionary of American Literary Biography,* Volumes 1-7
CDBLB before number: *Concise Dictionary of British Literary Biography,* Volumes 1-8
CDWLB before number: *Concise Dictionary of World Literary Biography,* Volumes 1-4

E

G

Logan, Martha Daniell 1704?-1779 . . . . . .DLB-200

Logan, William 1950- DLB-120

Logau, Friedrich von 1605-1655 . . . . . . .DLB-164

Logue, Christopher 1926- DLB-27

Lohenstein, Daniel Casper von
1635-1683 . . . . .DLB-168

Lo-Johansson, Ivar 1901-1990 . . . . .DLB-259

Lomonosov, Mikhail Vasil'evich
1711-1765. . . . . .DLB-150

London, Jack
1876-1916 . . . . .DLB-8, 12, 78, 212; CDALB-3

The London Magazine 1820-1829 . . . . .DLB-110

Long, David 1948- DLB-244

Long, H., and Brother DLB-49

Long, Haniel 1888-1956 . . . . .DLB-45

Long, Ray 1878-1935. . . . . .DLB-137

Longfellow, Henry Wadsworth
1807-1882 . . . . .DLB-1, 59, 235; CDALB-2

Longfellow, Samuel 1819-1892 . . . . .DLB-1

Longford, Elizabeth 1906- DLB-155

Longinus circa first century DLB-176

Longley, Michael 1939- DLB-40

Longman, T. [publishing house] DLB-154

Longmans, Green and Company DLB-49

Longmore, George 1793?-1867 . . . . .DLB-99

Longstreet, Augustus Baldwin
1790-1870. . . . . .DLB-3, 11, 74, 248

Longworth, D. [publishing house] DLB-49

Lonsdale, Frederick 1881-1954 . . . . .DLB-10

A Look at the Contemporary Black Theatre
Movement. DLB-38

Loos, Anita 1893-1981. . . . .DLB-11, 26, 228; Y-81

Lopate, Phillip 1943- Y-80

Lopez, Barry 1945- DLB-256

López, Diana
(see Isabella, Ríos)

López, Josefina 1969- DLB-209

Loranger, Jean-Aubert 1896-1942 . . . . . . .DLB-92

Lorca, Federico García 1898-1936. . . . . . .DLB-108

Lord, John Keast 1818-1872. . . . . .DLB-99

The Lord Chamberlain's Office and Stage
Censorship in England DLB-10

Lorde, Audre 1934-1992 . . . . .DLB-41

Lorimer, George Horace 1867-1939 . . . . . .DLB-91

Loring, A. K. [publishing house] DLB-49

Loring and Mussey DLB-46

Lorris, Guillaume de (see *Roman de la Rose*)

Lossing, Benson J. 1813-1891 . . . . .DLB-30

Lothar, Ernst 1890-1974 . . . . .DLB-81

Lothrop, D., and Company. DLB-49

Lothrop, Harriet M. 1844-1924. . . . . .DLB-42

Loti, Pierre 1850-1923 . . . . .DLB-123

Lotichius Secundus, Petrus 1528-1560. . . .DLB-179

Lott, Emeline ?-? DLB-166

Louisiana State University Press Y-97

The Lounger, no. 20 (1785), by Henry
Mackenzie. DLB-39

Lounsbury, Thomas R. 1838-1915 . . . . . . .DLB-71

Louÿs, Pierre 1870-1925 . . . . .DLB-123

Lovelace, Earl 1935- DLB-125; CDWLB-3

Lovelace, Richard 1618-1657. . . . . .DLB-131

Lovell, Coryell and Company. DLB-49

Lovell, John W., Company DLB-49

Lover, Samuel 1797-1868. . . . . . . .DLB-159, 190

Lovesey, Peter 1936- DLB-87

Lovinescu, Eugen
1881-1943 . . . . .DLB-220; CDWLB-4

Lovingood, Sut
(see Harris, George Washington)

Low, Samuel 1765-? DLB-37

Lowell, Amy 1874-1925. . . . . .DLB-54, 140

Lowell, James Russell 1819-1891
. . . . . .DLB-1, 11, 64, 79, 189, 235; CDALB-2

Lowell, Robert 1917-1977. . .DLB-5, 169; CDALB-7

Lowenfels, Walter 1897-1976. . . . . .DLB-4

Lowndes, Marie Belloc 1868-1947. . . . . . .DLB-70

Lowndes, William Thomas 1798-1843 . . .DLB-184

Lownes, Humphrey [publishing house]. . .DLB-170

Lowry, Lois 1937- DLB-52

Lowry, Malcolm 1909-1957. . . .DLB-15; CDBLB-7

Lowther, Pat 1935-1975. . . . . .DLB-53

Loy, Mina 1882-1966 . . . . .DLB-4, 54

Lozeau, Albert 1878-1924 . . . . .DLB-92

Lubbock, Percy 1879-1965. . . . . .DLB-149

Lucan A.D. 39-A.D. 65 . . . . .DLB-211

Lucas, E. V. 1868-1938 . . . . . . .DLB-98, 149, 153

Lucas, Fielding, Jr. [publishing house] DLB-49

Luce, Clare Booth 1903-1987 . . . . .DLB-228

Luce, Henry R. 1898-1967 . . . . .DLB-91

Luce, John W., and Company. DLB-46

Lucian circa 120-180 . . . . .DLB-176

Lucie-Smith, Edward 1933- DLB-40

Lucilius circa 180 B.C.-102/101 B.C.. . . . . .DLB-211

Lucini, Gian Pietro 1867-1914 . . . . .DLB-114

Lucretius circa 94 B.C.-circa 49 B.C.
. . . . .DLB-211; CDWLB-1

Luder, Peter circa 1415-1472 . . . . .DLB-179

Ludlam, Charles 1943-1987. . . . . .DLB-266

Ludlum, Robert 1927- Y-82

Ludus de Antichristo circa 1160 . . . . .DLB-148

Ludvigson, Susan 1942- DLB-120

Ludwig, Jack 1922- DLB-60

Ludwig, Otto 1813-1865 . . . . .DLB-129

Ludwigslied 881 or 882 . . . . .DLB-148

Luera, Yolanda 1953- DLB-122

Luft, Lya 1938- DLB-145

Lugansky, Kazak Vladimir
(see Dal', Vladimir Ivanovich)

Lugn, Kristina 1948- DLB-257

Lukács, Georg (see Lukács, György)

Lukács, György
1885-1971 . . . . .DLB-215, 242; CDWLB-4

Luke, Peter 1919- DLB-13

Lummis, Charles F. 1859-1928 . . . . .DLB-186

Lundkvist, Artur 1906-1991 . . . . .DLB-259

Lupton, F. M., Company. DLB-49

Lupus of Ferrières
circa 805-circa 862 . . . . .DLB-148

Lurie, Alison 1926- DLB-2

Lussu, Emilio 1890-1975 . . . . .DLB-264

Lustig, Arnošt 1926- DLB-232

Luther, Martin 1483-1546. . .DLB-179; CDWLB-2

Luzi, Mario 1914- DLB-128

L'vov, Nikolai Aleksandrovich 1751-1803 . .DLB-150

Lyall, Gavin 1932- DLB-87

Lydgate, John circa 1370-1450. . . . . .DLB-146

Lyly, John circa 1554-1606 . . . . .DLB-62, 167

Lynch, Patricia 1898-1972 . . . . .DLB-160

Lynch, Richard flourished 1596-1601 . . . .DLB-172

Lynd, Robert 1879-1949 . . . . .DLB-98

Lyon, Matthew 1749-1822. . . . . .DLB-43

Lyotard, Jean-François 1924-1998 . . . . . . .DLB-242

Lyric Poetry DLB-268

Lysias circa 459 B.C.-circa 380 B.C. DLB-176

Lytle, Andrew 1902-1995 . . . . .DLB-6; Y-95

Lytton, Edward
(see Bulwer-Lytton, Edward)

Lytton, Edward Robert Bulwer
1831-1891. . . . . .DLB-32

M

Maass, Joachim 1901-1972. . . . . .DLB-69

Mabie, Hamilton Wright 1845-1916 . . . . . .DLB-71

Mac A'Ghobhainn, Iain (see Smith, Iain Crichton)

MacArthur, Charles 1895-1956. . . . .DLB-7, 25, 44

Macaulay, Catherine 1731-1791. . . . . . . .DLB-104

Macaulay, David 1945- DLB-61

Macaulay, Rose 1881-1958 . . . . .DLB-36

Macaulay, Thomas Babington
1800-1859 . . . . .DLB-32, 55; CDBLB-4

Macaulay Company DLB-46

MacBeth, George 1932- DLB-40

Macbeth, Madge 1880-1965 . . . . .DLB-92

MacCaig, Norman 1910-1996 . . . . .DLB-27

MacDiarmid, Hugh
1892-1978 . . . . .DLB-20; CDBLB-7

MacDonald, Cynthia 1928- DLB-105

MacDonald, George 1824-1905. . . .DLB-18, 163, 178

MacDonald, John D. 1916-1986 . . . . .DLB-8; Y-86

MacDonald, Philip 1899?-1980. . . . . . . .DLB-77

Macdonald, Ross (see Millar, Kenneth)

Macdonald, Sharman 1951- DLB-245

MacDonald, Wilson 1880-1967. . . . . .DLB-92

Macdonald and Company (Publishers) . . .DLB-112

MacEwen, Gwendolyn 1941-1987. . . .DLB-53, 251

Macfadden, Bernarr 1868-1955. . . . . .DLB-25, 91

MacGregor, John 1825-1892 . . . . .DLB-166

MacGregor, Mary Esther (see Keith, Marian)

Machado, Antonio 1875-1939 . . . . .DLB-108

W

Weeks, Edward Augustus, Jr. 1898-1989 . . . . DLB-137

Weeks, Stephen B. 1865-1918 . . . . DLB-187

Weems, Mason Locke 1759-1825 . . . DLB-30, 37, 42

Weerth, Georg 1822-1856 . . . . DLB-129

Weidenfeld and Nicolson DLB-112

Weidman, Jerome 1913-1998 . . . . DLB-28

Weiß, Ernst 1882-1940 . . . . DLB-81

Weigl, Bruce 1949- DLB-120

Weinbaum, Stanley Grauman 1902-1935 . . DLB-8

Weiner, Andrew 1949- DLB-251

Weintraub, Stanley 1929- DLB-111; Y82

The Practice of Biography: An Interview with Stanley Weintraub Y-82

Weise, Christian 1642-1708 . . . . DLB-168

Weisenborn, Gunther 1902-1969 . . . . DLB-69, 124

Weiss, John 1818-1879 . . . . DLB-1, 243

Weiss, Peter 1916-1982 . . . . DLB-69, 124

Weiss, Theodore 1916- DLB-5

Weisse, Christian Felix 1726-1804 . . . . DLB-97

Weitling, Wilhelm 1808-1871 . . . . DLB-129

Welch, James 1940- DLB-175, 256

Welch, Lew 1926-1971? DLB-16

Weldon, Fay 1931- DLB-14, 194; CDBLB-8

Wellek, René 1903-1995 . . . . DLB-63

Wells, Carolyn 1862-1942 . . . . DLB-11

Wells, Charles Jeremiah circa 1800-1879 . . DLB-32

Wells, Gabriel 1862-1946 . . . . DLB-140

Wells, H. G. 1866-1946 . . . DLB-34, 70, 156, 178; CDBLB-6

Wells, Helena 1758?-1824 . . . . DLB-200

Wells, Robert 1947- DLB-40

Wells-Barnett, Ida B. 1862-1931 . . . . . DLB-23, 221

Welty, Eudora 1909- . . . . DLB-2, 102, 143; Y-87, Y-01; DS-12; CDALB-1

Eudora Welty: Eye of the Storyteller Y-87

Eudora Welty Newsletter Y-99

Eudora Welty's Funeral Y-01

Eudora Welty's Ninetieth Birthday Y-99

Wendell, Barrett 1855-1921 . . . . DLB-71

Wentworth, Patricia 1878-1961 . . . . DLB-77

Wentworth, William Charles 1790-1872 . . . . DLB-230

Werder, Diederich von dem 1584-1657 . . DLB-164

Werfel, Franz 1890-1945 . . . . DLB-81, 124

Werner, Zacharias 1768-1823 . . . . DLB-94

The Werner Company DLB-49

Wersba, Barbara 1932- DLB-52

Wescott, Glenway 1901- DLB-4, 9, 102

Wesker, Arnold 1932- DLB-13; CDBLB-8

Wesley, Charles 1707-1788 . . . . DLB-95

Wesley, John 1703-1791 . . . . DLB-104

Wesley, Mary 1912- DLB-231

Wesley, Richard 1945- DLB-38

Wessels, A., and Company DLB-46

Wessobrunner Gebet circa 787-815 . . . . DLB-148

West, Anthony 1914-1988 . . . . DLB-15

West, Cheryl L. 1957- DLB-266

West, Cornel 1953- DLB-246

West, Dorothy 1907-1998 . . . . DLB-76

West, Jessamyn 1902-1984 . . . . DLB-6; Y-84

West, Mae 1892-1980 . . . . DLB-44

West, Michelle Sagara 1963- DLB-251

West, Nathanael 1903-1940 . . . . DLB-4, 9, 28; CDALB-5

West, Paul 1930- DLB-14

West, Rebecca 1892-1983 . . . . DLB-36; Y-83

West, Richard 1941- DLB-185

West and Johnson DLB-49

Westcott, Edward Noyes 1846-1898 . . . . DLB-202

The Western Messenger 1835-1841 . . . . DLB-223

Western Publishing Company DLB-46

Western Writers of America Y-99

The Westminster Review 1824-1914 . . . . DLB-110

Weston, Arthur (see Webling, Peggy)

Weston, Elizabeth Jane circa 1582-1612 . . . DLB-172

Wetherald, Agnes Ethelwyn 1857-1940 . . . DLB-99

Wetherell, Elizabeth (see Warner, Susan)

Wetherell, W. D. 1948- DLB-234

Wetzel, Friedrich Gottlob 1779-1819 . . . . . DLB-90

Weyman, Stanley J. 1855-1928 . . . . DLB-141, 156

Wezel, Johann Karl 1747-1819 . . . . DLB-94

Whalen, Philip 1923- DLB-16

Whalley, George 1915-1983 . . . . DLB-88

Wharton, Edith 1862-1937 . . . . . DLB-4, 9, 12, 78, 189; DS-13; CDALB-3

Wharton, William 1920s?- Y-80

"What You Lose on the Swings You Make Up on the Merry-Go-Round" Y-99

Whately, Mary Louisa 1824-1889 . . . . . . DLB-166

Whately, Richard 1787-1863 . . . . DLB-190

From Elements of Rhetoric (1828; revised, 1846) DLB-57

What's Really Wrong With Bestseller Lists . . . Y-84

Wheatley, Dennis 1897-1977 . . . . DLB-77, 255

Wheatley, Phillis circa 1754-1784 . . . . . . DLB-31, 50; CDALB-2

Wheeler, Anna Doyle 1785-1848? DLB-158

Wheeler, Charles Stearns 1816-1843 . . DLB-1, 223

Wheeler, Monroe 1900-1988 . . . . DLB-4

Wheelock, John Hall 1886-1978 . . . . DLB-45

From John Hall Wheelock's Oral Memoir Y-01

Wheelwright, J. B. 1897-1940 . . . . DLB-45

Wheelwright, John circa 1592-1679 . . . . . DLB-24

Whetstone, George 1550-1587 . . . . DLB-136

Whetstone, Colonel Pete (see Noland, C. F. M.)

Whewell, William 1794-1866 . . . . DLB-262

Whichcote, Benjamin 1609?-1683 . . . . . . DLB-252

Whicher, Stephen E. 1915-1961 . . . . DLB-111

Whipple, Edwin Percy 1819-1886 . . . . . DLB-1, 64

Whitaker, Alexander 1585-1617 . . . . DLB-24

Whitaker, Daniel K. 1801-1881 . . . . DLB-73

Whitcher, Frances Miriam 1812-1852 . . . . DLB-11, 202

White, Andrew 1579-1656 . . . . DLB-24

White, Andrew Dickson 1832-1918 . . . . . DLB-47

White, E. B. 1899-1985 . . . DLB-11, 22; CDALB-7

White, Edgar B. 1947- DLB-38

White, Edmund 1940- DLB-227

White, Ethel Lina 1887-1944 . . . . DLB-77

White, Hayden V. 1928- DLB-246

White, Henry Kirke 1785-1806 . . . . DLB-96

White, Horace 1834-1916 . . . . DLB-23

White, James 1928-1999 . . . . DLB-261

White, Patrick 1912-1990 . . . . DLB-260

White, Phyllis Dorothy James (see James, P. D.)

White, Richard Grant 1821-1885 . . . . DLB-64

White, T. H. 1906-1964 . . . . DLB-160, 255

White, Walter 1893-1955 . . . . DLB-51

White, William, and Company DLB-49

White, William Allen 1868-1944 . . . . . DLB-9, 25

White, William Anthony Parker (see Boucher, Anthony)

White, William Hale (see Rutherford, Mark)

Whitchurch, Victor L. 1868-1933 . . . . . . DLB-70

Whitehead, Alfred North 1861-1947 . . . . DLB-100

Whitehead, James 1936- Y-81

Whitehead, William 1715-1785 . . . . . DLB-84, 109

Whitfield, James Monroe 1822-1871 . . . . DLB-50

Whitfield, Raoul 1898-1945 . . . . DLB-226

Whitgift, John circa 1533-1604 . . . . DLB-132

Whiting, John 1917-1963 . . . . DLB-13

Whiting, Samuel 1597-1679 . . . . DLB-24

Whitlock, Brand 1869-1934 . . . . DLB-12

Whitman, Albert, and Company DLB-46

Whitman, Albery Allson 1851-1901 . . . . . DLB-50

Whitman, Alden 1913-1990 . . . . Y-91

Whitman, Sarah Helen (Power) 1803-1878 . . . . DLB-1, 243

Whitman, Walt 1819-1892 . . . DLB-3, 64, 224, 250; CDALB-2

Whitman Publishing Company DLB-46

Whitney, Geoffrey 1548 or 1552?-1601 . . DLB-136

Whitney, Isabella flourished 1566-1573 . . DLB-136

Whitney, John Hay 1904-1982 . . . . DLB-127

Whittemore, Reed 1919-1995 . . . . DLB-5

Whittier, John Greenleaf 1807-1892 . . . . DLB-1, 243; CDALB-2

Whittlesey House DLB-46

Who Runs American Literature? Y-94

Whose Ulysses? The Function of Editing Y-97

Wickham, Anna (Edith Alice Mary Harper) 1884-1947 . . . . DLB-240

Wicomb, Zoë 1948- DLB-225

Wideman, John Edgar 1941- DLB-33, 143

Widener, Harry Elkins 1885-1912 . . . . . . DLB-140

Wiebe, Rudy 1934- DLB-60

Wiechert, Ernst 1887-1950 . . . . DLB-56

ISBN 0-7876-6013-2

90000

9 780787 660130